Understanding Behavior Disorders: A Contemporary Behavioral Perspective

Understanding Behavior Disorders: A Contemporary Behavioral Perspective

Edited by

Douglas W. Woods
University of Wisconsin, Milwaukee

Jonathan W. Kanter
University of Wisconsin, Milwaukee

CONTEXT PRESS
Reno, NV

Publisher's Note

Care has been taken to confirm the accuracy of the information presented and to describe generally accepted practices. However, the authors, editors, and publisher are not responsible for errors or omissions or for any consequences from application of the information in this book and make no warranty, express or implied, with respect to the contents of the publication.

Context Press
an imprint of New Harbinger Publications, Inc.
5674 Shattuck Avenue
Oakland, CA 94609
www.newharbinger.com

Library of Congress Cataloging-in-Publication Data
Understanding behavior disorders : a contemporary
    behavioral perspective / edited by Douglas W. Woods, Jonathan W. Kanter.
        p. ; cm.
    Includes bibliographical references and index.
    ISBN 978-1-878978-61-5 (pbk.)
1. Behavior therapy. 2. Cognitive therapy. 3. Behavioral assessment. 4. Behaviorism
(Psychology) I. Woods, Douglas W., 1971- II. Kanter, Jonathan.
    [DNLM: 1. Mental Disorders. 2. Behavioral Symptoms. 3. Mental Disorders—
therapy. 4. Models, Biological. 5. Models, Psychological. WM 140 U554 2007] I.
Title.
    RC489.B4U53 2007
    616.89'142—dc
                                            22 2007032081

Dedication

To the Woods family – Thanks for the inspiration
To Goldie, Buffy, Ralph, Lucy and my little Princess
D.W.W.

To my family, Gwynne and Zoe, with love (loving, as a verb)
J.W.K.

Acknowledgments

We would like to thank Steven Hayes for agreeing to publish this book and Emily Rodrigues at Context Press for her assistance in completing this project. We would also like to thank Sara Landes and Amanda Adcock for keeping us going. Finally, we would like to acknowledge the work of the authors. They took on a challenging task and were willing to behave in accordance with their values, despite the doubts, worries, and anxieties presented by both the task and deadlines.

Table of Contents

Preface x

Chapter 1 11
Introduction to Understanding Behavior Disorders:
A Contemporary Behavioral Perspective
Douglas W. Woods, Jonathan W. Kanter, & Sara J. Landes,
    University of Wisconsin, Milwaukee
Amanda C. Adcock, *University of North Texas*

Chapter 2 21
An Introduction to Principles of Behavior
Claudia Drossel, Thomas J. Waltz, & Steven C. Hayes,
    University of Nevada, Reno

Chapter 3 47
Applied Extensions of Behavior Principles:
Applied Behavioral Concepts and Behavioral Theories
Steven C. Hayes, Akihiko Masuda, Chad Shenk, James E. Yadavaia,
Jennifer Boulanger, Roger Vilardaga, Jennifer Plumb, Lindsay Fletcher,
Kara Bunting, Michael Levin, Thomas J. Waltz, & Mikaela J. Hildebrandt,
    University of Nevada, Reno

Chapter 4 81
From Normal Anxiety to Anxiety Disorders:
An Experiential Avoidance Perspective
Georg H. Eifert, *Chapman University*
John P. Forsyth, *University at Albany, SUNY*

Chapter 5 117
A Functional Contextual Account of Obsessive-Compulsive Disorder
Michael P. Twohig, *University of Nevada, Reno*
Daniel J. Moran, *Trinity Services, Inc./ MidAmerican Psychological Institute*
Steven C. Hayes, *University of Nevada, Reno*

Chapter 6 157
A Contemporary Behavior Analytic Model of Trichotillomania
Chad T. Wetterneck & Douglas W. Woods,
    University of Wisconsin, Milwaukee

Chapter 7 181
An Integrative Model of Depression Using Modern
Behavioral Principles
Jonathan W. Kanter, Sara J. Landes, Andrew M. Busch,
Laura C. Rusch, David E. Baruch, & Rachel C. Manos,
University of Wisconsin, Milwaukee

Chapter 8 217
Psychotic Disorders
Patricia A. Bach, *Illinois Institute of Technology*

Chapter 9 237
Addictive Behavior: An RFT-Enhanced Theory of Addiction
Kathleen M. Palm, *Brown Medical School / Butler Hospital*

Chapter 10 271
Eating Disorders: A New Behavioral Perspective and
Acceptance-Based Treatment Approach
Georg H. Eifert, *Chapman University*
Laurie A. Greco, *University of Missouri - St. Louis*
Michelle Heffner, *West Virginia University*
Ashleigh Louis, *Chapman University*

Chapter 11 297
Personality Disorders
Scott T. Gaynor & Susan C. Baird,
Western Michigan University

Chapter 12 341
Sexual Disorders
Bryan Roche, *National University of Ireland, Maynooth*
Ethel Quayle, *University College Cork, Ireland*

Chapter 13 369
Clinical Behavior Analysis and Health Psychology Applications
Ann D. Branstetter & Christopher C. Cushing,
Missouri State University

Chapter 14 389
A Behavioral Perspective on Adult Attachment Style, Intimacy,
and Relationship Health
Abigail K. Mansfield & James V. Cordova,
Clark University

Chapter 15 417
    Implications of Verbal Processes for Childhood Disorders:
    Tourette's Disorder, Attention Deficit Hyperactivity Disorder,
    and Autism
    Michael P. Twohig, Steven C. Hayes, & Nicholas M. Berens,
        University of Nevada, Reno

Index 445

Preface

We are clinical psychologists, drawn to the field because we wanted to help those with psychiatric impairments become better functioning individuals with a higher quality of life. We are also behavior analysts, drawn to this particular philosophical orientation because of its firm basis in the natural sciences. The blend of a clinical career with a behavior analytic orientation has been particularly rewarding as the translation from basic behavioral research to clinical practice is often quite clear and can be tremendously effective. The blend of clinical practice and behavior analysis has also, at times, been quite frustrating. We work with typically developing adults and children with various psychiatric impairments. Occasionally we felt clinically "stuck" because our traditional behavior analytic training could not adequately guide us in addressing our patient's distressing emotions or thoughts, which appeared to be quite important as targets of treatment. These concerns, along with the relatively recent development of a workable behavior analytic theory of language and cognition (i.e., Relational Frame Theory; RFT) and related "third wave" behavioral interventions (e.g., Acceptance and Commitment Therapy; ACT) set the stage, we felt, for a book that could potentially begin to lead to us and other behavior analytic clinical psychologists becoming "unstuck."

Understanding Behavior Disorders: A Contemporary Behavioral Perspective is a collection of chapters by different experts who agreed to undertake a unique challenge. These authors were asked to contribute chapters on specific psychiatric disorders. The chapters were to be both descriptive and innovative. All authors are behavior analytically trained and practice in the areas on which they write. The authors are also quite familiar with RFT and ACT. They were given the task of creating a contemporary behavioral model of a particular psychiatric disorder that incorporated, when appropriate, RFT concepts. They were asked to make the models experimentally testable and to discuss the treatment implications based on these theories.

This book does not fit nicely into any category. It is not a traditional psychopathology text, though psychopathology research is reviewed. It is not a traditional text reviewing treatment approaches, though treatment approaches are discussed. It is not a book on cognitive-behavior therapy, but traditional behavior analysts may believe it is. Our own understanding of the work is that it offers behavior analysis a chance to return to the mainstream world of clinical psychology. It is a translational work that offers a way for behavioral clinicians to reintegrate their clinical practice with an experimental analysis of behavior.

Douglas W. Woods
Jonathan W. Kanter
May 2007

Chapter 1

Introduction to Understanding Behavior Disorders: A Contemporary Behavioral Perspective

Douglas W. Woods, Jonathan W. Kanter, & Sara J. Landes
University of Wisconsin, Milwaukee
Amanda C. Adcock
University of North Texas

Behaviorally oriented clinical psychology has undergone transitional phases since its inception. Early behavioral clinicians were often dismissed by the proponents of rival grand theories (i.e., humanists, psychoanalysts), but they persisted and the resultant "first wave" of behavior therapy (Hayes, 2004; O'Donohue, 1998) produced some of the most enduring and effective treatments for various behavior problems. Examples include toilet training regimens (Foxx & Azrin, 1973), communication training programs for persons with developmental disabilities (e.g., Lovaas, 1987), and broad behavior management techniques (e.g., time out and token economies) that are widely used and have entered the popular lexicon. Empirical treatments for various psychiatric disturbances were also developed, including pleasant activity scheduling for depression (Lewinsohn & Graf, 1973), systematic desensitization for phobias (Wolpe, 1958), and habit reversal for a host of repetitive behavior problems (Azrin & Nunn, 1973).

Despite the early success of behavioral clinicians in developing effective treatments for psychiatric problems and the lasting and profound impact of these treatments in mental health practice and popular culture, their shared underlying theme of modifying solely the external environment eventually fell out of favor with the practicing community. In the 1960s-1970s behavioral clinical psychology transitioned from emphasizing and modifying only observable behavior to emphasizing and modifying internal behavior (e.g., thoughts). Clearly, the emergence of this "second wave" of behavior therapy reflected the dissatisfaction with the scope of "first wave" treatments (Hayes, 2004; Kohlenberg, Bolling, Kanter, & Parker, 2002; O'Donohue, 1998). A major source of dissatisfaction involved a lack of treatment development targeting affective and cognitive processes, a.k.a. private events, that were seen by many in the broader clinical community, clients and clinicians alike, as fundamental to the understanding and treatment of psychopathology.

Development of such interventions by early behavioral psychologists was hindered for both pragmatic and theoretical reasons. Pragmatically speaking, behaviorists have long argued that manipulable environmental events should be the focus of interventions rather than more difficult-to-access private events. Theoretically speaking, Skinner's writings on verbal behavior (1957) and private events (e.g., Skinner, 1945) were challenging for even the most advanced of scholars, unhelpful for most clinicians, and widely misunderstood. For example, Chomsky's (1959) widely cited critique of Skinner's *Verbal Behavior* resulted in the erroneous characterization of the behavioral view of verbal behavior as requiring direct experience with reinforcement in the presence of all stimuli toward which verbal behavior occurs. Chomsky made both the fundamental point that much of language cannot be attributed to such direct experiences and made the fundamental error of attributing this flawed position to Skinner. Others have been equally stymied by the behavioral view of private events, mischaracterizing the position as denying the very existence of private events at worst or denying any functional relation between affect, cognition, and overt behavior (e.g., that thoughts impact behavior) at best.

Such criticism and misunderstanding paved the way for individuals such as Beck (1967a, b) and Ellis (1962) to develop cognitive theories of language, cognition and private events that were easily translated into treatment techniques. Individuals with primarily behavioral orientations, such as David Barlow, abandoned the traditional behavior analytic position, recognized that thoughts *did* impact behavior in their patients, and logically began to incorporate cognitive therapy procedures into their behavioral practices. For example, by 1985, Lewinsohn, a pioneer in behavioral treatment for depression (e.g., Lewinsohn, 1974), had reformulated his model as an integrative cognitive-behavioral treatment approach (Lewinsohn, Hoberman, Teri, & Hautzinger, 1985). Lazarus (cf., 1968; 1976) and Seligman (cf., Overmier & Seligman, 1967; Seligman, 1975) are other notable CBT converts. The result of this exodus from traditional behavior analysis was another jump in treatment technologies. Brief manualized and packaged interventions were developed, efficacy established, and effectiveness for many determined. Indeed, these approaches are currently considered the standard of psychological care for many psychiatric disturbances (Chambless, Baker, Baucom, Beutler, Calhoun, Crits-Christoph et al., 1998).

It is interesting to note, however, that with the advent of behavior therapy's "second wave," something more than the creation of additional therapeutic options took place. In "first wave" treatments, the guiding principle was that observable abnormal behavior was controlled by one's external environment. However, with the onset of cognitive therapy, the guiding principle became one in which "...an individual's affect and behavior are largely determined by the way in which he or she structures the world" (Beck, Rush, Shaw, & Emery, 1979, p. 3). This change in underlying theoretical assumptions resulted in cognitive behavioral clinical psychologists stepping away from the basic laboratory in at least one very important way. The "first wave" was particularly powerful because replicated and rigorous investigations from basic laboratories yielded specific procedures that could be developed in the service of sound clinical practice. For example, it was not difficult to see how delivering an edible to an individual who emitted the word "dog" in the presence of a dog's picture was quite similar to how a rat may receive a food pellet contingent on a lever press in the presence of a green light. In contrast, basic research on cognition focused primarily on how the brain processed information. They did not experimentally demonstrate *how* thoughts actually come to control behavior, nor did the basic research in cognition provide a clear methodological example of how thoughts may be systematically modified in a way that results in behavior change. Without an understanding of these processes, any attempts at developing therapeutic strategies aimed at impacting the relationships between thoughts and behaviors were simply educated guesses.

Given these concerns, some behaviorally-oriented clinical psychologists remained committed to an approach in which treatments were highly informed by a basic science of behavior. This resulted in behavioral psychologists taking one of two paths of action. One group remained focused on utilizing and improving on variations of first-wave interventions and downplayed the importance or utility of cognitive interventions as an agent of change. It is interesting to note that those who followed this path may now be seeing some redemption. For some disorders, recent studies and meta-analyses are casting serious doubt that the cognitive therapy techniques created during the second-wave have any incremental validity above and beyond first-wave style treatments (Cuijpers, van Straten, & Warmerdam, 2007; Longmore & Worrell, 2007).

A second group, led by Steve Hayes at the University of Nevada, Reno, took on the first wave directly with a comprehensive overhaul of early behavior analytic thinking and a new research program on language and cognition. One major effort was the refinement and re-definition of the philosophical backbone of behavior analysis (i.e., radical behaviorism) into *functional contextualism*. Functional contextualism (Hayes, Hayes, & Reese, 1988) emphasizes (1) the need to provide functional definitions of behavior in terms of its contextual/historical determinants (i.e., the operant) thereby excluding mentalistic definitions or definitions of private behavior as the cause of public behavior, (2) the flexible nature of the operant as a unit of analysis (which readily allows for descriptions of abstract, molar, and generalized operants), and (3) a pragmatic rather than correspondence-based truth criterion. Hayes (1993), when coining the term, saw functional contextualism as stripping "needless mechanism and needless philosophical inconsistencies" (p. 11) from radical behaviorism.

Functional contextualism may have other benefits. First, simple avoidance of the term *radical behaviorism*, a term so misunderstood and maligned that ears close at its mention, may be useful in creating a larger audience for and better reception of work produced under the functional contextualistic umbrella. In addition, functional contextualism, compared to radical behaviorism, may be particularly useful for clinicians working with adult, outpatient populations, whose problems are at times too interrelated and abstract, and the histories involved are too distant and complex for useful mechanistic analyses. Finally, the growing body of research produced under this umbrella simply may call for a new label. As noted by Hayes (2005), "As the work deepens, it is becoming more and more obvious that the new behavior analysis that emerges...is at times almost unrecognizable, not because that was the purpose but because that is how profound the implications are to that tradition of an adequate account of language and cognition."

Hayes, in collaboration with Dermot Barnes-Holmes at the National University of Ireland, Maynooth, and others developed a research program to answer the question, "If thoughts can influence behavior, what behavioral processes must occur for this to happen?" They sought to address specific problems with the Skinnerian account of verbal behavior (e.g., that, technically speaking, a rat's lever press meets the definition of a verbal response according to Skinner) as well as address large gaps in the Skinnerian account. For example, while Skinner certainly noted that a long and complex history of reinforcement is necessary for the development of a normal verbal repertoire, he did not specify the nature of this history or suggest experimental procedures that would elucidate key variables in this history. Hayes and Barnes-Holmes began to build a basic behavior analytic model of language and cognition, incorporating earlier work by Sidman on stimulus equivalence (e.g., 1994), that was testable and that would foster a broadly applicable, philosophically coherent approach to treatment. The resulting theory of language and cognition is known as Relational Frame Theory (RFT; Hayes, Barnes-Holmes, & Roche, 2001), and the first approach to treatment that was conceptually linked to RFT is Acceptance and Commitment Therapy (ACT; Hayes, Strosahl, & Wilson, 1999).

Briefly, RFT describes a process through which humans learn to relate arbitrary stimuli to each other in multiple ways, within multiple contexts. This relating behavior—technically known as arbitrarily applicable relational framing—initially is reinforced using broadly available, socially generated conditioned reinforcers but eventually becomes self-reinforcing (i.e., sustained by the coherence of the relational networks produced by relational framing). The theory states that over time, individuals develop very strong, context-dependent relating repertoires involving functional stimulus classes of arbitrary stimuli, and this forms the basis for human language and cognition. Importantly, RFT describes a behavioral process through which language develops in the absence of direct reinforcement for every instance of language use, thereby addressing a primary gap in the Skinnerian account. Also, RFT suggests a behavioral process—technically the *transformation of stimulus functions*—through which thoughts may elicit and evoke feelings and other behaviors, providing a direct behavioral alternative to cognitive theory and therapy. RFT also suggests some compelling new directions for behaviorists, e.g., how an individual's painful emotional history can be brought into the present and play a functional role in the individual's current behavior. Likewise, it describes the conditions under which language might develop excessive control over behavior to the exclusion of real-time consequences for that same behavior. All of these issues have compelling clinical implications. Ultimately, RFT offers the promise of a basic behavioral science of language and cognition on which more effective behavioral interventions may be developed.

The work of Hayes and colleagues has not met with universal acclaim and appreciation. Some in the CBT community do not understand the implications of a functional contextual view of language and cognition vis-à-vis the mainstream cognitive model, and some in the behavior analysis community have disagreed with and misunderstood the theory themselves. Burgos (2003) simply called the theory "unintelligible." Palmer (2004) argued that it is an unnecessary and unparsimonious expansion of Skinner's (1957) treatment of verbal behavior, or at least Sidman's (e.g., 1994) formulation of stimulus equivalence (also see Stemmer, 1995). Others (Ingvarsson & Morris, 2004) have questioned specific RFT assertions (e.g., that relational framing is a *new* behavioral process). An additional concern is that it has not yet been widely researched by multiple independent research groups. Furthermore, it is often the case that at least some subjects in typical RFT preparations (e.g., match-to-sample) will not demonstrate the requisite component behaviors of mutual entailment, combinatorial entailment, and transformation of stimulus functions that are said to define relational framing, suggesting that alternate preparations need to be developed for the case to be made that RFT processes are ubiquitous in normal, adult, verbally-able humans.

All of these problems are being addressed. Cogent responses to Burgos (2003) and Palmer (2004) have been presented (Hayes & Barnes-Holmes, 2004) and direct RFT extensions of Skinner's theory have been advanced (Barnes-Holmes, Barnes-Holmes, & Cullinan, 2000). An increasingly diverse group of researchers are engaged in basic and applied RFT research. Alternate preparations for RFT research, such as the relational evaluation procedure, have been developed and are being used with increasing frequency. And most importantly, the clinical utility of the work is becoming increasingly clear, as the body of evidence in support of ACT and ACT processes is growing rapidly.

The rise of functional contextualism, RFT and ACT has led to the development of what is now being called the "third wave" of behavior therapy (Hayes, 2004), led by ACT but including several other important treatment approaches. Several of these approaches (including ACT but also Dialectical Behavior Therapy, Linehan, 1993) incorporate mindfulness, an Eastern spiritual approach that, when stripped of its spiritual associations, is surprisingly consistent with traditional behavior analytic philosophy and functional contextualism (Hayes, Follette, & Linehan, 2004). On a smaller scale, behavior analysts also addressed another weakness of the first wave—its lack of appreciation for or understanding of the therapeutic relationship—with the development of Functional Analytic Psychotherapy (FAP; Kohlenberg

& Tsai, 1991). Although diverse in form and technology, these approaches share an appreciation for the functional role of private events in psychiatric disorders.

Data in support of RFT and third wave treatments are accumulating at a rapid pace. Indeed, as this book nears publication well-designed studies are underway across the world evaluating ACT for various populations, components of ACT, RFT-ACT links, and basic RFT premises. The energy behind this research effort is intense and intelligent. Research on other contemporary approaches, notably DBT and Behavioral Activation (Martell, Addis, & Jacobson, 2001), is also occurring at a steady clip. At the same time, we are concerned that the promises of the third wave will not be fully realized. From contact with those in this area and from reading the literature on RFT and ACT, we noticed few explicit links between basic RFT research and the behavioral treatments for which RFT functions as the purported basic behavioral bedrock. For example, it is not uncommon for an ACT therapist to be unable to explain the basic tenets of RFT. Likewise, it is often difficult to see how particular ACT techniques may have the impact that would be necessary for behavior change to occur according to the RFT model, except in the most abstract sense. Given these concerns, we felt it would be useful to create a book that would allow clinicians versed in RFT and third wave treatments to tell the research community how cognition may play a functional role in various psychiatric disorders using an RFT model, and then to explain how treatment could be developed based on this model.

In the current book, we have assembled a collection of authors who coura-geously agreed to engage in this unique intellectual exercise. We invited individuals to review and critique the existing behavioral and cognitive behavioral models of a psychiatric disorder and then describe a contemporary behavior analytic theory, incorporating when warranted an RFT approach to private events. We specifically asked the authors to present testable theory, and when possible to describe what could be tested. We also asked the authors to describe the applied extensions of their theory. We recognized that the theories presented herein would find little current support from existing behavior analytic research, as most of these disorders have not been examined through a modern behavior analytic perspective. Thus, we encour-aged authors to present non-behavioral research that is consistent with the theory and to highlight work that still needs to be done. The overall purpose of the book was to present logical, plausible, and testable theories of common behavior disorders from a modern behavioral perspective. It is not a simple book on psychopathology, in which authors simply describe findings from other studies. Rather it is an attempt to synthesize, with a philosophical approach that is decidedly behavior analytic, how what is known about a disorder could be explained from what is known about basic behavioral processes in the creation of emotional, motoric, and language/cognitive behavior.

Many but not all of the chapters in this book emphasize functional contextualism, RFT, and ACT. In fact, a common theme emerges, and this theme will be familiar to those already familiar with ACT and its model of psychopathology. Specifically, a case is often made that relational language processes lead to the development of excessive rule governance and experiential avoidance, processes which ACT directly targets. This functional model plays out in different topographies that are represented by different psychiatric disorders. In other words, broad language processes underlie a broad functional psychopathological dimension (experiential avoidance), and ACT targets this process. Thus, ACT may be quite broadly applicable across a range of diagnostic categories and presenting problems, to the extent that language processes and experiential avoidance are at work. It is quite possible that this model is at the center of much psychopathology, and for readers who agree with it, this book will be an inspiration and confirmation. Collectively, the body of research accumulating in support of RFT and ACT may lead some to this conclusion.

It is also possible that the heavy focus on this model simply represents the still-infant status of the research community represented herein. We expect that subtle refinements, major expansions, and recognitions of previous erroneous omissions and wrong turns will all occur as this work evolves. Randomized clinical trials, with all the bells and whistles (e.g., adequate power, multiple sites representing expertise in all comparison conditions, medication and placebo controls, good adherence monitoring, good follow-up using blind evaluators, etc.) have not been done with ACT for several major disorders. Component analyses to identify necessary components of ACT are also lacking, and the links between RFT and ACT are not immune to alternate accounts. Thus, some of the theory will undoubtedly be proven false, as that is the nature of science. For readers who predict this outcome, this book—largely (but not entirely) written by devoted ACT clinicians and researchers—may be a provocation. In fact, we hope such readers are provoked, "but provoked…to test the theory empirically against alternative accounts" (Ingvarsson & Morris, 2004, p. 502) and provoked to critique the theory on logical, philosophical and empirical grounds. Only through such provocation and research may behavioral psychologists return to the point where basic laboratory research clearly influences our clinical practice.

References

Azrin, N. H., & Nunn, R. G. (1973). Habit reversal: A method of eliminating nervous habits and tics. *Behaviour Research and Therapy, 11*, 619-628.

Barnes-Holmes, D., Barnes-Holmes, Y., & Cullinan, V. (2000). Relational frame theory and Skinner's Verbal Behavior: A possible synthesis. *Behavior Analyst, 23*, 69-84.

Beck, A. T. (1967a). *Cognitive therapy and the emotional disorders*. New York: Meridian.

Beck, A.T. (1967b). *Depression: Clinical, experimental, and theoretical aspects*. New York: Harper & Row.

Beck, A. T., Rush, A. J., Shaw, B. F., & Emery, G. (1979). *Cognitive therapy of depression*. New York: Guilford Press.

Burgos, J. E. (2003). Laudable goals, interesting experiments, unintelligible theorizing: A critical review of Relational Frame Theory. *Behavior and Philosophy, 31*, 19-45.

Chambless, D. L., Baker, M. J., Baucom, D. H., Beutler, L. E., Calhoun, K. S., Crits-Christoph, P., et al. (1998). Update on empirically validated therapies, II. *The Clinical Psychologist, 51*, 3-16.

Chomsky, N. (1959). A review of B. F. Skinner's Verbal Behavior. *Language, 35*, 26-58.

Cuijpers, P., van Straten, A., & Warmerdam, L. (2007). Behavioral activation treatments of depression: a meta-analysis. *Clinical Psychology Review, 27,* 318-326.

Ellis, A. (1962). *Reason and emotion in psychotherapy.* New York: Institute for Rational Living.

Foxx, R. M., & Azrin, N. H. (1973). *Toilet training the retarded.* Champaign, IL: Research Press.

Hayes, S. C. (2003). Analytic goals and the varieties of scientific contextualism. In S. C. Hayes, L. J. Hayes, H. W. Reese, & T. R. Sarbin (Eds.). *Varieties of scientific contextualism* (pp. 11-27). Reno, NV: Context Press.

Hayes, S. C. (2004). Acceptance and commitment therapy, relational frame theory, and the third wave of behavior therapy. *Behavior Therapy, 35,* 639-665.

Hayes, S. C. (2005). *Basic foundations.* Retrieved April 24, 2007, from http://www.contextualpsychology.org/basic_foundations.

Hayes, S. C., & Barnes-Holmes, D. (2004). Relational operants: Processes and implications: A response to Palmer's review of relational frame theory. *Journal of the Experimental Analysis of Behavior, 82,* 213-224.

Hayes, S. C., Barnes-Holmes, D., & Roche, B. (Eds.). (2001). *Relational frame theory: A post-Skinnerian account of human language and cognition.* New York: Kluwer Academic/ Plenum Publishers.

Hayes, S. C., Follette, V. M., & Linehan, M. M. (Eds.). (2004). *Mindfulness and acceptance: Expanding the cognitive-behavioral tradition.* New York: Guilford.

Hayes, S. C., Hayes, L. J., & Reese, H. W. (1988). Finding the philosophical core: A review of Stephen C. Pepper's World Hypotheses. *Journal of the Experimental Analysis of Behavior, 50,* 97-111.

Hayes, S. C., Strosahl, K. D., & Wilson, K. G. (1999). *Acceptance and commitment therapy: An experiential guide to behavior change.* New York: Guilford.

Ingvarsson, E. T., & Morris, E. K. (2004). Post-Skinnerian, post-Skinner, or neo-Skinnerian? Hayes, Barnes-Holmes, and Roche's relational frame theory: A post-Skinnerian account of human language and cognition. *Psychological Record, 54,* 497-504.

Kohlenberg, R. J., Bolling, M. Y., Kanter, J. W., & Parker, C. R. (2002). Clinical behavior analysis: Where it went wrong, how it was made good again, and why its future is so bright. *The Behavior Analyst Today, 3,* 248-254.

Kohlenberg, R. J., & Tsai, M. (1991). *Functional analytic psychotherapy: Creating intense and curative therapeutic relationships.* New York: Plenum Press.

Lazarus, A. A. (1968). Learning theory and the treatment of depression. *Behavior Research and Therapy, 6,* 83-89.

Lazarus, A. A. (1976). Multimodal behavioral treatment of depression. In A. A. Lazarus (Ed.), *Multimodal behavior therapy* (pp. 97-102). New York: Springer.

Lewinsohn, P. M. (1974). A behavioral approach to depression. In R. J. Friedman & M. M. Katz (Eds.), *Psychology of depression: Contemporary theory and research* (pp. 157-178). Oxford, England: John Wiley & Sons.

Lewinsohn, P. M., & Graf, M. (1973). Pleasant activities and depression. *Journal of Consulting and Clinical Psychology, 41,* 261-268.

Lewinsohn, P. M., Hoberman, H. M., Teri, L. & Hautzinger, M. (1985). An integrative theory of depression. In S. Reiss & R. Bootzin (Eds.), *Theoretical issues in behavior therapy* (pp. 331-359). New York: Academic Press.

Linehan, M. M. (1993). *Cognitive-behavioral treatment of borderline personality disorder.* New York: Guilford.

Longmore, R. J., & Worrell, M. (2007). Do we need to challenge thoughts in cognitive behavior therapy? *Clinical Psychology Review, 27,* 173-187.

Lovaas, O. I. (1987). Behavioral treatment and normal educational and intellectual functioning in young autistic children. *Journal of Consulting and Clinical Psychology, 55,* 3-9.

Martell, C. R., Addis, M. E., & Jacobson, N. E. (2001). *Depression in context: Strategies for guided action.* New York: W. W. Norton & Co, Inc.

O'Donohue, W. (Ed.). (1998). *Learning and behavior therapy.* Boston: Allyn & Bacon.

Overmier, J. B., & Seligman, M. E. (1967). Effects of inescapable shock upon subsequent escape and avoidance responding. *Journal of Comparative & Physiological Psychology, 6,* 28-33.

Palmer, D. C. (2004). Data in search of a principle: A review of Relational Frame Theory: A post-Skinnerian account of human language and Cognition. *Journal of the Experimental Analysis of Behavior, 81,* 189-204.

Seligman, M. E. (1975). *Helplessness: On depression, development, and death.* Oxford, England: W. H. Freeman.

Sidman, M. (1994). *Equivalence relations and behavior: A research story.* Boston, MA: Authors Cooperative.

Skinner, B. F. (1945). The operational analysis of psychological terms. *Psychological Review, 52,* 270-277.

Skinner, B. F. (1957). *Verbal behavior.* East Norwalk, CT: Appleton-Century-Crofts.

Stemmer, N. (1995). Do we need an alternative theory of verbal behavior?: A reply to Hayes and Wilson. *Behavior Analyst, 18,* 357-362.

Wolpe, J. (1958). *Psychotherapy by reciprocal inhibition.* Stanford, CA: Stanford University Press.

Chapter 2

An Introduction to Principles of Behavior

Claudia Drossel, Thomas J. Waltz, & Steven C. Hayes
University of Nevada, Reno

Behavioral principles are not static. They develop systematically across the years. Perhaps more than any other approach to psychology, behavioral psychology is self-consciously committed to being a progressive science in which worthwhile earlier work is sustained even while new frontiers are explored. We are not speaking of conservatism for its own sake, but rather for the creation of a field that knows how to keep its hard won gains. A field that cannot do so will appear to renew itself by reinventing what was known earlier and forgotten. Scientific amnesia of that kind gives only the appearance of progress, not its essence.

Built upon a century of research in behavioral psychology, in the last decades a coherent and progressive approach to the topic of human language and cognition has emerged from within behavior analysis. This volume is designed to attempt to account for human psychopathology from the perspective of this comprehensive set of modern behavioral principles. To do that, it is necessary to describe these principles as well as the foundation upon which they rest.

The purpose of this chapter is to describe a workable core set of basic behavioral principles that can be used to understand complex human behavior. We will outline basic principles of learning and then extend those to the empirical analysis of human language and cognition. The next chapter will then describe how these fundamental principles are related to more middle-level constructs specifically focused on complex issues encountered in applied work, such as issues of relationship or sense of self.

Basic Behavioral Principles

Contingency Thinking

Everybody attempts to explain behavior: Parents ponder the reasons for their children's behavior; teachers attempt to influence their students' behavior; star-crossed lovers try to predict the behavior of their chosen one. This is both a blessing and a curse. It is a blessing because it is the source of public interest in psychological science. It is a curse because lay explanations of behavior strongly compete with scientific ones (Hineline, 1980).

Behavioral psychology emerges from a pragmatic and contextualistic philosophy of science that treats psychological events as the integrated action of a whole organism interacting in and with a context considered both historically and situationally (Hayes, Hayes, & Reese, 1988). These situated actions include all forms of psychological activity: moving, speaking, thinking, feeling, reasoning, problem-solving, and so on. It does not matter whether the action is publicly observable or observable only to the person engaging in it. Even private events can be studied scientifically, for reasons we will describe later (Skinner, 1945).

When behavior is approached in this pragmatic and contextualistic way, actions and their contexts are whole units. For example, going to the store implies a place to go from and to, a motivation to go, and a set of behavioral events that will accomplish that purpose. Going to the store is not just the action of a leg, or the twitches of muscle fibers. It is a whole event, but one with discernable aspects. Like a person looking at different sides of a box, behavioral psychologists look at different aspects of a whole behavioral episode to discern features that might help this entire event to be predicted and influenced. The rules that are abstracted to do that need to have precision (that is, only a certain number of things can be said about any episode), scope (that is, ways of speaking about one episode should apply to others), and depth (that is, successful ways of speaking at the level of psychological events should comport with successful analyses at the level of others sciences, such as biology, sociology, and so on).

The aspects – the "sides of the box" as it were – that are examined by behavioral psychology include the states of affairs that were present when an action occurred, the act itself, and the states of affairs that have been and are now produced by those actions. Broadly speaking, the first set of events is termed "antecedents," and the last set is called "consequences." These two considered together are all aspects of "context." The relationships among antecedents, actions, and consequences are called "contingencies."

These events can all be further divided for analytic purposes. Antecedents can include environmental events that have a psychological function (e.g., behavior occurs more or less frequently in their presence); conditions that alter the functions of other antecedent and consequential events (e.g., motivational events; drugs; augmentals); and the strength or occurrence of various other situated actions (e.g., repertoire; verbal rules). Consequences, on the other hand, include all events that have reliably followed behaviors in the past.

Although behavior only occurs in the moment, a snapshot of behavior does not reveal the stable antecedents or consequences nor the relationship among them. No one situation is ever exactly like another. Thus, when we examine behavioral patterns to predict or influence behavior in the future we focus on patterns that are evident over time. When we want to understand a particular behavior pattern, we try to determine those antecedents and consequences that help us predict and influence from situation to situation, that is, those that reveal reliable patterns and consistencies. For this reason, behavioral psychologists observe antecedents, behavior, and consequences repeatedly and then identify patterns of events that usually precede and follow an action.

All contingency streams are analyzed using the basic concepts in Figure 2.1. The dot denotes an emitive probabilistic relation between terms while the arrow indicates a contingent relation. Some analyses rely primarily on the terms in the top panel, Antecedents ● Behavior → Consequences. That integrated whole is called an operant "three-term contingency," simply because the behavior *operates* upon the environment, and the integrated unit consists of three terms. It is "integrated" because each can only be defined in terms of the other, and thus these are aspects of a whole, not a mechanical assemblage. Other analyses might keep track explicitly of the various events that alter these three events, any of which might be verbal. For example, when most organisms are food-deprived, food-related antecedents and consequences will come to the fore. The middle panel illustrates such a "four-term contingency" analysis. This is not the end of the complexity, however. There is now a good deal of evidence that the contingencies related to verbal behavior can vary in the degree to which they coincide with the contingencies for other behavior; at times, these contingencies may interact, compete with, or override one another. Excessive influence by verbal relations and consequent insensitivity to other contingencies is of particular interest in the clinical realm (see later chapters). For this reason, it is often necessary to keep track of multiple sets of contingencies – operating upon verbal and other behavior, and their interactions. When these variables are included, a contingency analysis involves the more complex set of considerations shown in the bottom panel of Figure 2.1.

Reinforcement and Punishment Contingencies

Although contingency analysis in a broad sense existed before the work of B. F. Skinner, he formalized this approach in 1938 and added a focus on whether specific contingencies resulted in an increase or decrease in the frequency of behavior over time. Reinforcement and punishment contingencies are distinguished by their effects on behavior.

Any behavior occurs in a given situation (the antecedent) and is followed by particular consequences. If, over time, the behavior increases in frequency (due to the contingency among antecedents, behavior, and consequences), the consequences are characterized as reinforcers and the operation is called reinforcement. If the behavior decreases in frequency (due to the contingencies), the consequences are characterized as punishers. "Reinforcement" and "punishment" are thus contingent relations (or dependencies) linking the frequency with which a behavior occurs, its antecedents, and its consequences. These "three-term-contingencies" constitute the simplest unit of analysis in behavioral psychology. It is important to remember that this unit encompasses not only the events preceding and following the behavior, but the dependent relations between them and resulting changes in the frequency of that behavior over time. Any one of the three terms (antecedents, behavior, or consequences) may be verbal.

Analysis in terms of the three-term contingency

Antecedents • Behavior → Consequences

Analysis in terms of the four-term contingency

Antecedents • Behavior → Consequences

↕

Establishing operations and setting events

Analysis in terms of direct and derived four-term contingencies

Antecedents • Behavior → Consequences

↕

Establishing operations and setting events

↕

Verbal Antecedents • Verbal Behavior → Verbal Consequences

↕

Verbal establishing operations and setting events

Figure 2.1. Forms of Contingency Analysis.

For convenience and simplification, Table 2.1 describes possible behavior-consequence outcomes in a binary fashion (that is, in terms of whether or not these events occur or do not occur).

(1) A behavior occurs →		(2) Following events are	
		Presented	Prevented/removed
(3) Over time, the frequency of behavior	Increases	Positive reinforcement	Negative reinforcement (avoidance, escape)
	Decreases	Positive punishment	Negative punishment (timeout, penalty)

Table 2.1. Reinforcement and punishment contingencies.

Other behavior-consequence relations are not describable as binary events but rather involve subtle changes in magnitude, duration, or quality. Thus, in a given state of affairs behavior occurs and is followed by a changed state of affairs. In Table 2.1 the changed state of affairs can be characterized either by the presentation of events or the prevention or removal of events. Skinner termed the presentation of events "positive," and their removal, postponement, prevention, or termination "negative." It helps to think of these terms arithmetically. Like a plus and minus sign, "positive reinforcement" is "positive" in the sense of being additive to the current state of affairs, while "negative" reinforcement is subtractive. The labels "positive" and "negative" are not evaluative (i.e., denoting good and bad; pleasant or unpleasant; or liked and disliked). This misunderstanding has caused a great deal of confusion.

The terms "positive" and "negative" only describe the contextual change that follows the behavior from the point of view of the observer. To determine whether the behavior was reinforced or punished, we have to look at the effects of the consequences over time. If behavior increases in rate, we speak of reinforcement, and if its frequency decreases, we speak of punishment.

Positive Reinforcement. Positive reinforcement is the strengthening of behavior due to a contingency that involves the presentation of particular consequences. Again, it is important to note that reinforcement is defined by the changing frequency of behavior, not by the presumed "pleasantness" or "unpleasantness" of events. This is part of why behavioral principles gain power over standard common-sense interpretations of behavior, because sometimes behavior may be reinforced by events that are usually thought to be aversive (e.g., access to restraints as a reinforcer, Rooker & Roscoe, 2005; chiding by a teacher as a reinforcer, Madsen, Becker, Thomas, Koser, & Plager, 1968).

When issues of what is "pleasant" or "desirable" become confused with positive reinforcement, detection of the functions of events become difficult, especially in applied situations. As this book emphasizes, applied behavioral approaches are grounded in an analysis based upon the *function* of behavior (Eifert, 1996; Follette, Naugle, & Linnerooth, 2000; O'Brien, McGrath, & Haynes, 2003). For example, clients often identify the particular behavioral patterns that are the sources of distress. The behavioral patterns that seemingly generate the problems have often persisted, sometimes for years. When what is "pleasant" or "desirable" becomes confused with what is reinforcing, this circumstance seems to contradict principles of behavior. Why doesn't distress—commonly conceptualized as an aversive event—lead to a reduction in the frequency of such behavior patterns? For example, suppose a client seeks therapy because of the occurrence of angry outbursts that continue despite their threat to the client's marriage. Just because the client characterizes these outbursts as distressing does not mean that they are not maintained by reinforcement (e.g., an intense interaction with the partner follows each angry outburst).

Analysis in terms of the three-term contingency

No spousal interaction • Behavior (angry outbursts) → Intense Interaction

Figure 2.2. Contingency analysis.

Even if they look negative or distressing themselves, these intense interactions might be reinforcing. They might be preferred to being ignored; they might prove that the partner cares; they might lead to a sense of closeness with an otherwise distant partner; they might feel alive; they might lead to sex; and so on. Thus, the angry outbursts may be positively reinforced by the subsequent intensive emotional engagement, whether or not it *looks* positive or reinforcing.

Negative Reinforcement (Avoidance, Escape). While positive reinforcement involves the presentation of events following behavior, negative reinforcement describes an increase in the rate of behavior if that behavior functions to escape or avoid particular events. Suppose a parent escapes from a child's tantrums at the checkout counter of a grocery store by buying the child candy. If the candy stops the tantrum, and this termination makes giving in to the child's demands in public situations more likely in the future, the parents' giving-in has been "negatively reinforced." If the term "negative" is thought of in the sense of "subtraction" it makes sense: the candy subtracts the tantrum from the parent's immediate environment.

When both persons are examined, a disturbing pattern can be created by interlocking contingencies of this kind. If tantruming increases in frequency over the next weeks or months because the candy was presented, the child's tantruming can be characterized as having been positively reinforced. Now caregiver and child have entered a "vicious cycle," "sick social cycle," or "coercive process" in which stopping the disruptive behavior reinforces patterns that actually escalate that behavior and, in turn, makes the caregiver's escape or avoidance even more likely (e.g., Patterson, 1982).

Because the functional definition and the common-sense approach to reinforcement often do not overlap, the identification of reinforcers is an integral and important part of behavior analysis. Reinforcer identification is exceptionally difficult when behavior is being maintained by negative reinforcement. In the case of avoidance, the event that maintains the behavior is postponed or prevented. It may rarely occur at all when the avoidance behavior is strong. A person's depressed behavior, for example, may serve to prevent angry interactions in the household (Hops, Biglan, Sherman, & Arthur, 1987). The long-standing success of the behavior pattern (i.e., the absence of angry interactions) may have made it impossible for the person to describe the relation between depressed behavior and familial disputes. By the time the person seeks therapy, it may seem that depressed behavior occurs "for no good reason." Consequently, from a current lack of identifiable maintaining factors it does not follow that problematic behavior patterns arose spontaneously or that they will be insensitive to situational changes.

Behaviors maintained by negative reinforcement are often less flexible than those maintained by positive reinforcement. Repertoires leading to successful avoidance or escape are both narrow and efficient. For one thing, aversive control tends to create a situation in which only a few behaviors are strong. For example, if something stops you from breathing, within seconds the *only* behaviors of interest are those that might lead to removal of the blockage. Furthermore, there is not much creativity and variability built into such actions. Likewise, if you now discovered that a certain behavior completely prevented the next episode, you would repeat whatever worked and not deviate or experiment much. If the negative reinforcement contingency were suddenly stopped under these conditions, your previously functional avoidance repertoire would become obsolete and may weaken eventually. Yet, you might continue to engage in the now non-functional avoidance behavior for quite some time. Concurrent verbal descriptions of these events (e.g., "reason-giving") may also serve to maintain behaviors that do not work. For these reasons, behavior that is negatively reinforced by avoidance or escape can be extraordinarily narrow, persistent, and out of contact with a more flexible, situationally appropriate repertoire.

Positive Punishment. As shown in Table 2.1 and parallel to the principle of reinforcement, the principle of punishment also describes a relation among antecedents, behavior, and consequences, such that behavior decreases in frequency following the reliable occurrence of certain events over time. The epitome of a positive punisher is the commonsense example of a hot stove: Touching the stove reliably leads to the presentation of scorching heat, and given these consequences, touching the stove will become less likely.

Punishment procedures, by definition, *do not* increase the rate of any specific target behavior. If an increase in the rate of a particular behavior is desired, reinforcement must be operative. Moreover, while punishment suppresses behavior, it is not clear what will occur in its place. That is one of the weaknesses of procedures based on punishment, and for this reason Skinner and other behavioral psychologists (e.g., Sidman, 1989) consistently have opposed its application (for a review of the ethical and effective use of punishment procedures, see Van Houten, 1983). The attractiveness of positive punishment often lies in its immediate effects: the annoying behavior stops. However, although the punished behavior has decreased in rate, the reinforcers that maintain the behavior are still effective. In this situation "symptom substitution" may occur (i.e., other problematic behavior patterns leading to the reinforcer may emerge). Thus, both pragmatics and ethics suggest that each punishment procedure be accompanied by the reinforcement of socially appropriate behavioral patterns. For example, parents have many demands upon their time. Especially if an infant is in the home, older siblings may receive the most attention when they engage in disruptive behavior. Punishment of a particularly disruptive behavior may quickly decrease its rate. However, if no appropriate means to get attention are established, it is likely that another disruptive behavior will emerge. Contrary to other approaches which may find fault with the child's need for attention, the behavioral perspective respects the child's need for attention as a given and focuses on providing access to attention by socially appropriate means.

Negative Punishment (Penalty, Timeout). While positive punishment procedures involve the presentation of an event, negative punishment procedures characterize a decrease in the rate of behavior because it is followed by the contingent removal, withdrawal, postponement, or termination of an event. Thus, a teenager may temporarily lose access to the family car as a consequence of breaking curfew. If, over time, incidences of breaking the curfew go down in frequency, then taking away car privileges functions as a negative punisher. Another example of negative punishment is the temporary withdrawal of access to social activities following behavior. If restless and agitated behavior with siblings at the dinner table, followed by temporary removal from the table to eat alone, leads to a decrease in the frequency of the problem behavior over time, then this procedure is correctly described as "time-out from family dinner."

Extinction

Importantly, for an event to be characterized as a reinforcer, not only does behavior have to increase in rate when consequences are made dependent upon the occurrence of the behavior, but withdrawal of the consequences has to eventually result in a *decrease* in the rate of behavior. "Extinction" is the term used for procedures that involve the breaking of a reinforcement contingency. To break a contingency, one may either withhold the consequences completely, or one may present those events regardless of the occurrence of particular behaviors. The same holds for extinction of punishment contingencies, where breaking the punishment contingency results in a subsequent *increase* in the rate of previously punished behavior.

Withdrawal of access to reinforcers often leads to a temporary escalation of behavior or increased variability (Morgan & Lee, 1996). The escalation is termed an "extinction burst," a common phenomenon when extinction procedures are in effect, which is then followed by a gradual decline in the behavior. In the case of social distress, for example, a client's social group may meet initial expressions with much sympathy, compassion, and understanding. There is a reinforcement contingency in effect. Accordingly, distress reports may increase in frequency, especially if the client does not have other repertoires to maintain social involvement. As time passes and behavior problems persist, the community may become less sympathetic and less attentive to the client's reports of distress. As a function of the community's withholding of attention, the client's reports may start escalating. After the burst and with extinction still in effect, the reports of distress are expected to decrease in rate over time.

Another effect sometimes seen during extinction is that other, previously extinguished behaviors or repertoires may "resurge" (e.g., Epstein, 1985; Wilson & Hayes, 1996). For example, alcohol-seeking may "resurge" (i.e., relapse may occur) when other, non-drug-related behaviors are extinguished (Podlesnik, Jimenez-Gomez, & Shahan, 2006). Like an extinction burst, resurgence needs to be expected as a normal indication that extinction is occurring.

The consistency with which behavior is reinforced or punished determines the persistence of the particular behavior under extinction conditions. If behavior always has been followed by reinforcement, discontinuing reinforcement will decrease the rate of behavior very quickly. In other words, the person quickly discerns that conditions have changed and that the behavior is not effective any more. A parent who consistently escaped from a child's tantruming by "giving in" and buying toys or candy, has arranged a continuous schedule of reinforcement. "Giving in" reinforces the child's behavior, i.e., it increases its rate over time. When extinction is implemented, and the parent remains firm in his or her decision to ignore the tantrum and refrain from buying candy, the child's behavior is expected to cease completely after only a few times at the checkout line. However, if behavior has been reinforced only once in a while, the parent has inadvertently established an intermittent reinforcement pattern. Under these circumstances, the behavior is expected to persist for quite some time. Intermittent reinforcement thus produces higher and more persistent rates. For this reason, extinction procedures should only be implemented if accidental reinforcement will not occur.

Motivation

The effectiveness of the reinforcer or punisher is measured in terms of the frequency of the behavior it supports, and the subject of motivation (also termed "establishing operations") addresses the ways by which the effectiveness of reinforcers or punishers may be changed. Food deprivation, for example, changes the effectiveness with which food supports behavior: While at the beginning of the day the items available in the lounge snack machine do not seem appealing, they may occasion a great deal of behavior (e.g., obtaining the necessary monetary change, operating the machine, devouring the items) in the middle of the afternoon, after missing lunch.

Rather than referring to a physical or internal state, "motivation" as used here refers to the practical procedures with which reinforcer or punisher effectiveness may be changed. Many drugs of abuse establish the effectiveness of social reinforcers: Ingestion of d-amphetamine increases the probability that a person will forego monetary reinforcers for monologues and instead speak to a same-sex confederate in a different room via a microphone (Higgins, Hughes, & Bickel, 1989). Other drugs decrease the effectiveness of punishers: Contrary to the popular perception of cannabis as an "amotivational" drug, experimental work has consistently shown that people under cannabis's influence are more likely to engage in non-preferred, repetitious, or strenuous tasks (Snycerski, Laraway, & Poling, 2000). One may speculate that cannabis may also make aversive social interactions more tolerable.

Motivational effects are not limited to drugs but may also emerge from the interaction of contingencies. For example, a basic research program that investigated the effects of activity on eating patterns showed that high-rate exercise schedules decrease the reinforcing effectiveness of food. This amotivational effect, in turn, leads to an increased engagement in exercising to the point at which the organism is close to starvation. Activity anorexia, empirically supported by animal models, seems to emerge from bidirectional and reciprocal changes in the effectiveness of reinforcers (for a review, see Pierce & Epling, 1991).

Other motivational effects arise from the interactions of verbal processes with other behavior and will be covered later in this chapter under the topics of "augmentals."

Practical Considerations

There is no fast-and-easy rule for the identification of components of the three or n-term contingency. Once the theoretically functional background is in place, the investigation is guided entirely by pragmatics. Skinner, alluding to the Jamesian conceptualization of a stream of consciousness, acknowledged that one might also speak of behavior as continuous (Skinner, 1953). The disruption of the stream and the formation of units of analysis that lend themselves to intervention are activities by the therapist or observer. Units are pragmatic, flexible, and dependent upon the therapist's conceptualization and purpose. Whether the therapist picked the "right" unit is an experimental question to be answered by its utility: if the intervention shows the desired results, an appropriate unit was chosen. Often there is a variety of levels of analysis one can choose. In the case of smoking, for example, the positive reinforcer may be conceptualized as the stimulation of cholinergic receptors and its physiological consequences. On another scale of analysis, smoking may be conceptualized as being maintained by the avoidance of withdrawal effects, where withdrawal effects function as a negative reinforcer. Alternatively, one may think of smoking as being maintained by the access to guaranteed social reinforcers, i.e., access to the smoking group that gathers on porches and balconies at parties and that provides an immediate commonality, smoking. In each case, the intervention differs. While nicotine replacement and slow titration of the dose may lead to abstinence in the first two examples, the last example requires an intervention that includes a social skills training component. Reinforcers and punishers thus can be conceptualized from a molecular to a molar scale, and so can behavior. As we shall see, however, adding an analysis of language to behavioral thinking focuses the analysis on a smaller set of likely possibilities, which is one of its sources of applied utility.

Behaviors that may look topographically different may belong to the same *functional* class. The opening of a door may be accomplished with many different topographies, such as turning a knob, pressing a bar, pulling a handle, nudging with one's hip, or pushing with a foot. In all cases the opening of the door, given a particular door type, will reinforce a variety of topographically dissimilar behaviors. The reader will note that this issue occurs repeatedly throughout this book. Behavioral patterns associated with post-traumatic stress disorder, for example, may be topographically dissimilar (say, drinking, unsafe sex, or social withdrawal) and yet all be maintained by the same avoidance or escape contingency (see also Hayes, Wilson, Gifford, Follette, & Strosahl, 1996).

Additionally, the topography of the class of behaviors that leads to particular consequences may vary within a lifetime. In a clinical example, a client's agoraphobic reaction may be conceptualized as a discrete behavioral event or as part of a larger pattern of behavior maintained by avoidance that permeates the client's life. While the first interpretation suggests exposure treatment in multiple settings, the second would call for the identification of reinforcers in the client's life that could be activated to establish or maintain alternative repertoires competing with avoidance. This pragmatic conceptual flexibility distinguishes behavior analytic from traditional approaches.

Respondent Conditioning

Respondent or "classical" conditioning refers to learning through stimulus-stimulus relations. The conceptualization of operant and respondent processes as distinct behavioral processes has not found empirical support (Jenkins, 1977). In general it seems to be more useful to think of these differences in terms of procedures.

In applied settings, respondent conditioning is most likely to be invoked post hoc to describe the acquisition of the psychological functions of a previously neutral event. For example, just as contiguous pairings of neutral with aversive events, such as shock, heat, or loud noise, can be used to establish events that support avoidance behavior in the laboratory, so too we can imagine how such histories might lead to aversive emotional responses in real life.

The reason that this chapter has focused almost entirely on operant procedures is that in practice, operant procedures are usually particularly effective in both establishing and undermining psychological functions of events, regardless of whether they are respondent or operant. If an event has acquired its discriminative or motivational function through respondent conditioning, this function can be modified through operant procedures (Allan, 1998; Engel, 1986a, 1986b). Exposure-based procedures, for example, may reinforce approach behaviors and extinguish escape or avoidance responding; the function of the event in question changes, regardless of whether it was established through respondent pairing or operant discriminative processes.

Sometimes researchers may refer to any procedure that does not explicitly arrange consequences as a respondent procedure. While the procedure may resemble that of respondent conditioning, the repertoires involved are often operant and have a long history of reinforcement that maintains them even in the absence of explicitly arranged consequences (e.g., Leader, Barnes, & Smeets, 1996).

Basic Behavioral Change Procedures

Reinforcing one behavior pattern while extinguishing another one is termed "differential reinforcement." Differential reinforcement accomplishes two goals: (1) it can shape novel behavior patterns, and (2) it can result in flexible and contextually appropriate repertoires.

Shaping. Shaping is the differential reinforcement of successive approximations to a target performance. A prototypical example for a shaping procedure is learning how to hit a baseball (Miller, 1997). First, a child will swing at a ball resting upon a tee. Once he or she reliably hits the ball in this stationary position, the coach will start throwing the ball to the child from a short distance with minimum speed. The criteria for distance and speed are systematically increased depending on the child's performance, i.e., after the child has met the preceding criterion reliably. Another example of shaping is children's "hot-and-cold" game, where orientation and approach to a target location are described as "hotter," while movement away from the target is labeled "colder."

Shaping also occurs in the therapeutic context. When five independent clinical psychologist raters judged interactions between Carl Rogers and a successful long-term therapy client, they found significant evidence of differential reinforcement in Rogers' client-centered therapy (Truax, 1966). Thus, therapist empathy, warmth, and acceptance systematically varied with the nature of the client's verbalizations, such that clarity of expression and positive self-statements were shaped over the duration of therapy. As with teaching a child to hit a baseball, the criterion for reinforcement might have been adjusted over time: While at first even the slightest indication of clarity or positive statement might have met with approval, the bar was raised ever so slightly throughout the therapeutic process. "Unconditional positive regard" indeed denotes the absence of punishment procedures and allows for gentle behavior change through differential reinforcement.

Discrimination training. While shaping implies a changing criterion for reinforcement, in discrimination training the delivery of reinforcers depends upon the context in which behavior occurs. When the behavior occurs more often in one situation than another, that behavior is "discriminated" or bound by context. Most, if not all, human behavior of interest to psychologists falls into this category. People implicitly assess whether others are behaving according to the social demands placed upon their behavior and evaluate behavior as appropriate to gender, age, specific roles, or socio-economic status, for example. It is important to note that this evaluation in turn has been differentially reinforced by the social or cultural context of the individual evaluator. Behavior can be contextual at several scales of analysis; and society, or on a smaller scale the therapist within session, is the arbiter of whether behavior is appropriate to the situation.

Social skills are prototypical examples of discriminated operants. Most individuals have learned to identify "a good time" to ask a favor, or "a bad time" to ask a boss for a promotion. "A good time" or "a bad time" may be substantiated by a "gut feeling," indicating that the relevant contextual variables that correlate with social success are often complex and subtle and not easily captured by instructions or rules. Because of the subtlety of the contextual cues, discrimination training usually requires the presentation of multiple examples of situations in which the behavior, or particular magnitudes of behavior, will be reinforced. These positive exemplars randomly alternate with situations in which reinforcement is not available. Multiple exemplar discrimination training is an integral component of most social skills training interventions. Interestingly, discrimination training is possible even in situations in which the coach or therapist cannot explicitly specify the criteria for reinforcement.

Azrin and Hayes (1984), for example, used multiple exemplar training to teach college-age men to identify whether similar-aged women were interested in their conversations with other men. Only the female speaker was videotaped during one-minute conversational interactions. Audio was omitted. During the baseline condition, the men gave estimates that did not closely match the degree of interest reported by the women. After a training condition consisting of feedback on the accuracy of each judgment, the accuracy of the men's estimates increased by over 50 percent and their actual social skills increased as well – even though the raters could not verbally say what they were picking up while learning to discriminate interest. Thus, discrimination training is especially useful when it is difficult to describe the detailed features upon which reinforcement is contingent, and explicit rules cannot be provided.

In addition to subtle features of events, relations among them may also discriminate the occurrence of behavior. Rapid approach of an object, for example, is one of the relations in the presence of which escape and avoidance behavior will be reinforced. Here, the relation between the position of observer and the gradually increasing occlusion of the observer's visual field governs stepping to the side, ducking, or catching the approaching object. As another example, the Doppler Effect reliably discriminates orientation to approaching or retreating vehicles. Music also provides countless examples of a relational context: Musical pieces can be identified regardless of their particular arrangement; or musical performances can be discriminated as "on" or "off key."

Most of our behavior occurs in a context that changes over time. Accordingly, regularities involved in these changes also constitute discriminanda: Facial changes due to aging, for example, occur with such specificity and regularity that we are able to replicate them with computer simulations ("morphing" faces from young to old). These regularities within change allow us to call particular changes "aging." Thus, the context to which behavior is bound does not have to be a discrete event. It can be a pattern of events dispersed in time or a relation among events.

Conditional discriminations. As the previous discussion of units of analysis showed, *n*-term contingencies can be nested at various scales. In conditional discriminations, the occurrence of a discriminated operant depends on an additional situational cue. To the chagrin of customers, for example, automated switchboards often allow the selection of a specific extension (a discriminated operant) only after a lengthy announcement has been followed by the instruction, "Select *now*." Selecting an extension before hearing this announcement is extinguished and thus often accompanied by some emotional behavior on the caller's part. Similarly, using touch screen monitors in airports, at automobile repair stores, or in banks involves the selection of specific options (itself a discriminated operant) only after the monitor's display has changed and added the relevant instructions.

Conditional discriminations can also involve relations among events. If instructed to choose the larger of three objects, a golf ball, a baseball, or a basketball, a person would choose the basketball over the baseball and the baseball over the golf ball. If asked to pick the smaller of these items, the correct choice would be different. Thus, how a relational choice is made depends or is conditional upon the presentation of the particular instruction. The training of a conditional discrimination of relations among events must present situations in such a way that the criterion for reinforcement is not tied to particular objects but to the relations among them. In other words, what remains stable and does not vary across multiple exemplars is the relationship of objects to each other based on their formal properties. Children's educational TV programs, such as Sesame Street, give countless examples of multiple exemplar training that illustrate relations, such as far-near, over-under, before-behind, or same-opposite. An extension of these conditional discriminations of events based on formal properties to abstract relations is at the heart of the modern behavior analytic account of language and cognition.

A Behavior Analysis of Language and Cognition

The Problem of Language

The modern behavior analytic account of language and cognition has emerged within the last decades and is built upon the principles described in the preceding pages. None of the principles are challenged or negated, but the unit of analysis is expanded, such that histories of conditional discrimination training relate synergistically to form complex repertoires, affecting the function of other events. While earlier attempts to provide an account of language and cognition did not emphasize the relational nature of verbal behavior (e.g., Skinner, 1957), the modern account explicitly asserts that behavior "usually labeled as verbal include[s] a referential quality [...] or generalized relations among arbitrary stimuli" (Chase & Danforth, 1991, p. 206). Thus, Skinner's (1957) analysis alluded to but failed to capture the "arbitrary, social or culturally determined relations among events in the world, symbols, pictures, gestures, and sounds" (Chase & Danforth, 1991, p. 206) that are the warp and weft of being verbal (see also Barnes-Holmes, Barnes-Holmes, & Cullinan, 2000; Sidman, 1994).

To illustrate this point, suppose a history of simple discrimination training (i.e., saying "x" in the presence of object "x" and not in the presence of object "y"). Skinner (1957) termed this behavior "tacting" and explained that "tacting" denotes that the speaker contacts the environment and provides the listener with access to events that previously only affected the speaker's behavior. The listener reinforces the speaker's tacting with social approval or by behaving with respect to the tacted events. Tacting is bound by antecedent events, but the consequences for tacting may vary.

According to Skinner, in its simplest case, the function of tacting is much like that of an instrument safety crosscheck that occurs between pilot and co-pilot in an airplane cockpit. Individuals are ascertaining that they are behaving with respect to similar events. Tacting increases in complexity as one thinks of complex social relations that occasion "crosschecks" with other members of the social group, especially if these relations only hold in certain contexts. However, problems with Skinner's definition arise when we are able to train a parrot to say "x" in the presence of object "x" and not in the presence of object "y" (e.g., Pepperberg, 2005). The parrot's behavior *looks* topographically as if it were verbal, but it does not have the common *functions* of human verbal behavior—to repeat, the "arbitrary, social or culturally determined relations among events in the world, symbols, pictures, gestures, and sounds" (Chase & Danforth, 1991, p. 206). This difference may be irrelevant to the parrot example, but it bears heavily on interventions in human language acquisition, when the establishment of rote responses in the presence of particular events may not lead to the sophisticated repertoire required for appropriate verbal functioning. Then, what other training might be necessary?

Relational Frame Theory (RFT)

RFT (Hayes, Barnes-Holmes, & Roche, 2001), supported by more than 70 studies to date (Hayes, Luoma, Bond, Masuda, & Lillis, 2006), builds upon a person's history of conditional discrimination training and adds four features capturing the function of human verbal behavior. These are arbitrary applicability, mutual entailment, combinatorial entailment, and transformation of stimulus functions.

Arbitrary applicability. There is substantial evidence that relational conditional discriminations, described above, may not only be based on the formal properties of events, but once the relation has been learned it can be applied to any situation based on contextual cues to do so. On a daily basis children ideally encounter thousands of training exemplars with feedback for these and other linguistic relations (see Moerk, 1996, for a review). For example, conditional discrimination training may lead to the identification of the larger object when presented with the word, "larger." After a prolonged conditional discrimination training history, a child will be able to tact the relations "larger" and "smaller," even when presented with other abstracted relations (e.g., the value of a nickel or "5" versus the value of a dime or "10"). Similarly, people who tact the relation "between" in a spatial context can also apply "between" to describe their political stance by noting that it is "between liberal and conservative." In other words, the relational nature of discriminations comes under the control of contextual cues other than the formal properties of the related events. The same relation applies, whether the context is concrete or abstract, but in one case it is control by formal properties and in the other by the relational context. The relation is arbitrarily applicable as a result (e.g., a nickel "is smaller than" a dime only by social convention).

Mutual entailment. A person will be able to behave with respect to relations (e.g., large-small, thick-thin, before-behind, far-near, over-under, same-opposite), even if only one of these relations is identified. Thus, a dime being larger than a nickel implies the nickel being smaller than the dime. This is called "mutual entailment" and is based on a particular history of reinforcement for behaving with respect to such entailed relations (e.g., Barnes-Holmes, Barnes-Holmes, Roche, & Smeets, 2001; Berens & Hayes, in press).

Combinatorial entailment. If multiple relations are presented, a person will be able to infer relations among these events. If, for example, one is told that A was the same as B, and B was the opposite of C, implied is that A is the opposite of C, and C is the opposite of A. Behaving with respect to the relationships among mutually entailed relations is called "combinatorial entailment." Again, regardless of the mutually entailed relation given (same-opposite, near-far, here-there, etc.), an overarching combinatorially entailed relation among common members is also implied. The emergence of explicitly untrained relations relies on an extensive training history that occurs as a matter of course in the rearing of typically developing children. This training history involves the explicit training of simple and conditional discriminations, and mutually entailed and combinatorial relations.

Transformation of stimulus functions. While a person may infer certain relations among events based upon the history just described, the events themselves may have a history of participating in operant relations, for example as punishers, reinforcers, motivators, or antecedent events. These psychological functions spread in accordance with mutually and combinatorially entailed relations: this is termed the transformation of stimulus functions. To revert to our previous example: If A functioned as a punisher, and a person were instructed that A was the same as B, and B was the opposite of C, then RFT would expect that A and B functioned as punishers while C remained neutral or functioned as a reinforcer if these stimuli were presented contingent upon behavior (Whelan & Barnes-Holmes, 2004). If, for example, a person was told that "bad," a word that presumably sets the context for social punishment contingencies, was the same as "böse," and "böse" was the

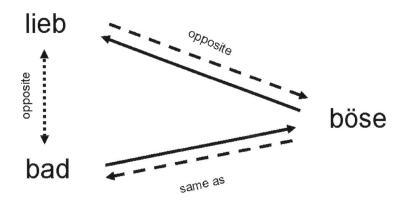

opposite of "lieb," being told that one was "lieb" would not occasion the same reaction as being told that one was "böse." Note that no further training would be necessary for these functions to emerge.

Figure 2.3 Behavior occasioned by emergent relations.

The solid arrows of Figure 2.3 depict directly trained relations; the dashed arrows depict mutually entailed relations; and the dotted double-headed arrow depicts combinatorially entailed relations. This emergence of consequential functions in accordance with the mutually and combinatorially entailed relations is called "transformation of stimulus function."

C_{rel}'s and C_{func}'s. Human language does not consist of isolated instances of utterances involving arbitrary applicability, mutual and combinatorial entailment, and transformation of stimulus function. Instead, each topographical unit (e.g., sentences, paragraphs, or chapters) contains multiple nested entailed relations and multiple possible functions, all of which differentially affect behavior. As in any discriminated operant, context regulates these actions. RFT distinguishes between two kinds of context: the relational context (C_{rel}) and the functional context (C_{func}) [the "C" stands for "context" in both abbreviations]. In the above example, the word "same" constitutes the relational context for a specific kind of relational response in the presence of "bad" and "böse" (the "relata"), while the word "opposite" sets the occasion for yet another type of relational response in the presence of "böse" and "lieb." Here, "same" and "opposite" function as C_{rel}'s. On the other hand, C_{func}'s refer to the context occasioning the transformation of behavioral functions in accordance with the entailed relations. Each event may have a history of multiple behavioral functions, and C_{func}'s are the contexts that govern the transformation. For example, told that "lieb" is also the same as "dear," being called "lieb" may reinforce behavior in a familial or romantic context but punish it in a professional context; or hearing the word may set the occasion for approach in the familial context and for escape or avoidance in the professional one. C_{func}'s would be necessary to disambiguate the behavioral functions.

C_{rel}'s and C_{func}'s are originally established directly, through a history of discrimination training; but as relational operants emerge they can be established indirectly, through entailed relations. Both C_{rel}'s and C_{func}'s can be identified in the context of larger functional verbal units, such as found in instructions (O'Hara, Barnes-Holmes, Roche, & Smeets, 2004), metaphors (Stewart & Barnes-Holmes, 2001), analogies (for a review see Stewart & Barnes-Holmes, 2004), logic, and problem-solving. C_{rel}'s and C_{func}'s locally regulate the continuously ongoing stream of behavior and become integrated with observed, sophisticated verbal repertoires. They are not limited to particular words or phrases, however. Tone of voice, pauses, gestures, whole conversations, or aspects of previous interactions with an individual can all function as C_{rel}'s and C_{func}'s for later interactions ("inside jokes" would be an example for the latter). According to RFT, without such abstracted contextual control, the automaticity of human language processes would be impossible.

The interaction of cognitions with other behavior. The processes of mutual and combinatorial entailment and transformation of stimulus function could be termed "automatic inferences," but the RFT account greatly improves upon traditional interpretations by providing an experimentally supported account of how cognitions and behavior may interact. Through transformation of stimulus function, RFT accounts for how events that have never been encountered obtain psychological meaning.

Suppose a person experiences a panic attack in a small local store and subsequently avoids leaving the home. During treatment, the client is asked to rank (C_{rel}) potential anxiety-provoking (C_{func}) locations, and paradoxically ranks the local store in which the first panic attack was experienced as less anxiety-provoking than Harrod's department store in London, which in fact the person has never visited. To the extent that the person has a history of describing Harrod's as "larger than" or "busier than" the local store, these multiple comparisons may come to bear upon the ranking of anxiety-provoking locations. "Ranking" (C_{rel}) provided the common context for application of the comparative relations. As a result, although never visited, Harrod's may occasion more avoidance behavior than the local store.

To illustrate how humans acquire such a complex repertoire of behaving with respect to entailed relations virtually "automatically," let us use imitation as a familiar example. Children's imitative behavior is shaped by first explicitly arranging reinforcement for "doing what the model does" in specific situations (clapping hands, stomping feet, tapping fingers, making faces). As the number of exemplars increases, the correspondence between the child's and the model's behavior starts to guide the child's behavior, for it is this relation that remains constant across opportunities for reinforcement.

As with imitative behavior, the relations that have frequently provided the criteria for reinforcement in conditional discrimination training situations come to govern behavior without additional environmental support, i.e., no particular prompts have to be given for the behavior to occur. However, the behavior continues to contact social and other reinforcers. The difference between imitative repertoires and the ones just described in the "Harrod's" example is that the criterion for reinforcement ("match the model") can be described in fewer words than the history of conditional discrimination training that leads to combinatorial entailment and transformation of stimulus function. Note that the ease of description by the psychologist is not an indicator for the ease with which these repertoires are acquired and performed. Describing the contingencies that operate upon "walking," for example, is a quite daunting task, yet walking is acquired by almost everybody.

RFT does not question or alter the history of conditional discrimination training necessary for the acquisition of complex repertoires; instead, it emphasizes that the criteria for reinforcement continue to govern behavior in the absence of explicitly arranged contingencies as the contexts influencing such responding (C_{rel}'s and C_{func}'s) become increasingly abstract. It posits that people's extensive verbal histories of reinforcement lead to an almost automatic application of mutual and combinatorial entailment to any encountered situation. The extensive history of trained conditional discriminations among relations bears on all verbal utterances, everything a person says or thinks. RFT is a logical extension of explicitly arranged conditional discrimination training and accounts for many verbal phenomena, such as generativity, figurative language in general, and vocabulary spurts in childhood in particular (Barnes-Holmes, Barnes-Holmes, & Cullinan, 2001; Stewart, Barnes-Holmes, Hayes, & Lipkens, 2001).

Rule-Governed Behavior

Because multiple contingencies operate upon behavior, the influence of emergent stimulus functions partly depends on the availability of alternative reinforcers that support behaviors competing with those functions. This interplay between multiple contingencies (such as that shown in the bottom panel of Figure 2.1) is studied under the topic of rule-governed behavior. Note that any instances of verbal behavior analyzed under this and the following rubrics involve arbitrary applicability, mutual entailment, combinatorial entailment, and transformation of stimulus function. These characteristics may not be independently verified or discussed but are implied by the scope of the analysis. As outlined above, transformation of stimulus function in accordance with entailed relations describes how events that have not been experienced come to affect behavior.

Behavior that is bound or discriminated by a particular verbal context is called "rule-governed." A person's typing repertoire quickly illustrates the difference between rule-governed and contingency-shaped behavior: When typing is first learned, a person may recite each letter and its respective keyboard position and tentatively move the respective fingers on the keyboard to produce the desired result. "Same" and "before/after" relations (O'Hara, Barnes-Holmes, Roche, & Smeets, 2004), as to what letter corresponds to the movement of which finger and to what effect, may guide the initial acquisition. As a person's repertoire becomes more fluent, it becomes less dependent on particular rules. Consequences in the forms of typos on the screen or annoying beeps by the computer shape proficiency, until thinking about which finger to move actually interrupts the now fluent performance. Behavior that was first entirely rule-governed gradually becomes more and more affected by the direct contingencies. Most skills are acquired in this fashion: An expert chef, for example, may not be able to state the rule by which he or she decides upon the final touches of a meal, although cooking was initially verbally instructed. Ideally, the degree of verbal control wanes.

Augmenting. An augmental is a particular type of instruction that changes the reinforcing or punishing effectiveness of an event through the transformation of stimulus functions according to entailed relations. Formative augmentals are those that establish events as reinforcers or punishers (e.g., being told that one is able to exchange a paper ticket for a promotional item; see also Whelan & Barnes-Holmes, 2004), while motivative augmentals increase or decrease the effectiveness of already established events. Again, whether the event actually comes to function as a reinforcer or a punisher is only evident by the effect on the behavior over time. To the degree that the augmental facilitates contact with the actual reinforcing or punishing contingencies, it might facilitate tracking which we discuss below.

Pliance. Rule-following can be conceptualized as two additional categories, pliance and tracking. Similarly to the earlier example of imitation, where "doing what the model does" is the occasion for reinforcement, in pliance the correspondence between a person's behavior and what that person has been told to do provides the context in which pliance is reinforced (Zettle & Hayes, 1982). Because only a social/verbal community could discriminate and differentially reinforce the rule-behavior correspondence, the reinforcers for pliance are always socially mediated, but it is the unit that is reinforced, not the type of reinforcer, that defines pliance. Pliance occurs across a variety of situations and is maintained by real or perceived social demands and not by the demands of the actual situation. Milgram's (1963) classic study of obedience, where nearly two-thirds of the subjects complied with instructions to administer increasing levels of shock to a confederate despite signs of the presumed victim's distress, illustrates how pliance can overwhelm appropriate social behavior. Although pliance is established by a rule-giver who reinforces correspondence with a particular rule or request, the verbal processes described above may extend pliance to self-generated demands that are maintained by verbally constructed social communities (e.g., "my mother is watching me from heaven"). For these reasons pliance can be greatly over-extended, and people may rigidly fulfill these demands even when they run counter to the actual contingencies. Hence, pliance can be a major source of clinical distress.

Tracking. Tracking is rule-governed behavior maintained by contingencies (Zettle & Hayes, 1982), that are contacted based upon the formal properties of behavior regulated by a rule. The consequences may be of any kind, including social consequences – what defines it as tracking is that the behavior itself (not the fact that the behavior was occasioned by a rule) produces the consequence. Closely following written driving directions, for example, may be necessary to find one's way for a first visit to a friend's home. Random driving may have led to the same result –the arrival at the friend's home is determined solely by the formal properties of the driving, however it was produced. In that sense, the reinforcers for tracking are not arbitrary.

It is impossible to determine whether a particular instance of following a rule constitutes pliance or tracking, because pliance and tracking are antecedent-behavior-consequent relations that occur over time. Generally speaking, pliance will persist regardless of the ultimate utility of the behavior because it involves an extensive history of reinforcement for rule-following per se that may compete with other available consequences. Conversely, tracking repertoires will adjust and be further refined by the situation at hand. Establishing repertoires may first require pliance; as the individual comes in contact with natural contingencies, tracking repertoires emerge. Such is the case when a couple engages in communication skill training during marriage counseling. The first few instances of following the rules may be maintained by the therapist's approval or praise. With practice, the couple may be able to use the skills dependent upon their impact in actual situations; the instructions from therapy have functioned to track the social utility of these communication skills. Similarly a young child may learn not to go into the street to avoid parental punishment; later, not going into the street may be a matter of avoiding cars.

In the absence of a skill deficit, excessive pliance may be implicated when it appears that an individual's verbal behavior is the only obstacle to more effective action in a particular situation. "Same" and "before/after" relations governing behavior maintained by avoidance are especially problematic, for–as long as the aversive event does not occur, regardless of its likelihood–the rule-following is reinforced. Additionally, if a person's verbal community has slowly shaped a person's description of his or her own performance without particular regard to the relevant behavior-environment contingencies, the performance itself is more likely to be consistent with the verbal description and less likely to track changes in the actually prevailing environmental contingencies (Catania, Matthews, & Shimoff, 1982). Thus, even when behavior looks as if it were tracking contingencies, only a change in those contingencies reveals whether the person's behavior is indeed flexible and adjusts to current demands (Hayes, Brownstein, Haas, & Greenway, 1986). Because of the risk of producing rigid rule-following given the social demand characteristics of the therapeutic setting, Hayes et al. (1986) advise considerable care when using instructions. As a general guideline, general, experiential, or metaphorical rules support more flexibility.

Other Behavior of Clinical Interest

Manding. While being vague may be advisable when providing instructions, manding benefits from conciseness and specificity. If a particular verbal utterance is always followed by the same listener-initiated consequences (Skinner, 1957) and, to be consistent with the modern account, participates in multiple "arbitrary, social or culturally determined relations" (Chase & Danforth, 1991, p. 206), the speaker is said to engage in "manding." Manding differs from "demanding" or "requesting" because it is defined by its function rather than syntactic properties of the utterance. Thus, if saying, "the food is bland," is always followed by an array of salts and spices on the table, the person is effectively manding these consequences. Like tacting, manding for novel events (as transformation of stimulus function) also occurs in accordance with a history of conditional discrimination training involving arbitrary and entailed relations (Murphy, Barnes-Holmes, & Barnes-Holmes, 2005). While Skinner posited a direct history of reinforcement for manding (but see "magical mands," Skinner, 1957, p. 48), the modern account allows for emergence through indirect and relational processes.

Because many individuals have difficulty expressing their needs, deficient mand repertoires are often therapeutic targets. Especially in couple therapy, one may observe one partner who consistently mands with statements that are not identifiable as demands or requests, and the other partner who displays excessive pliance. Under these conditions, the latter partner may complain of too heavy demands, while the former partner reports never asking for anything. Generally, non-specific and imprecise mands can be a source of much interpersonal tension.

Like all verbal operants, the frequency of a particular mand depends upon its effectiveness in producing consequences. If concise manding is occurring at a low rate, it may have been extinguished or punished. Assertiveness training is partially targeted at helping individuals to mand more effectively.

Tacting. As described earlier, Skinner's (1957) conceptualization of "tacting" as verbal behavior governed by a non-verbal event and reinforced by the social community does not explicitly reflect the relational aspects of human language studied by RFT. However, when "tacting" is considered more broadly (i.e., when a behavioral history of arbitrary applicability, mutual and combinatorial entailment, and transformation of stimulus function is assumed and behavior with respect to emergent—rather than directly trained—stimulus functions becomes possible), then the category of "tacting" is also one of clinical utility.

Tacting is verbal behavior bound by a specific non-verbal context that remains invariable (e.g., saying "table" in the presence of any table). The function of tacting may be to direct the listener to particular aspects of the context or of the speaker's behavior, to identify particular features of the situation, or to describe a situation that is inaccessible to the listener. The reinforcement contingencies for tacting involve nonspecific approval (e.g., praise, confirmation, or gratitude) for the accurate identification of particular events.

The correspondence between the described and the actual state of affairs is of special interest when events are inaccessible to the listener, or private. Given that inaccessibility, how do speakers learn to reliably report? Skinner (1945) suggested that correspondence is likely to be reinforced when the listener can rely on collateral events, collateral behavior, a history with similar events under accessible conditions, or metaphorical speech to determine the accuracy of the report (see also Stewart, Barnes-Holmes, Hayes, & Lipkens, 2001).

Private events are often accompanied by public collateral events, as when reports of nausea come with pallor. Collateral behavior may be holding one's stomach or vomiting. Both types of collaterals may make it more likely that a caregiver reinforces a child's report of nausea by keeping him or her home from school, thereby teaching the child to tact "nausea." Later, the history of speaking of nausea with public collaterals may lead to reliable tacting when these collaterals are not present. Alternatively, for more sophisticated speakers, relations applicable to different contexts may be used to describe one's ailment, e.g., "my stomach is churning." Importantly, private events participate in the relational processes described earlier (see also DeGrandpre, Bickel, & Higgins, 1992), suggesting that private events may be able to take on novel and emergent functions.

The verbal community shapes the tacting of private events in the same fashion as the tacting of public events. Note that the private-public distinction is defined by the observer's accessibility to the relations that occasion the tact; public and private events are not different in kind or differentially amenable to scientific study. In the therapeutic situation, the client's current out-of-session context and history constitute private events to which the therapist does not have access.

The interesting implication of tacting, as conceptualized above, is that an individual's skill of reliably tacting private events depends largely upon the practices of the social community. Social milieus that fail to establish correspondence between the reporting of private experiences and the social interpretation of the actual events have been characterized as invalidating: "An invalidating environment is one in which communication of private experience is met by erratic, inappropriate, and extreme responses" (Linehan, 1993, p. 49). In the absence of an effective tact repertoire for private experiences, individuals may present with flat or inappropriate affect, or they may escalate as responding shifts from tacting an event to manding for the audience to affirm the observation. Thus, an individual's social audience can unduly influence the reliability of tacting by imposing a threat of punishment, an opportunity to gain favors, or by reinforcing a particular report over another, regardless of correspondence (see Loftus, 2003, for a review of audience effects on memory). From this view, exaggerating, lying, or escalating are behaviors warranted by a client's history and current circumstances.

Conclusion

Behavior analysis (for a review see Baum, 1994; for philosophy, see Chiesa, 1994) is an evolving approach that involves verbally tacting antecedent-behavior-consequence relations. This job has become more complex with an appreciation of the important role of relational operants and rule-governance, but it is no less a form of behavior analysis.

All interventions in this book build upon the basic principles reviewed in this chapter. One can use them directly to facilitate contact with the larger antecedent-behavior-consequence patterns affecting clients' lives in order to relieve suffering and empower a more effective style of living. But applying these principles often is helped by middle level constructs that economically describe and integrate a wide range of behavioral concepts and their extension into the behavior analysis of language and cognition. These facilitative middle level constructs will be covered in the next chapter.

References

Allan, R. W. (1998). Operant-respondent interactions. In W. O'Donohue (Ed.), *Learning and behavior therapy* (pp. 146-168). Needham Heights, MA: Allyn & Bacon.

Azrin, R. D., & Hayes, S. C. (1984). The discrimination of interest within a heterosexual interaction: Training, generalization, and effects on social skills. *Behavior Therapy, 15,* 173-184.

Barnes-Holmes, D., Barnes-Holmes, Y., & Cullinan, V. (2000). Relational frame theory and Skinner's *Verbal Behavior*: A possible synthesis. *The Behavior Analyst, 23,* 69-84.

Barnes-Holmes, Y., Barnes-Holmes, D., & Cullinan, V. (2001). Education. In S. C. Hayes, D. Barnes-Holmes, & B. Roche (Eds.), *Relational frame theory: A post-Skinnerian account of human language* (pp. 181-195). New York: Kluwer Academic/Plenum Publishers.

Barnes-Holmes, Y., Barnes-Holmes, D., Roche, B., & Smeets, P. (2001). Exemplar training and a derived transformation of function in accordance with symmetry. *The Psychological Record, 51,* 287-308.

Baum, W. M. (1994). *Understanding behaviorism: Science, behavior, and culture.* New York: Harper Collins.

Berens, N. M., & Hayes, S. C. (in press). Arbitrarily applicable comparative relations: Experimental evidence for a relational operant. *Journal of Applied Behavior Analysis.*

Catania, A. C., Matthews, B. A., & Shimoff, E. (1982). Instructed versus shaped human verbal behavior: Interactions with nonverbal responding. *Journal of the Experimental Analysis of Behavior, 38,* 233-248.

Chase, P. N., & Danforth, J. S. (1991). The role of rules in concept learning. In L. J. Hayes & P. N. Chase (Eds.), *Dialogues on verbal behavior* (pp. 205-225). Reno, NV: Context Press.

Chiesa, M. (1994). *Radical behaviorism: The philosophy and the science.* Boston: Authors Cooperative, Inc.

DeGrandpre, R. J., Bickel, W. K., & Higgins, S. T. (1992). Emergent equivalence relations between interoceptive (drug) and exteroceptive (visual) stimuli. *Journal of the Experimental Analysis of Behavior, 58,* 9-18.

Eifert, G. H. (1996). More theory-driven and less diagnosis-based behavior therapy. *Journal of Behavior Therapy and Experimental Psychiatry, 27,* 75-86.

Engel, B. T. (1986a). An essay on the circulation as behavior. *Behavioral and Brain Sciences, 9,* 285-295.

Engel, B. T. (1986b). If it looks like a duck, walks like a duck, and quacks like a duck, it's a duck: Neurally mediated responses of the circulation are behavior. *Behavioral and Brain Sciences, 9,* 307-318.

Epstein, R. (1985). Extinction-induced resurgence: Preliminary investigations and possible implications. *Psychological Record, 35,* 143-153.

Follette, W. C., Naugle, A. E., & Linnerooth, P. J. N. (2000). Functional alternatives to traditional assessment and diagnosis. In M. J. Dougher (Ed.), *Clinical behavior analysis* (pp. 99-125). Reno, NV: Context Press.

Hayes, S. C., Barnes-Holmes, D., & Roche, B. T. (Eds.). (2001). *Relational frame theory: A post-Skinnerian account of human language and cognition.* New York: Plenum.

Hayes, S. C., Brownstein, A. J., Haas, J. R., & Greenway, D. E. (1986). Instructions, multiple schedules, and extinction: Distinguishing rule-governed from schedule-controlled behavior. *Journal of the Experimental Analysis of Behavior, 46,* 137-147.

Hayes, S. C., Hayes, L. J., & Reese, H. W. (1988). Finding the philosophical core: A review of Stephen C. Pepper's World Hypotheses. *Journal of the Experimental Analysis of Behavior, 50,* 97-111.

Hayes, S. C., Luoma, J. B., Bond, F. W., Masuda, A., & Lillis, J. (2006). Acceptance and commitment therapy: Model, processes and outcomes. *Behaviour Research and Therapy, 44,* 1-25.

Hayes, S. C., Wilson, K. G., Gifford, E. V., Follette, V. M., & Strosahl, K. D. (1996). Emotional avoidance and behavioral disorders: A functional dimensional approach to diagnosis and treatment. *Journal of Consulting and Clinical Psychology, 64,* 1152-1168.

Higgins, S. T., Hughes, J. R., & Bickel, W. K. (1989). Effects of d-amphetamine on choice of social versus monetary reinforcement: A discrete-trial test. *Pharmacology, Biochemistry and Behavior, 34,* 297-301.

Hineline, P. N. (1980). The language of behavior analysis: Its community, its functions, and its limitations. *Behaviorism, 8,* 67-86.

Hops, H., Biglan, A., Sherman, L., & Arthur, J. (1987). Home observations of family interactions of depressed women. *Journal of Consulting & Community Psychology, 55,* 341-346.

Jenkins, H. M. (1977). Sensitivity of different response systems to stimulus-reinforcer and response-reinforcer relations. In H. Davis & H. M. B. Hurwitz (Eds.), *Operant-Pavlovian interactions* (pp. 47-66). Mahwah, NJ: Lawrence Erlbaum Associates, Inc.

Leader, G., Barnes, D., & Smeets, P. M. (1996). Establishing equivalence relations using a respondent-type training procedure. *The Psychological Record, 46,* 685-706.

Linehan, M. M. (1993). *Cognitive-behavioral treatment of borderline personality disorder.* New York: Guilford.

Loftus, E. F. (2003). Make-believe memories. *American Psychologist, 58,* 867-873.

Madsen, C. H., Becker, W. C., Thomas, D. R., Koser, L., & Plager, E. (1968). An analysis of the reinforcing function of "sit-down" commands. In R. K. Parker (Ed.), *Readings in educational psychology* (pp. 265-278). Boston: Allyn & Bacon.

Milgram, S. (1963). Behavioral study of obedience. *Journal of Abnormal and Social Psychology, 67,* 371-378.

Miller, L. K. (1997). *Principles of everyday behavior analysis* (3rd ed.). New York: Brooks/Cole Publishing Company.

Moerk, E. L. (1996). Input and language learning processes in first language acquisition. In H. W. Reese (Vol. Ed.), *Advances in child development and behavior* (Vol. 26, pp. 181-228). New York: Academic Press.

Morgan, D. L., & Lee, K. (1996). Extinction-induced response variability in humans. *The Psychological Record, 46,* 146-160.

Murphy, C., Barnes-Holmes, D., & Barnes-Holmes, Y. (2005). Derived manding in children with autism: Synthesizing Skinner's *Verbal Behavior* with relational frame theory. *Journal of Applied Behavior Analysis, 38,* 445-462.

O'Brien, W. H., McGrath, J. J., & Haynes, S. N. (2003). Assessment of psychopathology with behavioral approaches. In J. R. Graham & J. A. Nagleri (Eds.), *Handbook of psychology: Vol. 10. Assessment psychology* (pp. 509-529). New York: John Wiley & Sons, Inc.

O'Hara, D., Barnes-Holmes, D., Roche, B., & Smeets, P. (2004). Derived relational networks and control by novel instructions: A possible model of generative verbal responding. *The Psychological Record, 54,* 437-460.

Patterson, G. R. (1982). *Coercive family process.* Eugene, OR: Castalia Publishing Co.

Pepperberg, I. M. (2005). An avian perspective on language evolution: Implications of simultaneous development of vocal and physical object combinations by a grey parrot (psittacus erithacus). In M. Tallerman (Ed.), *Language origins: Perspectives on evolution* (pp. 239-261). Oxford: Oxford University Press.

Pierce, W. D., & Epling, W. F. (1991). Activity anorexia: An animal model and theory of human self-starvation. In A. Boulton, G. Baker, & M. Martin-Iverson (Eds.), *Neuromethods: Vol. 18. Animal models in psychiatry I* (pp. 267-312). Clifton, NJ: Humana Press.

Podlesnik, C. A., Jimenez-Gomez, C., & Shahan, T. A. (2006). Resurgence of alcohol seeking produced by discontinuing non-drug reinforcement as an animal model of drug relapse. *Behavioural Pharmacology, 17,* 369-374.

Rooker, G. W., & Roscoe, E. M. (2005). Functional analysis of self-injurious behavior and its relation to self-restraint. *Journal of Applied Behavior Analysis, 38,* 537-542.

Sidman, M. (1989). *Coercion and its fallout.* Boston: Authors Cooperative, Inc.

Sidman, M. (1994). *Equivalence relations and behavior: A research story*. Boston: Authors Cooperative, Inc.

Skinner, B. F. (1938). *The behavior of organisms*. New York: Appleton-Century-Crofts.

Skinner, B. F. (1945). The operational analysis of psychological terms. *Psychological Review, 52,* 270-277.

Skinner, B. F. (1953). *Science and human behavior*. New York: Macmillan.

Skinner, B. F. (1957). *Verbal behavior*. Englewood Cliffs, NJ: Prentice Hall, Inc.

Snycerski, S., Laraway, S., & Poling, A. (2000). Basic research with humans. In A. Poling & T. Byrne (Eds.), *Introduction to behavioral pharmacology* (pp. 111-139). Reno, NV: Context Press.

Stewart, I., & Barnes-Holmes, D. (2001). Understanding metaphor: A relational frame perspective. *Behavior Analyst, 24,* 191-199.

Stewart, I., & Barnes-Holmes, D. (2004). Relational frame theory and analogical reasoning: Empirical investigation. *International Journal of Psychology & Psychological Therapy, 4,* 241-262.

Stewart, I., Barnes-Holmes, D., Hayes, S. C., & Lipkens, R. (2001). Relations among relations: Analogies, metaphors, and stories. In S. C. Hayes, D. Barnes-Holmes, & B. Roche (Eds.), *Relational frame theory: A post-Skinnerian account of human language and cognition* (pp. 73-86). New York: Kluwer Academic/Plenum Publishers.

Truax, C. B. (1966). Reinforcement and non-reinforcement in Rogerian psychotherapy. *Journal of Abnormal Psychology, 71,* 1-9.

Van Houten, R. (1983). Punishment: From the animal laboratory to the applied setting. In S. Axelrod & J. Apsche (Eds.), *The effects of punishment on human behavior* (pp. 13-42). New York: Academic Press.

Whelan, R., & Barnes-Holmes, D. (2004). The transformation of consequential functions in accordance with the relational frames of same and opposite. *Journal of the Experimental Analysis of Behavior, 82,* 177-196.

Wilson, K. G., & Hayes, S. C. (1996). Resurgence of derived stimulus relations. *Journal of the Experimental Analysis of Behavior, 66,* 267-281.

Zettle, R., & Hayes, S. C. (1982). Rule-governed behavior: A potential theoretical framework for cognitive-behavioral therapy. *Advances in Cognitive-Behavioral Research and Therapy, 1,* 73-118.

Chapter 3

Applied Extensions
of Behavior Principles:
Applied Behavioral Concepts
and Behavioral Theories

Steven C. Hayes, Akihiko Masuda, Chad Shenk,
James E. Yadavaia, Jennifer Boulanger, Roger Vilardaga,
Jennifer Plumb, Lindsay Fletcher, Kara Bunting, Michael Levin,
Thomas J. Waltz, & Mikaela J. Hildebrandt
University of Nevada, Reno

Behavioral principles are analytic concepts that allow us to parse complex situations into functional units. They have served us well in applied psychology, but in many situations higher level concepts are needed to provide effective guidance. For example, the principle of reinforcement tells us a major way that responses strengthen, but it does not tell us in the applied area which responses to focus on, what the reinforcers are, how best to change them, how multiple schedules will interact, and so on. The situation faced by a behavioral clinician is like a person wanting to build a house and having only a set of tools and rules about how to use them, but no architectural plans. Applied behavior analysts have developed methods to deal with some of these problems (e.g., functional analytic methods to identify functional reinforcers), but these have not always scaled into all areas of clinical work because when language and cognition intrude, the problems of target specification and contingency analysis increases exponentially.

In contrasts, empirical clinical psychology and related areas have attempted to avoid the need for linkage to basic principles merely by identifying techniques that work, but such efforts are unlikely to be successful as the basis of a clinical science for three major reasons (Hayes, 1998). Advances in clinical science are severely limited when they are based solely on specific formally-defined techniques because without theory we have (a) no basis for using our knowledge when confronted with a new problem or situation, (b) no systematic means to develop new techniques, and (c) no way to create a coherent and teachable body of knowledge.

In other areas of applied science, middle level concepts integrated into overarching theories help scale the most basic principles into complex situations. For example, a structural engineer can use knowledge about arches or triangulation of braces to build strong structures, knowing that these concepts are systematically linked to basic principles in physics, but without having to redo the work linking them each time a building is designed.

Middle-level concepts organized into a theory are relatively uncommon in behavior analysis. Previous attempts to define such concepts within behavioral psychology were held back by the unfortunate legacy of S-R learning theory. In the hands of S-R learning theorists, theory in behavioral psychology became a useless way station, systematically organized in a way that could not have applied impact.

Despite the fact that he was proposing a naturalistic concept, Tolman (1936) planted the seed for the difficulties with his concept of *intervening variables*. He proposed that "mental events may be conceived as objectively defined intervening variables... to be defined wholly operationally" (p. 101). As MacCorquodale and Meehl (1948) point out, Tolman's intervening variables were naturalistic, not mentalistic. They were merely short-hand for observed functional relations. But S-R learning theorists increasingly used the idea of intervening variables in a loose way, eventually arriving at true hypothetical constructs: Concepts that were *not* naturalistic descriptions of functional relations but were hypothetical entities. They explained the need for such concepts by claiming that if functional relations were "always the same ... then we would have no need of theory" (Spence, 1944, p. 51), and even adding the idea that theoretical constructs are "guesses as to what variables *other than the ones under the control of the experimenter* are determining the response" (Spence, 1944, p. 51, italics added).

In other words, in the hands of the S-R learning theorists, theory explicated what you could not see and could not manipulate. This definition of theory is useless to applied workers who theories that suggest how to manipulate events to change what they and their clients see. It is no wonder that Skinner rejected theory defined this way (1950), because it is antithetical to achieving prediction-and-influence as goals of behavioral science.

Behavior analytic psychology has a very different approach. It begins with careful *behavioral observations:* refined and precise descriptions of behavioral phenomena in well-characterized contexts. The functional relationship between behavioral phenomena and contextual events are organized into *behavioral principles:* ways of speaking about these relations that are precise and broad in scope, allowing behavioral phenomena to be both predicted *and* influenced. Specific complex phenomena are unpacked through *functional analysis:* the application of behavioral principles to a specific behavioral history and form. These are then organized into systematic and generally applicable sets of functional analyses of important classes of behavioral observations. When we have that level we have a *behavioral theory*. Theories of this kind are "analytic-abstractive" in that they are inductive generalizations that sit atop abstractions and analyses based on the observational level.

Behavioral theories of this kind have expanded the field of behavior analysis to the human problems to which behavior analysts have traditionally paid little attention. A prime example is the effort to expand behavioral approach to the experimental analysis of human language and cognition.

There are several reasons why the careful understanding of symbolic behavior and its application to behavioral problems are crucial in the field of clinical behavioral analysis. First, in many setting, such as adult outpatient work, behavior change is usually achieved through a verbal exchange between the client and therapist. Typically, the therapist does not have a direct or full access to the environment where the client's presenting problems occurs. Given this lack of environmental control, the therapist attempts to change the client's behavior somewhat indirectly through verbal interactions with the client (Anderson, Hawkins, & Scotti, 1997). Even in the context where the therapist has direct access to client's environment, verbal exchanges between client and therapist are inevitable.

Second, human verbal behavior is pervasive (Hayes, 2004; Hayes, Barnes-Holmes, & Roche, 2001; Skinner, 1957). Language-able individuals interact with the environment verbally and these verbal and cognitive processes become a significant source of behavior regulation. For instance, even a simple response such as burning one's hand on a stove most likely will generate a verbal rule to not touch the stove again when it is hot. Then, touching hot stoves with bare hands is avoided in the future based on both this painful experience and the generation of rule.

Third, a substantial body of evidence suggests that verbal processes change the function of other behavioral processes (Hayes et al., 2001; for a powerful experimental example of how relational learning alters classical and operant conditioning see Dougher, Hamilton, Fink, & Harrington, in press). For example, suppose a person who has a verbal rule "medication eliminates painful disease," experiences headache, takes medicine for it, and has the headache go away. If this person later has the thought "anxiety is painful disease" a prior history of relational learning may lead the person to take medication to control the anxiety. Anxiety become a kind of discriminative stimulus but its functions are *indirectly* learned.

Traditional behavior analysis and therapy focused on changing problematic overt behavior and emotional responses, or "first-order" change. Verbal and cognitive processes were construed entirely within the framework of direct applications of respondent and operant conditioning (Mowrer, 1947; Skinner, 1957). Given the lack of a more refined account of human language and cognition, cognitive therapy (CT) emerged in the 1970s and focused on the regulatory function of cognition interpreted in a more common sense or clinical way. Following the first-order change approach, CT attempted to replace problematic cognitions with more accurate and often more positive ones.

The recent emergence of acceptance- and mindfulness-based cognitive behavioral therapy have produced another alternative. Examples of third wave behavioral and cognitive therapies include Dialectical Behavior Therapy (DBT; Linehan, 1993a), Acceptance and Commitment Therapy (ACT; Hayes, Strosahl, & Wilson, 1999), Functional Analytic Psychotherapy (FAP; Kohlenberg & Tsai, 1991), Integrative Behavioral Couples Therapy (IBCT; Christensen, Jacobson, & Babcock, 1995; Jacobson, Christensen, Prince, Cordova, & Eldridge, 2000), Mindfulness Based Cognitive Therapy (MBCT; Segal, Williams, & Teasdale, 2002), and several others (e.g., Borkovec & Roemer, 1994; McCullough, 2000; Marlatt, 2002; Martell,

Addis, & Jacobson, 2001; Roemer & Orsillo, 2002). As a group they have ventured into areas traditionally reserved for the less empirical wings of psychotherapy, emphasizing such issues as acceptance, mindfulness, cognitive defusion, dialectics, values, and spirituality. An overarching theme that unite these therapies is an emphasis on contextual influences on human behavior and a functional approach to cognition and emotion in which the person's relationship to thoughts and feelings (or "second order" change) is targeted in addition to first order behavior change.

The emergence of these therapies not only provides alternative methods for psychological and behavioral problems but also expands the theoretical possibilities regarding the mechanisms of change in therapy. In the present chapter, we will first discuss a clinical behavioral account of psychopathology followed by its applied extensions in clinical practices. We will rely in particular on the middle level concepts from Relational Frame Theory (RFT; Hayes et al., 2001) reviewed in the previous chapter, and from third wave behavior therapy, especially ACT, DBT, and FAP. These will help explain the extensions discussed in other chapters in the present volume as authors attempt to consider how first and second wave behavioral and cognitive therapy can be extended to account more fully for psychopathology.

Clinical Behavioral Analytic Account of Psychopathology: Psychological Inflexibility

From a clinical behavior analytic perspective, psychopathology can be construed as an issue of the narrowness, rigidity, or imbalance of behavioral repertoires. From this perspective, the goal of treatment is to increase the expansion and flexibility in specific client's behavioral repertoires in a particular context. Behavioral flexibility, in this sense, is construed as the ongoing behavioral process of contacting the present situation (thought of both externally and internally) more fully and based on what the situation affords, changing or persisting in behavior in the service of chosen values not avoidance of experience (Hayes, 2004; Hayes, Strosahl, Bunting, Twohig, & Wilson, 2004).

A client's presenting problem(s) can be thought of in part as an unbalanced set of behavioral repertoires, including *behavioral excesses* of maladaptive or avoidance behaviors and *behavioral deficits* of skillful and rather adaptable behaviors (Martin & Pear, 1996). Clinical behavior analysis treats these problems functionally in order to understand how such behavior patterns are maintained and to find ways to alter these patterns (Hawkins, 1979; Hayes, Nelson, Jarrett, 1987).

As this perspective is expanded into the cognitive domain, clinical behavior analysis focuses more so on the impact of the behavior-regulatory *function* of cognition in a given contextual without directly challenging its occurrence and form, however. For example, the drinking behavior of an emotionally avoidant alcoholic responding to urges to drink is understood not just as too much drinking but also too much control by a verbally entangled antecedent (Wilson & Hayes, 2000), and by the excessive or unnecessary maintaining role of a reduction of negative emotional and cognitive events through alcohol.

Behavioral deficits of a particular type of behavior may occur due to the strong stimulus control of a verbal antecedent that occasion alternative or competing behavior. For example, a person with agoraphobia may not leave home because of rigid rules such as "If I leave my house by myself, I will lose control". The individual might have leaving their house in their repertoire in different context such as when his or her romantic partner is present, but not in a context of being alone, given the rule mentioned. Behavior of staying home may be negatively reinforced by the avoidance of potential danger that lies outside the home.

Behavioral deficits are also construed as the lack of behavioral repertoire (e.g., skill deficits). An example is a case of an individual who has a long history of self-injurious behavior such as cutting and burning in order to regulate emotions (Linehan, 1993). This may not simply be a problem of poor stimulus control. Rather, the individual may not have acquired healthy methods of dealing with emotion. In the absence of a broader repertoire, dangerous or lethal behaviors, negatively reinforced by the temporal reduction of distressing emotional arousal, may have become dominant.

The majority of behavioral problems in language-able individuals seem to involve verbal components, as these examples illustrate. The great majority of the psychological disorders listed in the Diagnostic and Statistical Manual of Mental Disorders-IV (DSM; American Psychiatric Association, 1994) involve cognition, verbally evaluated emotion, or behaviors regulated by verbal rules. From a clinical behavior analytic perspective, the problems are not so much the occurrence of these cognitions and emotions, but a person's response to these events (e.g., evaluating them, identifying with them, attempting to eliminate them). Even so-called problematic cognitions and emotions are not inherently negative or positive (Anderson et al., 1997; Hayes, et al., 2001). Again, these behavioral approaches are classified in terms of behavioral excesses or behavioral deficits.

Verbally regulated behavior is often very useful, but it also can create many problems. Verbal rules can limit behaviors available in a given context, and as a result, direct contingencies have limited opportunity to shape behavior (Hayes, 1989). In addition, verbal rules tend to be relatively rigid (Moxon, Keenan, & Hine, 1993; Watt, Keenan, Barnes, & Cairns, 1991) and once they are established they are likely to remain in one's repertoires (Rehfeldt & Hayes, 2000; Wilson & Hayes, 1996; Wilson, Lindsey, & Schooler, 2000). The insensitive nature of verbal behavior can lead an individual to spend time engaging in futile and unnecessary avoidance behaviors (e.g., Hayes, Wilson, Gifford, Follette, & Strosahl, 1996).

The focus of clinical behavior analysis is not just the elimination problems, but also the development of repertoires for constructive living (e.g., Goldiamond, 1974). Clients are exposed to diverse life contexts such as intimate relationships, family, friends, parenting, school, vocational activities, community services, physical health, and spirituality. The goal of therapy in clinical behavior analysis involves identifying, building, and maintaining new repertoires and strengthen existing repertoires aligned with personal values in diverse life contexts.

Applied Extension

Many of the techniques used in behavior therapy are drawn from behavior analytic principles. These traditional behavioral principles as well as modern behavioral principles focused on private events, such as emotions, cognitions, sensations, and memories.

Application of Contingency-Shaped Behavioral Principles

When a therapist has direct access to a client's environment where problematic behavior occurs, behavioral methods derived from traditional behavioral principles are feasible. By systematically manipulating the contingency of reinforcement in client life context, these methods directly influences behavioral excesses and behavioral deficits of both problematic and constructive repertoires. In addition, since verbal behavior is pervasive, the context of a therapy session can also be a context where verbal rules are elicited. This allows for the reconditioning and of antecedent events for the purpose of allowing alternative behavioral repertoires to be contingently shaped.

Shaping and Contingency Management. As was described in the previous chapter, contingency-shaped behavior is behavior whose antecedent stimulus is non-verbal and it is acquired through *direct exposure* to environmental consequences. In general, contingency-shaped behavior is developed and maintained by a gradual shaping of successive approximations to a goal. Many forms of human behavior, especially those learned at earlier ages, are understood to be acquired in this manner.

According to Martin and Pear (1996), shaping is a method of successive approximation that involves "the development of a new behavior by the successive reinforcement of closer approximations and the extinguishing of preceding approximations of the behavior" (p. 65). For example, English-speaking parents usually use shaping procedure to teach an infant to emit the vocal behavior "ma-ma". Some of the sounds the infant makes are similar to words in English. When this sound is occasioned, it is followed by reinforcement from the parents (e.g., kisses, caresses, and hugs). The sound that is similar to "mama" especially receives a large amount of this reinforcement. Eventually, the vocal behavior of "mama" is differentially reinforced and its primitive forms (e.g., "mmm") are extinguished. The infant's vocal behavior "mama" is developed, shaped, and maintained under the direct contingency of reinforcement.

According to Martin and Pear (1996), there are four dimensions of behavior that can be shaped; topography, amount (i.e., frequency, duration), latency (the time between the occurrence of antecedent stimulus and the beginning of a response), and intensity (the impact of behavior on the environment where it occurs). For example, social skills training can be thought of as an applied extension of the principle of differential reinforcement to build a client's interpersonal skills.. Through a careful assessment, a client's existing repertoires of interpersonal behavior are conceptualized based on the three-term contingency. Then, the final desired behavior is specified with respect to these four dimensions. For some behavioral concerns, a precise statement of the final desired behavior increases treatment adherence (e.g., when to reinforce). Regarding treatment adherence, another important factor is to choose the shaping steps with the correct pace. It is beneficial to identify the steps of successive approximations and to decide the completion criteria for moving to the next step.

Some of the contemporary behavior therapies also use the principles of successive approximation. For instance, Functional Analytic Psychotherapy (FAP; Kohlenberg & Tsai, 1991) places emphasis on therapeutic relationship between therapist and client in order to elicit and shape client interpersonal behaviors within a session. FAP assumes that client problematic interpersonal behaviors outside the therapy session occur more or less in the interaction with the therapist. Based on the principles of contingency of immediate reinforcement and generalization, FAP seeks to identify client problematic interpersonal behavior, and the therapist differentially reinforces successive approximations immediately after the emission of a behavior of this kind. Regarding the reinforcement from the therapist, a FAP therapist attempts to make the therapeutic relationship as natural as possible so that shaped behaviors are likely to be generalized to interpersonal contexts outside the session. FAP therapists do not provide verbal instruction (e.g., rules) of how to interact with the therapist. Rather, client interpersonal behavior is shaped by the therapist's natural reaction to the client's behavior. In many ways, FAP tries to avoid the paradoxical effect of didactic instruction (e.g., rule-governed behavior) and uses the therapeutic relationship as a vehicle for enhancing client progress through the principles of contingency-shaped behavior (Kohlenberg, Hayes, & Tsai, 1999).

Another method that is derived from the principles of contingency-shaped reinforcement is contingency management. There are a number of methods that fall into the category, such as reinforcement therapy, time-out, contingency contracting, token economy and others. Incorporating the direct contingencies, these methods are typically used as treatments for children and chronically institutionalized mental patients. For example, contingency management is used to treat a child's off-task behavior in class. After conducting a careful functional assessment, a teacher conceptualizes that the child's off-task behavior is reinforced by such events as her attention and/or escape from demands. Under such conditions, the teacher may directly arrange the contingency in such ways to extinguish child's off-task behavior (e.g., ignoring the child when the behavior is emitted), while at the same time differentially reinforcing his or her alternative behaviors (i.e., on-task behavior).

Two of the successful examples regarding contingency management are the treatment of institutionalized adult psychotics (Allyon & Azrin, 1968) and autistic children (Lovaas, 1987). Allyon and Azrin (1968) showed dramatic behavioral improvements among severe psychotic clients in the ward of a state mental hospital. Under the study, they changed staff behaviors so that they would differentially reinforce appropriate patient behavior and extinguish inappropriate ones. Their primary intervention included a token economy where patients were given tokens for their appropriate behavior, and then these tokens were later exchanged for certain goods. They found that after the intervention, patients functioned at a greater level than previously thought. Another successful case with the use of contingency management was its application to autistic children (Lovaas, 1987). Simply put, following years of intensive behavioral intervention, some autistic children showed improvements in their intellectual and educational abilities.

Dialectical Behavior Therapy (DBT; Linehan, 1993) also uses shaping and contingency management as ways to generalize skills building for managing distress, regulating emotions, and being effective in interpersonal situations, while at the same time reducing behavior excesses of particular types of behaviors such as parasuicide, alcohol abuse, and binging-and-purging. DBT views client behavior problems in part as behavioral deficits in the ability to safely and effectively manage emotional reactions to aversive stimuli. In individual and group therapies, alternative and more constructive emotional regulation skills are taught to clients. Then, when these skills are learned and maintained with proper topography, amount, latency, and intensity in therapy sessions or on telephone calls, clients are encouraged to use them outside the sessions to promote generalization. Skills trainings in DBT is a method derived from the principle of contingency-shaped behavior in that these emotional regulation skills are gradually shaped to the final desired behavior (Waltz & Linehan, 1999). These same skills are shaped for use with respect to behavioral excesses of problematic behaviors such as self-injurious behavior. Thus, the new skills that are shaped and managed are designed to alter a client's behavioral deficits as well as excesses in order to assist them in achieving personal goals and values.

In sum, shaping and contingency management are methods derived from the principles of contingency-shaped behavior. With the use of these methods, therapists can significantly control or help clients arrange their environment so that behavior excesses of problematic behaviors are unlikely to occur and that constructive behavior repertoires are likely to occur.

Application of Verbally-Governed Behavior Principles

As mentioned above, the application of rule-govern behavior principles is very important in the field of clinical behavior analysis. When therapists do not have direct access to client environment, behavior change of client is likely to be achieved through verbal interaction between client and the therapist. In addition, the core of psychopathology among language-able individuals is at human verbal activities. Presenting problems clients bring to session are often some form of cognitive and verbally entangled emotional experience. Their coping strategies for these problems are also verbally regulated, and often these are narrowing behavioral repertoires in a given context.

A number of middle level concepts, which we will in this chapter call "applied behavioral concepts," have been described within clinical behavior analysis in this area (Dougher, 1999) and the "third wave" of cognitive behavior therapy (Hayes, 2004). These behavioral concepts are not behavioral principles – they do not have that level of precision and scope. Instead they are higher level terms that orient practitioners and researchers to key aspects of an analytic domain viewed from a behavioral perspective.

The theory that underlies ACT (Hayes et al., 1999) is a good example of a theoretically organized set of applied behavioral concepts in the clinical. ACT is based on a hexagon model of psychopathology (see Figure 3.1) and treatment (see Figure 3.2). Psychopathology is argued (Hayes, Luoma, Bond, Masuda, & Lillis, 2006) to be the result, in large part, of excesses produced by human language and cognition. These include experiential avoidance and cognitive fusion – which we will define shortly. Literal language also leads to loss of contact with the present moment (both externally and internally) and focus on a conceptualized self. Lack of values clarity, or "values" in the service of pliance or avoidance, undermine the appetitive functions of verbal purpose, and inactivity, impulsivity, and avoidant persistence undermine committed action. Overall, the pathological core of problems from an ACT point of view is psychological inflexibility.

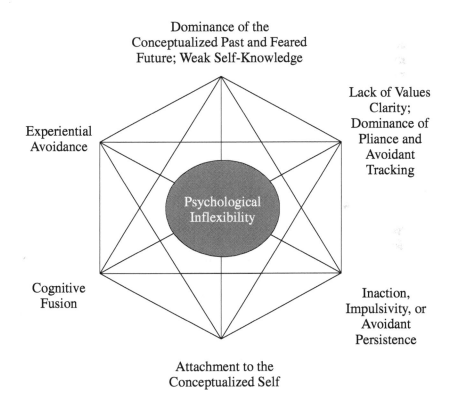

Figure 3.1. The ACT model of psychopathology.

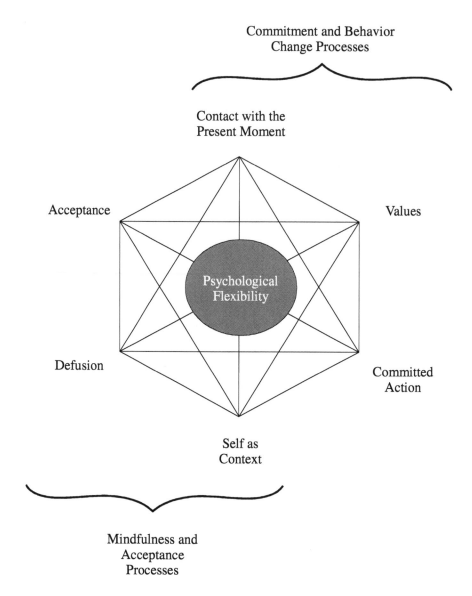

Figure 3.2. The ACT model of intervention.

These same interrelated functional processes are then targeted therapeutically in ACT: acceptance, defusion, self as context, contact with the present moment, values, and committed action (see Figure 3.2). The first four – the present moment, acceptance, defusion, and self as context – constitute the mindfulness and acceptance processes within the model. The last four – the present moment, self as context, values, and committed action – constitute the commitment and behavior change processes. The intended outcome of targeting these processes is psychological flexibility, which means the ability to experience events fully, consciously, and without defense, and to persist in or change behavior in a given situation in the service of chosen values. All of these concepts are middle-level conceptual terms, and we will walk through them and related concepts, as part of an effort to show how behavioral principles can give rise to applied behavioral concepts of direct use to applied workers.

Avoidance, Exposure, and Acceptance. In order to understand acceptance it is useful to first understand experiential avoidance, which Wilson, Hayes, Gregg, and Zettle (2001) have defined as "the tendency to attempt to modify the form, frequency, or situational sensitivity of private events (thoughts, feelings, memories, behavioral predispositions) even when this effort produces behavioral harm" (p. 215).

Let us first note the behavior of a non-verbal animal. Consider a rat that has been trained to press one lever for food if it has recently been shocked and a different lever for food if it has not recently been shocked. The rat can readily learn this discrimination and its selection of a lever can be thought of as a "report" of whether or not it has been shocked. But note that the rat does not avoid pressing the bar that accurately reports having been shocked. The rat has not acquired relational operants and the shock-bar press-food relations are direct and learned, not symmetrically entailed. Thus, the aversive effects of the shock do not spread via reporting about them or responding to them. There is no reason for the animal to avoid the effects of shock instead of the shock itself.

Due to the relational nature of language, human beings can re-experience aspects of an event simply by reporting it. It is therefore possible for the report of a trauma, for example, to evoke many of the emotions felt during the original event. In RFT terms, the event-report relation entails the report-event relation, and the functions of the event transfer to the report. This phenomenon is referred to as the "bidirectional transformation of stimulus functions" (Hayes & Hayes, 1992; Hayes & Wilson, 1993). It does not occur (or does not occur strongly) in classical and operant conditioning, both of which are dominantly unidirectional.

These reports include self-reports, memories, and the like, which means that anywhere a person goes, it is possible to revisit past painful events. In addition, in humans, thinking about or reporting emotions involves labeling them with words (Lazarus, 1982), and these words transform the functions of the emotions with which they are related. For example, the pain of trauma could be related to "bad." Although "bad" is an evaluation of the pain, not a formal property of it, the framing of "bad" with pain, in the context of cognitive fusion (discussed below), may result in functional equivalence between the two, as if "bad" is indeed a formal property of the pain. Further, pain may be related to "weak" or "I'll fall apart," as well as "bad" – in effect elaborating the aversive functions of painful events in accordance with the multiple relations involved.

The result is that avoidance processes can be far more extended and hard to limit in human beings. Nonhuman animals can successfully avoid aversive states by simply avoiding the situations where they occur. That cannot work with humans, who can re-experience an aversive event anywhere at any time simply by reporting it aloud or silently in the form of thinking. Because of that difficulty it is perfectly reasonable to extend the many ways of effectively avoiding negative external events to aversive internal events, like thoughts (Hayes, Strosahl et al., 2004; Hayes, Wilson, Gifford, Follette, & Strosahl, 1996). Further, because the aversiveness of emotions increases when they participate in relational frames with negative evaluations, we have even more reason to avoid thinking about emotional events, and we have increased motivation to try to avoid the emotions themselves (Hayes et al., 1996). Physical sensations may also be thrust into relational frames with labels and evaluations, thereby increasing the aversiveness of such sensations and evoking avoidance of thinking about or experiencing them. For example, chronic physical pain could be placed in an evaluative frame with "unbearable" and become more aversive through participation in this frame, making avoidance of the pain (unwillingness to remain in contact with it) more likely.

Unfortunately, attempts at avoidance of internal events are likely to fail. Thought suppression has been shown to temporarily decrease the frequency of the avoided thought, but later the frequency of the thought or distress regarding it increases (Gold & Wegner, 1995; Wegner, 1994a). This effect can be explained using RFT. Suppose someone is trying to avoid thinking about having a panic attack and decides simply to "think about something else," like being on vacation in a cozy cabin in the mountains. It is important to understand that the fully specified network is not simply the shorthand "think about the cabin" but rather "think about the cabin because it's not panic and doesn't make you anxious like thoughts about panic do." In other words, in addition to being verbally related to "pleasant vacation," the cabin is also verbally related to "panic and anxiety" and may evoke thoughts related to panic and anxiety. Thus, more and more neutral or pleasant things can be related to anxiety and panic (Wilson et al., 2001).

Further, the rebound effects of experiential avoidance are stronger in the contexts in which the suppression took place (Wegner, Schneider, Knutson, & McMahon, 1991). Thus, for example, if someone fears experiencing panic attacks in open spaces and therefore suppresses panic-related thoughts in those settings, the panic-related thoughts will become more likely in those settings. In addition, if thought suppression occurs during a particular mood, the thought will be more likely to return when that mood is reinstated. The suppressed thought, then, is most likely to return in contexts similar to those in which it was originally suppressed—exactly where it is least desired. From an RFT perspective, a bidirectional relation is established between the setting or mood and the suppressed thought, enabling the setting or mood to elicit the thought (Wilson et al., 2001).

Experiential avoidance is ineffective for three other reasons. First, checking whether it has been successful makes it unsuccessful. For example, in order to check to see whether one is avoiding thoughts related to the death of a spouse one has to think, "Have I thought about the death of my spouse?" This, of course, involves thinking about the death of the spouse. Second, efforts to eliminate thoughts strengthen a context in which thought will be treated literally. For example, suppressing a thought like "I'm bad" is treating the thought itself as "bad" and thus in an ironic way is confirming its "truth." Even if the thought is successfully avoided that very process makes it more likely that it will evoke avoidance in the future. In this way, avoided thoughts gradually become more fearsome or unacceptable (Wilson et al., 2001). Very similar RFT-based analyses apply to the avoidance and suppression of other private events, such as emotion or sensation. Third, avoidance narrows behavioral repertoires, and reduces flexible contact with available contingencies.

As a substantial body of evidence suggests that exposure and response prevention are helpful in the treatment of anxiety and related problems (Abramowitz, 1996). Experiential avoidance interferes with exposure however. An alternative response repertoire is acceptance. 'Acceptance' etymologically comes from a word meaning, "to take or receive what is offered". This definition implies that no matter what form of psychological event (i.e. thoughts, wants, emotions, etc.) is observed, we observe and experience it as it is, without a response effort to change or avoid the stimulus. Hayes (1994) defined acceptance as a behavioral process of exposure to the automatic or direct stimulus functions of events, without acting to reduce or manipulate those functions, and without acting on the basis of their derived or verbal function. Roemer and Orsillo (2002) treated acceptance as the process of "being experientially open to the reality of the present moment rather than being in a state of either belief or disbelief (or judging what is fair or unfair)" (p. 60). These definitions place the emphasis on contingencies of reinforcement in a given context and reduces the reliance on verbal rules that detract from direct experience.

Empirical data suggests that using acceptance instead of avoidance or thought suppression can have a positive effect (Gross & Levenson, 1997; Hayes et al., 2006; Kelly & Kahn, 1994). In many ways, acceptance can be characterized as an extension of traditional exposure and response prevention techniques, such as interoceptive exposure (Craske & Barlow, 1993). Acceptance methods may differ from traditional exposure exercises in that the stimuli that client's are exposed to include verbal events such as, thoughts and verbally evaluated emotions and memories. In other words, under a particular verbal antecedent, acceptance as an alternative behavior is strengthened by the extinction of stimulus function of these events.

Acceptance methods are usually experiential, rather than didactic. For example, a client is asked to close his or her eyes and to simply notice and experience physical sensation, emotion, & cognition without trying to control them. Or the client is encouraged to make contact with difficult psychological events in session that are usually avoided. In these exercises, the client is also asked to notice if he or she is caught by the literality of private events that previously lead to avoidance strategies. Another important thing to note is that acceptance is considered to be a behavioral skill. As the principle of successive approximation suggests, acceptance is to be built gradually depending on each client's strength of existing repertoire.

Fusion and Defusion. Through entailment and the transformation of functions, verbal constructions take on many of the psychological functions of the events they are related to, and do so to a degree that can over-extend their functions. Imagine putting your saliva into a sterilized glass until it is half full, and then chugging it all down. The repulsion that occurs as that sentence is read is inconsistent with the much larger amounts of saliva that are consumed each day, and the vastly positive effects of saliva in lubrication, digestion, and so on. The repulsion is a matter of *cognitive fusion* – the process by which particular verbal functions come to dominate over other directly and indirectly available psychological functions. Fusion is thus an overextension of relational functions due to a context of literality.

From an RFT point of view, the degree to which verbally-mediated or directly experienced events evoke the stimulus functions of other related events is determined by the context in which the relation between the two events occurs. It follows then that weakening the dominant stimulus functions of a verbal event involves changing the context in which verbal behavior has such functions (Barnes-Holmes, Hayes, Dymond, & O'Hora, 2001).

Blackledge (in press) notes that in normal language there is an attentional focus on the stimulus *products* of derived relational responding as opposed to the *process*. The verbal contexts that give rise to word meaning are both ubiquitous and subtle, and do not illuminate the fact that these meanings (functions) are due to arbitrary relations between events. Hayes et al. (1999) note that defusion seems to work in part by making the "ongoing process of framing events relationally evident in the moment" (p. 74). For example, talking about the "mind" as a third person, mindfulness exercises, or "cubbyholing" techniques in which thoughts are explicitly labeled as "thoughts" and emotions as "emotions" are all procedures that shift attention from relational products to relational processes.

Blackledge (in press) points to other aspects of a context of literality to identify other means of defusion. He notes that word meaning depends on "relatively standardized speech parameters involving the use of certain words to designate certain stimuli and relations, certain grammatical and syntactical sentence structures, [and] limited rates and frequencies of speech" and then observes that when any of these contextual features are removed, the transformation of stimulus functions is disrupted and speech temporarily loses some of its literal meaning. Examples of this process include cognitive defusion exercises such as repeatedly stating a negative thought aloud, singing a difficult thought or saying it in the voice of Donald Duck.

Because evaluative frames seem to be an especially troublesome aspect of cognitive fusion, another defusion approach attends to the distinction between descriptive and evaluative language–in close correspondence to the RFT distinction between formal and arbitrary stimulus properties (Blackledge, in press). Exercises that teach the distinction between the concrete dimensions of experience and evaluative dimensions (e.g., the difference between a round cup and an ugly one) may reduce the stimulus transformations that arise from hidden evaluative frames.

Noting that language relies on relational coherence as a reinforcer, Blackledge (in press) points out that defusion can also emerge by undermining reason-giving and relational coherence. For example, clients may be asked a series of "why" questions to demonstrate the ultimate arbitrary nature of rationality in many contexts or literal statements may be responded to in terms of function rather than form (e.g., "and what is saying that in the service of?") which undermines that context. Clients may be asked to rewrite their life history with the same factual events, thus undermining the coherence of the story, its believability and its basis as a justification for certain actions.

The goal of defusion is not to eliminate verbal stimulus functions but to bring behavior under more balanced and flexible forms of contextual control (Wilson & Murrell, 2004). It is not necessary (or even desirable) to disrupt all verbal functions of a specific event or to target all instances of verbal behavior for defusion. Defusion strategies can be used to target specific verbal content (e.g., "I'm a bad person") or broader classes of verbal behavior, such as excessive reason-giving. The immediate effects of defusion may last only a few moments and the client may repeatedly move between fusion and defusion. However, repeated exposure to contexts which support defusion may have long-lasting effects on a client's relationship to language by bringing fusion and defusion under more flexible and operant contextual control. Multiple exemplar training with defusion exercises may change an individual's learning history such that the individual is more likely to frame events in a way that is concordant with a level of fusion that fits the current situation. If a more flexible approach to framing verbal events confers an advantage in the client's environment, this behavior may generalize to contexts outside of therapy. Holding certain psychological functions lightly may lead to more effective ways of responding based on alternate relational frames or contact with direct contingencies.

The importance of this process with respect to verbal events is supported by both cognitive theories (e.g. Wells, 2002) as well as behavior analytic theories (e.g. Hayes, et al., 2001). For example, Mindfulness Based Cognitive Therapy (MCBT; Segal, Williams, & Teasdale, 2002) teaches a client to notice that they are having the thought that "things will never get better" and not to believe or fuse with this private event as a literal description of the future. This process of noticing thoughts as passing events of the here and now allows the client to detach from their certainty or literality, thereby reducing the likelihood of additional problematic thinking patterns such as ruminations about the future. Evidence suggests that this defusion approach may help clients in preventing the formation of negative thinking patterns that may contribute to relapse of a depressive episode (Teasdale, 1997; Teasdale et al., 2000) as well as improve autobiographical memory in these same clients (Williams et al., 2000).

Research has shown that mindfulness- and acceptance-based behavior therapies achieve positive results part by undermining the literal impact and behavior regulation function of verbal rules (Bach & Hayes, 2002; Bond & Bunce, 2000; Luciano, Gómez, Hernández, & Cabello, 2001; Zettle & Hayes, 1986; Zettle & Reins, 1989). In addition, laboratory studies also showed the connection between psychological health and cognitive defusion (e.g., Masuda, Hayes, Sackett, & Twohig, 2004).

The Contextual Self. There is a form of unhealthy fusion that is evident in the area of self– entanglement with the verbal descriptions, evaluations, predictions, and the like that make up the verbally conceptualized self (Hayes et al., 1999). Verbal abstraction and evaluation is constant and there is no way to prevent applying evaluations to the self. Attributes such as "I'm not a hard worker" or "deep down I'm mean" are linked to a coherent story that explains where these attributes came from and what their consequences are likely to be in the future. When we speak of our sense of self in this culture, it is most often of this conceptualized sense of self that we speak, and these verbal formulations are strongly reinforced by the social environment.

The problems with excessive entanglement with the conceptualized self are three fold. First, the analysis is something to be right about. For example a person may fuse with the thought that he or she is damaged and unlovable because he or she was abused. The coherence of the story is reinforcing but it comes at the cost of behavioral flexibility because any sudden change in behavior (without a change in the abuse history, which is impossible) violates the story. Second, the verbal formulations are mentalistic and fragmentary. Our stories are not and cannot themselves be well grounded in a scientific analysis of one's own life. The vast majority of the details in our lives are lost to history, and we would not know how best to formulate them even if they were known. Thus the formulations that arise are common-sense and often mentalistic constructions from fragmentary information. They are so incomplete that even when they are literally true they are virtually bound to be functionally false. But as the elements of our story cohere into a rigid verbal system, they prevent reformulation and flexibility outside of the limits of the story. Finally, features of the conceptualized self that link causes to behavioral solutions are generally missing, preventing the stories from having immediately useful implications. They do not effectively tell us what to *do*.

The contextual self is an extension of a traditional behavioral interpretation of self-awareness. Skinner (1974) argued that one becomes aware of his own behavior when the verbal community at large reinforces responding to one's own responding. When these second-order processes are established among non-humans, however (Lattal, 1975; Pliskoff & Goldiamond, 1966; Reynolds, 1966; Reynolds & Catania, 1962) none of the claimed benefits of self-awareness seem to arise. RFT argues that something is missing in the Skinnerian analysis (Barnes-Holmes, Stewart, Dymond, & Roche, 2000; Hayes, 1984). Specifically, self discrimination in humans and non-humans is functionally different because of the phenomena of derived relational responding (Barnes-Holmes, Hayes, & Dymond, 2001; Barnes-Holmes, Stewart, Dymond, & Roche, 2000; Hayes, Barnes-Holmes, & Roche 2001). Humans do not just respond to their own responding–they do so *verbally* (Hayes & Wilson, 1993). Furthermore, they learn to do so from a consistent locus or point of view in order to make consistently accurate verbal reports (Hayes, 1984). This is done through the acquisition of deictic relational frames.

Deictic frames can be shown only by demonstration and not by reference to formal or non-arbitrary counterparts. For example, a frame of comparison (say, "bigger than") can be shown non-arbitrarily in relata with relative size differences, but "mine" versus "yours" cannot be exemplified in this way. Similarly, there are no unique formal properties involved in what might be "here" relative to what might be "there", what might happen "now" relative to what might happen "then", or whoever is "I" relative to whoever is "you". The answers depend on the perspective of the speaker and thus can only be shown by demonstration.

RFT researchers have provided evidence that deictic frames are relational operants (Weil, 2007) that arise after a history of multiple exemplar training and follow a developmental profile (McHugh, Barnes-Holmes, & Barnes-Holmes, 2004). It is known both to be lacking in some disabled children without a sense of self and to be trainable (Rehfeldt, Dillen, Ziomek, & Kowalchuk, 2007).

For humans to respond accurately using deictic relations they seem to need a history of contact with multiple sets of exemplars that allow irrelevant content to be differentiated from the deictic perspective appropriate to the situation. For example, children are asked many questions about different content domains but correct self-reports require deictic frames to emerge as the invariants. For example, in response to the question, "What are you doing now?" a child may answer at different times "I am writing a note" or "I am taking a nap" or "I am eating my lunch." In these questions and answers "I" and "you" do not refer to the content, but to the perspective from which reports are made. As more and more such questions are asked, including questions about the past and the future ("What did you do yesterday?" "What are you doing *there?*"), the invariants (I/here/now) emerge as a kind of subtraction. The child does not just see, or see that he sees, the child sees seeing from a consistent perspective (Hayes, 1984; Hayes, 1989).

This form of self occurs whenever the speaker acknowledges that he (I) speaks about events occurring THERE and THEN, from HERE and NOW. In other words, I (located HERE and NOW) am the context where all the discriminations occur (located THERE and THEN) (Barnes-Holmes, Hayes, & Dymond, 2001; Hayes, 1989). This sense of self is important because it is the only self that is stable, unchangeable, and not dependent upon the content of our particular histories or emotional labeling (Hayes & Gregg, 2001).

Contact with the Present. Moment. In non-verbal organisms, the present moment is all there is. In verbal organisms it is otherwise. Verbal problem solving involves comparing present circumstances to a verbally constructed past or future. This act of relating the present to a constructed past or future means that events in the present moment are readily responded to within a context of the derived stimulus relations involving temporal and evaluative frames. Evaluative frames represent a particular type of comparative frame in which an event is compared to another event or an absolute standard (Wilson, Hayes, Gregg, & Zettle, 2001). Temporal frames involve comparing events along the dimension of time such as before/after and then/now (Hayes, Blackledge, & Barnes-Holmes, 2001).

The ability to relate events in terms of temporal and evaluative frames is adaptive and can be useful in many circumstances. The ability to construct hypothetical future events enables one to consider future problematic situations and the consequences of various actions without actually experiencing them. Potential problems can be anticipated beforehand and effective ways of responding can be developed. In addition, the delay in responding that occurs with the intrusion of verbally constructed contingencies can reduce the probability of emitting impulsive, maladaptive responses (Hayes, Gifford, Townsend, & Barnes-Holmes, 2001).

Although the ability to compare the present moment to past and future events can be adaptive, this process can become overextended and problematic. A lack of contact with the direct contingencies in one's current environment (Hayes, Zettle & Rosenfarb, 1989) can result in insensitive behavior. Verbally constructed contingencies can overwhelm those that are actually present. For example, someone who suffers from panic disorder may exhibit persistent anxiety and worry about the future occurrence or consequences of having a panic attack. This involves the relating of present circumstances to a verbally constructed past and future through temporal and evaluative frames. The person may relate the present situation to a hypothetical future circumstance in which a panic attack occurs. In addition, he may compare current physical sensations to sensations that have led to panic attacks in the past. The present moment and the actual contingencies present may not be aversive. However, instead of responding to the current situation in which there are no threatening cues he may act according to derived stimulus relations in which there is a direct threat of losing control or going insane or dying because of an imagined impending panic attack. This greatly narrows the potential behaviors that can be emitted and thus reinforced. Laughing, talking, going for a walk and a thousand other potential responses may sink to near zero probability in the face of impending doom and disaster.

Increasing contact with the present moment involves teaching the behavior of shifting attention to whatever thoughts, feelings, sensations or other events are occurring in the here and now (Fletcher & Hayes, 2005). Contact with the present moment alters the context of verbally constructed contingencies created through temporal and evaluative frames. This change in context does not directly reduce the occurrence of verbal relations, but does reduce the transformation of stimulus functions from these derived stimulus relations. Clients are taught to focus on what is occurring in the moment including the act of relating the present moment to a verbally constructed past or future. Thus, contact with the present moment includes noting the process of deriving stimulus relations as it occurs – a defusion process. Contact with the present moment is related to other concepts as well (Fletcher & Hayes, 2005). In order to be in contact with the present moment one has to accept what one may find there, for example. Furthermore, present moment awareness involves experiencing events from a position of I-Here-Now rather than I-There-Then. Thus, these processes are interrelated and inform each other (Fletcher & Hayes, 2005).

One particularly important form of contact with the present moment is contact with one's own experiences as an ongoing process. This "self as process" involves on-going observation and description of the continuous occurrence of thoughts, feelings, bodily sensations and the like. Access to internal as well as external events in the moment increases the flexibility, sensitivity, and effectiveness of behavior. For example, sensing that one is sad may make one more likely to seek a supportive social environment. This is why it is important that there is congruence between the ways we label the world within and the verbal community at large. Concepts such as empathy, self-knowledge and personality integration are the result of such processes (Barnes-Holmes, Hayes, & Dymond, 2001).

Mindfulness. Mindfulness, as the term may already imply, is not a method that was developed by behaviorally oriented psychologists. Mindfulness has been used as a method for enhancing awareness and attention for thousands of years, practiced religiously by Buddhist followers. Because of its mystical and spiritual foundations, a scientific definition of mindfulness has been difficult for empirical psychologists (Baer, 2003). For instance, Kabat-Zinn (2003) defines mindfulness as, "the awareness that emerges through paying attention on purpose, in the present moment, and nonjudgmentally to the unfolding of experience moment by moment (p. 145)." Teasdale et al. (2000) use mindfulness techniques to "teach individuals to become more aware of thoughts and feelings and to relate to them in a wider, decentered perspective as 'mental events' rather than as aspects of the self or as necessarily accurate reflections of reality (p. 616)." Mindfulness can be defined as "the defused, accepting, open contact with the present moment and the private events it contains as a conscious human being experientially distinct from the content being noticed" (Fletcher & Hayes, 2005, p. 322). This definition integrates several of the processes already described. Though there are discrepancies in several definitions of mindfulness, conceptual similarities are apparent (Dimidjian & Linehan, 2003).

A focus of deliberate contact with the present moment is parsimonious with a behavior analytic account of behavior and pathology. A mindfulness exercise is one particular method to help clients to increase the sensitivity to the contingency of reinforcement operating in the given moment. From clinical behavior analytic perspective, factors that prevent individuals from directly contacting with a given context is human linguistic practice. For instance, the image of self in a mirror may occasion verbal behavior of individuals who are diagnosed with eating disorder such as, "I'm too fat". This verbal rule with particular aversive function then occasions purging and excessive exercise followed by the reduction or temporal elimination of aversive private events (contingency of negative reinforcement).

For example, according to DBT (Linehan, 1993), the client diagnosed with eating disorder may not be aware of this behavioral process because of the literal impact of verbal rules. Given this problematic patterns, DBT is designed to help clients build and increase the repertoire of "observing" without judgment shaped to notice the stimulus control of verbally evaluated image in mirrors and related evaluative private events. Mindfulness is useful in applied settings problematic behavior patterns under the contingency of negative reinforcement. Thus, from a behavior analytic perspective, mindfulness is a method designed to increase alternative repertoire of awareness with respect to the stimulus control of particular verbal stimuli that occasion self-destructive behavior (Dinsmoor, 1985).

Furthermore, the alternative behavior of observing and experiencing events as they are in the present context is reinforced by altered functional relation of stimuli and behavior. In other words, given this experience, new verbal rules seem to be established. Once this skill of observing the present moment is shaped to a sufficient level, the client is able to observe the functional process of encountering a particular aversive stimulus, the tendency to emit escape or avoidance behavior, and the consequences of avoidance behaviors. This new rule may function as a verbal antecedent that is likely to occasion the alternative behavior that is followed by some sort of constructive consequences (e.g., the extinction of antecedent stimulus function). Therefore, the functional relationship between verbal antecedent and inflexible behavior is altered such that the antecedent stimuli no longer evoke avoidance behavior but now occasion more adaptable or flexible client behavior.

Mindfulness is a powerful agent of psychological change (e.g., Davidson, KabatZinn, Schumacher, Rosenkranz, Muller, Santorelli et al., 2003; Lutz, Greischar, Rawlings, Ricard, & Davidson, 2004) that has been adopted by many psychotherapy approaches (Hayes, Follette, & Linehan, 2004). Mindfulness is believed to be effective across many disorders (e.g. generalized anxiety, borderline personality, major depression, substance dependence, fibromyalgia, etc.) because of its focus of attending to stimuli in the present moment in order to alter the process through which people relate to private events. Mindfulness is useful when the desired outcome becomes a continual focus on the present moment by which we are purposely attending to in our current context, not one particular goal such as not being depressed (Teasdale et al., 2002). It is this changing in the arbitrary applicability of relational responding, not altering the content of a private event, that is believed to be responsible for the efficacy demonstrated across disorders:

> Any method that encourages non-evaluative contact with events that are here and now will also bring verbal regulatory strategies under better contextual control, because it will teach people the times and places to use literal, planful, evaluative skills and the times to use experiential, non-evaluative skills (Hayes & Wilson, 2003, p. 164).

Mindfulness processes foster behavioral flexibility in two ways: by increasing direct contact with contingencies in the environment and by reducing the impact of derived stimulus functions that are inherent in language by changing the context.

Problem-Solving. In behavior therapy, problem solving is roughly defined as a behavioral process to generate a variety of potentially effective responses to the problem situation and to increase the likelihood of selecting the most effective response from among these various alternatives (Goldfried & Davison, 1994). In other words, problem-solving is considered as the development of a new behavioral repertoire in a given situation where effective actions are absent as well as situations where there are some obstacles to prevent such actions. The term problem solving is also used as the name of a specific therapeutic technique that includes following behavioral sequences: define problem; gather information; identify possible solution; select plan; carry out plan; test outcome; change plan.

As a process, problem solving is not a technical term, rather it is one behavioral domain, including verbal behaviors. Hayes and his colleagues (Hayes, Gifford, Townsend, & Barnes-Holmes, 2001) defined problem-solving as "framing events relationally under the antecedent and consequential control of an apparent absent of effective actions" (p. 96). In some circumstance, the "problem" which is part of the relational activity remains verbal, such as the case of solving mathematical problems and existential concerns. In other circumstances, problem solving involves changes in nonverbal environment. Under such conditions, verbal problem solving is considered to be a pragmatic verbal analysis that alters the behavioral function of the non-verbal environment given the absence of effective action as an antecedent (Hayes, et al., 2001).

Problem-solving in this fashion is a core strategy of DBT (Linehan, 1993). Problem-solving is used to achieve many of the treatment goals set out by the client. This occurs on several levels, from the client initially seeking treatment for difficulties in life to defining specific problems that come up in the client's day to day life. DBT has outlined a number of strategies for problem-solving specific, day to day issues that often come up in treatment. For instance, the primary method used in DBT to identify problematic sequences of behavior is a behavior or chain analysis. A behavior analysis in DBT allows the client and therapist to identify behaviors (both public and private) that sequentially, and often historically, lead a client to the problem they are trying to solve. Identifying both the problem behavior (e.g. parasuicide) and the pattern of behaviors leading up to it, allows for the client and therapist to identify areas along the chain for the purposes of intervening. Intervention then is designed to disrupt problematic sequences of behavior so that the client can recondition discriminative stimuli to elicit more desirable chains of behavior.

Similarly, DBT uses what is called a "solution analysis" in order to identify a goal and the desired behaviors needed when attempting to achieve that goal. Like a behavior analysis, a solution analysis identifies specific behaviors, that have yet to occur, that would sequentially lead a client to the desired behavior or goal. After discussion between client and therapist, a plan is selected and skills for effectively carrying out the plan are identified and shaped in session. Once a clear plan is identified and practiced, identifying events that may reduce the ability of the client to adhere to the plan are then discussed. For example, a particular client may want a pay raise and she rehearsed how to appropriately ask her boss for the raise with her therapist. The client's employer may be angry that day and therefore less likely to give the client the raise. The boss' anger is then discussed and a plan for how to deal with that is then created.

Values. Values have been discussed in a variety of psychotherapies (e.g., Hayes et al., 1999; Miller & Rollnick, 2001). Simply put, "values are verbally constructed, globally-desired life directions: Values manifest themselves over time and unfold as an ongoing process rather than an outcome" (Wilson et al., 2001, p. 235). Values are unique for each client and each one usually identifies their own values in several life domains (e.g., intimate/family relationships, vocational and leisure activities, education, and others). From an applied behavior analytic perspective, values help augment verbally constructed appetitive consequences (Hayes et al., 1999; Hayes & Wilson, 1993; 1994).   Several studies have shown a relationship between value-oriented actions and client's psychological health (e.g. Heffner & Eifert, 2003; Luciano & Cabello, 2001). The very nature of behavioral treatment involves values and purpose (Wilson & Murrell, 2004). There would be no reason to focus on symptom reduction if the symptoms ameliorated were not preventing the sufferer from doing something in his or her life. Consequences are key to building new behaviors and maintaining them over time. In the case of complex human behavior, and in the face of pain and suffering, values are where we find the consequences of importance.

Skinner spoke about purpose (Skinner, 1974), but what he meant was reinforcement (Hayes & Wilson, 1993). For a nonverbal organism, the future we are speaking of is "the past as the future in the present" (Hayes, 1992, p. 113). That is, based on a history of reinforcement (the "past"), the animal is responding to present events in a way that in the past produced subsequent events. In this way reinforcement provides a kind of "purpose" or establishes a future event as a "valued" goal by a non-verbal organism.

For verbal organisms, purpose occurs in the context of arbitrarily applicable relational responding. Temporal and "if-then" relational frames allow humans to respond in terms of verbal relations among events that have never been experienced directly. Humans are able to construct a verbal "future" that they can work toward in the present. These are values or *verbally construed global desired life consequences* (Hayes et al., 1999, p. 206). Verbal relations of these kinds are important for human behavior, because very few human actions are shaped only by immediate direct consequences.

Values and augmentals. In a sense, we can think of values as a form of rule-following. When someone acts with "purpose," we are referring to self-directed rules. Rule-following based upon fusion and avoidance (forms of aversive control) leads to narrow and inflexible behavioral repertoires, whereas rule-following based upon acceptance and defusion (forms of appetitive control) leads to flexible behavioral repertoires that are likely to be maintained over time. Values are adaptive rules that help humans move toward a purpose that is meaningful and fulfilling, and that are likely to be maintained over time under appetitive, rather than aversive control. Values are both formative and motivative augmentals. Some values involve abstract consequences (such as justice or egalitarianism) that emerge as verbal consequences of importance entirely through relational networks—these are formative augmentals. Other values may impact the present moment by changing previously established consequential functions—these are motivative augmentals. Motivative augmentals are in essence verbal establishing operations. Motivative augmental control may be established for many adaptive rules, which function to increase the reinforcing features of the present moment linked to a "future" purpose. Consider a father who has heard and understood the rule "Exercise is part of a long healthy life" but has yet to follow this rule. By contacting the value of the importance of his children, the consequential functions of present stimuli may change. Exercise may be linked to images of seeing his children grow up, or being there to support them in difficult times. The disruptive effects of going to the gym now are not simply related to work not being done—they are related to loved one and to his deep sense of caring for his role as a father. Values allow this father to contact, in the moment, the direct contingencies related to his children that are aspects of an ongoing pattern of responding.

Values and tracks. Tracking refers to rule governed behavior under the control of a history of coordination between a rule and the environment independent of that rule (Barnes-Holmes, O'Hora, Roche, Hayes, Bissett, & Lyddy, 2001). In the above examples, the reinforcing properties of "love," "connectedness," and "being a good father" can be experienced in the moment, through relational responding that abstracts the relevant features of an on-going action and relates them to the overall chosen verbal purpose. This process sets the occasion for effective tracking. What are the other actions that might be supportive and loving and give rise to these same abstracted features? As these are formulated and tracked the impact of values expands.

Pliance. Pliance refers to rule-governed behavior under the control of a history of socially mediated reinforcement for coordination between behavior and the relevant rule (Barnes-Holmes, O'Hora, Roche, Hayes, Bissett, & Lyddy, 2001). Pliance generally undermines values because it shifts consequential control from chosen verbal purposes to the arbitrary social reactions of others. Thus identification of values should also undermine excessive pliance. This does not mean that values are individualistic or unconcerned with others. Indeed most values seem to be social, but they are chosen as a verbal operant, and are not justified by or turned over to the actions of others.

Committed Action

The majority of problematic behavioral patterns involve the failure to develop patterns of behavior that are regulated by delayed, probabilistic, and abstract outcomes as opposed to immediate, certain, and concrete ones. Said in another way, the problem of committed action is the problem of self-control. Psychopathology repeatedly presents itself as a failure not just of private experience but of action: A failure to act in ways that are in the person's long term interests.

Behavioral science has studied the variables influencing committed choices—shifts from patterns controlled by immediate, certain, and concrete outcomes to patterns regulated by or linked to delayed, probabilistic, and abstract outcomes. We will call the former impulsive choices, which is controversial. We will call the latter "valued choices," which does carry some risk of misunderstanding. We do so in part because delayed, probabilistic, and abstract outcomes are similar to values as we have just described, and in part because clinically the wording makes more salient the need for committed action experienced by so many clients. Note however that when dealing with non-verbal processes this label is purely metaphorical.

The dialectic between impulsive and valued choices seems central to many forms of psychopathology. For example, a focus on the immediate impact of one's behavior may lead to preferring a drink (an impulsive choice) to the discomfort of practicing the social skills needed to feel more at ease in social situations (a valued choice); to preferring a cigarette (an impulsive choice) over acting in accordance with long-term health goals (a valued choice); and to preferring to utter a harsh or rejecting remark (an impulsive choice) to the discomfort of developing an amicable compromise (a valued choice).

From a clinical perspective, individual instances of impulsive choices are of marginal interest (e.g., one isolated brash remark rarely ends a relationship and one cigarette does not lead to health problems). Problems of clinical interest typically arise when impulsive choices significantly outnumber valued ones. Indeed, the science of choosing between impulsive and valued alternatives suggests that without special efforts, behavior typically is disproportionately influenced by impulsive alternatives. There are, however a variety of ways to increase commitment to valued outcomes. Some of these processes have been modeled in the animal laboratory, through the use of direct consequences to build self-control. Others are linked to verbal processes of goal-setting and commitment, more formally justifying our convention in this chapter of speaking of such choices in values terms.

Contemporary researchers (e.g., Rachlin, 1995) conceptualize self-control as a "multiple influence" problem. Rachlin emphasizes that "self-control is developed [...] by restructuring behavior into wider patterns" (p. 117). Thus, if a drug user states that he or she values family, one can schedule a wide range of activities that fall into this category. The broader one conceptualizes the category, the more likely it is that the cumulative effect of the contacted reinforcers will compete with drug use. Keeping a job, making payments on time, and effectively resolving interpersonal conflicts within the home can all become part of the new pattern. As more and more activities occur that are in the service of "family," deviation from the pattern becomes less likely. When deviation occurs, it does not represent "weakness" or a "fatal flaw of character," but it can be interpreted as a "mere instance" as long as it does not disrupt the larger, more functional, pattern. Establishing or providing reinforcers that can effectively compete with easily available and potent reinforcers and contribute to the construction of broad patterns of effective action may be one of the keys to successful interventions (see also Lewinsohn, 1976).

Breaking patterns supported by impulsive outcomes

One way to prevent choosing impulsive alternatives is to avoid situations where impulsive choices are possible (e.g., no longer attend social gatherings where there is alcohol; avoid situations that evoke anxiety; or remove all high calorie foods from the home). However, such avoidance-based choice management often results in relapse when the preventive barriers are compromised (e.g., accidentally attending an event where alcohol is served; encountering high calorie food outside of the home). Prevention strategies of this kind are often met with temporary success, but typically lack the flexibility to maintain positive outcomes in the long run.

Another solution is to arrange situations where impulsive choices will be punished (e.g., abstinence-only support groups for addiction; enlisting others to "police" activities; pledging to pay penalties for impulsive choices). This strategy alone may also achieve some temporary success, but typically lacks the flexibility to curtail impulsive choices in the long run. As mentioned in the previous chapter, punishment contingencies may eliminate behavior, but they do not shape novel, more effective behavior. Furthermore, a focus on the impulsive choice has been correlated with persistent choosing of impulsive over valued alternatives (Mischel & Mischel, 1983). Thus, heavy emphasis on negatively evaluating one's impulsive choices may paradoxically increase the likelihood of making such choices in the future. A similar effect has been observed with experimental procedures that instruct subjects to deliberately control their thoughts (see Wegner, 1994b, for a review).

The choice of impulsive alternatives is often occasioned by contextual variables, such as smoking a cigarette after a meal. Maintaining a valued pattern (e.g., abstaining from smoking) is particularly difficult in situations where impulsive activities have been reinforced. One way to disrupt such contextual control is to deliberately undermine it. Cinciripini, Wetter, and McClure (1997) reviewed smoking interventions that scheduled smoking at the beginning while maintaining the number of cigarettes per day. These interventions were followed by greater abstinence rates than comparison conditions that focused exclusively on decreasing the number of cigarettes smoked daily because arbitrary scheduling broke the rigid smoking patterns that then were more susceptible to change.

Verbal relations often maintain impulsive choice patterns. Exposure to impulsive choice scenarios in the context of being willing, accepting, and/or defused from the variables influencing the choice (i.e., pre-committing to approaching the choice scenario without making an impulsive choice) can decrease the degree of control by such proximal verbal events. Generally, any activity that functions to broaden the context for choice will decrease the likelihood of choosing the impulsive alternative (Rachlin, 2000).

Building patterns supported by valued outcomes

Strategies for supporting valued choices fall under three categories: (a) increasing relative contextual control for the valued alternative, (b) pre-committing to choosing the valued alternative, and (c) directly training patterns of values engagement.

The probability of choosing a valued decision over the impulsive alternative may be increased by delaying the availability of the impulsive alternative (Rachlin, 1995; 2000). Even small delays can weaken the contextual control over impulsive choosing relative to more highly valued alternatives. For example, if listening to a band at a local pub at a late hour competed with being effective during an important business meeting early the next day, the temporal choice point can influence the decision to go to the pub. If a friend asks and the response is made immediately, then there is a strong contextual pull by the immediate social contingencies related to receiving an invitation from a friend, the rules of friendship, and belonging. The context makes the impulsive choice more probable. However, if the temporal choice point is delayed, the delay may weaken contextual control over choosing the impulsive alternative. Mindfulness exercises of the kind covered earlier can serve a similar function.

Another way to increase relative contextual control for choosing valued alternatives is to increase the salience of values-relevant events. Basic research related to impulsive and valued alternatives has demonstrated that signaling outcomes results in more frequent commitment to valued alternatives (Heyman, 1996; Heyman & Tanz, 1995). Clinical interventions that focus on the clarification of values and the identification of value-congruent goals and activities that can mark progress toward valued outcomes can accomplish the same function. Under such verbal augmentation, choosing between a high calorie and a healthy snack is more than a choice between isolated events, it becomes a choice between engaging in a pattern consistent with healthy living and deviating from that pattern with a high calorie snack. Here, values clarification and values pattern identification results in increasing the reinforcing effectiveness of the healthy snack relative to the high calorie snack. In effect, values clarification brings to bear multiple relations between values congruent and incongruent choice alternatives.

Social contexts can also be created to support committing to choosing values alternatives. Within therapy contexts, it appears that many interventions are effective due to specific social influence mechanisms. Sharing goals and commitments with others is known to produce much higher levels of goal-consistent behavior (Rosenfarb & Hayes, 1984) and the open discussion of values in a therapy context presumably has much the same effect. Commitments (e.g., literally asking a client to "take a stand") both make violations of valued choices more immediately aversive and progress toward them more salient, further encouraging and sustaining valued choices.

Self-monitoring of steps toward a valued end has broad and useful effects, in part because the self-monitoring process itself serves as a kind of commitment exercise, cuing remote and more valued consequences (Nelson & Hayes, 1981). Self-monitoring seems to be "reactive" for that reason, as is shown by the fact that reactivity does not depend on high levels of self-monitoring accuracy or the monitoring of high base-rate actions (Hayes & Nelson, 1983). Self-monitoring is also helpful because the client and the therapist gain access to operating contingencies, as well as the contextual factors important in creating a functional account for the problem behavior. Setting sub-goals and self-rewards for steps toward long term desired outcomes works similarly to self-monitoring, providing a kind of immediate social-standard against which valued choices can be evaluated (Hayes, Rosenfarb, Wulfert, Munt, Korn, & Zettle, 1985).

All of these methods are ways to begin to construct larger patterns of committed action, but they are more initial steps than maintenance steps. Larger patterns of committed action are most effective when they are multifaceted, flexible, broad, and virtually automatic. The goal is response integration, as individual behaviors cohere into robust patterns (Rachlin, 1995, 2000). This transitional process presents a practical challenge. In the early stages it is crucial to train engagement in valued choosing, arranging for supplemental consequences for engaging in valued patterns through social commitment, self-monitoring, goal-setting and multiple practical, accomplishable, low effort means of engaging in values-consistent patterns of behaving. But these patterns then need to shift to the natural contingencies when engagement has been of sufficient duration for their impact to be contacted (Ainslie & Monterosso, 2003; Kirby & Guastello, 2001; Siegel & Rachlin, 1995).

You can think of behavior activation as a procedure that relies on shaping and contingency management, although the contingencies are dominantly social contingencies within the therapeutic relationship. Behavioral activation in its various forms (e.g., activity scheduling) are among the most effective treatments for depression and several other problems, exceeding the impact of traditional CBT (Cuijpers, van Stratena, & Warmerdama, 2006; Dimidjian et al., 2006).

The Therapeutic Relationship

The therapeutic relationship is considered central in successful therapy of many orientations. There is a great deal of empirical support in the psychotherapy literature for a correlation between measures of therapeutic alliance and therapeutic outcome (Horvath, 2001; Martin, Garske, & Davis, 2000), but little systematic support for the specific relationship processes involved as causal processes that can be produced and trained (Martin, Garske & Davis, 2000). It is remarkable that a variable that is so frequently assumed to be central to therapeutic success is often not subject to detailed or explicit analysis in the training and manualization of therapies.

One reason this is the case may be the therapeutic relationship is a process that does not easily lend itself to analysis across types of therapy, individual therapies, or even the same therapy across time. Psychotherapy is a process of learning in the context of a relationship, but it is a functional process that at its best will be flexible in response to the variables present in each therapeutic relationship. For instance, one might assume that a useful therapeutic relationship is one that is warm and accepting. Although this may frequently be the case, we can easily make an argument for times when it might not be useful for the therapist to be warm or accepting. It seems likely that the most useful therapeutic relationship will be one that is psychologically flexible in response to the client's behavior and models the processes that it aims to teach. Going beyond that requires a more precise underlying model of the therapeutic relationship itself.

One model of the therapeutic relationship in modern clinical behavior analysis is that described in Functional Analytic Psychotherapy (Kohlenberg & Tsai, 1991). In this approach the focus is on detecting clinically relevant behaviors in session, using the therapeutic relationship to evoke them, using natural social reinforcers by the therapist to reinforce in-session improvements, and tracking and interpreting these relations. A second, complementary model of the therapeutic relationship is that of Acceptance and Commitment Therapy (Pierson & Hayes, 2007). In this approach a positive therapeutic relationship is defined as one that is accepting, defused, conscious, present focused, values-based, active, and flexible. The targeted goal is to establish these core processes, but that means that the therapist also needs to develop them and to use them in the therapeutic relationship itself. It is not possible to encourage acceptance in others, without being accepting of oneself and the client. As in FAP, the goal is to detect positive and negative client instances of these processes (e.g., acceptance or avoidance), and to model, instigate, and reinforce them. What the ACT model adds is that this very process of social reinforcement and shaping should be done using the self-same processes to evoke and reinforce gains: From ACT processes, target ACT processes, with ACT processes. For example, from an accepting stance with regard to oneself, the therapist needs to build acceptance skills in the client, by using acceptance, defusion, values-based actions and so on.

In both of these approaches the evolving therapeutic relationship may serve as a context in which different processes are learned and reinforced, undermining both current and historical contexts of social control. Even without conscious attention to the importance of these processes, most therapeutic relationships are going to provide a far more accepting context for client's thoughts, feelings and experiences than the majority of cultural and family contexts. Most therapies and therapists are also likely to take a less fused approach to verbal relations than most social contexts. As contact with immediate experience is encouraged and reinforced in the therapeutic relationship, the function of private experiences like thoughts and feelings begins to change.

New skills in dealing with private experience are established by the manner in which the therapist relates to his or her own thoughts and feelings as well as the thoughts and feelings of the client. This is why mere verbal content directed towards changing pathological processes is unlikely to be as useful as teaching within the process of a reinforcing therapeutic relationship. It is important that a therapist attend to these processes personally as well as in the relationship with the client.

If, for instance, a therapist is able to experience sadness alongside a client whose eyes begin to fill with tears without needing to change what the client is feeling in that moment, the client learns that his or her own experience of sadness is acceptable in a way that our broader culture does not support. The therapist may say "it seems like you are feeling sad now" as he or she models an affect congruent with that of the client. This simple statement, delivered empathically, functions to direct the attention of the client to his or her own present moment experiencing while modeling being present with the client. The "right now" also emphasizes the present moment nature of the client's experience. It reinforces acceptance by not attempting to change what the client is feeling in the moment and modeling the therapist accepting his or her own emotional response to the client's feelings. A therapist attuned to the client's experience may not even need to make any statement at all, if the client is present with the therapist and notices the therapist witnessing the beginning of tears in a way that is defused, accepting and present this mere presence may be very therapeutic. The nature of the development of relations is such that the influence of such a moment also has the potential to be quite broad, particularly as the client places increasing value on the therapeutic relationship and its value as a reinforcer increases.

Conclusion

The range of applied behavioral concepts of this kind is very large. In some ways this chapter is more a set of examples than an encyclopedic listing of the concepts that might be used to understand complex human behavior as behavioral principles are extended into the clinic. Terms such as exposure, psychological flexibility, skills development, active coping, and a long list of similar terms may be examined similarly. In the chapters that follow authors will use terms of this kind, often stopping to present shorthand descriptions of the ways that they may link to behavioral principles. Working through each and every such concept in technical detail is beyond the scope of this volume. It is more important to see that this is possible, natural, and useful. In general, clinical approaches long ago walked away from a vision of a unified discipline in which basic behavioral principles were the foundation of clinical innovation. That vision seems to be coming back in the modern era, as this volume testifies.

References

Abramowitz, J. S. (1996). Variants of exposure and response prevention in the treatment of obsessive-compulsive disorder: A meta-analysis. *Behavior Therapy, 27,* 583-600.

Ainslie, G., & Monterosso, J. R. (2003). Building blocks of self-control: Increased tolerance for delay with bundled rewards. *Journal of the Experimental Analysis of Behavior, 79,* 37-48.

American Psychiatric Association. (1994). *Diagnostic and statistical manual of mental disorders (4th ed.).* Washington, D.C.: American Psychiatric Press.

Anderson, C. M., Hawkins, R. P., & Scotti, J. R. (1997). Private events in behavior analysis: Conceptual basis and clinical relevance. *Behavior Therapy, 28,* 157-179.

Ayllon, T., & Azrin, N. H. (1968). *A motivating environment for therapy and rehabilitation.* New York: Appleton-Century-Crofts.

Bach, P., & Hayes, S.C. (2002). The use of acceptance and commitment therapy to prevent the rehospitalization of psychotic patients: A randomized controlled trial. *Journal of Consulting and Clinical Psychology, 70,* 1129-1139.

Baer, R. (2003). Mindfulness training as a clinical intervention: a conceptual and empirical review. *Clinical Psychology: Science & Practice, 10,* 125-143.

Barnes-Holmes, D., Hayes, S. C., & Dymond, S. (2001). Self and self-directed rules. In S. C. Hayes, D. Barnes-Holmes, & B. Roche (Eds.), *Relational frame theory: A post-Skinnerian account of human language and cognition* (pp. 119-139). Kluwer Academic/Plenum Publishers.

Barnes-Holmes, D., Hayes, S. C., Dymond, S., & O'Hora, D. (2001). Multiple stimulus relations and the transformation of stimulus functions. In S. C. Hayes, D. Barnes-Holmes, & B. Roche (Eds.), *Relational frame theory: A post-Skinnerian account of human language and cognition* (pp. 51-71). Kluwer Academic/Plenum Publishers.

Barnes-Holmes, D., O'Hora, D., Roche, B., Hayes, S. C., Bissett, R. T., & Lyddy, F. (2001). Understanding verbal regulation. In S. C. Hayes, D. Barnes-Holmes, & B. Roche (Eds.),

Relational frame theory: A post-Skinnerian account of human language and cognition (pp. 103-117). Kluwer Academic/Plenum Publishers.

Barnes-Holmes, D., Stewart, I., Dymond, S., & Roche, B. (2000). A behavior-analytic approach to some of the problems of the self: A relational frame analysis. In M. J. Dougher (Ed.), *Clinical behavior analysis* (pp. 47-74). Reno, NV: Context Press.

Blackledge, J. T. (2007). Disrupting verbal processes: Cognitive defusion in acceptance & commitment therapy and other mindfulness-based psychotherapies. *The Psychological Record, 57*.

Bond, F. W., & Bunce, D. (2000). Mediators of change in emotion-focused and problem-focused worksite stress management interventions. *Journal of Occupational Health Psychology, 5*, 156-163.

Borkovec, T. D., & Roemer, L. (1994). Generalized anxiety disorder. In R. T. Ammerman & M. Hersen (Eds.), *Handbook of prescriptive treatments for adults* (pp. 261-281). New York: Plenum.

Christensen, A., Jacobson, N. S., & Babcock, J. C. (1995). Integrative behavioral couple therapy. In N. S. Jacobson & A. S. Gurman (Eds.) *Clinical handbook of couples therapy* (pp. 31-64). New York: Guilford Press.

Cinciripini, P. M., Wetter, D. W., & McClure, J. B. (1997). Scheduled reduced smoking: Effects on smoking abstinence and potential mechanisms of action. *Addictive Behaviors, 22*, 759-767.

Craske, M. G., & Barlow, D. H. (1993). Panic disorder and agoraphobia. In D. H. Barlow (Ed.), *Clinical handbook of psychological disorders: A step-by-step treatment manual (2nd Ed.)* (pp. 1-47). New York: Guilford Press.

Cuijpers, P., van Stratena, A., & Warmerdama, L. (2007). Behavioral activation treatments of depression: A meta-analysis. *Clinical Psychology Review, 27*, 318-326.

Davidson, R. J., Kabat-Zinn, J., Schumacher, J., Rosenkranz, M., Muller, D., Santorelli, S., et al. (2003). Alterations in brain and immune function produced by mindfulness meditation. *Psychosomatic Medicine, 65*, 564-570.

Dimidjian, S., Hollon, S. D., Dobson, K. S., Schmaling, K. B., Kohlenberg, R. J., Addis, M. E., Gallop, R., McGlinchey, J. B., McGlinchey, J. B., Markley, D. K., Gollan, J. K., Atkins, D. C., Dunner, D. L., & Jacobson, N. S. (2006). Treatment of depression and anxiety - randomized trial of behavioral activation, cognitive therapy, and antidepressant medication in the acute treatment of adults with major depression. *Journal of Consulting and Clinical Psychology, 74*, 658-670.

Dimidjian, S. D., & Linehan, M. M. (2003). Mindfulness practice. In W. O'Donohue, J. Fisher, & S. Hayes (Eds.), *Cognitive behavior therapy: Applying empirically supported techniques in your practice* (pp. 229-237). New York: Wiley.

Dinsmoor, J. A. (1985). The role of observing and attention in establishing stimulus control. *Journal of the Experimental Analysis of Behavior, 43*, 365-381.

Dougher, M. (1999). *Clinical behavior analysis*. Reno, NV: Context Press.

Fletcher, L., & Hayes, S. C. (2005). Relational frame theory, acceptance and commitment therapy, and a functional analytic definition of mindfulness. *Journal of Rational Emotive and Cognitive Behavioral Therapy, 23*, 315-336.

Gold, D. B., & Wegner, D. M. (1995). Origins of ruminative thought: Trauma, incompleteness, nondisclosure, and suppression. *Journal of Applied Psychology, 25*, 1245-1261.

Goldiamond, I. (1974). Toward a constructional approach to social problems. *Behaviorism, 2*, 1-79.

Goldfield, M. R., & Davidson, G. C. (1994). *Clinical behavior therapy: Expanded edition*. New York: John Wiley & Sons, Inc.

Gross, J. J., & Levenson, R. W. (1997). Hiding feelings: The acute effects of inhibiting negative and positive emotion. *Journal of Abnormal Psychology, 106*(1), 95-103.

Hawkins, R. P. (1979). The functions of assessment: Implications for selection and development of devices for assessing repertoires in clinical, educational, and other settings. *Journal of Applied Behavior Analysis, 12*, 501-516.

Hayes, S. C. (1984). Making sense of spirituality. *Behaviorism, 12*, 99-110.

Hayes, S. C. (Ed.). (1989). *Rule-governed behavior: Cognition, contingencies, and instructional control*. New York: Plenum.

Hayes, S. C. (1992). Verbal relations, time and suicide. In S. C. Hayes & L. J. Hayes (Eds.), *Understanding verbal relations* (pp. 109-118). Reno, NV: Context Press.

Hayes, S. C. (1994). Content, context, and the types of psychological acceptance. In S. C. Hayes, N. S. Jacobson, V. M. Follette, & M. J. Dougher (Eds.), *Acceptance and change: Content and context in psychotherapy* (pp. 13-33). Reno, NV: Context Press.

Hayes, S. C. (1998). Understanding and treating the theoretical emaciation of behavior therapy. *The Behavior Therapist, 21,* 67-68.

Hayes, S. C. (2004). Acceptance and commitment therapy, relational frame theory, and the third wave of behavioral and cognitive therapies. *Behavior Therapy, 35,* 639-666.

Hayes, S. C., Barnes-Holmes, D., & Roche, B. (Eds.). (2001). *Relational frame theory: a post-Skinnerian account of human language and cognition.* New York: Plenum Press.

Hayes, S. C., Bissett, R. T., Zettle, R. D., Rosenfarb, I. S., Cooper, L. D., & Grundt, A. M. (1999). The impact of acceptance versus control rationales on pain tolerance. *The Psychological Record, 49,* 33-47.

Hayes, S. C., Blackledge, J. T., & Barnes-Holmes, D. (2001). Language and cognition: Constructing an alternative approach within the behavioral tradition. In S. C. Hayes, D. Barnes-Holmes, & B. Roche (Eds.), *Relational frame theory: A post-Skinnerian account of human language and cognition* (pp. 51-72). New York: Kluwer Academic/Plenum Publishers.

Hayes, S. C., Follette, V. M., & Linehan, M. M. (Eds.). (2004). *Mindfulness and acceptance: Expanding the cognitive-behavioral tradition.* New York: Guilford.

Hayes, S. C., Gifford, E. V, Townsend, R. C., Jr., & Barnes-Holmes, D. (2001). Thinking, problem-solving, and pragmatic verbal analysis. In S. C. Hayes, D. Barnes-Holmes, & B. Roche (Eds.), *Relational frame theory: A post-Skinnerian account of human language and cognition* (pp. 87-101). New York: Plenum Press.

Hayes, S. C., & Gregg, J. (2001). Functional contextualism and the self. In J. C. Muran (Ed.), *Self-relations in the psychotherapy process* (pp. 291-311). Washington, DC: American Psychological Association.

Hayes, S. C., & Hayes, L. J. (1992). Verbal relations and the evolution of behavior analysis. *American Psychologist, 47,* 1383-1395.

Hayes, S. C., Luoma, J. B., Bond, F. W., Masuda, A., & Lillis, J. (2006). Acceptance and commitment therapy: Model, processes and outcomes. *Behavior Research and Therapy, 44,* 1-25.

Hayes, S. C., & Nelson, R. O. (1983). Similar reactivity produced by external cues and self-monitoring. *Behavior Modification, 7,* 183-196.

Hayes, S. C., Nelson, R. O., & Jarrett, R. B. (1987). The treatment utility of assessment: A functional approach to evaluating assessment quality. *American Psychologist, 42,* 963-974.

Hayes, S. C., Rosenfarb, I., Wulfert, E., Munt, E. D., Korn, Z., & Zettle, R. D. (1985). Self-reinforcement effects: An artifact of social standard setting? *Journal of Applied Behavior Analysis, 18,* 201-214.

Hayes, S. C. Strosahl, K. D., & Wilson, K. G. (1999). *Acceptance and commitment therapy: An experiential approach to behavior change.* New York: Guilford Press.

Hayes, S. C., Strosahl, K. D., Bunting, K., Twohig, M., & Wilson, K. G. (2004). What is acceptance and commitment therapy? In S. C. Hayes & K. D. Strosahl (Eds.), *A practical guide to acceptance and commitment therapy* (pp. 3-29). New York: Springer-Verlag.

Hayes, S. C., & Wilson, K. G. (1993). Some applied implications of a contemporary behavior-analytic account of verbal events. *The Behavior Analyst, 16,* 283-301.

Hayes, S. C., & Wilson, K. G. (1994). Acceptance and commitment therapy: Altering the verbal support for experiential avoidance. *The Behavior Analyst, 17,* 289-303.

Hayes, S. C., & Wilson, K. G. (2003). Mindfulness: Method and process. *Clinical Psychology: Science and Practice, 10,* 161-165.

Hayes, S. C., Wilson, K. G., Gifford, E. V., Follette, V. M., & Strosahl, K. (1996). Emotional avoidance and behavioral disorders: A functional dimensional approach to diagnosis and treatment. *Journal of Consulting and Clinical Psychology, 64,* 1152-1168.

Hayes, S. C., Zettle, R. D., & Rosenfarb, I. (1989). Rule following. In S. C. Hayes (Ed.), *Rule-governed behavior: Cognition, contingencies, and instructional control* (pp. 191-220). New York: Plenum.

Heffner, M., & Eifert, G. H. (2003). Valued directions: Acceptance and Commitment Therapy in the treatment of alcohol dependence. *Cognitive and Behavioral Practice, 10,* 378-383.

Heyman, G. M. (1996). Resolving the contradictions of addiction. *Behavioral and Brain Sciences, 19,* 561-610.

Heyman, G. M., & Tanz, L. (1995). How to teach a pigeon to maximize overall reinforcement rate. *Journal of the Experimental Analysis of Behavior, 64,* 277-298.

Horvath, A. O. (2001). The alliance. *Psychotherapy: Theory, Research, Practice, Training, 38,* 365-372.

Jacobson, N. S., Christensen, A., Prince, S. E., Cordova, J., & Eldridge, K. (2000). Integrative behavioral couple therapy: An acceptance-based, promising new treatment for couple discord. *Journal of Consulting and Clinical Psychology, 68,* 351-355.

Kabat-Zinn, J. (2003). Mindfulness based interventions in context: Past, present, and future. *Clinical Psychology: Science & Practice, 10,* 144-156.

Kelly, A. E., & Kahn, J. H. (1994). Effects of suppression of personal intrusive thoughts. *Journal of Personality & Social Psychology, 66*(6), 998-1006.

Kirby, K. N., & Guastello, B. (2001). Making choices in anticipation of similar future choices can increase self-control. *Journal of Experimental Psychology: Applied, 7,* 154-164.

Kohlenberg, R., Hayes, S. C., & Tsai, M. (1993). Radical behavioral psychotherapy: Two contemporary examples. *Clinical Psychology Review, 13,* 579-592.

Kohlenberg, R. J., & Tsai, M. (1991). *Functional analytic psychotherapy: Creating intense and curative therapeutic relationships.* New York: Plenum.

Lattal, K. A. (1975). Reinforcement contingencies as discriminative stimuli. *Journal of the Experimental Analysis of Behavior, 23,* 241-246.

Lazarus, R. S. (1982). Thoughts on the relations between emotion and cognition. *American Psychologist, 37,* 1019-1024.

Lewinsohn, P. M. (1976). Activity schedules in treatment of depression. In J. D. Krumbotz & C. E. Thoresen (Eds.), *Counseling methods* (pp. 74-83). New York: Holt, Rinehart, and Winston.

Linehan, M. M. (1993). *Cognitive-behavioral treatment of borderline personality disorder.* New York: Guilford.

Lovaas, O. I. (1987). Behavioral treatment and normal intellectual and educational functioning in autistic children. *Journal of Consulting and Clinical Psychology, 55,* 3-9.

Luciano, S. M. C., & Cabello Luque, F. (2001). Trastorno de duelo y terapia de aceptacion y compromiso (ACT) [Bereavement and Acceptance and Commitment Therapy (ACT)]. *Analisis y Modificacion de Conducta, 27,* 399-424.

Luciano S. M. C., Gómez Martin, S., Hernández Lopez, M., & Cabello Luque, F. (2001). Alcoholismo, evitacion experiencial y terapia de aceptacion y compromiso [Alcoholism, Experiential Avoidance, and Acceptance and Commitment Therapy (ACT)]. *Análisis y Modificación de Conducta, 27,* 333-372.

Lutz, A., Greischar, L. L., Rawlings, N. B., Ricard, M., & Davidson, R. J. (2004) Long-term meditators self-induce high-amplitude gamma synchrony during mental practice. *Proceedings of the National Academy of Sciences, 101,* 16369-16373.

MacCorquodale, K., & Meehl, P. E. (1948). On a distinction between hypothetical constructs and intervening variables. *Psychological Review, 55,* 95-107.

Marlatt, G. A. (2002). Buddhist philosophy and the treatment of addictive behavior. *Cognitive & Behavioral Practice, 9,* 44-49.

Martell, C. R., Addis, M. E., & Jacobson, N. S. (2001). *Depression in context: Strategies for guided action.* New York: W. W. Norton.

Martin, D. J., Garske, J. P., & Davis, M. K. (2000). Relation of the therapeutic alliance with outcome and other variables: A meta-analytic review. *Journal of Consulting and Clinical Psychology, 68,* 438-450.

Martin, G., & Pear, J. (1996). *Behavior Modification: What it is and how to do it* (5th ed.), Upper Saddle River, NJ: Prentice-Hall.

Masuda, A., Hayes, S. C., Sackett, C. F., & Twohig, M. P. (2004). Cognitive defusion and self-relevant negative thoughts: Examining the impact of a ninety year old technique. *Behaviour Research and Therapy, 42,* 477-485.

McCullough, J. P., Jr. (2000). *Treatment for chronic depression: Cognitive Behavioral Analysis System of Psychotherapy (CBASP).* New York: Guilford Press.

McHugh, L., Barnes-Holmes, Y., & Barnes-Holmes, D. (2004). Perspective-taking as relational responding: A developmental profile. *Psychological Record, 54*, 115-144.

Miller, W. R., & Rollnick, S. (2001). *Motivational Interviewing: Preparing people for change (2nd ed.)*, New York: Guilford.

Mischel, H. N., & Mischel, W. (1983). The development of children's knowledge of self-control strategies. *Child Development, 54*, 603-619.

Mowrer, O. H. (1947). On the dual nature of learning: A re-interpretation of "conditioning" and "problem-solving". *Harvard Educational Review, 17*, 102-148.

Moxon, P. D., Keenan, M., & Hine, L. (1993). Gender-role stereotyping and stimulus equivalence. *The Psychological Record, 43*, 381-394.

Nelson, R. O., & Hayes, S. C. (1981). Theoretical explanations for reactivity in self-monitoring. *Behavior Modification, 5*, 3-14.

Pierson, H., & Hayes, S. C. (2007). Using acceptance and commitment therapy to empower the therapeutic relationship. In P. Gilbert & R. Leahy (Eds.), *The therapeutic relationship in cognitive behavior therapy* (pp. 205-228). London: Routledge.

Pliskoff, S. S., & Goldiamond, I. (1966). Some discriminative properties of fixed ratio performance in the pigeon. *Journal of the Experimental Analysis of Behavior, 9*, 1-9.

Rachlin, H. (1995). Self-control: Beyond commitment. *Behavioral and Brain Sciences, 18*, 109-159.

Rachlin, H. (2000). *The science of self-control*. Cambridge, MA: Harvard University Press.

Rehfeldt, R. A., & Hayes, L. J. (2000). The long-term retention of generalized equivalence classes. *The Psychological Record, 50*, 405-428.

Rehfeldt, R. A., Dillen, J. E., Ziomek, M. M., & Kowalchuk, R. K. (2007). Assessing relational learning deficits in perspective-taking in children with high-functioning autism spectrum disorder. *Psychological Record, 57*, 23-47.

Reynolds, G. S. (1966). Discrimination and emission of temporal intervals by pigeons. *Journal of the Experimental Analysis of Behavior, 9*, 65-68.

Reynolds, G. S., & Catania, A. C. (1962). Temporal discrimination in pigeons. *Science, 135*, 314-315.

Rosenfarb, I., & Hayes, S. C. (1984). Social standard setting: The Achilles heel of informational accounts of therapeutic change. *Behavior Therapy, 15*, 515-528.

Roemer, L., & Orsillo, S. M. (2002). Expanding our conceptualization of and treatment for generalized anxiety disorder: Integrating mindfulness/acceptance-based approaches with existing cognitive-behavioral models. *Clinical Psychology: Science & Practice, 9*, 54-68.

Segal, Z. V., Williams, J. M. G., & Teasdale, J. D. (2002). *Mindfulness-based cognitive therapy for depression: A new approach to preventing relapse*. New York: Guilford Press.

Siegel, E., & Rachlin, H. (1995). Soft commitment: Self-control achieved by response persistence. *Journal of the Experimental Analysis of Behavior, 64*, 117-128.

Skinner, B. F. (1950). Are theories of learning necessary? *Psychological Review, 57*, 193-216.

Skinner, B. F. (1957). *Verbal behavior*. New York: Appelton-Century-Crofts.

Skinner, B. F. (1974). *About behaviorism*. New York: Alfred A. Knopf.

Spence, K. W. (1944). The nature of theory construction in contemporary psychology. *Psychological Review, 51*, 48-68.

Teasdale, J. D. (1997). The relationship between cognition and emotion: The mind-in-place in mood disorders. In D. M. Clark & C. G. Fairburn (Eds.), *Science and practice of cognitive behaviour therapy* (pp. 67-93). London: Oxford University Press.

Teasdale, J. D., Moore, R. G., Hayhurst, H., Pope, M., Williams, S., & Segal, Z. V. (2002). Metacognitive awareness and prevention of relapse in depression: Empirical evidence. *Journal of Consulting and Clinical Psychology, 70*, 275-287.

Teasdale, J. D., Segal, Z. V., Williams, J. M., Ridgeway, V. A., Soulsby, J. M., & Lau, M. A. (2000). Prevention of relapse/recurrence in major depression by mindful-based cognitive therapy. *Journal of Consulting and Clinical Psychology, 68*, 615-623.

Tolman, E. C. (1936). Operational behaviorism and current trends in psychology. *Proceedings of the 25th Anniversary Celebration of Inauguration of Graduate Studies, University of Southern California*, 89-103.

Waltz, J., & Linehan, M. M. (1999). Functional analysis of borderline personality disorder behavioral criterion patterns. In J. Derksen & C. Maffei (Eds.), *Treatment of Personality Disorders* (pp.183-206). New York: Kluwer/Plenum.

Watt, A., Keenan, M., Barnes, D., & Cairns, E. (1991). Social categorization and stimulus equivalence. *The Psychological Record, 41,* 33-50.

Wegner, D. M. (1994a). *White bears and other unwanted thoughts.* New York: Guilford.

Wegner, D. M. (1994b). Ironic processes of mental control. *Psychological Review, 101,* 34-52.

Wegner, D. M., Schneider, D. J., Knutson, B., & McMahon, S. R. (1991). Polluting the stream of consciousness: The effect of thought suppression on the mind's environment. *Cognitive Therapy and Research, 15,* 141-151.

Weil, T. M. (2007). *The impact of training deictic frames on perspective taking in young children: A relational frame approach to theory of mind.* Unpublished doctoral dissertation, University of Nevada, Reno.

Wells, A. (2002). GAD, metacognition, and mindfulness: An information processing analysis. *Clinical Psychology-Science and Practice, 9,* 95-100.

Williams, J. M. G., Teasdale, J. D., Segal, Z. V., & Soulsby, J. (2000). Mindfulness-based cognitive therapy reduces overgeneral autobiographical memory in formerly depressed patients. *Journal of Abnormal Psychology, 109,* 150-155.

Wilson, K. G., & Hayes, S. C. (1996). Resurgence of derived stimulus relations. *Journal of the Experimental Analysis of Behavior, 66,* 267-281.

Wilson, K. G., &Hayes, S. C. (2000). Why it is crucial to understand thinking and feeling: An analysis and application to drug abuse. *The Behavior Analyst, 23,* 25-43.

Wilson, K. G., Hayes, S. C., Gregg, J., & Zettle, R. D. (2001). Psychopathology and psychotherapy. In S. C. Hayes, D. Barnes-Holmes, & B. Roche (Eds.), *Relational frame theory: A post-Skinnerian account of human language and cognition* (pp. 211-237). New York: Plenum Press.

Wilson, T. D., Lindsey, S., & Schooler, T. Y. (2000). A model of dual attitudes. *Psychological Review, 107,* 101-126.

Wilson, K. G., & Murrell, A. R. (2004). Values work in acceptance and commitment therapy: Setting a course for behavioral treatment. In S. Hayes, V. Follette, & M. Linehan (Eds.), *Mindfulness and acceptance: Expanding the cognitive-behavioral tradition* (pp. 120-151). New York: Guilford.

Zettle, R. D., & Hayes, S. C. (1986). Dysfunctional control by client verbal behavior: The context of reason-giving. *The Analysis of Verbal Behavior, 4,* 30-38.

Zettle, R. D., & Raines, J. C. (1989). Group cognitive and contextual therapies in treatment of depression. *Journal of Clinical Psychology, 45,* 438-445.

Chapter 4

From Normal Anxiety
to Anxiety Disorders:
An Experiential Avoidance Perspective

Georg H. Eifert
Chapman University
John P. Forsyth
University at Albany, SUNY

The goal of this chapter is to outline the role of experiential avoidance and other emotion regulation processes that are now considered crucial in explaining the genesis, maintenance, and alleviation of anxiety *disorders* rather than anxiety per se (Barlow, Allen, & Choate, 2004; Craske, 2003). In so doing, we draw attention to broad-band emotion regulatory processes for three reasons.

First, the emerging consensus is that experiential avoidance processes, namely the tendency to avoid, suppress, or escape from aversive emotional states and the contexts or cues that may evoke them, characterize virtually all anxiety disorders (Barlow, 2002; Barlow et al., 2004; Rosen & Schulkin, 1998). Second, findings from the field of emotion regulation suggest that experiential avoidance may be harmful when applied to aversive emotional states in that it serves as a general vulnerability variable that functions to transform normal anxiety and fear into disordered anxiety and potentiates other vulnerabilities (i.e., fear of fear or anxiety sensitivity) in predicting panic-related distress (Moses, Acheson, & Forsyth, 2006). That is, anxiety sensitivity mediates the relation between experiential avoidance and panic-related distress, but experiential avoidance does not mediate the relation between anxiety sensitivity and panic-related distress. Third, it is becoming increasingly clear that the application of emotional avoidance strategies in situations and contexts where they are unnecessary is largely responsible for the wide-ranging functional impairment typical of many persons with anxiety disorders. Indeed, rigid and inflexible forms of emotion regulation such as experiential avoidance, when juxtaposed with fear learning experiences and powerful competing approach contingencies that cannot be avoided without significant costs, likely function as an important predisposition for the development and maintenance of *disordered* fear (see Forsyth, Eifert, & Barrios, 2006, for a detailed account). Collectively, this work has led to a rethinking of the mastery and control agenda that has come to characterize many mainstream behavior therapies for the anxiety disorders (Barlow et al., 2004). Indeed, newer third generation behavior therapies either target experiential avoidance processes specifically (e.g., Acceptance and Commitment Therapy; Hayes, Strosahl, & Wilson, 1999), or target emotion regulation processes more broadly (e.g., Dialectical Behavior Therapy; Linehan, 1993). For these and other reasons, unified treatment protocols for persons suffering from anxiety disorders (see Eifert & Forsyth, 2005) now target emotion regulation processes explicitly in therapy.

Our intent here is to provide a broad overview of this work with an eye on how it may help advance our understanding of anxiety disorders and lead to improved clinical interventions, including modifications to the most effective aspects of cognitive-behavioral treatments. To set a context for the discussion, we begin with a brief overview of the anxiety disorders, followed by a critical evaluation of behavioral and cognitive-behavioral accounts of anxiety and fear learning within an emotion regulation context. The remaining sections describe findings from emotion regulation research that are germane to understanding the maintenance of anxiety-related problems and some applied implications that follow from this account.

Part I. Overview of Anxiety Disorders

This section is designed to give the reader a brief overview of the central features of the major anxiety disorders except for obsessive-compulsive disorder, which is discussed elsewhere (see Moran & Twohig, this volume) as currently defined by the Diagnostic and Statistical Manual of Mental Disorders, 4th Edition, Text Revision (DSM-IV-TR; American Psychological Association, 2000).

Fear and Anxiety

Fear is a present-oriented state that occurs in response to an imminent real or imagined danger or threat. Anxiety, by contrast, is a future-oriented mood state that is accompanied by anxious apprehension, worry, increased muscle tension, restricted peripheral autonomic arousal, and marked increases in EEG beta activity reflecting intense cognitive processing in the frontal lobes (Borkovec, Alcaine, & Behar, 2004; Craske, 1999). Experiencing fear and anxiety is in many instances healthy and adaptive. Both emotions serve a purpose, namely, to keep us alive and out of trouble.

Panic Attacks

Barlow (2002) noted that clinical manifestation of the basic emotion of fear is most evident in panic attacks. In addition to a strong autonomic surge that typically occurs within ten minutes, and sometimes in as little as two minutes, individuals experiencing a panic attack report extreme fear and terror, thoughts of dying and losing control, and an overwhelming urge to escape and get away from wherever they are. Such fear responses are emergency alarm reactions. The main function of such responses is to prepare humans and other mammals for self-preserving actions that may prevent or minimize harm resulting from contact with a potentially harmful environmental stimulus or event. The core of that response is a fight or flight action tendency. It is that strong urge to escape that leads people to avoid places where escape could be difficult (e.g., movie theaters, large shopping malls, formal social gatherings). If the action tendency is blocked, then the intensity of fear tends to increase.

Panic Disorder and Agoraphobia

Panic Disorder (PD) is characterized by recurrent panic attacks, fear of bodily sensations associated with autonomic arousal, and anxiety concerning the possibility of future panic attacks. Current diagnostic criteria for a diagnosis of PD require documenting recurrent and unexpected attacks (APA, 2000). At least one of the attacks must be followed by at least one month of persistent worry about future attacks, worry about the consequences of the attacks, or a behavioral change because of the attacks (e.g., some type of avoidance). At the core, panic disorder is a fear of experiencing fear (Chambless & Gracely, 1989). People are literally afraid of panic attacks and the potential consequences of such attacks. Agoraphobia is essentially a fear of having a panic attack in particular places, not a fear of those places as was previously thought. Accordingly, agoraphobia may best be viewed as a complication of panic disorder, where people attempt to avoid future panic attacks by staying in "safe" areas and avoiding stimuli and places that have previously been associated with panic. Nearly all persons who develop agoraphobia do so after first experiencing panic attacks.

Specific Phobias

A specific phobia is a marked and persistent fear of a specific object or situation that is excessive or unreasonable. Exposure to the feared object usually produces an immediate and intense fear reaction (i.e., a panic attack). This alarm response is accompanied by a strong urge to flee from the object or situation and may be accompanied by significant impairment and distress about fear evoking events and their emotional consequences. Persons suffering from specific phobias will often make great efforts to avoid future encounters with the feared object. Nonetheless, they typically recognize that their fear is excessive or unreasonable. This knowledge, however, has no impact on the urge to escape and avoid feared objects or the ability to control physiological and subjective responses that follow.

Social Phobia

Social phobia is characterized by an excessive and persistent fear and avoidance of situations that involve social interaction and evaluation by others. Persons typically show heightened personal awareness of autonomic activity in social situations, experience real or perceived social inadequacy, and typically avoid and escape from social situations as much as they can. The main feature of social phobia is not so much a fear of the actual social situation but rather having a panic attack or somehow failing and being humiliated or embarrassed while being in a social situation. Thus, as with the other anxiety disorders, the core issue for individuals with social phobia appears to revolve around avoiding the experience of negative affect.

Post Traumatic Stress Disorder (PTSD)

PTSD is the only psychological problem with a clear etiological marker, namely a traumatic event. Although problem responses may manifest within three to six months after the trauma, they also can arise years after a traumatic event. Yet a traumatic experience does not always result in PTSD; about two-thirds of trauma victims never go on to develop PTSD (Jaycox & Foa, 1998). The major clinical features of PTSD fall into three broad clusters: reexperiencing of the traumatic event, avoidance of trauma-related stimuli, and chronically elevated bodily arousal. Heightened concerns regarding threats of personal safety (e.g., death) are central to the disorder.

The most personally distressing feature of PTSD is reexperiencing aspects of the traumatic events triggered by trauma-related stimuli. This reexperiencing results in heightened somatic activity and behavioral manifestations of extreme terror such as immobility (Jaycox & Foa, 1998; Marx, Forsyth, Heidt, Fusé, & Gallup, in press). During flashbacks and nightmares people with PTSD can relive traumatic experiences vividly and in a way that seems very realistic to them. Persons with PTSD typically go to great lengths to avoid any cues or situations that may serve as reminders of the event. The central function of such avoidance is to prevent reexperiencing the negative affect and psychological pain associated with the trauma.

Generalized Anxiety Disorder (GAD)—The Prototypical Anxiety Disorder?

The clinical features of Generalized Anxiety Disorder (GAD) are (a) excessive worry about a number of events and activities occurring more days than not for at least six months causing clinically significant distress or impaired functioning; (b) unsuccessful attempts to stop or control worrying and to reduce anxiety by means of worrying; and (c) a number of central nervous system (CNS) problems such as muscle tension, restlessness, fatigue, difficulty concentrating, irritability, and sleep disturbance.

In recent years, the recognition of worry and anxious apprehension as core processes in GAD has led to the notion that GAD may in fact be *the* "basic" anxiety disorder. Barlow (2002) defines anxious apprehension as a future-oriented mood state in which an individual becomes ready for, or prepares to cope with, upcoming negative events. This state is associated with heightened negative affect, chronic overarousal, a sense of unpredictability and uncontrollability, and attentional focus for signs of threat or danger. Barlow views anxious apprehension as a core process that can serve as a platform for the genesis and maintenance of all anxiety disorders. That is, the process of anxious apprehension is present in all anxiety disorders, but the specific content of that apprehension varies from disorder to disorder.

GAD tends to be associated with indiscriminant avoidance of negative affect. Such avoidance, in turn, tends to be rather automatic or habitual (Mennin, Heimberg, Turk, & Fresco, 2002), with worry serving as the main cognitive avoidance response to threatening material. Specifically, the function of worry is to avoid imagery and physiological arousal associated with anxiety and negative affect (Borkovec et al., 2004). When people worry they are mostly talking to themselves, that is, worry involves abstract verbal thinking as opposed to imagery (Borkovec & Newman, 1998). Hence, worry allows people to approach emotional topics from an abstract conceptual perspective and thereby avoid aversive images and intense negative emotions. In the short run, such strategies account for autonomic restriction or blunted emotional reactivity commonly seen in GAD sufferers. In the long run, however, this strategy is ineffective. In fact, individuals tend to experience even more intense anxiety over the long haul, which is usually followed by efforts to reduce anxiety by engaging in more worrying. Our greatly improved understanding of GAD gives us important clues as to what behavioral processes may make anxiety a clinically significant problem, and those processes will then become important treatment targets.

Anxiety Disorders Have Much in Common

The splitting approach of the DSM has focused too much on the differences between anxiety disorders (Barlow et al., 2004). Such differences are obvious at the phenomenological level, particularly if one focuses on events that elicit fear and anxiety across the anxiety disorders. Yet anxiety disorders share some striking commonalities. For instance, although panic attacks occur most frequently in persons with PD, they also can and do occur in persons with all other anxiety disorders (Barlow, 2002). Most importantly, the tendency to avoid and escape from fear and anxiety is characteristic of just about every individual diagnosed with an anxiety-related disorder (Salters-Pedneault, Tull, & Roemer, 2004). The form of escape and avoidance behavior may differ at a phenomenological level, but the basic function of those behaviors is the same: they serve to reduce fear and anxiety and get the person out of the situation where they experience fear and anxiety.

There is also considerable overlap between anxiety disorders and major mood disorders (see Mineka, Watson, & Clark, 1998, for a review). For instance, Barlow and colleagues (2004) report that 55% of patients with a principal anxiety or mood disorder had at least one other additional anxiety or depressive disorder at the time of assessment. In the majority of cases of coexisting anxiety and depression, anxiety disorders precede rather than follow the onset of mood disorders.

The observable overlapping features of the various anxiety disorders, as well as the large co-occurrence of anxiety and mood disorders, point to a more basic fundamental and functional overlap at the process level that is at the heart of all anxiety disorders: rigid and excessive attempts to avoid experiencing anxiety and unpleasant private content. In subsequent sections, we present empirical evidence suggesting that avoiding negative affect may be a core pathological process that is involved in many anxiety-related problems.

Part II. Current Models of Anxiety Disorders

In this section we briefly review the traditional behavioral and cognitive-behavioral accounts of anxiety. We then describe the core features of a model, described in more detail elsewhere (see Forsyth et al., 2006), that outlines a new functional behavioral approach. In this model, emotion regulation strategies and language processes are at the core of the transformation from normal experiences of fear and anxiety to disordered experiences of fear and anxiety. We do not address biological theories here because psychological and biological theories of anxiety have largely pursued their own agenda. Rachman (2004) also points out that, with few exceptions, biological theories seek to explain particular disorders. They do not provide broad theories of anxiety that have been the hallmark of behavioral models.

Behavioral Views

Ivan Pavlov (1903, 1927, 1941) is best known within the field of psychology for his serendipitous discovery of classical or respondent conditioning. Yet, Pavlov's most interesting later work involved use of classical conditioning procedures as a litmus test to elucidate variables and processes that contribute to abnormal behavior. Experimental neurosis is a good example of this work, for it illustrates how Pavlov and his colleagues used both appetitive and aversive procedures to induce persistent abnormal behavior in laboratory animals. Such procedures, in turn, involved complex contingencies that went well beyond simple classical conditioning contingencies (Gantt, 1944; Liddell, 1947). Much of this work also sought to relate genetic and biological individual difference vulnerabilities (e.g., excitation and inhibition) with conditioning processes to account for how conditioning could result in psychopathology. Though Pavlov maintained a keen interest in classical conditioning throughout his career, he never thought of it as a model of clinically disordered processes. Instead, he viewed classical conditioning as a highly adaptive process that allowed organisms to interface effectively with and adapt to environmental demands.

Early behavior therapy owes much of its success to the conditioning account of the etiology and maintenance of anxiety disorders. In this account, anxiety disorders are learned or acquired via a process of classical conditioning (Eysenck, 1987; Marks, 1969, 1981; Wolpe, 1958; Wolpe & Rachman, 1960) and maintained via negative reinforcement through operant escape and avoidance behaviors (Mowrer, 1939, 1960). Consistent with this view, phobias and anxiety disorders were conceptualized in fear conditioning terms. Thus, when an otherwise benign stimulus occurs in close contingency with an anxiety-inducing event, it becomes highly likely that the stimulus will later elicit anxiety and fear without further trauma. In fact, a relation between otherwise neutral stimuli and a false alarm (i.e., a panic attack) may be enough to set this learning in motion (Barlow, 1988; Bouton, Mineka, & Barlow, 2001; Chambless & Gracely, 1989; Forsyth & Eifert, 1996a, 1998a; Wolpe & Rowan, 1988).

For instance, several analog studies out of our lab group have shown that panic attacks (induced by inhalations of 20% CO_2-enriched air as a UCS) can function as conditioning events in the etiology of anxiety disorders (Forsyth, Eifert, & Thompson, 1996; Forsyth & Eifert, 1996a, 1998a, 1998b). This work suggests that fear conditioning involves, at least from an individual's perspective, a relation between bodily and environmental cues and a highly unpleasant false alarm response (i.e., a panic attack; Barlow, 2002; Forsyth & Eifert, 1996a; Wolpe & Rowan, 1988). More interesting still was our finding that human fear learning is fully mediated by the magnitude of the unconditioned response rather than the intensity of the UCS designed to evoke it (i.e., 20% versus 13% CO_2-enriched air; see Forsyth, Daleiden, & Chorpita, 2000). This work is consistent with earlier observations by Eysenck (1967) who suggested that the false alarm response is what humans experience as traumatic (see also McNally & Lukach, 1992), not necessarily an aversive stimulus capable of evoking it. This view is also at the core of contemporary thinking about the critical processes involved in fear learning, wherein experiencing panic attacks or panic-like responses function as critical conditioning events in the genesis of panic and other anxiety disorders (Bouton et al., 2001).

Cognitive-Behavioral Views

One logical consequence of the conditioning account was that successful treatment needs to involve helping clients to confront feared stimuli and contexts in a safe therapeutic environment so as to (a) counter the powerful action tendency to avoid or escape fear evoking stimuli and situations and thereby (b) allow for new corrective emotional learning via extinction of excessive fear and anxiety (Wolpe, 1958). This view, based largely on extinction as a process, survived more or less intact until the 1970s, when criticisms mounted suggesting that fear conditioning cannot adequately explain the etiology and maintenance of anxiety disorders (Rachman, 1977, 1991).

Growing dissatisfaction with nonmediational behavioral accounts, coupled with limited behavioral research addressing the relation between language and emotional meaning, set the stage for cognitive theories and constructs. The cognitive view emerged to account for the relation between feeling, affect, and cognitive processes. This cognitive information-processing view of the anxiety disorders uses mediational constructs (e.g., networks, nodes, expectancies, appraisals, and schemata) borrowed from information and computer science. It emphasizes the role of memory, attention, catastrophic thinking patterns, irrational beliefs, unrealistic self-statements and appraisals, and the like in the etiology, maintenance, and treatment of anxiety disorders. These notions have had great appeal and were quickly integrated within behavior therapy and became known as cognitive-behavior therapy (Beck & Emery, 1985).

Recognizing the importance of language and emotion in human affairs, cognitive psychologists have emphasized the inextricable relation between language and emotive functions, that is, how language-symbolic processes convey emotional meaning and how emotions depend on such processes.

The fundamental idea is that emotions are experienced as a result of the way in which events are interpreted or appraised. It is the meaning of events that triggers emotions rather than the events themselves. The particular appraisal made will depend on the context in which an even occurs, the mood the person is in at the time it occurs, and the person's past experiences... Effectively this means that the same event can evoke a different emotion in different people, or even different emotions in the same person on different occasions (Salkovskis, 1996, p. 48).

From a practical clinical perspective, the cognitive approach is intriguing and points to the importance of helping clients with anxiety disorders develop a different relation to their thoughts and evaluations. At a conceptual level, however, the cognitive view appeals to one behavior (e.g., particular thoughts or beliefs) in order to explain another behavior (e.g., excessive avoidance). In the process, virtually all of these accounts fail to recognize that behavior is a dependent variable that is itself in need of explanation. This perspective sets up a conceptual and practical dilemma that is not easy to get around. Thus, if we were to accept core beliefs and faulty schema as explanations, we still need to answer the crucial question of how one dependent variable can cause another, including how a dependent variable can become an independent variable (Forsyth, Lejuez, Hawkins, & Eifert, 1996; Skinner, 1953). The contemporary behavior analytic account, by contrast, tends to treat such events as real behavior-behavior relations that are situated in and within a context (Hayes & Brownstein, 1986). This stance has allowed behavior analysts to study events that people experience within the skin (e.g., thinking and feeling) and directs attention away from problematic private content as the problem. Instead, it focuses on contextual variables and processes of which such behavior-behavior relations are a function. Such contextual variables, in turn, can be manipulated directly, and thus provide important insights as to how we can best treat problems associated with these behaviors.

Toward a New Behavioral Perspective

Numerous criticisms have been raised about the clinical relevance of fear conditioning research as a model of anxiety disorders. Most of these have followed from an oversimplified view of conditioning preparations and processes. Our intent here is not to redress all of these criticisms (e.g., Marks, 1981; Menzies & Clarke, 1995; Rachman, 1977, 1991), as none of them hold up in light of contemporary learning theory (Bouton et al., 2001; Forsyth & Eifert, 1996a, 1996b, 1998a, 1998b; Mineka & Zinbarg, 1996). That is, all but one. As we see it, the chief challenge facing Pavlovian conditioning research is in explaining how an entirely functional and ubiquitous learning process (i.e., conditioning) coupled with equally functional and ubiquitous emotional responses (i.e., fear and anxiety) would send some individuals down the path to an anxiety disorder and not others (Forsyth et al., 2006). This issue is a bit different than asking whether individual differences moderate fear learning (Eysenck, 1967; 1976; Mineka & Zinbarg, 1996), including events occurring before, during, and following conditioning (e.g., latent inhibition, context). Rather, the question here is about how conditioning itself, when placed in the context of fear, would yield an anxiety disorder and not simply conditioned fear, anxiety, or avoidance that most humans have experienced at some point in their lives. Put simply, what makes fear conditioning helpful in some contexts and problematic in others?

When fear is evoked, for instance, the typical acute consequence is disruption and narrowing of ongoing behavior. Such disruptions function to ready organisms to take immediate action to prepare for, and subsequently escape from or avoid, potential sources of threat. It makes sense to learn to fear stimuli that have been associated with aversive consequences, and particularly aversive emotional states, even when people are exposed to contingencies between arbitrary stimuli and aversive UCSs. In fact, evolutionarily it would be exceedingly costly for organisms to fail to show conditioned fear and hence fail to learn from aversive experiences. These actions function to mobilize all mammals to take appropriate action in response to threat or danger, and thus contribute in some sense to survival. Following aversive experiences, most mammals will actively avoid exposing themselves to stimuli that predict aversive responses, in part, because it makes adaptive sense to do so. Our challenge then is to explain the parameters and processes that transform such behavior from being adaptive in some contexts to maladaptive or dysfunctional in others.

What makes fear learning a problem? Classical fear conditioning emerged as a model of anxiety disorders largely because of Watson and Raynor's (1920) dramatic demonstration of fear acquisition in Little Albert. The correspondence between the behavior of Albert and the phobias and other anxiety problems was striking and led to the recognition of a process by which fear could be acquired. Yet, the recognition of a process should not be confused with saying that fear learning itself is problematic, or that fear learning is an adequate analog of phobias or anxiety disorders. Under the circumstances, Albert behaved in accord with the history he was provided. There were no costs associated with his conditioned fear or his avoidant behavior. By contrast, fear learning and avoidance across the anxiety disorders are typically associated with costs, in large part, because such behavior is set within a context of powerful competing approach contingencies (see Hayes, 1976). Such competing contingencies are typically reflected in the reasons anxious clients seek treatment (e.g., "My fear of driving is driving my husband crazy," or "I just don't like feeling anxious," or "I can't drive to work because I might have a panic attack").

This dual-component view suggests that fear learning becomes problematic only when it (a) removes access to reinforcing events, and/or (b) puts the individual in contact with aversive events. The resulting avoidance, in turn, becomes disruptive when competing contingencies supporting (a) and/or (b) are present. Thus, a pedestrian who hears the blare of a horn of an oncoming car and jumps out of the way clearly demonstrates fear, conditioning, and avoidance. Yet, this person would not be considered phobic, in part, because there are few or no approach contingencies in this situation (Costello, 1970; Hayes, 1976). In fact, approach in this context (running into the street) would be extremely punishing. This situation is analogous to animal avoidance learning paradigms wherein a signal is followed by the emission of an avoidance response or else the onset of an aversive stimulus. Such behaviors, as Hayes (1976) points out, are not phobic because there is no competing approach element in the situation. Though etiologically all phobic behavior is avoidance behavior, it is not true that all avoidance behavior is phobic behavior (see Hayes, 1976), nor is it true that all fear learning is phobic learning (cf. Forsyth et al., 2006).

From a more functional process-oriented perspective, classical fear conditioning is recognized as an enormously powerful means of altering the functions of a range of events and directing behavior as a consequence. Yet, such learning cannot account for the development of an anxiety disorder except under the most extreme and unusual circumstances. If there are no strong approach contingencies in the situation (i.e., approach-avoidance conflict), then fear learning is just fear learning and avoidance is simply avoidance, not a phobia or an anxiety disorder. The implications of this account have yet to be fully tested in human fear conditioning analogs, but have been demonstrated reliably in animal research (e.g., see Hayes, Lattal, & Myerson, 1979). Such tests in humans present a challenge, in part, because humans can expand the range and scope of approach-avoidance contingencies, including classical conditioning processes, via language and verbal behavior.

The role of language in disordered fear. As with nonhuman animals, humans can learn fear directly through aversive conditioning experiences. In addition, humans may be punished for showing fear—for instance, a child may be scolded by a parent for displaying fearful behavior. Humans can also respond to approach-avoidance contingencies verbally and symbolically without being confronted with the actual contingencies directly. Thus, a person who learns that fear is bad and must be managed before being able to do important tasks (e.g., go to work, attend a child's play; all approach contingencies) may, in turn, struggle to manage the emotional response first in order to engage in effective actions second. This type of learning can take approach-avoidance conflict to a new level of complexity and requires consideration of what humans do to manage the experience and expression of emotions. As we will indicate, this is a key difference between nonhuman animals and humans and one that is accounted for, in large part, by social contingencies and the capacity for humans to engage in complex verbally-mediated relations, including rule-governed verbal behavior. Such capacities make it possible for humans to engage in self and emotion regulatory actions that are not possible to the same degree in nonverbal organisms, including primates.

Despite ample evidence (e.g. Cook & Mineka, 1991; Suomi, 1999) that primates experience and express pain and chronic states of anxious arousal, there is no indication that they *suffer about the experience of having pain and anxiety*. For instance, rhesus monkeys exposed to uncontrollable and unpredictable aversive stimulation experience alarm responses followed by long-term anxious arousal.

Primates will also learn to avoid the source and context of aversive stimulation, but as best we can tell, they do not act deliberately and purposefully to regulate their emotional experience. Humans, by contrast, can and do suffer about their own emotional pain and histories by responding to conditioned responses with evaluative verbal behavior and thinking (e.g., "God, this is awful," "I'm going to pass out") and by engaging in efforts to suppress, avoid, or escape from their emotional pain and related thoughts. Thus, humans can become fearful of fear, depressed about anxiety, worried about the future, agonized about the past. They also engage in struggles to avoid and escape from unpleasant thoughts, images, sensations, feelings, behavioral tendencies, and the circumstances that have evoked them in the past or *may* evoke them in the future. The capacity of language, coupled with powerful social contingencies regarding the experience and expression of emotion, may make this possible.

The experience and expression of emotion as well as the implications of regulating emotional experience for success and personal happiness are largely shaped by social and cultural conventions and contact with other human beings (Gross, 1998a; Hayes et al., 1999). According to relational frame theory (Hayes, Barnes-Holmes, & Roche, 2001), much of this learning is heavily dependent on complex forms of relational learning that is entailed in language and verbal-symbolic behavior (Forsyth, 2000; Forsyth et al., 2006; Forsyth & Eifert, 1996b; Friman, Hayes, & Wilson, 1998). Language serves important symbolic functions by providing humans with emotional experiences without exposure to the actual physical stimuli or events that ordinarily elicit those responses (Staats & Eifert, 1990). For instance, humans can re-experience, countless times and with great intensity, emotions associated with a traumatic event that may have happened years ago, simply by thinking about or visualizing the event.

Such verbal-relational tendencies are socialized and emerge by about the age of two and are fundamentally built into human language and cognition (for a more detailed account of relational learning processes, see Hayes et al., 2001). Such learning begins with an extensive history of reinforcement for relating many stimuli in many different ways based largely on their formal stimulus properties (e.g., beachball is a ball, a basketball is a ball), and thereafter through more indirect relations (e.g., spoken word "ball" is the same as written word ball and other physical examples of balls and not balls). Such a history, in turn, makes it possible for humans to relate other, novel stimuli in numerous ways without being taught to do so (see Blackledge, 2003). For instance, suppose that a person has learned to associate heart palpitations with subsequent panic. Suppose also that this person has learned from others that heart palpitations could mean a heart attack. Depending on the context, and without further training, this person may derive "I'm having a heart attack" when in the middle of a panic attack. Moreover, because a heart attack is associated with other psychological functions that are abstract (e.g., death), this person may also think "I'm dying" when having a panic attack or benign heart palpitations. Such learning, in this example, was established directly and indirectly, with the abstract verbal functions being established via arbitrary verbal relations. Arbitrary here simply means that the new relations are not dependent on the stimulus properties of the relation (e.g., a felt beating heart does not entail heart disease or death, or necessarily panic for that matter), but rather established by social convention.

Language entangles humans in a struggle with emotions. The language-based capacity for humans to evaluate, and respond relationally to their own evaluations, thoughts, and feelings with more evaluations, may make it possible for humans to get entangled in a struggle with their own emotions while acting not to have them. With the above example, one can quite literally try to run away from the experience of fear and a host of events with which it might be arbitrarily related without being taught to do so. That is, the experience of fear can now be established via derived relations with many other events, including those that entail strong approach contingencies. Indeed, several studies have shown transfer of fear and avoidance functions as well as respondent eliciting and extinction functions following a history of learning relations between arbitrary stimuli (Augustson & Dougher, 1997; Dougher, Augustson, Markham, Greenway, & Wulfert, 1994). What is interesting about this work is that it shows how language can establish relations between events that are not taught directly. Thus, if one has been taught verbally that A equals B equals C, and painful shock is associated with C, it is likely that A and B will also evoke conditioned emotional responses. This has been demonstrated with several relational classes (e.g., same, opposite, greater than, less than) and both appetitive and aversive functions (see Hayes et al., 2001, for a detailed account).

Collectively, this work points to the kinds of histories that may transform the experience of a sudden quick movement of the heart into "this is dangerous" and "I might be dying" without direct contact with the aversive contingency (i.e., death). It also points to how language may function to fuse verbal processes with the formal properties of private and public events. When such fusion occurs, a thought is no longer just a thought, and a word is no longer just a sound; rather, actual events can become entailed with the words used to describe them, and thus humans can respond to words about some event as if they were responding to the actual event itself. Consequently, humans can establish contingencies almost entirely through verbal processes (e.g., "don't touch the hot stove or you'll get burned") and can respond to those verbal constructions even when the faced with powerful contradictory natural contingencies (e.g., "I might get 'burned' if I trust that person," meaning hurt).

Though there is evidence that nonverbal organisms can learn relational responses based on the formal properties of relata (e.g., pick a larger object when presented with multiple different objects of varying size and shape), they cannot make more complex relational responses (e.g., pick the *most dangerous* object when presented with a picture of the moon, a tree, and a small wasp). A nonverbal animal would not be able to respond above chance, whereas a verbally sophisticated human would likely chose the wasp simply because they have learned from the social verbal community that bees can be dangerous (cf. Blackledge, 2003; Staats & Eifert, 1990).

One outcome of this process of relational learning through language is the tendency to regulate aversive emotional experience so as to suppress, control, avoid, or escape from it. Another outcome is that language processes can greatly expand the scope of fear learning beyond learning through direct experiences. Both point to the powerful role of socially-mediated contingencies in shaping the experience and expression of emotion. When such contingencies are juxtaposed with classical conditioning contingencies, otherwise adaptive fear learning processes can lead some individuals down the path of developing an anxiety disorder (Forsyth et al., 2006). It is to a discussion of this view that we now turn.

Part III: A Functional Emotional Regulation Perspective of Anxiety Disorders

Numerous accounts have been put forth to explain the shift from normal to clinically disordered fear and anxiety. Most accounts share two notions. First, fear and anxiety are somehow dysregulated, such that either an emotional response occurs too frequently, too intensely, or for too long a time period. Second, anxiety and fear are often evoked or elicited by bodily or environmental cues and situations that do not demand such responses. That is, fear and anxiety are evoked in the absence of real threat or danger. This combination of dysregulated emotions occurring in contexts that do not call for an anxious response may result in wide ranging functional impairment. Cognitive-behavior therapies for anxiety disorders target these emotion regulation and context sensitivity problems with some combination of cognitive restructuring and exposure-based strategies (Barlow, 2002; Barlow et al., 2004).

The Nature of Emotion Regulation

Emotion regulation simply refers to a heterogeneous set of actions that are designed to influence "which emotions we have, when we have them, and how we experience and express them" (Gross, 2002, p. 282; see also Gross, 1998a). Such actions include, but are not limited to, phenomena captured by terms such as reappraisal, distraction, avoidance, escape, suppression, emotion and problem-focused coping, and use of substances to enhance or blunt emotional experience. Each of these domains subsumes numerous actions that can be applied to both positive and negative emotional states (Parrott, 1993). In the context of aversive emotional states, emotion regulatory processes share a common functional goal, namely to avoid or minimize the frequency, intensity, duration, or situational occurrence of internal feeling states, associated thoughts, and physiological processes (e.g., fear and anxiety). Some regulatory processes may be relatively autonomic or habitual occurring in or outside of awareness (e.g., selective attention), whereas others may be more purposeful or deliberate (e.g., blame, rumination, suppression, avoidance). Most processes, however, can be characterized by actions (i.e., automatic or controlled) that aim to alter the form or frequency of events that may precede an emotional response, the consequences of emotional responding, or the emotional response itself. The former has been described as antecedent-focused emotion regulation, whereas the later refers to response-focused emotion regulation.

The emerging field of emotion regulation research and theory aims to bring together numerous processes that are involved in the experience, expression, and modulation of emotion, including the positive and negative consequences of emotion regulation itself (e.g., achievement of goals, restriction in life functioning). That is, emotion regulation is best thought of as a broad term that characterizes a range of well-established psychological phenomena that have been shown to influence the experience and expression of emotion. Though emotion regulation is itself not a dysfunctional process, it can become dysfunctional when the emotions concerned cannot and need not be regulated, and when the very act of emotion regulation gets in the way of meaningful life activities (i.e., regulation that competes with powerful approach contingencies; see Hayes, 1976). It is for these and other reasons that the very topic of emotion regulation is gaining currency in psychopathology research (Barlow et al., 2004; Eifert & Forsyth, 2005) and mental health care more generally (Blackledge & Hayes, 2001; Gross & Muñoz, 1995).

Our consensual model of emotion regulation in a fear learning context (see Forsyth et al., 2006, for details) suggests that humans may regulate the antecedents and consequences of emotions. Antecedents, in the case of anxiety disorders, may include situations where anxiety and fear are likely to occur, bodily and environmental cues that tend to evoke such reactions, whether emotionally relevant information is attended to, and how such information is evaluated or appraised (e.g., "this isn't so bad," or "I can't get through this"). In Pavlovian conditioning terms, the relevant antecedents would be conditional stimuli or CSs and quite possibly unconditioned stimuli or UCSs and the contexts where both may occur. Strategies used to regulate emotions on the front end are important precisely because how one responds to emotional inputs, and particularly the verbal evaluation of those inputs (i.e., "this is dangerous, awful, harmful"), affect the emotional consequences that may follow. Thus, escalation of the emotional sequence can be attenuated or avoided altogether depending on how one manages the antecedents that may evoke or occasion emotional experience.

Once the emotion occurs, regulation efforts tend to focus on the intensity, duration, and general quality of the conditioned or unconditioned emotional response and its consequences. Such response-focused regulation strategies may involve taking a break, relaxation, deep breathing, distraction, affiliating with others, or doing something pleasant. There is nothing particularly problematic about such strategies when they are applied in a context sensitive and flexible manner. Problems may arise when persons make rigid and inflexible efforts to (a) down-regulate the cognitive, physiological, or behavioral components of negative emotions (e.g., anxiety, fear, depressed mood) when such efforts are (b) unnecessary to engage powerful competing approach contingencies. Such down regulation strategies are often subtle and idiosyncratic in persons suffering from anxiety disorders, and usually take the form of suppression, control, avoidance, or escape (Barlow, 2002; Barlow et al., 2004).

Healthy and Unhealthy Varieties of Emotion Regulation

Historically the field of emotion regulation research and theory has remained agnostic with regard to the positive and negative consequences of various emotion regulation strategies and their implications for psychological health and wellness. Increasingly, however, we are learning that certain forms of emotion regulation may be healthier than others, and that some strategies tend to yield human suffering. Here we briefly summarize experimental and correlational findings from this literature that seem relevant to a more complete understanding of how fear and fear learning may become problematic.

Antecedent-focused regulation. Recall that antecedent forms of emotion regulation characterize actions that occur before emotional response tendencies are fully engaged. The most extensively studied of these strategies is reappraisal; a strategy referring to verbal-linguistic actions that function to change the meaning of an emotion-eliciting situation for the better or for the worse (Lazarus & Alfert, 1964). Several lines of research suggest that positive reappraisal is one of the more flexible and effective means of minimizing the negative impact of an aversive event (Gross, 1998b, 2002; Ochsner, Bunge, Gross, & Gabrieli, 2002). This strategy, in turn, includes numerous other actions (e.g., refocusing on the positive in a situation, sense making, acceptance) with the goal being to reframe an emotion-eliciting situation in less emotional terms. Other obvious and less functional antecedent focused strategies include behavioral and cognitive avoidance, distraction, suppression, and even escape.

Several studies suggest that positive reappraisal strategies are much less likely to be used by depressed and anxious persons relative to healthy controls (Garnefski et al., 2002), and that infrequent use of such strategies in healthy adolescents is associated with more depressive and anxious symptoms (Garnefski & Spinhoven, 2001). Others have shown that reappraisal tends to be less costly emotionally and cognitively relative to suppression and avoidance, and that chronic use of suppression impairs memory for emotional information even after controlling for neuroticism and social desirability (e.g., see Richards & Gross, 1999, 2000). The neurobiological circuitry underlying reappraisal is also being worked out. For instance, recent studies by Ochsner and colleagues (2002, 2004) showed that reappraisal appears to activate regions of the prefrontal cortex involved in working memory and cognitive control, and regions involved in active monitoring of performance (i.e., dorsal anterior cingulated) and self evaluation and self-monitoring of emotion (i.e., dorsal medial prefrontal cortex). This work suggests that reappraisal, like other emotion regulatory strategies, draws heavily upon verbal linguistic processes and that these processes may up or down regulate amygdala activity. This circuitry, in turn, is strongly implicated in emotion fear and fear learning (LeDoux, 1996, 2000).

Response and consequence-focused regulation. Several studies have demonstrated that suppression of aversive emotions, including expressive outward suppression, does not provide relief from the psychological experience of that emotion. In fact, just the opposite tends to occur. The emotion becomes stronger and more salient, resulting in increased sympathetic nervous system activity (e.g., peripheral vasoconstriction, cardiovascular and electrodermal response; see Gross, 1998a; Gross & Levenson, 1993, 1997; Richards & Gross, 1999) and a range of undesired psychological content in the suppressor, and interestingly in those interacting with him or her (see Butler & Gross, 2004, for a review).

Several other independent lines of research suggest that attempts to suppress and control unwanted thoughts and feelings can result in more (not less) unwanted thoughts and emotions (Clark, Ball, & Pape, 1991; Gold & Wegner, 1995; Lavy & van den Hout, 1990; Wegner, Schneider, Carter, & White, 1987; Wegner, Schneider, Knutson, & McMahon, 1991; Wegner & Zanakos, 1994; see also Purdon, 1999, for a review). Moreover, emotion suppression has been shown to impair memory and problem solving (e.g., Baumeister, Bratslavsky, Muraven, & Tice, 1998; Richards & Gross, 1999, 2000), contribute to suffering and pain (Cioffi & Holloway, 1993; Gross & Levenson, 1997; McCracken, 1998; McCracken, Spertus, Janeck, Sinclair, & Wetzel, 1999), increase distress and restrict life functioning (Marx & Sloan, 2002), diminish contact with meaningful and valued life activities, and reduce overall quality of life (see Hayes, Luoma, Bond, Masuda, & Lillis 2006, p. 11 for a summary of outcome studies and quality of life measures used in studies). Individuals who chronically engage in expressive suppression also tend to report more negative experiences and less positive experiences (Gross & John, 2002, 2003). Interestingly, such relations appear to be completely mediated by perceived inauthenticity (John & Gross, 2004); a construct that denotes an approach-avoidance conflict and is similar to diminished self-acceptance (Blackledge & Hayes, 2001). The emerging consensus here is that response-focused emotion regulation requires considerable effort, only works to a point, and is counterproductive when the emotions are intense and highly aversive. Thus, reacting to our own reactions can actually amplify those reactions in a vicious self-perpetuating cycle, resulting in an increase of the very emotion that is not desired, and particularly in contexts or situations where the regulation of emotion would be most desired (Craske, Miller, Rotunda, & Barlow, 1990).

The importance of flexibility. Functional accounts of emotion regulation and other behavioral processes demand attention to contextual factors. In this view, the utility of emotion regulation depends on whether it works or not to achieve desired outcomes, and whether it can be flexibly applied depending on the context. That is, because emotion regulation characterizes socially acquired behaviors (not immutable traits) it ought to be sensitive to contextual determinants. For instance, positive reappraisal seems like a useful strategy to defuse or minimize the impact of an aversive emotion compared to avoidance, suppression, and control. Yet, this does not mean that positive reappraisal should be uniformly applied where it does not work. For example, it would not seem advantageous for a person to remain in a highly aversive situation using positive reappraisal when other behavioral options are clearly more viable. Flexibility, or the ability to discriminate between a range of stimuli in and outside a context, seems crucial in any account of the functional utility of emotion regulation strategies in a fear learning context. In fact, the failure of discrimination—or the tendency to regulate emotions indiscriminately or chronically in a trait-like fashion—is emerging as a core theme that appears to distinguish problematic from more functional forms of emotion regulation and poorer long-term adjustment (Bonanno, Papa, LaLande, Westphal, & Coifman, 2004; John & Gross, 2004).

The tendency for language processes to facilitate or interfere with discrimination and contingency shaped responding is well established (see Hayes, 2004c, for a detailed account). For instance, rules can either make learning contingencies more rapid, or rules can interfere with learning contingency relations (e.g., Hayes & Brownstein, 1986). The behavioral account of inflexibility in humans has focused on how language processes diminish contact with powerful approach contingencies by setting up patterns of self and emotion regulation as a prerequisite for effective action (Zettle & Hayes, 1982). Experiential avoidance is a more recent term that has been used to describe this tendency. Experiential avoidance, like the term emotion regulation, refers to behaviors where the focus is to alter the frequency, duration, or form of unwanted private events (i.e., thoughts, feelings, physical sensations, and memories) and the cues and situations that occasion them (Hayes, 1994; Hayes, Wilson, Gifford, Follette, & Strosahl, 1996). This is a technical definition as much as it is a functional definition. It characterizes a set of actions that tend to be more rule-governed than contingency shaped. Thus, it yields behaviors that appear more rigid and inflexible than circumstances would warrant.

Because experiential avoidance entails the very same set of processes that can make emotion and thought regulation problematic, it is thought to contribute to numerous problems associated with unwanted psychological and emotional content (Hayes et al., 1996). In fact, persons so predisposed will likely experience approach-avoidance conflicts across numerous situations for the simple reason that experiential avoidance is rigidly and inflexibly applied and is thus pitted up against numerous life contingencies (verbally and nonverbally derived) that demand approach (e.g., going to work, running errands, taking a vacation, being with people). For instance, persons who use chronic suppression tend to report feeling a sense of incongruence between their private and outer behavior, fear being accepted by others, and thus use suppression in relationships they care about and are afraid to lose (see John & Gross, 2004, for a review). This example illustrates how emotion regulation interfaces with several verbally derived approach-avoidance conflicts. It also suggests how this tendency may be a potentially self-destructive process that is associated with significant costs and a range of negative outcomes, including functional impairment in interpersonal, social, and occupational domains, and overall poorer quality of life (Gross, 1998a; Hayes et al., 1996; Pennebaker & Beall, 1986; Quilty, Van Ameringen, Mancini, Oakman, & Farvolden, 2003), and even illness and greater mortality risk (Denollet et al., 1996).

The question, then, is why do we avoid feelings and thoughts as if they were the enemy? As we described earlier, social learning creates a context where forms of experiential avoidance and non-acceptance can thrive. As a result, we typically do not question what life might be like if unpleasant emotions and thoughts were treated simply as events to be experienced as part of being fully human, and not as events that must be managed and controlled (cf. Blackledge & Hayes, 2001). We do not question the cultural mandate that equates failures of emotional regulation with suffering and misery and connects "positive" thoughts and feelings with an ability to engage life to its fullest. In this cultural context, anxious thoughts and feelings become obstacles to living and the achievement of valued goals. They are reasonable justifications for inaction and quite often fused with a sense of self-worth (e.g., "I'm not good enough," "I am broken"). It follows that unwanted feelings and thoughts must be managed and controlled (e.g., "My anxiety and depression need to be fixed before I can do what matters to me"), even if that control comes at significant cost to the individual. Paradoxically, the first step toward healthier and more flexible uses of emotional regulation may involve fostering greater discrimination and less rule-governed behavior, particularly as applied to regulating unwanted emotional experiences. Evidence suggest that this stance puts humans (and most nonverbal organisms) in a much better position to exert control where they have it, namely, in responding to natural contingencies. We expand on this below, by showing how experiential avoidance may function to maintain disordered experiences of anxiety and fear, and serve as an experiential risk factor for the development and maintenance of anxiety disorders.

Experiential Avoidance: A Learned and Potentially Toxic Form of Emotion Regulation

Experiential avoidance is thought to function as a core psychological diathesis--a way of relating with oneself and the world--underlying the development and maintenance of anxiety disorders and several other forms of psychopathology (Blackledge & Hayes, 2001; Hayes et al., 1996; Hayes & Wilson, 1993, 1994). It is a process related to how we go about influencing the emotions we have, when we have them, and how we experience and express them. As such, experiential avoidance is best described as an overarching emotion regulation strategy (see Gross, 1998a) that differs from largely inherited biological individual differences that may make persons more vulnerable to developing an anxiety disorder (e.g., an overly active behavioral inhibition system, Gray, 1990; temperament, Kagan, 1989; neuroticism, Eysenck, 1967; Eysenck & Rachman, 1965).

Though Gray (1990) and Kagan and Snidman (1999) readily acknowledge the importance of environmental variation in activating and modulating the influence of behavioral inhibition and temperament, they emphasize the strong heritable components and identified a number of associated brain structures and neurophysi-ological correlates (see Fox, Henderson, Marshall, Nichols, & Ghera, 2005, for a recent review). Neuroticism is likewise thought of as an important individual difference predisposition—a proxy for biological dysregulation—that covaries with the tendency to be more or less emotionally reactive (Eysenck, 1967; Flint, 2004; Gross, Sutton, & Ketelaar, 1998; Larsen & Ketelaar, 1991; Tellegen, 1985). Such tendencies describe emotionality, whereas emotion regulation describes how and why emotions direct or disrupt a range of psychological, physiological, and sociobehavioral processes (Blair, Denham, Kochanoff, & Whipple, 2004).

Though few would dismiss the role of temperament and other biological individual differences in conferring risk for anxiety pathology, it is important to recognize that the tendency to be more or less emotional is not necessarily problematic, unless one is willing to claim that emotions are somehow problematic. Indeed, the tendency to regulate emotions is only modestly related with baseline individual difference domains such as neuroticism (Gross & John, 2003) and extraversion (John & Srivastava, 1999). Such weak relations suggest that the tendency to suppress, and to engage in experiential avoidance more generally, does not occur simply because persons experience more negative affect or negative emotions that need to be regulated. Estimates of the additive and non-additive heritability of neuroticism are low and comparable to other complex human traits (27-31% and 14-17%, respectively; see Flint, 2004, for a review). Nonetheless, it remains to be seen whether temperamental factors (e.g., neuroticism, behavioral inhibition) interface with (a) contingencies that help establish less functional forms of emotion regulation, such as a rigid use of avoidance-oriented coping strategies when faced with aversive life events (Leen-Feldner, Zvolensky, Feldner, & Lejuez, 2004), and (b) concomitant strong approach contingencies that may make emotion and its regulation problematic.

Evidence supporting experiential avoidance as a toxic diathesis. To show that emotional avoidance functions as a behavioral diathesis and risk factor for anxiety-related pathology, it is important to demonstrate that this predisposition functions to exacerbate aversive emotional responding in individuals with no known history of psychopathology. Consistent with this view, we have shown that greater predispositions toward emotional avoidance (as assessed using the Acceptance and Action Questionnaire; Hayes et al., 2004), including the deliberate application of instructed emotion regulation strategies (i.e., emotion suppression), results in more acute emotional distress, but not greater autonomic reactivity (Feldner, Zvolensky, Eifert, & Spira, 2003). This study shows that emotional avoidance strategies potentiate experimentally-induced acute episodes of emotional distress in healthy individuals with no known psychopathology.

We have since replicated these findings and found that emotional avoidance, but not other psychological risk factors for panic (e.g., anxiety sensitivity), tends to covary with more severe panic response, even in healthy individuals (Karekla, Forsyth, & Kelly, 2004; see also Spira, Zvolensky, Eifert, & Feldner, 2004). After several trials of inhaling CO_2-enriched air, individuals high in experiential avoidance endorsed more panic symptoms, more severe cognitive symptoms, and more fear, panic, and uncontrollability than their less avoidant counterparts.

Interestingly, as in all previous studies we conducted in our labs, the magnitude of autonomic responses did not discriminate between groups.

Only one study that we know of has shown a relation between experiential avoidance and physiological reactivity to pleasant, unpleasant, and neutral film clips. In that study, persons with a greater predisposition toward experiential avoidance tended to experience their positive and negative emotions more intensely, but also showed greater heart rate suppression to unpleasant stimuli relative to their less avoidant counterparts (Sloan, 2004). These studies provide further evidence that experiential avoidance exacerbates aversive emotional responses and may constitute a risk factor for emotional learning and thus play a role in the development and maintenance of anxiety disorders. Collectively, the work discussed above and other related studies (Hayes et al., 1996) suggest that a rigid repertoire of experiential avoidance may constitute an important psychological diathesis and risk factor for the development, maintenance, and potential exacerbation of anxiety-related problems (see Feldner, Zvolensky, & Leen-Feldner, 2004, for a review). It is for this reason that experiential avoidance has increasingly become a primary treatment target in newer behavior therapies.

Experiential acceptance: An example of a broad-band deregulation strategy. There have been increasing efforts to examine alternative strategies designed to undo and counter experiential avoidance. Acceptance means having an experience without engaging in efforts to somehow change it. We refer to it as an emotion deregulation strategy because its purpose is not to regulate (in the sense of changing or calming) an emotional experience such as fear. The purpose of acceptance strategies is to foster willingness to stay in contact with aversive private experiences without acting on them, or because of them, so they can move forward with their lives. In our own research lab, for instance, we compared the effects of creating an acceptance versus an emotion control context on avoidance behavior and reported fear in women scoring high in anxiety sensitivity (Eifert & Heffner, 2003). All women were asked to breathe 5.5% CO_2-enriched air for two 10-minute periods. This challenge procedure reliably produces involuntary and largely uncontrollable physiological sensations that are similar to those experienced by people during panic attacks (see Forsyth & Eifert, 1998a). Prior to the inhalation trials, half of the participants were taught how not to fight their reactions but to accept and make space for them, whereas the remaining participants were taught a special breathing skill and were encouraged to use it to control their reactions. Nearly half of the participants instructed to control their fear worried that they would lose control. Interestingly, quite a few of them (20%) actually did lose control—they dropped out of the study altogether. In contrast, participants taught to accept their reactions reported less intense fear and fewer catastrophic thoughts and were less avoidant behaviorally (0% drop out rate).

Our results were replicated in a study examining the effects of accepting versus suppressing the effects of a panicogenic CO_2 challenge in persons suffering from panic disorder (Levitt, Brown, Orsillo, & Barlow, 2004). Participants in that study were simply instructed to either accept or suppress their responses to the CO_2 challenge. The acceptance group was significantly less anxious and less avoidant than the suppression or no-instruction control groups. Yet, the groups did not differ in terms of self-reported panic symptoms or physiological responses. It is important to reiterate that people in these studies, just like people with panic attacks in natural life, had no choice about having or not having the physical sensations. People cannot choose not to have emotions such as fear and anxiety, and quite often fear conditioning episodes. They can, however, choose whether or not to down-regulate fear and anxiety when it shows up.

There are also a number of clinical studies suggesting that client attempts to control anxiety may have negative paradoxical effects (Ascher, 1989). For example, Wegner (1994) found that attempts to control anxiety in the face of ongoing stress exacerbate physiological arousal. Additional work, though based largely on retrospective self-report, confirms that the tendency to suppress thoughts is strongly related to the extent of anxiety, OCD complaints, and depression in healthy persons and OCD sufferers (McLaren & Crowe, 2003). Indeed, healthy individuals that tend to suppress personally relevant intrusive thoughts experience more depression, obsessionality, and anxiety compared with their counterparts who tend to accept such thoughts (Marcks & Woods, 2005). Additionally, Heide and Borkovec (1983) found that many of their participants who went through a relaxation exercise experienced increases rather than the targeted decreases in anxiety. A study by Craske, Rowe, Lewin, and Noriega-Dimitri (1997) also showed that adding slow diaphragmatic breathing did not increase the effectiveness of interoceptive exposure treatment for panic disorder. In fact, breathing retraining--itself a form of emotion regulation--can lead to poorer outcomes compared to treatment without such training (Schmidt et al., 2000).

In a more general way, active coping efforts that attempt to minimize the experience of anxiety may (paradoxically and unintentionally) maintain pathological anxiety and increase the anxiogenic effects of interoceptive stimulation (Craske, Street, & Barlow, 1989). For instance, Spira, Zvolensky, Eifert, and Feldner (2004) found that avoidant coping strategies (e.g., denial, mental disengagement, substance abuse) predicted more frequent and intense CO_2-induced physical and cognitive panic symptoms than acceptance-based coping strategies. These findings are consistent with earlier studies showing that attempts to avoid aversive private events are largely ineffective and may be counterproductive (Cioffi & Holloway, 1993; McLaren & Crowe, 2003; Pennebaker & Beall, 1986). Together these findings suggest that hiding, actively suppressing, escaping from, or avoiding negative thoughts and emotions is not helpful in the long term. In fact, purposefully trying to control feeling anxious may increase the very anxiety one wants to control (Gross & Levenson, 1997), while also increasing the probability that unwanted emotional responses will recur (often in a more severe form) in the future (Cox, Swinson, Norton, & Kuch, 1991; Hayes, 2004a; Hayes et al., 1996, 1999). Worse yet, anxiety suppression and control efforts can act to decrease positive emotional experiences

(Gross, 2002). The result is more anxiety, not less, which will likely be followed by more effort to control the anxiety, in a self-perpetuating cycle.

Fear Learning in an Emotion Regulation Context

Fear learning provides an important experiential foundation for stimuli and situations to acquire aversive functions. Verbal processes, in turn, can expand the range of events that may evoke fear, including avoidance, following aversive learning. Thus, any point in the emotion generative process could, in principal, be a target of emotion regulation within and outside a fear learning context (see Forsyth et al., 2006). For instance, persons may act to avoid or escape from antecedents that may evoke or occasion fearful responding (i.e., CSs, occasion setters, discriminative stimuli), aversive stimuli that may evoke fear and anxiety (i.e., UCSs, punishers), and contexts or situations that may reliably predict a relation between antecedents and emotional consequences. Persons may also act to avoid or escape from the very experience of fear itself and any accompanying thoughts, sensations, behavioral tendencies, or consequences.

Although fear learning may temporarily disrupt ongoing behavior (e.g., avoidance or escape), certain emotion regulation strategies may take this basic form of learning to a whole new level. Specifically, we have proposed (cf. Forsyth et al., 2006) that fear and fear learning may shift from being a normative process to a disordered process when persons: (a) do not accept the reality that they experience certain emotions, thoughts, memories, or physical sensations they do not like; (b) are unwilling to be in contact with them as they are; (c) take deliberate steps to alter their form and frequency or the circumstances that occasion those experiences, and (d) do so rigidly and inflexibly even at significant personal and interpersonal cost (cf. Forsyth, 2000; Forsyth & Eifert, 1996b, 1998b; Friman, et al., 1998; Hayes et al., 1996). We suggest that these four behavioral predispositions, and the verbal-cognitive processes that guide them, are at the core of understanding the development and maintenance of anxiety disorders and figure prominently in several contemporary behavioral approaches to treatment such as *Acceptance and Commitment Therapy* (ACT; Hayes et al., 1999), *Dialectical Behavior Therapy* (Linehan, 1993), and *Integrative Behavioral Couples Therapy* (Jacobson, Christensen, Prince, Cordova, & Eldridge, 2000).

An important element of this model is the idea that rigid emotion regulation (i.e., control, suppression, avoidance, distraction, escape) may emerge as a consequence of fear learning. Another is that language may transform fear learning into anxiety pathology. The very processes that establish and shape experiential avoidance may, in turn, function as an important predisposition for fear and fear learning to become problematic (Forsyth et al., 2006). There are at least two ways this could happen. First, language processes can expand the range of stimuli relevant to previous (adaptive) learning, including logically related events (e.g., "I was afraid in the mall," "I felt trapped," "I could be trapped in an elevator or an open field or a marriage," etc.), imagined futures, or fear itself. Second, language can create self-amplifying loops (e.g., rules about how not to think of fearful things, which when followed evoke thinking about fearful things). Language and social learning also establish rules that set up self-regulation as a prerequisite for effective action: *To live well, I must first think and feel well.* Experiential avoidance is a life constricting behavior precisely because humans cannot avoid their psychological experience of the world while at the same time engaging powerful approach contingencies in that world.

If this account is at least partly correct, then it points to several key processes that may turn emotional and psychological pain, whether conditioned or not, into suffering. One such process is the tendency to self-regulate unpleasant emotions, including associated thoughts, feelings, and behavioral tendencies with avoidance strategies. The second process points to the role of language in maintaining such regulation tendencies. Wilson, Hayes, Gregg, and Zettle (2001) point out that changing verbal relations by adding new verbal relations elaborates rather than eliminates the existing network, because verbal relational learning is typically additive not subtractive. Verbal relational learning can therefore function to expand the range of events that evoke fear based on limited learning and the range of events for which emotional avoidance is applied. Often such relations take the form of rules such as "I can't fly in a plane because I will have a panic attack," "I don't want to go out because I'm depressed," or "I get too anxious when I'm around people." These examples, and many others like them, hint at the kinds of approach-avoidance relations described earlier. They also highlight how excessive experiential avoidance may act to facilitate or impair functioning and turn fear and fear learning into a clinical disorder.

Contrast the above relations with "I can fly and may have a panic attack," "I will go out along with my depression," and "I can be anxious or have an upsetting thought and be around people." These latter examples include only approach-approach contingencies. Fear, fear learning, and approach contingencies are facts of life that need not be changed. The purpose of this acceptance strategy is to help individuals whose lives have been scarred by excessive experiential avoidance behavior develop a new way of relating to their emotional experience. We ask clients to accept what they cannot control because non-acceptance has not worked in their lives and held them back on their journey toward a meaningful life. The ultimate criterion for choosing one strategy over another is workability: what strategy is more helpful in moving people in directions that are truly meaningful to them. Such a posture of acceptance may also be a key preventive mechanism that protects persons from developing anxiety disorders.

Part IV: Clinical Implications

Up to this point, we have provided a broad outline of our recent arguments for conceptualizing fear learning in an emotion regulation context (see Forsyth et al., 2006). This perspective does not diminish the relevant work regarding the nature of fear learning itself. Rather, this view suggests that it is critical to evaluate what people do about fear learning processes when attempting to develop more clinically relevant conditioning analogues of anxiety disorders. Below we briefly highlight some applied implications of an emotion regulation account in the context of recent efforts to develop more unified treatments for anxiety disorders.

General Treatment Implications

The literature on experiential avoidance suggests a number of related clinical strategies that target the experiential avoidance agenda itself and the verbal processes supporting it (e.g., Eifert & Forsyth, 2005; Hayes et al., 1999). For instance, experiential exercises based on metaphor and paradox may be used to teach clients how to experience their anxious thoughts and feelings from a mindful, detached, observer perspective, while learning to make space for anxious thoughts and feelings and other unwanted facets of their private world (e.g., physical sensations, images, memories). The goal here would be to foster greater experiential openness and psychological flexibility and less rule-governed behavior. By weakening powerful verbally-regulated avoidance contingencies that might set up approach-avoidance conflicts in the natural environment, an acceptance posture also may help free up clients to use their hands and feet to change how they respond to unwanted experiences, and thus transform problematic fear and anxiety into just fear and anxiety. This is potentially important, for it suggests that interventions that reduce experiential avoidance may result in more approach-approach relations in a client's natural environment, and a broader range of functioning. It also suggests that therapists should attend to approach-avoidance contingencies in the therapeutic setting and thus frame exposure in a way that it models such contingencies, and not simply avoidance contingencies (for a detailed treatment guide, see Eifert & Forsyth, 2005).

Additionally, the verbal-relational properties entailed in language and emotion regulation are additive and expansive, and heavily dependent on context (Hayes et al., 2001). The basic animal and human literature, for instance, suggests that extinction is not unlearning, but new learning. In fact, it is becoming increasingly clear that contextual factors are important in fear renewal and relapse (Craske, 2003). Language processes also serve as an important context that may function to occasion fear relapse and fear renewal. For instance, suppose a person has learned a relation between panic attacks, elevators, and avoidance. These relations, in turn, are reliably evoked in the context of going to work (approach contingency) and other important activities where closed spaces may be involved. Interoceptive and exteroceptive exposure may be quite successful in altering such relations, including altering the functions of other events that might be part of this network.

Yet exposure may not result in extinction of all stimuli that have had their functions transformed verbally through participation in relational frames with the targeted stimuli. When this happens, other unchecked elements of the network may function to reactivate and solidify previously altered relations, including the very agenda of emotion regulation itself. For instance, suppose this person later finds herself in a relationship and feels "trapped." This feeling, in turn, may evoke panic and avoidance, and because both were related to closed spaces before, she may subsequently experience renewal of fear to elevators and other closed spaces without further panic attacks in those contexts. Unfortunately, we know little about how verbal processes function in exposure therapy and fear renewal. Yet, basic research on verbal processes suggests that such outcomes are likely and may be difficult to prevent entirely (Hayes et al., 2001). This again highlights why disrupting the experiential avoidance agenda may be critical, in part, because it helps hold together and make toxic aversive emotional states in the context of competing environmental demands.

Specific Implications for Cognitive-Behavioral Therapies

Mainstream cognitive-behavioral therapies (CBT) for anxiety disorders tend to conceptualize unwanted anxiety-related private events as problems that warrant clinical attention (Beck & Emery, 1985). Accordingly, the therapeutic solution is to alleviate symptoms by getting clients to confront feared objects or aversive bodily events in a safe therapeutic context to facilitate corrective emotional learning and fear reduction (e.g., Barlow, 2002). Techniques used include exteroceptive or interoceptive in vivo exposure, imaginal exposure, thought stopping, response prevention, flooding, systematic desensitization, worry control and decatastrophizing, cognitive restructuring, systematic desensitization, guided imagery, breathing retraining, and progressive muscle relation. Comprehensive treatment manuals incorporating such techniques are available for all major anxiety disorders: panic disorder (*Mastery of Your Anxiety and Panic*; Barlow & Craske, 2000), specific phobias (*Mastery of Your Specific Phobia*; Antony, Craske, & Barlow, 1997), obsessive-compulsive disorder (*Mastery of Obsessive-Compulsive Disorder*; Foa & Kozak, 1997), and generalized anxiety disorder (*Mastery of Your Anxiety and Worry*; Zinbarg, Craske & Barlow, 1993).

The word "mastery" in the titles of such manuals is not accidental and reflects the underlying philosophy and approach of such treatments. These treatments suggest, either explicitly or implicitly, that having catastrophic or other "maladaptive" thoughts is part of the problem and a cause of human suffering that may interfere with living a successful life. Otherwise, it would make no sense to target them for change in therapy. The goal is to assist clients in becoming better at controlling (i.e., mastering) their thoughts and emotional experiences by teaching them more effective regulation strategies. This is indeed what many anxious clients expect from psychotherapy: They want to learn more effective ways of reducing unwanted private events. That is, they want to learn better forms of emotion regulation.

A key problem of traditional CBT is that it tends to play into this system by suggesting to clients that pursuing a control and mastery approach may indeed be a long-term workable solution and by attempting to teach clients more effective management strategies than they may have used in the past. The literature on the effects of experiential avoidance, however, suggests that this approach itself may be flawed and points to a different strategy. This strategy involves helping clients give up the struggle to control and avoid unwanted thoughts and feelings. Thus far, people have often desperately tried to relax *away* fear and anxiety by pushing their unwanted thoughts and feelings away. Instead, an acceptance-based behavior therapy approach aims to help people relax *with* their anxiety––whether conditioned or not––by being and moving with it. Anxious thoughts and feelings are not considered "symptomatic" of anything, but rather normal facets of human experience. The task for clients then is no longer to down-regulate anxiety and fear because anxiety and fear in and of themselves are not the problem.

Targeting unwanted private experiences in therapy has been shown to be quite efficacious and can produce symptom reduction and relief. This strategy, however, may also keep clients entangled in their struggle with their painful psychological and emotional experiences, in part, because targeting them in treatment implies that they are problematic and the cause of life problems. Thus, when anxious thoughts and feelings occur again (and they will occur again), clients will be inclined to engage in efforts to change or reduce them in order to live better. Alternately, we could aim to teach people how to experience a wide range of emotional experiences, willingly and without defense, and behave effectively despite what they may think or feel. *Willing* here is not about brute force of will. It means being open and having what is. It is about finding a way to live a meaningful and productive life *and* taking personal pains and joys along for the ride instead of living to avoid or manage psychological pain.

Acceptance and Commitment Therapy for Anxiety Disorders

Third-wave behavior therapies (Hayes, 2004a, 2004b) tend to focus on domains of human experience that go well beyond symptom alleviation and control as therapeutic goals. Instead, they emphasize topics traditionally reserved for less empirical wings of psychology such as acceptance, mindfulness, values, spirituality, meaning and purpose, relationships, and quality of life. These approaches challenge the symptom and syndrome-focused change agenda that has come to characterize much of mainstream CBT. They offer a unique and expanded view of human suffering and what it means to foster psychological health and wellness. To illustrate, we outline briefly the basic elements of an ACT approach to the treatment of anxiety disorders (for a more detailed session-by-session treatment guide, see Eifert & Forsyth, 2005).

First, within a coherent theoretical and philosophical framework, ACT illuminates the ways that language entangles clients into futile attempts to wage war against their own inner lives. This war is fundamentally about the application of emotion regulation efforts in contexts where such regulation efforts are unnecessary or unworkable. Addressing the struggle head on is what an ACT approach to treatment is about because non-acceptance and struggle with anxiety is the toxic process that makes anxiety a clinically significant problem. ACT tries to undermine and loosen the hold that excessive, rigid, and inflexible emotion regulation has on the lives of anxiety sufferers. With anxiety disorders, this form of regulation usually centers on anxious thoughts and feelings that are unwanted or undesired, including the situations that might occasion them. In short, anxious sufferers devote enormous time and effort so as not to experience anxiety and fear, rather than doing what is most important to them. Through experiential exercises based on metaphor and paradox, clients learn how to experience their anxious thoughts and feelings from a mindful observer perspective, as they are rather than as how they evaluate them. Learning to make space for anxious thoughts and feelings and other unwanted facets of their private world (e.g., physical sensations, images, memories) is a step toward greater experiential openness and psychological flexibility. This acceptance posture frees up clients to use their hands and feet to regulate how they live their lives consistent with their values and goals.

Second, cognitive-behavioral interventions typically focus on narrow-band clinical outcomes in the form of symptom reduction and relief. To get there, however, clients typically must go through quite a bit of pain by confronting anxiety and fear-evoking cues and situations during in vivo or imaginal exposure exercises. Interestingly, this is the point at which more than a few anxious clients drop out of therapy (Becker & Zayfert, 2001). Two recent studies from our labs showed the positive effects of an acceptance context for preventing dropout. The first study (Karekla & Forsyth, 2004) showed significant differences in the pattern of attrition rates between CBT vs. ACT-enhanced CBT for persons suffering from panic disorder. Prior to introducing the rationales for interoceptive and exteroceptive exposure, none of the CBT clients and only three ACT clients dropped out of therapy prematurely. However, following the introduction of the exposure rationales, five persons discontinued therapy in the CBT group and only one person discontinued in the ACT group.

The main difference between the exposure rationales was in how they were framed (i.e., mastery and control of panic versus mastery of experiencing panic) and for what purpose (i.e., controlling panic symptoms versus living more fully and consistently with what one values). The results of this study suggest that exposure conducted in the service of feeling better is somewhat limiting and not very inspiring. All the pain of therapy and for what? The hope of feeling less anxious? At some level, anxious persons recognize that feeling less anxious does not mean that they will be anxiety free, or that somehow their lives will be better, richer, or more meaningful. In the second related study with highly anxious females (Eifert & Heffner, 2003) who experienced panic-like responses in an acceptance or a control context, we found that 20% of control participants dropped out of the study, whereas none of the acceptance participants did. Here, too, by giving up their efforts to gain control, people had actually gained control and strength.

While ACT allows room for symptom alleviation, it is not a main target or *the* therapeutic goal. Rather, the focus is on what we call broad-band outcomes. Such outcomes are about helping the client move in life directions that they truly care about. For instance, a client may value having deep and meaningful relationships with her children, but is letting her anxiety regulation efforts get in the way of that. Within ACT, the focus would be about removing barriers to having that kind of relationship with her children (e.g., unnecessary emotion regulation strategies). Anxiety reduction may occur as a consequence, but it is not an explicit target. Rather, the explicit targets are in areas that most readers will associate with a life lived well, namely living in a manner consistent with meaningful values and goals. Making and keeping value-guided commitments are an important part of an ACT approach to anxiety disorders (Eifert & Forsyth, 2005). Valued living dignifies the treatment, and makes the hard work of therapy worthwhile.

Traditional CBT exposure interventions for anxiety have a different feel when used within an ACT approach. Exposure, for instance, is no longer cast as an eliminative technique within a mastery and control of anxiety framework because it sends a message to the client that anxiety is the problem and must be reduced or managed before a client can live better. Rather, exposure within ACT is framed as one of several experiential exercises, with the goal being to *feel* better (i.e., become better at feeling), not to feel *better* (i.e., feeling less anxiety). This "mastery of experience" framework for ACT exposure exercises is about helping clients develop willingness to experience thoughts and feelings for what they are. Thus, exposure exercises within ACT are framed in the service of fostering greater psychological flexibility, experiential willingness, and openness. They are about growth and are always done in the service of client values and goals. This approach, which we describe in detail elsewhere (Eifert & Forsyth, 2005), is very much about altering how clients with anxiety respond to their emotional and psychological experiences, not the structure or content of those experiences. We are trying to help clients make room for those experiences, while freeing up psychological and behavioral space for clients to get on with the task of living their lives consistent with and in the direction of their chosen values.

Conclusions

When viewed historically, behavior therapy has been an enormously successful experiment. Its success, in turn, is based in large part on the simple principle of conducting clinical science with at least one eye on practical utility. The utility of fear conditioning research as a clinical analog of anxiety-related suffering is a good news, bad news story. The good news is that Pavlovian fear conditioning research and theory, despite numerous criticisms regarding its scope and clinical relevance, remains at the core of contemporary behavioral accounts of the origins, maintenance, and amelioration of anxiety disorders. The bad news is that earlier behavior therapies represented classical conditioning as a sufficient model to account for the development of anxiety disorders. This led to the notion that anxiety-related suffering is about excessive physiological responding or other psychological content, including avoidance.

This chapter introduced the notion that fear and its conditioned basis are not disordered processes per se, but rather become so when humans act on them and because of them so as to alter their form, frequency, or occurrence. The regulation of anxiety and fear using any number of strategies may result in temporary relief (e.g., anxiety reduction via negative reinforcement). Yet, the cumulative effect over time of such actions may be life constriction and long-term suffering. Such actions, when rigidly and inflexibly applied, can take over a person's life and turn the experience of fear and fear learning into an emotional experience that is a problem, not simply a painful experience that can be had.

The emerging consensus is that such regulation tends to make aversive emotions more intense and more likely to occur: *if you don't want it, you've got it.* This outcome, when coupled with powerful approach contingencies, may function as a predisposing and maintaining factor for anxiety pathology. As clients learn to give up the struggle and control agenda and focus on life-goal related activities, they are no longer owned by their unwanted experiences. After developing greater clarity about personal values and committing to needed behavior change, we encourage clients to embark on the journey and put those commitments into action. They are free to live.

References

American Psychiatric Association. (2000). *Diagnostic and statistical manual of mental disorders,* (4th ed., text revision). Washington, DC: Author.

Antony, M. M., Craske, M. G., & Barlow D. H. (1997). *Mastery of your specific phobia.* Boulder, CO: Graywind Publications.

Ascher, L. M. (1989). Paradoxical intention and recursive anxiety. In L. M. Ascher (Ed.), *Therapeutic paradox* (pp. 93-136). New York: Guilford.

Augustson, E. M., & Dougher, M. J. (1997). The transfer of avoidance evoking functions through stimulus equivalence classes. *Journal of Behavior Therapy and Experimental Psychiatry, 28,* 181-191.

Barlow, D. H. (1988). *Anxiety and its disorders: The nature and treatment of anxiety and panic.* New York: Guilford.

Barlow, D. H. (2002). *Anxiety and its disorders: The nature and treatment of anxiety and panic,* (2nd ed). New York: Guilford.

Barlow, D. H., Allen, L. B., & Choate, M. L. (2004). Toward a unified treatment for emotional disorders. *Behavior Therapy, 35,* 205-230.

Barlow, D. H., & Craske, M. G. (2000). *Mastery of your anxiety and panic* (3rd ed.). Boulder, CO: Graywind Publications.

Baumeister, R. F., Bratslavsky, E., Muraven, M., & Tice, D. (1998). Ego depletion: Is the active self a limited resource? *Journal of Personality and Social Psychology, 74,* 1252-1265.

Beck, A. T., & Emery, G. (1985). *Anxiety disorders and phobias: A cognitive perspective.* New York: Basic Books.

Becker, C. B., & Zayfert, C. (2001). Integrating DBT-based techniques and concepts to facilitate treatment for PTSD. *Cognitive and Behavioral Practice, 8,* 107-122.

Blackledge, J. T. (2003). An introduction to relational frame theory: Basics and applications. *The Behavior Analyst Today, 3,* 421-433.

Blackledge, J. T., & Hayes, S. C. (2001). Emotion regulation in acceptance and commitment therapy. *JCLP/In session: Psychotherapy in Practice, 57,* 243-255.

Blair, K. A., Denham, S. A., Kochanoff, A., & Whipple, B. (2004). Playing it cool: Temperament, emotion regulation, and social behavior in preschoolers. *Journal of School Psychology, 42,* 419-443.

Bonanno, G. A., Papa, A., LaLande, K., Westphal, M., & Coifman, K. (2004). The importance of being flexible: The ability to both enhance and suppress emotional expression predicts long-term adjustment. *Psychological Science, 15,* 482-487.

Borkovec, T. D., Alcaine, O., & Behar, E. (2004). Avoidance theory of worry and generalized anxiety disorder. In R. G. Heimberg, C. L. Turk, & D. S. Mennin (Eds.), *Generalized anxiety disorder: Advances in research and practice* (pp. 77-108). New York: Guilford.

Borkovec, T. D., & Newman, M. G. (1998). Worry and generalized anxiety disorder. In A. S. Bellack & M. Hersen (Series Eds.), *Comprehensive Clinical Psychology, Vol. 6* (pp. 439-459). New York: Elsevier.

Bouton, M. E., Mineka, S., & Barlow, D. H. (2001). A modern learning theory perspective on the etiology of panic disorder. *Psychological Review, 108,* 4-32.

Butler, E. A., & Gross, J. J. (2004). Hiding feelings in social contexts: Out of sight is not out of mind. In P. Philippot & R. S. Feldman (Eds.), *The regulation of emotion* (pp. 101-126). Mahwah, NJ: Erlbaum.

Chambless, D. L., & Gracely, E. J. (1989). Fear of fear and the anxiety disorders. *Cognitive Therapy and Research, 13,* 9-20.

Cioffi, D., & Holloway, J. (1993). Delayed costs of suppressed pain. *Journal of Personality and Social Psychology, 64,* 274-282.

Clark, D. M., Ball, S., & Pape, D. (1991). An experimental investigation of thought suppression. *Behaviour Research and Therapy, 29,* 253-257.

Cook, M., & Mineka, S. (1991). Selective associations in the origins of phobic fears and their implications for behavior therapy. In P. R. Martin (Ed.), *Handbook of behavior therapy and psychological science* (pp. 413-434). New York: Pergamon.

Costello, C. G. (1970). Dissimilarities between conditioned avoidance responses and phobias. *Psychological Review, 77,* 250-254.

Cox, B. J., Swinson, R. P., Norton, G. R., & Kuch, K. (1991). Anticipatory anxiety and avoidance in panic disorder with agoraphobia. *Behaviour Research and Therapy, 29,* 363-365.

Craske, M. G. (1999). *Anxiety disorders: Psychological approaches to theory and treatment.* Denver, CO: Westview Press/Basic Books.

Craske, M. G. (2003). *Origins of phobias and anxiety disorders: Why more women than men?* Oxford, England: Elsevier.

Craske, M. G., Miller, P. P., Rotunda, R., & Barlow, D. H. (1990). A descriptive report of features of initial unexpected panic attacks in minimal and extensive avoiders. *Behaviour Research and Therapy, 28,* 395-400.

Craske, M. G., Rowe, M., Lewin, M., & Noriego-Dimitri, R. (1997). Interoceptive exposure versus breathing retraining within cognitive-behavioural therapy for panic disorder with agoraphobia. *British Journal of Clinical Psychology, 36,* 85-99.

Craske, M. G., Street, L., & Barlow, D. H. (1989). Instructions to focus upon or distract from internal cues during exposure treatment of agoraphobic avoidance. *Behaviour Research and Therapy, 27,* 663-672.

Denollet, J., Sys, S. U., Stoobant, N., Rombouts, H., Gillebert, T. C., & Brutsaert, D. L. (1996). Personality as an independent predictor of long-term mortality in patients with coronary heart disease. *The Lancet, 347,* 417-421.

Dougher, M. J., Augustson, E., Markham, M. R., Greenway, D. E., & Wulfert, E. (1994). The transfer of respondent eliciting and extinction functions through stimulus equivalence. *Journal of the Experimental Analysis of Behavior, 62,* 331-351.

Eifert, G. H., & Forsyth, J. P. (2005). *Acceptance and commitment therapy for anxiety disorders: A practitioner's treatment guide to using mindfulness, acceptance, and value-based behavior change strategies.* Oakland, CA: New Harbinger.

Eifert, G. H., & Heffner, M. (2003). The effects of acceptance versus control contexts on avoidance of panic-related symptoms. *Journal of Behavior Therapy and Experimental Psychiatry, 34,* 293-312.

Eysenck, H. J. (1967). *The biological basis of personality.* Springfield, IL: C. C. Thomas.

Eysenck, H. J. (1976). The learning theory model of neurosis – A new approach. *Behaviour Research and Therapy, 14,* 251-267.

Eysenck, H. J. (1987). Behavior therapy. In H. J. Eysenck & I. Martin (Eds.), *Theoretical foundations of behavior therapy* (pp. 3-34). New York: Plenum.

Eysenck, H. J., & Rachman, S. (1965). *Causes and cure of neurosis.* London: Routledge and Kagan Paul.

Feldner, M. T., Zvolensky, M. J., Eifert, G. H., & Spira, A. P. (2003). Emotional avoidance: An experimental test of individual differences and response suppression during biological challenge. *Behaviour Research and Therapy, 41,* 403-411.

Feldner, M. T., Zvolensky, M. J., & Leen-Feldner, E. W. (2004). A critical review of the empirical literature on coping and panic disorder. *Clinical Psychology Review, 24,* 123-148.

Flint, J. (2004). The genetic basis of neuroticism. *Neuroscience and Biobehavioral Reviews, 28,* 307-316.

Foa, E. B., & Kozak, M. J. (1997). *Mastery of obsessive-compulsive disorder (OCD): A cognitive-behavioral approach.* Boulder, CO: Graywind.

Forsyth, J. P. (2000). A process-oriented behavioral approach to the etiology, maintenance, and treatment of anxiety-related disorders. In M. J. Dougher (Ed.), *Clinical behavior analysis* (pp. 153-180). Reno, NV: Context Press.

Forsyth, J. P., Daleiden, E., & Chorpita, B. F. (2000). Response primacy in fear conditioning: Disentangling the contributions of the UCS vs. the UCR. *The Psychological Record, 50,* 17-33.

Forsyth, J. P., & Eifert, G. H. (1996a). Systemic alarms in fear conditioning I: A reappraisal of what is being conditioned. *Behavior Therapy, 27,* 441-462.

Forsyth, J. P., & Eifert, G. H. (1996b). The language of feeling and the feeling of anxiety: Contributions of the behaviorisms toward understanding the function-altering effects of language. *The Psychological Record, 46,* 607-649.

Forsyth, J. P., & Eifert, G. H. (1998a). Response intensity in content-specific fear conditioning comparing 20% versus 13% CO_2-enriched air as unconditioned stimuli. *Journal of Abnormal Psychology, 107,* 291-304.

Forsyth, J. P., & Eifert, G. H. (1998b). Phobic anxiety and panic: An integrative behavioral account of their origin and treatment. In J. J. Plaud & G. H. Eifert (Eds.), *From Behavior Theory to Behavior Therapy* (pp. 38-67). Needham, MA: Allyn & Bacon.

Forsyth, J. P., Eifert, G. H., & Barrios, V. (2006). Fear conditioning research as a clinical analog: What makes fear learning disordered? In M. G. Craske, D. Hermans, & D. Vansteenwegen (Eds.), *Fear and learning: Basic science to clinical application* (pp. 133-153). Washington, DC: American Psychological Association.

Forsyth, J. P., Eifert, G. H., & Thompson, R. N. (1996). Systemic alarms in fear conditioning II: An experimental methodology using 20% carbon dioxide inhalations as an unconditioned stimulus. *Behavior Therapy, 27,* 391-415.

Forsyth, J. P., Lejuez, C., Hawkins, R. P., & Eifert, G. H. (1996). A critical evaluation of cognitions as causes of behavior. *Journal of Behavior Therapy and Experimental Psychiatry, 27,* 369-376.

Fox, N. A., Henderson, H. A., Marshall, P. J., Nichols, K. E., & Ghera, M. M. (2005). Behavioral inhibition: Linking biology and behavior within a developmental framework. *Annual Review of Psychology, 56,* 235-262.

Friman, P. C., Hayes, S. C., & Wilson, K. G. (1998). Why behavior analysts should study emotion: The example of anxiety. *Journal of Applied Behavior Analysis, 31,* 137-156.

Gantt, W. H. (1944). *Experimental basis for neurotic behavior: Origin and development of artificially produced disturbances of behavior in dogs.* New York: Paul B. Hoeber.

Garnefski, N., & Spinhoven, K. P. (2001). Negative life events, cognitive emotion regulation, and emotional problems. *Personality and Individual Differences, 30,* 1311-1327.

Garnefski, N., van den Kommer, T., Kraaij, V., Terrds, J., Legerstee, J., & Onstein, E. (2002). The relationship between cognitive emotion regulation strategies and emotional problems: Comparison between a clinical and non-clinical sample. *European Journal of Personality, 16,* 403-420.

Gold, D. B., & Wegner, D. M. (1995). Origins of ruminative thought: Trauma, incompleteness, nondisclosure, and suppression. *Journal of Applied Social Psychology, 25,* 1245-1261.

Gray, J. A. (1990). Brain systems that mediate both emotion and cognition. *Cognition and Emotion, 4,* 269-288.

Gross, J. J. (1998a). The emerging field of emotion regulation: An integrative review. *Review of General Psychology, 2,* 271-299.

Gross, J. J. (1998b). Antecedent- and response-focused emotion regulation: Divergent consequences for experience, expression, and physiology. *Journal of Personality and Social Psychology, 74,* 224-237.

Gross, J. J. (2002). Emotion regulation: Affective, cognitive, and social consequences. *Psychophysiology, 39,* 281-291.

Gross, J. J., & John, O. P. (2002). Wise emotion regulation. In P. Salovey & L. F. Barrett (Eds.), *The wisdom in feeling: Psychological processes in emotional intelligence* (pp. 297-319). New York: Guilford.

Gross, J. J., & John, O. P. (2003). Individual differences in two emotion regulation processes: Implications for affect, relationships, and well-being. *Journal of Personality and Social Psychology, 85,* 348-362.

Gross, J. J., & Levenson, R. W. (1993). Emotional suppression: Physiology, self-report, and expressive behavior. *Journal of Personality and Social Psychology, 64,* 970-986.

Gross, J. J., & Levenson, R. W. (1997). Hiding feelings: The acute effects of inhibiting negative and positive emotion. *Journal of Abnormal Psychology, 106,* 95-103.

Gross, J. J., & Muñoz, R. F. (1995). Emotion regulation and mental health. *Clinical Psychology: Science and Practice, 2,* 151-164.

Gross, J. J., Sutton, S. K., & Ketelaar, T. (1998). Relations between affect and personality: Support for the affect-level and affect-reactivity views. *Personality and Social Psychology Bulletin, 24,* 279-288.

Hayes, S. C. (1976). The role of approach contingencies in phobic behavior. *Behavior Therapy, 7,* 28-36.

Hayes, S. C. (1994). Content, context, and the types of psychological acceptance. In S. C. Hayes, N. S. Jacobson, V. M. Follette, & M. J. Dougher (Eds.), *Acceptance and change: Content and context in psychotherapy* (pp. 13-32). Reno, NV: Context Press.

Hayes, S. C. (2004a). Acceptance and commitment therapy and the new behavior therapies: Mindfulness, acceptance, and relationship. In S. C. Hayes, V. M., Follette, & M. Linehan (Eds.), *Mindfulness and acceptance: Expanding the cognitive-behavioral tradition* (pp. 1-29). New York: Guilford.

Hayes, S. C. (2004b). Acceptance and commitment therapy, relational frame theory, and the third wave of behavioral and cognitive therapies. *Behavior Therapy, 35,* 639-666.

Hayes, S. C. (Ed.) (2004c). *Rule-governed behavior: Cognition, contingencies, and instructional control.* Reno, NV: Context Press.

Hayes, S. C., Barnes-Holmes, D., & Roche, B. (2001). Relational frame theory: A post-Skinnerian account of human language and cognition. New York: Kluwer.

Hayes, S. C., & Brownstein, A. J. (1986). Mentalism, private events, and scientific explanation: A defense of B. F. Skinner's view. In S. Modgil & C. Modgil (Eds.), *B. F. Skinner: Consensus and controversy* (pp. 207-218). Sussex, England: Falmer Press.

Hayes, S. C., Lattal, K. A., & Myerson, W. A. (1979). Strength of experimentally induced phobic behavior in rats: Avoidance versus dual-component formulations. *Psychological Reports, 44,* 891-894.

Hayes, S. C., Luoma, J. B., Bond, F. W., Masuda, A., & Lillis, J (2006). Acceptance and commitment therapy: Model, process, and outcomes. *Behaviour Research and Therapy, 44,* 1-25.

Hayes, S. C., Strosahl, K. D., & Wilson. K. G. (1999). *Acceptance and commitment therapy: An experiential approach to behavior change.* New York: Guilford.

Hayes, S. C., Strosahl, K. D., Wilson, K. G., Bissett, R. T., Pistorello, J., Toarmino, D., et al. (2004). Measuring experiential avoidance: A preliminary test of a working model. *Psychological Record, 54,* 553-578.

Hayes, S. C., & Wilson, K. G. (1993). Some applied implications of a contemporary behavior-analytic account of verbal events. *The Behavior Analyst, 16,* 283-301.

Hayes, S. C., & Wilson, K. G. (1994). Acceptance and commitment therapy: Altering the verbal support for experiential avoidance. *The Behavior Analyst, 17,* 289-303.

Hayes, S. C., Wilson, K. G., Gifford, E. V., Follette, V. M., & Strosahl, K. (1996). Experiential avoidance and behavioral disorders: A functional dimensional approach to diagnosis and treatment. *Journal of Consulting and Clinical Psychology, 64,* 1152-1168.

Heide, F. J., & Borkovec, T. D. (1983). Relaxation-induced anxiety: Paradoxical anxiety enhancement due to relaxation training. *Journal of Consulting and Clinical Psychology, 51,* 171-182.

Jacobson, N. S., Christensen, A., Prince, S. E., Cordova, J., & Eldridge, K. (2000). Integrative behavioral couple therapy: An acceptance-based, promising new treatment for couple discord. *Journal of Consulting and Clinical Psychology, 68,* 351-355.

Jaycox, L. H., & Foa, E. B. (1998). Post-traumatic stress disorder. In A. S. Bellack & M. Hersen (Series Eds.), *Comprehensive Clinical Psychology, Vol. 6* (pp. 499-517). New York: Elsevier.

John, O. P., & Gross, J. J. (2004). Healthy and unhealthy emotion regulation: Personality processes, individual differences, and life span development. *Journal of Personality, 72,* 1301-1333.

John, O. P., & Srivastava, S. (1999). The big five trait taxonomy: History, measurement, and theoretical perspectives. In L. A. Pervin & O. P. John (Eds.), *Handbook of personality: Theory and research* (2nd ed., pp. 102-138). New York: Guilford.

Kagan, J. (1989). Temperamental contributions to social behavior. *American Psychologist, 44,* 668-674.

Kagan, J., & Snidman, N. (1999). Early childhood predictors of adult anxiety disorders. *Biological Psychiatry, 46,* 1536-1541.

Karekla, M., & Forsyth, J. P. (2004, November). A comparison between acceptance enhanced cognitive behavioral and panic control treatment for panic disorder. In S. M. Orsillo (Chair), *Acceptance-based behavioral therapies: New directions in the treatment development across the diagnostic spectrum.* Paper presented at the 38th annual meeting of the Association for Advancement of Behavior Therapy, New Orleans, LA.

Karekla, M., Forsyth, J. P., & Kelly, M. M. (2004). Emotional avoidance and panicogenic responding to a biological challenge procedure. *Behavior Therapy, 35,* 725-746.

Larsen, R. J., & Ketelaar, T. (1991). Extraversion, neuroticism, and susceptibility to positive and negative mood induction procedures. *Personality and Individual Differences, 10,* 1221-1228.

Lavy, E. H., & van den Hout, M. A. (1990). Thought suppression induces intrusions. *Behavioural Psychotherapy, 18,* 251-258.

Lazarus, R. S., & Alfert, E. (1964). Short-circuiting of threat by experimentally altering cognitive appraisal. *Journal of Abnormal and Social Psychology, 69,* 195-205.

LeDoux, J. E. (1996). *The emotional brain.* New York: Simon & Schuster.

LeDoux, J. E. (2000). Emotion circuits in the brain. *Annual Review of Neuroscience, 23,* 155-184.

Leen-Feldner, E. W., Zvolensky, M. J., Feldner, M. T., & Lejuez, C. W. (2004). Behavioral inhibition: Relation to negative emotion regulation and reactivity. *Personality and Individual Differences, 36,* 1235-1247.

Levitt, J. T., Brown, T. A., Orsillo, S. M., & Barlow, D. H. (2004). The effects of acceptance versus suppression of emotion on subjective and psychophysiological response to carbon dioxide challenge in patients with panic disorder. *Behavior Therapy, 35,* 747-766.

Linehan, M. M. (1993). *Skills training manual for treating borderline personality disorder.* New York: Guilford.

Liddell, H. S. (1947). The experimental neurosis. *Annual Review of Physiology, 9,* 569-580.

Marcks, B. A., & Woods, D. W. (2005). A comparison of thought suppression to an acceptance-based technique in the management of personal intrusive thoughts: A controlled evaluation. *Behaviour Research and Therapy, 43,* 433-445.

Marks, I. M. (1969). *Fears and phobias.* New York: Academic Press.

Marks, I. (1981). *Cure and care of neurosis.* New York: Wiley.

Marx, B., Forsyth, J. P., Heidt, J. M., Fusé, T., & Gallup, G. G., Jr. (in press). Tonic immobility as an evolved predator defense: Implications for sexual assault survivors. *Clinical Psychology: Science and Practice.*

Marx, B. P., & Sloan, D. M. (2002). The role of emotion in the psychological functioning of adult survivors of childhood sexual abuse. *Behavior Therapy, 33,* 563-577.

McCracken, L. M. (1998). Learning to live with pain: Acceptance of pain predicts adjustment in persons with chronic pain. *Pain, 74,* 21-27.

McCracken, L. M., Spertus, I. L., Janeck, A. S., Sinclair, D., & Wetzel, F. T. (1999). Behavioral dimensions of adjustment in persons with chronic pain: Pain-related anxiety and acceptance. *Pain, 80,* 283-289.

McLaren, S., & Crowe, S. F. (2003). The contribution of perceived control of stressful life events and thought suppression to the symptoms of obsessive-compulsive disorder in both non-clinical and clinical samples. *Journal of Anxiety Disorders, 17,* 389-403.

McNally, R. J., & Lukach, B. M. (1992). Are panic attacks traumatic stressors? *American Journal of Psychiatry, 149,* 824-826.

Mennin, D. S., Heimberg, R. G., Turk, C. L., & Fresco, D. M. (2002). Applying an emotion regulation framework to integrative approaches to generalized anxiety disorder. *Clinical Psychology: Science and Practice, 9,* 85-90.

Menzies, R. G., & Clarke, J. C. (1995). The etiology of phobias: A non-associative account. *Clinical Psychology Review, 15,* 23-48.

Mineka, S., Watson, D., & Clark, L. A. (1998). Comorbidity of anxiety and unipolar mood disorders. *Annual Review of Psychology, 49,* 377-412.

Mineka, S., & Zinbarg, R. (1996). Conditioning and ethological models of anxiety disorders: Stress-in-dynamic context anxiety models. In D. A. Hope (Ed.), *Perspectives on anxiety, panic, and fear: Volume 43 of the Nebraska symposium on motivation* (pp. 135-210). Lincoln, NE: Nebraska University Press.

Moses, E. B., Acheson, D. T., & Forsyth, J. P. (2006). *Does anxiety sensitivity mediate the relation between experiential avoidance and acute panicogenic distress? An experimental evaluation.* Paper presented at 40th Annual Convention of the Association for Behavioral and Cognitive Therapies, Chicago, IL.

Mowrer, O. H. (1939). A stimulus-response analysis of anxiety and its role as a reinforcing agent. *Psychological Review, 46,* 553-565.

Mowrer, O. H. (1960). *Learning Theory and Behavior.* New York: Wiley.

Ochsner, K. N., Bunge, S. A., Gross, J. J., & Gabrieli, J. D. (2002). Rethinking feelings: An fMRI study of the cognitive regulation of emotion. *Journal of Cognitive Neuroscience, 14,* 1215-1229.

Ochsner, K. N., Ray, R. D., Cooper, J. C., Robertson, E. R., Chopra, S., Gabrieli, J. D. E., et al. (2004). For better or for worse: Neural systems supporting cognitive down- and up-regulation of negative emotion. *Neuroimage, 23,* 483-499.

Parrott, W. G. (1993). Beyond hedonism: Motives for inhibiting good moods and for maximizing bad moods. In D. M. Wegner & J. W. Pennebaker (Eds.), *Handbook of mental control* (pp. 278-308). Englewood Cliffs, NJ: Prentice-Hall.

Pavlov, I. P. (1903). Experimental psychology and psychopathology in animals. *Herald of the Military Medical Academy, 7,* 109-121.

Pavlov, I. P. (1927). *Conditioned reflexes: An investigation of the physiological activity of the cerebral cortex.* Oxford, England: Oxford University Press.

Pavlov, I. P. (1941). *Conditioned reflexes and psychiatry.* New York: International Publishers.

Pennebaker, J. W., & Beall, S. K. (1986). Confronting a traumatic event: Toward an understanding of inhibition and disease. *Journal of Abnormal Psychology, 95,* 274-281.

Purdon, C. (1999). Thought suppression and psychopathology. *Behaviour Research and Therapy, 37,* 1029-1054.

Quilty, L. C., Van Ameringen, M., Mancini, C., Oakman, J., & Farvolden, P. (2003). Quality of life and the anxiety disorders. *Journal of Anxiety Disorders, 17,* 405-426.

Rachman, S. (1977). The conditioning theory of fear acquisition: A critical examination. *Behaviour Research and Therapy, 15,* 375-387.

Rachman, S. (1991). Neo-conditioning and the classical theory of fear acquisition. *Clinical Psychology Review, 11,* 155-173.

Rachman, S. (2004). *Anxiety* (2nd ed.). New York: Psychology Press.

Richards, J. M., & Gross, J. J. (1999). Composure at any cost? The cognitive consequences of emotion suppression. *Personality and Social Psychology Bulletin, 25,* 1033-1044.

Richards, J. M., & Gross, J. J. (2000). Emotion regulation and memory: The cognitive costs of keeping one's cool. *Journal of Personality and Social Psychology, 79,* 410-424.

Rosen, J. B., & Schulkin, J. (1998). From normal fear to pathological anxiety. *Psychological Review, 105,* 325-250.

Salkovskis, P. M. (1996). The cognitive approach to anxiety: Threat beliefs, safety seeking behavior, and the special case of health anxiety and obsessions. In P. M. Salkovskis (Ed.), *Frontiers of cognitive therapy* (pp. 49-74). New York: Guilford.

Salters-Pedneault, K., Tull, M. T., & Roemer, L. (2004). The role of avoidance of emotional material in the anxiety disorders. *Applied and Preventive Psychology, 11*, 95-114.

Schmidt, N. B., Woolaway-Bickel, K., Trakowski, J., Santiago, H., Storey, J., Koselka, M., et al. (2000). Dismantling cognitive-behavioral treatment for panic disorder: Questioning the utility of breathing retraining. *Journal of Consulting and Clinical Psychology, 68*, 417-424.

Skinner, B. F. (1953). *Science and human behavior.* New York: Macmillan.

Sloan, D. M. (2004). Emotion regulation in action: Emotional reactivity in experiential avoidance. *Behaviour Research and Therapy, 42*, 1257-1270.

Spira, A. P., Zvolensky, M. J., Eifert, G. H., & Feldner, M. T. (2004). Avoidance-oriented coping as a predictor of anxiety-based physical stress: A test using biological challenge. *Journal of Anxiety Disorders, 18*, 309-323.

Staats, A. W., & Eifert, G. H. (1990). The paradigmatic behaviorism theory of emotions: Basis for unification. *Clinical Psychology Review, 10*, 539-566.

Suomi, S. J. (1999). Attachment in rhesus monkeys. In J. Cassidy & P. R. Shaver (Eds.), *Handbook of attachment: Theory, research, and clinical application* (pp. 181-197). New York: Guilford.

Tellegen, A. (1985). Structures of mood and personality and their relevance to assessing anxiety, with an emphasis on self-report. In A. H. Tuma & J. Maser (Eds.), *Anxiety and the anxiety disorders* (pp. 681-706). Hillsdale, NJ: Lawrence Erlbaum.

Watson, J. B., & Raynor, R. (1920). Conditioned emotional reactions. *Journal of Experimental Psychology, 3*, 1-14.

Wegner, D. M. (1994). Ironic processes of mental control. *Psychological Review, 101*, 34-52.

Wegner, D. M., & Zanakos, S. (1994). Chronic thought suppression. *Journal of Personality, 62*, 615-640.

Wegner, D. M., Schneider, D. J., Knutson, B. & McMahon, S. R. (1991). Polluting the stream of consciousness: The effect of thought suppression on the mind's environment. *Cognitive Therapy and Research, 15*, 141-152.

Wilson, K. G., Hayes, S. C., Gregg, J., & Zettle, R. D. (2001). Psychopathology and psychotherapy. In S. C. Hayes, D. Barnes-Holmes, & B. Roche (2001), *Relational frame theory: A post-Skinnerian account of human language and cognition* (pp. 211- 237). New York: Kluwer.

Wolpe, J. (1958). *Psychotherapy by reciprocal inhibition.* Stanford, CA: Stanford University Press.

Wolpe, J., & Rachman, S. (1960). Psychoanalytic "evidence": A criticism based on Freud's case of Little Hans. *Journal of Nervous and Mental Disease, 131*, 135-148.

Wolpe, J., & Rowan, V. C. (1988). Panic disorder: A product of classical conditioning. *Behaviour Research and Therapy, 26*, 441-450.

Zettle, R. D., & Hayes, S. C. (1982). Rule governed behavior: A potential theoretical framework for cognitive-behavior therapy. In P. C. Kendall (Ed.), *Advances in cognitive-behavioral research and therapy, Vol. 1* (pp. 73-118). New York: Academic.

Zinbarg, R. E., Craske, M. G., & Barlow D. H. (1993). *Mastery of your anxiety and worry.* Boulder, CO: Graywind Publications.

Chapter 5

A Functional Contextual Account of Obsessive-Compulsive Disorder

Michael P. Twohig
University of Nevada, Reno
Daniel J. Moran
Trinity Services, Inc. / MidAmerican Psychological Institute
Steven C. Hayes
University of Nevada, Reno

Obsessive-compulsive disorder (OCD) is classified in the *Diagnostic and StatisticalManual of Mental Disorders* (DSM-IV-TR; APA, 2000) as an anxiety disorder and is characterized by distressing intrusive thoughts and unwanted repetitive behaviors. Scientific investigation of the possible basis for obsessive-compulsive behavior began to solidify in the 1950's (Solomon, Kamin, & Wynne, 1953; Solomon & Wynne, 1954), and these seminal studies on traumatic avoidance learning influenced future research investigating the effectiveness of behavior therapy applications (Rachman, Marks, & Hodgson 1973). Empirically supported psychosocial treatments for obsessive-compulsive disorder (Clark, 2004; Steketee & Barlow, 2002) are drawn from a large literature of learning principles and cognitive-behavioral theory, but more recent advances in a behavior analytic approach to language and cognition have not yet been integrated into behavioral and cognitive approaches to OCD. The focus of this chapter is to clarify how these advances might increase our understanding of OCD and possibly our success in treating it.

The Nature and Prevalence of OCD

OCD is comprised of obsessions and corresponding compulsions. *Obsessions* are defined in the DSM-IV-TR as "persistent ideas, thoughts, impulses, or images that are experienced as intrusive and inappropriate and that cause marked anxiety or distress; they are not worries about real-life problems; they are accompanied by attempts to ignore, suppress, or neutralize (i.e., subjective resistance); and they are acknowledged as a product of the person's mind" (APA, 2000, p. 457). *Compulsions* are defined as "repetitive behaviors (e.g., hand washing, ordering, checking) or mental acts (e.g., praying, counting, repeating words silently) that the person feels compelled to perform in response to an obsession or certain rigidly applied rules;

and the functions of the behaviors or mental acts is to prevent or reduce distress or some dreaded event or situation. The rituals either are not connected in a realistic way with what they are intended to neutralize or are clearly perceived as excessive" (p. 457). Foa and Kozak (1995) report that over 90% of persons with OCD exhibit both obsessions *and* compulsions and that 90% of the sample admitted performing the compulsion in order to reduce distress from the obsession.

According to the DSM-IV criteria, the individual must also find the obsessions or compulsions to be excessive, time consuming or unreasonable, cause distress, or significantly interfere with daily activities or with social or occupational functioning. Most individuals with OCD can recognize that their obsessions and compulsions are interfering with their lives, but many also report that they do not find their obsessions to be unreasonable (Foa & Kozak, 1995; Rachman & de Silva, 1978). In some instances the obsession can be difficult to distinguish from delusional thinking. To differentiate OCD from schizophrenic cognitive activity, the individual must be able to recognize that the obsessions are a product of his or her mind and not from an external source.

Lifetime prevalence rates for OCD are documented at approximately 2.3% in the United States (Weissman, Bland, Canino, Greenwand, Hwo, Newman et al., 1994). Typically, the onset of OCD is in the teens and early twenties and the mean age of onset is estimated to be 21 years for men and 22 years for women (Rasmussen & Eisen, 1992), although later assessments found a later onset with the mean age in the United States being 26 (Weissman et al., 1994). Weissman et al. (1994) also found prevalence estimates and ages of onset to be relatively uniform across samples from various cultures. Rasmussen and Eisen's (1992) review of demographic variables showed that 53% of obsessive-compulsive patients were women and 47% were men, but pediatric samples show a 2:1 male-female ratio (Hanna, 1995). There have been reports of OCD onset being associated with other life events such as the loss of a loved one, severe medical illness, major financial problems, or the onset of pregnancy (Lensi, Cassano, Correddu, Ravagli, Kunovac, & Akishal, 1996; Neziroglu, Anemone, & Yaryura-Tobias, 1992). Nevertheless, it is important to note that many individuals cannot identify an event that generated their OCD (Rasmussen & Tsuang, 1986).

There is poor clinical prognosis for those diagnosed with OCD who do not seek treatment. A long-term follow-up study showed (*M*=47 years) that OCD is a chronic condition with periodic waxing and waning in severity (Skoog & Skoog, 1999). In the same study, nearly half of the sample continued to experience clinically significant features and one-third had subclinical features, although 83% showed improvement in the 40-year period. Complete recovery only occurred in 20% of the sample. These findings are consistent with other studies of the natural course of OCD (e.g., Demal, Lenz, Mayrhofer, Zapotoczky, & Zitterl, 1993).

At first glance, the clinical presentations of OCD seem quite diverse in comparison to other disorders. However, despite the appearance of different manifestations, the types of obsessions and compulsions are fairly consistent.

Typical reports of obsessions and corresponding compulsions include: harming/religious/sexual obsessions, which occur with checking rituals; contamination obsessions, which occur with washing /cleaning rituals; and symmetry/ordering/certainty obsessions, which occur with counting/repeating/checking compulsions (as reported in Steketee & Barlow, 2002). Additionally, the majority of clients diagnosed with OCD have multiple obsessions and compulsions. These general types of obsessions and compulsions are fairly consistent across cultures and the content of the obsession seems fit the context. For example, reported fears of contamination of sexually transmitted diseases such as syphilis and gonorrhea have been replaced with AIDS in recent years. Although overt activity is commonly considered the hallmark of compulsions, these behaviors can occur privately.

Private compulsions (also called "covert rituals or compulsions") are common in OCD samples. Mavissakalian, Turner, and Michelson (1985) reported that approximately 25% of individuals diagnosed with OCD seem to have no visible compulsions; their compulsions are done privately (e.g., praying, counting, repeating a certain phrase). Private compulsions seem to function the same way as public compulsions; they are done in response to a certain obsession and function to reduce that obsession or its associated feelings (Salkovskis & Westbrook, 1989). The distinction between public and private compulsions is important from a treatment effectiveness standpoint. It has been shown that private compulsions are more difficult to treat than public ones (Salkovskis & Westbrook, 1989), although they respond to exposure and extinction procedures in the same way as public compulsions (de Silva, Menzies, & Shafran, 2003). As with private compulsions, hoarding compulsions have been found to be more difficult to treat than other overt compulsions (Black, Monahan, Gable, Blum, Clancy, & Baker, 1998).

OCD has a high rate of co-occurrence of other psychological disorders. Most studies show that 50 to 75% of individuals diagnosed with OCD will have another diagnosable disorder (Antony, Downie, & Swinson, 1998; Brown, Campbell, Lehman, Grisham, & Mancill, 2001; Karno, & Golding, 1991), and this rate is even higher when lifetime comorbidity is assessed with fewer than 15% having a sole diagnosis of OCD (Brown et al., 2001; Crino & Andrews, 1996).

The most common psychiatric diagnoses co-occurring with OCD are other anxiety disorders and mood disorders. Approximately 50% of those with OCD also have another anxiety disorder (Weisman et al., 1994). Of all the anxiety disorders, OCD has the highest co-occurrence of depression, with 27% of individuals diagnosed with OCD meeting criteria for major depression (Weisman, et al., 1994). Interestingly, it has been found that comorbid anxiety disorders tended to precede the onset of OCD whereas depression tended to occur after (Brown et al., 2001). Other notable relations with OCD include eating disorders and hypochondriasis, which have a 10% or lower rate of co-occurrence with OCD (Formea & Burns, 1995; Savron, Fava, Grandi, Rafanelli, Raffi, & Belluardo, 1996). Lifetime comorbidity of OCD and body dysmorphic disorder has been found to be 12% (Simon, Hollander, Stein, Cohen, & Aronowitz, 1995). Tourette's disorder (TD) has a special link with

OCD in that TD often occurs with OCD symptoms (King, Leckman, Scahill, & Cohen, 1999). Reviews have found that OCD symptoms are present in 11 to 80% of those diagnosed with TD, with more recent studies finding higher rates (King et al., 1999), but the converse is not true. Only a small proportion of those diagnosed with OCD exhibit tics (Eisen, Goodman, Keller, Warshaw, DeMarco, Luce et al., 1999).

Individuals diagnosed with OCD have been found to have a high rate of personality disorders with most individuals meeting criteria for at least one (Baer & Jenike, 1992; Black, Noyes, Pfohl, Goldstein, & Blum, 1993; Mavissakalian, Hamann, & Jones, 1990; Steketee, Chambless, & Tran, 2001). OCD is most commonly related to the Cluster C - the "anxious" group, particularly avoidant, dependent, and obsessive-compulsive personality disorders. Possibly surprisingly to some, OCD does not have a higher prevalence with obsessive-compulsive person- ality disorder than with other personality disorders.

Models of OCD

OCD is one of the more highly studied psychiatric disorders. An informal search of PsychINFO© shows over 3,500 entries that indicate "obsessive compul- sive disorder" as a key concept compared to "trichotillomania" and "body dysmorphic disorder" which both have around 300 entries; depression has just over 4,400 entries. Additionally there are many authored and edited volumes on the disorder. Despite all this research there is no accepted model of OCD, and treatment improvements are needed. In this section we will review briefly some of the available models of OCD.

Behavioral Models of Etiology

According to some proponents of the behavioral model, obsessions and compulsions are learned coping responses to aversive situations that are reinforced by their consequences (Maher, 1966; Meyer & Chesser, 1970). Mowrer's two-stage theory of fear and avoidance is typically used to explain the etiology of phobias, but has been applied to OCD, as well. According to Mowrer (1939, 1960), physiological fear responses are learned through classical conditioning, and avoidance responses are operantly conditioned. In the classic example of this theory, animals received repeated pairings of a warning tone, the neutral stimulus (NS), and an aversive shock, the unconditioned stimulus (UCS). After repeated pairings, the tone acquires aversive conditioned stimulus (CS) properties eliciting physiological anxiety, the conditioned response (CR), in the presence of the tone, even when no shock is given. In this first stage, anxiety is conditioned to a previously neutral stimulus. In the second stage, the animal avoids the tone, the CS, by making operant escape responses. This reduces contact with the anxiety-provoking stimulus and negatively reinforces the avoidance behavior. In OCD, the obsession can be conceptualized as the CS that elicits fear/anxiety, and the compulsion can serve as an avoidance response which reduces the obsession.

Behavioral researchers have long questioned the duality of Mowrer's theory. One approach has been to remove the first stage in which a CS is classically conditioned. Sidman (1962) delivered a shock to rats without an explicit stimulus to signal the shock was coming. The inescapable shock was delivered every fifteen seconds, as long as the animal failed to make a bar press response. The lever response postponed the next shock for another fifteen seconds. When the animal did not respond, it would be shocked fifteen seconds later and continually shocked at fifteen second intervals, unless it emitted another response which would postpone the shock. In Sidman's procedure, the conditioned stimulus was purposefully absent, but his procedure maintains high levels of avoidance. Pavlovian ingredients can be reintroduced by inference because anything the rat does, aside from pressing the lever, is paired with shock (Herrnstein, 1969, p. 56).

Herrnstein (1969) extended Sidman's dispute of the two-factor theory. He contended that the CS termination was an unnecessary or untestable feature in an avoidance responding paradigm. Herrnstein cited several studies where avoidance occurs when the CS has been eliminated as a factor (Bolles, Stokes & Younger, 1966; Herrnstein & Hineline, 1966; Taub & Berman, 1963). He also pointed out that Mowrer may have overlooked situations as a whole functioning as a CS.

While two-factor theory is often used to explain the onset and maintenance of this disorder (Carr, 1974; Dollard & Miller, 1950; Hodgson & Rachman, 1972; Maher, 1966; Roper, Rachman, & Hodgson, 1973), similar criticisms came from clinical researchers. Emmelkamp (1987) suggested that the first stage of the theory is superfluous:

> Typically, ritualistic activities have powerful anxiety-reducing effects in stressful periods. Although patients sometimes give a detailed account of one or more traumatic experiences associated with the development of the obsessive-compulsive behavior, the traumatic situation by itself rarely leads directly to the obsessive-compulsive behavior. (p. 312)

Emmelkamp also added that with many obsessional patients, different obsessions and compulsions exist simultaneously, while Mowrer's theory would seem to require many different traumatic experiences to explain the different obsessions. This led Emmelkamp (1987) to assert that "there is little or no evidence that classical conditioning provides an adequate account of the development of obsessional problems" (p. 312). As Tynes, Salins, Skiba, and Winstead (1992) stated, "the first stage is perhaps less defensible in actuality, but the second stage forms the basis for behavioral therapy and is readily observable in OCD patients' behavior" (p. 198).

It is worth noting that some criticisms of two-factor theory do not address issues of generalization, higher-order conditioning, or relational framing. The neutral stimulus that becomes a CS for anxiety is not strictly the only stimulus that can evoke anxiety responses. Stimuli that are similar to the original CS can take on its stimulus properties due to generalization. Higher-order conditioning, the process of pairing a new stimulus to a well-established CS, also makes it possible for the individual to exhibit anxiety responses to different stimuli. Different stimuli that are relationally framed with conditioned stimuli can also elicit conditioned responses (Wulfert, Greenway, Farkas, Hayes, & Dougher, 1994). These processes could allow fear responses to be distributed to a wider range of stimuli and do not necessarily require many different traumatic experiences to explain the fear responses.

Another theory positing that it is not reduction of anxiety that maintains OCD behavior is Gray's (1975) safety signal theory. Gray proposed that the "safety signals" resulting from the compulsive acts reinforce these behaviors. Avoiding a certain anxiety-provoking situation puts the person in a different environment, one with stimuli that can be considered reinforcing. Behavior bringing about this "different environment" is reinforced, and perhaps increases the likelihood of ritualizing.

Social learning theory also suggests how rituals are conditioned and maintained. Millon (1981) emphasized the role of excessive parental control. The social learning theory suggests that a parent/child relationship characterized by punishment of the child who fails to meet "rigid parental expectations and standards for acceptable behavior" (Pollak, 1987, p. 254) may result in later OCD behavior. The child learns what to do and what not to do in order to avoid punishment. Social learning theory suggests that the child is conditioned to emphasize his/her own responsibility for other people's situations and feel guilty when such responsibility is not recognized.

Cognitive Models of Etiology

The cognitive approach to anxiety disorders in general is usually credited to Beck (1976), who proposes that affective disturbance observed in anxiety disorders is produced by negative automatic thoughts (NAT's), which are produced by dysfunctional assumptions. There are a variety of explanations of the role of cognitions in OCD (e.g., Clark, 2004; Rachman, 1997, 1998; Salkovskis, 1998). These models differ in the specific constructs that are presumed to play a role in the disorder. For example, Salkovskis (1998) stresses the role a feeling of "inflated responsibility" has with regard to controlling the obsessions; Rachman (1998) writes that those diagnosed with OCD misinterpret the intrusive thought as personally important and threatening, and Clark (2004) stresses that obsessions are experienced as contrary to core values or one's identity. In general, they all tend to stress the negative role of certain maladaptive cognitions in OCD.

Most of these models indicate that the unwanted intrusive thought is the starting place of the disorder, and the unwanted intrusive thoughts are produced by some stimuli. All models seem to agree that faulty appraisals and beliefs are necessary but not sufficient for creating obsessions (Rachman, 1997; Salkovskis, 1985). Consistent with this view, it has been found that individuals diagnosed with OCD assign a more negative valence to their obsessions, find them more meaningful, and find them more distressing, lengthier, and more intense and frequent (Rachman & de Silva, 1978). According to these cognitive theories, the individual's attempts to control these unwanted intrusive thoughts (e.g., neutralizations and compulsions) plays an important role in the exacerbation of the disorder.

The two processes - faulty appraisals of the obsessions and escape behaviors - produce an escalation of the unwanted intrusive thoughts. This will result in an immediate decrease in the obsession, but can strengthen the frequency and intensity of the obsession in the long term.

Biomedical Etiology

The medical model attempts to explain the etiology of OCD using genetic factors (Carey & Gottesman, 1981; Nestadt, Lan, Samuels, Riddle, Bienvenu, Liang et al., 2000; Swedo, Leonard, Garvey, Mittleman, Allen, Perlmutter et al. 1989), neurochemistry (Hollander, De Caria, & Liebowitz, 1989; Yaryura-Tobias, 1977; Zohar & Insel, 1987) and neuropsychological functioning (Behar, Rapoport, Berg, Denckla, Mann, Cox et al., 1984). According to Jenike (1986), head injuries, encephalitis, and brain tumors have all been associated with the development of obsessive-compulsive disorder.

In a study by Nestadt et al. (2000), well-trained diagnosticians were blinded as to whether participants were OCD probands or relatives and whether they were from case or control families. It was found that first-degree relatives of probands diagnosed with OCD had a nearly five times higher lifetime prevalence of OCD. Additionally, obsessive behaviors were more similar in families than compulsive behaviors, and relatives of OCD probands were at greater risk for both obsessions and compulsions than relatives of controls, and there was again a greater likelihood of obsessions than compulsions. A recent meta-analysis (Hettema, Neale, & Kendler, 2001) suggests significant familial aggregation for OCD behaviors, and a considerable familial relationship among relatives with obsessive-compulsive spectrum disorders, such as trichotillomania and other tic disorders (Leckman, King, & Cohen, 1999; Miltenberger, Rapp, & Long, 2001). While there may be some support for genetic influences on the likelihood of exhibiting OCD behaviors, "current behavioral genetics have done little to thoughtfully address the way nonbiological factors may lead to an expression of any genotype" (Follette & Houts, 1996, p. 1127).

Neurobiological hypotheses for OCD behavior suggest small structural abnormalities in the caudate nucleus, as well as functional dysregulation of neural circuits comprising orbitofrontal cortex, cingulate cortex, and the caudate nucleus in OCD. According to Dougherty, Rauch, and Jenike (2002), OCD can be conceptualized as a disease involving cognitive and corticostriatal networks. Baxter (1990) posits that the cortex-striatum functioning is scattered in the OCD patient. Some research suggests that childhood onset of OCD/ Tourette's Disorder can stem from streptococcal infections which lead to autoimmune processes that may damage striatal neurons (Swedo, Schapiro, Grady, Cheslow, Leonard, Kumar et al., 1989; Swedo et al., 1998). The prevailing neurochemical description of OCD hypothesizes pathological uptake of serotonin as an important part of the behavioral concerns, but this description is criticized as being inconclusive by other medical and behavioral researchers (Griest, Jefferson, Kobak, Katzelnick, & Serlin, 1995;

Insel, Murphy, Cohen, Alterman, Kilts, & Linnoila, 1983; Weizman, Carmi, Hermesh, Shahar, Apter, Tyano et al., 1986).

OCD Treatment Research

Exposure with ritual prevention (ERP) is the best validated treatment for OCD, with effectiveness rates that range from 60-85% (Abramowitz, 1997). ERP has notable limitations, however. In addition to the 15-40% of individuals who do not respond to ERP, another 25% will refuse the treatment and another 3-12% will drop out (Foa, Steketee, Grayson, & Doppel, 1983). This finding led Foa, Franklin, and Kozak (1998) to write that a "current criticism if EX/RP is that its overall effectiveness is limited by the fact that many patients reject it because they are too afraid. Future research should explore methods to decrease refusals" (p. 271). Furthermore, particular subgroups do not do as well. Treatment is less effective with individuals with private or hoarding compulsions (Clark, 2004). Clients who are poorly motivated or noncompliant also tend to have diminished treatment gains (Foa et al., 1998).

There are treatment options available beyond psychosocial interventions, but the data are not impressive. Clomipramine and selective serotonin reuptake inhibitors, such as sertraline, fluvoxamine, fluoxetine, paroxetine, and citalopram, are evidence based pharmacological treatments for OCD (see Dougherty et al., 2002 for a review) but their effects are no larger and in some studies less robust than the best psychosocial interventions (Stanley & Turner, 1995). These medications provide serotonergic reuptake blocking properties and are the mainstay of pharmacological treatment for OCD. In practice, pharmacotherapy and psychotherapy are often jointly used (Baer & Minichiello, 1998), but here too the data are equivocal. Some researchers conclude that the combination of behavior therapy with pharmacotherapy is more effective than either treatment alone (Hohagen, Winkelmann, Rasche-Räuchle, Hand, König, Munchau et al., 1998), but others conclude that the addition of psychiatric medication does not enhance cognitive therapy or behavior therapy for OCD (van Balkom, de Haan, van Oppen, Spinhoven, Hoogduin, & van Dyck, 1998). Neurosurgery has been used with severe cases (Rapoport & Inoff-Germain, 1997) but it has not been studied in controlled trials and raises a wide variety of concerns (Albucher, Curtis, & Pitts, 1999; Bejerot, 2003).

Recently, attention has been directed toward the addition of cognitive procedures to ERP. Unfortunately, this does not make ERP more effective (Franklin & Foa, 2002), which creates a paradox: cognitions seem to be involved in OCD, but targeting them in the way that cognitive therapists do, does not seem to add to treatment effectiveness.

Recently a new "third wave" of behavioral and cognitive therapy has emerged (Hayes, 2004) that provides new options for expanding beyond ERP. These new methods also address emotion and cognition, but are believed to do so in a fundamentally different way. The third wave treatments, in general, focus on altering the function of one's private events (e.g., thoughts and feelings) rather than changing their form, frequency, or situational sensitivity, as is usually seen in traditional CBT. This chapter seeks to provide an analysis of OCD from a third wave or functional contextual standpoint that incorporates findings from the OCD literature and recent advances in the understanding of language and cognition.

Relevant Findings Surrounding OCD

In developing a model of OCD it is helpful first to consider the available evidence on some of its psychological features. We will review those data in this section.

Frequency of Intrusive Thoughts

Intrusive thoughts *per se* are not unusual. It has been found that 80-90% of the population experiences unwanted intrusive thoughts (Clark & de Silva, 1985; Freeston, Ladoucer, Thibodeau, & Gagnon, 1991; Parkinson & Rachman, 1981; Purdon & Clark, 1993; Salkovskis & Harrison, 1984). Rachman and de Silva (1978) compared a nonclinical population to a group diagnosed with OCD on their experiences with unwanted, obsessive-like intrusive thoughts, and images, and found that 84% of their nonclinical population experienced unwanted intrusive thoughts that were similar in form and content to the OCD group. In addition, the OCD group reported their obsessions to be more frequent, intense, and uncontrollable, and more likely associated with neutralization responses. Thus, it seems that any model of OCD needs to account for the different function of intrusive thoughts for individuals with OCD. Possible influences on these differences that have been examined include thought suppression, thought action fusion, and memory deficits.

Thought Suppression

There is emerging and strong evidence that human beings' abilities to remove unwanted intrusive thoughts from consciousnesses are mediocre at best and poor at worst. This difficulty was originally shown with nonclinical populations using emotionally neutral thoughts. Wegner and colleagues (e.g., Wegner, 1994; Wegner, Schneider, Carter, & White, 1987) have demonstrated that deliberate suppression can result in increases in neutral thoughts once suppression attempts have been terminated. This paradox - that attempting to control one's thoughts might make them less controllable - might be central to OCD.

The literature on thought suppression with OCD patients is still somewhat inconsistent. When investigated with unwanted intrusive thoughts, it has been found that deliberate suppression of intrusive thoughts in nondiagnosed individuals results in increased occurrence and disturbances of the thoughts (Rutledge, 1998; Salkovskis & Campbell, 1994; Trinder & Salkovskis, 1994), although these results are not always consistent (Purdon & Clark, 2001). While investigating individuals diagnosed with OCD, Janeck and Calamari (1999) did not find evidence of an enhancement or rebound effect at the group level when suppression was applied to obsessions, but they did find that a greater number of individuals in the OCD group showed a rebound effect than those in the control group. Conversely, Tolin,

Abramowitz, Przeworski, and Foa (2002) found only the OCD group, and not a control group, showed an immediate enhancement effect when suppressing a neutral thought. Recent research with 50 individuals diagnosed with OCD did not find a rebound effect after attempts at suppression; however, attempts at suppression did result in greater discomfort with the thoughts that did occur and a greater negative mood (Purdon, Rowa, & Antony, 2005). Finally, Tolin, Abramowitz, Hamlin, Foa, and Synodi (2002) found that individuals diagnosed with OCD were more likely to attribute their difficulties with thought control to internal rather than external reasons. Thus, while the literature is still somewhat unclear, it does appear that thought suppression in patients with OCD is a moderately ineffective and disturbing coping strategy.

Thought Action Fusion

Considering the function of one's thoughts has been central to theories of OCD for some time. Rachman (1993) indicated that individuals diagnosed with OCD commonly believed that an unacceptable thought, impulse, or image could actually cause harm to happen to someone else. Similarly, Salkovskis (1985) wrote that "thinking this is as bad as doing it" (p. 573) and that "having a thought about an action is like performing the action" (p. 579). These notions are at the center of the construct of thought action fusion (TAF; Rachman, 1993).

Factor analyses of the TAF construct have consistently found two different forms of this phenomenon (Rachman, Thordarson, Shafran, & Woody, 1995; Rassin, Merckelback, Muris, & Schmidt, 2001). Likelihood TAF refers to the belief that having a thought, such as an obsession, increases the likelihood that that specific event will occur. Moral TAF refers to the belief that having an unacceptable thought is the moral equivalent to acting on that thought. Research has found that TAF is highly related to OCD (Amir, Freshman, Ramsey, Neary, & Brigidi, 2001; Rachman et al., 1995; Shafran, Thordarson, & Rachman, 1996), other anxiety disorders (Abramowitz, Whiteside, Lynam, & Kalsy, 2003; Rassin, Diepstraten, Merckelbach, & Muris, 2001; Rassin, Merckelbach, Muris, & Schmidt, 2001), and depression (Abramowitz et al., 2003). Research is conflicting as to whether TAF is related to worry or not (Coles, Mennin, & Heimberg, 2001; Hazlett-Stevens, Zucker, & Craske, 2002). One study found that the TAF scales were related to obsessions but not to worry (Coles et al., 2001), and another found that likelihood TAF but not moral TAF was related to scores of worry (Hazlett-Stevens et al., 2002). TAF likelihood was a significant predictor of one's believed controllability of upsetting sexual and nonsexual intrusive thoughts (Clark, Purdon, & Byers, 2000), and TAF moral was significantly, positively related to religiosity (Rassin & Koster, 2003).

Rachman, Shafran, Mitchell, Trant, and Teachman (1996) developed a manipulation that evoked TAF by asking the participant to write the sentence "I hope ____ is in a car accident in the next 24 hours" and placing the name of a close friend or family member in the blank. This preparation has been found to result in increases in TAF Likelihood and increased urges to neutralize and anxiety (Rachman et al.,

1996; van den Hout, van Pol, & Peters, 2001; van den Hout, Kindt, Weiland, & Peters, 2002). Those who neutralized their thought were more likely to feel guilty, more immoral, and experience a greater sense of responsibility after writing the thought compared to those who did not neutralize (Zucker, Craske, Barrios, & Holguin, 2002). There is evidence that directly confronting TAF before engaging in this experimental writing exercise can reduce anxiety and TAF (Zucker et al., 2002). Research suggests that a course of cognitive behavior therapy can reduce TAF (Rassin, Diepstraten, Merckelbach, & Muris, 2001).

In a separate experimental manipulation, high school students were told that if they thought of the word "apple" they would cause a person in a different room to be shocked. Mock electrical equipment was attached to the subjects so they would believe their thoughts were being detected. It was found that those who were told their thought would cause the shock had higher frequency of the thought, more discomfort, and more resistance to the intrusion as compared to a group who was told to "relax and sit quietly" (Rassin, Merckelbach, Murris, & Spaan, 1999). Overall, the literature is suggesting that there are more and less effective ways to respond to obsessions.

Memory Deficits

There has been a considerable amount of research on the role of memory impairment in OCD, as it appears the repetitive behavior stems from not remembering if the action was performed. Individuals with high levels of checking have been found to be impaired in their memory for complex verbal information (Deckersbach, Otto, Savage, Baer, & Jenike, 2000; Sher, Mann, & Frost, 1984; Zitterl, Urban, Linzmayer, Aigner, Demal, Semler et al., 2001), although other studies failed to find this relation (e.g., Rubenstein, Peynircioglu, Chambless, & Pigott, 1993). Research has been more consistent in finding limitations in remembering experimentally presented non-verbal stimuli in individuals with OCD (e.g., Savage, Baer, Keuthen, Brown, Rauch, & Jenike, 1999; Sher, Frost, Kushner, Crews, & Alexander, 1989; see Muller & Roberts, 2005 for a review).

Those diagnosed with OCD seem to have greater difficulties remembering if they performed an action or not (Ecker & Engelkamp, 1995; Rubenstein et al., 1993; Sher, Frost, & Otto, 1983; Sher et al., 1984, 1989), although most of this research has been conducted with checking compulsions and it is unclear whether this applies to other forms. Individuals diagnosed with OCD do not have faith in their memories as to whether the behavior was performed or not (Muller & Roberts, 2005). For example, when participants are presented with varying types of stimuli (e.g., words, objects) and asked to recall the items, those diagnosed with OCD performed as well as controls but were less confident in their answers (Foa, Amir, Gershuny, Molnar, & Kozak, 1997; Hermans, Martens, De Cort, Pieters, & Eelen, 2003; McNally & Kohlbeck, 1993; Tolin, Abramowitz, Kozak, & Foa, 2001). This finding was also confirmed by slower reaction times by individuals with checking compulsions (MacDonald, Anthony, MacLeod, & Richter, 1997).

A Functional Contextual Account of OCD

What might account for the range of features seen in OCD? The present model views OCD as a disorder of verbal regulation based on biological vulnerability, characteristics of language development, and an inappropriate use of verbal regulatory strategies particularly as targeted toward private events. A diagram of this model is provided in Figure 5.1.

Biological Vulnerabilities

When looking at how OCD develops it seems appropriate to start from the beginning. Humans are born with certain biological predispositions that make things more and less likely. For example, professional basketball players are taller rather than shorter. It is possible that there is a similar situation in OCD. In broad terms, some biological basis seems possible because OCD is more common in relatives of those diagnosed with OCD (e.g., Nestadt et al., 2000).

The present model emphasizes problems in the application of verbal regulation strategies to private events, particularly negatively valenced and anxiety-producing thoughts. This would be more of a problem if there was a biological influence to relate negative events. Indeed, the available evidence suggests that this is the case.

Pediatric and adult OCD has been associated with dysfunction in the ventral prefrontal cortical (VPFC)-striatal-thalamic neural circuits in the brain (Saxena, Brody, & Schwartz, 1998). This area includes the anterior cingulate cortex, the area that is targeted in neurosurgery for OCD (Rapoport & Inoff-Germain, 1997), and has been shown to be more active in those diagnosed with OCD as compared to others (Ursu, Stenger, Shear, Jones, & Carter, 2004). This region of the brain is associated with emotions and one's experience of pain or other uncomfortable private events. It can be activated by hearing words associated with pain (Naoyuki, Osaka, Masanao, Hirohito, & Hidenao, 2004), pain related emotion (Gao, Ren, Zhang, & Zhao, 2004), feeling or witnessing a pinprick (Morrisaon, Lloyd, Di Pellegrino, & Roberts, 2004), and memory for contextual fear conditioning (Frankland, Bontempi, Talton, Kaczmarek, & Silva, 2004). Excessive activity in VPFC could make one more likely to be aware of and respond to potential and experienced aversive events. Taken together it seems possible that persons likely to develop OCD start with a greater ability to bring anxiety into a given context, including through language and conditioning.

Early Language Conditioning

According to the functional contextual approach, mere biological vulnerability is not enough to develop OCD. Inappropriate use of verbal regulatory strategies is necessary and these processes must be learned.

Parents of anxious children tend to show greater control and are less granting of autonomy for their children (Dumas, LaFreniere, & Serketich, 1995; Krohne & Hock, 1991; Siqueland, Kendall, & Steinberg, 1996). They also encourage avoidance of potentially difficult situations (Dadds, Barrett, Rapee, & Ryan, 1996). Parents

An ACT Model of Obsessive-Compulsive Disorder

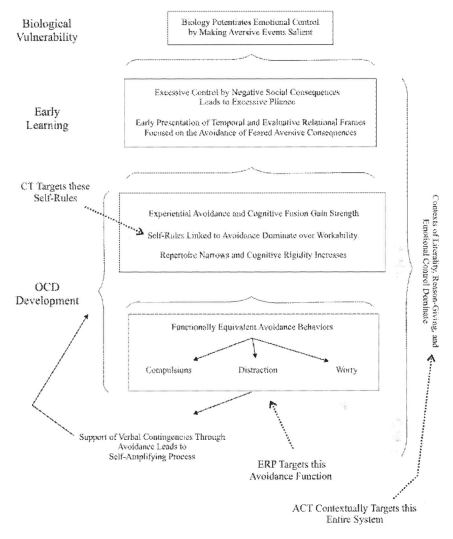

Figure 5.1. A Functional Contextual Model of OCD.

of children with OCD likewise model avoidance and fearfulness (Henin & Kendall, 1997) and link this fear to verbal processes. For example, Hibbs, Hamburger, Lenane, Rapoport, Kruesi, Keysor et al. (1991) found that parents of children diagnosed with OCD showed higher levels of criticism and over-involvement of their child's performance in a task than a control group. These parents tend to be strict (Merkel, Pollard, Weiner, & Staebler, 1993; O'Connor & Freeston, 2002), over-involved (Merkel et al., 1993), and less confident in their children's abilities, less rewarding of independence, and less likely to use positive problem solving strategies with their children (Barrett, Shortt, & Healy, 2002).

This history may lead to several verbal regulatory processes. Criticism, lack of autonomy, over-involvement, and lower independence may lead to high levels of pliance - rule governed behavior based on arbitrary reinforcement for a correspon-dence between rules and specified behavior (Barnes-Holmes, O'Hora, Roche, Hayes, Bissett, & Lyddy, 2001) - and channel those rules toward patterns of avoidance. Pliance is the earliest form of rule-governance, and seems to be a necessary condition for acquisition of rule-governed behavior. Because the child is also learning to focus on and predict negative outcomes, and because these children are already predisposed to notice and experience aversive feelings and to learn based on fear conditioning, rule control would tend gradually shift from pure pliance, to tracking. Tracking is rule-governed behavior produced by a history of obtaining non-arbitrary consequences (i.e., those that are present independently of the delivery of the rule) specified in a rule by bringing behavior under control of the rule. In one sense this is desirable, because it strengthens the ability to achieve reinforcers through verbally planned actions. In this case, however, tracking can considerably expand the scope of avoidance learning. Instead of just learning to avoid criticism, the child may begin to avoid anxiety, uncertainty, or vulnerability. This expands avoidance learning because events of this kind are available to motivate behavior in virtually all situations.

An example would be a child who has a biological predisposition to increased anxiety responses being reared by parents who are constantly telling her that the world is dangerous, that she cannot handle the stress of the world, and teach her not to do things "because Mommy said so." Such an environment could shape a rigid pliance repertoire, and such inflexibility may be maladaptive in the future. Further, being in the parents' good graces is an important influence on her behavior and she may not only have an inappropriate "because Mommy said so" pliance repertoire, but also track that "I need to avoid risk, possible danger, and stress" whether Mommy said so or not. The child could grow up generalizing and framing new avoidance rules in fresh environments. It should be noted that broadly similar models have been proposed by previous OCD researchers. Rachman (1976) has proposed an "over-control" model where the child has a predisposition that is fostered by over-control by the parents.

Because both aversive control and excessive rule-control result in relatively narrow and inflexible repertoires, early establishment of such patterns could make reduction of these patterns difficult. Said another way, individuals who develop OCD are more likely to notice and experience certain private events as aversive and seem to be taught by their parents to avoid these events through pliance and tracking based rule-following, which could result in a relatively rigid pattern that is difficult to test and to change. All of these features will be discussed in more detail later.

Development of Language-Based Psychopathological Patterns

The present analysis is based on Relational Frame Theory (RFT; Hayes, Barnes-Holmes, & Roche, 2001) which provides a unique way to look at the manner in which environmental events (public and private) are experienced. According to RFT, the core of human language is the learned ability to arbitrarily relate one event to another (mutually and in combination) and to alter the functions of these events as a result. Two forms of contextual control are important: contexts that control how events are related (e.g., same, opposite, better, and so on) and contexts that control which functions are altered by these relations. Specific relational operants of this kind are called relational frames.

Two types of relational frames that are of particular importance in the analysis and treatment of OCD are temporal and evaluative frames. Temporal frames involve responding to stimuli in terms of relations of time and sequence; they allow us to predict the future, construct an imagined future, and reconsider the past. Comparative frames allow us to evaluate one event in reference to another. For example, we can assess if "this one" is *better than* "that one" or which "one" we would want more. The combination of these two frames allows us to compare and evaluate predicted outcomes to present situations or other predicted future outcomes. For that reason they are critical to problem solving of all kinds, according to an RFT analysis.

The problem occurs when conditioned private events are targeted. For example, the obsession, "If I think about killing my girlfriend, then I must take a shower otherwise I might actually do it," possesses both of these frames. There is an IF-THEN temporal relation that shows the future consequences of a behavior: killing one's girlfriend. Comparative relations are also evident in the possible outcomes of this obsession: 1) take a shower and not kill her, and 2) do not take a shower and possibly kill her. Through a transformation of stimulus function, one is able to experience psychologically and physically some of what each of these outcomes would be like. We can experience the verbally constructed future in the present.

Cognitive theories generally suggested that these thoughts are experienced as part of an "OCD schemata." Specifically, that the individual possesses faulty appraisals and beliefs associated with the obsession (Clark, 2004). Stated another way, they follow their thoughts and their thoughts do not accurately track reality.

From an RFT point of view, the combination of predisposition to more intense anxiety responses, a strong avoidance learning repertoire, and excessive pliance and tracking linked to elimination of private events gives normal unwanted intrusive thoughts greater functional impact. Individuals diagnosed with OCD develop a particularly heightened awareness to situations that could possibly have aversive consequences that are dealt with through selected rule-following repertoires. Once the relation is formed that this event might possibly end in an aversive consequence, the possible aversive event can be experienced intensely by the individual. The individual applies avoidant and rule-based learning to these feelings and thoughts, which serves as a context that greatly increases their functional impact. Compulsions decrease aversive feelings but negatively reinforce the whole process, so this way of relational framing gets strengthened and further increases avoidance. The process begins to build on itself.

From this functional viewpoint, unlike dualistic cognitive perspectives, obsessive thoughts are not just *believed* to be real, but rather that they have *real* impact. The functional impact of obsessions is not directly due to a faulty *appraisal* or *belief*–rather it is a faulty form of contextual control over relational frames and the functions they evoke.

Cognitive Fusion

As these relational framing processes develop, language becomes highly entangled in the regulation of our behavior. The process of being verbally entangled makes it difficult for verbal humans to experience the world directly - as nonverbal organisms do - because stimulus relations and verbal rules dominate over other forms of behavioral regulation. This process has been termed "cognitive fusion" (Hayes, 2004). While being verbal is useful in most situations in our lives, it also can make human behavior rigid and inflexible even when our verbal rules do not match the changing real world contingencies (Hayes, 1989; Hayes, Strosahl, & Wilson, 1999; Shimoff, Catania, & Matthews, 1981; Wilson & Hayes, 1996).

This is similar to the concept of TAF, which is highly related to OCD (Amir et al., 2001; Rachman et al., 1995; Shafran et al., 1996). TAF involves: 1) the belief that thinking about an unacceptable or disturbing event makes it more likely that that event will occur in real life, and 2) that having unacceptable thoughts, images, or impulses are morally equivalent to actually engaging in the behavior. In the cognitive literature, these events are described as catastrophic misinterpretations (Shafran et al., 1996). These misinterpretations are usually corrected, at least in the case of OCD, by engaging in some type of neutralizing behavior. Neutralizing is used by cognitive theorists as support for TAF because of the belief that neutralizing will affect the real world in the opposite way the obsessions did.

There is generally wide agreement that TAF occurs and is an important component of OCD, but a technical account of TAF has not been provided. TAF is more an outcome than a description of a process. The psychological outcomes described in TAF research are consistent with an RFT analysis of verbal behavior.

Transformation of stimulus functions can produce the physiological and psychological sensations of engaging in a behavior through derived relations, provided a functional context evokes these functions. One can experience the outcome of a compulsion indirectly, simply by thinking about it. It is not a large step to the view that thinking about doing something is just as bad as doing it.

We normally do not experience the related feelings or bodily sensations whenever a thought occurs. For example, if someone not diagnosed with OCD thinks about hurting one's mother he or she might have a small feeling of sorrow or repulsion, but it is likely to be fleeting and small – nothing like what might be felt if it actually occurred. This is the result of the contextual control over the functions of our relational actions: if this thought is experienced as a transient thought or in a context that would not support the stimulus functions of the thought (such as not having access, method or motive for hurting one's mother), few of the emotional functions will be elicited. Without the literal and important contextual variables, the relational network is not sufficient enough to transform stimulus functions. It is when thoughts are taken in a literal context that the functions will be much greater.

The context determines what functions are transferred. For example, the physiological reaction one would have if someone yelled "Car!" while you were sitting at your desk would be different than while you were crossing a street. The same verbal stimulus is experienced differently in these different contexts. Those diagnosed with OCD likely experience their obsessions in a much more literal context in anxiety provoking situations than those who are not diagnosed.

The primary context could be referred to as a *context of literality*–a verbally constructed environment where thoughts and feelings, and the environment as structured by those thoughts and feelings, are experienced with greater adherence to the arbitrary relations than the direct contingencies. In RFT, once a relational network forms it is easier to change functions than relations themselves (Wilson, Hayes, Gregg, & Zettle, 2001) because these networks are historical and there are no processes that truly eliminate well-established behaviors (even extinction only inhibits but does not remove previous learning, as is shown for example, in reacquisition effects in operant and classical conditioning, Catania, 1997). Ironically, the relational contexts one would use to attempt to change the form of the relational network also tend to be functional contexts in which the impact of that network is increased. For example, any attempt to reduce the obsession - by the client or therapist - paradoxically supports this context of literality, as well as other contexts such as a context of emotional control, or of reason giving (because obsessions are the focus of both control efforts and explanations for behavior). Targeting these thoughts for change strengthens such contexts because change efforts imply that these thoughts are meaningful and *should* be addressed - that they are true and believable. Also, it likely strengthens the temporal and evaluative frames involved, which may increase rule following and behavioral rigidity, and narrow one's repertoire. Thus, from this perspective, any attempt to prove this thought incorrect or to change it only strengthens the contexts that provide obsessions with their behavior regulatory power. This possibility is supported by the thought suppression literature showing that attempts to decrease many types of thoughts can result in such paradoxical results (Purdon & Clark, 2002).

Emotional Avoidance

As individuals diagnosed with OCD become more fused with their thoughts, they begin to experience the possible consequences of their thoughts more readily.

Individuals who experience the aversive sensations associated with obsessions have been reported to engage in a number of different compulsions, the most common being checking, washing, repeating, ordering, counting, and hoarding (Antony et al., 1998). In addition to these common compulsions, individuals with OCD engage in a number of different escape or avoidance responses to obsessions including: covert compulsions, neutralizing, magical thinking, assurance strategies (such as calling one's family members to make sure they are not injured), rationalizing, and avoiding situations that evoke the obsession. With OCD, compulsions have been found to reduce the private event immediately (Hornsveld, Kraaimaat, & van DamBaggen, 1979), but not for long durations of time because the obsessions recur later. For individuals diagnosed with OCD, engaging in the compulsions is about not experiencing the aversive feelings associated with experiencing the obsession; checking the lock is about not feeling uncomfortable, not about seeing if the door is locked or not.

As can be seen from the diagnostic criteria, these attempts to avoid or prevent aversive private events are a very large part of the disorder. The diagnostic criteria for OCD specify that "the person attempts to ignore or suppress the thoughts, impulses, or images, or to neutralize them with another thought or action" (APA, 2000, p. 462). Similarly for compulsions, "the behaviors or mental acts are aimed at preventing or reducing distress or preventing some dreaded event or situation" (APA, 2000, p. 462). It can be argued that it is not the obsessions that are problematic *per se*, but what the person does with the obsessions that are at the core of OCD. It is the checking, cleaning, and ritualistic behaviors that interfere with social functioning. A person with OCD will continue to engage in these behaviors even though there are impairments on one's quality of life (Koran, Theinemann, & Davenport, 1996), probable troubles maintaining employment (Leon, Portera, & Weisman, 1995), and difficulties in relationships (Emmelkamp & Beens, 1991).

In addition to interfering socially, attempts to escape or avoid one's obsessions have been found to sometimes increase their frequency, severity, or situational sensitivity with nondiagnosed individuals (Wenzlaff & Wegner, 2000) and individuals diagnosed with OCD (Purdon & Clark, 2002). Hayes, Wilson, Gifford, Follette, and Strosahl (1996) provided a possible explanation for this occurrence.

> Deliberate attempts to rid oneself of a thought involves following the verbal rule 'I must not think thought X.' However, such a rule, by specifying 'thought X' produces contact with 'thought X' and thus thoughts of 'thought X.' Whether by ritual, distraction, or suppression, experiential avoidance in OCD seems to be more the source of the life-constricting effects of the disorder than unwanted thoughts per se (p. 1160).

Escape or avoidance of unpleasant private events been implicated as a central function of many psychological disorders including OCD and defined as "experiential avoidance" (Hayes et al., 1996). Experiential avoidance is the attempt to fix and control the form, frequency, or situational sensitivity of private events (e.g., thoughts, feelings, bodily sensations, and memories), even when attempts to do so cause psychological harm. Experiential avoidance can be understood in RFT terms. For example the statement, "if I get rid of my anxiety then I can live the life I want," is an example of an IF-THEN relation that often occasions behavior aimed at reducing anxiety. If this thought is taken literally, there is only one way to live the life one wants - get rid of the anxiety. Unfortunately, following this rigid prescription will increase the functional context for the impact of thoughts about anxiety, and anxiety tends to increase. There is some empirical support for this position. The Acceptance and Action Questionnaire (AAQ; Bond & Bunce, 2000; Hayes, Strosahl, Wilson, Bissett, Pistorello, Toarmino et al., 2004), a key measure of experiential avoidance, has been found to be related to several well-known fear and anxiety measures in the .4 to .6 range, and these correlations are still significant even after controlling for related concepts such as thought suppression per se, or for response sets such as social desirability (Hayes, Strosahl, Wilson, Bissett, Pistorello, Toarmino et al., 2004). The role of experiential avoidance has been illustrated with trichotillomania, an OCD-spectrum disorder. Adults suffering from trichotillomania who score high on the AAQ have more frequent and intense urges to pull, less ability to control urges, and more pulling-related distress than persons who score low in experiential avoidance as measured by the AAQ (Begotka, Woods, & Wetterneck, 2004).

The notion that the avoidance of the aversive private event is a major factor in the disorder is also supported in the treatment literature. ERP has been found to be the most supported psychological intervention of OCD (Chambless, Baker, Baucom, Beutler, Calhoun, Crits-Cristoph et al., 1998), and its effectiveness could arguably be the result of limiting the client's ability to avoid the obsession and associated aversive private events. Research has shown that when one engages in any level of experiential avoidance when participating in ERP, it hinders the long-term outcome of the treatment (Foa & Kozak, 1986). Similarly, individuals with private obsessions and compulsions are more difficult to treat than individuals with overt avoidance strategies (Salkovskis & Westbrook, 1989), presumably because their methods of experiential avoidance are more difficult to prevent.

Rule Governed Behavior, Rigidity, and Narrowness

The effects of being verbal organisms extend beyond our abilities to draw psychological and physiological functions from our thoughts. The ability to frame events relationally allows us to behave in response to socially constructed contingencies in addition to "real-world" contingencies. We can create antecedent-behavior-consequence contingencies, evaluate and cognitively experience the possible outcomes, and then behave in response to those verbally created contingencies. This process of rule-governance has a large amount of basic research behind it (Baron & Galizio, 1983; Baron, Kaufman, & Stauber, 1969; Hayes, Brownstein, Haas, & Greenway, 1986; Shimoff et al., 1981). Following rules can limit interaction with environmental contingencies, which can have adaptive and/ or maladaptive consequences. Following rules can obviously be very adaptive. For instance, many people have never been burned by a stove when it is hot because they were "told." However, some of the rules passed down from "those in the know," might lead to problematic functioning (ex. "Son, don't call a girl for a week after your first date. It'll make you look desperate."). Clinically, the most notable outcome of following verbal contingencies over real-world contingencies is that it interferes with the natural shaping process (Baron & Galizio, 1983; Baron et al., 1969; Hayes, Brownstein, Zettle, Rosenfarb, & Korn, 1986) and that sensitivity occurs when the behavior becomes predominantly governed by natural contingencies, instead of solely by verbal contingencies (Galizio, 1979). The person will often rigidly and inflexibly follow a verbal rule even in the face of contradictory evidence from the environment (Hayes et al., 1986).

The function of a verbal rule can be explained and demonstrated by RFT. IF-THEN temporal relations are used to specify the relation between the behavior and the consequence specified in the rule. Additionally, the components of the statement gain meaning through their participation in relational frames. For example, "valuables" are valuable because of their participation in frames of sameness with things like money and the work it takes to earn the money. Conditionality and causality link multiple IF-THEN relations together such as: "If I do not check my door, then someone might break in and trash my house and steal all my 'valuables,' and I will have to call the police, and they might not believe me," etc. This verbal statement, through transformation of stimulus function, will allow the person to verbally experience the results of not following the rule, possibly leading to anxiety responses and fear. Accordingly, 40% of those diagnosed with OCD reported that the only result of not following the compulsion was discomfort (Tolin, Abramowitz, Kozak, & Foa, 2001).

Environmental insensitivity is seen in OCD. For example, if burglaries are common in an area, and the person has experienced a break-in, then extra vigilance when locking the door lock is consistent with the environmental contingency. But, when no such events have ever been experienced and the real-world contingencies do not indicate that such a behavior is necessary, rigidly sticking with behavior patterns such as checking a lock multiple times may be indicative of following a verbal rule and not a real-world contingency. The ability to follow rules and not have to learn everything experientially is likely in human's best interest. For example, it is good we do not have to be burned by a hot stove to learn that it is dangerous. But, rule following is often too strongly supported in certain contexts, as seen in those diagnosed with OCD.

Empirical support for this position exists. It has been found that high levels of behavioral rigidity are related to laboratory assessments of rule-governed insensitivity (Wulfert et al., 1994). An assessment of rigidity used recently in the behavioral literature (Wulfert et al., 1994) is the Scale for Personality Rigidity (SPR; Rehfisch, 1958a, 1958b). Wulfert et al. (1994) found that high scores on the SPR suggested a more rigid response style in natural settings and the individuals tended to adhere more to instructions and previously adopted response patterns. Additionally, the rigidity scores positively correlate with social anxiety scores (Naftulin, Donnelly, & Wolkon, 1974; Sinha, 1992). Other researchers have used rigidity to describe the behavior and personality of people with OCD specifically (Emmelkamp, 1987; Millon, 1981; Pollak, 1987; Shapiro, 1965). Moran (1999) demonstrated a positive correlation between SPR and Yale-Brown Obsessive Compulsive Scale (Y-BOCS; Goodman, Price, Rasmussen, Mazure, Fleischman, Hill et al., 1989) scores in a sample of OCD and non-OCD participants, $(r = .42, p < .01)$, although he was not able to demonstrate the presence of greater rule following in individuals diagnosed with OCD in an experimental setting (Moran, 1999).

A problematic result of rigid rule following and a reduced sensitivity to environmental contingencies is the narrow set of responses exhibited in particular contexts (Hayes, 2004). For example, in the case of OCD, during an obsession the client almost always avoids or escapes, and is likely following a rule that "if I have this thought or feeling and do not do certain behaviors, something bad will occur." Avoidance itself is not a problematic response - it is actually quite adaptive, but it can become problematic when it is the only response and as a result the flexibility needed for contingency-shaped learning is undermined. It would not be much of a problem if the person only engaged in the compulsion occasionally when the obsession occurs, but most people engage in the compulsion almost every time the obsession occurs.

Therapeutically, and somewhat deviant from many mainstream approaches, the individual does not necessarily need to stop having the obsession. Rather, he or she needs to develop some *flexibility* - the ability to engage in many different behaviors when the obsession is present. This is a relatively new theory of the processes that underlie exposure procedures (Wilson & Murrell, 2004), and is consistent with basic animal research on classical extinction (Bouton, 2002) and RFT (Hayes et al. 2001).

In summary, it is proposed that those diagnosed with OCD rigidly follow rules as specified in the obsession, and generally follow rules suggesting that "experiencing discomfort such as anxiety is bad." This type of rigid rule following results in a narrowed repertoire in the presence of the obsession. Increasing one's attention to real-world contingencies and broadening one's behavioral repertoire beyond the compulsion in the presence of the obsession becomes the target of treatment.

Verbal Consequences - Self Amplifying Processes

It is apparent that engaging in the compulsion in response to the obsession is not effective at decreasing the disorder in the long run. Research has shown that the prognosis for someone with OCD is poor without some type of intervention (Skoog & Skoog, 1999). The obsession never seems to decrease in frequency even as the individual engages in the compulsion (Clark, 2004). RFT argues this is because the individual is following a verbal contingency that does not need to comport with the real world contingency. For example, if a person has the obsession "if I think about killing my girlfriend then I need to take a shower, otherwise I might actually kill her," taking the shower reinforces this verbal contingency. This contingency does not represent the way the world actually works. Because the contingency is verbal and does not exist non-arbitrarily in the world, continuing to follow it can hinder appropriate functioning and possibly increase the strength of the disorder. Each time the verbal contingency is followed it is reinforced and strengthened, thus, it maintains itself.

The processes that have been described are likely involved in many psychological disorders and social problems (Hayes, 2004; Hayes et al., 1996) and are not specific to OCD. They can be manifested in different ways for different individuals, and obsessions and compulsions are just one example. Those with OCD have been found to engage in many other disorders that are functionally similar including: anxiety disorders and OCD spectrum disorders such as tic disorders and trichotillomania (Clark, 2004). Additionally, those diagnosed with OCD engage in many functionally similar avoidance behaviors beyond just compulsions including: distraction, social control, worry, punishment, and re-appraisal (Wells, 1997).

How Other Interventions Target This Processes

The present model has implications for new forms of intervention but it is worth noting how existing empirically supported interventions fit within the model. Research has shown that a number of different psychological interventions are effective treatments for OCD, namely ERP, CT, and CBT. As described by other researchers, these interventions should produce change through different processes (Abramowitz, 1997): ERP should create larger decrease in physiological measures of anxiety, and those who receive cognitive therapy should respond better on psychological measures of cognitive change; although, as Abramowitz indicates, these interventions are often difficult to disentangle.

Research has not shown that ERP alone produces greater physiological decreases than CBT. When measures of irrational thinking are examined, CBT and ERP do not differ at posttreatment, but in most (Emmelkamp & Beens, 1991; Emmelkamp, Visser, & Hoekstra, 1998; van Oppen, de Haan, van Balkom, Spinhoven, Hoogduin, & van Dyck, 1995) but not all (McLean, Whittal, Sochting, Koch, Paterson, Thordarson et al., 2001) studies the CBT group is more likely to show a change across time on such measures. Conversely, Rheaume and Ladouceur (2000) found that sometimes changes in compulsive behavior will precede changes in cognitive variables in both ERP and cognitive therapy. Thus, although the processes through which these changes occur are not clear, there is evidence that cognitive therapy produces greater cognitive change than ERP.

ERP likely decreases compulsive behavior by directly stopping compulsive actions (response prevention), but cognitively, "it seems likely that extended periods of exposure permit emotional discomfort (usually anxiety) to dissipate, so that the feared situations provoke less reaction. This in turn may alter the person's attitudes toward the situation and the expected outcomes" (Steketee & Barlow, 2002, p. 540). On the other hand, cognitive interventions *directly address* the attitudes associated with negative emotions like anxiety, embarrassment, and guilt (Rachman, 1997,

1998; Salkovskis, 1989). Thus, while the data are not totally clear, theoretically these two interventions are meant to target different areas.

It is possible that, while both these treatments are targeting their assumed areas, they are also engaging the processes described in this theory. For example, in ERP the client is told that if he or she sits with the discomfort long enough, the feelings will subside. On the one hand, sitting with discomfort may undermine experiential avoidance and may broaden the repertoire available while feeling anxiety. On the other hand, this rule may subtly strengthen functional importance of the obsessions and it supports the rules that ultimately these feelings should not be felt. Similarly, cognitive therapy directly addresses the cognitive fusion or the TAF aspect of this model, but also does so in a way that might paradoxically strengthen some putatively pathological processes, such as the temporal and evaluative relations engaged by the obsession. Therapeutically, cognitive interventions attempt to decrease this process by directly attacking the obsession at the level of content. Research has shown that once a relational frame is developed it is very difficult to make it go away (Wilson & Hayes, 1996), if not impossible. Cognitive restructuring directly trains the client to evaluate and compare possible outcomes, which is exactly the same process this theory suggests might be dangerous in obsessions. The concern, from this theoretical standpoint, is that what is being taught in these interventions may be both therapeutic and countertherapeutic. If so, a new approach to the handling of one's cognitions may be helpful.

ACT-Enhanced Exposure for OCD - Increasing Behavioral Flexibility

Previous research has illustrated that exposure is the central procedure for the effective treatment of OCD; the more exposure, the better the outcomes (Abramowitz, 1996). This is a robust finding that is consistent with the treatment of most anxiety disorders (Barlow, 2002) and should not be forgotten when developing new treatment approaches for OCD. But, before we proceed we should clarify the difference between exposure as a *procedure* and exposure as a *process*.

Exposure as a therapeutic *procedure* is generally discussed as any procedure that assists the individual in confronting the feared object. This could be through imagination, live exposure, or interoceptive exposure. The therapist finds events or situations that will evoke the bodily states of interest and helps the client approach them. But this is not all that is needed to create "successful" exposure; the individual must also be experientially in contact with this event (Craske, Street, Jayaraman, & Barlow, 1991). This is not an experimental or theoretical concern with animal preparations. When the properties of classically conditioned extinction are studied in nonhuman animals, the results are quite consistent (Rescorla, 1967). But humans have the ability to avoid experientially even if they appear to be orienting to the feared stimulus. Thus, in order for exposure to be effective the person must experience the traumatic memory, feel the garbage in the trashcan, or sense the shortness of breath or increased heart rate.

Researchers seem to generally be in agreement with exposure as a *procedure* as described, but they are less clear about what exposure the *process* is. What is occurring when the person is in contact with these feared events that makes it therapeutic? There are generally three different proposed functions of exposure: extinction, cognitive restructuring, and broadening of repertoire theory. Extinction in classical conditioning refers to a decrease in conditioned responding that occurs when conditioning is terminated. This explanation is at the core of many explanations of the effectiveness of exposure (Foa & Kozak, 1986). Cognitive theorists, largely in the OCD area, have also implicated cognitive change as a factor in reduction of OCD symptomatology. Most OCD researchers have indicated that ERP-type exposure has a cognitive correcting function. They write that when the client experiences the obsession without engaging in the compulsion and experiences that the hypothesized consequence does not occur, that cognitive restructuring takes place. The experience corrects their thinking and they learn that their thinking was irrational. Currently, most OCD researchers write that exposure works through both these processes. Both these processes are control procedures focused on helping the client gain control over private events.

The final proposed function of extinction is the broadening of repertoire theory (Wilson & Murrell, 2004). This differs from the two processes described above because it does not focus on controlling one's private events. It is solely based on changing one's overt behavior. It focuses on helping the individual move toward valued goals and objectives while in the presence of the feared stimulus. This theory is based on animal research that shows that conditioned aversives suppress responding (Geller, 1960) and that extinction results in *not only* the decrease in the target behavior but also the increase in other behaviors in a particular context (Bouton, 2002).

Research has generally supported the aforementioned extinction and cognitive change model, although not in all cases. There are examples where behavioral change occurs but the individual does not experience a decrease in physiological responsiveness or cognitive change as a result of exposure (Rheaume & Ladoucer, 2000). Additionally, there is a growing body of literature indicating behavioral change can precede both cognitive and physiological changes (Ilardi & Craighead, 1994; Rheaume & Ladoucer, 2000). Researchers still need to uncover the exact process involved in exposure or if many of these processes are involved.

Thus, the repertoire broadening theory is inherently an exposure-based procedure but as one will notice its goals are more focused on "effective living" and less so on the effects of the procedures on one's private events. The goal is to help the client continue responding while in the presence of the feared stimulus (e.g., obsessions). The focus is not to help the client decrease his or her anxiety or obsessions—although that may occur. If treatment is done in this fashion, then exposure and its function must be rethought, and the function of these procedures must be recontextualized. The outcome or dependent variable that one would be looking for from this perspective would be increased behavioral flexibility. For instance, the Yale-Brown Obsessive Compulsive Inventory (Y-BOCS; Goodman et al., 1989) the most commonly used assessment instrument for outcome studies in the treatment of OCD, has questions regarding "time occupied by obsessive thoughts," "distress associated with obsessive thoughts," and "degree of control over obsessive thoughts." Some of these questions regarding obsessions are clearly unnecessary for a repertoire broadening theory of extinction. There are no good standardized measures of change from the repertoire broadening perspective; the most useful type of measure would be overt behavioral measures such as decreases in compulsive behavior and increases in clinically relevant goal-oriented behavior.

ACT for OCD

Acceptance and Commitment Therapy (ACT; Hayes, Strosahl, & Wilson, 1999) in general, or for addressing OCD, is inherently an exposure-based treatment, but the function of the exposure is not to help the client control his or her obsessions or related anxiety. The goal is to recontextualize these private events from ones that constrict behavior to commonplace private events that do not limit daily and valuable life functioning. If this is difficult to grasp, imagine an individual who, every 30 minutes, has the thought that he needs to wash his hands or he will contaminate the whole city, and feels really uncomfortable if he does not wash. Is this a problem? We would say no. It could be a problem is he did wash his hands every 30 minutes and it severely interfered with his life. According to the ACT approach, living the life one wants is not dependent on feeling a certain way—it is about doing what one finds important. To help the person live the life he or she wants ACT works to change the function of private events so that they are less constricting, but not so that they occur less often or are less scary.

A complete protocol of ACT as a treatment for OCD is not possible given the space limitations (for an ACT for OCD treatment protocol see Twohig, Hayes, Plumb, Pruitt, Sailer, & Torch, 2006). There are six core processes in ACT: acceptance, defusion, contact with the present moment, self as context, values, and committed action. We will explain how each of these core areas targets the behavioral inflexibility.

Acceptance. Acceptance involves an active and undistorted recognition of private events including feelings of anxiety and obsessions. Acceptance is not the same as tolerance; acceptance involves choosing to experience these events wholly—as they are. Acceptance is the opposite of control. Most cognitive style interventions focus on changing the form, frequency, or situational sensitivity of one's private events, and acceptance is a different approach.

Acceptance is a central component in ACT as a treatment of OCD. First, it assists in shifting the client's focus from controlling the obsession to observing real environmental contingencies. Second, acceptance directly challenges the client's rules that he or she must not experience the obsession and that steps must be taken to decrease it. This helps the client shift his or her focus from decreasing the obsession to learning how to live a valuable life while experiencing the obsession.

Third, acceptance is in direct contradiction to experiential avoidance. Finally, as indicated by the thought suppression data, ceasing attempts to control the obsessions should stop the self-amplifying processes that may be responsible for the downward spiral in OCD.

Many of the empirically supported treatments for OCD involve some type of focus on acceptance. For example, Foa and Wilson's (1991) self-help method suggests, among other control alternatives, the acceptance of one's obsessions during response prevention methods: "Accept the anxious thought. So even though your ultimate goal is to stop obsessing, the way to best reach that goal is to develop the attitude of acceptance" (p. 80). While there are no data yet indicating that acceptance will increase the *effectiveness* of exposure, there is evidence that it increases the *acceptability* of exposure, which might indirectly foster effectiveness (Eifert & Heffner, 2003; Levitt, Brown, Orsillo, & Barlow, 2004). Similar results have been shown for pain tolerance (e.g., see Hayes, Bissett, Korn, Zettle, Rosenfarb, Cooper et al., 1999 for one of several similar studies). Acceptance of private events has also been shown to mediate the impact of ACT in several studies and to differentiate it from other interventions (e.g., Bond & Bunce, 2000; Gifford, Kohlenberg, Hayes, Antonuccio, Piasecki, Rasmussen-Hall et al., 2004) including OCD (Twohig, Hayes, & Masuda, 2006a).

Cognitive Defusion. Cognitive defusion in the treatment of OCD involves changing the function of the client's private events from the actual events they are related to, to what they actually are - only thoughts and feelings. Defusion involves stepping back from one's private events including obsessions and anxiety, and experiencing the ongoing process of relating rather than merely the products of relating. An example of a defusion exercise used in the treatment of OCD involves repeating the obsession over and over until it has lost all of its meaning. The function is not to decrease its effect on the individual diagnosed with OCD per se, but assist the person in seeing that the thought has additional functions besides eliciting fear. It is also just a sound.

Technically, cognitive defusion is the process of undermining the transformation of stimulus functions and thus the behavior regulatory impact of verbally entangled private events. In clinical situations, defusion is measured by assessing the literal believability of thoughts or the need to comply with or alter thoughts as distinct from the mere occurrence of thoughts. ACT seeks to alter the context under which some verbal events are experienced. In the case of obsessions, the goal is to increase the ability to accept these thoughts (as thoughts) and to undermine the need to respond to them in any way beyond mere observation.

Defusion exercises affect all of the processes described earlier because they are all verbal in nature, but they most directly target cognitive fusion or TAF. If defusion methods are successful, the obsession will still likely occur for the person, but it will be experienced more as just a thought or a feeling – much as individuals without OCD experience such intrusive thoughts when they occur.

Evidence for the effectiveness of cognitive defusion interventions comes from several sources including basic research in the form of a comparison of one ACT defusion exercise with traditional thought control techniques (Masuda, Hayes, Sackett, & Twohig, 2004) and through its effectiveness in a pain tolerance task (Gutiérrez, Luciano, Rodríguez, & Fink, 2004). Finally, ACT process research has consistently shown that ACT is uniquely effective in decreasing the believability of private events even when they continue to occur, and that these changes help explain the impact of ACT (e.g., Bach & Hayes, 2002; Hayes, Bissett, Korn, Zettle, Rosenfarb, Cooper et al., 2004; Zettle & Hayes, 1987), including the treatment of OCD (Twohig et al. 2006a).

Self as Context. Self as context involves discriminating the difference between oneself as a conscious person and one's thoughts and feelings. The great advantage of this sense of self is that self is experienced as an arena in which the content of consciousness is not threatening. The individual can experience the obsession, even a highly threatening one such as stabbing one's children, and not be as threatened by it because there is a separation of these thoughts and feelings and the individual. A metaphor for this position is to think of oneself as a chessboard and the pieces on it as one's thoughts and concerns about oneself. The chessboard is not affected, moved, or harmed by the activities of the pieces.

Self as context is helpful with a particularly destructive form of fusion: attachment to the self as verbally constructed, not the self that is experienced in the present moment. This includes individuals who experience their OCD as something *they are* rather than something that *they experience*. For example, there is very little flexibility in the thought, "I think about stabbing my children, so I'm a bad person." From this stance the person will likely engage in behaviors that paradoxically confirm this belief of "badness" (e.g., to perform rituals to rid oneself of evil thoughts because otherwise the inherent badness will emerge). The focus of self as context is to help the person into a position where he or she is more willing to move forward as a whole, valid person. ACT operates under the assumption that the person can move forward just as he or she is and that no change to "self" is needed – just a change in behavior.

Being Present. Humans have a very difficult time stepping out of their verbal activity and being present. Our verbal practices are incredibly useful in most situations, especially with external environment concerns. Yet, there are times when verbal practices *are* the problem instead of the solution. For example, when a person is struggling with an obsession regarding killing one's spouse, he or she does not need additional verbal entanglement to decide what to do with that thought. The person needs skills to be able to "step back" from that thought, perceive it differently, and come into contact with real-world contingencies rather than the insensitive and arbitrarily applicable contingencies. Being present in ACT shares similarities with mindfulness practices in other psychological interventions (Hayes & Shenk, 2004). An example of an exercise that would foster being present involves closing one's eyes and picturing one's thoughts float past on a stream. The person is asked to not stick with any one thought, but to let the thought pass by one after another. The function is to be in the present moment rather than in one's thoughts. The function of this exercise is not to stop or avoid difficult thoughts, but to develop a sense of an experience as it is, rather than an experience manipulated by our verbal behavior.

Exposure methods ask clients to be present with their reactions in the moment without engaging in their typical approaches to avoidance. Data suggest that clients diagnosed with OCD who are less compliant with this component of traditional cognitive-behavioral therapy benefit less from treatment than do other clients (Franklin, Abramowitz, Kozak, Levitt, & Foa, 2000). Training the client to stay in contact with the present moment in a broader, more open and more flexible way, may establish general skills that are useful in such circumstances.

Research on generalized anxiety disorder (GAD) is consistent with this stance. For example, Borkovek (2002) wrote "People suffering from generalized anxiety disorder (GAD) live in a strange world. Actually, they do not live in the world very much at all" (p. 77). He further writes that their constant worrying increases their overall anxiety and decreases their attention to the real world. For this exact reason, his treatment of GAD includes procedures such as relaxation to assist the client in coming into contact with the present moment (e.g., Borkovek, Newman, Pincus, & Lytle, 2002). ACT for OCD contains functionally similar work to help the client come into greater contact with the present moment and be less focused on their thoughts.

Values. In general, individuals with OCD are working under the verbal agenda that they need to get rid of the obsessions before they can start living the life that they want. ACT assumes that these attempts to control the obsession are themselves part of the problem and that obsessions do not need to change before significant life changes can occur. Values work in ACT involves working toward things that are important to the client while shifting the focus away from changing one's private events as a primary target. The point is to focus on meaningful endeavors that may or may not compete with the compulsive behaving. An example of a values exercise in ACT might be, "Would you be willing to not engage in your compulsion during dinner tonight so that you can truly be there interacting with your family?"

Values statements make certain behaviors more appetitive and other behaviors more aversive. This increases certain behaviors that compete with undesirable behaviors, such as avoidance (Hayes, Strosahl, & Wilson, 1999). Values work can enhance a client's motivation to engage in treatment and provide direction. Values work generally enhances all the processes that were described before. For example, moving toward valued activities will directly contradict experiential avoidance because movement toward these values is done regardless of one's feelings or attitudes at the time. This may be especially true for exposure work, which can be very difficult for individuals with anxiety.

Although the experimental analysis of values is still in its infancy, there are indications that values focused ACT protocols can have a strong impact of the role of difficult private events. For example, a small randomized controlled trial by Dahl,

Wilson, and Nilsson (2004) demonstrated the effectiveness of a brief, values-oriented ACT intervention with individuals with chronic pain who were at risk for long-term unemployment.

Committed Action. Committed action is directly linked to values work. The commitments that are agreed upon are done in response to one's stated values. For example, a client who spends her days cleaning the house in response to an obsession that involves her children getting poisoned might agree to only cleaning for one hour so that she has more time to spend with her children. In the treatment of OCD, commitments are specified periods of time that the client agrees to engage in valued behavior, without regard for one's thoughts or feelings at the time, while practicing defusion and acceptance. Committed action work is likely to be enhanced after a thorough functional analysis of the client's avoidance behaviors.

Committed action in ACT can formally be similar to exposure as done in ERP or CBT, but the focus of the intervention is different. The client would still be asked to approach the feared stimuli without experientially avoiding, but in ACT as a treatment for OCD, the goal would not be to decrease anxiety or the obsession (although that may occur), it would be done as a willingness exercise done in the service of the client's values. It would help the client to be able to function with the obsession and anxiety present. This will assist the individual in increasing his or her behavioral repertoire in the presence of the obsessions and anxiety. The client in exposure-based therapy who learns to "sit with the anxiety" rather than to escape or avoid it may similarly be learning to do other things with the obsession and anxiety present. Furthermore, as larger and larger patterns of committed action are constructed, basic research shows that emotional impulses and control by short term contingencies at the cost of long term contingencies are reduced (Rachlin, 1997).

The empirical support for not engaging in the compulsion while in the presence of the obsession is substantial. It is arguably the core component in the treatment of OCD (Abramowitz, 1996). Nevertheless, we are still not clear what process is occurring during such exercises. There are many different theories including decreases in obsessions and anxiety (Steketee & Barlow, 2002), changes in cognitions (Rachman, 1997, 1998), or increases in behavioral flexibility (Wilson & Murrell, 2004). While agreement on the exact process involved in this procedure does not exist, there is evidence that exposing the client to situations that elicit the obsession and having the client not engage in the compulsion is therapeutically useful to decrease obsessions and compulsions. The process through which it works will need to be investigated.

Empirical Support for ACT as a Treatment for OCD

ACT has been shown to be an effective treatment for a variety of disorders (Hayes, Masuda, Bissett, Luoma, & Guerrero, 2004) including anxiety disorders and stress. Zettle (2003) found that a six hour ACT intervention as effective as systematic desensitization as a treatment for math anxiety. Results were maintained at two-month follow-up with high experiential avoiders showing larger gains at follow-up in the ACT condition. Block (2002) found that ACT was equally effective when compared to Cognitive Behavioral Group Therapy on measures of willingness to experience anxiety and anxiety during the exposure exercises. Both treatments were more effective than a control condition. ACT participants also remained longer in the post-treatment behavioral exposure task than participants in the CBGT group after controlling for pretreatment scores. Additionally, ACT has been shown to reduce worksite stress (Bond & Bunce, 2000; Hayes, Bissett et al., 2004), and anxiety and stress experienced by parents of disabled children (Blackledge, 2004).

Additionally, there are uncontrolled case studies (Hayes, 1987) and controlled single subject design studies (Twohig et al., 2006a) showing ACT to be an effective treatment for OCD. ACT alone is helpful as a treatment for skin picking (Twohig, Hayes, & Masuda, 2006b), and trichotillomania when used in combination with Habit Reversal (Twohig & Woods, 2004). Process data in these latter two studies showed that both interventions caused expected decreases in experiential avoidance indicating that the interventions had the presumed effect.

ACT was evaluated as a treatment for OCD with four individuals diagnosed with OCD–including an individual with a hoarding compulsion–in a multiple baseline across participants design (Twohig et al., 2006a). Results showed almost complete cessation of the compulsions for all participants by the end of treatment, with concurrent reductions in a standardized measure of OCD, anxiety, depression, and experiential avoidance at posttreatment, with continued or maintained gains on all measures at three-month follow-up. Additionally, on a face valid measure of treatment process, all participants indicated they were more willing to experience the obsessions and that the obsession was less believable at as a result of the intervention. Interestingly, these gains were achieved while receiving high ratings on a measure of treatment acceptability. Thus, while the empirical evidence for ACT as a treatment for OCD is limited, it is also promising.

Preliminary evidence supporting this approach is mounting as part of a large randomized clinical trial comparing ACT and progressive relaxation training (PRT) in the treatment of adult OCD. Preliminary results are showing a favorable effect for ACT over PRT from pre to post, with results being maintained at three month follow-up (Twohig et al., 2006a). Although this study is still in progress, it adds additional support for the use of ACT with this population.

Summary and Conclusions

OCD is a highly researched disorder and effective psychological treatments have been developed, namely ERP or CBT. Yet, these treatments are not completely effective and continued work is necessary. Therefore, this chapter provided an account of OCD from a functional contextual perspective in the hopes of increasing our abilities to successfully treat individuals diagnosed with this disorder. This chapter proposed a model of OCD that demonstrates how verbal abilities, while useful in some contexts, can severely restrict one's behavior especially in contexts where strong emotional responses occur. This model proposes that processes such as rule governance, experiential avoidance, and cognitive fusion support a narrowing of one's repertoire in fear producing contexts, such as when one is experiencing an obsession. This model is different in that it suggests an increased effort at behavioral change over cognitive change. This position comes from the finding that cognitive change may not be necessary or can be counterproductive for behavioral change to occur.

From an applied perspective, this model suggests helping the individual "step back" from his or her obsessions and focus on behavior change that is associated with one's values. It is also proposed that exposure is a central process in this treatment of OCD, and that the functional process of exposure is to broaden the individual's repertoire in the presence of the obsession. Being able to step back from one's thoughts assists in creating a verbal context where the individual can more readily engage in valued behavior.

Because this account is from a functional contextual perspective, the ultimate "truth" of this model will be based of its successfulness. The goal of this account is to create a more successful treatment and if it assists in doing that, then it is worthwhile. If this does not result in a more successful treatment then this theory is not useful. Preliminary data indicates that there is something that is useful in this procedure. Future research will have to determine the extent.

References

Abramowitz, J. S. (1996). Variants of exposure and response prevention in the treatment of obsessive-compulsive disorder: A meta-analysis. *Behavior Therapy, 27,* 583-600.

Abramowitz, J. S. (1997). Effectiveness of psychological and pharmacological treatments of obsessive-compulsive disorder: A quantitative review. *Journal of Consulting and Clinical Psychology, 65,* 44-52.

Abramowitz, J. S., Whiteside, S., Lynam, D., & Kalsy, S. (2003). Is thought-action fusion specific to obsessive-compulsive disorder?: A mediating role of negative affect. *Behaviour Research and Therapy, 41,* 1069-1079.

Albucher, R. C., Curtis, G. C., & Pitts, K. (1999). Neurosurgery for obsessive-compulsive disorder: Problems with comorbidity. *American Journal of Psychiatry, 156,* 495-496.

American Psychiatric Association. (2000). *Diagnostic and statistical manual of mental disorders (4th ed., text revision).* Washington, DC: Author.

Amir, N., Freshman, M., Ramsey, B., Neary, E., & Brigidi, B. (2001). Thought-action fusion in individuals with OCD symptoms. *Behaviour Research and Therapy, 39,* 765-776.

Antony, M. M., Downie, F., & Swinson, R. P. (1998). Diagnostic issued and epidemiology in obsessive-compulsive disorder. In R. P. Swinson, M. M. Antony, S. Rachman, & M. A. Richter (Eds.), *Obsessive-compulsive disorder: Theory, research, and treatment* (pp. 3-32). New York: Guilford.

Bach, P., & Hayes, S. C. (2002). The use of acceptance and commitment therapy to prevent the rehospitalization of psychotic patients: A randomized controlled trial. *Journal of Consulting and Clinical Psychology, 70,* 1129-1139.

Baer, L., & Jenike, M. (1992). Personality disorders: Obsessive-compulsive disorders. *Psychiatric Clinics of North America, 15,* 803-812.

Baer, L., & Minichiello, W. (1998). Behavior therapy for obsessive-compulsive disorder. In M. Jenike, L. Baer, & W. Minichiello (Eds.), *Obsessive-compulsive disorders: Practical management.* St. Louis, MO: Mosby.

Barlow, D. H. (2002). *Anxiety and its disorders: The nature and treatment of anxiety and panic.* New York: Guilford.

Barnes-Holmes, D., O'Hora, D., Roche, B., Hayes, S. C., Bissett, R. T., & Lyddy, F. (2001). Understanding and verbal regulation. In S. C. Hayes, D. Barnes-Holmes, & B. Roche (Eds.), *Relational frame theory: A post-Skinnerian account of human language and cognition* (pp. 103-117). New York: Plenum Press.

Baron, A., & Galizio, M. (1983). Instructional control of human operant behavior. *Psychological Record, 33,* 495-520.

Baron, A., Kaufman, A., & Stauber, K. A. (1969). Effects of instructions and reinforcement-feedback on human operant behavior maintained by fixed-interval reinforcement. *Journal of the Experimental Analysis of Behavior, 12,* 701-712.

Barrett, P., Shortt, A., & Healy, L. (2002). Do parents and child behaviours differentiate families whose children have obsessive-compulsive disorder from other clinic and non-clinic families? *Journal of Child Psychology and Psychiatry, 43,* 597-607.

Baxter, L. (1990). Brain imaging as a tool in establishing a theory of brain pathology in obsessive-compulsive disorder. *Journal of Clinical Psychiatry, 51,* 22-25.

Beck, A. T. (1976). *Cognitive therapy and the emotional disorders.* New York: International/University Press.

Begotka, A. M., Woods, D. W., & Wetterneck, C. T. (2004). The relationship between experiential avoidance and the severity of trichotillomania in a nonreferred sample. *Journal of Behavior Therapy and Experimental Psychiatry, 35,* 17-24.

Behar, D., Rapoport, J., Berg, C., Denckla, M., Mann, L., Cox, C., et al. (1984). Computerized tomography and neuropsychological test measures in adolescents with obsessive-compulsive disorder. *American Journal of Psychiatry, 141,* 363-369.

Bejerot, S. (2003). Psychosurgery for obsessive-compulsive disorder: Concerns remain. *Acta Psychiatrica Scandinavica, 107,* 241-243.

Black, D. W., Noyes, R., Pfohl, B., Goldstein, R., & Blum, N. (1993). Personality disorder in obsessive-compulsive volunteers, well comparison subjects, and their first-degree relatives. *American Journal of Psychiatry, 150,* 1226-1232.

Black, D. W., Monahan, P., Gable, J., Blum, N., Clancy, G., & Baker, P. (1998). Hoarding and treatment response in 38 nondepressed subjects with obsessive-compulsive disorder. *Journal of Clinical Psychiatry, 59,* 420-425.

Blackledge, J. T. (2004). *Using acceptance and commitment therapy in the treatment of parents of autistic children.* Unpublished doctoral dissertation, University of Nevada, Reno.

Block, J. A. (2002). Acceptance or change of private experiences: A comparative analysis in college students with public speaking anxiety. *Dissertation Abstracts International: Section B: The Sciences & Engineering, 63*(9-B), 4361.

Bolles, R. C., Stokes, L. W., & Younger, M. S. (1966). Does CS termination reinforce avoidance behavior? *Journal of Comparative and Physiological Psychology, 62,* 201-207.

Bond, F. W., & Bunce, D. (2000). Mediators of change in emotion-focused and problem-focused worksite stress management interventions. *Journal of Occupational Health Psychology, 5,* 156-163.

Borkoveck, T. D. (2002). Life in the future versus life in the present. *Clinical Psychology: Science and Practice, 9,* 76-80.

Borkoveck, T. D., Newman, M. G., Pincus, A. L., & Lytle, R. (2002). A component analysis of cognitive-behavioral therapy for generalized anxiety disorder and the role of interpersonal problems. *Journal of Clinical and Consulting Psychology, 70,* 288-298.

Bouton, M. E. (2002). Context, ambiguity, and unlearning: Sources of relapse after behavioral extinction. *Biological Psychiatry, 52,* 976-986.

Brown, T. A., Campbell, L. A., Lehman, C. L., Grisham, J. R., & Mancill, R. B. (2001). Current and lifetime comorbidity of the DSM-IV anxiety and mood disorders in a large clinical sample. *Journal of Abnormal Psychology, 110,* 585-599.

Carey, G., & Gottesman, I. I. (1981). Twin and family studies of anxiety, phobic and obsessive disorders. In D. F. Klein & J. G. Rabkin (Eds.), *Anxiety: New research and changing concepts.* New York: Raven Press.

Carr, A. T. (1974). Compulsive neurosis: A review of the literature. *Psychological Bulletin, 81,* 311-318.

Catania, C. A. (1997). *Learning (4th ed.)*. Englewood Cliffs, NJ: Prentice Hall.

Chambless, D. L., Baker, M. J., Baucom, D. H., Beutler, L. E., Calhoun, K. S., Crits-Christoph, P., et al. (1998). An update on empirically validated therapists II. *The Clinical Psychologist, 51,* 3-21.

Clark, D. A. (2004). *Cognitive-behavioral therapy for OCD.* New York: Guilford.

Clark, D. A., & de Silva, P. (1985). The nature of depressive and anxious thoughts: Distinct or uniform phenomena? *Behaviour Research and Therapy, 23,* 383-393.

Clark, D. A., Purdon, C., & Byers, S. (2000). Appraisal and control of sexual and non-sexual intrusive thoughts in university students. *Behaviour Research and Therapy, 38,* 439-455.

Coles, M., E., Mennin, D. S., & Heimberg, R. G. (2001). Distinguishing obsessive features and worries: The role of thought-action fusion. *Behaviour Research and Therapy, 39,* 947-960.

Craske, M. G., Street, L. L., Jayaraman, J., & Barlow, D. H. (1991). Attention versus distraction during in vivo exposure: Snake and spider phobias. *Journal of Anxiety Disorders, 5,* 199-211.

Crino, R. D., & Andrews, G. (1996). Obsessive-compulsive disorder and Axis I comorbidity. *Journal of Anxiety Disorders, 10,* 37-46.

Dadds, M. R., Barrett, P. M., Rapee, R. M., & Ryan, S. (1996). Family process and child anxiety and aggression: An observational analysis. *Journal of Abnormal Child Psychology, 24,* 715-735.

Dahl, J., Wilson, K. G., & Nilsson, A. (2004). Acceptance and commitment therapy and the treatment of persons at risk for long-term disability resulting from stress and pain symptoms: A preliminary randomized trial. *Behavior Therapy, 35,* 785-802.

Deckersbach, T., Otto, M. W., Savage, C. R., Baer, L., & Jenike, M. A. (2000). The relationship between semantic organization and memory in obsessive-compulsive disorder. *Psychotherapy and Psychosomatics, 69,* 101-107.

Demal, U., Lenz, G., Mayrhofer, A., Zapotoczky, H. G., & Zitterl, W. (1993). Obsessive-compulsive disorder and depression: A retrospective study on the course and interaction. *Psychopathology, 26,* 15-150.

de Silva, P., Menzies, R. G., & Shafran, R. (2003). Spontaneous decay of compulsive urges: The case of covert compulsions. *Behaviour Research and Therapy, 41,* 129-137.

Dollard, J., & Miller, N. (1950). *Personality and psychotherapy.* New York: McGraw-Hill.

Dougherty, D. D., Rauch, S. L., & Jenike, M. A. (2002). Pharmacological treatments from obsessive-compulsive disorder. In P. E. Nathan & J. M. Gorman (Eds.), *A guide to treatments that work (2nd ed.)* (pp. 387-410). New York: Oxford University Press.

Dumas, J. E., Lafreniere, P. J., & Serketich, W. J. (1995). 'Balance of Power': A transactional analysis of control in mother-child dyads involving socially competent, aggressive, and anxious children. *Journal of Abnormal Psychology, 104,* 104-113.

Ecker, W., & Engelkamp, J. (1995). Memory for actions in obsessive-compulsive disorder. *Behavioural and Cognitive Psychotherapy, 23,* 349-371.

Eifert, G. H., & Heffner, M. (2003). The effects of acceptance versus control contexts on avoidance of panic-related symptoms. *Journal of Behavior Therapy and Experimental Psychiatry, 34,* 293-312.

Eisen, J. L., Goodman, W. K., Keller, M. B., Warshaw, M. G., DeMarco, L. M., Luce, D. D., et al. (1999). Patterns of remission and relapse in obsessive-compulsive disorder: A 2-year prospective study. *Journal of Clinical Psychiatry, 60,* 346-351.

Emmelkamp, P. M. G. (1987). *Obsessive-compulsive disorders.* New York: Guilford.

Emmelkamp, P. M. G., & Beens, H. (1991). Cognitive therapy with obsessive-compulsive disorder: A comparative evaluation. *Behaviour Research and Therapy, 29,* 293-300.

Emmelkamp, P. M. G., Visser, S. & Hoekstra, R. J. (1998). Cognitive therapy vs. exposure in vivo in the treatment of obsessive-compulsive disorder. *Cognitive Therapy and Research, 12,* 103-114.

Foa, E. B., Amir, N., Gershuny, B., Molnar, C., & Kozak, M .J. (1997). Implicit and explicit memory in obsessive-compulsive disorder. *Journal of Anxiety Disorders, 11,* 119-129.

Foa, E. B., Franklin, M. E., & Kozak, M. J. (1998). Psychosocial treatments for obsessive-compulsive disorder: Literature review. In R. P. Swinson, M. M. Anthony, S. Rachman, & A. Richter (Eds.), *Obsessive-compulsive disorder: Theory, research, and treatment* (pp. 258-276). New York: Guilford.

Foa, E. B., & Kozak, M. S. (1986). Emotional processing of fear: Exposure to corrective information. *Psychological Bulletin, 99,* 20-35.

Foa, E. B., & Kozak, M. J. (1995). DSM-IV field trial: Obsessive-compulsive disorder. *American Journal of Psychiatry, 152,* 90-94.

Foa, E. B., Steketee, G., Grayson, J. B., & Doppelt, H. G. (1983). Treatment of obsessive- compulsives: When do we fail? In E. B. Foa & P. M. G. Emmelkamp (Eds.), *Failures in behavior therapy* (pp. 10-34). New York: Wiley.

Foa, E. B., & Wilson, R. (1991). *Stop obsessing! How to overcome your obsessions and compulsions.* New York: Bantam Doubleday Dell.

Follette, W. C., & Houts, A. C. (1996). Models of scientific progress and the role of theory in taxonomy development: A case study of the DSM. *Journal of Consulting and Clinical Psychology, 64,* 1120-1132.

Formea, G., & Burns, L. (1995). Relation between the syndromes of bulimia nervosa and obsessive-compulsive disorder. *Journal of Psychopathology and Behavioral Assessment, 17,* 167-176.

Frankland, P. W., Bontempi, B., Talton, L. E., Kaczmarek, L., & Silva, A. J. (2004). The involvement of the *anterior cingulate cortex* in remote contextual fear memory. *Science, 304,* 881-883.

Franklin, M. E., Abramowitz, J. S., Kozak, M. J., Levitt, J. T., & Foa, E. B. (2000). Effectiveness of exposure and ritual prevention for obsessive-compulsive disorder: Randomized compared with nonrandomized samples. *Journal of Consulting and Clinical Psychology, 68,* 594-602.

Franklin, M. E., & Foa, E. B. (2002). Cognitive behavioral treatments for obsessive-compulsive disorder. In P. E. Nathan & J. M. Gorman (Eds.), *A guide to treatments that work (2nd ed.)* (pp. 367-386). New York: Oxford University Press.

Freeston, M. H., Ladouceur, R., Thibodeau, N., & Gagnon, F. (1991). Cognitive intrusions in a non-clinical population. I. Response style, subjective experience, and appraisal. *Behaviour Research and Therapy, 29,* 585-597.

Galizio, M. (1979). Contingency-shaped and rule-governed behavior: Instructional control of human loss avoidance. *Journal of the Experimental Analysis of Behavior, 31,* 53-70.

Gao, Y., Ren, W., Zhang, Y., & Zhao, Z. (2004). Contributions of the anterior cingulate cortex and amygdala to pain- and fear-conditioned place avoidance in rats. *Pain, 110,* 343-353.

Geller, I. (1960). The acquisition and extinction of conditioned suppression as a function of the base-line reinforcer. *Journal of the Experimental Analysis of Behavior, 3,* 235-240.

Gifford, E. V., Kohlenberg, B. S., Hayes, S. C., Antonuccio, D. O., Piasecki, M. M., Rasmussen-Hall, M. L., et al. (2004). Acceptance theory-based treatment for smoking cessation: An initial trial of acceptance and commitment therapy. *Behavior Therapy, 35,* 689-706.

Goodman, W. K., Price, L. H., Rasmussen, S. A., Mazure, C., Fleischman, R. L., Hill, C. L., et al. (1989). The Yale-Brown Obsessive Compulsive Scale: Development, use, and reliability. *Archives of General Psychiatry, 46,* 1006-1011.

Gray, J. A. (1975). *Elements of a two-process theory of learning.* New York: Academic Press.

Griest, J. H., Jefferson, J. W., Kobak, K. A., Katzelnick, D. J., & Serlin, R. C. (1995). Efficacy and tolerability of serotonin transport inhibitors in obsessive-compulsive disorder: A meta-analysis. *Archives of General Psychiatry, 52,* 53-60.

Gutiérrez, O., Luciano, C., Rodríguez, M., & Fink, B. C. (2004). Comparison between an acceptance-based and a cognitive-control-based protocol for coping with pain. *Behavior Therapy, 35,* 767-784.

Hanna, G. L. (1995). Demographic and clinical features of obsessive-compulsive disorder in children and adolescents. *Journal of the American Academy of Child Adolescent Psychiatry, 34,* 19-27.

Hayes, S. C. (1987). A contextual approach to therapeutic change. In N. Jacobson (Ed.), *Psychotherapists in clinical practice: Cognitive and behavioral perspectives* (pp. 327-387). New York: Guilford.

Hayes, S. C. (Ed.). (1989). *Rule-governed behavior: Cognition, contingencies, and instructional control.* New York: Plenum.

Hayes, S. C. (2004). Acceptance and commitment therapy, relational frame theory, and the third wave of behavioral and cognitive therapies. *Behavior Therapy, 35,* 639-665.

Hayes, S. C., Barnes-Holmes, D., & Roche, B. (2001). *Relational frame theory: A post-Skinnerian account of human language and cognition.* New York: Kluwer Academic/ Plenum Publishers.

Hayes, S. C., Bissett, R., Korn, Z., Zettle, R. D., Rosenfarb, I., Cooper, L., et al. (1999). The impact of acceptance versus control rationales on pain tolerance. *The Psychological Record, 49,* 33-47.

Hayes, S. C., Brownstein, A. J., Haas, J. R., & Greenway, D. (1986). Instructions, multiple schedules, and extinction: Distinguishing rule-governed from schedule-controlled behavior. *Journal of the Experimental Analysis of Behavior, 46,* 137-147.

Hayes, S. C., Brownstein, A. J., Zettle, R. D., Rosenfarb, I., & Korn, Z. (1986). Rule-governed behavior and sensitivity to changing consequences of responding. *Journal of the Experimental Analysis of Behavior, 45,* 237-256.

Hayes, S. C., Masuda, A., Bissett, R., Luoma, J., & Guerrero, L. F. (2004). DBT, FAP, and ACT: How empirically oriented are the new behavior therapy technologies? *Behavior Therapy, 35,* 35-54.

Hayes, S. C., & Shenk, C. (2004). Operationalizing mindfulness without unnecessary attachments. *Clinical Psychology: Science and Practice, 11,* 249-254.

Hayes, S. C., Strosahl, K. D., & Wilson, K. G. (1999). *Acceptance and commitment therapy: An experiential approach to behavior change.* New York: Guilford.

Hayes, S. C., Strosahl, K. D., Wilson, K. G., Bissett, R. T., Pistorello, J., Toarmino, et al. (2004). Measuring experiential avoidance: A preliminary test of a working model. *The Psychological Record, 54,* 553-578.

Hayes, S. C., Wilson, K. G., Gifford, E. V., Follette, V. M., & Strosahl, K. (1996). Emotional avoidance and behavior disorders: A functional dimensional approach to diagnosis and treatment. *Journal of Consulting and Clinical Psychology, 64,* 1152-1168.

Hazlett-Stevens, H., Zucker, B. G., & Craske, M .G. (2002). The relationship of thought-action fusion to pathological worry and generalized anxiety disorder. *Behaviour Research and Therapy, 40,* 1199-1204.

Henin, A., & Kendall, P. C. (1997). Obsessive-compulsive disorder in childhood and adolescence. *Advances in Clinical Child Psychology, 19,* 75-131.

Hermans, D., Martens, K., De Cort, K., Pieters, G., & Eelen, P. (2003). Reality monitoring and metacognitive beliefs related to cognitive confidence in obsessive-compulsive disorder. *Behaviour Research and Therapy, 41,* 383-401.

Herrnstein, R. J. (1969). Method and theory in the study of avoidance. *Psychological Review, 76,* 49-69.

Herrnstein, R. J., & Hineline, P. N. (1966). Negative reinforcement as shock frequency reduction. *Journal of the Experimental Analysis of Behavior, 9,* 421-430.

Hettema, J. M., Neale, M.C., & Kendler, K. S. (2001) A review and meta-analysis of the genetic epidemiology of anxiety disorders. Invited special article. *American Journal of Psychiatry, 158,* 1568-1578.

Hibbs, E. D., Hamburger, S. D., Lenane, M., Rapoport, J. L., Kruesi, M. J. P., Keysor, C. S., et al. (1991). Determinants of expressed emotion in families of disturbed and normal children. *Journal of Child Psychology and Psychiatry, 32,* 757-770.

Hodgson, R., & Rachman, S. (1972). The effects of contamination and washing in obsessional patients. *Behaviour Research and Therapy, 10,* 111-117.

Hohagen. F., Winkelmann, G., Rasche-Räuchle, H., Hand, I., König, A, Munchau, N., et al. (1998). Combination of behaviour therapy with fluvoxamine in comparison with behaviour therapy and placebo: Results of a multicentre study. *British Journal of Psychiatry, 173,* 71-78.

Hollander, E., De Caria, C., & Liebowitz, M. (1989). Biological aspects of obsessive-compulsive disorder. *Psychiatric Annals, 19,* 80-87.

Hornsveld, R. H. J., Kraaimaat, F. W. K., & van DamBaggen, R. M. J. (1979). Anxiety/discomfort and handwashing in obsessive-compulsive and psychiatric control patients. *Behaviour Research and Therapy, 17,* 223-228.

Ilardi, S. S., & Craighead, W. E. (1994). The role of nonspecific factors in cognitive-behavior therapy for depression. *Clinical Psychology: Science & Practice, 1,* 138-156.

Insel, T. R., Murphy, D. L., Cohen, R. M., Alterman, I. S., Kilts, C., & Linnoila, M. (1983). Obsessive-compulsive disorder: A double-blind trial of clomipramine and clorgyline. *Archives of General Psychiatry, 40,* 605-612.

Janeck, A. S., & Calamari, J. E. (1999). Thought suppression in obsessive-compulsive disorder. *Cognitive Therapy & Research, 23,* 497-509.

Jenike, M. A. (1986). Somatic treatments. In M. Jenike, L. Baer, & W. Minichiello (Eds.), *Obsessive compulsive disorders: Theory and management.* Littleton, MA: PSG Publishing Co.

Karno, M., & Golding, J. M. (1991). Obsessive compulsive disorder. In L. N. Robinson & D. A. Regier (Eds.), *Psychiatric disorders in America: The Epidemiologic Catchment Area study* (pp. 204-219). New York: Free Press.

King, R. A., Leckman, J. F., Scahill, L., & Cohen, D. J. (1999). Obsessive-compulsive disorder, anxiety, and depression. In. L. F. Leckman & D. J. Coher (Eds.), *Tourette's syndrome - tics, obsessions, compulsions: Developmental psychopathology and clinical care* (pp. 43-63). New York: John Wiley and Sons.

Krohne, H. W., & Hock, M. (1991). Relationships between restrictive mother-child interactions and anxiety of the child. *Anxiety Research, 4,* 109-124.

Koran, L. M., Theinemann, M., & Davenport, R. (1996). Quality of life in patients with obsessive compulsive disorder. *American Journal of Psychiatry, 156,* 783-788.

Leckman, J. F., King, R. A., & Cohen, D. J. (1999). Tics and tic disorders. In J. F. Leckman & D. J. Cohen (Eds.), *Tourette's syndrome - Tics, obsessions, compulsions: Developmental psychopathology and clinical care.* New York: Wiley & Sons.

Lensi, P., Cassano, G. B., Correddu, G., Ravagli, S., Kunovac, J. L., & Akiskal, H. S. (1996). Obsessive-compulsive disorder: Familial-developmental history, symptomology, comorbidity and course with special reference to gender-related differences. *British Journal of Psychiatry, 169,* 101-107.

Leon, A. C., Portera, L., & Weisman, M. M. (1995). The social costs of anxiety disorders. *British Journal of Psychiatry, 166,* 19-22.

Levitt, J. T., Brown, T. A., Orsillo, S. M., & Barlow, D. H. (2004). The effects of acceptance versus suppression of emotion on subjective and psychophysiological response to carbon dioxide challenge in patients with panic disorder. *Behavior Therapy, 35,* 747-766.

MacDonald, P. A., Antony, M. M., MacLeod, C. M., & Richter, M. M. (1997). Memory and confidence in memory judgments among individuals with obsessive compulsive disorder and nonclinical controls. *Behaviour Research and Therapy, 35,* 497-505.

Maher, B. A. (1966). *Principles of psychopathology: An experimental approach.* New York: McGraw-Hill.

Masuda, A., Hayes, S. C., Sackett, C., & Twohig, M. P. (2004). Cognitive defusion and self-relevant negative thoughts: Examining the impact of a ninety year old technique. *Behaviour Research and Therapy, 42,* 477-485.

Mavissakalian, M. R., Hamann, M., & Jones, B. (1990). Correlates of DSM-III personality disorders in obsessive compulsive disorder. *Comprehensive Psychiatry, 31,* 481-489.

Mavissakalian, M. R., Turner, S. M., & Michelson, L. (1985). Future directions in the assessment and treatment of obsessive-compulsive disorder. In M. R. Mavissakalian, S. M. Turner, & L. Michelson (Eds.), *Psychological and pharmacological treatment of obsessive-compulsive disorder.* New York: Plenum Press.

McLean, P. D., Whittal, M. L., Sochting, I., Koch, W. J., Paterson, R., Thordarson, D. S., et al. (2001). Cognitive versus behavior therapy in the group treatment of obsessive compulsive disorder. *Journal of Consulting and Clinical Psychiatry, 69,* 205-214.

McNally, R. J., & Kohlbeck, P. A. (1993). Reality monitoring in obsessive-compulsive disorder. *Behaviour Research and Therapy, 31,* 249-253.

Merkel, W. T., Pollard, C. A., Weiner, R. L., & Staebler, C. R. (1993). Perceived parental characteristics of patients with obsessive-compulsive disorder, depression, and panic disorder. *Child Psychiatry ad Human Development, 24,* 49-57.

Meyer, V., & Chesser, E. S. (1970). *Behavior therapy in clinical psychiatry.* New York: Science House, Inc.

Millon, T. (1981). *Disorders of personality: DSM-III: Axis II.* New York: Wiley & Sons.

Miltenberger, R. G., Rapp, J. R. & Long, E. S. (2001). Characteristics of trichotillomania. In D. Woods & R. Miltenberger (Eds.), *Tic disorders, trichotillomania and repetitive behavior disorders: Behavioral approaches to analysis and treatment* (pp. 133-150). Norwell, MA: Kluwer.

Moran, D. J. (1999). Rules and reinforcement contingency changes in persons with obsessive-compulsive disorder. *Dissertation Abstracts International: Section B: The Sciences and Engineering, 59*(9-B), 5100.

Morrisaon, I., Lloyd, D., Di Pellegrino, G., & Roberts, N. (2004). Vicarious responses to pain in *anterior cingulate cortex*: Is empathy a multisensory issue? *Cognitive, Affective, & Behavioral Neuroscience, 4,* 270-274.

Mowrer, O. H. (1939). A stimulus-response analysis of anxiety and its role as a reinforcing agent. *Psychological Review, 46,* 553-565.

Mowrer, O. H. (1960). *Learning theory and behavior.* New York: Wiley.

Muller, J., & Roberts, J. E. (2005). Memory and attention in obsessive-compulsive disorder. *Anxiety Disorders, 15,* 1-28.

Naftulin, D. H., Donnelly, F. A., & Wolkon, G. H. (1974). Selection of nuns for training as mental health counselors. *Journal of Community Psychology, 2,* 366-369.

Naoyuki, O., Osaka, O., Masanao, M., Hirohito, K., & Hidenao, F. (2004). A word expressing affective pain activates the *anterior cingulate cortex* in the human brain: An fMRI study. *Behavioural Brain Science, 153,* 123-127.

Nestadt, G., Lan, T., Samuels, J., Riddle, M., Bienvenu, O. J., III, Liang, K. Y., et al. (2000). Complex segregation analysis provides compelling evidence for a major gene underlying obsessive-compulsive disorder and for heterogeneity by sex. *American Journal of Human Genetics, 67,* 1611-1616.

Neziroglu, F., Anemone, R., & Yaryura-Tobias, J. A. (1992). Onset of obsessive-compulsive disorder in pregnancy. *American Journal of Psychiatry, 149,* 947-950.

O'Connor, T. L., & Freeston, M. A. (2002). Recollection of parent-child relationships in patients with obsessive-compulsive disorder and panic disorder with agoraphobia. *Acta Psychiatrica Scandinavica, 105,* 310-316.

Parkinson, L., & Rachman, S. (1981). Part I. The nature of intrusive thoughts: Distinct or uniform phenomena? *Behaviour Research and Therapy, 23,* 383-393.

Pollak, J. (1987). Relationship of obsessive-compulsive personality to obsessive-compulsive disorder: A review of the literature. *Journal of Psychology, 121,* 137-148.

Purdon, C., & Clark, D. A. (1993). Obsessive intrusive thoughts in nonclinical subjects. Part I. Content and relation with depressive, anxious and obsessional symptoms. *Behaviour Research and Therapy, 31,* 712-720.

Purdon, C., & Clark, D. A. (2001). Suppression of obsession-like thoughts in nonclinical individuals: Impact on thought frequency, appraisal and mood state. *Behaviour Research and Therapy, 39,* 1163-1181.

Purdon, C., & Clark, D. A. (2002). The need to control thoughts. In R. O. Frost & G. Steketee (Eds.), *Cognitive approaches to obsessions and compulsions: Theory, assessment, and treatment* (pp. 29-43). Oxford, UK: Elsevier.

Purdon, C., Rowa, K., & Antony, M. M. (2005). Thought suppression and its effects on thought frequency and mood state in individuals with obsessive-compulsive disorder. *Behavior Research and Therapy, 43,* 93-108.

Rachlin, H. (1997). The teleological science of self-control. *Behavioral and Brain Sciences, 20,* 367-369.

Rachman, S. (1976). Obsessional-compulsive checking. *Behavior Research and Therapy, 14,* 269-277.

Rachman, S. (1993). Obsessions, responsibility and guilt. *Behavior Research and Therapy, 31,* 149-154.

Rachman, S. (1997). A cognitive theory of obsessions. *Behavior Research and Therapy, 35,* 793-802.

Rachman, S. (1998). A cognitive theory of obsessions: Elaborations. *Behavior Research and Therapy, 36,* 385-401.

Rachman, S., & de Silva, P. (1978). Abnormal and normal obsessions. *Behavior Research and Therapy, 16,* 233-248.

Rachman, S., Marks, I., & Hodgson, R. (1973). The treatment of obsessive-compulsive neurotics by modeling and flooding in vivo. *Behavior Research and Therapy, 11,* 463-471.

Rachman, S., Shafran, R. Mitchell, D., Trant , J., & Teachman, B. (1996). How to remain neutral: An experimental analysis of neutralization. *Behavior Research and Therapy, 34,* 889-898.

Rachman, S., Thordarson, D. S., Shafran, R., & Woody, S. R. (1995). Perceived responsibility: Structure and significance. *Behavior Research and Therapy, 33,* 779-784.

Rapoport, J. L., & Inoff-Germain, G. (1997). Medical and surgical treatment of obsessive compulsive disorder. *Neurologic Clinics of North America, 15,* 421-428.

Rasmussen, S. A., & Eisen, J. L. (1992). The epidemiology and clinical features of obsessive-compulsive disorder. *Psychiatric Clinics of North America, 15,* 743-758.

Rasmussen, S. A., & Eisen, J. L. (1994). The epidemiology and differential diagnosis of obsessive-compulsive disorder. *Journal of Clinical Psychiatry, 55*, 5-14.

Rasmussen, S. A., & Tsuang, M. T. (1986). Clinical characteristics and family history in DSM-III obsessive-compulsive disorder. *American Journal of Psychiatry, 143*, 317-322.

Rassin, E., Diepstraten, P., Merckelbach, H., & Muris, P. (2001). Thought-action fusion and thought suppression in obsessive-compulsive disorder. *Behavior Research and Therapy, 39*, 757-764.

Rassin, E., & Koster, E. (2003). The correlation between thought-action fusion and religiosity in a normal sample. *Behavior Research and Therapy, 41*, 361-368.

Rassin, E., Merckelbach, H., Muris, P., & Schmidt, H. (2001). The thought-action fusion scale: Further evidence for its reliability and validity. *Behavior Research and Therapy, 39*, 537-544.

Rassin, E., Merchelbach, H., Muris, P., & Spaan, V. (1999). Thought-action fusion as a causal factor in the development of intrusions. *Behavior Research and Therapy, 37*, 231-237.

Rehfisch, J. M. (1958a). A scale for personality rigidity. *Journal of Consulting Psychology, 22*, 11-15.

Rehfisch, J. M. (1958b). Some scale and test correlates of a personality rigidity scale. *Journal of Consulting Psychology, 22*, 372-374.

Rescorla, R. A. (1967). Pavlovian conditioning and its proper control procedures. *Psychological Review, 74*, 71-80.

Rheaume, J., & Ladouceur, R. (2000). Cognitive and behavioural treatments of checking behaviours: An examination of individual cognitive change. *Clinical Psychology and Psychotherapy, 7*, 1-12.

Roper, G., Rachman, S., & Hodgson, R. (1973). An experiment in obsessional checking. *Behaviour Research and Therapy, 11*, 271-277.

Rubenstein, C. S., Peynircioglu, Z. F., Chambless, D. L., & Pigott, T. A. (1993). Memory in subclinical obsessive-compulsive checkers. *Behavior Research and Therapy, 31*, 759-765.

Rutledge, P. C. (1998). Obsessionality and the attempted suppression of unpleasant personal intrusive thoughts. *Behaviour Research and Therapy, 36*, 403-416.

Salkovskis, P. M. (1985). Obsessional-compulsive problems: A cognitive-behavioral analysis. *Behavioral Research and Therapy, 23*, 549-552.

Salkovskis, P. M. (1989). Cognitive-behavioral factors and the persistence of intrusive thoughts in obsessional problems. *Behavioral Research and Therapy, 27*, 677-682.

Salkovskis, P. M. (1998). Psychological approaches to the understanding of obsessional problems. In R. P. Swinson, M. M. Anthony, S. Rachman, & M. A. Richter (Eds.), *Obsessive-compulsive disorder: Theory, research, and treatment* (pp. 33-50). New York: Guilford.

Salkovskis, P. M., & Campbell, P. (1994). Thought suppression induces intrusion in naturally occurring negative intrusive thoughts. *Behaviour Research and Therapy, 32*, 1-8.

Salkovskis, P. M., & Harrison, J. (1984). Abnormal and normal obsessions: A replication. *Behaviour Research and Therapy, 22*, 1-4.

Salkovskis, P. M., & Westbrook, D. (1989). Behavior therapy and obsessional ruminations: Can failure be turned into success? *Behaviour Research and Therapy, 27*, 149-160.

Savage, C. R., Baer, L., Keuthen, N. J., Brown, H. D., Rauch, S. L., & Jenike, M. A. (1999). Organizational strategies mediate nonverbal memory impairment in obsessive-compulsive disorder. *Biological Psychiatry, 45*, 905-916.

Savron, G., Fava, G. A., Grandi, S., Rafanelli, C., Raffi, A. R., & Belluardo, P. (1996). Hypochondriacal fears and beliefs in obsessive-compulsive disorder. *Acta Psychiatrica Scandinavica, 93*, 345-348.

Saxena, S., Brody, A. L., & Schwartz, J. M. (1998). Neuroimaging and frontal-subcortical circuitry in obsessive-compulsive disorder. *British Journal of Psychiatry, 173*, 26-37.

Shafran, R., Thordarson, D. S., & Rachman, S. (1996). Thought-action fusion in obsessive-compulsive disorder. *Journal of Anxiety Disorders, 10*, 370-391.

Shapiro, D. (1965). *Neurotic styles*. New York: Basic Books, Inc.

Sher, K. J., Frost, R. O., Kushner, M., Crews, T. M., & Alexander, J. E. (1989). Memory deficits in compulsive checkers: Replication and extension in a clinical sample. *Behavior Research and Therapy, 27*, 65-69.

Sher, K. J., Frost, R. O., & Otto, R. (1983). Cognitive deficits in compulsive checkers: An exploratory study. *Behavior Research and Therapy, 21*, 357-363.

Sher, K. J., Mann, B., & Frost, R. O. (1984). Cognitive dysfunction in compulsive checkers: Further explorations. *Behavior Research and Therapy, 22*, 493-502.

Shimoff, E., Catania, A. C., & Matthews, B. A. (1981). Uninstructed human responding: Sensitivity of low-rate performance to schedule contingencies. *Journal of the Experimental Analysis of Behavior, 36,* 207-220.

Simon, G., Hollander, E., Stein, D., Cohen, L., & Aronowitz, B. (1995). Body dysmorphic disorder in the DSM-IV field trial for obsessive-compulsive disorder. *American Journal of Psychiatry, 152,* 352-357.

Sinha, D. (1992). Sinha's anxiety test three decades later. *Journal of Personality and Clinical Studies, 8,* 1-6.

Siqueland, L., Kendall, P. C., & Steinberg, L. (1996). Anxiety in children: Perceived family environment and observed family interaction. *Journal of Clinical Child Psychology, 25,* 225-237.

Skoog, G., & Skoog, I. (1999). A 40-year follow-up of patients with obsessive-compulsive disorder. *Archives of General Psychiatry, 56,* 121-127.

Solomon, R., Kamin, L., & Wynne, L. C. (1953). Traumatic avoidance learning: The outcomes of several extinction procedures with dogs. *The Journal of Abnormal and Social Psychology, 48,* 291-302.

Solomon, R., & Wynne, L. (1954). Traumatic avoidance learning: The principles of anxiety conservation and partial irreversibility. *The Psychological Review, 61,* 352-385.

Stanley, M. A., & Turner, S. M. (1995). Current status of pharmacological and behavioral treatment of obsessive-compulsive disorder. *Behavior Therapy, 26,* 163-186.

Steketee, G., & Barlow, D. H. (2002). Obsessive-compulsive disorder. In D. H. Barlow (Ed.), *Anxiety and its disorders: The nature and treatment of anxiety and panic.* (pp.516-550). New York: Guilford.

Steketee, G., Chambless, D. L., & Tran, G. Q. (2001). Effects of Axis I and II comorbidity on behavior therapy outcome for obsessive disorder and agoraphobia. *Comprehensive Psychiatry, 42,* 76-86.

Swedo, S. E., Schapiro, M., Grady, C., Cheslow, D., Leonard, H., Kumar, A., et al. (1989). Cerebral glucose metabolism in childhood onset obsessive-compulsive disorder. *Archives of General Psychiatry, 46,* 518-523.

Swedo, S. E., Leonard, H. L., Garvey, M., Mittleman, B., Allen, A. J., Perlmutter, S., et al. (1998). Pediatric autoimmune neuropsychiatric disorders associated with streptococcal infections: Clinical description of the first 50 cases. *American Journal of Psychiatry, 155,* 264-271.

Taub, E., & Berman, A. J. (1963). Avoidance conditioning in the absence of relevant proprioceptive and exteroceptive feedback. *Physiological Psychology, 56,* 1012-1016.

Tolin, D. F., Abramowitz, J. S., Hamlin, C., Foa, E. B., & Synodi, D. S. (2002). Attributions for thought suppression failure in obsessive-compulsive disorder. *Cognitive Therapy and Research, 26,* 505-517.

Tolin, D. F., Abramowitz, J. S., Kozak, M. J., & Foa, E. B. (2001). Fixity of belief, perceptual aberration, and magical ideation in obsessive-compulsive disorder. *Journal of Anxiety Disorders, 15,* 501-510.

Tolin, D. F., Abramowitz, J. S., Przeworski, A., & Foa, E. B. (2002). Thought suppression in obsessive-compulsive disorder. *Behaviour Research and Therapy, 40,* 1251-1270.

Trinder, H., & Salkovskis, P. M. (1994). Personally relevant intrusions outside the laboratory: Long-term suppression increases intrusion. *Behaviour Research and Therapy, 32,* 833-842.

Twohig, M. P., Hayes, S. C., & Masuda, A. (2006a). Increasing willingness to experience obsessions: Acceptance and commitment therapy as a treatment for obsessive-compulsive disorder. *Behavior Therapy, 37,* 3-13.

Twohig, M. P., Hayes, S. C., & Masuda, A. (2006b). A preliminary investigation of acceptance and commitment therapy as a treatment for chronic skin picking. *Behaviour Research and Therapy, 44,* 1513-1522.

Twohig, M. P., Hayes, S. C., Plumb, J., Pruitt, L., Sailer, A., & Torch, M. (2006). *A randomized clinical trial of acceptance and commitment therapy for OCD.* Paper presented at the annual conference of the Association for Behavior and Cognitive Therapies, Chicago, IL.

Twohig, M. P., & Woods, D. W. (2004). A preliminary investigation of acceptance and commitment therapy and habit reversal as a treatment for trichotillomania. *Behavior Therapy, 35,* 803-820.

Tynes, L. L., Salins, C. Skiba, W., & Winstead, D. K. (1992). A psychoeducational and support group for obsessive-compulsive disorder patients and their significant others. *Comprehensive Psychiatry, 33,* 197-201.

Ursu, S., Stenger, A. V., Shear, K. M., Jones, M. R., & Carter, C. S. (2004). Overactive action monitoring in *obsessive-compulsive disorder*: Evidence from functional magnetic resonance imaging. *Psychological Science, 14,* 347-353.

van Balkom, A. J. L. M., de Haan, E., van Oppen, P., Spinhoven, P., Hoogduin, K. A. L., & van Dyck, R. (1998). Cognitive and behavioral therapies alone versus in combination with fluvoxamine in the treatment of obsessive-compulsive disorder. *Journal of Nervous and Mental Disease, 186,* 492-499.

van den Hout, M., Kindt, M., Weiland, T., & Peters, M. (2002). Instructed neutralization, spontaneous neutralization and prevented neutralization after and obsession-like thought. *Journal of Behavior Therapy and Experimental Psychiatry, 33,* 177-189.

van den Hout, M., van Pol, M., & Peters, M. (2001). On becoming neutral: Effects of experimental neutralizing reconsidered. *Behaviour Research and Therapy, 39,* 1439-1448.

van Oppen, P., de Haan, E., van Balkom, A. J. L. M., Spinhoven, P., Hoogduin, K., & van Dyck, R. (1995). Cognitive therapy and exposure in vivo in the treatment of obsessive-compulsive disorder. *Behaviour Research and Therapy, 33,* 379-390.

Weisssmann, M. M., Bland, R. Canino, G., Greenwand, S., Hwo, H., Newman, S., et al. (1994). The cross national epidemiology of obsessive compulsive disorder. *Journal of Clinical Psychiatry, 55,* 5-10.

Weizman, A., Carmi, M., Hermesh, H., Shahar, A., Apter, A., Tyano, S., et al. (1986). High-affinity imipramine binding and serotonin uptake in platelets of eight adolescent and ten adult obsessive-compulsive patients. *American Journal of Psychiatry, 143,* 335-339.

Wegner, D. M. (1994). Ironic processes of mental control. *Psychological Review, 101,* 34-52.

Wegner, D. M., Schneider, D. J., Carter, S. R., & White, T. L. (1987). Paradoxical effects of thought suppression. *Journal of Personality and Social Psychology, 53,* 5-13.

Wells, A. (1997). *Cognitive therapy of anxiety disorders: A practice manual and conceptual guide.* Chichester, UK: Wiley.

Wenzlaff, R. M., & Wegner, D. M. (2000). Thought suppression. *Annual Review of Psychology, 51,* 59-91.

Wilson, K. G., & Hayes, S. C. (1996). Resurgence of derived stimulus relations. *Journal of the Experimental Analysis of Behavior, 66,* 267-281.

Wilson, K. G., Hayes, S. C., Gregg, J., & Zettle, R. D. (2001). Psychopathology and psychotherapy. In S. C. Hayes, D. Barnes-Holmes, & B. Roche (Eds.), *Relational frame theory: A post-Skinnerian account of human language and cognition* (pp. 211-237). New York: Plenum Press.

Wilson, K. G., & Murrell, A. R. (2004). Values work in acceptance and commitment therapy: Setting a course for behavioral treatment. In S. C. Hayes, V. M. Follette, & M. M. Linehan (Eds.), *Mindfulness and acceptance: Expanding the cognitive behavioral tradition* (pp. 120-151). New York: Guilford.

Wulfert, E., Greenway, D. E., Farkas, P., Hayes, S. C., & Dougher, M. J. (1994). Correlation between self-reported rigidity and rule-governed insensitivity to operant contingencies. *Journal of Applied Behavior Analysis, 27,* 659-671.

Yaryura-Tobias, J. A. (1977). Obsessive-compulsive disorders: A serotonergic hypothesis. *Journal of Orthomolecular Psychiatry, 6,* 1-10.

Zettle, R. D. (2003). Acceptance and commitment therapy (ACT) vs. systematic desensitization in treatment of mathematics anxiety. *Psychological Record, 53,* 197-215.

Zettle, R. D., & Hayes, S. C. (1987). Component and process analysis of cognitive therapy. *Psychological Reports, 64,* 939-953.

Zitterl, W., Urban, C., Linzmayer, L., Aigner, M., Demal, U., Semler, B., et al. (2001). Memory deficits in patients with DSM-IV obsessive-compulsive disorder. *Psychopathology, 34,* 113-117.

Zohar, J., & Insel, T. R. (1987). Drug treatment of obsessive-compulsive disorder. Special Issue: Drug treatment of anxiety disorders. *Journal of Affective Disorders, 13,* 193-202.

Zucker, B. G., Craske, M. G., Barrios, V., & Holguin, M. (2002). Thought-action fusion: Can it be corrected? *Behaviour Research and Therapy, 40,* 653-664.

Chapter 6

A Contemporary Behavior Analytic Model of Trichotillomania

Chad T. Wetterneck
Douglas W. Woods
University of Wisconsin, Milwaukee

Trichotillomania (TTM) involves chronic hair pulling that results in significant hair loss (Miltenberger, Rapp, & Long, 2001). An individual must also meet the following criteria to be diagnosed with TTM: (a) an increasing level of tension immediately prior to hair pulling or during attempts to avoid pulling, (b) a sensation of relief, pleasure, or gratification during hair pulling, (c) the pulling is not better explained by a general medical condition or other mental disorder, and (d) significant distress or impairment in occupational, social, or other areas of functioning is experienced as a result of the pulling (American Psychiatric Association, 2000).

Prevalence and Onset

Exact prevalence rates of TTM are unavailable, but a survey of 2600 college students estimated that 0.6% of the population met DSM diagnostic criteria for the disorder (Christenson, Pyle, & Mitchell, 1991). However, in the same sample, 2.5% of students engaged in clinically significant hair pulling (i.e., pulling that resulted in hair loss regardless of antecedent tension or subsequent tension relief). More recent research has suggested that 2% (Rothbaum, Shaw, Morris, & Ninan, 1993) to 3% (Woods, Miltenberger, & Flach, 1996) of college students experience pulling with resultant significant hair loss. According to Christenson, Mackenzie, and Mitchell (1994), TTM is more common in females than males, but the gender difference found in adults may not be as significant in children (Miltenberger et al., 2001).

Chronic hair pulling has been found to begin as early as one year of age and as late as 70 years, with the average age of onset being approximately 13 years (Mansueto, Townsley-Stemberger, McCombs-Thomas, & Goldfinger-Golomb, 1997). The youngest reported sample in the TTM literature was a group of 10 toddlers, whose average age was 26 months with an average age of onset around 18 months (Wright & Holmes, 2003).

Comorbidity

TTM can lead to personal distress and interpersonal/social difficulties as a result of avoiding social or pleasant activities (Diefenbach, Mouton-Odum, & Stanley, 2002). For example, Stemberger, Thomas, Mansueto, and Carter (2000) found that over 60% of adults with TTM avoided swimming and getting haircuts, over 20% avoided well-lit public places, and over 30% were uncomfortable with windy weather. Additionally, over 50% reported low self-esteem, depression, irritability, and feelings of unattractiveness. Combined, these findings indicate that TTM may contribute to significant distress in one's daily functioning.

In addition to these concerns, a variety of psychological disorders often occur in conjunction with TTM. As many as 55% of individuals with TTM have comorbid psychiatric diagnoses, most commonly mood and anxiety disorders (Diefenbach et al., 2002). For example, Schlosser, Black, Blum, and Goldstein (1994) found that 27% of a sample with TTM had a diagnosis of mood disorder, 26% had an obsessive-compulsive disorder diagnosis, 23% had a diagnosis of another anxiety disorder, and 55% had a comorbid personality disorder diagnosis. Similar comorbidity rates were found by Christenson et al. (1991) who found that 23% of the sample also had major depression and 18% also had panic disorder.

Patterns of Hair pulling

The location and method of pulling, as well as the objects used to pull can differ among individuals. Persons with TTM may pull hair from any body region, but typically pull from the scalp, eyelashes, beard, eyebrows, and/or the pubic region (Woods et al., in press). Hairs are typically pulled from more than one area and are commonly pulled one at a time rather than in clumps (Stein, Christenson, & Hollander, 1999).

Hair pulling is central to TTM, but individuals with the disorder often engage in a variety of behaviors before, during, and after the actual pulling. Mansueto et al. (1997) state that behaviors preceding actual pulling can involve finding an appropriate place for pulling, preparing instruments to aid in pulling (e.g., tweezers, pins, brushes, and combs), choosing the area on the body to pull, and choosing the specific hairs to pull. According to Miltenberger et al. (2001), behaviors such as hair stroking or touching are commonly exhibited before an individual pulls the hair. Pulling itself often involves gripping hairs with the index and thumb finger or wrapping longer hair around the index finger and pulling it from the body, usually with the predominant hand (Stein et al, 1999).

According to Mansueto et al. (1997), post-pulling behaviors may involve manipulating the pulled hair using the mouth, hands, or face. These manipulating behaviors may include rubbing the hair on the face or mouth, or biting, chewing, or ingesting the hair. The pulled hair might also be saved for later use or simply be discarded.

Hair Pulling in Children

Few studies exist regarding the phenomenology of TTM in children. Although TTM generally starts between the ages of 11 to 13, Wright and Holmes (2003) note that younger children may not meet medical criteria for TTM as the feeling of tension and relief from tension may not be reported. Although Wright and Holmes' sample consisted of toddlers, similar findings have been noted in adolescents (King et al., 1995). King and colleagues studied 15 adolescents with TTM whose ages ranged from 9 to 17. When the sample was divided into those above and those below the mean age, those in the younger group were significantly more likely to omit rising tension prior to pulling and relief or gratification after pulling. Hanna (1997) found similar results in a sample of 11 children and adolescents with chronic hair pulling. In this study, 55% of participants did not report increasing tension prior to hair pulling or when attempting to resist, and only 36% endorsed pleasure, relief, or gratification during pulling (Hanna, 1997).

In addition to not meeting all diagnostic criteria, some researchers have suggested that early childhood-onset hair pulling is a separate, time-limited problem, which does not progress to a later disorder (Swedo & Leonard, 1992). Nevertheless, psychiatric comorbidity appears to be evident in some younger children with TTM, with recent research on toddlers showing that 50% of the toddlers in the sample met requirements for a comorbid anxiety disorder, 40% displayed developmental problems, 20% had chronic pediatric concerns, and 100% of the sample had family stressors such as parental separation, homelessness, unemployment, or parent mental illness (Wright & Holmes, 2003).

Although early childhood-onset hair pulling appears to last for a shorter duration and often runs its course without treatment or with minimal intervention (Swedo & Leonard, 1992; Winchel, 1992), individuals who display hair pulling for at least six months typically have a more chronic case that is more resistant to treatment (Mansueto, et al., 1997). This may imply that hair pulling in very young children is a benign habit separate from TTM (Friman, 1992), but does not rule out the possibility that early-onset hair pulling represents an early phase of TTM for some individuals. Regardless, chronic pulling can fluctuate in severity and is reported to be precipitated by multiple factors such as stressful life events, significant alterations in environmental conditions, the opportunity to pull, childhood illness, injury to the scalp, and academic stress (Stein et al., 1999).

Current Research on Etiology

Comparative Findings

Evidence for the biological underpinnings of TTM stems from both comparative and neurobiological research. Researchers have attempted to use body-focused repetitive behaviors in animals as a model for understanding human habitual behaviors. In animal models, repetitive grooming problems are viewed as fixed action patterns that are affected by specific environmental variables (Moon-Fanelli,

Dodman, & O'Sullivan, 1999). Avian feather picking, in which a seemingly healthy bird removes feathers to the point of noticeable feather loss, has been found in captive birds (Moon-Fanelli et al., 1999). Similar to some individuals with TTM, birds with avian feather picking disorder will often target feathers that appear to be different from other feathers. Bordnick, Thyer, and Ritchie (1994) also found that such birds manipulate their feathers before they are discarded; an action similar to that seen in some humans with TTM. To date, there have been no well supported etiologies for feather picking disorder, although there is speculation that neurotransmitter deficiencies, operant factors (e.g., attention given to damaged areas), and stressors similar to those found in humans (e.g., stress, periods of inactivity, lack of companionship) may play a role in the disorder (Bordnick et al., 1994).

Moon-Fanelli and colleagues also found excessive licking of the body in both cats and dogs to the point of noticeable hair loss. This behavior was found to be more prevalent with indoor animals, female cats, and animals experiencing higher levels of distress. Moon-Fanelli and colleagues noted that there was often a medical or organic basis for this excessive licking such as parasites, allergies, food, medications, or skin problems. In such cases, amelioration of the underlying medical condition often alleviated the excessive licking, but stress then produced an increase in the frequency of such behaviors.

Animal models appear similar to descriptions of TTM, but there are facets of the models that do not map well on to humans. First, grooming behavior in humans does not appear to be an innate sequence of behavior, but rather an operantly acquired set of behaviors. Second, although environmental stressors appear to play a primary role in the development of "animal trich," a number of human cases have not reported the presence of environmental stressors preceding the onset of the disorder (Graber & Arndt, 1993). Because of these factors and general interspecies differences, animal models should be approached with caution. Although they may offer a useful tool for understanding some aspects of TTM, humans add unique capabilities and experiences that could alter the behavioral expression of TTM, beyond what is found in the comparative models.

Genetic/Neurobiological Findings

Genetic Findings. A genetic foundation for TTM has been suggested by showing that the problem is more common in family members of TTM probands (Lenane et al., 1992), but neither a specific gene location nor mode of inheritance has been identified in humans. However, a promising animal genetics model has recently been published, which may aid in understanding the potential genetic underpinnings of TTM. McGrath, Campbell, and Burton (1999) created mice that contained a neuropotentiating transgene in the cortical and amygdala neurons known to trigger some of the same central nervous system regions hypothesized to be hyperactive in OCD-spectrum disorders. Constant release of cholera toxin within these neurons induced behaviors in mice such as motor tics, periods of repetition of normal behaviors, and biting, pulling or plucking at the skin of other mice and themselves.

The McGrath study concluded the basis for this behavior was not a primary defect in cognitive or affective processing; instead it was believed to be caused by hyper-responsiveness to afferent stimuli. The finding also implied that the neural origin of these symptoms is excessive forebrain glutamate release onto the striatum.

A separate line of research has investigated how specific genes may affect grooming behaviors in animals. Greer and Capecchi (2002) examined mice in which the Hoxb8 gene was disrupted. These mice demonstrated excessive grooming that led to hair removal and lesions, as well as the excessive grooming of cagemates. This study is the first to relate a specific genetic sequence to hair-removing behavior.

Neurochemical Findings. There have been few studies on the neurobiological basis of TTM, but because of favorable responses to clomipramine, there is a belief that TTM may be related to a dysregulation of the serotonin system (Swedo et al., 1989). Likewise, Stein and Hollander (1992) found SSRI's and dopamine blockers to be effective in reducing hair pulling, suggesting excessive dopamine activity may also be a contributing factor to TTM.

Another line of inquiry has investigated the endogenous opiate system. Given the findings that people with TTM appear not to experience pain at the site of pulling (Ristvedt & Christenson, 1996) and the finding that naltrexone (an opioid blocker) successfully reduced hair pulling (Christenson et al., 1994), it has been hypothesized that persons with TTM, have a heightened endogenous opioid sensitivity when pulling. The result of this sensitivity would be a decrease in pain sensitivity and/or an increase in pleasurable sensations. However, the one study to systematically evaluate this hypothesis failed to confirm this effect in persons with TTM as compared to a psychiatrically healthy population (Frecscka & Arato, 2002).

Neuroanatomical/Neuropsychological Findings. Through the use of neuroimaging techniques, evidence for neurostructural deficits in persons with TTM is beginning to emerge. Functional and morphological brain studies in patients with TTM have found that patients with TTM have significantly reduced left putamen and left ventriculate volumes compared to healthy controls and concluded that these findings more closely resemble patterns found in patients with Tourette's disorder, and not patterns found in OCD patients (Breiter et al., 1996; Jenike et al., 1996; Robinson et al., 1995).

Likewise, Swedo, Rapoport, Leonard, and Schapiro (1991) conducted PET scans on a small group of TTM patients at rest. Results showed increased right and left cerebellar and right superior parietal functioning. Subsequent SPECT scans by Stein et al. (2002) showed that people with more severe hair pulling experienced a greater decrease of activity in frontal and parietal regions and left caudate. Likewise, Stein et al. showed that the SSRI treatments for TTM had the effects of reducing activity in frontal areas dealing with language processing and emotional perception, and in the putamen, an area involved in habitual motor patterns. Thus, such findings suggest that improvement in TTM may come after decreasing brain activity involved in language processing, emotional perception, and habitual motor activity.

Neuropsychological Findings. A number of studies have attempted to identify the neuropsychological correlates to TTM. However, the findings have been mixed. In one of the early neuropsychological studies, Rettew et al. (1991) found that persons with TTM exhibited impaired spatial processing. Keuthen et al. (1996) found deficits in nonverbal memory and executive functioning, as well as deficits in subjects' ability to maintain a mental set. More recently, Stanley, Hannay, and Breckenridge (1997) found that persons with TTM performed more poorly on divided attention tasks than normal controls. The authors also found that poor performance on the divided attention tasks was significantly correlated with increases in anxiety and depression, suggesting that the experience of anxiety or depression may result in a decreased ability to attend to behavioral alternatives.

Clearly, findings from the neurobiological perspective remain scarce and inconclusive. Combining the evidence, it does appear that TTM has some type of genetic foundation, though specific details are unavailable. Likewise, it appears that both a habitual motor pattern and language/emotional processing components are involved. Finally, it appears that persons with TTM have difficulty dividing their attention between tasks, and that doing so is made more difficult when experiencing states of anxiety or depression. Nevertheless, it remains to be seen whether the neurobiological variables are genetically fixed from birth or are acquired as a result of environmental/brain interactions over extended periods of time.

Behavioral/Psychological Research on TTM

Existing psychological research into the etiology and maintenance of TTM has fallen into two separate categories; phenomenological description and experimental psychopathology.

Phenomenology. The phenomenological research on TTM typically has been conducted by interviewing persons with TTM about various behavioral and affective correlates of hair pulling. Generally, these correlates can be interpreted within a functional analytic format focusing on antecedents and consequences. Although not every individual with TTM experiences or is functionally impacted by each of the variables described below, it should be understood that these are commonly implicated in many with TTM.

Antecedents. Antecedents to pulling can be broken down into three categories; settings, specific sensory stimuli, and private events.

Settings or activities in which pulling is more likely are typically found in the individual's home. Pulling commonly takes place in one's bedroom and/or bathroom. Other setting events in which pulling is more likely include driving, reading, and watching television (Mansueto et al., 1997). These settings may serve as conditioned stimuli or cues that have been repeatedly paired with the impulse or urge to pull.

Specific physical, visual, and tactile stimuli may also frequently serve as antecedents to pulling. The majority of hair pullers seek out target hairs that possess specific physical qualities. Mansueto et al. (1997) state that individuals with TTM may focus on specific color, shape, and/or texture of hairs as targets for removal. According to Stein et al. (1999), hairs described as coarse, thick, wiry, or stubbly are often pulled because of the texture of the hairs and stimulation experienced from them. Other stimuli that precipitate pulling involve the use of implements (e.g., tweezers or mirrors; Mansueto et al., 1997). Similar to the settings and activities in which people often pull, the specific characteristics of hair or presence of an implement may also evoke the pulling.

Private Events. According to Mansueto et al. (1997), various private events have been suggested as hair pulling triggers including affective states and cognitions. Research identifying internal cues for pulling has primarily focused on negative affective states such as anxiety and tension, but a wide variety of affective states may play a role. Reports suggest loneliness, fatigue, guilt, anger, indecision, frustration, and excitement (Mansueto et al., 1997) may also function to elicit hair pulling. Woods and Miltenberger (1996) examined habits (i.e., hair manipulation, object manipulation, etc.) in a sample of university students exposed to conditions designed to elicit either states of anxiety, boredom, or emotional neutrality. Subjects' hair and face manipulation were found to increase in the anxiety condition, while object manipulation increased in the boredom condition, suggesting that certain private events may evoke habitual behavior.

Diefenbach, et al. (2002) examined the occurrence and intensity of different affective states reported by those with TTM prior, during, and after pulling episodes. Boredom was found to significantly decrease from pre- to post-pulling, suggesting activities that promote boredom may function as an establishing (i.e., motivative) operation (Michael, 1993). Immediate decreases in reported states of anxiety and tension were also found after pulling occurred suggesting that increased levels of anxiety and tension may also function as establishing operations that make anxiety/ tension reducing behaviors more rewarding. Although some affective states seemed to diminish across the hair pulling episode, others increased in salience (Diefenbach et al., 2002). Self-reported relief, sadness, anger, and guilt significantly increased through the pulling sequence, suggesting that some affective stimuli may be involved in reinforcement or punishment of hair pulling.

Research from our laboratory has found that a number of private events may serve as antecedents to hair pulling. A nonreferred sample of hair pullers reported that physical symptoms (i.e., accelerated heart rate, tingling feelings), bodily sensations (i.e., general tension, sensations localized to specific areas), and general uncomfortableness (i.e., vague urges, inner pressure, or feeling not "just right") preceded a majority of the hair pulling episodes (Wetterneck and Woods, 2005).

The final group of private events that may trigger pulling include cognitions or specific thoughts about pulling. According to Mansueto et al. (1997), specific cognitions about hair pulling are not predominant triggers to pulling for the majority of individuals with TTM, but when these cognitions occur, they resemble obsessive thought patterns similar to those reported by individuals with Body Dysmorphic Disorder and Obsessive-Compulsive Disorder. Although the behavioral function of specific cognitions is unclear, they could evoke rule-governed behavior or could produce a conditioned response whose resultant stimuli function as establishing operations (EO). For example, seeing a coarse or gray hair in the mirror may evoke thoughts that lead to the removal of the hair (e.g., "My eyebrows should be symmetrical" or "Gray hairs are bad, and I need to remove them."). Likewise, a thought such as "This hair is out of place and ugly," could function as a conditioned stimulus that elicits a strong negative emotion (e.g. anxiety), which then serves as an EO for pulling. Norberg, Wetterneck, Woods, & Conelea (in press) examined the relationship between a number of cognitions and hair pulling in a nonreferred sample of hair pullers. The results indicated that dysfunctional beliefs about appearance, thoughts of shame, and fears about being evaluated in a negative manner was positively correlated with hair pulling severity (i.e., greater endorsement of these thoughts correlated with higher levels of hair pulling).

Consequences. A variety of consequences to hair pulling have been described in the phenomenological literature. These can generally be broken down into three areas: tangible reinforcement, automatic positive reinforcement, and automatic negative reinforcement.

Tangible Reinforcement. Mansueto et al. (1997) and Rapp, Miltenberger, Galensky, Ellingson, and Long (1999) state that specific tangible features of the hair may actually reinforce pulling or prepulling behaviors (e.g., stroking hair or otherwise twisting hair). The pulled hair may be rubbed against a person's body, often the face or between fingers, or certain types of hairs, such as coarse hair or those with plump roots may be more appealing to the puller. A number of studies have investigated the amount of time spent on hair pulling and manipulation of the pulled hair (Miltenberger, Long, Rapp, Lumley, and Elliot, 1998; Rapp et al., 1999; Rapp, Dozier, Carr, Patel, & Enloe, 2000). These studies have found that the amount of time spent on the manipulation of pulled hair was equal to or greater than the time spent pulling hair. Rapp et al. (1999) suggested that the manipulation of hair, which consisted of rubbing between the participant's fingers or against her lips, may positively reinforce hair pulling.

Automatic Positive Reinforcement. According to Mansueto et al. (1997), there may be a sensation that is immediately experienced during pulling sequences that positively reinforces hair pulling. These sensations have been labeled as a satisfying feeling, pleasure, desired pain, or other pleasant sensations. Experiencing recurrent pleasurable sensations from pulling can lead to the development of a motivative operation when such sensations are absent. These states of deprivation from such reinforcers then evoke pulling and produce additional sensations.

Automatic Negative Reinforcement. Mansueto et al. (1997) state that hair pulling may also be reinforced by distracting an individual from a stressful event, undesired emotions, or boredom. In this case, hair pulling is negatively reinforced by temporarily removing these aversive private stimuli. Inherent in the definition of TTM is that pulling results in a decrease in antecedent tension, but pulling can also be negatively reinforced by reducing unpleasant sensations at the pulling site (e.g., burning, itching, or tingling). As a result, when these unpleasant experiences or sensations occur, an individual may be more likely to pull to reduce the aversive sensation.

Diefenbach et al. (2002) found feelings such as relief, guilt, sadness, and anger to increase across the course of a hair pulling session. An increase in relief supports the view of hair pulling as a negatively reinforced behavior, however, increases in unpleasant feelings may also have a punishing effect on the behavior. Similar results were found by Woods et al. (2006). This contradiction in consequences (i.e., a behavior that has both negatively reinforcing and punishing properties), may help to explain why any one pulling episode comes to an end. At the initiation of a pulling episode, the negative reinforcers (e.g., tension, anxiety) are strong, and the punishers (e.g., guilt, sadness, anger) are weak. However, as the pulling progresses, the negative reinforcer will weaken and the punisher will strengthen. Eventually, the person will reach a point where the pulling stops as the punishers become stronger than the reinforcers.

Experimental Psychopathology Research on TTM

The aforementioned descriptive research on TTM suggests a number of possible controlling variables. Recent research in our lab has begun to look more closely at these and other areas of psychological functioning to clarify the functional impact of these variables. These findings are reviewed below.

Developmental Changes In Antecedent Experiences of Those with TTM. Phenomenological descriptions of pulling in children and adults, and studies describing how the pulling experience changes over time suggest that pulling, and presumably its controlling variables, are different at the onset of TTM when compared to later in the course of the disorder. Recently, our lab asked 329 individuals with TTM to complete a survey about phenomenological changes in their TTM over the course of the disorder. Results showed approximately 43% did not recall an urge or impulse to pull during initial hair pulling experiences and that the presence of the antecedent urge or impulse to pull hair increased over the course of the disorder for 71% of the respondents. Likewise, antecedent anxiety had increased for 65% of the sample. Other studies have noted that many children with TTM do not report feeling an urge or impulse prior to pulling, nor relief as a result of the pulling (Hanna, 1997; King et al., 1995; Wright & Holmes, 2003). It is unclear at this time whether the children are unable to identify these private events as they occur or if this feeling is initially absent and develops over time.

Focused vs. Automatic Pulling. This change in pulling phenomenology from one in which pulling does not occur in the presence of an urge, impulse, or other unpleasant private event to one in which pulling is done in reaction to such a stimulus points to a potentially important distinction in different types of pulling. Indeed evidence suggests that there are at least two unique patterns of pulling in which those with TTM engage. Focused pulling seems to be preceded a private internal event such as an urge, bodily sensation (i.e., itching or burning), or cognition. In cases of focused pulling, the actual pulling appears to be done to moderate this internal event. In contrast, automatic pulling seems to occur outside of one's awareness, often during sedentary activities (i.e., watching television, reading, or driving) and without any identifiable private (e.g., urge, emotion, specific cognition) antecedent. Early estimates suggest that approximately 75% of pulling episodes are automatic and 25% are focused (Christenson & Mackenzie, 1994).

The existence and utility of the focused and automatic distinction is still debatable, but recent research conducted in our lab validates the distinction. In this research, a 10- item survey designed to measure focused and automatic pulling, was administered to 43 adults with TTM. A factor analysis was conducted using a varimax rotation, and separate focused and automatic factors emerged. Results showed that the two factors were unrelated (r=-.092, p>.05), thus increasing the validity of the focused/automatic construct. In addition, the focused factor, but not the automatic factor was significantly and positively correlated with measures of negative affect, including the BDI (r=.31, p<.05), and the STAI (r=.33, p<.05).

Although the focused/automatic distinction has growing research support, the reader should not mistake these patterns of pulling as substitutes for causal variables. In other words, a person is not aware of their pulling and pulling to reduce unpleasant private stimuli because they are a focused puller. Rather, focused pulling is a label for a particular behavior pattern, which itself needs explained. Possible variables controlling both automatic and focused pulling, and the sequence in which each may develop is described in more detail below in the Contemporary Behavioral Theory section.

Role of Acceptance. As discussed previously, persons with TTM often report the existence of unpleasant private events that precede pulling, and the increasing frequency or intensity of these events predicts greater pulling severity (Begotka, Woods, & Wetterneck, 2004). Unfortunately, research attempting to link specific aversive private events to overt behavioral outcomes often fail to account for the possibility that some individuals enter the situation with histories that are more likely to result in escape or avoidance behavior in the presence of such private events. The tendency to act in accordance with this history in a given situation is known as experiential avoidance. Experiential avoidance and its opposite, experiential acceptance, should be considered when trying to establish functional relationships between aversive private events and actual pulling. Research in our lab has begun to investigate the relationship between the willingness to experience unpleasant private events and the current severity of TTM. 436 participants completed surveys measuring experiential avoidance (i.e., escape or avoidance of unwanted thoughts or emotions) and TTM severity (Begotka et al., 2004). A significant correlation was found between the two constructs indicating that higher experiential avoidance is associated with more severe TTM. The authors concluded that addressing experiential avoidance may be an important focus of treatment with TTM.

Subsequently, Wetterneck and Woods (2005) found that individuals with TTM who reported verbally based anxiety (e.g., worrying) or autonomic arousal prior to pulling have significantly higher TTM severity. However, when this relationship was reexamined using the level of experiential avoidance as a constant, the former relationship was no longer significant. Thus, it appears that experiential avoidance or the response tendency to avoid unpleasant private stimuli, may mediate the relationship between antecedent private events and TTM severity.

Norberg et al. (in press) found similar results when investigating the effects of specific cognitions on TTM severity. In this study, high levels of dysfunctional beliefs about appearance, shameful thoughts, and fears of negative evaluation were significantly related to higher levels of TTM severity. However, these relationships diminished or disappeared when controlling for experiential avoidance. The results of these studies again suggest the need for treatments that increase acceptance of various private events.

With regards to the "types" of pulling, Begotka, Woods, and Wetterneck (2003) found that self-reported levels of focused pulling was significantly positively correlated with experiential avoidance. However, automatic pulling was not related to experiential avoidance, providing further evidence that the two types of pulling may be maintained by two separate behavioral processes.

Summary of the Experimental Psychopathology Research. The early research in TTM has focused on the biological underpinnings and phenomenological experiences of persons with TTM. Little work has been done, however, in terms of experimental psychopathology. Recent work in this area has focused on the importance of understanding both the public and private controlling environmental stimuli, and especially the possibility that relationships between private evens and pulling may be mediated by a third factor, a contextual variable known as psychological acceptance. To further advance the psychopathology work in TTM, we propose the Contemporary Behavior Analytic Model of TTM.

Contemporary Behavior Analytic Model of TTM

The contemporary behavior analytic model seeks to (1) present a theoretical rationale for the development of TTM that can explain both focused and automatic pulling, (2) explain how the two would differ in terms of controlling variables and phenomenology, and (3) provide implications for treatment. A broad summary of the contemporary behavior analytic model of TTM is provided below, followed by a more detailed account in specific areas.

Summary of the Contemporary Behavior Analytic Model of TTM

Early in the development of TTM, underlying biological susceptibility factors (e.g., susceptibility to specific tactile reinforcers, damaged inhibitory regions of the brain) combined with operantly learned grooming behavior, results in the emergence of repeated hair manipulation. While engaging in the repeated stroking or manipulation of hair, the tactile or visual effects of the manipulation reinforces the behavior. As a result of the specific reinforcement, the grooming behavior eventually may be shaped into pulling. The maintaining consequence (e.g., visual or tactile stimulation) could vary by individual but likely occurs out of the verbal awareness.

Situations in which competing stimuli are absent (e.g., boredom) should increase the reinforcing value of any automatic sensory stimulation, and thus pulling should increase in such circumstances (e.g., Lindberg, Iwata, & Kahng, 1999).

However, the individual eventually begins to tact his or her pulling behavior, its antecedents and consequences. For example, when asked by a parent, "What are you doing?" the child, either overtly or covertly, may say "I'm rubbing and pulling my hair out, and now I'm dropping it on the floor." As such, the overt motoric event leads to a private verbal event. Combining this tacting repertoire with an adequately trained relational framing repertoire (Hayes, Strosahl, & Wilson, 1999) may result in these verbal descriptions of the pulling sequence (i.e., antecedent, behavior, consequence) being related to other stimuli. The result of this relating behavior will be a myriad of antecedent and consequent stimuli that can exert functional control over pulling.

In addition, given an adequately developed rule-generating repertoire, verbal rules emerge to describe the effects of pulling. Hayes et al. (1999) refer to this type of rule as tracking. At this point, the tracking rule accurately describes the delivery of the direct contingencies. However, given the tracking rules and the aforementioned relational framing, pulling can quickly begin to occur in situations that would not be predicted by the direct contingencies.

Essentially, the contemporary model of TTM describes how pulling can develop and be maintained by direct contingency control and influenced by language via a transformation of stimulus functions and verbal rules. The contemporary model suggests that nearly all cases of TTM begin as learned grooming behaviors that are highly reinforced through a host of possible direct contingencies. However, as the pulling experience becomes a verbally described event, the types of antecedents and consequences controlling the behavior will expand, and with the emergence of a rule-governed repertoire, some pulling may become rule-controlled as opposed to contingency controlled. To understand how this process occurs and its implications, a discussion of initial pulling and the way in which it becomes a verbal event must occur.

Initial Pulling. Little is known about the variables surrounding the first hair pulling experiences or how this behavior develops into TTM. However, results from developmental research on TTM supports the notion that the disorder may begin with pulling that is controlled by automatic direct contingencies, often out of verbal awareness. In such cases, the reinforcer is automatically delivered, and may represent an early learning history combined with biologically established specific neurostructural anomalies, and/or abnormalities in neurochemical functioning. Indeed, early functional analytic research on children with TTM have shown specific automatic reinforcers to maintain pulling in a limited number of cases (Miltenberger et al., 1998; Rapp et al., 1999; Rapp et al., 2000). The process by which this occurs is probably very similar to the processes involved in the comparative models of TTM.

Given a biological predisposition and an appropriate learning history, a habitual pattern of automatically reinforced behavior develops. Eventually such behavior will come under the control of specific antecedent setting events (e.g., bathrooms or low activity environments and the absence of scolding parents), and will thus be more likely to occur in such situations. For example, riding in a car may occasion pulling simply because there are no competing activities to engage in, making any physical stimulation a more potent reinforcer. As a result, the pulling may be more likely to occur, and as such, the car may eventually develop antecedent control over the pulling.

The Origin of the Urge/Tension/Unpleasant Private Event. At this point, the person may have little awareness the behavior is occurring and may have no urge or tension prior to pulling. Nevertheless, the origin of these antecedent phenomena must be explained. In adults with TTM, the urge appears to serve as one of many antecedents for hair pulling. As stated earlier, not all individuals with TTM experience an urge and it is believed that younger children do not report experiencing this same urge as often as adults (Hanna, 1997; King et al., 1995; Wright & Holmes, 2003). Given these findings, an explanation is needed for what the urge is, how it develops and why it is present for some and not others.

The limited research on individuals with TTM suggests that the origins of the disorder may be related to various neurobiological dysfunctions. If this is true, it is possible that the precursor sensation may represent cortical activation early in the neural circuitry underlying the pulling behavior. Perhaps as a result of completing the neuronal circuit, the sensation may change (e.g., reduce or disappear) after the behavior is performed. A more behavioral interpretation of the urge is that the "urge" is simply the phenomenological result of being deprived of a very powerful reinforcer for a period of time in the presence of specific antecedents with a history of pulling being reinforced in its presence. When deprived of the automatically reinforcing consequences (e.g., activity, scalp stimulation) for a period of time and when in certain antecedent situations, the sensations become more powerful reinforcers, and the organism may experience a visceral sensation (an analogy would be hunger pangs as a result of food deprivation) that intensifies until the reinforcer is delivered. In either case, these processes can occur without explicit awareness (i.e., ability to tact the sensation) of the feeling by the person. Given that the behavior of detecting one's own bodily states (e.g., proprioception) may not fully develop until almost 8 years of age (Sigmundsson, Whiting, & Loftesnes, 2000), it is not surprising that many younger children with TTM report no urge prior to or a relief of tension after the hair pulling.

Developing Awareness of Pulling. In verbally competent humans, it is unlikely that the urge and pulling experiences can occur for long outside of the person's awareness. Because verbal awareness of the pulling can significantly alter the variables controlling the behavior, a brief discussion is necessary of how awareness of pulling and the urge develops. However, we must begin by defining the term "awareness." By "awareness" we refer to accurately emitting a specific verbal behavior (e.g., "I'm pulling, or I've just pulled.") contingent on the pulling. Assuming the child has developed a strong tacting (Skinner, 1957), and deitic relational framing repertoire (e.g., I-YOU; Hayes, Barnes-Holmes, & Roche, 2001), he or she should be able to quickly learn to be "aware" of his or her behavior when consequences (e.g., being told to stop pulling; physical pain, etc.) are delivered contingent on pulling. Although this type of awareness should be quite easy to develop, a number of other variables could influence its development. For example, when pulling, a person with TTM is often engaged in other activities such as watching TV, riding in a car, or reading a book. Engaging in such behaviors, may weaken the tacting repertoire (especially in persons who exhibit deficits in divided attention ability; see Neuropsychological Findings above), and may make "awareness" of specific pulling episodes more difficult. Such an analysis may help explain why "awareness" is lacking during many sedentary activities (e.g., television watching or driving). In such cases, the hands are not engaging in competing behaviors, and the activity itself may be competing with one's self-tacting repertoire.

Awareness of the Urge. Along with an increasing awareness of the pulling, research indicates sensory experiences can be brought into awareness (i.e., can be tacted) with reinforcement or feedback (Cameron, 2001). Therefore it is possible that people develop awareness of the precursor sensation (urge, tension, etc) as a result of the environmental reactions to their hair pulling. For example, as others notice and point out that a girl is pulling her hair, the antecedent sensations may become more salient to her as they predict the onset of pulling. Along with feedback from others, the verbal recognition of antecedent sensations may result from pain or other interoceptive feedback stemming from the act of pulling.

Even though a precursor sensation may exist, it is not necessarily the case that verbal awareness of this sensation will develop. A number of factors may inhibit such processes. First, individuals who do not have an adequate tacting repertoire would not be expected to report urges or tension to pull. Second, specific topographies of pulling that occur without salient physical or social consequences would not be expected to have an associated urge. As such, it is possible that some topographies of pulling may be more associated with a reported urge/tension than others.

In those cases where an urge does develop and enter into awareness, it must be understood that the consequences, which aid in the establishment of urge awareness, will also transfer their stimulus functions to the antecedent urge. For example, if the consequence of the hair pulling is initially negative feedback from the environment, the private antecedent sensation may also begin to acquire a negative function. A child who is berated by a parent for hair pulling may exhibit a transfer of stimulus function from the feelings in the situation (upset by negative feedback) to the experience of the private sensation. In such cases, the private antecedent stimulus comes to develop aversive properties and is established as a potential negative reinforcer. The potential for this process may be even greater for those with a strong history of escaping from or reducing aversive private experiences (i.e., those high in experiential avoidance).

At this point in the model of TTM, pulling is still controlled by direct contingencies, and in verbally competent adolescents and adults, it is likely that the behavior and its antecedent urges can be tacted. Nevertheless, the fact that pulling has now been tacted may have a significant impact on how it is controlled. Next, we turn our attention to the implications of pulling becoming a verbal event. At the heart of this discussion are the effects of relational framing.

The Effects of Relational Framing

The Pervasiveness of the Urge. As described above, the urge or other private antecedents to pulling can be evoked by a variety of directly trained situations. However, the urge to pull can also seemingly be evoked at any time, and may occur in novel situations in which pulling has never been reinforced or punished. To understand how this might work, one needs to undersand the transfer of stimulus function concept. As discussed in earlier chapters, the transfer of stimulus function refers to a stimulus' acquisition of another stimulus' functional properties (e.g., reinforcer, SD, EO, etc) as a result of being framed relationally with that stimulus. The result of framing and subsequent transfer of stimulus function yields an almost unlimited number of stimuli that could evoke, elicit, or reinforce pulling behavior without pulling ever having had occurred in that situation.

Using the transfer of function concept, RFT would predict that stimuli that were verbally related to (e.g., in frames of coordination with) an urge-evoking stimulus would also evoke the urge. For example, in our clinic, we often ask persons with TTM to imagine themselves in a high-risk situation (e.g., driving in a car). This purely verbal activity (imagining) is typically quite effective in producing the reported urge to pull. One must keep in mind that pulling (and the consequences that created the urge to pull, or made that urge aversive) has never occurred in the presence of "imagined driving," but only in the presence of actual driving. As such, one would predict that actual, but not imagined driving, may evoke the urge. However, because the arbitrary stimuli (e.g., words or images) used to describe the driving have been framed relationally with the actual driving event, the stimulus function of the actual event (e.g., evocation of the urge) may transfer to the arbitrary stimuli.

A second way in which relational framing may affect pulling with respect to the urge involves the emergence of the urge itself into relational frames. After awareness of the urge emerges, a verbal stimulus will exist, which has the same functional properties as the actual urge. As such, the verbal stimuli used to describe the urge (e.g., urge, tense, anxiety, bad, unpleasant, etc), will enter into a variety of relational frames (e.g., coordination, opposition, etc.) with other verbal stimuli. If this occurs, in certain contexts, these related stimuli may have the same function as the original words used to describe the urge. For example, words in a frame of coordination with the original urge-describing words (e.g., "unpleasant" or "painful") may produce subtle elicitative effects with respect to pulling. If the antecedent sensation is tacted as "tension," then pulling may be more likely to be evoked in situations whose elements are also in a relational frame with "tension," such as a stressful day at work or a fight with a significant other.

A separate way in which relational framing can impact pulling is through establishing specific stimuli as reinforcing. For example, most individuals would feel pain contingent on pulling a hair, but over time, many people with TTM experience the removal of hair as gratifying or pleasurable. In some cases, this may occur because certain hairs (e.g., gray or coarse hairs) have been tacted as "bad." As a result, specific features of hairs have entered into relational frames with "bad," and as such may obtain the various stimulus functions of "bad" (e.g., becomes a negative reinforcer), such that its removal is "good" (assuming "bad" has been framed in opposition with "good").

By now in the development of TTM, the person has established pulling maintained by direct contingencies, is aware of the behavior and its phenomenology, and in persons with intact relational framing ability, it is likely that this pulling is beginning to be impacted by relationally-derived stimuli, either as an antecedent or consequence variable or both. At this point, rule-governed hair pulling may develop.

Rule-Governed Pulling Emerges. Rule-governed pulling differs functionally, but not necessarily topographically from pulling controlled through direct contingencies. Directly controlled pulling is elicited by a direct or relationally derived antecedent stimulus and reinforced via an automatic consequence (either direct or derived). In contrast, rule-governed pulling is elicited by a contextually-bound rule and maintained by the generalized conditioned reinforcers inherent in rule-following. It is important to understand that the consequences maintaining the automatic pulling (e.g., tactile stimulation, reduction in physiological arousal) are not entirely the same consequences maintaining the tracking rule underlying focused pulling (i.e., following tracking rules is also controlled by generalized conditioned reinforcers for rule following). Because the tracking rule described the actual contingency and is likely to be implemented in similar circumstances, it may often be difficult to differentiate between focused and automatic pulling. However, there are pieces of anecdotal evidence that at least some pulling may be rule governed. This evidence comes from two areas. First, it is sometimes the case that pulling continues despite changes in the contingency that would predict a decrease in pulling. For example, a client is given a substitute tactile stimulus that should decrease the reinforcing value of pulling, but still continues to pull. As another example, you may find that as you increase response effort involved in pulling (making the client wear gloves or mittens, or putting Vaseline on their fingers) it may not result in a decrease in pulling (although it may limit the amount of hair removed). The second line of evidence comes from the fact that pullers will often describe rules such as "I have to pull until I get the right hair," or "I have to get one that feels right," even though there is no discernible stimulus features that might predict the "right" hair or the "right" feeling. Combined, these pieces of evidence suggest that direct reinforcement *may not maintain all instances of hair pulling*. The failure of hair pulling to stop despite changes in the automatic contingencies can be explained by the maintenance of the behavior via rule-control. A substantial amount of research has been conducted to demonstrate that rule-governed behavior will not easily change despite changes in the direct contingencies surrounding the behavior (Galizio, 1979; Hayes, Brownstein, Haas, and Greenway, 1986; Matthews, Shimoff, Catania, and Sagvolden, 1977; Shimoff, Catania, and Matthews, 1981). That some pulling becomes rule-governed may help explain why people with TTM keep pulling in the presence of aversive consequences. The current model offers an interesting paradox. Essentially, the pulling continues when it is still met with strong aversive stimuli (e.g., pain, shame, teasing, etc). Directly reinforced pulling may decrease with such consequences, but rule-governed pulling may continue, if not worsen, in the face of such consequences.

How does Pulling Decrease the "Urge, and Other Unpleasant Private Events?" The mechanism by which pulling actually decreases the urge or other aversive emotional or cognitive experiences is unclear. There may be a number of different processes. First, it may be the case that pulling simply corresponds to termination of movement-related neural activity and the offset of the urge is correlated with the offset of this activity. A second possibility is that the urge reflects a state of sensory deprivation, and after the behavior has produced enough stimulation, the state of deprivation has been eliminated. Similarly for pulling triggered by unpleasant private events, it is quite possible that the pulling functions to distract or offers a behavioral alternative to private verbal activity. In other words, pulling may be reinforced by distracting one from thinking thoughts that produce aversive stimulation.

Automatic vs. Focused Pulling-Revisited

Given the two existing patterns of pulling identified in the psychopathology literature, it would be worthwhile to consider how the possible controlling variables described above map onto the automatic/focused distinction. Given that the focused/automatic pulling distinction hinges primarily on whether or not an individual is aware of (i.e., person can verbally report) pulling (and it's antecedents/consequences), it may be tempting to simply define automatic pulling as contingency-controlled pulling, and focused pulling as verbally mediated.

Unfortunately, this simple distinction is likely inadequate for two primary reasons. First, it is possible that particular stimuli having a functional effect on pulling, have acquired their functions through relational (i.e., verbal) processes (e.g., an image may create the EO of boredom, which then evokes pulling). In this example, verbal processes are in play, but the behavior is still maintained by automatic positive reinforcement. Would this be automatic or focused? It is unclear.

Second, it is possible that a person can be verbally aware of a behavior, but that behavior is not necessarily controlled by verbal rules. For example, just because a person can accurately report that they pull to reduce tension does not mean that the rule plays a functional role in that person's pulling. The pulling still may be maintained by simple negative reinforcement processes rather than rule control.

Given these unclear distinctions, the utility of the automatic/focused distinction should be considered. Our opinion is that despite its potential for confusion, the focused-automatic distinction should be maintained for the time being. There are two reasons for this recommendation. First, we believe the distinction generally points to distinctions between contingency controlled and rule-governed pulling, although grey areas remain. Second, we believe that in the absence of an effective way to measure rule-governed pulling, the focused concept is useful for treatment planning purposes.

Problems with Contemporary Model and Verifiable Hypotheses it Generates

Perhaps the largest problem with the contemporary model is the lack of empirical evidence based on clinical samples of those with TTM. In order to study the hypothesized development of focused and automatic pulling in a naturalistic setting, one would have to follow the progression of the disorder from the onset for a number of years. A second difficulty with the current model involves distinguishing between pulling that is controlled by a rule and pulling that is controlled by direct contingencies. As a general guideline, the behavior can be assumed to be rule governed if there appear to be no directly controlling contingencies, or if the withholding of these stimuli contingent on pulling has a negligible effect on pulling frequency. Although similar logical "by default" assumptions have been made in applied behavior analysis with respect to controlling variables of self injurious behavior (e.g. automatic reinforcement; Oliver, Murphy, Crayton, and Corbett, 1993) such practices are still not desirable, and until a contextually-specific test for rule control is developed, the rule control by default approach will have to suffice.

Despite these concerns, this new model was designed to be testable, and as such does generate a number of verifiable hypotheses. First, a number of developmental predictions stemming from the current model could be evaluated. First, pulling prior to the onset of significant rule-following repertoires should always be controlled by direct contingencies, and as such should be more successfully treated through contingency management procedures than after rule-following repertoires have developed. For example very young children or individuals with profound verbal disabilities should follow this pattern. Second, at the onset of pulling, there should be little demonstrated ability to verbally describe the pulling event, but this description should emerge as the child meets greater consequences for pulling and learns specific words to describe private events, and should emerge rapidly in children for whom pulling begins after the age of 8 (i.e., when interoceptive skills are more formally developed). Third, minimizing the negative social and physical consequences for the pulling at the beginning of the disorder should minimize the severity of the disorder in a verbally competent child. Fourth, it should be the case that all people who demonstrate rule-governed pulling will report an urge or some type of private antecedent sensation, but not all persons reporting some type of private antecedent sensation will demonstrate rule-governed pulling.

In addition to these developmental predictions, the model yields a number of other testable areas for research. A model of how the urge is maintained and increases as a result of relational framing may be tested using stimulus equivalence paradigms. Discriminative stimuli that reliably elicit feelings defined as urges can be trained relationally with neutral stimuli to determine whether a transfer of stimulus function occurs. Other aspects of relational framing (i.e., whether training classes of greater than/less than affect reports of stimulus function severity) could also be studied in this manner.

Analog models of aversive experiences (i.e., exposure to unpleasant noises, mild shocks, the cold pressor task, etc.) could be set up to investigate whether individuals with TTM react differently than those without the disorder. For example, one could introduce a negative reinforcement paradigm in which an aversive experience can be avoided by performing an action (i.e., button press) for a short period of time or endure the aversive experience for a slightly longer initial period with a longer absence in between aversive experiences. One would predict that persons with TTM (especially those with a focused pulling repertoire) may be more likely to choose the immediate elimination of the aversive sound when compared to normal controls.

Treatment Implications from the Contemporary Model

Despite the various limitations of the current model, and the obvious need for further empirical testing, it does suggest a number of treatment recommendations and highlights possible areas of intervention development. During the assessment phase of treatment, a complete functional assessment should be conducted to determine the antecedent conditions that are likely to elicit hair pulling as well as the automatic consequences that may maintain pulling. In addition to assessing these variables, an attempt should be made to evaluate the possibility that rules may be controlling the pulling.

Given a proper functional assessment, treatment can occur on three domains. First, stimulus control procedures can be (and traditionally have been) used to eliminate or alter the various discriminative stimuli that elicit pulling such as the removal of mirrors, tweezers, or shaving hair from the body. Unfortunately, typical stimulus control interventions often ignore key relevant controlling variables resulting from relational framing behavior. As stated earlier, when pulling becomes a verbal event, a vast number of other antecedent stimuli can be established as controlling variables. Thus, the behavioral psychologists efforts to identify such stimuli may be difficult, and such stimuli may not be easily amenable to traditional stimulus control procedures.

The second domain in which treatment can occur is at the level of consequence manipulations. For elimination of both positive and negatively reinforced behavior, extinction is the treatment of choice. However, because pulling is often maintained by automatic reinforcement, and because extinction involves withholding reinforcement contingent on behavior, it is often not a feasible procedure in TTM as the removal of the hair creates functional impairment, and it would be difficult if not impossible to withhold the reinforcer (see Miltenberger, 2001). As such, a procedure such as habit reversal may be useful. Habit reversal tries to teach the client a behavior that competes with pulling, and reinforce the competing behavior with social praise.

Habit reversal may also lead to habituation to aversive antecedent experiences, whether the aversiveness of these experiences were obtained either through direct conditioning or established through relational framing. As such, habit reversal executed faithfully, may address the effects relational framing has on establishing pulling-eliciting antecedents in a way that typical stimulus control procedures cannot. Unfortunately, compliance with habit reversal is often difficult, and the intervention does nothing to directly effect rule-governed pulling.

As such, the third possible domain of treatment involves more directly targeting the effects of pulling becoming a verbal event (e.g., the effects of relational framing and rule governance). As stated previously, with faithful compliance, HRT may alter the derived functions of some stimuli through a habituation process. However, poor compliance with HRT will decrease this treatment effect. Likewise, HRT does not address rule-governed behavior directly.

Some have attempted to deal with the issues relevant to relational framing and rule following via cognitive therapy. Essentially, attempts are made to directly change the rule or alter the frequency of an identified verbal stimulus through cognitive techniques (e.g., cognitive restructuring, thought stopping). However, such attempts ignore the findings, which demonstrate that cognitive events are only related to pulling in the context of an experientially avoidant repertoire. In other words, individuals who tend not to act on unpleasant private experiences (i.e., are experientially accepting) are less likely to be impacted by verbal events than those who are more experientially avoidant (i.e., engage in escape or avoidance behavior contingent on such stimuli). As such, it appears that problems derive from relational framing or rule-governed behavior are better addressed by an intervention that attempt to establish an experientially accepting and non-rule governed context with respect to private events.

Given that the Contemporary Behavior Analytic Model would predict that pulling in older adolescents and adults is a mix of directly controlled and rule-controlled behavior, with the stimulus-altering effects of relational framing playing a relevant role in both types, it may be useful to combine interventions designed to address as many relevant controlling variables as possible. As such, it may make sense to combine stimulus control procedures with habit reversal. Functionally, this combination alone should address the directly controlled pulling, and may even begin to disrupt some stimulus effects of relational framing if treatment compliance is consistent. The addition of another intervention, such as Acceptance and Commitment Therapy (ACT; Hayes, Strosahl, & Wilson, 1999) may be useful in further decreasing the negative stimulus functions created through relational framing, and may be useful in decreasing the rule-governed behavior.

Two studies from our research laboratory have shown good success in significantly reducing hair pulling by combining these treatment elements. The first study employed two separate three-subject multiple baseline across subjects design and a seven session manual combining ACT and Habit Reversal to treat hair pulling (Twohig & Woods, 2004). Five of the six participants demonstrated significant reductions in self-reported hair pulling and independent social validity ratings of pre to post photographs showed significant improvement of damage produced by pulling. Furthermore, the authors showed that as the subjects showed a greater decrease in a measure of experiential avoidance, they showed a greater decrease in pulling severity across time.

The second study was a randomized controlled trial comparing a ten session ACT and Habit Reversal treatment package to a wait-list control group for adults with TTM (Woods, Wetterneck, & Flessner, 2006). Results indicate a significant improvement in reducing hair pulling in the treatment group over that of the control condition. Also, there was a significant correlation between a reduction in TTM severity across time and a reduction in self-reported experiential avoidance. This finding is the first indicator that procedures associated with ACT may be beneficial in reducing hair pulling in combination with behavioral techniques such as Habit Reversal.

Summary

The current chapter has provided one possible behavioral model of TTM and attempts were made to link it to treatment options. Of course, the model and proposed mechanisms of change underlying treatment may prove to be wholly correct, wholly incorrect, or somewhere in between. Only empirical testing of the model, its derived treatments, and the underlying mechanism of change will answer these questions. Although the model is admittedly speculative, it is testable, and as such offers a starting point.

References

American Psychiatric Association. (2000). *Diagnostic and statistical manual of mental disorders* (4th ed. Text Revision). Washington, DC: Author.

Begotka, A. M., Woods, D. W., & Wetterneck, C. T. (2003, November). The relationship between experiential avoidance and the severity of trichotillomania in a nonreferred sample. In M. E. Franklin & N. J. Keuthen (Co-Chairs). *New Developments in Trichotillomania Research*. Symposium presented at the 37th Annual Convention of the Association for Advancement of Behavior Therapy. Boston, MA.

Begotka, A. M., Woods, D. W., & Wetterneck, C. T. (2004). The relationship between experiential avoidance and the severity of Trichotillomania in a nonreferred sample. *Journal of Behavior Therapy and Experimental Psychiatry, 35*, 17-24.

Bordnick, P. S., Thyer, B. A., & Ritchie, B. W. (1994). Feather picking disorder and trichotillomania: An avian model of human psychopathology. *Journal of Behavior Therapy and Experimental Psychiatry, 25*, 189-196.

Breiter, H. C., Rauch, S. L., Kwong, K. K., Baker, J. R., Weisskoff, R. M., Kennedy, D. N., et al (1996). Functional magnetic resonance imaging of symptom provocation in obsessive-compulsive disorder. *Archives of General Psychiatry, 53,* 595-606.

Cameron, O. G. (2001). Interoception: The inside story- A model for psychosomatic process. *Psychosomatic Medicine, 63,* 697-710.

Christenson, G. A., Crow, S. J., MacKenzie, T. B., et al. (1994, May). *A placebo controlled double-blind study of naltrexone for trichotillomania.* Paper presented at the 150th Annual Meeting of the American Psychiatric Association. Philadelphia, PA.

Christenson, G. A., & Mackenzie, T. B. (1994). Trichotillomania. In M. Hersen & R. T. Ammerman (Eds.), *Handbook of prescriptive treatment for adults* (pp.217-235). New York, NY: Plenum Press.

Christenson, G. A., Mackenzie, T. B., & Mitchell, J. (1994). Adult men and women with trichotillomania: a comparison of male and female characteristics. *Psychosomatics, 35,* 365-370.

Christenson, G. A., Pyle, R. L., & Mitchell, J. E. (1991). Estimated lifetime prevalence of trichotillomania in college students. *Journal of Clinical Psychology, 52,* 415-417.

Diefenbach, G. J., Mouton-Odum, S., & Stanley, M. A. (2002). Affective correlates of trichotillomania. *Behaviour Research and Therapy, 40,* 1305-1315.

Frecska, E., & Arato, M. (2002). Opiate sensitivity test in patients with stereotypic movement disorder and trichotillomania. *Progress in Neuro-Psychopharmacology & Biological Psychiatry, 26,* 909-912.

Friman, P. C. (1992). Letter to the Editor. *American Journal of Psychiatry, 149,* 284.

Galizio, M. (1979). Contingency-shaped and rule-governed behavior: Instructional control and human loss avoidance. *Journal of the Experimental Analysis of Behavior, 31,* 53-70.

Graber, J., & Arndt, W. B. (1993). Trichotillomania. *Comprehensive Psychiatry, 34,* 340-346.

Greer, J. M., & Capecchi, M. R. (2002). Hoxb8 is required for normal grooming behavior in mice. *Neuron, 33,* 23-34.

Hanna, G. L. (1997). Trichotillomania and related disorders in children and adolescents. *Child Psychiatry and Human Development, 27,* 255-268.

Hayes, S. C., Barnes-Holmes, D., & Roche, B. (2001). *Relational frame theory: A post-Skinnerian account of human language and cognition.* New York: Kluwer Academic/Plenum Publishers.

Hayes, S. C., Brownstein, A. J., Haas, J. R., & Greenway, D. E. (1986). Instructions, multiples schedules, and extinction: Distinguishing rule-governed from schedule controlled behavior. *Journal of the Experimental Analysis of Behavior, 46,* 137-147.

Hayes, S. C., Strosahl, K. D., & Wilson, K. G. (1999). *Acceptance and commitment therapy: An experiential approach to behavior change.* New York: Guilford Press.

Jenike, M. A., Breiter, H. C., Baer, L., Kennedy, D. N., Savage, C. R., Olivares, M. J., et al. (1996). Cerebral structural abnormalities in obsessive-compulsive disorder: A qualitative morphometric magnetic resonance imaging study. *Archives of General Psychiatry, 53,* 625-632.

King, R.A., Scahill, L., Vitulano, L. A., Schwab-Stone, M., Tercyak, K. P., & Riddle, M. A. (1995). Childhood trichotillomania: Clinical phenomenology, comorbidity, and family genetics. *Journal of the American Academy of Child and Adolescent Psychiatry, 34,* 1451-1459.

Keuthen, N. J., Savage, C. L., O'Sullivan, R. L., Brown, H. D., Shera, D. M., Cyr, P., et al. (1996). Neuropsychological functioning in trichotillomania. *Biological Psychiatry, 39,* 747-749.

Lenane, M. C., Swedo, S. E., Rapoport, J. L., Leonard, H., Sceery, W., & Guroff, J. J. (1992). Rates of obsessive compulsive disorder in first degree relatives of patients with trichotillomania: A research note. *Journal of Child Psychiatry, 33,* 925-933.

Lindberg, J. S., Iwata, B. A., & Kahng, S. (1999). On the relation between object manipulation and stereotypic self-injurious behavior. *Journal of Applied Behavior Analysis, 32,* 51-62.

Mansueto, C. S., Townsley-Stemberger, R. M., McCombs-Thomas, A., & Goldfinger-Golomb, R. (1997). Trichotillomania: A comprehensive behavioral model. *Clinical Psychology Review, 17,* 567-577.

Matthews, B. A., Shimoff, E., Catania, A. C., & Sagvolden, T. (1977). Uninstructed human responding: Sensitivity to ratio and interval contingencies. *Journal of the Experimental Analysis of Behavior, 27,* 453-467.

McGrath, M. J., Campbell, K. M., & Burton, F. H. (1999). The role of cognitive and affective processing in a transgenic mouse model of cortical-limbic neuropotentiated compulsive behavior. *Behavioral Neuroscience, 113,* 1249-1256.

Michael, J. (1993). "Establishing operations." Response. *Behavior Analyst, 16,* 229-236.

Miltenberger, R. G. (2001). Behavior Modification: Principles and Procedures (2nd Edition). Belmond, CA: Wadsworth Publishing.

Miltenberger, R. G., Long, E. S., Rapp, J. T., Lumley, V., & Elliot, A. J. (1998). Evaluating the function of hair pulling: A preliminary investigation. *Behavior Therapy, 29,* 211-219.

Miltenberger, R. G., Rapp, J. T., & Long, E. S. (2001). Characteristics of Trichotillomania. In D. W. Woods & R. G. Miltenberger (Eds.), *Tic Disorders, trichotillomania, and other repetitive behavior disorders* (pp. 133-150). New York: Kluwer Academic Publishers.

Moon-Fanelli, A. A., Dodman, N. H., & O'Sullivan, R. L. (1999). Veterinary models of compulsive self-grooming: Parallels with trichotillomania. In D. J. Stein, G. A. Christenson, & E. Hollander (Eds.), *Trichotillomania* (pp. 63-92). Washington, DC: American Psychiatric Press.

Norberg, M. M., Wetterneck, C. T., Woods, D. W., & Conelea, C. A. (in press). Examination of the mediating role of psychological acceptance in relationships between cognitions and the severity of chronic hairpulling. *Behavior Modification.*

Oliver, C., Murphy, G. H., Crayton, L., & Corbett, J. A. (1993). Self-injurious behavior in Rett syndrome: Interactions between features of Rett syndrome and operant conditioning. *Journal of Autism and Developmental Disorders, 23,* 91-109.

Rapp, J. T., Dozier, C. L., Carr, J. E., Patel, M. R., & Enloe, K. A. (2000). Functional analysis of hair manipulation: A replication and extension. *Behavioral Interventions, 15,* 121-133.

Rapp, J. T., Miltenberger, R. G., Galensky, T. L., Ellingson, S. A., & Long, E. S. (1999). A functional analysis of hair pulling. *Journal of Applied Behavior Analysis, 32,* 329-337.

Rettew, D. C., Cheslow, D. L., Rapoport, J. L., Leonard, H. L., Lenane, M. C., Black, B., et al. (1991). Neuropsychological test performance in trichotillomania: A further link with obsessive-compulsive disorder. *Journal of Anxiety Disorders, 5,* 225-235.

Ristvedt, S. L., & Christenson, G. A. (1996). The use of pharmacologic pain sensitization in the treatment of repetitive hair pulling. *Behavior Research and Therapy, 34,* 647-648.

Robinson, D., Wu, H., Munne, R. A., Ashtari, M., Alvin, J. M., Bilder, R. M., et al. (1995). Reduced caudate nucleus volume in obsessive-compulsive disorder. *Archives of General Psychiatry, 52,* 393-398.

Rothbaum, B., Shaw, L., Morris, R., & Ninan, P. (1993). Prevalence of trichotillomania in a college freshman population (Letter). *Journal of Clinical Psychiatry, 54,* 72.

Schlosser, S., Black, D. W., Blum, N., & Goldstein, R. B. (1994). The demography, phenomenology, and family history of 22 persons with compulsive hair pulling. *Annals of Clinical Psychiatry, 6,* 147-152.

Shimoff, E., Catania, A. C., & Matthews, B. A. (1981). Uninstrcuted human responding: Sensitivity of low rate performance to schedule contingencies. *Journal of the Experimental Analysis of Behavior, 36,* 207-220.

Sigmundsson, H., Whiting, H. T. A., & Loftesnes, J. M. (2000). Development of proprioceptive sensitivity. *Experimental Brain Research, 135,* 348-352.

Skinner, B. F. (1957). *Verbal Behavior.* New York, NY: Appleton-Century-Crofts, Inc.

Stanley, M. A., Hannay, H. J., & Breckenridge, J. K. (1997). The neuropsychology of trichotillomania. *Journal of Anxiety Disorders, 11,* 473-488.

Stein, D. J., Christenson, G. A., & Hollander, E. (1999). Trichotillomania. Washington, DC: American Psychiatric Press.

Stein, D. J., & Hollander, E. (1992). Low-dose pimozide augmentation of serotonin reuptake blockers in the treatment of trichotillomania. *Journal of Clinical Psychiatry, 53,* 123-126.

Stein, D. J., van Heerden, B., Hugo, C., van Kradenburg, J., Warwick, J., Zungu-Dirwayi, N., et al. (2002). Functional brain imaging and pharmacotherapy in trichotillomania single photon emission computed tomography before and after treatment with the selective serotonin reuptake inhibitor citalopram. *Progress in Neuro-Psychopharmacology & Biological Psychiatry, 26,* 885-890.

Stemberger, R. M. T., Thomas, A. M., Mansueto, C. S., & Carter, J. G. (2000). Personal toll of trichotillomania: Behavioral and interpersonal sequelae. *Journal of Anxiety Disorders, 14,* 97-104.

Swedo, S. E., & Leonard, H. L. (1992). Trichotillomania an obsessive compulsive spectrum disorder. *Psychiatric Clinics of North America, 15,* 777-791.

Swedo, S. E., Leonard, H. L., Rapoport, J. L., Lenane, M. C., Goldberger, E. L., & Cheslow, D. L. (1989). A double-blind comparison of clomipramine and despramine in the treatment of trichotillomania (hair pulling). *New England Journal of Medicine, 321,* 497-501.

Swedo, S. E., Rapoport, J. L., Loenard, H. L., & Schapiro, M. B. (1991). Regional cerebral glucose metabolism of women with trichotillomania. *Archives of General Psychiatry, 48,* 828-833.

Twohig, M. P., & Woods, D. W. (2004). A preliminary investigation of acceptance and commitment therapy as a treatment for trichotillomania. *Behavior Therapy, 35,* 803-820.

Wetterneck, C. T., & Woods, D. W. (2005). *Hair pulling antecedents in trichotillomania: Their relationship with experiential avoidance.* Manuscript submitted for publication.

Winchel, R. M. (1992). Trichotillomania: Presentations and treatment. *Psychiatric Annals, 22,* 84-89.

Woods, D. W., Flessner, C. A., Franklin, M. E., Keuthen, N. J., Goodwin, R. D., Stein, D. J., Walther, M. R., & TLC-SAB. (2006). The trichotillomania impact project (TIP): Exploring phenomenology, functional impairment, and treatment utilization. *Journal of Clinical Psychiatry, 67,* 1877-1888.

Woods, D. W., & Miltenberger, R. G. (1996). Are persons with nervous habits nervous? A preliminary examination of habit function in a nonreferred population. *Journal of Applied Behavior Analysis, 29,* 259-261.

Woods, D. W., Miltenberger, R. G., & Flach, A. D. (1996). Habits, tics, and stuttering: Prevalence and relation to anxiety and somatic awareness. *Behavior Modification, 20,* 216-225.

Woods, D. W., Wetterneck, C. T., & Flessner, C. A. (2006). A controlled evaluation of acceptance and commitment therapy plus habit reversal as a treatment for trichotillomania. *Behaviour Research and Therapy, 44,* 639-656.

Wright, H. H., & Holmes, G. R. (2003). Trichotillomania (hair pulling) in toddlers. *Psychological Reports, 92,* 228-230.

Chapter 7

An Integrative Model of Depression Using Modern Behavioral Principles

**Jonathan W. Kanter, Sara J. Landes, Andrew M. Busch,
Laura C. Rusch, David E. Baruch, & Rachel C. Manos**
University of Wisconsin, Milwaukee

The behavioral approach to depression presented in this chapter represents an extension of traditional behavioral models in terms of derived relational responding and resulting transformations of function, experiential avoidance, and several other factors. These extensions address several weaknesses of the traditional model which largely led to its stagnation for several decades, and hopefully will spur a renewal of behavior analytic research on this topic. Before we present the current model, we review the diagnostic categories of depression, relevant biological and psychological findings, and the traditional behavioral and cognitive-behavioral models. We will not address mania or depressive episodes that occur in the context of bipolar disorders in this chapter, as they require a different model than the one presented herein.

Diagnostic Categories

Before discussing the diagnostic categories of depression as defined by the Diagnostic and Statistical Manual of Mental Disorders (DSM-IV-TR; American Psychiatric Association, 2000), a brief caveat is in order. While clinical behavior analysts are careful to avoid reifying a descriptive label, such as Major Depressive Disorder, into a thing and using it to explain the symptoms it describes, we are interested in the patterns of behavior that occasion usage of the label and the pragmatic utility of such labeling (Follette & Houts, 1996; Friman, Hayes, & Wilson, 1998; Hayes & Follette, 1992). Our assumption is that the label is pragmatically useful for communication purposes, although it does not refer to a thing nor does it have an essential composition.

DSM-IV-TR parses depression into various subcategories, each with similar and overlapping characteristics. The two primary depressive disorders are Major Depressive Disorder and Dysthymic Disorder. To be diagnosed with current Major Depressive Disorder (MDD) an individual must be in a Major Depressive Episode (MDE). To meet criteria for an MDE, an individual must present with at least five of the following nine symptoms: depressed mood; anhedonia (markedly diminished interest or pleasure in all, or almost all, activities); significant increase or decrease in weight or appetite; insomnia or hypersomnia; psychomotor agitation or retardation; fatigue or loss of energy; feelings of worthlessness or inappropriate guilt; impaired concentration or ability to make decisions; and recurrent thoughts of death, recurrent suicidal ideation, or a suicide plan or attempt. At least one of the symptoms must be depressed mood or anhedonia. In addition, the symptoms must co-occur during the same two-week period, be present most of the day, nearly every day (except for thoughts of death or suicidal ideation, which simply can be recurrent, or a suicide plan or attempt, which need not occur more than once), and cause clinically significant distress or impairment in social, occupational, or other important areas of functioning.

As the symptom list suggests, the symptom profiles of specific individuals with MDD vary markedly (e.g., Líndal & Stefánsson, 1991). The "vegetative" symptoms of depression (decreased appetite and insomnia) tend to correlate positively with depression severity (Buchwald & Rudick-Davis, 1993), while the "reversed vegetative" symptoms (increased appetite and hypersomnia) are less common and do not correlate with severity. Similarly, psychomotor retardation is more common while agitation is less common, but both may be demonstrated by the same individual at different times. In general, past behavioral accounts (e.g., Lewinsohn, 1974) have tended to focus on symptoms that can be described as reductions in behavioral frequency or flexibility, and have not addressed the substantial heterogeneity of symptom profiles and seemingly contradictory presentations where some behaviors are increasing and some are decreasing.

A diagnosis of Dysthymic Disorder (DD) requires depressed mood most of the day, more days than not, for at least two years, and at least two of the following six symptoms: poor appetite or overeating, insomnia or hypersomnia, low energy or fatigue, low self-esteem, poor concentration or difficulty making decisions, and feelings of hopelessness. A quick comparison shows that the symptoms for DD and MDD are quite similar. Both include depressed mood, appetite changes, sleep changes, fatigue or loss of energy, and poor concentration or difficulty making decisions. DD includes low self-esteem while MDD includes "feelings of worthlessness or inappropriate guilt;" upon inspection these appear to be referring to quite similar conditions. Finally, DD includes "feelings of hopelessness" which is not included in the symptom list for MDD although it is considered indicative of MDD's "depressed mood" criterion. The primary point is that the two symptom lists are similar and the two disorders can only be reliably distinguished by the number of symptoms necessary for the diagnosis and chronicity.

In addition to DD, there are an increasing number of diagnostic categories of depressive disorders or problems involving sad or irritable affect. In fact, Appendix B of DSM-IV-TR lists seventeen proposed disorders for further study, six of which deal with disorders of mood: Postpsychotic Depressive Disorder of Schizophrenia, Premenstrual Dysphoric Disorder, Minor Depressive Disorder, Recurrent Brief Depressive Disorder, Mixed Anxiety-Depressive Disorder, and Depressive Personality Disorder (DPD). The latter four have several criteria that overlap with Major

Depressive Disorder, differing only in duration or number of symptoms. While a quick glance at these subcategories suggests that these indeed may be different disorders with different etiologies and corresponding treatment implications, a behavior analytic view holds that the current proliferation of depressive disorders is largely unnecessary. Therefore, a behavioral model of depression must account not for several distinct disorders but a phenomenon of depression with great variability in time course, symptom severity, and correlated conditions.

Epidemiology

It has been estimated that up to 25 million people in the United States meet criteria for some type of depressive disorder (Keller, 1994). Depressive disorders also result in considerable financial expenditure including time spent away from the workplace and an increase in health care costs. Estimates of the economic cost of depressive disorders in the United States range between 2.7 to 5.6 billion dollars annually in service provision (Rost, Zhang, Fortney, Smith, & Smith, 1998; see also McCombs, 1993) and rises to 44 billion dollars annually based on larger indices that include work absenteeism, treatment costs, and other factors (Antonuccio, Thomas, & Danton, 1997).

Prevalence rates for Major Depressive Disorder differ by gender, with rates for women approximately double those for men, and this gender difference appears to emerge in early adolescence (Hammen & Rudolph, 2003). Contrary to previous belief, it is now widely recognized that adolescents manifest and report problems with depression similar to those of adults and in high enough numbers to be a significant mental health problem (e.g., Kovacs & Goldston, 1991). In addition, rates of adolescent MDD have been rising over the past several decades and these changes are not generally attributed to methodological issues; adolescents appear to be experiencing more depression than in the past (Kessler, 2002). In adulthood, point prevalence estimates range from 5-9% in women and 2-3% in men, and the lifetime prevalence of MDD may be as high as 25% in women and 12% in men (American Psychiatric Association, 2000).

Etiology

Biology and Biological Vulnerability

The role of biological vulnerabilities to depression cannot be dismissed, although most agree that environmental variables are equally-to-more important. Family, twin, and adoption studies produce heritability estimates ranging from 20-45% for milder depression and possibly higher for moderate to severe depression (Wallace, Schneider, & McGuffin, 2002). Biologists generally believe depression is likely a product of multiple genes and a complex gene-environment interaction. Evidence for inherited biological systems, either at the neurochemical or neuroanatomical level, is lacking. In addition, the validity of heritability estimates has been challenged for many years by researchers and theorists from a variety of perspectives (Ceci & Williams, 1999), with the strong suggestion that the estimates are biased towards higher probability of heritability (e.g., Marshall & Pettitt, 1985). Behavioral theorists have questioned the notion of heritability as a tautology that leads to the banal conclusion that all behavior is ultimately based in the genotype and brain (Hayes, 1998; Turkheimer, 1998), which is a given but irrelevant conclusion if the goal of science is the influence of behavior. However, the identification of depression susceptibility genes and the development of biological treatments based on these findings—if that potentiality becomes reality at some point in the future—certainly will bolster the relevance of such genetic research for preventing and treating depression (Wallace et al., 2002). More sophisticated behavioral genetic models recently have been advanced that focus on the interaction between stressful life events and serotonin transporter gene alleles, which have been implicated in antidepressant response for some patients (Caspi, Sugden, Moffitt, Taylor, Craig, Harrington et al., 2003).

The neurochemistry of depression is a complex and evolving field. Early biogenic amine theories of depression that postulated either a serotonin or norepinephrine deficiency, or a problem with the balance of these neurotransmitters, were the cause of depression, have not been supported (Thase, Jindal, & Howland, 2002). Most depressed individuals evidence no such deficiencies, although subgroups do. The timing of antidepressant action on these neurotransmitter levels does not fit the quick response to drugs that patients often exhibit (reviewed in Valenstein, 1998). However, this early theory is still propagated by the mainstream media and pharmaceutical industry, with graphics in television advertisements depicting a reduced flow of cartoon-ish serotonin bubbles in the synaptic cleft, unable to reach their receptor sites. Later theories that attempt to correct these problems also have produced mixed results (Valenstein, 1998). Current research suggests that noradrenergic, serotoninergic, and dopaminergic pathways may all play a role in depression (Thase et al., 2002). Norepinephrine and serotonin are mostly found in neurons with cell bodies located in the pons, but dopaminergic neurons are found in several brain regions. Furthermore, these neurons collectively have very broad and diffuse distributions to multiple brain regions.

Current theories acknowledge the complexity of the neurochemical, neuroendocrine, neurophysiological, and structural systems that participate in depressed behavior. There are mixed findings of structural and functional abnormalities in several brain regions, including the prefrontal cortex (PFC), anterior cingulate cortex, hippocampus, and amygdala (Davidson, Pizzagalli, Nitschke, & Putnam, 2002). These findings are quite variable and only a minority of depressed individuals demonstrates the full package of deficits, leading researchers to conclude that depression refers to a heterogeneous group of disorders. There are no longitudinal studies showing that brain abnormalities precede depression so it is not known if they are a cause, correlate, or consequence of depression (Davidson et al., 2002).

Neuroscience and Personality

As imaging and other measurement techniques have increased in sophistication, affective neuroscientists have become interested in the neurobiological basis of personality dimensions, with increasing emphasis on the prefrontal cortex (PFC) as the focal structure in personality dimensions related to depression. In particular, Gray (1972, 1981) posited two broad personality dimensions underlying learning and affect, which have come to be known as the *behavioral inhibition system* (BIS) and *behavioral activation system* (BAS). The BAS in particular is said to be sensitive to reward (positive reinforcement), organizes approach and goal directed behavior, and is responsible for the experience of positive emotions such as hope and happiness (Carver & White, 1994). Regarding depression, research has found that hypoactivation of the left PFC characterizes individuals with lower self-reported BAS sensitivity (Coan & Allen, 2003; Harmon-Jones & Allen, 1997; Sutton & Davidson, 1997). BAS deficits also have been found to correlate with current depression (Kasch, Rottenberg, Arnow, & Gotlib, 2002; Pinto-Meza, Caseras, Soler, Puigdemont, Perez, & Torrubia, 2006) and predict the course of depression (Kasch et al., 2002; McFarland, Shankman, Tenke, Bruder, & Klein, 2006). Furthermore, depression has been repeatedly found to correlate with hypoactivation of the left PFC (Davidson et al., 2002; Henriques & Davidson, 1991; Must, Szabó, Bódi, Szász, Janka, & Kéri, 2006). Finally, two well-used neuropsychological tasks—the Wisconsin Card Sort (Heaton, Chelune, Talley, Kay, & Curtiss, 1993) and the Iowa Gambling Task (Bechara, Damasio, Damasio, & Anderson, 1994)—also activate the PFC (with varying degrees of specificity within the PFC) and show consistent deficits in depression. Both of these tasks assess executive functioning when confronted with reinforcement and punishment and changes in schedules of reinforcement and punishment.

Current theories of the functional neural circuitry of depression also include (among many brain regions not discussed herein) the anterior cingulate cortex (ACC) and the basal ganglia (BG), both of which appear to be involved in sensitivity and reaction to reinforcement, especially response-contingent reinforcement. Thus, a functional neuroanatomical model of depression is growing that involves a complex neural circuitry of sensitivity and responding to reinforcement. Given that a defining symptom of MDD, anhedonia, may be characterized as a diminished capacity to experience rewards, this model may have broad implications. As we discuss below, this functional neuroanatomical model is completely consistent with the traditional behavioral model of depression, which also highlights deficits in positive reinforcement, but the behavioral model locates the problem in environmental contingencies rather than in an underlying personality or neuroanatomical defect.

An alternate affective neuroscience model of depression has been presented by Thase and colleagues (2002). They review research findings which implicate depression as a dysregulation of the body's stress response system (the limbic-hypothalamic-pituitary-adrenal, or HPA axis) for a significant number of individuals. Research indicates that individuals with higher stress reactivity will be more likely to withdraw in stressful situations, and stress reactivity has a heritable component (Sloman, Gilbert, & Hasey, 2003). The HPA axis findings parallel conclusions from personality/temperament research indicating a broad temperamental dimension that works in concert with the BAS- the BIS (Gray, 1994). The BIS is sensitive to punishment, organizes withdrawal behavior, may be hyperactive in depression and anxiety disorders, and may be partially localized in the left PFC (Gray, 1972, 1981). Alternately, a similar construct has been labeled *negative affectivity*, and self-report assessments of this construct suggest that it may underlie both anxiety and depressive disorders (Mineka, Watson, & Clark, 1998). Thus, some cases of depression may be a function of HPA axis dysfunction, especially in chronic cases with many years of living with stress and anxiety. It is important to note that while HPA axis dysfunction may be implicated in chronic depression, HPA axis dysfunction is not understood as a cause of depression. Environmental determinants that produce HPA axis dysfunction are still at play and would need to be identified for a full behavioral analysis of this model.

Psychological Findings

Thousands of research studies on the psychopathology of depression have been conducted. We do not attempt to review them here. Instead, we briefly summarize four bodies of research that have particular relevance to behavioral models of depression: antecedent environmental events, interpersonal problems, cognitive vulnerability, and avoidance and anxiety.

Antecedent environmental events. It is well known that both major stressful life events (e.g., death, divorce, loss of job) and the accrual of multiple chronic mild stressors (e.g., work-related stress, homemaking demands, financial trouble) predict the onset, maintenance, and relapse of depressive episodes (Billings & Moos, 1984; Kessler, 1997; Mazure, 1998; Monroe & Depue, 1991; Paykel, 1982). Likewise, it is common for clients with chronic depression to report childhood histories of prolonged and inescapable traumatic experiences (Bifulco, Brown, & Adler, 1991; Levitan, Parikh, Lesage, Hegadoren, Adams, Kennedy et al., 1998; Sedney & Brooks, 1984). It is important to keep in mind that while the evidence clearly establishes stressful life events as precursors to depression, the relationship is reciprocal in that depressed behavior also elicits and exacerbates stressful life events (Kessler, 1997). This overwhelming evidence for the role of stressful life events in depression became the foundation of the traditional behavioral model (Lewinsohn, 1974) that posited that such events are best viewed as losses of major sources of positive reinforcement. Similarly, Seligman's early learned helplessness model (Overmier & Seligman, 1967; Seligman, 1975) emphasized the role of punishment in depression. These models will be described in more detail below.

Interpersonal problems. Research is also clear that interpersonal problems, a subset of antecedent environmental events, predict and characterize depression (Barnett & Gotlib, 1988). Loss of, and low, social support have been found to increase risk for depression (Brown & Harris, 1978; Monroe & Depue, 1991). Depressed individuals engage in fewer social activities, fewer positive social interactions, and display deficits in social skills (Libet & Lewinsohn, 1973). Intimate relationships maintained by depressed individuals are poor compared to those of non-depressed controls (Zlotnick, Kohn, Keitner, & Della Grotta, 2000), and problems with intimate relationships are maintained after the depression remits (Hammen & Brennan, 2002). As with antecedent environmental events, the causal relationship between interpersonal problems and depression is reciprocal (Coyne, 1976), as the evidence is also clear that depression influences social support (Gotlib & Lee, 1989; Joiner & Metalsky, 2001) and psychosocial functioning in general (Barnett & Gotlib, 1988).

Cognitive vulnerability. While interpersonal problems and environmental stressors often precipitate depression, many depressed individuals are not able to clearly identify either acute or chronic problems prior to the onset of a depressive episode. In some of these instances the issue may be lack of a repertoire for identifying and describing problems, but in some instances it appears that depression occurs in the absence of objectively-defined problems, at least as typically defined. Similarly, not all individuals who experience depressogenic antecedent events become depressed. Both lines of evidence have led cognitive researchers to claim that the true source of depression is the nature of an individual's interpretation of events, rather than the events themselves. Two cognitive theories have been advanced. Both theories incorporate a diathesis-stress model that acknowledges the importance of negative life events in triggering depression, but also focuses on cognitive vulnerabilities that must be present for a negative life event to be interpreted in a depressogenic manner and have a detrimental effect.

According to Beck's (1967; Beck, Rush, Shaw, & Emery, 1979; Clark, Beck, & Alford, 1999) theory of depression, during childhood depressed individuals develop a negative schema as a result of negative events, such as a loss of a parent, peer rejection, or having a depressed family member. This negative schema is activated when the individual encounters a negative event and influences information processing in a negative and biased fashion. The negative bias is described as the cognitive triad—a negative view of the world (the impossibility of overcoming current obstacles), self (personal deficiency), and future (hopelessness that things will change). These biases are expressed in terms of automatic thoughts in specific situations that result in depression and other negative feelings. The construct of self-esteem incorporates the negative view of self important to the cognitive model, and low self-esteem repeatedly been found to be a strong correlate of depression (Bernet, Ingram, & Johnson, 1993).

Similarly, the hopelessness theory of depression (Abramson, Metalsky, & Alloy, 1989) emphasizes the importance of a specific negative inferential style for cause (e.g., "I did poorly on the test because I am dumb."), self (e.g., "If I do not succeed in school, I am worthless."), and consequence (e.g., "Because I am a bad test taker, I will never get into graduate school.") which contributes to a sense of hopelessness and depression. The vast majority of research on the hopelessness theory of depression has focused on a negative inferential style for cause, also referred to as negative attributional style. Compared to Beck's model, the hopelessness theory of depression has less scope (the authors only claim it applies to a subset of depressed individuals) and involves fewer hypothetical constructs (the construct of the depressogenic schemas is replaced by cognitive style). However, only Beck's model was developed into a set of treatment techniques and interventions (described below).

Beck and other cognitive researchers (reviewed in Clark et al., 1999) interpret a vast body of research as supportive of their cognitive model of depression, but there have been many active and vocal critics of the model. In general, an extremely large and unquestionable body of research establishes the presence of negative cognitive content during depression; the problem has been difficulty establishing the causal role of cognitive variables independent of, and in advance of, depressive episodes in longitudinal research (Ingram, Miranda, & Segal, 1998). Unlike research on antecedent environmental events and interpersonal problems, which establishes reciprocal causal relationships, researchers of cognitive content have failed to demonstrate that the putative causal factors are present in those vulnerable to depression prior to an episode of depression. Recent revisions of cognitive theory have advanced the notion that cognitive risk factors are largely inactive, and thus inaccessible to researchers, until triggered by negative life events. Persons and Miranda (1992) have labeled this the "mood state hypothesis," in that cognitive vulnerability exists but a person's ability to report it depends on current mood state.

Despite the wealth of research on cognitive distortions in depression, a body of research on depressive realism proposes an alternate model. This literature posits that depressed individuals, rather than experiencing distortions in thinking, fail to show many of the self-serving biases common in nondepressed individuals (Msetfi, Murphy, Simpson, & Kornbrot, 2005). In the seminal depressive realism study (Alloy & Abramson, 1979), depressed and nondepressed participants were exposed to a series of response-contingent or event-contingent outcomes, after which they were asked to make judgments about the degree to which the response or event predicted the outcome. Participants' judgments were then compared to the actual degree of contingency. Results indicated an unrealistic, optimistic bias among nondepressed individuals and, conversely, a tendency toward more realistic perceptions among depressed individuals.

Recent research has found limitations to the depressive realism phenomenon. Specifically, there tend to be few differences between depressed and nondepressed individuals when positive, uncontrollable contingencies are being evaluated, indicating that findings in this area do not reflect a general difference in contingency learning between depressed and nondepressed individuals (Alloy, Abramson, & Kossman, 1985; Carson, 2001; Lennox, Bedell, Abramson, Raps, & Foley, 1990; Vasquez, 1987). The depressive realism effect appears to be limited to situations in which the outcome is not contingent upon an event (e.g., a participant response) and situations in which negative outcomes occur at high rates (Msetfi et al., 2005).

Avoidance and anxiety. Considerable psychopathology research supports the relation between avoidance and depression (reviewed by Ottenbreit & Dobson, 2004). Avoidant coping and avoidant problem-solving styles have been found to predict future depressed moods (Blalock & Joiner, 2000; Londahl, Tverskoy, & D'Zurilla, 2005), correlate with current depressive episodes (Kuyken & Brewin, 1994), and predict lack of remission of depression (Holahan & Moos, 1986). Ottenbreit and Dobson (2004) distinguished between cognitive avoidance strategies (denial, minimization, or cognitive distraction) and behavioral avoidance strategies (escape from situation or engagement in alternative/distracting activities), and found that both correlated with depressed mood.

Recent research on rumination also shows a clear relation to depression. Behaviorists have argued that rumination functions as a type of cognitive avoidance (Martell, Addis, & Jacobson, 2001), and there is some initial research to support this contention (Kanter, Mulick, Busch, Berlin, & Martell, in press). A ruminative cognitive style has been found to predict the onset (Just & Alloy, 1997; Nolen-Hoeksema, 2000), length (Umberson, Wortman, & Kessler, 1992), and severity (Nolen-Hoeksema, Parker, & Larson, 1994) of depressive episodes. In addition, rumination leads to decreased social involvement and increased social isolation (Umberson et al., 1992). Finally, some research suggests that rumination may be particularly relevant to mixed anxiety and depression (Nolen-Hoeksema, 2000).

There is substantial co-morbidity of depressive disorders and anxiety disorders (reviewed in Mineka et al., 1998)—a set of disorders for which avoidance is the central feature (Barlow, 2002). As noted above, considerable personality and genetic research supports the notion that a broad tempermental dimension underlies depression and anxiety, particularly depression and Generalized Anxiety Disorder, and biological models of depression and anxiety in terms of HPA axis dysfunction have been developed in parallel with these findings. In fact, pure cases of depression without at least some co-morbid anxiety are relatively rare, and the onset of anxiety problems often precedes the onset of depression longitudinally (Mineka et al., 1998). Barlow, Allen and Choate (2004) recently proposed a unified model of anxiety and depression based on these findings. We further discuss avoidance and anxiety below.

Behavioral and Cognitive Models of Depression

The focus of this chapter is to present an integrative model of depression using behavior analytic principles. In order to present a modern model, we first present the traditional behavioral models and identify their shortcomings. The modern model builds upon and is an integration of these earlier models. Therefore, we spend considerable time and detail on traditional models of depression.

Lewinsohn's Reinforcement Deprivation Model

The traditional behavioral model of depression has been dominated by the view of Lewinsohn (Lewinsohn, 1974; Lewinsohn & Graf, 1973), largely because this view led to an active research program and specific treatment techniques and was incorporated into Cognitive Therapy (Beck et al., 1979), which became the most common of the modern cognitive-behavioral approaches. (For historical overviews of the development of the behavioral model, see Hopko, Lejuez, Ruggiero, & Eifert, 2003; Jacobson, Martell, & Dimidjian, 2001; Kanter, Callaghan, Landes, Busch, & Brown, 2004; Martell et al., 2001.). Similar to Ferster (1973), Lewinsohn described depression as characterized primarily by a low rate of *response-contingent positive reinforcement* (RCPR).

According to Lewinsohn (1974), RCPR is a function of three factors: the number of events that are potentially reinforcing to the individual, the availability of these reinforcing events in the environment, and whether or not the individual has in his/her repertoire the instrumental behavior necessary to obtain this reinforcement from the environment. Lewinsohn's model emphasized situations involving social skills deficits that produce chronic deficits in RCPR or environmental changes that produce losses of major sources of RCPR. If the social skills deficits are clear enough, the losses large enough, and the resulting deficits in positive reinforcement are clearly identifiable, no additional explanatory factors are necessary for the onset of depression. Likewise, as posited by Lewinsohn, maintenance of depression requires an inability to reacquire old sources or acquire new sources of reinforcement. This may be due to continued social skills or environmental deficits, among other factors.

According to Lewinsohn (1974), a low rate of RCPR produces a low rate of social and other behaviors because the lack of reinforcement effectively extinguishes the behaviors contingent on such reinforcement. In addition, the low rate of RCPR is assumed to act as an eliciting stimulus for additional depressive behaviors, such as dysphoria, fatigue, and other somatic symptoms. Finally, cognitive symptoms of depression such as low self-esteem, pessimism, and guilt are assumed to be secondary elaborations of other symptoms which have been elicited or evoked by the low rate of RCPR. In other words, the cognitive symptoms may be inaccurate tacts or causal explanations for the observed private and public experiences of depression. For example, "I am sick" may be evoked by somatic symptoms, "I am unlikable" may be evoked by social isolation and poor interpersonal relations, and "I am bad" may be evoked by feelings of guilt.

Research on Lewinsohn's approach was mixed at best (reviewed in Blaney, 1977, 1981), and some research contradicted Lewinsohn's model. For example, Cole and Milstead (1989) found that social skills deficits were a consequence, not a cause, of depression, and Lewinsohn himself showed that the frequency of RCPR (as operationalized in terms of pleasant or unpleasant events) did not predict the later occurrence of depression (Lewinsohn & Hoberman, 1982). Although there is now general consensus that both interpersonal problems and negative life events are both causes and consequences of depression, at the time it was thought that an acceptable theory of depression would have to address more than deficits in positive reinforcement and social skills. Other causal variables and the role of cognitive variables would have to be addressed (Dobson & Block, 1988). Lewinsohn subsequently abandoned his behavioral theory in favor of an integrative theory that combined behavioral and cognitive factors (Lewinsohn, Hoberman, Teri, & Hautzinger, 1985). Lewinsohn's integrative theory led to "Coping with Depression," a group treatment that includes relaxation training, pleasant activity monitoring and scheduling, social skills training, and cognitive restructuring (Lewinsohn, Antonuccio, Breckenridge, & Teri, 1984; Lewinsohn, Muñoz, Youngren, & Zeiss, 1986).

Seligman's Learned Helplessness Model

If depression is to be interpreted literally, as in behavior being "pressed down" or reduced, then the relationship between punishment and depression is clear, as punishment by definition reduces behavior. The role of punishment in depression was first explicated by Seligman in a series of learned helplessness experiments with dogs (Overmier & Seligman, 1967; Seligman, 1975). Like loss of RCPR in the reinforcement deprivation model, punishment contingencies can be seen as reducing behavior directly and eliciting dysphoria.

Seligman's original learned helplessness model in which inescapable punishment led directly to learned helplessness, a subtype of depression, also was criticized as inadequate (e.g., Costello, 1978) and the model grew increasingly cognitive over time (Abramson, Seligman, & Teasdale, 1978). The current formulation (Abramson et al., 1989) has largely abandoned punishment contingencies as integral to the model and instead focuses on cognitive constructs, such as hopelessness and inferential styles. However, learned helplessness may be taken as a model for some forms of depression without endorsing related hypotheses about causal cognitive concepts. As described above, childhood histories involving generalized and severe punishment contingencies should be of particular importance in this regard (Bifulco et al., 1991; Levitan et al., 1998; Sedney & Brooks, 1984). No behavioral treatments based on a punishment model have been developed, although punishment was incorporated somewhat into Lewinsohn's cognitive-behavioral expansion of his early treatment approach (Lewinsohn et al., 1984).

Beck's Cognitive Model

As described above, the cognitive model of depression evolved in response to concerns that behavioral (and psychodynamic) models of depression were inadequate (Dobson & Block, 1988). In fact, Cognitive Therapy (CT; Beck et al., 1979) is quite similar to "Coping with Depression." Both treatments are a combination of cognitive and behavioral interventions. However, CT's behavioral interventions are embedded in a staunchly cognitive conceptualization in that the overarching function of behavioral interventions is cognitive change. For example, the CT manual states, "The term *behavioral techniques* may suggest that the immediate therapeutic attention is solely on the patient's overt behavior...[but] the ultimate aim of these techniques in cognitive therapy is to produce change in the negative attitudes so that the patient's performance will continue to improve" (p. 118). The cognitive therapist, especially early in treatment and for severely depressed individuals, identifies behavior problems and activates the client in his/her natural environment with daily activity monitoring and scheduling as well as graded behavioral homework assignments. Social skills training and problem solving interventions also are encouraged throughout treatment as appropriate. However, the overwhelming focus of treatment is on cognitive restructuring and cognitive change. CT has garnered considerable empirical support in group trials, and has become the most widely-researched and widely-used of the cognitive-behavioral treatments (DeRubeis & Crits-Christoph, 1998). However, evidence suggests that it is not as effective as initially thought. For example, in two large-scale studies supporting the efficacy of CT for depression (Elkin, Shea, Watkins, Imber, Sotsky, Collins et al., 1989; Hollon, DeRubeis, Evans, Wiemer, Garvey, Grove et al., 1992), of those clients who entered treatment only 64-68% completed treatment and only 50-51% of those who completed treatment were classified by clinical interviewers as recovered (see also Westen & Morrison, 2001).

Although CT is widely used, cognitive researchers have had great difficulty finding evidence to support cognitive mechanisms of change when CT is effective. A major challenge came from a component analysis by Jacobson and colleagues (1996). In this study, CT was broken into three additive components. The first component (Behavioral Activation, BA) prescribed behavioral interventions for the full course of treatment and proscribed any attempts at cognitive modification. The second component prescribed behavioral interventions and attempts to identify, monitor, challenge, and modify automatic thoughts but proscribed work on underlying schemas. The third component allowed behavioral interventions, work on automatic thoughts, and work on underlying schemas and thus represented the full and complete CT package. Jacobson and colleagues (1996) reasoned that if BA was as effective in treating depression as were the other components, this could be taken as evidence that cognitive interventions were unnecessary in the treatment of depression. Jacobson and colleagues (1996) found no evidence that the complete CT package produced better outcomes, despite a large sample, excellent adherence and competence by therapists in all conditions, and a clear bias by the study therapists favoring CT. Also, CT was no more effective than BA in preventing relapse at a two-year follow-up (Gortner, Gollan, Dobson, & Jacobson, 1998). Therefore, this study suggests that the full CT package is not necessary and that BA alone may account for client improvement in CT.

Problems with Traditional Behavioral and Cognitive Models

For a model to be adequate, it must account for the major research findings in the area. Our review of the research on depression suggests several themes that need to be addressed. First, depression as defined by the DSM-IV-TR is a heterogeneous group of problems, characterized by considerable variability in time course, symptom severity, and correlated conditions. No current model accounts for this complexity. The traditional behavioral model could have addressed these issues somewhat if it encouraged functional assessment to determine treatment targets, yet it did not (Kanter et al., 2004). Instead, it presented a unitary model and corresponding treatment, as did Beck's cognitive model. But how does a unitary model explain both the individual whose sleep and appetite have decreased and the individual whose sleep and appetite have increased? If sleeping and eating are to be considered as behavioral repertoires, it is difficult if not impossible to envision a history that can produce both increases and decreases in these repertoires. Although the DSM-IV-TR allows one to code Melancholic versus Atypical Depression to capture these and other individual variations in symptom profiles, psychotherapeutic treatments in general have ignored this behavioral variability in favor of unitary models. As described below, a modern behavioral model can address this concern by emphasizing functional assessment to determine treatment targets, and assuming no essential composition to depression.

Second, environmental, interpersonal, and cognitive mediational factors are all important to depression, and the causal relationships between these variables and depression are complex and probably variable. Depression is sometimes clearly precipitated by negative life events, either in the form of major losses, chronic punishment, or the accrual of multiple, daily stressors. Likewise, research on interpersonal problems clearly establishes them as both causes and consequences of depression. While traditional behavioral models have addressed these two factors, it is also clear that depression is characterized by negative, biased cognitive content and a ruminative cognitive style; both of these, while not necessarily causal to depression, clearly exacerbate and maintain it. A behavioral model that ignores cognitive variables is rightly criticized, as is a cognitive model that emphasizes cognitive content to the neglect of other important variables. Again, a modern behavioral model that emphasizes functional assessment to determine relevant variables and incorporates cognitive variables into an overall behavioral conceptualization appears to be necessary.

Finally, the role of avoidance and anxiety in behavioral models of depression has been relatively neglected (Barlow et al., 2004; Ottenbreit & Dobson, 2004). Ferster (1973), in his seminal functional analysis of depression, noted that the depressed repertoire is characterized by high frequency escape and avoidance behaviors, topographically seen as complaining, crying, and withdrawing, and that these behaviors both preempt positively reinforced behavior and lead to additional reductions in positive reinforcement. Traditionally, behaviorists have considered a particular depressed affective state as related to low rates of positive reinforcement and an anxious affective state as related to high rates of negative reinforcement, thus allowing for separate conceptualizations of the two disorders. However, it is difficult to conceive of realistic environment-behavior relations that could be adequately characterized by either low rates of positive reinforcement or high rates of negative reinforcement but not some combination of the two. Ferster (1973) described the problem well:

> It may not be possible to say whether the reason a depressed person is agitated, disturbed, and complaining is because of the absence of positively reinforced behavior or because the aversively motivated behavior is prepotent over and hence prevents positively reinforced behavior. A repertoire that efficiently avoids aversive stimuli may still lack sufficient

amounts of positive reinforcement. Conversely, the aversively motivated behavior of some depressed persons may come from the absence of positively reinforced behavior or a sudden reduction in it (p. 859).

Thus, the co-occurrence of anxiety with depression may be re-stated as the potential for losses of positive reinforcement in any situation involving excessive aversive control. Skinner (1948, 1953, 1971, 1986) consistently emphasized aversive control as our fundamental social problem and the development and support of repertoires associated with natural positive reinforcement as our ideal. His brief but formal characterization of depression was in terms of aversive social control (1953, p. 363), and Ferster's (1973) analysis emphasized aversive control as well. With this in mind, it is possible that Lewinsohn's original formulation of depression in terms of RCPR may have mistakenly neglected the role of anxiety and aversive control in depression (Barlow et al., 2004), and the modern model offered below addresses this omission.

Modern Behavioral Model of Depression

To summarize, a modern behavioral model of depression must address three weaknesses in previous models: lack of functional assessment and appreciation of the heterogeneity of the relevant phenomena, inability to conceptualize cognitive variables as part of a behavioral framework, and neglect of the role of avoidance in depression. Behavior analysis has the capacity to address these issues without abandoning its principles. In fact, additional behavioral principles relevant to depression already have been described in several places (Dougher & Hackbert, 1994; 2000; Kanter, Cautilli, Busch, & Baruch, 2005; see also Eifert, Beach, & Wilson, 1998, for an alternative, paradigmatic behavioral model). Readers are referred to the above sources for discussion of several of these behavioral principles, including ratio strain, reinforcement erosion, stimulus control, and deficits in rule-governed behavior. Below we focus on two broad content areas: relational stimulus control and avoidance. We feel these two areas address two of the weaknesses in previous models, lack of appreciation for cognitive variables and avoidance, but leave the third weakness, lack of functional assessment and appreciation of heterogeneity, unaddressed.

Relational Stimulus Control

We offer a brief summary of the characteristics of verbal behavior according to Relational Frame Theory (RFT). A more detailed summary is provided in this volume and in Hayes, Barnes-Holmes, and Roche (2001). According to RFT, verbal behavior (including thinking) is technically seen as the behavior of framing events relationally: responding to one stimulus in terms of its given or inferred relation to other stimuli. Relational framing is characterized as generalized (or abstracted) operant behavior (although this has been debated, see Barnes-Holmes & Hayes, 2003; Galizio, 2003) and a description of relational framing in terms of the three-term operant contingency is illuminative. First, regarding discriminative control, the contextual cues that occasion relational framing and its content may themselves be relational and arbitrary in nature; thus, other than previous verbal behavior (which may be private) little environmental support is necessary to occasion verbal behavior and control its content (although non-arbitrary features of the environment certainly may play a role and are important). However, verbal contextual cues have obtained their discriminative functions historically through interaction with the social community, so the environmental origins of stimulus control important to behavior analysis are not lost in RFT. Second, the relational response itself has complex properties and effects on other stimuli including entailment and transformation of functions. Like discriminative control, these stimulus functions may also be quite arbitrary and unrelated to current environmental features. Thus, the behavior of relational framing has a potentially transformative effect on the environment; environmental stimuli that would otherwise control behavior may not do so and new stimuli, idiosyncratic to the individual's verbal learning history, may exert control. Third, regarding reinforcement, RFT posits that verbal behavior is reinforced automatically by "sense making," "coherence," "being right," and other related verbal reinforcers. Thus, it is maintained with very little direct environmental input, but like the contextual cues, these reinforcing functions have also been obtained historically (e.g., early and repeated social reinforcement for the coherence of relational networks leads eventually to coherence itself becoming reinforcing). In summary, these characteristics of relational framing highlight how verbal behavior, when it occurs, may be quite relentless in overpowering, transforming, and reducing environmental control.

RFT and traditional behavioral models. Traditional behavioral models emphasized the effects of reinforcement deprivation and punishment on behavior, but little attention was paid to how events and circumstances acquire reinforcing and punishing functions. RFT suggests that these functions may be acquired and augmented verbally, and these effects may be quite destructive. Consider a depressed individual attending a social event who has verbally categorized certain party goers as "losers" and others as "winners." In this case, socializing may only be reinforcing if it occurs with those categorized as "winners." However, the criteria that established the categories may be quite arbitrary and idiosyncratic to the verbal learning history of that individual. For example, winners may solely consist of male athletes. Thus, an arbitrarily-defined winner, established as reinforcing through relational transformations of function, may or may not be otherwise naturally reinforcing. Likewise, the individual may be quite naturally compatible with an arbitrarily-defined "loser" but either will avoid conversation with this person or find conversation boring due to the dominance of the verbally-derived functions. In terms of Lewinsohn's model, such a verbal learning history may limit the number of potential reinforcing agents available to the individual, and contribute to deficits in positive reinforcement.

Likewise, deficits in positive reinforcement can be established verbally. Consider a depressed individual who categorizes himself as a "loser." In this situation, anything the person does, if related verbally to the core "loser" quality, may have functions transformed in accordance with the derived relation. Thus, a potentially reinforcing social event may become aversive and depressing simply because the individual attended it. (Groucho Marx demonstrated this possibility with his line, "I wouldn't want to be a member of any club that would have me as a member.")

Cognitive researchers were correct in noting that negative thinking can produce negative mood; the research is clear on this (reviewed in Clark et al., 1999). They further posited that core depressogenic schemas were responsible for the negative thinking, and, along with the environmental events that trigger them, serve as the distal and proximal causes of depression (see research on cognitive vulnerability reviewed by Ingram et al., 1998). RFT provides behavioral psychologists a vocabulary and theory with which cognitive variables can be conceptualized and understood. Negative self-statements so often seen in depression acquire their meanings and functions through bi-directional and combinatorial transformations of function.

Criticisms of early behavioral models often focused on their inability to integrate cognitive variables. Lewinsohn's original model did account for negative self-statements as inaccurate or faulty tacts but the treatment techniques derived from the model ignored any implications of this tacting. Thus, RFT adds a necessary expansion to the treatment conceptualization. Specifically, it predicts that simple behavioral activation should fail for individuals with verbal repertoires character-ized by generalized negative self-statements such as "I'm a loser." Potentially reinforcing events may be rendered ineffective by inclusion in a dominant relational network that transforms their functions. Thus, the depressed person complains that "nothing is fun anymore." Because of relational transformations of function, the degree of global anhedonia in depression should correlate with the strength and frequency of this repertoire, and this is not easily addressed by simply scheduling contact with "fun" or once-reinforcing events.

A similar analysis may be conducted with Seligman's punishment model. While it is clear that histories of chronic, severe, and global punishment may produce depression through a variety of behavioral mechanisms, it is also clear that many people feel "punished" in the absence of such a history. Once again, traditional behavioral models had some difficulty conceptualizing such circum-stances while a contemporary behavioral model handles them easily. Punishment contingencies may be established verbally (see Augustson & Dougher, 1997, for an analogue demonstration of this effect).

To summarize the implications of RFT for depression, RFT adds to the traditional model a conceptualization of how cognition may play a role in depression. Specifically, through verbally-mediated transformation of function, environmental stimuli that do not function naturally to elicit sadness and depression may obtain these functions. Thus a history involving relational networks dominated by themes of loss, punishment, and negativity has the potential to greatly expand the range and diversity of stimuli that may occasion negative affect and depression. It is important to note that RFT does not diminish the importance of

RCPR to depression; rather it expands the range of environmental histories that can result in loss of RCPR. Verbal repertoires can produce functional losses in RCPR, even if the environmental reinforcing stimuli have not changed or been lost.

Avoidance

The second primary consideration of the modern behavioral model of depression is avoidance. Two relevant models of avoidance have been advanced: the model of *experiential avoidance* by Hayes and colleagues (Hayes, 2004; Hayes, Wilson, Gifford, Follette, & Strosahl, 1996) that has been incorporated into Acceptance and Commitment Therapy (ACT; Hayes, Strosahl, & Wilson, 1999) and a simpler model of avoidance that has been incorporated into Behavioral Activation (BA; Martell, Addis, & Jacobson (2001). These models have been fully compared by Kanter, Baruch, and Gaynor (under review).

Experiential avoidance. Hayes and colleagues (Hayes, 2004; Hayes et al., 1996) have developed a model of experiential avoidance: an unwillingness to remain in contact with particular private experiences coupled with attempts to escape or avoid these experiences. Experiential avoidance is not an account of depression; rather, it is posited as a functional diagnostic category (Hayes & Follette, 1992) that identifies a psychological process key to many topographically-defined diagnostic categories, including depressive disorders. In fact, little has been written specifically about experiential avoidance and depression other than Zettle (2004). Regarding depression, as pointed out by Zettle, although the term experiential avoidance accommodates both escape and avoidance behavior, *experiential escape* may be more appropriate for depression in that the depressed individual may more likely be preoccupied with terminating psychological events that have already been experienced and are currently being endured, such as guilt, shame, and painful memories of loss experiences, rather than those that are anticipated and avoided. We will use the more general term *experiential avoidance* as it is more consistent with ACT usage.

It is important to note that, according to theoretical expositions on the historical conditions necessary for the development of experiential avoidance (e.g., Hayes et al., 1996; Hayes, Strosahl, & Wilson, 1999), aversive stimulus functions that evoke experiential avoidance are not innate to private stimuli but are obtained historically through interaction with the social/verbal community and through verbal transformations of function. The experience of complex emotions, such as depression, can be understood by describing the history through which the term "depression" has been learned, corresponding bodily states identified, and both labeled as "bad" (Friman et al., 1998). Assuming that "bad" functions as a conditioned punisher, the functions of other stimuli (e.g., bodily states labeled "depressed") that are relationally framed with "bad" are transformed accordingly. Subsequently, these stimuli evoke experiential avoidance.

For example, consider an individual with an extensive generalized experiential avoidance repertoire and a chronic self-report of low self-esteem. This repertoire may have been obtained during a history of abuse and neglect by caregivers, specifically punishment for expressing negative emotions and no reinforcement for successfully regulating emotions. Any uncomfortable feeling may be evaluated and labeled negatively. This evaluation participates in a relational network that transforms the functions of the original feelings and, as such, they become more aversive through the process. For example, sadness is a common emotional experience that probably serves adaptive functions. As Zettle (2004) points out, an individual may interpret an experience of sadness as "being bad" because it reflects the quality of their life (e.g., "I must be doing something wrong.") or worth as human beings (e.g., "Normal people don't feel this way so there must be something wrong with me."), and it is held as a cause for other behaviors (e.g., "I tend to drink more when I'm feeling down.") or their absence (e.g., "When I feel this bad I can't even get out of bed to go to work."). Functionally, these statements may result in additional avoidance and loss of positive reinforcers. Thus, a verbal response to a normal, adaptive feeling can render it maladaptive and start the cycle of depression.

While RFT suggests how private events become aversive due to a verbal history and may evoke avoidance, experiential avoidance itself is described as a verbal (i.e., rule-governed) process. It is not just that private events evoke avoidance and such avoidance is maintained by immediate negative reinforcement, it is that these aversive private events occasion verbal rules that occasion a repertoire of behavior that functions to control and minimize aversive private events. More succinctly stated, verbal rules dictate experiential avoidance. However, some recent studies have found evidence that those with depression may be less rule-governed than those without depression (Baruch, Kanter, Busch, Richardson, & Barnes-Holmes, 2006; Rosenfarb, Burker, Morris, & Cush, 1993). This issue deserves further study.

Conceptualizing experiential avoidance as rule-governed, however, suggests that it may be particularly pernicious, leading to decreased contact with contingencies that would otherwise control and modify behavior in more functional directions (Hayes, 1998). According to ACT, experiential avoidance often does not work, as the events (thoughts and feelings) targeted for avoidance often are respondent or, as described above, have acquired aversive respondent functions through participation in verbal relational networks. However, the rule-governed nature of experiential avoidance repertoires obscures contact with the failure of the rule. In addition, experiential avoidance may work in the short-term but leads paradoxically to a subsequent increase in the events targeted for avoidance and produce chronic aversive private events in the long term. When experiential avoidance does work in the short-term, a generalized avoidance repertoire may be reinforced which may result in poor problem solving and restricted change efforts when needed in the future.

Avoidance in Behavioral Activation. BA's theory of avoidance, unlike ACT's, does not highlight verbal processes either in the development or maintenance of avoidance. Largely based on Ferster (1973), BA suggests that aversive private events are unconditioned responses, elicited by contingencies involving loss or deprivation or high levels of aversive control (Jacobson et al., 2001; Martell et al., 2001).

Avoidance of these aversive private events, in the form of inactivity, inertia, and withdrawal and other topographies, is evoked by the events themselves or by their environmental determinants/correlates; a rule-governed process is not posited. These avoidance patterns are maintained by short-term negative reinforcement. The avoidance patterns deny the individual access or opportunity to contact positive reinforcement, solve the problems that caused the aversive events in the first place, and result in an overall narrowing and restricting of the behavioral repertoire.

Avoidance and depression. As described above, one gap in the traditional behavioral model of depression is the lack of appreciation for the role of aversive contingencies in depression, and a focus on avoidance fills that gap. Taken together and de-emphasizing their differences for our current purposes, we can see how the two models of avoidance add considerably to the traditional model. Consider an individual with a large environmental change such as a divorce and loss of employment. A decrease in response-contingent positive reinforcement and an increase in elicited dysphoria follow. Note that the traditional behavioral model is adequate at this point but it stops here. The current model also considers whether there is a relevant history that has established avoidance as a response to these difficult events. This may lead to short-term attempts to feel better (e.g., an increase in sleeping and eating to avoid the dysphoria with no active attempts to re-establish positive reinforcement). This starts the cycle of depression and the individual feels worse. The person's history may also have established negative self-critical cognitions as elicited responses, which evoke further avoidance, distraction, and thought suppression efforts to avoid the elicited cognitions. This may produce thought rebound and rumination, which increasingly disrupts problem solving, leads to poor sleep, and strengthens the depression. Alternately, the individual could react with adaptive coping methods such as active problem solving and support seeking, which would break the cycle and ameliorate the depression.

Whether avoidance of aversive private events is rule-governed (ACT's model) or not (BA's model), the emphasis on avoidance is clearly warranted. In line with an idiographic conceptualization of depression, we suggest that clients may vary on this dimension, and intra-client behavior may vary as well. The strength of an avoidance repertoire (whether experiential and rule-governed or not) should be a function of degree of contact with the historical contexts responsible for the development of the repertoire and should vary on a continuum accordingly. Specification of these histories to predict and control the development of avoidance is an important area for future research. The development of assessment strategies to determine whether clinically-relevant repertoires are more rule-governed or directly contingency shaped are thus necessary.

Model Summary

As a reminder, the current model of depression does not treat depression as an entity. It is important not to associate this condition with a specific pattern of physiological responding or reify it as a particular emotional state. We accept

Skinner's (1953) view of emotional states as simply co-occurring behavioral responses (elicited unconditioned reflexes, conditioned reflexes, operant predispositions) which appear integrated because the behaviors are occasioned by common discriminada and controlled by common consequences. The particular quality of an emotional state labeled "depression" should vary with the characteristics of the environmental triggers. As implied by our discussion of RFT above, the quality of the emotional state also should vary depending on the characteristics of the reinforcing community that shaped usage of the term for a particular individual. With that in mind, the current model of depression combines several factors:

1. The traditional view that losses of, reductions in, or persistently insufficient levels of positive reinforcement elicit the respondent affective states and produce the reductions in behavior associated with the tact "depression" remains important. Lewinsohn emphasized environmental events that produce losses of major sources of reinforcement and skills deficits that limit an individual's ability to obtain reinforcement. It is clear that some cases of depression are best described by this model, particularly when the losses are clear and obvious or the skills deficits are immediately apparent. However, this model needs to be elaborated and expanded in several ways.

2. It is important to keep in mind that a myriad of factors can produce a dearth of positive reinforcement. Many other factors besides those highlighted by Lewinsohn are relevant, including ratio strain and reinforcement erosion (Dougher & Hackbert, 1994, 2000; Kanter, Schildcrout, & Kohlenberg, 2005). Indeed, the field of behavior analysis, if nothing else, has established how behavior can be increased or decreased. All functional processes that decrease behavior are potentially relevant to depression, if the behavioral reductions produced are large and generalized, and elicited dysphoria is assumed to occur concomitantly with the behavioral reductions. Many of these processes, especially those that are historically distant from the current depression, may best be seen as establishing operations (Dougher & Hackbert, 2000).

On a related note, as described more fully by the developers of *Brief Behavioral Activation Treatment for Depression* (BATD; Lejuez, Hopko, & Hopko, 2001) which we discuss below, a complete behavioral model of depression must also account for not only reductions in non-depressive behavior due to loss of contingent positive reinforcement and other factors, but increases in depressive behavior due to application of contingent positive reinforcement (e.g., increased attention for being "sick"). However, as described by Coyne (1976), social interactions that initially reinforce depressive behavior may over time become punitive, resulting in more global reductions in behavior and increased severity of depression. The role of positive reinforcement in maintaining depressive behavior may be minimal but should not be ignored if a complete conceptualization is sought.

3. Less emphasized by Lewinsohn's traditional model but of particular importance to our current model are persistent punishment and high levels of chronic aversive stimulation (Dougher & Hackbert, 1994; Ferster, 1973; Hopko, Lejuez, Ruggiero, & Eifert, 2003). Extreme persistent punishment may lead to depression as per Seligman's early learned helplessness model (Overmier & Seligman, 1967), but also important are less extreme punishment and negative reinforcement contingencies that evoke increases in escape and avoidance behavior before the onset of helplessness and the extinction of effort. These situations may be seen as respondent elicitors for anxiety, and may result in decreased contact with positive reinforcement over time. Thus, environmental events resulting in increases in punishment and negative reinforcement may also be seen as depression-eliciting stimuli.

The co-morbidity of anxiety and depression should be a function of the degree to which anxious avoidance also results in a loss of positive reinforcement. Given how quickly an event can acquire multiple functions through relational networks, it is easy to see how anxiety and depression co-occur so readily. If, however, there is no loss of positive reinforcement, we expect anxiety but not depression. If there is a loss, we expect both. Likewise, situations in which there is a loss of positive reinforcement but no aversive control should generate depression but not anxiety. It is difficult to conceive of such situations. At first glance, uncomplicated grief may be an example of a pure problem of a dearth of positive reinforcement without avoidance, but upon inspection a grief situation also presents multiple aversive stimuli to occasion escape and avoidance behavior. Nonetheless, grief may present a relatively pure model of depression in terms of loss of reinforcement.

4. Aversive stimulation may be public or private. Including a functional role for private aversive stimulation is a departure from the traditional model, but it seems clearly important to depression. Two models of this type of avoidance have been advanced (Kanter, Baruch, & Gaynor, 2006): ACT's model of experiential avoidance in which avoidance is seen as mediated by a relational history through which private events have obtained aversive functions, and BA's model that does not specify how private events become aversive, but assumes that they can be so naturally. ACT's model further specifies that experiential avoidance is rule-governed, while BA again more simply proposes that it is maintained by negative reinforcement. We believe both models are viable and potentially useful to a full conceptualization of depression.

5. Through participation in relational frames and given a history which has established high strength relational networks of "loss," "abandonment,"

"helplessness," or similar networks, new environmental stimuli can take on properties of depression-eliciting and depression-maintaining stimuli. For example, a fight with one's husband may elicit a depression response, but that response is useful only if the husband has died or been lost permanently, not if the husband is still present but seen as "lost." This must be verbally-mediated because the person has not directly experienced the death of a husband, thus classical conditioning of the fight (CS) with the death (UCS) could not have occurred. Clinical observations of these relational networks, and the lack of a direct training history to support simple conditioning explanations for the behavior associated with these networks, led Beck to develop the cognitive model of depression (Beck, 1964, 1967). Via RFT, behaviorists now can address these issues without abandoning behavioral principles. RFT vastly expands the range of situations that can function as depression-eliciting and depression-maintaining stimuli, as the functions of the stimuli may be largely determined by one's idiosyncratic verbal learning history.

Treatment Implications

Assessment

Our conceptualization is that depression is a varied, multifaceted, and imprecise behavioral phenomenon caused by multiple historical and contextual factors that may vary from individual to individual. Thus, a treatment for depression that starts with functional assessment to determine treatment targets should be effective for a wider range of individuals than should a treatment that assesses and intervenes on a more limited range of targets. Simply put, flexibility seems paramount in treating depression. Current cognitive-behavioral treatment packages tend to provide a limited array of potential treatment targets, and assessment strategies are limited to assess those targets specified by the treatment. These treatments rarely acknowledge the possibility that treatment may most successfully target variables not specified by the treatment. More specifically, treatments do not provide a functional assessment strategy to determine when a given therapeutic technique is appropriate or when to try a different one.

In fact, such an assessment strategy has yet to be developed, particularly one that takes into account the complexities of contextual control once verbal transformations of function are involved (Hayes & Follette, 1992). One important area for future research may be the development of broader functional assessment strategies that include assessment of verbal variables and rule governance. These assessments should be conducted at the start of treatment and continue over the course of treatment to determine treatment targets and treatment utility. In the meanwhile, as described by Kanter and colleagues (2004), we believe that any level of individualized behavioral assessment would be an improvement over the application of treatments based on topographically defined responses rather than functional response classes. In line with the pragmatic nature of radical behaviorism, a complete and exhaustive analysis is not necessary to begin an intervention, and functional assessments need not rely solely on experimental manipulations. As suggested by Skinner (1953), clinical case material and clinical interviews are also appropriate to determine the relevant history and guide the choice of interventions.

We recommend starting behavior analytic treatment for depression with such a proxy functional assessment, and continuing to assess targeted response classes throughout treatment. In this regard, clinical behavior analysts may benefit from learning the chain analysis procedures of Dialectical Behavior Therapy (DBT; Linehan, 1993), the functional assessment procedures of Behavioral Activation (BA; Martell et al., 2001), and the Functional Idiographic Assessment Template (FIAT; Callaghan, 2001; Callaghan, Summers, & Weidman, 2003) developed for Functional Analytic Psychotherapy (FAP; Kohlenberg & Tsai, 1991). More general discussions of assessment strategies for clinical behavior analysis include Hayes and Follette (1992) and Follette, Naugle, and Linnerooth (1999).

Treatment

Several behavior analytic treatments for depression have been developed, including Brief Behavioral Activation Treatment for Depression (BATD; Lejuez, Hopko, & Hopko, 2001), Behavioral Activation (BA; Martell et al., 2001), Acceptance and Commitment Therapy (ACT; Hayes et al., 1999) and Functional Analytic Psychotherapy (FAP; Kohlenberg & Tsai, 1991).

Brief Behavioral Activation Treatment. In this chapter we have emphasized that the traditional behavioral model may still apply and this must be assessed on a case-by-case basis. When assessment suggests that the traditional model applies (i.e., the client's depression appears to be a product of a specific loss of situational positive reinforcement), it is quite possible that targeted efforts to address deficits in positive reinforcement will be sufficient. A current treatment approach that does exactly this is Brief Behavioral Activation Treatment for Depression (BATD; Lejuez, Hopko, & Hopko, 2001). BATD is structured around the use of activity logs to monitor and schedule behavior. Of note is that BATD departs from the traditional behavioral treatment approach of pleasant events scheduling by borrowing a value assessment procedure from ACT (Hayes et al., 1999; discussed below). Based on this individualized assessment, an activity hierarchy is created that guides activity scheduling. This departure addresses the oft-cited weakness in Lewinsohn's original approach (Kanter et al., 2004; Martell et al., 2001) that pleasant events scheduling (Lewinsohn & Graf, 1973) was not based on idiographic assessment but rather pleasant events were topographically defined and assumed to be reinforcing. BATD has been evaluated through several cases studies (Hopko, Lejuez, & Hopko, 2004; Hopko, Bell, & Armento, 2005; Lejuez, Hopko, & LePage, 2001) and a small randomized controlled trial on an inpatient unit (Hopko, Lejuez, LePage, Hopko, & McNeil, 2003). In this trial, BATD produced significantly greater self-reported reductions in depression from pre-treatment to post-treatment compared to general supportive therapy.

Acceptance and Commitment Therapy. As described above, RFT highlights how verbal behavior, when it occurs, may be quite relentless in overpowering, transforming, and reducing environmental control. Cognitive therapists traditionally had an advantage over behavior therapists in that they had a conceptualization for this important phenomenon and a linked set of treatment techniques for depression. ACT provides a solution for behavior analysts. The distinction between ACT and CT remains clear, however, as ACT does not attempt to change clients' negative thoughts in order to change depression, as does CT. Instead, ACT targets the believability of or connection to (in ACT parlance, "literality of" or "fusion with") thoughts. As described above, ACT posits that the aversive functions of thoughts are obtained historically, through interaction with the social/verbal community and through verbal transformations of function as per RFT. ACT interventions target believability by highlighting this environmental context with a series of related defusion, mindfulness, and acceptance interventions (Hayes & Wilson, 2003).

ACT also targets depressogenic thinking with its focus on experiential avoidance. Indeed, the overriding ACT conceptualization is that experiential avoidance underlies a host of psychological disorders in addition to depression. Important to our discussion is that ACT emphasizes that experiential avoidance itself is fueled by a verbal, rule-governed process. Such rules may take many forms, such as "I can't stand to feel this way," "Having feelings makes one weak and vulnerable," or "I need to be happy." In the *creative hopelessness* phase of ACT, clients are guided toward recognizing the unworkability of the experiential avoidance agenda that underlies these rules. Then, their functional control over avoidance behavior is targeted with defusion, mindfulness, and acceptance strategies. Thus, ACT targets both cognitive variables and avoidance, and thus is potentially a strong treatment option in terms of our current model of depression.

It is important to note that ACT, when successful, involves much more than the simple reduction in depression as its goal. ACT explicitly enters a world of values, purpose, and meaning that the typical behavioral treatment does not enter. A guiding principle of ACT is that human suffering and the language context that drives suffering are ever-present, and this may be particularly true with depression. ACT distinguishes itself by challenging psychiatric and mainstream psychological orthodoxy with the notion that perhaps the ubiquity of the problem suggests that our attempts to solve the problem may in fact be part of the problem. ACT proposes that clients may be best served by not focusing on trying to change the distressing symptoms with which they present; instead ACT endeavors to help clients identify values and behave according to those values, regardless of distressing symptoms. While this somewhat grand vision that questions and changes the fundamental goals of psychotherapy may be appealing to many clinical behavior analysts, and scary or disturbing to others, it is consistent with Skinner and his original vision for behavior analysis (Skinner, 1948, 1971).

Data on ACT for depression are limited (reviewed by Kanter, Baruch, & Gaynor, 2006). Two small randomized studies of *Comprehensive Distancing* (CD), an early, approximate version of ACT that interestingly included pleasant events scheduling (see Zettle, 2004, for comparisons of ACT and CD), found that CD performed better than CT when administered individually (Zettle & Hayes, 1986) and equivalently to CT when conducted in a group setting. With regards to the current form of ACT, as of this date, there is no randomized outcome or process research published examining its efficacy with respect to depressive clients, although a third study has been completed but is not yet published (Folke & Parling, 2004) and a fourth study comparing ACT to CT, in which non-responders midway through therapy are re-assigned to the other therapy, is ongoing (Zettle, 2005). Substantial research on ACT for other problems (reviewed in Hayes, Masuda, Bissett, Luoma, & Guerrero, 2004) often included co-morbid depressed clients, so a significant number of depressed clients have been treated in positive research trials on ACT. This research, however, does not permit us to identify outcomes for depressed clients per se. Evaluating modern ACT for depression compared to other active treatments is an important area for future research.

Behavioral Activation. BA (Martell et al., 2001) also targets cognitive variables and avoidance. BA is largely designed to identify and block avoidance and generate more effective alternate coping repertoires. Disruptive negative thinking, when it occurs, is conceptualized as rumination, an avoidance strategy, and is then submitted to the same strategies that target other forms of avoidance. A simple acronym often guides treatment: Clients are taught to increase awareness of *TRAPs*: functional relationships between internal and external triggers (*T*), resulting negative emotional responses (*R*), and avoidance patterns (*AP*). Then, clients are taught to monitor avoidance patterns and instead activate alternate, more effective coping responses. In this way, activation is focused and specifically targets avoidance. BA, in addition to the increased focus on activation instead of avoidance, also includes problem-solving strategies, assertiveness and other social skills training strategies, mindfulness training, therapist modeling, and mental rehearsal strategies. Thus, BA casts a wide net in terms of treatment components and potential mechanisms of change.

Data on BA are difficult to assess because the treatment conceptualization and components keep changing. Early data on pleasant events scheduling (reviewed above) are more relevant to BATD than current BA, and current BA has been changed considerably since the component analysis of CT, described above, that provided initial support for BA (see Jacobson et al., 2001). BA in its current form appears very promising based on a recently completed randomized trial. This study compared BA, CT, Paroxetine (Paxil), and a medication placebo in a large sample with well-trained clinicians providing treatment in all conditions. All treatments performed well for mildly depressed clients, but BA performed surprisingly well for the traditionally difficult-to-treat moderately-to-severely depressed clients, outperforming CT and performing equivalently to Paroxetine (Dimidjian, Hollon, Dobson, Schmaling, Kohlenberg, Addis et al., 2006). In addition, Paroxetine evidenced a very large drop-out rate and problems with relapse and recurrence when the medication was discontinued (Dobson, Hollon, Dimidjian, Schmaling, Kohlenberg, Rizvi et al., 2004), so BA appears to be the superior treatment when all is considered.

Functional Analytic Psychotherapy. Finally, we believe it is important to mention Functional Analytic Psychotherapy (FAP; Kohlenberg & Tsai, 1991). FAP does not present a conceptualization of depression; in fact, FAP does not present a conceptualization of psychopathology at all. Instead, FAP provides a set of treatment recommendations based on Skinnerian functional analyses (e.g., Skinner, 1953, 1957, 1969) of complex clinical phenomena that are directly relevant to depression, including emotion, memory, cognition, and an understanding of the self. These analyses are largely theoretical rather than empirical but nonetheless provide the behavior therapist with a consistent behavioral conceptualization for working with these issues.

The important distinction between FAP and the other treatments presented in this chapter is that FAP harkens back to basic behavior analytic principles of reinforcement and assumes that clinically-relevant target behaviors can be observed and modified during the outpatient office visit (Follette, Naugle, & Callaghan, 1996; Kohlenberg & Tsai, 1991). Thus, while the typical FAP session includes the same kind of client-therapist verbal interaction that characterizes most psychotherapy, key to FAP is that the therapist is shaping behavior while this talk is occurring. This assumption recontextualizes the office visit from one characterized mainly by verbal behavior about target behaviors to one during which target behaviors can be directly assessed and modified. Problem behaviors will occur during the therapy session due to formal similarities between qualities of the therapist, the therapy, and the therapy setting and qualities of the outside environments that elicit and evoke problem behaviors. The therapist's goal in FAP is to watch for and purposefully evoke in-session instances of the targeted operants and differentially reinforce more effective client responding (see also Callaghan, Naugle, & Follette, 1996). Of particular relevance to depression is that this strategy focuses therapy on interpersonal problems, which our review above highlighted as key to our model of depression.

FAP is intended as a stand-alone treatment and as a process by which an existing treatment can harness behavior analytic principles and be made more powerful. For example, to maximize the impact of BATD interventions we also recommend incorporating FAP into BATD, thereby providing the therapist a framework within which in-session occurrences of depressive and non-depressive behavior may be assessed and targeted. For example, the therapeutic relationship provides a valuable source of support, caring, and feedback for many clients, but a particular depressed client's interpersonal repertoire may have been sufficiently extinguished by previous outside losses such that supportive and caring responses from the therapist are not evoked or elicited. Therapy work could focus on specific activation of support-seeking, asking for help, revealing discomfort, and other intimacy-enhancing behaviors in the therapeutic relationship as well as in outside relationships.

Several single-case reports on stand-alone FAP have been published (Callaghan et al., 2003; Kanter, Landes, Busch, Rusch, Brown, Baruch, & Holman, in press; Kohlenberg & Tsai, 1994; Paul, Marx, & Orsillo, 1999; see also Cordova & Koerner, 1993; Vandenberghe, Ferro, & Furtado da Cruz, 2003). However, a convincing empirical case for the benefits of stand-alone FAP has yet to be made (Corrigan, 2001; Hayes et al., 2004). As an adjunct to existing treatment, promising treatment development data exist supporting the utility of FAP enhancements to cognitive-behavioral therapy for adult depression (Kohlenberg, Kanter, Bolling, Parker & Tsai, 2002; Kanter, Kohlenberg & Schildcrout, 2005) and group cognitive-behavioral treatment for adolescent depression (Gaynor & Lawrence, 2002). Regarding FAP enhancements to behavior analytic treatments, preliminary data support the efficacy of a combined FAP and ACT treatment for smoking cessation (Gifford, Kohlenberg, Hayes, Antonuccio, Piasecki, Rasmussen-Hall et al., 2004), but the potential of FAP as an enhancement to behavior analytic treatments for depression is unexplored.

Conclusion

We believe the clinical behavior analyst working with adult outpatient depression should be familiar with the treatment approaches described above. However, as implied above, the ideal clinical behavior analytic treatment for depression would not entail choice and delivery of a particular treatment approach. Rather, an ongoing process of functional assessment over the course of treatment would inform the choice of treatment targets and corresponding interventions based on a theoretical fit between problem conceptualization and the underlying principles of an intervention. BATD, ACT, and BA interventions may all be important in this regard, but as of yet there is no integrated strategy. FAP offers some hope for integration, but there is a long and complex research and theory development road to be traveled before clinical behavior analysis reaches that state. For the time being, those who write about treatment for depression largely write from the perspective of one treatment package or another. Attempts to describe a broad functional conceptualization of depression and link this conceptualization to a set of intervention techniques, allowing for individual differences between and within clients, are largely left to the individual clinician. As our goal in this chapter was to present a model of depression, not a model of corresponding treatment, we did not attempt a comprehensive solution here either.

Whether an integrated, functional treatment approach we eluded to here will prove superior to simpler, more focused approaches is an empirical question. To the extent that depression in different individuals is characterized by different functional processes, a treatment approach that includes heavy idiographic functional assessment and a variety of techniques for intervention on different processes may be maximally beneficial. To the extent that depression is characterized by multiple functional processes within individuals, an approach that provides this variety in an integrated fashion may be maximally beneficial. However, to the extent that most depression consistently is functionally related to one or two core processes, such as experiential avoidance or loss of positive reinforcement, an approach that neglects idiographic assessment in favor of interventions focused on these assumed processes will be fine for most people. However, clinicians trained only in specific treatments rather than functional assessment and intervention will have little in their repertoire for what to do when treatment fails, other than to pick a different specific treatment. While at the level of theory this more eclectic approach may appear unappealing to many behavior analysts, the burden of proof for the superiority of a functional approach is functional outcomes with individual clients.

Establishing the superiority of a functional approach to depression treatment will not be an easy task. Research on depression treatment is marked by repeated failures to demonstrate the superiority of one treatment over another, including apparent equivalence of behavioral and cognitive approaches (Gloaguen, Cottraux, Cucherat, & Blackburn, 1998). Similarly, convincing evidence for specific mechanisms of change is lacking, with several component analyses suggesting apparent equivalence of various cognitive and behavioral treatment components (Jacobson et al., 1996; Jarrett & Nelson, 1987; Zettle & Rains, 1989). Likewise, process analyses often find theoretically inconsistent and contradictory results (e.g., Jacobson et al., 1996; Shaw, Elkin, Yamaguchi, Olmstead, Vallis, Dobson et al., 1999). For example, many clients report improvements in depression before the implementation of any specific techniques, highlighting the importance of "nonspecific" factors (Busch, Kanter, Landes, & Kohlenberg, 2006; Ilardi & Craighead, 1994). These factors, such as the therapeutic alliance, have yet to be specified with much precision (Castonguay & Holtforth, 2005), much less the precision necessary for an adequate behavior analysis (although FAP may be quite important with regard to specification of the active mechanisms of the therapeutic relationship).

An additional complication that the field historically has wrestled with is the relative ease with which acute depression is treated, at least for mildly-to-moderately depressed individuals, versus the difficulty preventing recurrence of symptoms. Thus, research designs must include large samples of severely depressed clients and clients should be followed for several years post-treatment for an adequate assessment of recurrence prevention. Cognitive therapy has recently shown some strength in these areas in comparison to medication (DeRubeis, Hollon, Amsterdam, Shelton, Young, Salomon et al., 2005; Fava, Rafanelli, Grandi, Conti, & Belluardo, 1998; Paykel, Scott, Teasdale, Johnson, Garland, Moore et al., 1999), notwithstanding the recent BA study (Dimidjian et al., 2006). Thus, behavior analysis has considerable work to do if it aims to make a lasting contribution to the field in this area.

References

Abramson, L. Y., Metalsky, G. I., & Alloy, L. B. (1989). Hopelessness depression: A theory-based subtype of depression. *Psychological Review, 96,* 358-372.

Abramson, L. Y., Seligman, M. E., & Teasdale, J. D. (1978). Learned helplessness in humans: Critique and reformulation. *Journal of Abnormal Psychology, 87,* 49-74.

Alloy, L. B., & Abramson, L. Y. (1979). Judgment of contingency in depressed and nondepressed students: Sadder but wiser? *Journal of Experimental Psychology: General, 108,* 441-485.

Alloy, L. B., Abramson, L. Y., & Kossman, D. A. (1985). The judgment of predictability in depressed and nondepressed college students. In F. R. Brush & J. B. Overmier (Eds.), *Affect, conditioning, and cognition: Essays on the determinants of behavior* (pp. 229-246). Hillsdale, NJ: Erlbaum.

American Psychiatric Association. (2000). *Diagnostic and statistical manual of mental disorders* (4th ed., text revision). Washington, DC: Author.

Antonuccio, D. O., Thomas, M., & Danton, W. G. (1997). A cost-effectiveness analysis of cognitive behavior therapy and fluoxetine (Prozac) in the treatment of depression. *Behavior Therapy, 28,* 187-210.

Augustson, E. M., & Dougher, M. J. (1997). The transfer of avoidance evoking functions through stimulus equivalence classes. *Journal of Behavior Therapy & Experimental Psychiatry, 28,* 181-191.

Barlow, D. H. (2002). *Anxiety and its disorders: The nature and treatment of anxiety and panic* (2nd ed.). New York: Guilford.

Barlow, D. H., Allen, L. B., & Choate, M. L. (2004). Toward a unified treatment for emotional disorders. *Behavior Therapy, 35,* 205-230.

Barnes-Holmes, D., & Hayes, S. C. (2003). A reply to Galizio's "The abstracted operant: A review of Relational Frame Theory: A post-Skinnerian account of human language and cognition." *Behavior Analyst, 26,* 305-310.

Barnett, P. A., & Gotlib, I. H. (1988). Psychosocial functioning and depression: Distinguishing among antecedents, concomitants, and consequences. *Psychological Bulletin, 104,* 97-126.

Baruch, D. E., Kanter, J. W., Busch, A. M., Richardson, J. V., & Barnes-Holmes, D. (2006). *The differential effect of instructions on dysphoric and non-dysphoric individuals.* Manuscript submitted for publication.

Bechara, A., Damasio, A. R., Damasio, H., & Anderson, S. W. (1994). Insensitivity to future consequences following damage to human prefrontal cortex. *Cognition, 50,* 7-15.

Beck, A. T. (1964). Thinking and depression: II. Theory and therapy. *Archives of General Psychiatry, 10,* 561-571.

Beck, A. T. (1967). *Depression: Clinical, experimental, and theoretical aspects.* New York: Harper and Row.

Beck, A. T., Rush, A. J., Shaw, B. F., & Emery, G. (1979). *Cognitive therapy of depression.* New York: Guilford.

Bernet, C. Z., Ingram, R. E., & Johnson, B. R. (1993). Self-esteem. In C. G. Costello (Ed.), *Symptoms of depression* (pp. 141-159). New York: John Wiley & Sons.

Bifulco, A., Brown, G. W., & Adler, Z. (1991). Early sexual abuse and clinical depression in adult life. *British Journal of Psychiatry, 159,* 115-122.

Billings, A. G., & Moos, R. H. (1984). Chronic and nonchronic unipolar depression: The differential role of environmental stressors and resources. *Journal of Nervous & Mental Disease, 172,* 65-75.

Blalock, J. A., & Joiner, T. E. (2000). Interaction of cognitive avoidance coping and stress in predicting depression/anxiety. *Cognitive Therapy & Research, 24,* 47-65.

Blaney, P. H. (1977). Contemporary theories of depression: Critique and comparison. *Journal of Abnormal Psychology, 86,* 203-223.

Blaney, P. H. (1981). The effectiveness of cognitive and behavioral therapies. In L. P. Rehm (Ed.), *Behavior therapy for depression: Present status and future directions* (pp. 1-32). New York: Academic Press.

Brown, G. W., & Harris, T. (1978). Social origins of depression: A reply. *Psychological Medicine, 8,* 577-588.

Buchwald, A. M., & Rudick-Davis, D. (1993). The symptoms of major depression. *Journal of Abnormal Psychology, 102,* 197-205.

Busch, A. M., Kanter, J. W., Landes, S. J., & Kohlenberg, R. J. (2006). Sudden gains and outcome: A broader temporal analysis of Cognitive Therapy for depression. *Behavior Therapy, 37,* 61-68.

Callaghan, G. M. (2001). Demonstrating clinical effectiveness for individual practitioners and clinics. *Professional Psychology: Research & Practice, 32,* 289-297.

Callaghan, G. M., Naugle, A. E., & Follette, W. C. (1996). Useful constructions of the client-therapist relationship. *Psychotherapy: Theory, Research, Practice, Training, 33,* 381-390.

Callaghan, G. M., Summers, C. J., & Weidman, M. (2003). The treatment of histrionic and narcissistic personality disorder behaviors: A single-subject demonstration of clinical effectiveness using Functional Analytic Psychotherapy. *Journal of Contemporary Psychotherapy, 33,* 321-339.

Carson, R. C. (2001). Depressive realism: Continuous monitoring of contingency judgments among depressed outpatients and non-depressed controls. (Doctoral dissertation, Vanderbilt University). *Dissertation Abstracts International, 62*(2-B), 1070.

Carver, C. S., & White, T. L. (1994). Behavioral inhibition, behavioral activation, and affective responses to impending reward and punishment: The BIS/BAS scales. *Journal of Personality and Social Psychology, 67,* 319-333.

Caspi, A., Sugden, K., Moffitt, T. E., Taylor, A., Craig, I. W., Harrington, H., et al. (2003). Influence of life stress on depression: Moderation by a polymorphism in the 5-HTT gene. *Science, 301,* 386-389.

Castonguay, L. G., & Holtforth, M. G. (2005). Change in psychotherapy: A plea for no more "nonspecific" and false dichotomies. *Clinical Psychology: Science & Practice, 12,* 198-201.

Ceci, S. J., & Williams, W. M. (1999). *The nature-nurture debate: The essential readings.* Malden, MA: Blackwell Publishers.

Clark, D. A., Beck, A. T., & Alford, B. A. (1999). *Scientific foundations of cognitive theory and therapy of depression.* New York: John Wiley & Sons.

Coan, J. A., & Allen, J. J. B. (2003). Frontal EEG asymmetry and the behavioral activation and inhibition systems. *Psychophysiology, 40,* 106-114.

Cole, D. A., & Milstead, M. (1989). Behavioral correlates of depression: Antecedents or consequences? *Journal of Counseling Psychology, 36,* 408-416.

Cordova, J. V., & Koerner, K. (1993). Persuasion criteria in research and practice: Gathering more meaningful psychotherapy data. *Behavior Analyst, 16,* 317-330.

Corrigan, P. W. (2001). Getting ahead of the data: A threat to some behavior therapies. *Behavior Therapist, 24,* 189-193.

Costello, C. G. (1978). A critical review of Seligman's laboratory experiments on learned helplessness and depression in humans. *Journal of Abnormal Psychology, 87,* 21-31.

Coyne, J. C. (1976). Toward an interactional description of depression. *Psychiatry: Journal for the Study of Interpersonal Processes, 39,* 28-40.

Davidson, R. J., Pizzagalli, D., Nitschke, J. B., & Putnam, K. (2002). Depression: Perspectives from affective neuroscience. *Annual Review of Psychology, 53,* 545-574.

DeRubeis, R. J., & Crits-Christoph, P. (1998). Empirically supported individual and group psychological treatments for adult mental disorders. *Journal of Consulting & Clinical Psychology, 66,* 37-52.

DeRubeis, R. J., Hollon, S. D., Amsterdam, J. D., Shelton, R. C., Young, P. R., Salomon, R. M., et al. (2005). Cognitive therapy vs. medications in the treatment of moderate to severe depression. *Archives of General Psychiatry, 62,* 409-416.

Dimidjian, S., Hollon, S. D., Dobson, K. S., Schmaling, K., Kohlenberg, R. J., Addis, M. E., et al. (2006). Randomized trial of behavioral activation, cognitive therapy, and antidepressant medication in the acute treatment of adults with major depression. *Journal of Consulting and Clinical Psychology, 74, 658-670.*

Dobson, K. S., & Block, L. (1988). Historical and philosophical bases of the cognitive-behavioral therapies. In K. S. Dobson (Ed.), *Handbook of cognitive-behavioral therapies* (pp. 387-414). New York: Guilford.

Dobson, K. S., Hollon, S. D., Dimidjian, S. A., Schmaling, K. B., Kohlenberg, R. J., Rizvi, S., et al. (2004, May). Prevention of relapse. In S. D. Hollon (Chair), *Behavioral Activation, Cognitive Therapy, and Antidepressant Medication in the Treatment of Major Depression.* Symposium conducted at the annual meeting of the American Psychiatric Association, New York, NY.

Dougher, M. J., & Hackbert, L. (1994). A behavior-analytic account of depression and a case report using acceptance-based procedures. *Behavior Analyst, 17,* 321-334.

Dougher, M. J., & Hackbert, L. (2000). Establishing operations, cognition, and emotion. *Behavior Analyst, 23,* 11-24.

Eifert, G. H., Beach, B. K., & Wilson, P. H. (1998). Depression: Behavioral principles and implications for treatment and relapse prevention. In J. J. Plaud & G. H. Eifert (Eds.), *From behavior theory to behavior therapy.* (pp. 68-97). Needham Heights, MA: Allyn & Bacon.

Elkin, I., Shea, M. T., Watkins, J. T., Imber, S. D., Sotsky, S. M., Collins, J. F., et al. (1989). National Institute of Mental Health Treatment of Depression Collaborative Research Program: General effectiveness of treatments. *Archives of General Psychiatry, 46,* 971-982.

Fava, G. A., Rafanelli, C., Grandi, S., Conti, S., & Belluardo, P. (1998). Prevention of recurrent depression with cognitive behavioral therapy: Preliminary findings. *Archives of General Psychiatry, 55,* 816-820.

Ferster, C. B. (1973). A functional analysis of depression. *American Psychologist, 28,* 857-870.

Folke, F., & Parling, T. (2004). *ACT in group format for individuals who are unemployed and on sick leave suffering from depression: A randomized controlled trial.* Unpublished master's thesis, University of Uppsala.

Follette, W. C., & Houts, A. C. (1996). Models of scientific progress and the role of theory in taxonomy development: A case study of the DSM. *Journal of Consulting & Clinical Psychology, 64,* 1120-1132.

Follette, W. C., Naugle, A. E., & Callaghan, G. M. (1996). A radical behavioral understanding of the therapeutic relationship in effecting change. *Behavior Therapy, 27,* 623-641.

Follette, W. C., Naugle, A. E., & Linnerooth, P. J. N. (1999). Functional alternatives to traditional assessment and diagnosis. In M. J. Dougher (Ed.), *Clinical behavior analysis* (pp. 99-125). Reno, NV: Context Press.

Friman, P. C., Hayes, S. C., & Wilson, K. G. (1998). Why behavior analysts should study emotion: The example of anxiety. *Journal of Applied Behavior Analysis, 3,* 137-156.

Galizio, M. (2003). The abstracted operant: A review of relational frame theory: A post-Skinnerian account of human language and cognition. *Behavior Analyst, 26,* 159-169.

Gaynor, S. T., & Lawrence, P. S. (2002). Complementing CBT for depressed adolescents with Learning through In Vivo Experience (LIVE): Conceptual analysis, treatment description, and feasibility study. *Behavioural & Cognitive Psychotherapy, 30,* 79-101.

Gifford, E. V., Kohlenberg, B. S., Hayes, S. C., Antonuccio, D. O., Piasecki, M. M., Rasmussen-Hall, M. L., et al. (2004). Acceptance-based treatment for smoking cessation. *Behavior Therapy, 35,* 689-705.

Gloaguen, V., Cottraux, J., Cucherat, M. A., & Blackburn, I. M. (1998). Meta-analysis of the effects of cognitive therapy in depressed patients. *Journal of Affective Disorders, 49,* 59-72.

Gortner, E. T., Gollan, J. K., Dobson, K. S., & Jacobson, N. S. (1998). Cognitive-behavioral treatment of depression: Relapse prevention. *Journal of Consulting and Clinical Psychology, 66,* 377-384.

Gotlib, I. H., & Lee, C. M. (1989). The social functioning of depressed patients: A longitudinal assessment. *Journal of Social & Clinical Psychology, 8,* 223-237.

Gray, J. A. (1972). The psychophysiological basis of introversion-extraversion: A modification of Eysenck's theory. In V. D. Nebylitsyn & J. A. Gray (Eds.), *The biological bases of individual behaviour* (pp. 182-205). San Diego: Academic Press.

Gray, J. A. (1981). A critique of Eysenck's theory of personality. In H. J. Eysenck (Ed.), *A model for personality* (pp. 246-276). Berlin: Springer-Verlag.

Gray, J. A. (1994). Three fundamental emotion systems. In P. Ekman & R. J. Davidson (Eds.), *The nature of emotion: Fundamental questions* (pp. 243-247). New York: Oxford University Press.

Hammen, C., & Brennan, P. A. (2002). Interpersonal dysfunction in depressed women: Impairments independent of depressive symptoms. *Journal of Affective Disorders, 72,* 145-156.

Hammen, C., & Rudolph, K. D. (2003). Childhood mood disorders. In E. J. Mash & R. A. Barkley (Eds.), *Child psychopathology,* (2nd ed., pp. 233-278). New York: Guilford.

Harmon-Jones, E., & Allen, J. J. B. (1997). Behavioral activation sensitivity and resting frontal EEG asymmetry: Covariation of putative indicators related to risk for mood disorders. *Journal of Abnormal Psychology, 106,* 159-163.

Hayes, S. C. (1998). Resisting biologism, *The Behavior Therapist, 21,* 95-97.

Hayes, S. C. (2004). Acceptance and commitment therapy, relational frame theory, and the third wave of behavioral and cognitive therapies. *Behavior Therapy, 35,* 639-665.

Hayes, S. C., Barnes-Holmes, D., & Roche, B. (2001). *Relational frame theory: A post-Skinnerian account of human language and cognition.* New York: Kluwer/Plenum.

Hayes, S. C., & Follette, W. C. (1992). Can functional analysis provide a substitute for syndromal classification? *Behavioral Assessment, 14,* 345-365.

Hayes, S. C., Masuda, A., Bissett, R., Luoma, J., & Guerrero, L. F. (2004). DBT, FAP, and ACT: How empirically oriented are the new behavior therapy technologies. *Behavior Therapy, 35,* 35-54.

Hayes, S. C., Strosahl, K. D., & Wilson, K. G. (1999). *Acceptance and commitment therapy: An experiential approach to behavior change.* New York: Guilford.

Hayes, S. C., & Wilson, K. G. (2003). Mindfulness: Method and process. *Clinical Psychology: Science & Practice, 10,* 161-165.

Hayes, S. C., Wilson, K. G., Gifford, E. V., Follette, V. M., & Strosahl, K. D. (1996). Emotional avoidance and behavioral disorders: A functional dimensional approach to diagnosis and treatment. *Journal of Consulting and Clinical Psychology, 64,* 1152-1168.

Heaton, R. K., Chelune, G. J., Talley, J. L., Kay, G. G., & Curtiss, G. (1993). *Wisconsin Card Sorting Test Manual: Revised and expanded.* Odessa, FL: Psychological Assessment Resources.

Henriques, J. B., & Davidson, R. J. (1991). Left frontal hypoactivation in depression. *Journal of Abnormal Psychology, 100,* 535-545.

Holahan, C. J., & Moos, R. H. (1986). Personality, coping, and family resources in stress resistance: A longitudinal analysis. *Journal of Personality & Social Psychology, 51,* 389-395.

Hollon, S. D., DeRubeis, R. J., Evans, M. D., Wiemer, M., Garvey, M. J., Grove, W. M., et al. (1992). Cognitive therapy and pharmacotherapy for depression: Singly and in combination. *Archives of General Psychiatry, 49,* 774-781.

Hopko, D. R., Bell, J. L., & Armento, M. E. A. (2005). Behavior therapy for depressed cancer patients in primary care. *Psychotherapy: Theory, Research, Practice, Training, 42,* 236-243.

Hopko, D. R., Lejuez, C. W., & Hopko, S. D. (2004). Behavioral activation as an intervention for coexistent depressive and anxiety symptoms. *Clinical Case Studies, 3,* 37-48.

Hopko, D. R., Lejuez, C. W., LePage, J. P., Hopko, S. D., & McNeil, D. W. (2003). A brief behavioral activation treatment for depression: A randomized pilot trail within an inpatient psychiatric hospital. *Behavior Modification, 27,* 458-469.

Hopko, D. R., Lejuez, C. W., Ruggiero, K. J., & Eifert, G. H. (2003). Contemporary behavioral activation treatments for depression: Procedures, principles and progress. *Clinical Psychology Review, 23,* 699-717.

Ilardi, S. S., & Craighead, W. E. (1994). The role of non-specific factors in cognitive-behavior therapy for depression. *Clinical Psychology: Science and Practice, 1,* 138-156.

Ingram, R. E., Miranda, J., & Segal, Z. V. (1998). *Cognitive vulnerability to depression.* New York: Guilford.

Jacobson, N. S., Dobson, K. S., & Truax, P. A. (1996). A component analysis of cognitive-behavioral treatment for depression. *Journal of Consulting & Clinical Psychology, 64,* 295-304.

Jacobson, N. S., Martell, C., & Dimidjian, S. (2001). Behavioral activation treatment for depression: Returning to contextual roots. *Clinical Psychology: Science and Practice, 8,* 255-270.

Jarrett, R. B., & Nelson, R. O. (1987). Mechanisms of change in cognitive therapy of depression. *Behavior Therapy, 18,* 227-241.

Joiner, T. E., & Metalsky, G. I. (2001). Excessive reassurance seeking: Delineating a risk factor involved in the development of depressive symptoms. *Psychological Science, 12,* 371-378.

Just, N., & Alloy, L. A. (1997). The response styles theory of depression: Tests and an extension of the theory. *Journal of Abnormal Psychology, 106,* 221-229.

Kanter, J. W., Baruch, D. E., & Gaynor, S. T. (2006). Acceptance and commitment therapy and behavioral activation for the treatment of depression: Description and comparison. *The Behavior Analyst, 29,* 161-185.

Kanter, J. W., Callaghan, G. M., Landes, S. J., Busch, A. M., & Brown, K. R. (2004). Behavior analytic conceptualization and treatment of depression: Traditional models and recent advances. *The Behavior Analyst Today, 5,* 255-274.

Kanter, J. W., Cautilli, J. D., Busch, A. M., & Baruch, D. E. (2005). Toward a comprehensive functional analysis of depressive behavior: Five environmental factors and a possible sixth and seventh. *Behavior Analyst Today, 6,* 65-81.

Kanter, J. W., Landes, S. J., Busch, A. M., Rusch, L. C., Brown, K. R., Baruch, D. E., & Holman, G. I. (in press). The effect of contingent reinforcement on target variables in outpatient psychotherapy for depression: A successful and unsuccessful case using functional analytic psychotherapy. *Journal of Applied Behavior Analysis.*

Kanter, J. W., Mulick, P. Busch, A. M., Berlin, K. S., & Martell, C. R. (in press). The behavioral activation for depression scale (BADS): Psychometric properties and factor structure. *Journal of Psychopathology and Behavioral Assessment.*

Kanter, J. W., Schildcrout, J. S., & Kohlenberg, R. J. (2005). In vivo processes in cognitive therapy for depression: Frequency and benefits. *Psychotherapy Research, 15,* 366-373.

Kasch, K. L., Rottenberg, J., Arnow, B. A., & Gotlib, I. H. (2002). Behavioral activation and inhibition systems and the severity and course of depression. *Journal of Abnormal Psychology, 111,* 589-597.

Keller, M. B. (1994). Depression: A long-term illness. *British Journal of Psychiatry, 165,* 9-15.

Kessler, R. C. (1997). The effects of stressful life events on depression. *Annual Review of Psychology, 48,* 191-214.

Kessler, R. C. (2002). Epidemiology of depression. In I. H. Gotlib & C. L. Hammen (Eds.), *Handbook of depression* (pp. 23-42). New York: Guilford.

Kohlenberg, R. J., Kanter, J. W., Bolling, M. Y., Parker, C. R., & Tsai, M. (2002). Enhancing cognitive therapy for depression with functional analytic psychotherapy: Treatment guidelines and empirical findings. *Cognitive and Behavioral Practice, 9,* 213-229.

Kohlenberg, R. J., & Tsai, M. (1991). *Functional analytic psychotherapy: Creating intense and curative therapeutic relationships.* New York: Plenum Press.

Kohlenberg, R. J., & Tsai, M. (1994). Improving cognitive therapy for depression with functional analytic psychotherapy: Theory and case study. *Behavior Analyst, 17,* 305-320.

Kovacs, M., & Goldston, D. (1991). Cognitive and social cognitive development of depressed children and adolescents. *Journal of the American Academy of Child and Adolescent Psychiatry, 30,* 388-392.

Kuyken, W., & Brewin, C. R. (1994). Stress and coping in depressed women. *Cognitive Therapy & Research, 18,* 403-412.

Lejuez, C. W., Hopko, D. R., & Hopko, S. D. (2001). A brief behavioral activation treatment for depression: Treatment manual. *Behavior Modification, 25,* 255-286.

Lejuez, C. W., Hopko, D. R., & LePage, J. P. (2001). A brief behavioral activation treatment for depression. *Cognitive & Behavioral Practice, 8,* 164-175.

Lennox, S. S., Bedell, J. R., Abramson, L. Y., Raps, C., & Foley, F. W. (1990). Judgment of contingency: A replication with hospitalized depressed, schizophrenic and normal samples. *Journal of Social Behavior and Personality, 5,* 189-204.

Levitan, R. D., Parikh, S. V., Lesage, A. D., Hegadoren, K. M., Adams, M., Kennedy, S. H., et al. (1998). Major depression in individuals with a history of childhood physical or sexual abuse: Relationship to neurovegetative features, mania, and gender. *American Journal of Psychiatry, 155,* 1746-1752.

Lewinsohn, P. M. (1974). A behavioral approach to depression. In R. J. Friedman & M. M. Katz (Eds.), *Psychology of depression: Contemporary theory and research* (pp. 157-178). Oxford, England: John Wiley & Sons.

Lewinsohn, P. M., Antonuccio, D. O., Breckenridge, J. S., & Teri, L. (1984). *The coping with depression course.* Eugene, OR: Castalia.

Lewinsohn, P. M., & Graf, M. (1973). Pleasant activities and depression. *Journal of Consulting & Clinical Psychology, 41,* 261-268.

Lewinsohn, P. M., & Hoberman, H. M. (1982). Depression. In A. S. Bellack, M. Hersen, & A. E. Kazdin (Eds.), *International handbook of behavior modification and therapy* (pp. 126-148). New York: Plenum.

Lewinsohn, P. M., Hoberman, H. M., Teri, L., & Hautzinger, M. (1985). An integrative theory of depression. In S. Reiss & R. Bootzin (Eds.), *Theoretical issues in behavior therapy,* (pp. 331-359). New York: Academic Press.

Lewinsohn, P. M., Muñoz, R. F., Youngren, M. A., & Zeiss, M. A. (1986). *Control your depression.* Englewood Cliffs, NJ: Prentice-Hall.

Libet, J. M., & Lewinsohn, P. M. (1973). Concept of social skill with special reference to the behavior of depressed persons. *Journal of Consulting & Clinical Psychology, 40,* 304-312.

Líndal, E., & Stefánsson, J. G. (1991). The frequency of depressive symptoms in a general population with reference to DSM-III. *International Journal of Social Psychiatry, 37,* 233-241.

Linehan, M. M. (1993). *Cognitive-behavioral treatment of borderline personality disorder.* New York: Guilford.

Londahl, E. A., Tverskoy, A., & D'Zurilla, T. J. (2005). The relations of internalizing symptoms to conflict and interpersonal problem solving in close relationships. *Cognitive Therapy and Research, 29,* 445-462.

Marshall, J. R., & Pettitt, A. N. (1985). Discordant concordant rates. *Bulletin of the British Psychological Society, 38,* 6-9.

Martell, C. R., Addis, M. E., & Jacobson, N. E. (2001). *Depression in context: Strategies for guided action.* New York: W. W. Norton & Co, Inc.

Mazure, C. M. (1998). Life stressors as risk factors in depression. *Clinical Psychology: Science & Practice, 5,* 291-313.

McCombs, B. L. (1993). Learner-centered psychological principles for enhancing education: Applications in school settings. In L. A. Penner & G. M. Batsche (Eds.), *Challenge in mathematics and science education: Psychology's response* (pp. 287-313). Washington, DC: American Psychological Association.

McFarland, B. R., Shankman, S. A., Tenke, C. E., Bruder, G. E., & Klein, D. N. (2006). Behavioral activation system deficits predict the six-month course of depression. *Journal of Affective Disorders, 91,* 229-234.

Mineka, S., Watson, D., & Clark, L. A. (1998). Comorbidity of anxiety and unipolar mood disorders. *Annual Review of Psychology, 49,* 377-412.

Monroe, S. M., & Depue, R. A. (1991). Life stress and depression. In J. Becker & A. Kleinman (Eds.), *Psychosocial aspects of depression* (pp. 1101-1130). Hillsdale, NJ: Erlbaum.

Msetfi, R. M., Murphy, R. A., Simpson, J., & Kornbrot, D. E. (2005). Depressive realism and outcome density bias in contingency judgments: The effect of the context and intertrial interval. *Journal of Experimental Psychology: General, 134,* 10-22.

Must, A., Szabó, Z., Bódi, N., Szász, A., Janka, Z., & Kéri, S. (2006). Sensitivity to reward and punishment and the prefrontal cortex in major depression. *Journal of Affective Disorders, 90,* 209-215.

Nolen-Hoeksema, S. (2000). The role of rumination in depressive disorders and mixed anxiety/depressive symptoms. *Journal of Abnormal Psychology, 109,* 504-511.

Nolen-Hoeksema, S., Parker, L. E., & Larson, J. (1994). Ruminative coping with depressed mood following loss. *Journal of Personality and Social Psychology, 67,* 92-104.

Ottenbreit, N. D., & Dobson, K. S. (2004). Avoidance and depression: The construction of the Cognitive-Behavioral Avoidance Scale. *Behaviour Research & Therapy, 42,* 293-313.

Overmier, J. B., & Seligman, M. E. (1967). Effects of inescapable shock upon subsequent escape and avoidance responding. *Journal of Comparative & Physiological Psychology, 6,* 28-33.

Paul, R. H., Marx, B. P., & Orsillo, S. M. (1999). Acceptance-based psychotherapy in the treatment of an adjudicated exhibitionist: A case example. *Behavior Therapy, 30,* 149-162.

Paykel, E. S. (1982). Psychopharmacology of suicide. *Journal of Affective Disorders, 4,* 271-273.

Paykel, E. S., Scott, J., Teasdale, J. D., Johnson, A. L., Garland, A., Moore, R., et al. (1999). Prevention of relapse in residual depression by cognitive therapy: A controlled trial. *Archives of General Psychiatry, 56,* 829-835.

Persons, J. B., & Miranda, J. (1992). Cognitive theories of vulnerability to depression: Reconciling negative evidence. *Cognitive Therapy & Research, 16,* 485-502.

Pinto-Meza, A., Caseras, X., Soler, J., Puigdemont, D., Perez, V., & Torrubia, R. (2006). Behavioural inhibition and behavioural activation systems in current and recovered major depression participants. *Personality and Individual Differences, 40,* 215-226.

Rosenfarb, I. S., Burker, E. J., Morris, S. M., & Cush, D. (1993). Effects of changing contingencies on the behavior of depressed and nondepressed individuals. *Journal of Abnormal Psychology, 102,* 642-646.

Rost, K., Zhang, M., Fortney, J., Smith, J., & Smith, G. R. (1998). Expenditures for the treatment of major depression. *American Journal of Psychiatry, 155,* 883-888.

Sedney, M. A., & Brooks, B. (1984). Factors associated with a history of childhood sexual experience in a nonclinical female population. *Journal of the American Academy of Child Psychiatry, 23,* 215-218.

Seligman, M. E. (1975). *Helplessness: On depression, development, and death.* Oxford, England: W. H. Freeman.

Shaw B. F., Elkin, I., Yamaguchi, J, Olmstead, M., Vallis, T., Dobson, K., et al. (1999). Therapist competence ratings in relation to clinical outcome in cognitive therapy of depression. *Journal of Consulting & Clinical Psychology, 67,* 837-846.

Skinner, B. F. (1948). *Walden Two.* Oxford, England: Macmillan.

Skinner, B. F. (1953). *Science and human behavior.* Oxford, England: Macmillan.

Skinner, B. F. (1957). *Verbal Behavior.* East Norwalk, CT: Appleton-Century-Crofts.

Skinner, B. F. (1969). *Contingencies of reinforcement: A theoretical analysis.* New York: Appleton-Century-Crofts.

Skinner, B. F. (1971). *Beyond Freedom and Dignity.* New York: Knopf.

Skinner, B. F. (1986). What is wrong with daily life in the western world? *American Psychologist, 41,* 568-574.

Sloman, L., Gilbert, P., & Hasey, G. (2003). Evolved mechanisms in depression: The role and interaction of attachment and social rank in depression. *Journal of Affective Disorders, 74,* 107-121.

Sutton, S. K., & Davidson, R. J. (1997). Prefrontal brain asymmetry: A biological substrate of the behavioral approach and inhibition systems. *Psychological Science, 8,* 204-210.

Thase, M. E., Jindal, R., & Howland, R. H. (2002). Biological aspects of depression. In I. H. Gotlib & C. L. Hammen (Eds.), *Handbook of depression* (pp. 192-218). New York: Guilford.

Turkheimer, E. (1998). Heritability and biological explanation. *Psychological Review, 105,* 782-791.

Umberson, D., Wortman, C. B., & Kessler, R. C. (1992). Widowhood and depression: Explaining long-term gender differences in vulnerability. *Journal of Health and Social Behavior, 33,* 10-24.

Valenstein, E. S. (1998). *Blaming the brain: The truth about drugs and mental health.* New York: The Free Press.

Vandenberghe, L., Ferro, C. B. L., & Furtado da Cruz, A. C. (2003). FAP-enhanced group therapy for chronic pain. *The Behavior Analyst Today, 4,* 369-375.

Vasquez, C. (1987). Judgment of contingency: Cognitive biases in depressed and nondepressed subjects. *Journal of Personality and Social Psychology, 52,* 419-431.

Wallace, J., Schnieder, T., & McGuffin, P. (2002). Genetics of depression. In I. H. Gotlib & C. L. Hammen (Eds.), *Handbook of depression* (pp. 169-191). New York: Guilford.

Westen, D., & Morrison, K. (2001). A multidimensional meta-analysis of treatments for depression, panic, and generalized anxiety disorder: An empirical examination of the status of empirically supported therapies. *Journal of Consulting & Clinical Psychology, 69,* 875-899.

Zettle, R. D. (2004). ACT with affective disorders. In S. C. Hayes & K. D. Strosahl (Eds.), *A practical guide to acceptance and commitment therapy* (pp. 77-102). New York: Springer Science + Business Media, Inc.

Zettle, R. D. (July, 2005). *ACT and depression.* Presentation at the Acceptance and Commitment Therapy (ACT) Summer Institute. Philadelphia, PA.

Zettle, R. D., & Hayes, S. C. (1986). Dysfunctional control by client verbal behavior: The context of reason-giving. *The Analysis of Verbal Behavior, 4,* 30-38.

Zettle, R. D., & Rains, J. C. (1989). Group cognitive and contextual therapies in treatment of depression. *Journal of Clinical Psychology, 45,* 436-445.

Zlotnick, C., Kohn, R., Keitner, G., & Della Grotta, S. A. (2000). The relationship between quality of interpersonal relationship and major depressive disorder: Findings from the National Comorbidity Survey. *Journal of Affective Disorders, 59,* 205-215.

Chapter 8

Psychotic Disorders

Patricia A. Bach
Illinois Institute of Technology

Historically, the psychotic disorders have been regarded as especially intractable mental health problems. The Diagnostic and Statistical Manual, fourth edition, text revision (DSM-IV-TR; American Psychiatric Association, 2000) defines as psychotic, any prominent hallucinations, delusional beliefs, or disorganized speech or behavior. Psychotic disorders include schizophrenia, schizophreniform disorder, schizoaffective disorder, delusional disorder, brief psychotic disorder, shared psychosis, psychotic disorder not otherwise specified, psychotic disorder due to a general medical condition, and substance induced psychosis. These disorders share the presence of one or more of the above symptoms, however the etiologies and courses of the disorders varies considerably (APA, 2000). Schizophrenia is the most prevalent of the psychotic disorders and has a relatively early onset, poor prognosis and chronic course. For these reasons there has been considerably more research on schizophrenia than on the other psychotic disorders, and it is therefore the focus of this chapter.

Course and Prevalence

Schizophrenia is usually first diagnosed in late adolescence or early adulthood. It is equally prevalent across many different cultures (Walker, Kestler, Bollini, & Hochman, 2004) and is among the 10 leading causes of disability world wide (World Health Organization Division of Mental Health and Prevention of Substance Abuse, 1998). The disorder is characterized by a period of at least six months with three prominent symptom clusters: positive symptoms, negative symptoms, and cognitive deficits, and impairment in social or occupational functioning during a significant portion of the time symptoms are prominent. Positive symptoms include delusions, hallucinations, and disorganized or catatonic behavior. Negative symptoms include blunted affect, ahedonia, avolition, and alogia. Cognitive deficits include impairments in attention, memory, executive functions and abstract thinking (Meuser & Salyers, 2003). The course of schizophrenia is usually chronic, consisting of periods of acute psychosis with intermittent periods of remission, usually without a return to pre-morbid level of functioning. Due to cognitive deficits associated with schizophrenia, persons with the disorder are less likely to develop lasting relationships, have poorer social and independent living skills, and have lower educational and occupational attainment as compared to persons without schizophrenia (Corrigan & Penn, 2001).

Eighty percent of those diagnosed with schizophrenia will relapse if treatment is stopped after their first acute psychotic episode (Vauth, Loschmann, Rusch, & Corrigan, 2004). Relapse rates are 20% per *year* among patients who receive psychosocial treatment and antipsychotic medication, nearly 40% per *year* among persons receiving medication only, and approach 10% per *month* in unmedicated individuals (Gorman, 1996). Though new pharmacological innovations continue to offer promise in the amelioration of symptoms of psychosis, between 25 and 50% of persons with symptoms of psychosis continue to experience symptoms even while taking antipsychotic medication (Garety, Fowler, & Kuipers, 2000). How a person responds to symptoms of psychosis, including the extent to which symptom content is believed and the degree of distress associated with symptoms, also plays a role in relapse (Bach & Hayes, 2002; Gaudiano, 2005).

Current Research on Etiology of Schizophrenia

Today few doubt that genetics and neurobiology play a role in the etiology of schizophrenia. The literature on the biology of psychopathology generally and schizophrenia in particular has become so vast and so technical that entire books have been written about it (e.g., Lieberman, Stroup, & Perkins, 2006; McGuffin, Owen, & Gottesman, 2004; Murray, Jones, van Os, & Cannon, 2003). Thus, the review of biological contributions to the disorder will be limited to general findings in genetics, neurodevelopment, and neurobiology.

Genetic Findings

The lifetime prevalence of schizophrenia among unrelated individuals in the general population is about 1%. As the degree of genetic relatedness to persons with schizophrenia increases, the prevalence of schizophrenia increases. Among third degree relatives of persons with schizophrenia (e.g., first cousins), the prevalence of schizophrenia doubles to 2%. The concordance rate is about 5% among second degree relatives (e.g., grandparents, nephews/nieces, and half siblings). The concordance rate doubles again among siblings (9%) and parents (13%) of persons with schizophrenia. Among dizygotic twins, the concordance rate is 17%. Children with two parents with schizophrenia and monozygotic twins where one is diagnosed with schizophrenia show the highest concordance rates, 46% and 48% respectively (Gottesman, 1991). The high concordance among monozygotic twins suggests that schizophrenia has a genetic basis and at the same time, the less than 100% concordance rate suggests a complex etiology.

The complicated genetic etiology of schizophrenia makes it difficult for researchers to develop specific genetic models of the disorder. For instance specific genes often fail to distinguish between family members who do and do not develop the disorder, or fail to correlate with specific symptoms of schizophrenia (Schneider & Deldin, 2001). On the other hand, even while microgenetic features of schizophrenia may fail to distinguish individuals with the disorder, they may be useful for identifying precursors of schizophrenia and thus for developing more specific neurobiological models (Bassett, Chow, Abdel-Malik, Gheorgiu, Husted, & Weksberg, 2003).

Another area of research examines the genetic relationships among schizophrenia and other disorders within susceptible populations. There is substantial evidence that schizotypal personality disorder is genetically related to schizophrenia. That is, biological relatives of those with schizophrenia are more likely to be diagnosed with schizotypal personality disorder as compared to persons without close relatives with schizophrenia. A recent adoption study suggests that children adopted from mothers with schizophrenia are at greater risk for schizophrenia, schizotypal personality disorder, and for all non-schizophrenia psychotic disorders, while not having an increased prevalence of other personality disorders, affective disorders, or substance abuse (Tienari, Wynne, Laksy, Moring, Niemenen, Sorri et al., 2003). This line of research suggests possible relations between the etiology of schizophrenia and the etiologies of other psychotic disorders.

Neurodevelopmental Research

Neurodevelopmental etiological theories link psychotic disorders to adverse events in the prenatal and neonatal environment. Such events are hypothesized to cause brain abnormalities during development, which may then lead to later psychopathology (Weinberger, 1996). Various factors have been associated with an increased risk of developing schizophrenia, including exposure to famine (Hoek, Brown, & Susser, 1998), rH factor incompatibility (Hollister, Laing, & Mednick, 1996), and maternal influenza and other infections occurring during prenatal development (e.g., Buka, Tsuang, Torrey, Klebanoff, Bernstein, & Yolken, 2001).

Like genetic models of schizophrenia, environmental research also fails to fully account for the etiology of psychotic disorders. Persons with psychotic disorders are more likely to have experienced adverse prenatal and neonatal events, however not all who experience such events develop a psychotic disorder. While intriguing, the question of whether genetic and environmental etiologies are separate or interactive has not been resolved.

Neurobiological Research

Whether the causes of schizophrenia are genetic/biological, environmental, or both, recent advances in brain imaging techniques have led researchers to identify structural and functional differences in the neuroanatomy and neurophysiology of persons with the disorder. Recent evidence suggests that persons with schizophrenia have larger than average brain ventricles, a related increased volume of cerebral spinal fluid, decreased frontal lobe volume, and decreased gray matter volume in the temporal and occipital lobes (Mitelman, Shihabuddin, Brickman, Hazlett, & Buchsbaum, 2003). These and other brain abnormalities have been associated with some of the cognitive deficits seen in schizophrenia (Heinrichs, 2005), such as memory, attention, planning and sensory and motor integration. Although it is clear that there are structural neurological differences in persons with schizophrenia, a major limitation of biological assessment is that it does not suggest causes for the observed abnormalities or inform diagnosis or treatment (Meuser & Salyers, 2003).

Research on the physiological etiology of psychotic disorders primarily uses functional brain imaging technology and drug studies, often to elucidate the role of neurotransmitters. Though dopamine and glutamate have received the most attention, other neurotransmitters including gamma aminobutyric acid (GABA), acetylcholine and serotonin have also been implicated in the etiology and pharmacological treatment of schizophrenia (Tamminga, 2006). This line of research has been especially fruitful in developing psychopharmacological treatments for psychotic disorders. For instance, dysfunction in specific glutamate receptors is associated with some of the abnormalities observed in schizophrenia (Goff & Coyle, 2001), and a higher than normal density of specific dopamine receptors is associated with both schizotypal personality disorder and schizophrenia (Siever & Davis, 2004). Research findings suggest that many antipsychotic medications work by altering specific types of dopamine and glutamate receptors (Walker et al., 2004). Furthermore, drugs such as PCP, which alter glutamate receptors, often produce symptoms of psychosis in persons without schizophrenia (Goff & Coyle, 2001).

While neurophysiological research is promising, further research is needed to clarify the relationships among gluatamate, dopamine, other neurotransmitters and the specific phenotype. To date, the exact etiological mechanisms underlying the relationships among neurotransmitters and psychosis is unknown. While this line of research may be fruitful for development of pharmacological interventions and useful to basic researchers, it remains limited for diagnosing schizophrenia or for making specific treatment recommendations.

The Diathesis-stress Model

The diathesis-stress model first proposed by Zubin and Spring (1977) suggests that neither genetic nor environmental factors alone are sufficient to account for schizophrenia and associated disability. Instead it is hypothesized that a person with a genetic predisposition (i.e., diathesis) will only develop schizophrenia if also exposed to stressful environmental events. Corrigan (2000) added the dimension of social stigma, positing that reactions of the social group to persons with schizophrenia contributes to disability associated with schizophrenia. Thus, the diathesis-stress model is the broadest etiological model of mental illness and explores interactions among biological, environmental and social factors. Much current research is aimed at increasing the specificity of this model.

Psychosocial and Cognitive Research

Until fairly recently symptoms of psychosis received limited attention from cognitive and behavior therapy researchers, with schizophrenia being described in the mid 1980's as 'the forgotten child of behavior therapy' (Tarrier & Wykes, 2004). Since then, awareness of medications' limited efficacy, and the success of cognitive behavior therapy in treating other psychiatric disorders has led to an increase of interest in developing effective psychological treatments for psychosis (Haddock, Tarrier, Spaulding, Yusupoff, Kinney, & McCarthy, 1998). Relatedly, there has been an increase in understanding the role of cognitive, psychosocial and behavioral factors in the etiology of these disorders. Most attention has been focused on the etiologies of hallucinations and delusions specifically and more recently on understanding cognitive deficits seen in schizophrenia.

Persons with schizophrenia show deficits in almost all areas of cognitive functioning including sensory information processing, attention, memory, planning, and abstract reasoning (Walker et al., 2004). Delusions and auditory hallucinations are clearly cognitive phenomena; both are largely verbal phenomena that occur in the absence of the nonverbal stimuli that would normally produce such verbal responding. For example, the hallucinating patient hears voices in the absence of a speaker, and the delusional individual reports beliefs unsupported by external events. Also, attributional biases appear to play a role in both the phenomenology of hallucinations (Heilbrun, 1980) and in the formation and maintenance of delusional beliefs (Bentall, Kinderman, & Kaney, 1994). Both verbal and neurological processes appear to play a role in the etiology of auditory hallucinations. Some posit that auditory hallucinations occur when an individual fails to distinguish self-generated thoughts from external verbal events. That is, individuals fail to attribute their voices to themselves (Bentall, Haddock, Slade, & Peter, 1994). Hoffman (1986) suggested that individuals misattribute voices as being outside of themselves when their thoughts and conscious intentions are discordant. The hypothesis that auditory hallucinations are in fact self-generated thoughts is supported by the finding that auditory hallucinations are accompanied by sub-vocal activity of the speech musculature similar to that experienced by individuals who are "talking to themselves" (Green & Preston, 1981). Others propose that hallucinations are a failure of discourse planning, that is an individual's planned discourse, which usually remains unconscious, intrudes into conscious awareness and is experienced as voices (Hoffman & Satel, 1993). Still others hypothesize that hallucinations are produced by attentional deficits in making use of contextual cues (Maher, 1980). Salzinger (1984) has a similar theory that auditory hallucinations can be accounted for by the tendency of persons with schizophrenia to respond to more immediate rather than remote stimuli.

Research also suggests that persons with delusional beliefs interpret ambiguous information as confirming their delusional beliefs (Lowe & Chadwick, 1990). Similarly, Bentall and colleagues (1994) suggest that attentional and attributional biases operate in the formation and maintenance of delusional beliefs. While neuroimaging studies point to activation of particular brain areas and to neurophysiological activity co-occurring with delusional thinking, none of these studies suggest an entirely biological explanation for or cause of delusional beliefs (Bentall, Corcoran, Howard, Blackwood, & Kinderman, 2001). Studies of cognition and delusions indicate that individuals with persecutory delusions pay increased attention to threat related stimuli and make excessively global, stable, and external attributions about the causes of negatively evaluated events. Finally, delusional subjects are excessively confident in their social judgments. Thus, the processes involved in maintaining delusions are in many ways similar to the processes maintaining all beliefs whether delusional or non-delusional. While no one theory of delusions is universally accepted, Bentall and colleagues (2001) propose an integrated model of delusions, which posits that attributional style, self-representation, and adverse early experience interact and all play a role in maintaining delusional beliefs.

When the function of delusions is considered, some posit that delusional beliefs, and especially grandiose and paranoid delusions, are defenses against low self-esteem (Bentall & Kinderman, 1999). For example, a person who has failed in many endeavors might maintain self-esteem by concluding that, "I have failed because others are plotting against me" instead of merely concluding that "I am a failure", or in the case of grandiose delusions may counter the thought "I am a failure" with the belief that "I am the president" or "I am a recording star." Other theories (see Bentall & Kinderman, 1999; Maher, 1988) posit that delusions are faulty attributions that function as explanations for unusual events. For example, when delusions and hallucinations occur together they are often related, and delusions usually function to explain the hallucinations. For instance, when a man hears voices, he might believe that there is a radio in his head.

Social Cognition and Theory of Mind

Social cognition can be described as the investigation of what social behavioral events people attend to, how they interpret and evaluate social behavior, and how and to what end they organize, represent, remember, and recall social information (Newman, 2001). Theory of mind specifically presumes that individuals understand, cooperate with or deceive others based on an implicit theory that others have minds and act based on the content of their minds. While believed by some to be present in other social organisms to a limited degree, theory of mind ability is believed to be most advanced in humans (Corcoran, 2001). Deficits in social cognitive skills, including theory of mind, have been proposed to account for symptoms of autism (Baron-Cohen, 1995) and schizophrenia (Corcoran, 2001).

According to a social cognitive model of psychosis, positive and negative symptoms of schizophrenia can be understood as arising from an inability to represent intentional mental states of the self and others (Corcoran, 2001). Frith (1992) proposed that negative symptoms, hallucinations, and delusions of control or thought insertion result from deficits in monitoring ones own mental state and intentions while paranoid delusions, and delusions of reference and thought insertion result from deficits in the mental representation of other's thoughts, beliefs and intentions. A series of experiments conducted by Corcoran and Frith and reported by Corcoran (2001) led them to conclude that theory of mind originates from a combination of representation of autobiographical memory and conditional reasoning and that symptoms of schizophrenia can be understood in terms of deficits in one or both of these skills. More specifically, they suggest that negative symptoms of schizophrenia result from deficits in both autobiographical memory and conditional reasoning, that paranoia is an outcome of recalling only unusual and negatively evaluated events from the past, that disorganized speech is an outcome of conditional reasoning deficits and a failure to appreciate the relationship between the speaker and listener's knowledge, and that delusions generally result from an inability to accurately infer others intentions. Other research suggests that, as compared to control participants, persons with schizophrenia perform poorly on theory of mind tasks even when general cognitive deficits are controlled for (Brune, 2005).

Cognitive and social cognitive models of symptoms of psychosis aim to describe the etiology of symptoms of psychosis. Other models of psychosis aim instead to describe responses to symptoms of psychosis no matter what their origin. A functional contextual approach to cognition is not entirely inconsistent with theory of mind, and offers slightly more precision in formulating an etiology for delusions and hallucinations and problems in living associated with them. Further, such an approach has lead to novel treatment approaches that may be adapted to the treatment of psychotic symptoms.

A Functional Contextual Approach to Psychosis

The account presented below begins at the more basic level of cognition and cognitive deficits that may play a role in the etiology of symptoms of psychosis. However, consideration of cognitive deficits alone is not adequate to account for symptoms of psychosis or their treatment. Thus, an exploration of cognitive deficits is followed by consideration of the social and historical context of the individual and how cognitive deficits may lead to specific symptoms and problematic responses to such symptoms. Finally, specific treatment approaches, and the evidence base for them are discussed.

Perspective Taking

Within a functional contextual approach the same phenomena explicated in terms of theory of mind can be described in terms of perspective taking, which in relational frame theory (RFT) terms requires an understanding of deictic, or perspective-taking, relations. Briefly, RFT holds that the core of human language involves learning relations between stimuli, such as relations of correspondence, hierarchy, opposition, and comparison. Deictic or perspective-taking relations involve relations between me and you, here and there, and now and then. According to RFT, individuals always act from the perspective ME/HERE/NOW but perspective taking requires relating ME to YOU, HERE to THERE, and NOW to THEN (Hayes, Fox, Gifford, Wilson, Barnes-Holmes, & Healy, 2001). The ability to relate oneself in time and space to alternate persons, times and spaces allows one to understand past events, consider the future including future consequences of past and present behavior, appreciate the differences between one's own perspective and the perspectives of others, and respond to others in a socially appropriate manner. In this light, deficits in perspective taking could have devastating consequences.

Failure to appreciate the perspective of others might lead one to give little thought to the social consequences of one's behavior or to make erroneous conclusions about the intentions of others including the formation of beliefs of persecution. Failure to consider the implications of behavior (HERE-NOW) in terms of its consequences (THERE-THEN) might be associated with amotivation. Failure to appreciate how one's past behavior (THERE-THEN) is associated with one's present circumstances might lead one to describe the self in terms of prevailing verbal contingencies even in the absence of a history that supports one's present self-description including grandiose delusions. Failure to see one's self (ME-HERE-NOW) as the source of verbal stimulation could lead to hallucinations and delusions of reference falsely attributed to sources outside of the self. In short, failure to adequately relate stimuli in terms of the perspectives of person, place, and time could account for both positive and negative symptoms of psychosis.

Barnes-Holmes, McHugh, and Barnes-Holmes (2006) demonstrated a developmental trend in perspective-taking ability through a series of experiments in which persons of different ages were asked to answer a series of progressively more difficult perspective-taking questions. Subjects responded to several questions that encompassed the perspective-taking frames of ME-YOU, HERE-THERE, and NOW-THEN in simple, combined and reverse form. More simple questions required consideration of only a single frame of perspective, for instance, "I have a red brick and you have a green brick. If I was you and you were me, which brick would you have?" More complicated questions involved two frames of perspective. For instance, "Yesterday you were sitting there on the blue chair and today you are sitting here on the black chair. If here was there and there was here and if now was then and then was now where would you be sitting now?" They found that children made more errors than adults, that subjects of all ages had more difficulty with the perspectives of time and place than the perspective of person and that subjects with autism made many more errors than normally developing subjects.

Evidence for the role of such perspective-taking deficits in psychosis is preliminary and promising. Specifically, Bach (2006) administered this same questionnaire to persons diagnosed with a psychotic disorder and experiencing delusions or hallucinations Subjects made many more errors than the normally developing sample tested by Barnes-Holmes and colleagues (2006) and the number of errors was positively correlated with symptom severity as measured by the Brief Psychiatric Rating Scale (Overall & Gorham, 1962).

There is also evidence that persons with schizophrenia fail to make use of contextual information in adjusting behavior. Such contextual insensitivity may lead persons to misinterpret the meaning of words with multiple meanings and to require excessive contextual information before such information is used to adjust behavior (Titone, Levy, & Holzman, 2000). Research shows that those with delusional beliefs make less use of relevant contextual cues in forming hypotheses about the world and that making judgments with minimal information may lead to erroneous hypotheses about the world and to overestimating that one's hypothesis is correct (McGuire, Junginger, Serrhel, Burright, & Donovick, 2001). The research on contextual insensitivity provides indirect support for perspective-taking deficits in schizophrenia, in that perspective-taking ability would be required for understanding social contextual cues and deficits in this skill would make contextual-insensitivity likely.

In itself, the observation that persons with psychotic symptoms make more perspective-taking errors is interesting but as yet, has not influenced treatment practices. However, promising treatment protocols for teaching perspective taking skills are in development and have promising preliminary results (Barnes-Holmes, Barnes-Holmes, & McHugh, 2004). Extensions of this work for psychosis are underway (Bach, 2006). A primary difference between the perspective-taking versus theory of mind approach is that the perspective-taking approach has greater generalizability; a theory of mind account limits perspective taking to noting that other's have a different perspective from one's self. A relational frame theory account of perspective taking considers the multiple perspectives of person, place, and time.

Acceptance and Avoidance

Overt behavior associated with hallucinations and delusions often has more negative consequences for the individual than do the symptoms themselves. For example, when someone commits a crime while following a command hallucination, it is the crime that is consequated, not the hallucination. If someone disturbs neighbors with paranoid behavior or by 'talking back' to voices (Bach & Shawyer, 2006), the neighbor will report the disturbing behavior to the police, not the voices. Practically speaking, hallucinations and delusions are usually problematic when they cause subjective distress to the individual experiencing them, or when the individual responds to the content of a hallucination or delusional belief in ways that have negative social consequences or threaten the safety of one's self or others. These secondary symptoms are viewed as important targets of intervention within the field of psychosocial rehabilitation (Bachrach, 1992), in Acceptance and Commitment Therapy (Bach & Hayes, 2002; Gaudiano & Herbert, 2006), and in some cognitive behavioral approaches (Turkington & Siddle, 2000).

Many approaches to understanding psychiatric symptoms emphasize the verbal *content* of private events and treatment approaches emphasize trying to change unwanted or faulty content (Hayes, 1994). For instance, cognitive therapies for delusions and hallucinations emphasize eliminating delusional thoughts or hallucinations through testing reality and challenging beliefs (Gaudiano, 2005). Reduction of private symptoms (e.g., frequency of hallucinations or delusions) is the primary outcome measure in most trials of CBT for schizophrenia (Tarrier & Wykes, 2004). Such approaches appear to presume that delusional beliefs and hallucinations per se are problematic and that normal functioning will resume if the symptoms and/or associated distress are decreased. A functional contextual approach places less emphasis on the content of symptoms and more emphasis on the function of symptoms. For instance, research on psychosis using Acceptance and Commitment Therapy has suggested that even in the absence of significant reduction in delusions and hallucinations functioning can improve as measured by decreased hospitalization (Bach & Hayes, 2002).

While delusions and hallucinations may appear bizarre and are often regarded as more 'severe' than other symptoms of mental illness (Corrigan & Holzman, 2001), there is much evidence that they are on a continuum with 'normal' psychological phenomena (Turkington, & Siddle, 2000). All beliefs may be characterized as interactions between ones thoughts and the environment (Bentall, Kinderman, & Kaney, 1994). Beliefs are influenced and evaluated as "true" through one's thoughts and by one's actions and the consequences one experiences as a result of these actions. Strauss (1969) has advocated that beliefs be characterized on a continuum rather than being regarded as merely delusional or non-delusional. Bentall (2001) raises important philosophical questions about the ability to prove that many beliefs are false, as such claims presume that one can definitively identify reality, incontrovertible proof, and correct versus incorrect inferences. The finding that there is no evidence of a reasoning impairment in deluded subjects when compared to normal subjects also supports the notion that normal and delusional beliefs are continuous phenomena (Kozak & Foa, 1994). It is well known that, when interpreting environmental events, individuals tend to use information in a way that confirms their existing beliefs. Delusional individuals are also likely to hold these reasoning biases.

Other evidence for the continuity of delusional and non-delusional beliefs is based on the theory that delusional beliefs result from attempts to make sense of anomalous sensory experiences, which occurs commonly in those with delusions (Maher, 1988). This may explain why delusions so often occur secondary to hallucinations; the delusional belief functions to explain the abnormal sensory experience of the hallucination (Chadwick & Lowe, 1994). Further, normal subjects also develop irrational beliefs when exposed to anomalous experiences under experimental conditions (Kozak & Foa, 1994), and most individuals occasionally make attributions about events that are later proved false and have thoughts that may be evaluated by others as paranoid or grandiose without being regarded as delusional. Even beliefs that may be evaluated as delusional are not always associated with adverse consequences. Persons with delusional beliefs usually only present for treatment when they are significantly distressed by delusional thought content, or when they behave inappropriately in response to delusional thought content and are involuntarily hospitalized (e.g., after they call the police, shout at or threaten others, or claim money or property that does not belong to them). Maher (1988) points out that delusional beliefs and related overt behaviors are no more difficult to modify than are beliefs and practices regarded as 'non-delusional' such as political or spiritual beliefs.

Auditory hallucinations may also be regarded as continuous with ordinary perceptual experience. Normal individuals can be induced to experience hallucinations under conditions of sensory or sleep deprivation (Oswald, 1974), and most individuals misattribute or misidentify auditory stimuli at times (Turkington & Siddle, 2000), for instance hearing one's name being called in the absence of a person calling one's name or misidentifying the source of a noise. Further, clinical subjects experiencing auditory hallucinations often respond to hallucinatory content in a manner similar to those experiencing self-generated thoughts. When an individual's relation to the content of auditory hallucinations is considered, they are similar to the experience of unwanted intrusive thoughts (Wells & Davies, 1994). The primary distinction between the experience of hallucinations and intrusive thoughts is that the hallucinating person experiences the source of the thought as an external voice, while the normal subject recognizes an intrusive thought as being self-generated (Heilbrun, 1980). Also, the majority of persons who report hallucinations have no mental health problems at all (Tien, 1991), and while most persons with schizophrenia make negative evaluations about auditory hallucinations, 50% also make positive evaluations, such as the voices keep them company or say nice things about them (Miller, O'Connor, & DiPasquale, 1993).

Considering delusional beliefs and hallucinations as points on a continuum rather than as discontinuous with normal experience has both clinical and theoretical implications. Symptoms that are seen as abnormal are more likely to be rejected. As will be discussed further below, normalizing symptoms may facilitate acceptance of them.

Thought Suppression and Avoidance

The literature on thought suppression—deliberately attempting to control or suppress thought content—may be useful in understanding symptoms of psychosis and responses to symptoms of psychosis. Persons experiencing auditory hallucinations appear to respond to thought content in a manner similar to unwanted thoughts experienced as self-generated (a perspective-taking error perhaps). Research suggests that many attempt to control unwanted thoughts by trying to suppress them. However, there is much evidence that when one attempts to suppress a thought, a rebound effect occurs in which the frequency of the thought increases following an initial reduction in symptom frequency (Wegner, Schneider, Carter, & White, 1987). Further, when an individual tries to control private events in one domain of behavior, it is more difficult to exert conscious control over other simultaneously occurring behaviors, which suggests that the capacity to exert conscious control over one's own behavior is fairly limited (Bargh & Chartrand, 1999). Since many individuals experiencing hallucinations, and some of those experiencing delusions, try to suppress the unwanted material, thought suppression may be a factor in the etiology of hallucinations and delusions. Thought suppression would not impact the genesis of hallucinations, but might paradoxically increase their frequency.

There is also evidence that engaging in verbal worry following exposure to a stressful stimulus is associated with an increase in intrusive images about the stressor (Wells & Papageoriou, 1995). Individuals with schizophrenia are known to talk more about issues related to disordered thinking, to make more frequent references to their own cognitions (Rosenberg & Tucker, 1979), and to experience more frequent hallucinations during periods of anxiety and stress (Slade, 1972) as compared to normal controls. As a result, increased attention to their own verbal behavior may paradoxically lead to an increase in the occurrence of thoughts the individual is attempting to suppress.

Other negative consequences of thought suppression have been found. For example, research indicates that suppressed thought content and mood become associated, such that the occurrence of one leads to the occurrence of the other (Wenzlaff, Wegner, & Klein, 1991). For example, an individual feeling depressed and experiencing hallucinations would be more likely to experience hallucinations when depressed and/or to become depressed when hallucinating if he has tried to suppress hallucinatory content when depressed.

For many reasons, individuals with delusions and hallucinations may engage in avoidance strategies such as thought suppression to control them. First, individuals are more likely to use avoidance strategies to cope with thoughts that are evaluated as being subject to high social disapproval or as indicating that one might cause harm to one's self or another (Freeston & Ladouceur, 1993; Purdon & Clark, 1994). Delusions, and command auditory hallucinations often have content that would elicit social disapproval. Further, positive symptoms of schizophrenia are associated with negative-self evaluation. That is, as negative self-evaluation increases so do positive symptoms of schizophrenia (Barrowclough, Tarrier, Humphreys, Ward, Gregg, & Andrews, 2003). Also, compared to normal controls, persons experiencing hallucinations have stronger beliefs that it is not normal to have intrusive or unwanted thoughts (Lobban, Haddock, Kinderman & Wells, 2002). Hallucinating subjects also report less confidence in their cognitive processes and believe that consistency of thought is very important.

Researchers hypothesize that meta-cognitive beliefs such as confidence in cognitive processes may play a role in the genesis of hallucinations. However, a functional analytic view would suggest that meta-cognitive beliefs may play a role in the responses an individual makes in relation to hallucinations rather than the genesis of hallucinations. For example, hallucinating subjects who reported decreased believability in their hallucinations after ACT therapy reported a higher frequency of hallucinations (Bach & Hayes, 2002), suggesting that decreased believability leads to decreased attempts to suppress symptoms and/or to increased willingness to report symptoms.

In summary, perspective-taking deficits may contribute to the formation of false beliefs, play a role in the subjective experience of hallucinations, and contribute to negative symptoms such as avolition. Furthermore, focusing on the content of the symptoms rather than one's response to the symptoms may foster non-acceptance of symptoms, and attempts to avoid and control symptoms which may exacerbate rather than solve the problem. Increased distress, dysfunctional behavior and poor social competence are likely outcomes. Treatment approaches informed by the above formulation of psychosis are a relatively new and promising approach to the treatment of symptoms.

Acceptance and Commitment Therapy in the Treatment of Psychosis

Traditional cognitive therapies focus on changing or eliminating undesirable thoughts, feelings and bodily sensations. In the case of delusions and hallucinations, most cognitive therapies emphasize eliminating delusional thoughts or hallucinations through challenging beliefs or testing reality (Gaudiano, 2005). Such approaches to the treatment of delusions and hallucinations are based upon an implicit assumption that the false beliefs per se are the problem, and that once these private events no longer occur, the individual will again function normally. However, many persons with schizophrenia are described as treatment resistant, a significant minority are not responsive to medication (Tarrier & Wykes, 2004), and 75% experience residual symptoms even while taking antipsychotic medication (Brier, Schreiber, Dyer, & Pickar, 1991).

Since hallucinations and delusions appear to be highly resistant to permanent elimination, a more pragmatic approach might be to teach individuals to respond differently to their own private events. As stated earlier, from a functional contextual perspective, it is not the occurrence of the symptoms (i.e., hallucinations or delusions) so much as the individual's interaction with them that leads to dysfunction. As discussed above, attempts to avoid and control hallucinations and delusional beliefs appears to play a key role in dysfunctional behaviors associated with symptoms. Individuals who believe psychotic symptom content is real also demonstrate *cognitive fusion* with the content. In contrast, individuals who approach their thoughts in the context that symptom content does not describe reality may see their mental illness or the process of symptoms as the problem (e.g., the problem is schizoaffective disorder, or the problem is hearing voices). When an individual is cognitively fused with hallucinations or delusions, behavior done to avoid such stimuli becomes more likely, and when cognitively defused, such avoidance behavior becomes less likely. Likewise, when cognitively fused, those with schizophrenia may be more likely to act in accordance with the private events. For example, when an individual experiencing voices telling him to kill himself actually makes a suicide attempt or when the individual experiencing a voice telling her to kill someone attempts homicide, he or she demonstrates fusion with the cognition.

From a functional-contextualistic perspective, a variety of therapeutic strategies are employed to create a context that supports (a) acceptance rather than avoidance of psychotic symptoms, (b) defusion from the literal meaning of the symptoms, and (c) engagement in behaviors that are in accordance with one's own unique set of values, despite the content of the psychotic symptoms.

Acceptance and Commitment Therapy (ACT; Hayes, Strosahl, & Wilson, 1999) is a functional contextualistic treatment that attempts to train these core therapeutic strategies. Empirical support for ACT in the treatment of psychosis is growing. Two randomized controlled trials of a brief ACT intervention with psychiatric inpatients showed reduced rates of rehospitalization during a four month follow-up period (Bach & Hayes, 2002: Gaudiano & Herbert, 2006) and case studies (e.g., see García & Pérez, 2001) and interventions combining ACT interventions with more traditional cognitive therapy have yielded impressive preliminary outcomes (Bach & Shawyer, 2006). Below, the basic therapeutic targets when using ACT to treat psychotic disorders are briefly described.

Acceptance Rather than Avoidance

To specifically counter the destructive response tendencies to avoid or otherwise control hallucinatory/delusional symptoms and or the various emotions such symptoms evoke, various therapeutic strategies are used to promote the acceptance of private events. According to ACT, willingness to experience all private events without avoidance and to behave according to the consequences of the overt behavior rather than to the evaluation of private events or their verbal stimulus functions allows for more behavioral options. Acceptance is not viewed as a feeling or belief, but is an action or stance one takes in relation to ones thoughts and feelings including delusional beliefs and hallucinations. Acceptance of symptoms of psychosis can now be assessed using a recently developed instrument for assessing acceptance of symptoms of psychosis (Shawyer, Ratcliff, Mackinnon, Farhall, Hayes, & Copolov, in press).

Throughout ACT, the client is exposed to his own private events including hallucinatory and delusional content when applicable. This allows the individual to practice experiencing the emotions they have tried to avoid in the safe environment of the therapy room. Clients usually experience that the worst consequence of exposure to the feared content is feeling uncomfortable, and clients also have the opportunity to observe that they can act in spite of experiencing subjectively unpleasant thoughts, emotions, or bodily sensations.

Cognitive Defusion

A variety of therapeutic strategies may be utilized to promote cognitive defusion. First, normalizing symptoms such as hallucinations may reduce distress and increase attention to process and willingness to report symptoms when they occur. When symptoms are normalized, an individual experiencing hallucinations also may be more able to separate or defuse from such maladaptive cognitions as "I am bad." For example, when the voices say "You are bad," the patient may have a more functional response of "I feel bad when I hallucinate" or "I don't like hallucinations," rather than guilt or aversive feelings elicited by the hallucination.

A second therapeutic approach designed to decrease cognitive fusion involves training deliteralization. The ACT therapist teaches the individual to focus more on the process of thinking and the workability of behavior tied to particular thoughts, and less on the content of private events. For example, hearing voices say "you are a bad person" does not mean that one is actually a bad person. Individuals are taught to distance themselves from their thoughts by using language conventions such as talking about private events by emphasizing the type of verbal event rather the content of that event through using the phrase, "I'm having the thought that...", or "I'm having the feeling..." (Hayes & Wilson, 1994). For example, the individual with paranoid delusions would be taught to say, "I'm having the thought that they're out to get me", instead of saying, "They're out to get me." Deliteralization is similar to the concept of disidentification described by Teasdale (1999) as a component of some cognitive therapies.

A third defusion technique involves training the client that he or she need not act on his or her thoughts. People have a tendency to attribute automatic behaviors and behaviors outside their control to acts of will (Wegner & Wheatley, 199). For example, the person hearing voices saying, "don't go to your appointment" may inform treatment providers that the voices "made me" skip the appointment. In ACT, the hallucinating individual is reminded that he can go to his appointment even when voices tell him not to. The individual is instructed to "just notice" the thought, feeling, or sensation, rather than acting to avoid it or acting on its content (Hayes et al., 1996). Clients are encouraged to distance from thoughts and to behave in the service of attaining valued outcomes. Most clients will find that avoidance strategies keep them from many valued experiences they would like to have, and that deliteralization allows for more effective behavior.

Values

Both acceptance strategies and therapeutic techniques designed to promote cognitive defusion are done with the long-term goal of engaging in a more functional and productive life. Not unlike various other therapeutic approaches, a focus on an individual's goals in all life domains considered important to the consumer (e.g., social, occupational, or spiritual) is an important component of a functional-contextualistic approach. In ACT clients are encouraged to explore their goals and values so that they may identify behaviors that might lead to the accomplishment of desired goals and are consistent with these values (Hayes et al., 1999). Avoidance behaviors that function to reduce unpleasant private events are often inconsistent with one's stated goals and values. Also, overt behavior in relation to symptom content may also hinder goal attainment. Persons who talk aloud to voices or pursue perceived enemies may find it difficult to establish and maintain employment or meaningful social relationships. Values clarification and goal setting may increase the individual's willingness to engage in new behavior patterns and learn new skills; broadly speaking, to increase approach behaviors and decrease avoidance behaviors.

Goal-focused interventions also may impact symptoms of psychosis by changing the context of personally relevant aspects of the individual's verbal environment. For example, as discussed above, delusions may function as a defense against low self-esteem in the face of failure (Bentall et al., 2001). Instead of attributing failure to one's self the paranoid individual attributes failure to the evil intentions of others. An individual who is taking steps towards attaining goals may report increased self-esteem in the absence of explanatory fictions. The individual does not need to avoid negative self-evaluation if self-evaluations are more positive, thus delusional thought content may show up less in the context of goal attainment. Goal setting and subsequent goal attainment may allow for the establishment of new verbal relations among stimuli previously associated with danger. Persons with serious mental illness often have a lack of social roles beyond that of 'mental patient'. New social roles such as 'friend' or 'coworker' may allow for the establishment of new verbal relations such that a person who previously functioned as a potential malevolent other may have new stimulus functions that allow for the emergence of new verbal relations that control new overt behavior patterns. Similarly, persons reporting hallucinations may find that as they increase behavior associated with goal attainment attention to internal stimulation decreases as there are more opportunities for external stimulation.

Considering psychosis from a functional contextual perspective offers a means of considering the etiology of psychotic disorders behaviorally in a manner useful for developing psychosocial interventions for their treatment. Early trials of functional contextual treatment approaches are so far promising and several studies building on this foundation are now underway.

References

American Psychiatric Association. (2000). *Diagnostic and Statistical Manual of Mental Disorders* (4th Ed., Text Revision). Washington, D.C.: American Psychiatric Association.

Bach, P. (2006). *Perspective-taking and psychosis*. Paper presented at the Second World Conference on ACT, RFT, and Contextual Behavioural Science. London, United Kingdom.

Bach, P., & Hayes, S. C. (2002). The use of acceptance and commitment therapy to prevent rehospitalization of psychotic patients: a randomized controlled trial. *Journal of Consulting and Clinical Psychology, 70*, 1129-1139.

Bach, P., & Shawyer, F. (2006). *Acceptance and psychosis*. Paper presented at the second world conference on ACT, RFT, and contextual behavioural science. London, United Kingdom.

Bachrach, L. L. (1992). Psychosocial rehabilitation and psychiatry in the care of long-term patients. *The American Journal of Psychiatry, 149*, 1455-1463.

Bargh, J. A., & Chartrand, T. L. (1999) The unbearable automaticity of being. *American Psychologist, 54*, 462-479.

Barnes-Holmes, Y., Barnes-Holmes, D., & McHugh, L. (2004). Teaching derived relational responding to young children. *Journal of Early and Intensive Behavioral Intervention, 1*, 4-10.

Barnes-Holmes, Y., McHugh, L., & Barnes-Holmes, D. (2006). Perspective-taking and theory of mind: A relational frame account. *The Behavior Analyst Today, 5*, 15-25.

Baron-Cohen, S. (1995). *Mindblindness: An essay on autism and theory of mind*. Cambridge, MA: MIT Press.

Barrowclough, C., Tarrier, N., Humphreys, L., Ward, J., Gregg, L., & Andrews, B. (2003). Self-esteem in schizophrenia: Relationships between self-evaluation, family attitudes, and symptomatology. *Journal of Abnormal Psychology, 112*, 92-99.

Bassett, A. S., Chow, E. W. C., Abdel Malik, P., Gheorgiu, M., Husted, J., & Weksberg, R. (2003). The schizophrenia phenotype in 22q11 deletion syndrome. American Journal of Psychiatry, *160*, 1580–1586.

Bentall, R. P. (2001). Social cognition and delusional beliefs. In P. W. Corrigan & D. L. Penn (Eds.), *Social cognition and schizophrenia* (pp. 123-148). Washington, D. C.: American Psychological Association.

Bentall, R. P., Corcoran, R., Howard, R, Blackwood, N., & Kinderman, P. (2001). Persecutory delusions: A review and theoretical integration. *Clinical Psychology Review, 21,* 1143-1192.

Bentall, R. P., Haddock, J. G., Slade, P., & Peter, D. (1994). Cognitive behavior therapy for persistent auditory hallucinations: From theory to therapy. *Behavior Therapy, 25,* 51-66.

Bentall, R. P., & Kinderman, P. (1999). Self-regulation, affect, and psychosis: The role of social cognition in paranoia and mania. In T. Daglish & M. J. Power (Eds.), *Science and practice of cognitive behavior therapy* (pp. 353-381). Chinchester, England: Wiley.

Bentall, R. P., Kinderman, P., & Kaney, S. (1994). The self, attributional processes, and abnormal beliefs: Towards a model of persecutory delusions. *Behaviour Research and Therapy, 32,* 331-341.

Brier, A., Schreiber, J. L., Dyer, J., & Pickar, D. (1991). National Institute of Mental Health longitudinal study of chronic schizophrenia: Prognosis and predictors of outcome. *Archives of General Psychiatry, 48,* 239-246.

Brune, M. (2005). "Theory of mind" in schizophrenia: A review of the literature. *Schizophrenia Bulletin, 31,* 21-42.

Buka, S. L., Tsuang, M. T., Torrey, E. F., Klebanoff, M. A., Bernstein, D., & Yolken, R. H. (2001). *Maternal infections and subsequent psychosis among offspring. Archives of General Psychiatry, 58,* 1032-1037.

Chadwick, P. D. J., & Lowe, C. F. (1994). A cognitive approach to measuring and modifying delusion. *Behaviour Research and Therapy, 32,* 355-367.

Corcoran, R. (2001). Theory of mind in schizophrenia. In D. Penn & P. Corrigan (Eds.), *Social cognition in schizophrenia* (pp. 149-174). Washington, D.C.: American Psychiatric Association.

Corrigan, P. W. (2000). Mental health stigma as social attribution: Implications for research methods and attitude change. *Clinical Psychology: Science and Practice, 7,* 48-67.

Corrigan, P. W., & Holzman, K. L. (2001). Do stereotype threats influence social cognitive deficits in schizophrenia? In P. W. Corrigan & D. L. Penn (Eds.), *Social cognition and schizophrenia* (pp. 175-194). Washington, D.C.: American Psychological Association.

Corrigan, P. W., & Penn, D. L. (2001). Introduction: framing models of social cognition and schizophrenia. In P. W. Corrigan & D. L. Penn (Eds.), *Social cognition and schizophrenia* (pp. 3-37). Washington, D. C.: American Psychological Association.

Freeston, M. H., & Ladouceur, R. (1993). Appraisal of cognitive intrusions and response style: Replication and extension. *Behaviour Research and Therapy, 31,* 185-191.

Frith, C. D. (1992). *The cognitive neuropsychology of schizophrenia.* Hillsdale, NJ: Erlbaum.

García, J. M. M., & Pérez, M. A. (2001). ACT as a treatment for psychotic symptom. The case of auditory hallucinations. *Analisis y Modificación de Conducta, 27,* 455-472.

Garety, P. A., Fowler, D., & Kuipers, E. (2000). Cognitive-behavioral therapy for medication-resistant symptoms. *Schizophrenia Bulletin, 26,* 73-81.

Gaudiano, B. A. (2005). Cognitive behavior therapies for psychotic disorders: Current empirical status and future directions. *Clinical Psychology: Science and Practice, 12,* 33-49.

Gaudiano, B. A., & Herbert, J. D. (2006). Believability of hallucinations as a potential mediator of their frequency and associated distress in psychotic inpatients. *Behavioural and Cognitive psychotherapy, 34,* 497-502.

Goff, D. C., & Coyle, J. T. (2001). The emerging role of glutamate in the pathophysiology and treatment of schizophrenia. *American Journal of Psychiatry, 158,* 1367-1377.

Gorman, J. M. (1996). *The new psychiatry.* New York: St. Martin's Press.

Gottesman, I. I. (1991). *Schizophrenia genesis.* New York: Freeman.

Green, P., & Preston, M. (1981). Reinforcement of vocal correlates of auditory hallucinations by auditory feedback: A case study. *British Journal of Psychiatry, 139,* 204-208.

Haddock, G., Tarrier, N., Spaulding, W., Yusupoff, L., Kinney, C., & McCarthy, E. (1998). Individual cognitive-cehaviour therapy in the treatment of hallucinations and delusions. *Clinical Psychology Review, 18,* 821-838.

Hayes, S. C. (1994). Content, context, and the types of psychological acceptance. In S. C. Hayes, N. S. Jacobson, V. M. Follette, & M. J. Dougher (Eds.), *Acceptance and change: Content and context in psychotherapy* (pp. 13-32). Reno, NV: Context Press.

Hayes, S. C., Fox, E., Gifford, E. V., Wilson, K. G., Barnes-Holmes, D., & Healy, O. (2001). Derived relational responding as learned behavior. In S. C. Hayes, D. Barnes-Holmes, & B. Roche (Eds.). *Relational frame theory: A post-Skinnerian account of human language and cognition* (pp. 21-50). New York: Plenum Press.

Hayes, S. C., Strosahl, K. D., & Wilson, K. G. (1999). *Acceptance and commitment therapy: An experiential approach to behavior change.* New York: Guilford Press.

Hayes, S. C., & Wilson, K. G. (1994). Acceptance and commitment therapy: Altering the verbal support for experiential avoidance. *The Behavior Analyst, 17,* 289-303.

Heilbrun, A. B. (1980). Impaired recognition of self-expressed thoughts in patients with auditory hallucinations, *Journal of Abnormal Psychology, 89,* 728-736.

Heinrichs, R. W. (2005). The primacy of cognition in schizophrenia. *American Psychologist, 60,* 229-242.

Hoek, H. W., Brown, A. B., & Susser, E. (1998) The Dutch famine and schizophrenia spectrum disorders. *Social Psychiatry and Psychiatric Epidemiology, 33,* 373-379.

Hoffman, R. E. (1986) Verbal hallucinations and language production processes in schizophrenia. *Behavioral and Brain Sciences, 9,* 503-517.

Hoffman, R. E., & Satel, S. L. (1993). Language therapy for schizophrenic patients with persistent 'voices'. *The British Journal of Psychiatry, 162,* 755-758.

Hollister, J. M., Laing, P., & Mednick, S. A. (1996). Rhesus incompatibility as a risk factor for schizophrenia in male adults. *Archives of General Psychiatry, 53,* 19-24.

Kozak, M. J., & Foa, E. B. (1994). Obsessions, overvalued ideas, and delusions in obsessive-compulsive disorder. *Behaviour Research and Therapy, 32,* 343-353.

Lieberman, J. A., Stroup, T. S., & Perkins, D. O. (Eds.) (2006) *The American Psychiatric Publishing textbook of schizophrenia.* Washington, D.C.: American Psychiatric Publishing.

Lobban, F., Haddock, G., Kinderman, P., & Wells, A. (2002). The role of metacognitive beliefs in auditory hallucinations. Personality and Individual Differences, *32,* 1351-1363.

Lowe, C. F., & Chadwick, P. D. J. (1990). Verbal control of delusions. *Behavior Therapy, 21,* 461-479.

Maher, B. A. (1988). Anomalous experience and delusional thinking: The logic of explanations. In T. F. Oltmanns & B. A. Maher (Eds.), *Delusional beliefs.* New York: Wiley and Sons Inc.

Maher, B. A. (1980). Contextual constraint and the recall of verbal material in schizophrenia: The effect of thought disorder. *British Journal of Psychiatry, 137,* 69-73.

McGuffin, P., Owen, M. J., & Gottesman, I. I. (Eds.) (2004). *Psychiatric genetics and genomics.* Oxford, England: Oxford University Press.

McGuire, L., Junginger, J., Adams, S. G., Burright, R., & Donovick, P. (2001). Delusions and delusional reasoning. *Journal of Abnormal Psychology, 110,* 259-266.

Meuser, K. T., & Salyers, M. P. (2003). Schizophrenia. In M. Hersen & S. M. Turner (Eds.) *Adult psychopathology and diagnosis* (4th ed.). Hoboken, N. J.: John Wiley & Sons, Inc.

Miller, L. J., O'Connor, E., & DiPasquale, T. (1993). Patients' attitudes toward hallucinations. *American Journal of Psychiatry, 150,* 584-588.

Mitelman, S. A., Shihabuddin, L., Brickman, A. M., Hazlett, E. A., & Buchsbaum, M. S. (2003). MRI assessment of gray and white matter distribution in Brodmann's areas of the cortex in patients with schizophrenia with good and poor outcomes. *American Journal of Psychiatry, 160,* 2154-2168.

Murray, R. M., Jones, P. B., van Os, J., & Cannon, M. (2003). *The epidemiology of schizophrenia.* Cambridge, England: Cambridge University Press.

Newman, L. (2001). What is "social cognition?" Four approaches and their implications for schozophrenia research. In P. Corrigan & D. Penn (Eds.), *Social cognition and schizophrenia* (pp. 41-72). Washington, D.C.: American Psychiatric Association.

Oswald, I. (1974). *Sleep* (3rd ed.). Harmondsworth, England: Penguin.

Overall, J. E., & Gorham, J. R. (1962). The brief psychiatric rating scale. *Psychological Reports, 10,* 799-812.

Purdon, C., & Clark, D. A. (1993) Obsessive intrusive thoughts in non-clinical subjects. Part I: Content and relation with depressive, anxious and obsessional symptoms. *Behaviour Research and Therapy, 31,* 713-720.

Rosenberg, S. D., & Tucker, G. J. (1979). Verbal behavior and schizophrenia: The semantic dimension. *Archives of General Psychiatry, 36*, 1331-1337.

Salzinger, K. (1984). The immediacy hypothesis in a theory of schizophrenia. In W. D. Spaulding & J. K. Cole (Eds.), *Nebraska symposium on motivation: Theories of schizophrenia and psychosis.* Lincoln, Nebraska: University of Nebraska Press.

Schneider, F., & Deldin, P. J. (2001). Genetics and schizophrenia. In H. E. Adams & P. B. Sutker (Eds.), *Comprehensive handbook of psychopathology* (3rd ed.) (pp. 371-402). New York: Kluwer Academic/Plenum Publishers.

Siever, L. J., & Davis, K. L. (2004). The pathophysiology of schizophrenia disorders: Perspectives from the spectrum. *American Journal of Psychiatry, 161*, 398-413.

Shawyer, F., Ratcliff, K., Mackinnon, A., Farhall, J., Hayes, S., & Copolov, D. (In press). The Voices Acceptance and Action Scale (VAAS): Pilot data. *Journal of Clinical Psychology.*

Slade, P. D. (1972). The effects of systematic desensitization on auditory hallucinations. *Behaviour Research and Therapy, 10*, 85-91.

Strauss, J. S. (1969). Hallucinations and delusions as points on continua function. *Archives of General Psychiatry, 21,*581-586.

Tamminga, C. A. (2006). The neurobiology of cognition in schizophrenia. *The Journal of Clinical Psychiatry, 67*, 9-13.

Tarrier, N., & Wykes, T. (2004). Is there evidence that cognitive behaviour therapy is an effective treatment for schizophrenia? A cautious or cautionary tale? *Behaviour Research and Therapy, 42*, 1377-1401.

Teasdale, J. D. (1999). The relationship between cognition and emotion: The mind-in-place in mood disorders. In D. M. Clark & C. G. Fairburn (Eds.), *Science and practice of cognitive behaviour therapy* (pp. 67-93). New York: Oxford University Press Inc.

Tien, A. Y. (1991). Distributions of hallucinations in the population. *Social Psychiatry and Psychiatric Epidemiology, 26*, 287-292.

Tienari, P., Wynne, L. C., Laksy, K., Moring, J., Niemenen, P., Sorri, A., et al. (2003). Genetic boundaries of the schizophrenia spectrum: Evidence from the Finnish adoptive family study of schizophrenia. *American Journal of Psychiatry, 160*, 1587-1594.

Titone, D., Levy, D. L., & Holzman, P. S. (2000). Contextual insensitivity in schizophrenic language processing: Evidence from lexical ambiguity. *Journal of Abnormal Psychology, 109*, 761-767.

Turkington, D., & Siddle, R. (2000). Improving understanding and coping in people with schizophrenia. *Psychiatric Rehabilitation Skills, 4*, 300-320.

Vauth, R., Loschmann, C., Rusch, N., & Corrigan, P. W. (2004). Understanding adherence to neuroleptic treatment in schizophrenia. *Psychiatry Research, 125*, 43-49.

Walker, E., Kestler, L., Bollini, A., & Hochman, K. M. (2004). Schizophrenia: Etiology and course. *Annual Review of Psychology, 55*, 401-430.

Wegner, D. M., Schneider, D. J., Carter, S. R., & White, T. L. (1987). Paradoxical effects of thought suppression. *Journal of Personality and Social Psychology, 53*, 5-13.

Wegner, D. M., & Wheatley, T. P. (1999). Apparent mental causation: Sources of the experience of will. *American Psychologist, 54*, 480-492.

Weinberger, D. R. (1996). On the plausibility of "the neurodevelopmental hypothesis" of schizophrenia. *Neuropsychopharmacology. 14*, 1S-11S.

Wells, A., & Davies, M. I. (1994). The Thought Control Questionnaire: A measure of individual differences in the control of unwanted thoughts. *Behaviour Research and Therapy, 32*, 871-878.

Wells, A., & Papageorgiou, C. (1995) Worry and the incubation of intrusive images following stress. *Behaviour Research and Therapy, 33*, 579-583.

Wenzlaff R. M., Wegner, D. M., & Klein, S. B. (1991). The role of thought suppression in the bonding of thought and mood. *Journal of Personality and Social Psychology, 60*, 500-508.

World Health Organization Division of Mental Health and Prevention of Substance Abuse (1998). *Schizophrenia and public health.* Geneva, Switzerland: World Health Organization.

Zubin, J., & Spring, B. (1977). Vulnerability: A new view of schizophrenia. *Journal of Abnormal Psychology, 86*, 103-126.

Chapter 9

Addictive Behavior:
An RFT-Enhanced Theory of Addiction

Kathleen M. Palm
Brown Medical School / Butler Hospital

Substance use disorders are the most frequently occurring mental health problem in the United States (Regier, Farmer, Rae, Locke, Keith, Judd et al., 1990). Researchers estimate that the prevalence of lifetime alcohol dependence ranges from 8% to 14% (Grant, Dawson, Stinson, Chou, Dufour, & Pickering, 2004; Grant, Stinson, Dawson, Chou, Dufour, Compton et al., 1994; Narrow, Rae, Robins, & Regier, 2002). According to the 2004 National Household Survey on Drug Abuse, an estimated 22.5 million people met criteria for substance dependence or abuse in the past year, with 18.2 million dependent on or abusing alcohol, and 3.4 million dependent on or abusing both alcohol and illicit drugs (Substance Abuse and Mental Health Services Administration [SAMHSA], 2006). Unfortunately, the incidence of substance use and associated problems has been increasing. Researchers found that between 1990 and 1998, there was a 63% increase for marijuana, a 37% increase for cocaine, a 92% increase for hallucinogens, a 154% increase for inhalants, a 181% increase for pain relievers, a 132% increase for tranquilizers, a 165% increase for stimulants, and a 90% increase for sedatives (SAMHSA, 1998).

Along with the increased incidence of substance use, there has been an increase in associated mortality and morbidity. In 2000, some of the leading causes of death in the United States included tobacco (435,000 deaths; 18.1%), alcohol (85,000 deaths; 3.5%), and illicit drug use (20,000 deaths; Mokdad, Marks, Stroup, & Gerberding, 2004). Substance abuse is associated with significant medical problems (e.g., neurocognitive dysfunction, heart disease, cancer, alcohol-related liver disease, and pancreatitis; Weintraub, Dixon, Delahanty, Schwartz, Johnson, Cohen et al., 2001) and soaring health care costs (Kranzler, Babor, & Lauerman, 1990). Accounting for treatment and prevention, healthcare, lost job productivity and earnings, and other costs related to crime and social welfare, the annual cost of alcohol and drug abuse in the United States is estimated to be $245.7 billion (National Institute on Drug Abuse [NIDA], 2004).

Substance Use Disorders

Some researchers have conceptualized substance involvement as a progression of substance use that ranges in severity from occasional use to problem use to substance abuse to substance dependence (Sanchez-Craig, 1986; Sobell, Wagner,

& Sobell, 2003), with more severe diagnoses being associated with tolerance and withdrawal. However, researchers have also found that some individuals can meet criteria for substance dependence without meeting criteria for abuse (Hasin, Hatzenbueler, Smith, & Grant, 2005). The *Diagnostic and Statistical Manual of Mental Disorders* (DSM-IV-TR; American Psychiatric Association [APA], 2000) defines substance dependence as a pattern of cognitive, behavioral, and physiological phenomena that persist despite exposure to repeated negative consequences. This repeated pattern usually involves compulsive drug-taking behavior, tolerance, and withdrawal. Substance dependence is also characterized by unsuccessful efforts at controlling substance use, a significant amount of time spent engaging in activities related to obtaining or using the substance, and impaired functioning in social, occupational, and recreational activities.

Tolerance typically involves either a need for a markedly increased amount of the substance in order to achieve intoxication or the desired effect, or a markedly diminished effect with continued use of the same amount of the substance (APA, 2000). The degree to which tolerance develops varies across substances. For example, as tolerance to a substance develops, individuals may be at an increased risk of serious harm or death due to a compromised capacity to notice the increasing toxicity associated with continued substance use. Acute lethal toxicity has been reported most frequently in cases of heroin and methadone overdose (Gable, 2004).

Withdrawal is marked by either a characteristic withdrawal syndrome for the substance, or the same substance being taken to relieve or avoid withdrawal symptoms (APA, 2000). Symptoms of withdrawal vary, with some substances having much more severe symptoms than others. For example, common nicotine withdrawal symptoms include depressed mood, insomnia, anxiety, irritability, difficulty concentrating, and restlessness, while alcohol withdrawal symptoms can include anxiety, insomnia, increased hand tremor, hallucinations, and grand mal seizures. Although there are individual variations on the experience of withdrawal, negative affect (i.e., irritability, depressed mood, sadness) is a common symptom across most withdrawal syndromes (Baker, Piper, McCarthy, Majeskie, & Fiore, 2004).

Etiology of Substance Use Disorders

Substance use disorders are complex and influenced by biological, psychological, and sociocultural variables. Over time, researchers have studied many underlying mechanisms in efforts to understand substance abuse and dependence. These lines of research have resulted in a great deal of information regarding biological etiology, gender differences, comorbidity, and environmental influences of addictive behaviors. Presently, there is a general consensus in the field that substance use problems are multi-determined and that theoretical models should address how biological, psychological, and sociocultural factors mutually influence each other in the development, maintenance, and cessation of addictive behavior.

Biological etiology. Research examining the biological etiology of substance dependence has largely focused on genetic factors. Familial studies have illustrated concordance rates of substance use disorders among family members, particularly twins; while more recent molecular genetics research has identified specific genetic components associated with substance dependence. Approximately 50% of alcohol dependent individuals have close relatives with alcohol dependence, while another 20% report alcoholism in extended family members (Schuckit, 1994, 1999). Similarly, evidence from twin studies suggests substantial genetic influence on the development of substance use disorders (Heath, Madden, Bucholz, Dinwiddie, Slutske, Bierut et al., 1999; Kendler, Walters, Neale, Kessler, Heath, & Eaves, 1995; Slutske Heath, Madden, Bucholz, Statham, & Martin, 2002; Tsuang, Bar, Harley, & Lyons, 2001). For example, in a study including 2,708 twin pairs, Knopik and colleagues (Knopik, Heath, Madden, Bucholz, Slutske, Nelson et al., 2004) found that genetic influences accounted for approximately 50% of the variance in alcohol dependence diagnoses.

Although there is likely no specific addiction gene, there are genetic influences on factors related to substance use. Inherited factors affecting absorption, distribution, and metabolism place individuals on a continuum of sensitivity to substances (Kreek, Bart, Lilly, LaForge, & Nielsen, 2005; Schuckit, 1994, 1999). For example, research has shown that in Asian populations, there is an inherited variation in the ability to metabolize acetaldehyde into acetic acid, which influences the risk for alcohol dependence (Harada, Agarwal, Goedde, Tagaki, & Ishikawa, 1982; Wall, Shea, Chan, & Carr, 2001). Thus, some individuals may require three to five drinks to achieve the same level of intoxication that others get from one to two drinks. Additionally, genetic influences on personality may impact risk-taking, sensation-seeking, or impulsive behaviors, which may increase the likelihood that a person will be in contact with illicit substances (Slutske et al., 2002).

Genes associated with dopamine, serotonin, endogenous opioids, anandamide, GABA, and glutamate have also been examined in relation to the neurobiological aspects of addiction and the reinforcing qualities of substances. For example, in a meta-analysis of 64 studies including 10,000 participants, Young, Lawford, Nutting, and Noble (2004) found that the A_1 allele of the DRD2 is a marker of substance use and even a stronger marker of severe misuse. DRD2 polymorphisms have been reported across a range of substance use disorders, including nicotine, stimulants, opiates, and alcohol (Young et al., 2004). Research indicates that the underlying brain processes associated with this genetic marker influence various neurotransmitter systems, particularly the dopaminergic system which is believed to play a role in drug-related reinforcement (Kreek et al., 2005).

The research examining the molecular genetics of addiction has grown exponentially in recent years. Some researchers have speculated that individuals' genetic composition may be responsible for the types of environments they seek out (Evans, Gillespie, & Martin, 2002). For example, the DRD2 A_1 allele, which has been associated with alcohol dependence and other substance use disorders, has also been associated with extraversion (Cohen, Young, Baek, Kessler, & Ranganath, 2005) and novelty seeking (Berman, Ozkaragoz, Young, & Noble, 2002). In other words, some individuals may have a genetic predisposition toward particular personality characteristics, which in turn may lead to a greater risk for substance abuse and dependence. Although this is an intriguing possibility, most researchers agree that it is an interaction of biological and environmental factors that lead to the development of substance abuse and dependence (e.g., Berman & Noble, 1997; Kendler et al., 1995; Tsuang et al., 2001; Young et al., 2004). Thus, individuals who have genetic risk factors will not necessarily develop substance dependence, but given additional psychological and environmental factors, they may be at an even greater risk than individuals who do not have a genetic predisposition. Genetics account for a portion of the variance in substance dependence diagnoses, but other psychological and environmental factors influence the manifestation of symptoms.

Gender differences. Substance use disorders are more commonly diagnosed in males than females (Anthony, Warner, & Kessler, 1994). According to data from the National Comorbidity Study (Anthony et al., 1994), the odds of having alcohol dependence for men versus women were 2.81, and for drug dependence were 1.62. Cross-national studies have replicated these findings (Wilsnack, Vogeltanz, Wilsnack, Harris, Ahlstrom, Bondy et al., 2000). Although the causes of these gender differences continue to be investigated and debated, several speculations include differences in metabolism, women's more restricted social roles, sensitivity to the effects of substances, and frequency and rate of substance consumption (Wilsnack et al., 2000).

Comorbid psychopathology and personality characteristics. The National Comorbidity Study (Kessler, 1994) indicated that 13.7% of the United States population suffers from concurrent substance use and mental health disorders within their lifetime. Approximately 78% of alcohol dependent men and 86% of alcohol dependent women met criteria for a lifetime diagnosis of another psychiatric disorder (Kessler, 1994), particularly affective and anxiety disorders (Grant, Stinson et al., 2004; Kessler, 1994; Kilpatrick, Ruggiero, Acierno, Saunders, Resnick, & Best, 2003; Regier et al., 1990). Some researchers have found that comorbid diagnoses may influence the course of substance dependence. Among children and adolescents, conduct disorder is associated with an increased risk for both onset and progression of substance use disorders (Caspi, Moffitt, Newman, & Silva, 1996; Clark, Parker, & Lynch, 1999). Hasin and colleagues (Hasin, Liu, Nunes, McCloud, Samet, & Endicott, 2002) examined the temporal relationship of major depressive disorder (MDD) to substance dependence in adults. They examined substance use and remission patterns among individuals with no history of MDD, current substance-induced MDD, current MDD while abstinent from substance use, and history of MDD prior to lifetime onset of substance dependence. They found that a prior history of MDD and substance-induced MDD were associated with a reduced likelihood of remission from substance dependence, and that current abstinence MDD was associated with relapse after a stable remission.

While the notion of an addictive personality has achieved some popular acceptance, research has failed to identify a specific pattern of personality traits that consistently characterize individuals who abuse substances (Nathan, 1988). However, there are several personality characteristics that may be risk factors, including emotionality and impulsivity (Dom, D'Haene, Hulstijn, & Sabbe, 2006; Sher &

Trull, 1994). Emotionality is a temperament trait that refers to the tendency to be easily and intensely aroused. Research suggests that many individuals diagnosed with substance use disorders demonstrate high emotionality (Sher & Trull, 1994). Impulsivity is also highly correlated with substance dependence (Hawkins, Catalano, & Miller, 1992) and with early experimentation with substances and a high susceptibility to developing substance use disorders (Tarter, Kirisci, Mezzich, Cornelius, Pajer, Vanyukov et al., 2003). Other characteristics that have been associated with substance use disorder diagnoses include a decreased ability to inhibit behaviors, insensitivity to consequences, perception that time has slowed, and perseverance of negatively reinforced actions (Dom et al., 2006).

In summary, substance use disorders are associated with a variety of co-morbid conditions and personality traits, particularly those associated with negative affect and impulsivity. The temporal relationship between these characteristics and substance use disorders can be variable; however, research suggests that these conditions may exacerbate each other when co-occurring.

Environmental factors related to substance use. Researchers have identified a number of environmental risk factors associated with substance use disorders. The age of onset of substance abuse and dependence is typically in mid-adolescence (Parra, O'Neill, & Sher, 2003; Vega, Aguilar-Gaxiola, Andrade, Bijl, Borges, Caraveo-Anduaga et al., 2002), and as age of first intoxication decreases, the risk for future dependence tends to increase (Grant, Stinson, & Harford, 2001). The presence of family problems and poor family relationships increases the likelihood of early onset of use (De Micheli & Formigoni, 2002), and the interaction between deficient parental monitoring and peer influence predicts even poorer outcomes (Chassin, Pillow, Curran, Molina, & Barrera, 1993). Substance use among peers is a powerful socio-environmental risk factor (Greenberger, Chen, Beam, Wang, & Dong, 2000; Jessor, Turbin, Costa, Dong, Zhang, & Wang, 2003; Kandel, 1985), in that peers provide immediate access to substances, encourage participation in substance use, and reinforce conformity (Costa, Jessor, & Turbin, 1999). On the other hand, there are characteristics of family environments that seem to serve as protective factors against substance involvement. That is, greater parental support, predictable parental sanctions, higher parental education, parental intolerance of deviance, and greater religiosity predict less substance use (Jessor et al., 2003; Stice, Barrera, & Chassin, 1993; Vakalahi, 2001). Factors associated with the maintenance of substance abuse are similar to those listed above and can include greater access to substances, more life stressors, limited social resources, and family problems (Moos, Nichol, & Moos, 2002).

Theoretical Models of Addiction

There are many theoretical models of addiction. While an exhaustive list and explanation of all existing models is beyond the scope of this chapter, the significant concepts of several prominent addiction theories are discussed briefly. For comprehensive reviews of significant addiction theories, the reader is referred to Leonard & Blane (1999) and West (2006).

Before the biological etiology of addiction was understood, substance abuse was viewed as the result of volitional decision-making. Such *moral models* purported that the individual person is the causal agent of substance abuse and treatment of such people should involve legal or social sanctions, as their behavior represented a willful violation of social codes (Fingarette, 1988). Over time, *temperance models* replaced earlier notions of addiction (Miller & Hester, 1995). From this perspective, the cause of addiction was the substance itself and treatment implications focused on controlling the supply of substances (i.e., prohibition). Eventually, addiction came to be conceptualized as a disease or a characterological flaw (e.g., lifetime diagnosis, addictive personality). From such perspectives, the cause of addiction was said to be the physical or psychological makeup of the individual. In treatment, individuals were told that it was imperative that they accept the label of "alcoholic" or "addict," and abstain from all substances.

Elements of the above models persist today and influence the current culture of addiction research and treatment. For example, McLellan and colleagues (McLellan, Lewis, O'Brien, & Kleber, 2000) recently described drug dependence as a chronic medical illness. It is within this context that newer *behavioral* and *cognitive social learning* models have emerged. While some of these models primarily focus on one aspect of addictive behavior (e.g., craving, withdrawal, relapse), most have broader implications for addiction. Some of these models are explained below.

Traditional Behavioral Models

Behavioral accounts of addiction can be roughly classified as classical conditioning, positive reinforcement, and negative reinforcement models. It should be noted, however, that most models incorporate principles of both classical and operant conditioning.

Classical conditioning models. Models of drug dependence highlighting classical conditioning, or Pavlovian conditioning, are well established (Eissenberg, 2004; Wikler, 1984). Classical conditioning accounts of drug-taking describe how environmental cues that are repeatedly paired with drug-taking and drug effects can come to evoke the response of drug-taking. That is, when the drug (the unconditioned stimulus; UCS) and the pleasure experienced as a result of drug-taking (the unconditioned response; UCR) are repeatedly paired with drug-associated stimuli (conditioned stimuli; CS), the drug-associated stimuli can elicit the same reactions as the drugs themselves. For example, given a history in which drugs were reliably paired with the presence of a drug dealer's car, it would be likely that a heroin addict would experience conditioned craving when he or she sees a car similar to the one driven by the drug dealer (Wilson & Hayes, 2000). Thus, after repeated pairings between the drug and the drug dealer's car, the car itself elicits some of the responses that the drug elicits. This phenomenon has been observed among opiate addicts returning to their old neighborhoods after detoxification (Wikler, 1977) and in animal studies (for a review, see McDonald & Siegel, 2004).

Evidence also suggests that interoceptive pre-drug cues, in addition to environmental cues, can elicit CRs that contribute both to tolerance and to withdrawal (Siegel, 2005). In such an account, the UCS is the drug's direct effect (e.g., physiological reaction) and the cues that accompany the primary drug effect are CS's. Prior to a history of learning, the pharmacological stimulation elicits responses that compensate for drug-induced disturbances (i.e., UCR). After repeated pairings between the drug's direct effect (UCS) and cues that accompany the drug (CS), the drug-compensatory responses are elicited as conditioned responses to the cues (Siegel, 1999, 2005). Siegel (2001; Siegel & Ramos, 2002) argued that as CRs strengthen, they function to oppose the main effects of the drug. As a result, tolerance develops and greater amounts of the drug are necessary to achieve the same UCR (i.e., drug effect). When a CS (i.e., drug cue) occurs in the absence of the drug, the CR occurs without the opposing UCR. Thus, when a drug-associated CS occurs in the absence of the drug, the CS may evoke the experience of withdrawal symptoms.

Positive reinforcement models. Decades of animal research have repeatedly shown that most drugs of abuse function as reinforcing stimuli (for a review, see Glautier, 2004). Positive reinforcement accounts of addictive behavior are often emphasized in describing the initiation of drug use, but have also been used to describe relapse and maintenance of drug use (e.g., de Wit & Stewart, 1981; Shiffman, Ferguson, & Gwaltney, 2006). Two recent positive reinforcement models that have been used to describe addictive behavior are behavioral economics and incentive sensitization theory.

Behavioral economics is a behavioral theory of choice that describes the allocation of behavior among available potential positively reinforcing activities (Vuchinich & Heather, 2003). This account predicts that drug use will increase in contexts lacking non-drug sources of reinforcement and will decrease if access to alternative reinforcers is increased (Higgins, Heil, & Plebani-Lussier, 2003). A number of empirical animal and human studies have illustrated how changes in substance use depends on the availability of other reinforcers (for reviews, see Higgins et al., 2003; Vuchinich & Tucker, 1988). For example, research suggests that the ratio of reinforcement from drugs relative to the total reinforcement from a number of potential reinforcers is more predictive of drug-taking than reinforcement from drugs alone (Correia & Carey, 1999; Murphy, Correia, Colby, & Vuchinich, 2005).

Bickel and Marsch (2001) suggested two behavioral economics concepts that may be particularly useful in understanding drug dependence: elasticity of demand and delay discounting. These concepts describe drugs as positive reinforcers, but also include an emphasis on the context in which the reinforcers are presented. With regard to elasticity of demand, inelastic consumption refers to decreases in consumption that are proportionally less than increases in price, while elastic consumption refers to decreases in consumption that are proportionally greater than increases in price. In other words, among drug dependent individuals, drugs are less sensitive to price, or more "inelastic," than other reinforcers (Jacobs & Bickel, 1999;

Petry & Bickel, 1998). So, for example, smokers may continue to smoke cigarettes despite large increases in the dollar cost of cigarette packs.

Delay discounting refers to the notion that given the opportunity for more than one reward, the reward that is delivered immediately will have a greater influence on behavior than the one presented later in time (i.e., at a delay). That is, the reinforcer effectiveness of rewards that are presented on a delayed schedule may be discounted, or reduced. For example, individuals who are abusing drugs rather than engaging in activities with greater long-term benefit (e.g., employment, relationships, education) may be discounting these delayed rewards and opting for the immediate rewards associated with drug use. In fact, substance dependence has been associated with greater discounting of delayed rewards in a number of studies across different substances of abuse (e.g., Bickel, Odum, & Madden, 1999; Kirby & Petry, 2004; Ohmura, Takahashi, & Kitamura, 2005; Petry, 2001). Elasticity of demand and delay discounting provide useful behavioral explanations of previous findings regarding the behaviors and personality characteristics (e.g., impulsivity, disinhibition) associated with substance dependence (Bickel & Marsch, 2001).

Incentive sensitization theory (Robinson & Berridge, 2001) also focuses on the positive reinforcing effects of drug-taking. This theory incorporates classical and operant conditioning but emphasizes neuroadaptations that occur through repeated drug administrations (Glautier, 2004). The developers of this model explain that traditional positive and negative reinforcement models of substance dependence are inadequate (Berridge & Robinson, 1995; Robinson & Berridge, 2001). They assert that previous models do not provide sufficient explanation for why individuals continue to seek drugs in instances in which no pleasure or withdrawal exists, nor why craving can be highest immediately after drug use (Berridge & Robinson, 1995). According to Berridge and Robinson (2003; Robinson & Berridge, 2001), incentive sensitization can be summarized in four points: (1) potentially addictive drugs produce long-lasting changes in brain organization, (2) systems that are changed are those typically involved in motivation and reward, (3) these neuroadaptations leave brain reward systems hypersensitive to drugs and drug-associated stimuli, and (4) the sensitized systems do not mediate pleasurable effects of drugs, but instead mediate a subcomponent of reward termed "incentive salience" or "wanting." Researchers have found support for this theoretical model in human and animal studies (for a review, see Berridge & Robinson, 2003).

Negative reinforcement models. While numerous negative reinforcement models have been described in the literature, three classic models include withdrawal-based accounts, self-medication, and opponent-process theory. Eissenberg (2004) provided a thorough review of these theories as they relate to nicotine dependence; however, most have been described across different drugs of abuse.

Withdrawal-based negative reinforcement models emphasize the role that a withdrawal syndrome plays in maintaining drug use. According to these models, drug-taking is reinforced through the avoidance or relief of drug withdrawal, thus increasing the likelihood of future drug consumption. Although this model is one of the oldest accounts of addictive behavior, it has fallen out of favor in recent years, as accumulating evidence indicates that neither the presence of a physiological withdrawal syndrome nor withdrawal severity predict substance use (e.g., Bradley, Phillips, Green, & Gossop, 1989; Patten & Martin, 1996).

Self-medication and tension-reduction models of drug dependence highlight the role that drugs of abuse play in escaping or avoiding pre-existing emotional distress or negative affect (Cappell & Greeley, 1987; Crutchfield & Gove, 1984; Khantzian, 1997). These accounts address criticisms of previous negative reinforcement models that did not account for initial drug use. Khantzian (1997) proposed that individuals who abuse substances feel overwhelmed by emotions. He stated that substance abuse could provide relief from painful emotions or enhance the perception of control over emotions. There is mixed evidence for self-medication models of abuse. Evidence supporting the models comes primarily from studies of stress reduction in substance abusers with comorbid conditions, particularly under certain conditions such as prior experience with substances (Breslau, 1995; Grant, Stinson et al., 2004). However, it is possible that the expectation of stress reduction may be a stronger predictor of substance use than the actual experience of stress reduction (for a review, see Pohorecky, 1991).

Solomon and Corbit (1974) used opponent process theory to explain addiction. According to an opponent process conceptualization, the initial effects of drugs are appetitive, but the maintenance of drug use is explained by a negative reinforcement account. Initial drug use violates an affective homeostasis. It is this disruption in homeostasis and the body's efforts to regain balance that lead to the development of substance dependence. Solomon and Corbit asserted that a single drug administration may alter the organism by temporarily reducing its reward threshold. Thus, stimuli that were neutral seem rewarding and stimuli that were mildly rewarding seem very rewarding. Over time, other internal processes begin to oppose the drug-induced reduction in reward threshold by working to increase reward threshold, thus returning to the pre-drug state. This increase in threshold is said to mark the beginning of drug dependence. Newer models using this framework also include elements of other negative-reinforcement accounts and neurobiological effects of drug use. The work of Koob and colleagues (e.g., Koob, 1996; Koob & Le Moal, 1997; Koob, Stinus, Le Moal, & Bloom, 1989) has been particularly influential. These researchers assert that addiction is a process of hedonic homeostatic dysregulation (Koob & Le Moal, 1997) in which certain neurotransmitters, hormones, and neurobiological sites mediate hedonic dysregulation and provide risk for or protection from the development of drug dependence.

Traditional Behavioral Principles

Behavior-consequence relations. To start, there is a general consensus among addiction researchers that drug-taking is operant behavior and drugs function as reinforcers (Eissenberg, 2004; Glautier, 2004; McSweeney, Murphy, & Kowal, 2005; Schuster & Thompson, 1969). As stated earlier, drug-taking is a complex behavior that may be controlled by negative reinforcement (escape and avoidance) in some contexts and positive reinforcement in others. Regardless of function, as an operant behavior, particular predictions can be made about the effectiveness of drugs as reinforcers of drug-taking behavior. For example, reinforcer effectiveness is influenced by schedules of reinforcement and the magnitude of the reinforcer.

Schedules of reinforcement are patterns by which reinforcers are delivered contingent upon a given behavioral response. As with other operant behaviors, reinforcement schedules for drug-taking impact the persistence of the behavioral pattern, and drug-taking that occurs on a variable ratio schedule appears to be most resistant to extinction (e.g., Panlilio, Weiss, & Schindler, 2000). For example, smokers frequently report that they continue to smoke cigarettes when cigarettes are no longer enjoyable in the hopes of getting that one cigarette that is enjoyable. Laboratory research has found that changes in schedules of reinforcement can change drug-taking behavior. For example, increasing a fixed ratio schedule of reinforcement can decrease consumption of cigarettes (DeGrandpre, Bickel, Higgins, & Hughes, 1994).

As with behavioral economics models described above, concurrent schedules of reinforcement may also influence the effectiveness of drugs as reinforcers. Whether or not a particular operant behavior, such as drug-taking, is emitted may depend on the concurrent availability of reinforcers for that behavior versus the reinforcers for another behavior. Laboratory and treatment research supports the notion that the availability of non-drug reinforcers should decrease drug-taking if the non-drug reinforcers are of a sufficient magnitude and are delivered according to a schedule that does not support drug-taking (Carroll, Lac, & Nygaard, 1989; Nader & Woolverton, 1991). Animal drug self-administration studies show how when there is a "choice" situation, or concurrent schedules of reinforcement, injections that are available more frequently in time maintain behavior more strongly than less frequently available reinforcers (Woolverton, 1996). Contingency management treatments, such as voucher-based reinforcement, capitalize on these findings and have been effective in increasing abstinence (Higgins, Alessi, & Dantona, 2002; Rawson, Huber, McCann, Shoptaw, Farabee, Reiber et al., 2002).

The effectiveness of a reinforcer also can be related to its magnitude. The experience of a drug's magnitude may be related to the actual potency of the drug itself, sensitization to the drug, and habituation. First, certain drugs have a greater abuse potential than less reinforcing drugs. Length of time between onset of abuse to dependence is sometimes used as a measure of abuse potential for a given drug. For example, Ridenour and colleagues (Ridenour, Maldonado-Molina, Compton, Spitznagel, & Cottler, 2005) found that the length of time between onset of abuse to dependence differs across drug classes. They observed a shorter length of time for cocaine and opiates, followed by cannabis and alcohol. Additionally, the route of administration, dose, and absorption rate may influence the magnitude of drug effects (Farre & Cami, 1991).

Second, biological and historical variables influence sensitivity to drug effects. As described above, some individuals are more biologically sensitive to drug effects, such that one person may experience intoxication with a smaller amount of a substance than another person. Interestingly, a history with drugs as reinforcers can increase sensitization in some contexts while decreasing sensitization (i.e., habituation) in others. Animal and human studies have illustrated how responsiveness to a drug can increase when it is repeatedly presented (for a review, see McSweeney et al., 2005). Similarly, priming studies have shown that there is an increase in the rate of operant responding for a drug when individuals experience a pre-dose of that drug (Bigelow, Griffiths, & Liebson, 1977; Chutuape, Mitchell, & de Wit, 1994). Sensitization also might explain reinstatement, which involves the recovery of extinguished responding after the presentation of some part of a conditioning episode. This phenomenon has been observed across many drugs (e.g., Chiamulera, Borgo, Falchetto, Valerio, & Tessari, 1996; de Wit & Stewart, 1981). McSweeney and colleagues (2005) argued that if sensitization is responsible for reinstatement, then one might predict that any strong stimulus could occasion reinstatement, not only those involved in conditioning. This notion might partially explain how many individuals relapse in the presence of significant stressors.

Finally, the magnitude of a drug as a reinforcer may be related to habituation, a decrease in responsiveness to reinforcers with repeated presentations. Baker and Tiffany (1985) described tolerance in terms of a habituation model. They speculated that delivering large doses of a drug at short inter-dose intervals would promote the development of tolerance. Accumulating research supports this claim. A series of studies by McSweeney and colleagues (e.g., McSweeney, 1992; McSweeney, Hinson, & Cannon, 1996) illustrated how the rate of reinforcement delivery during a session impacts responding, such that there is more frequent responding at the beginning, with fewer responses over time. These effects do not seem to be explained by satiety. Roll, McSweeney, Johnson, and Weatherly (1995; as cited in Roll & McSweeney, 1999) varied the deprivation level and magnitude of a food reinforcer without changing the pattern of delivery and found no differences in the pattern of responding across these conditions.

Stimulus-behavior relations. Characteristics of stimulus conditions also influence drug-taking. Some researchers have found that stimulus conditions have a significant impact on operant behavior, even after controlling for the role of consequences (Nevin, Smith, & Roberts, 1987). Three characteristics of stimulus conditions that have been examined in relation to drug use include the roles of discriminative stimuli, establishing operations, and stimulus generalization. Below is a description of how stimulus conditions have been examined in relation to drug taking, followed by a stimulus control analysis of drug-related cognitions.

Researchers have illustrated the role of discriminative stimuli, or stimuli that set the occasion for an operant behavior, in drug-taking and drug-seeking behaviors. Discriminative stimuli can be interoceptive (de Wit & Stewart, 1981; DeGrandpre & Bickel, 1993), non-drug (e.g., a noise; Stretch, Gerber, & Wood, 1971), and distal from the actual drug-taking behavior (DeGrandpre & Bickel, 1993). Social cognitive research also supports an association between discriminative stimuli (i.e., drug cues) and drug-taking. For example, drug dependent individuals exhibit an attentional bias toward stimuli associated with drug use (Franken, Kroon, Wiers, & Jansen, 2000; Lubman, Peters, Mogg, Bradley, & Deakin, 2000), and attentional bias is related to greater cravings (Waters, Shiffman, Bradley, & Mogg, 2003).

Establishing operations. Establishing operations are environmental events or operations that influence the saliency of discriminative stimuli and the effectiveness of reinforcers (Michael, 1982, 1983). Several research studies suggest that certain establishing operations influence whether or not drug effects will function as reinforcers. For example, animal studies have shown that when a drug is provided only in specific stimulus conditions, the drug effects will occur only in those conditions (Anagnostaras & Robinson, 1996; Stewart & Vezina, 1991; Wang & Hsiao, 2003). Additionally, studies with humans have shown that tolerance is more pronounced in the presence of drug-associated environments than in alternative environments (for reviews see Baker & Tiffany, 1985; Siegel & Ramos, 2002). This phenomenon has been described as the "situational-specificity of tolerance" (Siegel, 2001). Some theorists have speculated that this phenomenon may increase the risk of overdose when using drugs in an unfamiliar environment (e.g., Siegel, 2001). Researchers have also found that affective states can function as establishing operations as well. Yetnikoff and Arvanitogiannis (2005) found that in addition to showing sensitization in a paired environment and no response in a non-drug paired environment, rats exhibited drug effects in a positive affect, non-drug environment. These researchers suggested that the positive affective state, which may have been associated with drug effects in the past, modulated the expression of the drug effects.

Stimulus generalization. Stimulus generalization occurs when there is no differential responding across different environmental stimuli (Plaud & Plaud, 1998). Generally speaking, stimulus generalization is likely with stimuli that are physically similar to each other, and as stimuli begin to physically differ less responding to the second stimulus occurs (see Stokes & Baer, 1977). Due to stimulus generalization, drug-taking may be evoked by an increasing number of discriminative stimuli and could become more pervasive as this process occurs. Response generalization may also occur. For example, DeGrandpre and Bickel (1993) described how discriminative stimuli for coffee drinking could also become discriminative stimuli for cigarette smoking, especially when cigarette smoking is repeatedly paired with coffee drinking in the presence of the given discriminative stimuli. Another way generalization may occur is through relational responding, which is discussed below.

Cognitive Social Learning Models

Cognitive social learning models of addiction have been influenced by social learning theory and principles of learning (for a review, see Brandon, Herzog, Irvin, & Gwaltney, 2004). Cognitive social learning models suggest that drug use is not responsible for addiction, but rather it is the meaning that drug use has for the individual, the coping skills available to the person, and the persistence of engaging in coping behavior that is responsible for addiction. Although there are many different cognitive social learning models of addiction, most of these accounts include a description of how self-efficacy, outcome expectancies, situational factors, social modeling, and coping skills influence substance use. Examples of prominent cognitive social learning models in the field of addictions include Goldman's (Goldman, Brown, & Christiansen, 1987) model of drug expectancies, Marlatt and Gordon's (1985) model of relapse, and Tiffany's (1990) cognitive processing theory of drug use.

One cognitive social learning model of addiction is Goldman's model of drug expectancies (Goldman et al., 1987). Expectancies are beliefs about the anticipated outcome of engaging in a particular behavior (Del Boca, Darkes, Goldman, & Smith, 2002). Expectancies have been described as structures in long-term memory that influence cognitive processes and, ultimately, govern behavior (Jones, Corbin, & Fromme, 2001). There is a growing literature of empirical support indicating that addictive behavior is significantly and positively associated with positive expectancies and inversely associated with negative expectancies (for a review, see Jones et al., 2001). That is, when individuals have outcome expectancies that using substances will have positive and desirable effects, they are more likely to use. Individuals diagnosed with substance dependence tend to report stronger outcome expectancies than non-dependent individuals and these expectancies increase as a function of patterns of use (Brown, Goldman, & Christiansen, 1985). Further, drug use enhances expectancies and as an individual develops substance dependence, the activation of expectancies becomes more automatic and expectancy networks become more complex (e.g., Darkes, Greenbaum, & Goldman, 2004; Reich & Goldman, 2005).

According to Marlatt and Gordon's (1985) social learning theory of relapse, the likelihood of a person engaging in substance use depends on the interaction between a given a particular high-risk situation, self-efficacy, outcome expectancies, and coping skills. Additionally, the attributions individuals make regarding their drug use after a period of abstinence are important determinants of whether they will experience full-blown relapse. Specifically, a single violation of abstinence may result in a full-blown relapse if the individual makes internal, stable, and global attributions for the occurrence of the violation (i.e., the Abstinence Violation Effect). Research supporting this theory has shown that in the presence of positive outcome expectancies and low self-efficacy, substance use is likely (Blume, Schmaling, & Marlatt, 2003; Gwaltney, Shiffman, Paty, Liu, Kassel, Gnys et al., 2002). Additionally, stressful (i.e., high risk) situations predict substance use (Seeman & Seeman, 1992), and coping skills and self-efficacy can buffer the effects of stress on substance use (Abrams, Niaura, Carey, Monti, & Binkoff, 1986). This model has been applied across different drugs of abuse and dependence (for a review, see Marlatt & Donovan, 2005).

Tiffany's (1990; Tiffany & Conklin, 2000) cognitive processing theory is primarily a model of drug use maintenance and relapse, and describes drug use behavior as largely controlled by automatic processes that are not necessarily related to classical conditioning. According to this model, drug acquisition and use can become an automatic process that is relatively fast and efficient, effortless, completed without intention or awareness, and difficult to impede in the presence of triggers (Tiffany, 1990). Over time the procedures associated with this automatic process are stored in memory in the form of action plans that include (1) stimulus configurations necessary for elicitation of actions, (2) procedures for enactment of actions (e.g., finding a vein for injection), (3) coordination of actions into sequences, (4) alternative actions in the event of an obstacle, (5) support physiology for action components, and (6) generation of physiological adjustments in anticipation of drug intake (i.e., tolerance; Tiffany, 1990; Tiffany & Conklin, 2000). If this automatic process is disrupted (e.g., the individual is unable to obtain the drug of abuse), then non-automatic cognitive processes take over and give rise to urges and cravings. In this way, drug urges and craving are conceptualized as theoretically distinct from drug-use behavior itself.

Integrative Models of Addiction

More recent accounts of addiction tend to be integrative theories that incorporate components of traditional behavioral and cognitive social learning models (e.g., Baker et al., 2004; Brown, Lejuez, Kahler, Strong, & Zvolensky, 2005; Otto, Powers, & Fischmann, 2005). For example, Baker et al. (2004) described an integrative "affective processing" model in which drug use occurs to relieve or avoid negative affect. According to this model, the presence of negative affect decreases the amount of "cool information processing," such that the likelihood of delaying immediate relief in favor of long-term benefit is decreased. Other contemporary models also emphasize the role of drug-taking in relieving distress (Brown et al., 2005; Otto et al., 2005), and suggest that deficits in distress tolerance skills are related to substance abuse.

Although new accounts of addiction include a synthesis of the empirically supported components of previous theories, there are several limitations to these theories. First, despite the abundance of research supporting both positive and negative reinforcement functions, there has been an emphasis on specifying one solitary function of drug taking behavior; for example, appetitive versus escape/avoidance. Second, over time, limitations of previous classical and operant conditioning models have been addressed by adding components of other popular theories, such as cognitive theory. While it is useful to consider the scientific findings on human behavior across literatures, theoretical eclecticism may limit progress in understanding addiction by preventing the field from exploring and testing new theories that may better account for addictive behaviors. This may lead to a lack of behavioral treatment innovation and understanding of treatment process. Contemporary models of substance use disorders could benefit from a unifying conceptualization that could guide future research and treatment endeavors.

A Contemporary Behavioral Model of Substance Use

This contemporary behavioral model adds an analysis of language to the traditional behavioral model. It focuses on Relational Frame Theory (RFT; Hayes, Barnes-Holmes, & Roche, 2001), experiential avoidance, and rule governance. Below, a brief overview of RFT is provided, and then examples are given to demonstrate how RFT may account for previous findings that have been traditionally explained by more cognitive conceptualizations (e.g., expectancies). This RFT-enhanced description of addictive behavior describes how cognition and language may function to enhance reinforcer effectiveness and increase stimulus generalization. Then, an analysis of language, particularly rules that dictate experiential avoidance, is provided to suggest how rule-governed experiential avoidance may be seen as a particular instantiation of RFT that can result in increased problems with alcohol and drug use.

Cognitions and Drug-taking

In order to provide a behavior analytic account of cognitions related to drug taking, it is useful to describe some of the core principles of Relational Frame Theory (RFT; Hayes et al., 2001). According to RFT, a key to understanding human language and cognition is relational responding – a process in which two or more events are related along some dimension such as "same as," "bigger than," or "weaker than." Furthermore, humans appear to engage in *derived relational* responding, in which relational responding occurs with events that have not been trained directly and that are not related formally. Accumulating research suggests that relational responding has characteristics of an operant (Barnes-Holmes, Barnes-Holmes, Smeets, Strand, & Friman, 2004; Healy, Barnes-Holmes, & Smeets, 2000), and as such, traditional behavioral principles can apply.

From an RFT perspective, events that are not physically present or aversive can become psychologically present and acquire aversive functions through relational responding. That is, not only can actual events cause pain, but self-reports of such events can also cause pain. For example, drug-users often report experiencing cravings when they talk about drug use (Drobes & Tiffany, 1997). An RFT perspective suggests that a process akin to stimulus generalization can occur across verbal events via the transformation of stimulus function, expanding the number of contexts that occasion drug-taking behavior. Suppose an individual has no history of seeing or using cocaine, but has learned the relation that cocaine equals fine, white powder. One day, the person snorts cocaine at a party and consequently experiences increased energy, heightened alertness, and feelings of exhilaration. Later, when someone asks the person if they have any "blow," the person experiences cravings. Although the individual did not experience a high in the direct presence of the word "blow" in the past, through derived relational responding, the word "blow" acquired stimulus functions of the actual drug. Thus, as more verbal and environmental relations are added to his or her history, the person has cravings in response to more events. In order to escape or avoid the feeling of craving, the individual may consume the drug and, in doing so, reinforce drug-taking and strengthen the new associations with other stimuli.

Derived relational responding and the transformation of stimulus functions might also inform our understanding of relapse. Relapse situations may be more likely when high-risk behaviors are regarded as positive (e.g., "I don't have to avoid the bar anymore because I have quit drinking"), when social support for the association of "actual abstinence equals actual reinforcement" is disrupted (e.g., a drug addict is arrested on an old charge and has the thought that "It doesn't matter how hard I try"), and when verbal relations seemingly justify substance use ("I can't stand these cravings;" Wilson & Hayes, 2000). On the other hand, these same processes of derived relational responding can also support abstinence. For example, the thought "I'm abstinent" can become reinforcing and the individual may engage in behaviors that would increase the likelihood of making such a verbalization (e.g., attending an AA or NA meeting).

As is the case in learning overt behavior, it may be difficult to unlearn relational responding. In fact, due to the transfer of stimulus functions, the relational network may be so extensive that it would be difficult to develop new learning for every relation. Research has repeatedly shown that even when responses are extinguished in one context, they can re-emerge in other contexts (Collins & Brandon, 2002; Garcia-Gutierrez & Rosas, 2003). Some researchers have speculated that the equivocal findings of extinction treatment studies (e.g., cue exposure; Drummond, Cooper, & Glautier, 1990) could be a result of treatments not extinguishing the full network of relations involved (see Siegel & Ramos, 2002). Additionally, the work by Bouton and colleagues (for a review, see Bouton, 2004) illustrates how stimulus-behavior relations are not un-learned in extinction, but rather new relations are learned.

Research examining attempts to suppress cognitions illustrates that it is difficult to suppress relational responding. In fact, attempting to change or control relations directly may expand the relational network rather than extinguish previous learning. That is, the thought "do not think about alcohol" may become related to the relational network associated with drinking, thus increasing thoughts of drinking rather than decreasing those thoughts. For example, Wenzlaff and colleagues (Wenzlaff, Wegner, & Klein, 1991) found that reinstating the mood in which participants were instructed to suppress particular thoughts resulted in the return of the suppressed thoughts. In another study, Palfai, Colby, Monti, and Rohsenow (1997) exposed 50 daily smokers, who were also social drinkers, to their favorite alcoholic drink and told them to either monitor or suppress urges for alcohol. Following this procedure, participants were permitted to smoke while smoking behaviors were assessed. Results indicated that those who were instructed to suppress urges showed significantly more intense smoking behavior than those who were not instructed to suppress.

As described above, a large literature has explored the role of cognitions, particularly expectancies, in maintaining drug consumption. Much of this research can be interpreted from an RFT conceptualization. Some researchers predict that expectancies facilitate behavior change through disrupting learned associations among content, behavior, and experience (see Del Boca et al., 2002). In a typical expectancy challenge design, participants are invited into a simulated bar. Some participants are provided with actual alcohol, while others are provided with a non-alcoholic beverage that looks and tastes similar to the alcoholic beverage. Researchers have found that participants respond to non-alcoholic beverages in a manner consistent to alcoholic beverages (Darkes & Goldman, 1993, 1998; Dunn, Lau, & Cruz, 2000). Although these findings can be explained without reference to RFT (e.g., the physical stimulus properties of the lab and the beverages evoked drunk behavior), RFT highlights the possibility that how the participant was thinking about the situation may have been influential as well. For example, thoughts such as "this is beer," and "If I drink several drinks, then I feel drunk" may also set the occasion for particular behavioral responses; for example, behavioral disinhibition.

The notion of expectancies may also explain treatment effects of some drug dependence interventions. For example, pharmacological interventions, such as disulfiram, produces nausea after drinking, thus they alter the consequential functions of alcohol and drugs from positive to punishing. This intervention is frequently effective even if the person never drinks (for a review, see Kranzler, 2000). That is, in order for treatment to be effective, it is not necessary to expose the patient to alcohol while describing the effects of the medication, nor is it necessary to have the patient experience actual illness. In this situation, the functions of alcohol must be transformed from positive to punishing verbally (Wilson & Hayes, 2000).

Researchers also have found that expectancies play a role in the experience of withdrawal (Tate, Stanton, Green, Schmitz, Le, & Marshall, 1994). For example, dependent smokers who believed they were receiving an active nicotine gum used more gum, reported fewer withdrawal symptoms, and smoked fewer cigarettes during their first week of quitting, regardless of actual nicotine content (Gottlieb, Killen, Marlatt, & Taylor, 1987). From an RFT perspective, the belief "if I wear the patch, then I will not experience withdrawal," may change the function of physiological experiences associated with actual withdrawal, thus not occasioning the behavior of smoking.

Alcohol expectancies have also been demonstrated in children. Wiers, Sergeant, and Gunning (2000) examined the responses of 395 school-age children who completed a questionnaire inquiring about positive and negative alcohol expectancies and found that the inclusion of a puppet-reference in the questionnaire was related to increases in positive alcohol expectancies over time. RFT suggests that positive associations between the puppet and thoughts about alcohol might have influenced the stimulus functions of alcohol-related stimuli. An important implication of this work is that when one is conducting research, treatments, or assessments for drug use, the stimulus functions of verbal events can support either drug-taking or abstinence related behaviors, and the actual functions may be quite specific to the individuals' particular verbal learning histories.

Rule Governance and Experiential Avoidance

For decades, researchers have repeatedly found a relationship between avoidant coping styles and poor clinical outcomes in cases of substance abuse and dependence (e.g., Cooper, Russell, & George, 1988; Ireland, McMahon, Malow, & Kouzekanani, 1994; Wills & Cleary, 1996). Hayes and colleagues (Hayes, Wilson, Gifford, Follette, & Strosahl, 1996) have highlighted the notion of experiential avoidance, which occurs when a person is "unwilling to remain in contact with particular private experiences (e.g., bodily sensations, emotions, thoughts, memories, behavioral predispositions) and takes steps to alter the form or frequency of these events and the contexts that occasion them" (p. 1154). In other words, in efforts to control cravings, emotions, or thoughts, individuals sometimes create rules for how to avoid or control these experiences.

Rigid use of rules aimed at controlling or avoiding private experiences (i.e., thoughts, feelings, cravings, etc.) can be problematic. From a logical standpoint, it can be shown how rules that specify controlling private experience can lead paradoxically to continued drug use. First, such rules can ironically increase the likelihood of experiencing the aversive functions of the avoided event. For example, a person who experiences urges to use heroin might try to think about something else. Functionally, however, the full rule is "think about something else not related to heroin because that makes you want to use." Perhaps the "something else" is a thought about walking the dog. Now the full rule is "think about walking the dog and not heroin because that makes you want to use and the dog makes you happy." Now the dog is verbally related to happy, but also to "not heroin" and "not using." In time, through derived relational responding, the dog and the word "dog" may paradoxically evoke thoughts of using heroin. According to this analysis, avoidance rules can foster more and more relations between neutral stimuli and heroin, thus increasing thoughts of heroin rather than decreasing them. Further, in order to evaluate whether or not "think about something else" is effective at decreasing thoughts of heroin use, one must necessarily think about heroin use (Wilson & Hayes, 2000).

Such logical analysis suggests that it is difficult for humans to avoid aversive private experiences because language allows them to occur in many situations. To cope with this pain, people attempt to avoid cravings, thoughts, memories, and feelings and learn to apply verbal rules regarding the need to avoid those private experiences (i.e., "I can't stand feeling this way," "I have to stop thinking about using"). Attempts to avoid or suppress these feelings may become associated with the aversive feelings themselves such that, when individuals have the thought "do not think about using," they automatically think of using and may experience the feelings associated with using in the past.

Rule-governance may also influence drug taking by decreasing behavioral flexibility. Considerable research suggests that excessive verbal behavior—when individuals are responding to verbally constructed contingencies—may interfere with contacting actual environmental contingencies (Joyce & Chase, 1990; Kudadjie-

Gyamfi & Rachlin, 2002; Lippman, 1994). This pattern can lead to a limited response class and insensitivity to changing contingencies. Although research in this area specifically as it applies to drug use is limited, the implications are clear. For example, when one tries to avoid thoughts of drinking, the avoidance behavior itself may strengthen the behavior regulatory effect of the avoided thought. In other words, when a person tries not to think about drinking and he in fact does not drink, then the evaluation might be made that avoiding that particular thought caused him to remain abstinent. Thus, successful avoidance of the thought of drinking as a fearful event increases the likelihood that the person will avoid the thought in the future and decreases the likelihood that the individual will contact more productive sources of control (see Wilson, Hayes, Gregg, & Zettle, 2001). Future research to support this pattern is needed.

In summary, according to an RFT model, efforts to avoid or change private experiences can be counterproductive in that they may inadvertently maintain the stimulus functions they are designed to remove. Avoidance efforts also can redirect focus away from effective behaviors and toward struggles with less controllable events (e.g., "I have to get rid of this thought in order to not drink") and perpetuate rules about the linear, causal connection between private events and drinking (e.g., "I have to get rid of this in order to not drink because this is why I drink") thereby reinforcing the inflexibility of the relationship between internal stimuli and drinking. As drinking or drugging continues to occasion these internal stimuli, and as avoidance continues to exacerbate these internal stimuli and connect them to drinking, the sequence strengthens, and the stimulus-drinking relation is reinforced (Gifford, Kohlenberg, Hayes, Antonuccio, Piasecki, Rasmussen-Hall et al., 2004).

Limitations and Future Research Directions

Although there is accumulating evidence for some of the basic tenets of RFT (Hayes, Barnes-Holmes, & Roche, 2001), research on how verbal processes result in experiential avoidance, which in turn creates a self-perpetuating dysfunctional cycle, is in its infancy. Furthermore, research on how these processes relate to addiction is lacking. Hayes and Wilson (1996) have argued that RFT is an extension of behavior analytic principles to a different kind of operant (relational responding), however the incremental validity of this theory is an empirical question that researchers should continue to explore. Alternately, others have argued that RFT is ambiguous, complex, and contradictory, and therefore difficult to understand and test (Galizio, 2003; Osbourne, 2003; Salzinger, 2003).

The current model provides an interesting theoretical framework that could guide future research aimed at understanding substance abuse and dependence. Future research should further examine the role of relational responding in addictions. Comparisons of human and animal models may provide more insight into the importance cognition and language in substance use. For example, an RFT model would predict similar drug self-administration between animals and humans when there are external manipulations to the environment, but greater stimulus generalization among humans due to relational responding. Additionally, an RFT model would predict that extinction to drug cues would be less effective in humans compared to animal models because through relational responding and increased stimulus generalization more contexts would be associated with drug effects.

Given that expectancies have been studied a great deal in the field of addictions, future research could examine predictions of an RFT model using traditional expectancy laboratory challenges. It would be interesting to compare attempts to directly alter expectancies to attempts to alter the stimulus functions of expectancies (e.g., the believability of expectancies). As suggested by Wilson and colleagues (2001), self-report instruments that include ratings of the believability of given statements may be helpful here. For example, one study (Zettle & Hayes, 1986) used a modified Automatic Thoughts Questionnaire (Hollon & Kendall, 1980) that examined both the frequency and believability of depressive thoughts. Similar modifications could be made to existing scales that assess outcome expectancies for alcohol and drugs. An RFT perspective would predict that drug-taking would be more strongly associated with believability of expectancies compared to frequency of expectancies.

Another interesting test could be to examine how relational responding in a laboratory setting predicts drug use prospectively and in naturalistic settings. Researchers in the field of addiction have been exploring more naturalistic assessment devices in order to understand the phenomena of craving, drug use, and relapse more completely. For example, several researchers have used ecological momentary sampling devices in which individuals record cravings, behavioral inclinations, mood, and drug use throughout the course of the day (e.g., Shiffman, Waters, & Hickcox, 2004; Shiffman & Waters, 2004). It would be interesting to examine prospectively how moment-to-moment changes in drug use and cravings are associated with relational responding. Researchers could include questions about thoughts and believability of thoughts in momentary sampling devices.

Treatment Implications of New Behavioral Model

Functional Assessment of Substance Use

The theoretical account of addictive behavior described in this chapter points to important assessment and treatment implications. As is the case with most behavior analytic approaches, idiographic functional assessment is very important. Assessment should include information about the abused substance, the function of the substance for that person, positive and negative consequences of use, environments in which the person is likely to use, and rules the person has about use, quitting, and aversive private experiences. Although there are similarities between individuals' histories of substance use, behaviors may serve different functions across different contexts. For example, drug taking may function as positive reinforcement at parties, but negative reinforcement when done alone at home. Understanding the functional dimensions of one's behavior can help treatment providers tailor treatments to address the individual's struggles more appropriately. Also, assessment should be on-going throughout treatment. Humans are constantly adding to their histories, and the current model suggests that it is important to understand how new relations are being derived as individuals progress through their recovery. For example, individuals may attempt to use new therapy techniques to help with an old agenda of avoiding thoughts of using.

Treatment as Altering Context

Substance use disorders are chronic, relapsing conditions with significant mortality, morbidity, and disability. Research has repeatedly shown that few individuals are able to maintain continuous abstinence, regardless of treatment participation (Brownell, Marlatt, Lichtenstein, & Wilson, 1986; Witkiewitz & Marlatt, 2004). However, a recent meta-analysis suggests that participation in substance abuse treatments is associated with better outcomes than receiving no treatment (Prendergast, Podus, Chang, & Urada, 2002). It is anticipated that future research testing the predictions of the current RFT-enhanced model will enhance the field's understanding of addictive behavior and provide direct implications for the development of incrementally efficacious behavioral treatments.

An RFT-enhanced behavioral model of addiction provides a unifying conceptualization of factors influencing substance abuse and dependence. Given that this model builds on previous behavioral models, many existing empirically supported behavioral treatments would be consistent with the current conceptualization. However, for the sake of clarity, one useful distinction that can be made in treatment is the difference between altering the external versus the internal environment. For the external environment, treatment should target altering the behavior-consequence and the stimulus-behavior relations associated with drug-taking. This can be done by changing reinforcement schedules such that alternative behaviors are reinforced more strongly and frequently than drug-taking, and by altering the stimuli associated with drug-taking. For example, two interventions might be the use of a community reinforcement approach for abstinence-supportive behaviors (Higgins, Wong, Badger, Ogden, & Dantona, 2000; Smith, Meyers, & Delaney, 1998) or behavioral marital therapy (Fals-Stewart, Birchler, & O'Farrell, 1996; O'Farrell & Fals-Stewart, 2000). Involvement in 12-step programs may also facilitate reinforcement of abstinence-supportive behaviors and engender a new social environment not associated with use (Morgenstern, Labouvie, McCrady, Kahler, & Frey, 1997; Ouimette, Finney, & Moos, 1997). Further, although there is debate about the actual mechanisms of some pharmacological agents, there are several that may work through altering the function of drug-taking, including disulfiram and acamprosate for alcohol; buprenorphine and methadone for opiates; and nicotine replacement and bupropion for nicotine (for a review, see Kleber, Weiss, Anton, Rounsaville, George, Strain et al., 2006).

In regards to treatment implications for the internal environment (i.e., cognition, emotion), behavior change could be facilitated through changing the consequences of drug-related cognitions and changing the stimulus functions of cognitions. Examples of strategies that target altering the verbal context include acceptance, defusion, and values clarification. Analog studies examining these techniques among non-clinical populations have shown promising results (Hayes, Bissett, Korn, Zettle, Rosenfarb, Cooper et al., 1999; Gutiérrez, Luciano, Rodríguez, & Fink, 2004; Masuda, Hayes, Sackett, & Twohig, 2004) and data from treatment research using these strategies for clinical populations is beginning to emerge. Acceptance describes the process of approaching aversive stimuli while behaving effectively in one's environment. Individuals are guided through exposure to difficult feelings, thoughts, or urges, in the service of practicing new, effective behaviors that are more consistent with their values. In non-substance abusing populations, researchers have shown that acceptance strategies alter the verbal context of rules through decreasing their believability (Bach & Hayes, 2002; Zettle & Hayes, 1987). In using these acceptance strategies, it is important to focus on the function of verbal behavior and not the content of what people are saying. Accumulating research supports the idea that it is not the change in form or frequency of thoughts, but rather it is the way individuals relate to cognitions that is associated with better outcomes (Teasdale, Scott, Moore, Hayhurst, Pope, & Paykel, 2001; Zettle & Hayes, 1987).

Defusion is the process of disrupting the ordinary meaning functions of language such that the believability of thoughts and the impact those thoughts have on behavior is undermined (Hayes, Strosahl, & Wilson, 1999). For example, if an individual states "I need a hit," defusion would be aimed at having the person change how they relate to that thought as a description of personal identity to a description of a process, which is "I am a person who is having the thought 'I need a hit' at this moment." Another strategy is Titchener's (1916) classic "milk, milk, milk" exercise. The word "milk" elicits a range of associations (e.g., white, cold, creamy, glass, cow, etc), as does the word "cigarette" (e.g., calm, relaxed, smoke). If you repeat either of these words in rapid succession, it soon becomes a different sound – dissociated from the previously mentioned associations. Defusion is not aimed at changing the thought but changing the context in which the thought emerges, thus altering the stimulus functions.

Values clarification and other motivational techniques (e.g., Motivational Interviewing; Miller & Rollnick, 2002) may alter the stimulus functions of behavior through increasing the value of alternative verbally constructed consequences. Values clarification also capitalizes on rule-governed insensitivity to the benefit of the patient, to persist in values-guided action in the face of competing contingencies (e.g., withdrawal symptoms). The goals of these strategies are to bring individuals into emotional contact with these alternative consequences and to have them behave in response to alternative verbal behavior. These treatment strategies may alter the verbally constructed consequences from, "I will feel bad if I don't use," to "Not using will help me be a better mother." Behaviors are directed toward areas where control is effective (instead of toward changing private experiences) and evaluated in terms of their effectiveness in achieving valued goals. Motivational interviewing, which includes a values clarification component, has shown good effects in clinical trials across a variety of substance use disorders (e.g., Burke, Arkowitz, & Dunn, 2002; Burke, Arkowitz, & Menchola, 2003; Project MATCH Research Group, 1997).

Research on self-change among substance dependent individuals illustrates how developing a new verbal context can influence behavior in non-treatment settings. Sobell, Ellingstad, and Sobell (2000) found that reasons for self-change primarily involved negative health consequences and personal issues (e.g., shame about use in a particular incident), followed by changes in how individuals viewed substance use (e.g., substance abuse was incompatible with a role they were assuming) and influence from a significant other (e.g., partner, family, friend). These accounts of self-change can be explained from an RFT perspective (see Barnes-Holmes, O'Hora, Roche, Hayes, Bissett, & Lyddy, 2001). For example, say that a person who abuses alcohol does not behave in response to the rule "if you stop drinking, you will have a long and happy life." Now, say that this person is hospitalized and is told by a doctor that he is in liver failure and his life is in immediate danger. It is possible that he quits permanently, even though he has failed to do so before. From an RFT perspective, the function of the phrase "long and happy life" may have been transformed by the doctor's statement and this event. The doctor's statement may have functioned to increase the value of a "long and happy life" by describing how it is in immediate risk. Further, "I do not stop drinking" may become associated with the aversive consequences of being sick, while "I do stop drinking" is evaluated less negatively. Although the individual's belief in the rule remains unchanged (he always believed that excessive drinking was dangerous), he now follows the previously ineffective rule because he values the specified consequences ("long and happy life") more highly.

Acceptance and Commitment Therapy (ACT; Hayes et al., 1999), a treatment that combine acceptance, defusion, and values clarification has shown promising outcomes. For example, in one study ACT plus methadone was more effective in decreasing substance use among polysubstance dependent participants compared to methadone alone (Hayes, Wilson, Gifford, Bissett, Piasecki, Batten et al., 2004). In another study, smokers who received ACT had better one-year abstinence rates than those receiving nicotine replacement therapy (Gifford et al., 2004). Although there are only a few published studies examining ACT for substance use disorders, emerging evidence for the efficacy of this intervention across a variety of clinical problems is promising (for a review, see Hayes, Luoma, Bond, Masuda, & Lillis, 2006).

Conclusion

Substance use disorders and their associated problems continue to be significant public health concerns. Over time, numerous theories have been developed to explain the phenomenology of addictive behavior, however many of these models offer either incomplete or theoretically eclectic accounts. The present RFT-enhanced behavioral analysis of addictive behavior provides a theoretically consistent account of factors associated with substance abuse and dependence, with specific predictions for research and treatment. Although the data on RFT is preliminary, it is growing.

References

Abrams, D. B., Niaura, R. S., Carey, K. B., Monti, P. M., & Binkoff, J. A. (1986). Understanding relapse and recovery in alcohol abuse. *Annals of Behavioral Medicine, 8*, 27-32.

Anagnostaras, S. G., & Robinson, T. E. (1996). Sensitization to the psychomotor stimulant effects of amphetamine: Modulation by associative learning. *Behavioral Neuroscience, 110*, 1397-1414.

American Psychiatric Association. (2000). *Diagnostic and statistical manual of mental disorders (4th ed., text revision).* Washington, D.C.: Author.

Anthony, J. C., Warner, L. A., & Kessler, R. C. (1994). Comparative epidemiology of dependence on tobacco, alcohol, controlled substances, and inhalants: Basic findings from the National Comorbidity Survey. *Experimental and Clinical Psychopharmacology, 2*, 244-268.

Bach, P., & Hayes, S. C. (2002). The use of acceptance and commitment therapy to prevent the rehospitalization of psychotic patients: A randomized controlled trial. *Journal of Consulting and Clinical Psychology, 70*, 1129-1139.

Baker, T. B., Piper, M. E., McCarthy, D. E., Majeskie, M. R., & Fiore, M. C. (2004). Addiction motivation reformulated: An affective processing model of negative reinforcement. *Psychological Review, 111*, 33-51.

Baker, T. B., & Tiffany, S. T. (1985). Morphine tolerance as habituation. *Psychological Review, 92*, 78-108.

Barnes-Holmes, D., O'Hora, D., Roche, B., Hayes, S. C., Bissett, R., & Lyddy, F. (2001). Understanding and verbal regulation. In D. Barnes-Holmes, S. C. Hayes, & B. Roche (Eds.), *Relational frame theory: A post-Skinnerian account of human language and cognition* (pp. 103-117). New York: Kluwer Academic/Plenum Publishers.

Barnes-Holmes, Y., Barnes-Holmes, D., Smeets, P. M., Strand, P., & Friman, P. (2004). Establishing relational responding in accordance with more-than and less-than as generalized operant behavior in young children. *International Journal of Psychology and Psychological Therapy, 4*, 531-558.

Berman, S. M., & Noble, E. P. (1997). The D2 dopamine receptor (DRD2) gene and family stress; interactive effects on cognitive functions in children. *Behavior Genetics, 27*, 33-43.

Berman, S. M., Ozkaragoz, T., Young, R., & Noble, E. P. (2002). D2 dopamine receptor gene polymorphism discriminates two kinds of novelty seeking. *Personality and Individual Differences, 33*, 867-882.

Berridge, K. C., & Robinson, T. E. (1995). The mind of the addicted brain: Neural sensitization of wanting versus liking. *Current Directions in Psychological Science, 4*, 71-76.

Berridge, K. C., & Robinson, T. E. (2003). Parsing reward. *Trends in Neuroscience, 26*, 507-513.

Bickel, W. K., & Marsch, L. A. (2001). Toward a behavioral economic understanding of drug dependence: Delay discounting processes. *Addiction, 96*, 73-86.

Bickel, W. K., Odum, A. L., & Madden, G. J. (1999). Impulsivity and cigarette smoking: Delay discounting in current, never, and ex-smokers. *Psychopharmacology, 146*, 447-454.

Bigelow, G. E., Griffiths, R. R., & Liebson, I. A. (1977). Pharmacological influences upon human ethanol self-administration. *Advances in Experimental Medicine and Biology, 85B*, 523-538.

Blume, A. W., Schmaling, K. B., & Marlatt, A. G. (2003). Predictors of change in binge drinking over a 3-month period. *Addictive Behaviors, 28*, 1007-1012.

Bouton, M. E. (2004). Context and behavioral processes in extinction. *Learning and Memory, 11*, 485-494.

Bradley, B. P., Phillips, G., Green, L., & Gossop, M. (1989). Circumstances surrounding the initial lapse to opiate use following detoxification. *British Journal of Psychiatry, 154*, 354-359.

Brandon, T. H., Herzog, T. A., Irvin, J. E., & Gwaltney, C. J. (2004). Cognitive and social learning models of drug dependence: Implications for the assessment of tobacco dependence in adolescents. *Addiction, 99*, 51-77.

Breslau, N. (1995). Psychiatric comorbidity of smoking and nicotine dependence. *Behavior Genetics, 25*, 95-101.

Brown, R. A., Lejuez, C. W., Kahler, C. W., Strong, D. R., & Zvolensky, M. J. (2005). Distress tolerance and early smoking lapse. *Clinical Psychology Review, 25*, 713-733.

Brown, S. A., Goldman, M. S., & Christiansen, B. A. (1985). Do alcohol expectancies mediate drinking patterns of adults? *Journal of Consulting and Clinical Psychology, 53*, 512-519.

Brownell, K. D., Marlatt, G. A., Lichtenstein, E., & Wilson, G. T. (1986). Understanding and preventing relapse. *American Psychologist, 41*, 765-782.

Burke, B. L., Arkowitz, H., & Dunn, C. (2002). The efficacy of motivational interviewing and its adaptations: What we know so far. In W. R. Miller & S. Rollnick (Eds.), *Motivational interviewing: Preparing people for change (2nd ed.)* (pp. 217-250). New York: Guilford.

Burke, B. L., Arkowitz, H., & Menchola, M. (2003). The efficacy of motivational interviewing: A meta-analysis of controlled clinical trials. *Journal of Consulting and Clinical Psychology, 71*, 843-861.

Cappell, H., & Greeley, J. (1987). Alcohol and tension reduction: An update on research and theory. In H. T. Blane & K. E. Leonard (Eds.), *Psychological theories of drinking and alcoholism* (pp. 15-54). New York: Guilford.

Carroll, M. E., Lac, S. T., & Nygaard, S. L. (1989). A concurrently available non-drug reinforcer prevents the acquisition or decreases the maintenance of cocaine-reinforced behavior. *Psychopharmacology, 97*, 23-29.

Caspi, A., Moffitt, T. E., Newman, D. L., & Silva, P. A. (1996). Behavioral observations at age 3 years predict adult psychiatric disorders. *Archives of General Psychiatry, 53*, 1033-1039.

Chassin, L., Pillow, D. R., Curran, P. J., Molina, B. S., & Barrera, M., Jr. (1993). Relation of parental alcoholism to early adolescent substance use: a test of three mediating mechanisms. *Journal of Abnormal Psychology, 102*, 3-19.

Chiamulera, C., Borgo, C., Falchetto, S., Valerio, E., & Tessari, M. (1996). Nicotine reinstatement of nicotine self-administration after long-term extinction. *Psychopharmacology, 127*, 102-107.

Chutuape, M. A., Mitchell, S., & de Wit, H. (1994). Dynamic changes in reinforcer effectiveness. *Journal of Applied Behavior Analysis, 36*, 421-438.

Clark, D. B., Parker, A. M., & Lynch, K. G. (1999). Psychopathology and substance-related problems during early adolescence: A survival analysis. *Journal of Clinical Child Psychology, 28*, 333-341.

Cohen, M. X., Young, J., Baek, J. M., Kessler, C., & Ranganath, C. (2005). Individual differences in extraversion and dopamine genetics predict neural reward responses. *Cognitive Brain Research, 25*, 851-861.

Collins, B. N., & Brandon, T. H. (2002). Effects of extinction context and retrieval cues on alcohol cue reactivity among nonalcoholic drinkers. *Journal of Consulting and Clinical Psychology, 70*, 390-397.

Cooper, M. L., Russell, M., & George, W. H. (1988). Coping, expectancies, and alcohol abuse: A test of social learning formulations. *Journal of Abnormal Psychology, 97*, 218-230.

Correia, C. J., & Carey, K. B. (1999). Applying behavioral theories of choice to substance use in a sample of psychiatric outpatients. *Psychology of Addictive Behaviors, 134*, 207-212.

Costa, F. M., Jessor, R., & Turbin, M. S. (1999). Transition into adolescent problem drinking: The role of psychosocial risk and protective factors. *Journal of Studies on Alcohol, 60*, 480-490.

Crutchfield, R. D., & Gove, W. R. (1984). Determinants of drug use: A test of the coping hypothesis. *Social Science and Medicine, 18*, 503-509.

Darkes, J., & Goldman, M. S. (1993). Expectancy challenge and drinking reduction: Experimental evidence for a mediational process. *Journal of Consulting and Clinical Psychology, 61*, 344-353.

Darkes, J., & Goldman, M. S. (1998). Expectancy challenge and drinking reduction: Process and structure in the alcohol expectancy network. *Experimental and Clinical Psychopharmacology, 6*, 64-76.

Darkes, J., Greenbaum, P. E., & Goldman, M. S. (2004). Alcohol expectancy mediation of biopsychosocial risk: Complex patterns of mediation. *Experimental and Clinical Psychopharmacology, 12*, 27-38.

De Micheli, D., & Formigoni, M. L. (2002). Are reasons for the first use of drugs and family circumstances predictors of future use patterns? *Addictive Behaviors, 27*, 87-100.

de Wit, H., & Stewart, J. (1981). Reinstatement of cocaine reinforced responding in the rat. *Psychopharmacology, 75,* 134-143.

DeGrandpre, R. J., & Bickel, W. K. (1993). Stimulus control and drug dependence. *Psychological Record, 43,* 651-666.

DeGrandpre, R. J., Bickel, W. K., Higgins, S. T., & Hughes, J. R. (1994). A behavioral economic analysis of concurrently available money and cigarettes. *Journal of the Experimental Analysis of Behavior, 61,* 191-201.

Del Boca, F. K., Darkes, J., Goldman, M. S., & Smith, G. T. (2002). Advancing the expectancy concept via the interplay between theory and research. *Alcohol: Clinical and Experimental Research, 26,* 926-935.

Dom, G., D'Haene, P., Hulstijn, W., & Sabbe, B. (2006). Impulsivity in abstinent early- and late-onset alcoholics: Differences in self-report measures and a discounting task. *Addiction, 101,* 50-59.

Drobes, D. J., & Tiffany, S. T. (1997). Induction of smoking urge through imaginal and in vivo procedures: Physiological and self-report manifestations. *Journal of Abnormal Psychology, 106,* 15-25.

Drummond, D. C., Cooper, T., & Glautier, S. P. (1990). Conditioned learning in alcohol dependence: Implications for cue exposure treatment. *British Journal of Addiction, 85,* 725-743.

Dunn, M. E., Lau, H. C., & Cruz, I. Y. (2000). Changes in activation of alcohol expectancies in memory in relation to changes in alcohol use after participation in an expectancy challenge program. *Experimental and Clinical Psychopharmacology, 8,* 566-575.

Eissenberg, T. (2004). Measuring the emergence of tobacco dependence: The contribution of negative reinforcement models. *Addiction, 99,* 5-29.

Evans, D. M., Gillespie, N. A., & Martin, N. G. (2002). Biometrical genetics. *Biological Psychology, 61,* 33-51.

Fals-Stewart, W., Birchler, G. R., & O'Farrell, T. J. (1996). Behavioral couples therapy for male substance-abusing patients: Effects on relationship adjustment and drug-using behavior. *Journal of Consulting and Clinical Psychology, 64,* 959-972.

Farre, M., & Cami, J. (1991). Pharmacokinetic considerations in abuse liability evaluation. *British Journal of Addiction, 86,* 1601-1606.

Fingarette, H. (1988). Alcoholism: The mythical disease. *Public Interest, 91,* 3-22.

Franken, I. H., Kroon, L. Y., Wiers, R. W., & Jansen, A. (2000). Selective cognitive processing of drug cues in heroin dependence. *Journal of Psychopharmacology, 14,* 395-400.

Gable, R. S. (2004). Comparison of acute lethal toxicity of commonly abused psychoactive substances. *Addiction, 99,* 686-696.

Galizio, M. (2003). The abstracted operant: A review of relational frame theory: A post-Skinnerian account of human language and cognition. *The Behavior Analyst, 26,* 159-169.

Garcia-Gutierrez, A., & Rosas, J. M. (2003). Context change as the mechanism of reinstatement in causal learning. *Journal of Experimental Psychology: Animal Behavior Processes, 29,* 292-310.

Gifford, E. V., Kohlenberg, B. S., Hayes, S. C., Antonuccio, D. O., Piasecki, M. M., Rasmussen-Hall, M. L., et al. (2004). Acceptance-based treatment for smoking cessation. *Behavior Therapy, 35,* 689-706.

Glautier, S. (2004). Measures and models of nicotine dependence: Positive reinforcement. *Addiction, 99,* 30-50.

Goldman, M. S., Brown, S. A., & Christiansen, B. A. (1987). Expectancy theory: Thinking about drinking. In H. T. Blane & K. E. Leonard (Eds.), *Psychological theories of drinking and alcoholism* (pp. 181-226). New York: Guilford.

Gottlieb, A. M., Killen, J. D., Marlatt, G. A., & Taylor, C. B. (1987). Psychological and pharmacological influences in cigarette smoking withdrawal: Effects of nicotine gum and expectancy on smoking withdrawal symptoms and relapse. *Journal of Consulting and Clinical Psychology, 55,* 606-608.

Grant, B. F., Dawson, D. A., Stinson, F. S., Chou, S. P., Dufour, M. C., & Pickering, R. P. (2004). The 12-month prevalence and trends in DSM-IV alcohol abuse and dependence: United States, 1991-1992 and 2001-2002. *Drug and Alcohol Dependence, 74,* 223-234.

Grant, B. F., Stinson, F. S., Dawson, D. A., Chou, S. P., Dufour, M. C., Compton, W., et al. (2004). Prevalence and co-occurrence of substance use disorders and independent mood and anxiety disorders: Results from the National Epidemiologic Survey on alcohol and related conditions. *Archives of General Psychiatry, 61,* 807-816.

Grant, B. F., Stinson, F. S., & Harford, T. C. (2001). Age at onset of alcohol use and DSM-IV alcohol abuse and dependence: A 12-year follow-up. *Journal of Substance Abuse, 13,* 493-504.

Greenberger, E., Chen, C., Beam, M., Wang, S., & Dong, Q. (2000). The perceived social contexts of adolescents' misconduct: A comparative study of youths in three cultures. *Journal of Research on Adolescence, 10,* 365-388.

Gutiérrez, O., Luciano, C., Rodríguez, M., & Fink, B. C. (2004). Comparison between an acceptance-based and a cognitive-control-based protocol for coping with pain. *Behavior Therapy, 35,* 767-784.

Gwaltney, C. J., Shiffman, S., Paty, J. A., Liu, K. S., Kassel, J. D., Gnys, M., et al. (2002). Using self-efficacy judgments to predict characteristics of lapses to smoking. *Journal of Consulting and Clinical Psychology, 70,* 1140-1149.

Harada, S., Agarwal, D. P., Goedde, H. W., Tagaki, S., & Ishikawa, B. (1982). Possible protective role against alcoholism for aldehyde dehydrogenase isozyme deficiency in Japan. *Lancet, 2,* 827.

Hasin, D. S., Hatzenbueler, M., Smith, S., & Grant, B. F. (2005). Co-occurring DSM-IV drug abuse in DSM-IV drug dependence: results from the National Epidemiologic Survey on alcohol and related conditions. *Drug and Alcohol Dependence, 80,* 117-123.

Hasin, D. S., Liu, X., Nunes, E., McCloud, S., Samet, S., & Endicott, J. (2002). Effects of major depression on remission and relapse of substance dependence. *Archives of General Psychiatry, 59,* 375-380.

Hawkins, J. D., Catalano, R. F., & Miller, J. Y. (1992). Risk and protective factors for alcohol and other drug problems in adolescence and early adulthood: Implications for substance abuse prevention. *Psychological Bulletin, 112,* 64-105.

Hayes, S. C., Barnes-Holmes, D., & Roche, B. (2001). *Relational frame theory: A post-Skinnerian account of human language and cognition.* New York: Kluwer Academic/Plenum Publishers.

Hayes, S. C., Bissett, R. T., Korn, Z., Zettle, R. D., Rosenfarb, I. S., Cooper, L. D., et al. (1999). The impact of acceptance and control rationales on pain tolerance. *Psychological Record, 49,* 33-47.

Hayes, S. C., Luoma, J. B., Bond, F. W., Masuda, A., & Lillis, J. (2006). Acceptance and commitment therapy: Model, processes and outcomes. *Behavior Research and Therapy, 44,* 1-25.

Hayes, S. C., Strosahl, K., & Wilson, K. G. (1999). *Acceptance and commitment therapy: An experiential approach to behavior change.* New York: Guilford.

Hayes, S. C., & Wilson, K. G. (1996). Criticisms of relational frame theory: Implications for a behavior analytic account of derived stimulus relations. *Psychological Record, 46,* 221-236.

Hayes, S. C., Wilson, K. G., Gifford, E. V., Bissett, R., Piasecki, M., Batten, S. V., et al. (2004). A preliminary trial of twelve-step facilitation and acceptance and commitment therapy with polysubstance-abusing methadone-maintained opiate addicts. *Behavior Therapy, 35,* 667-688.

Hayes, S. C., Wilson, K. G., Gifford, E. V., Follette, V. M., & Strosahl, K. (1996). Experiential avoidance and behavioral disorders: A functional dimensional approach to diagnosis and treatment. *Journal of Consulting and Clinical Psychology, 64,* 1152-1168.

Healy, O., Barnes-Holmes, D., & Smeets, P. M. (2000). Derived relational responding as generalized operant behavior. *Journal of the Experimental Analysis of Behavior, 74,* 207-227.

Heath, A. C., Madden, P. A., Bucholz, K. K., Dinwiddie, S. H., Slutske, W. S., Bierut, L. J., et al. (1999). Genetic differences in alcohol sensitivity and the inheritance of alcoholism risk. *Psychological Medicine, 29,* 1069-1081.

Higgins, S. T., Alessi, S. M., & Dantona, R. L. (2002). Voucher-based incentives: A substance abuse treatment innovation. *Addictive Behaviors, 27,* 887-910.

Higgins, S. T., Heil, S. H., & Plebani-Lussier, J. (2003). Clinical implications of reinforcement as a determinant of substance use disorders. *Annual Review of Psychology, 55,* 1-31.

Higgins, S. T., Wong, C. J., Badger, G. J., Ogden, D. E. H., & Dantona, R. L. (2000). Contingent reinforcement increases cocaine abstinence during outpatient treatment and 1 year of follow-up. *Journal of Consulting and Clinical Psychology, 68,* 64-72.

Hollon, S. D., & Kendall, P. C. (1980). Cognitive self-statements in depression: Development of an automatic thoughts questionnaire. *Cognitive Therapy and Research, 4,* 383-395.

Ireland, S. J., McMahon, R. C., Malow, R. M., & Kouzekanani, K. (1994). Coping style as a predictor of relapse to cocaine abuse. In L. S. Harris (Ed.), *Problems of drug dependence, 1993: Proceedings of the 55th annual scientific meeting, National Institute of Drug Abuse monograph series no. 141.* Washington, D.C.: U.S. Government Printing Office.

Jacobs, E. A., & Bickel, W. K. (1999). Modeling drug consumption in the clinic using simulation procedures: Demand for heroin and cigarettes in opioid-dependent outpatients. *Experimental and Clinical Psychopharmacology, 7,* 412-426.

Jessor, R., Turbin, M. S., Costa, F. M., Dong, Q., Zhang, H., & Wang, C. (2003). Adolescent problem behavior in China and the United States: A cross-national study of psychosocial protective factors. *Journal of Research on Adolescence, 13,* 329-360.

Jones, B. T., Corbin, W., & Fromme, K. (2001). A review of expectancy theory and alcohol consumption. *Addiction, 96,* 57-72.

Joyce, J. H., & Chase, P. N. (1990). Effects of response variability on the sensitivity of rule-governed behavior. *Journal of the Experimental Analysis of Behavior. Special Issue: The experimental analysis of human behavior, 54,* 251-262.

Kandel, D. B. (1985). On processes of peer influences in adolescent drug use: a developmental perspective. *Advances in Alcohol and Substance Abuse, 4,* 139-163.

Kendler, K. S., Walters, E. E., Neale, M. C., Kessler, R. C., Heath, A. C., & Eaves, L. J. (1995). The structure of the genetic and environmental risk factors for six major psychiatric disorders in women. *Archives of General Psychiatry, 52,* 374-383.

Kessler, R. C. (1994). The National Comorbidity Survey of the United States. *International Review of Psychiatry, 6,* 365-376.

Khantzian, E. J. (1997). The self-medication hypothesis of substance use disorders: A reconsideration and recent applications. *Harvard Review of Psychiatry, 4,* 231-244.

Kilpatrick, D. G., Ruggiero, K. J., Acierno, R., Saunders, B. E., Resnick, H. S., & Best, C. L. (2003). Violence and risk of PTSD, major depression, substance abuse/dependence, and comorbidity: Results from the National Survey of Adolescents. *Journal of Consulting and Clinical Psychology, 71,* 692-700.

Kirby, K. N., & Petry, N. M. (2004). Heroin and cocaine abusers have higher discount rates for delayed rewards than alcoholics or non-drug-using controls. *Addiction, 99,* 461-471.

Kleber, H. D., Weiss, R. D., Anton, R. F., Rounsaville, B. J., George, T. P., Strain, E. C., et al. (2006). Treatment of patients with substance use disorders. *American Journal of Psychiatry, 163,* 5-82.

Knopik, V. S., Heath, A. C., Madden, P. A., Bucholz, K. K., Slutske, W. S., Nelson, E. C., et al. (2004). Genetic effects on alcohol dependence risk: re-evaluating the importance of psychiatric and other heritable risk factors. *Psychological Medicine, 34,* 1519-1530.

Koob, G. F. (1996). Drug addiction: The yin and yang of hedonic homeostasis. *Neuron, 16,* 893-896.

Koob, G. F., & Le Moal, M. (1997). Drug abuse: Hedonic homeostatic dysregulation. *Science, 278,* 52-58.

Koob, G. F., Stinus, L., Le Moal, M., & Bloom, F. E. (1989). Opponent process theory of motivation: Neurobiological evidence from studies of opiate dependence. *Neuroscience and Biobehavioral Reviews, 13,* 135-140.

Kranzler, H. R. (2000). Pharmacotherapy of alcoholism: Gaps in knowledge and opportunities for research. *Alcohol and Addiction, 35,* 537-547.

Kranzler, H. R., Babor, T. F., & Lauerman, R. J. (1990). Problems associated with average alcohol consumption and frequency of intoxication in a medical population. *Alcohol: Clinical and Experimental Research, 14,* 119-126.

Kreek, M. J., Bart, G., Lilly, C., LaForge, K. S., & Nielsen, D. A. (2005). Pharmacogenetics and human molecular genetics of opiate and cocaine addictions and their treatments. *Pharmacological Reviews, 57,* 1-26.

Kudadjie-Gyamfi, E., & Rachlin, H. (2002). Rule-governed versus contingency-governed behavior in a self-control task: Effects of changes in contingencies. *Behavioural Processes, 57,* 29-35.

Leonard, K. E., & Blane, H. T. (1999). *Psychological theories of drinking and alcoholism (2nd ed.).* New York: Guilford.

Lippman, L. G. (1994). Rule-governed performance and sensitivity to contingencies: What's new? *Journal of General Psychology, 121,* 353-360.

Lubman, D. I., Peters, L. A., Mogg, K., Bradley, B. P., & Deakin, J. F. W. (2000). Attentional bias for drug cues in opiate dependence. *Psychological Medicine, 30,* 169-175.

Marlatt, A. G., & Donovan, D. M. (2005). *Relapse prevention: Maintenance strategies in the treatment of addictive behaviors (2nd ed.).* New York: Guilford.

Marlatt, G. A., & Gordon, J. R. (1985). *Relapse prevention: Maintenance strategies in the treatment of addictive behaviors.* New York: Guilford.

Masuda, A., Hayes, S. C., Sackett, C. F., & Twohig, M. P. (2004). Cognitive defusion and self-relevant negative thoughts: Examining the impact of a ninety year old technique. *Behaviour Research and Therapy, 42,* 477-485.

McDonald, R. V., & Siegel, S. (2004). Intra-administration associations and withdrawal symptoms: Morphine-elicited morphine withdrawal. *Experimental and Clinical Psychopharmacology, 12,* 3-11.

McLellan, A. T., Lewis, D. C., O'Brien, C. P., & Kleber, H. D. (2000). Drug dependence, a chronic medical illness: Implications for treatment, insurance, and outcomes evaluation. *Journal of the American Medical Association, 284,* 1689-1695.

McSweeney, F. K. (1992). Rate of reinforcement and session duration as determinants of within-session patterns of responding. *Animal Learning and Behavior, 20,* 160-169.

McSweeney, F. K., Hinson, J. M., & Cannon, C. B. (1996). Sensitization-habituation may occur during operant conditioning. *Psychological Bulletin, 120,* 256-271.

McSweeney, F. K., Murphy, E. S., & Kowal, B. P. (2005). Regulation of drug taking by sensitization and habituation. *Experimental and Clinical Psychopharmacology, 13,* 163-184.

Michael, J. (1982). Distinguishing between discriminative and motivating functions of stimuli. *Journal of the Experimental Analysis of Behavior, 37,* 149-155.

Michael, J. (1983). Evocative and repertoire-altering effects of an environmental event. *The Analysis of Verbal Behavior, 2,* 19-21.

Miller, W. R., & Hester, R. K. (1995). Treatment for alcohol problems: Toward an informed eclecticism. In R. K. Hester & W. R. Miller (Eds.), *Handbook of alcoholism treatment approaches: Effective alternatives.* Boston: Allyn & Bacon.

Miller, W. R., & Rollnick, S. (2002). *Motivational interviewing: Preparing people for change. (2nd ed.).* New York: Guilford.

Mokdad, A. H., Marks, J. S., Stroup, D. F., & Gerberding, J. L. (2004). Actual causes of death in the United States, 2000. *Journal of the American Medical Association, 291,* 1238-1245.

Moos, R. H., Nichol, A. C., & Moos, B. S. (2002). Risk factors for symptom exacerbation among treated patients with substance use disorders. *Addiction, 97,* 75-85.

Morgenstern, J., Labouvie, E., McCrady, B. S., Kahler, C. W., & Frey, R. M. (1997). Affiliation with Alcoholics Anonymous after treatment: A study of its therapeutic effects and mechanisms of action. *Journal of Consulting and Clinical Psychology, 65,* 768-777.

Murphy, J. G., Correia, C. J., Colby, S. M., & Vuchinich, R. E. (2005). Using behavioral theories of choice to predict drinking outcomes following a brief intervention. *Experimental and Clinical Psychopharmacology, 13,* 93-101.

Nader, M. A., & Woolverton, W. L. (1991). Effects of increasing the magnitude of an alternative reinforcer on drug choice in a discrete-trials choice procedure. *Psychopharmacology, 105,* 169-174.

Narrow, W. E., Rae, D. S., Robins, L. N., & Regier, D. A. (2002). Revised prevalence estimates of mental disorders in the United States: Using a clinical significance criterion to reconcile 2 surveys' estimates. *Archives of General Psychiatry, 59,* 115-123.

Nathan, P. E. (1988). The addictive personality is the behavior of the addict. *Journal of Consulting and Clinical Psychology, 56,* 183-188.

National Institute on Drug Abuse. (2004). The economic costs of alcohol and drug abuse in the United States; 1992. http://www.nida.nih.gov/EconomicCosts/Index.html.

Nevin, J. A., Smith, L. D., & Roberts, J. (1987). Does contingent reinforcement strengthen operant behavior? *Journal of the Experimental Analysis of Behavior, 48,* 17-33.

O'Farrell, T. J., & Fals-Stewart, W. (2000). Behavioral couples therapy for alcoholism and drug abuse. *Journal of Substance Abuse Treatment, 18,* 51-54.

Ohmura, Y., Takahashi, T., & Kitamura, N. (2005). Discounting delayed and probabilistic monetary gains and losses by smokers of cigarettes. *Psychopharmacology, 182,* 508-515.

Ouimette, P. C., Finney, J. W., & Moos, R. H. (1997). Twelve-step and cognitive-behavioral treatment for substance abuse: A comparison of treatment effectiveness. *Journal of Consulting and Clinical Psychology, 65,* 230-240.

Osbourne, J. G. (2003). Beyond Skinner? A review of relational frame theory: A post-Skinnerian account of human language and cognition. *The Analysis of Verbal Behavior, 19,* 19-27.

Otto, M. W., Powers, M. B., & Fischmann, D. (2005). Emotional exposure in the treatment of substance use disorders: Conceptual model, evidence, and future directions. *Clinical Psychology Review, 25,* 824-839.

Palfai, T. P., Colby, S. M., Monti, P. M., & Rohsenow, D. J. (1997). Effects of suppressing the urge to drink on smoking topography: A preliminary study. *Psychology of Addictive Behaviors, 11,* 115-123.

Panlilio, L. V., Weiss, S. J., & Schindler, C. W. (2000). Effects of compounding drug-related stimuli: Escalation of heroin self-administration. *Journal of the Experimental Analysis of Behavior, 73,* 211-224.

Parra, G. R., O'Neill, S. E., & Sher, K. J. (2003). Reliability of self-reported age of substance involvement onset. *Psychology of Addictive Behavior, 17,* 211-218.

Patten, C. A., & Martin, J. E. (1996). Does nicotine withdrawal affect smoking cessation? Clinical and theoretical issues. *Annals of Behavioral Medicine, 18,* 190-200.

Petry, N. M. (2001). Pathological gamblers, with and without substance use disorders, discount delayed rewards at high rates. *Journal of Abnormal Psychology, 110,* 482-487.

Petry, N. M., & Bickel, W. K. (1998). Polydrug abuse in heroin addicts: A behavioral economic analysis. *Addiction, 93,* 321-335.

Plaud, J. J., & Plaud, D. M. (1998). Clinical behavior therapy and the experimental analysis of behavior. *Journal of Clinical Psychology, 54,* 905-921.

Pohorecky, L. A. (1991). Stress and alcohol interaction: An update of human research. *Alcohol: Clinical and Experimental Research, 15,* 438-459.

Prendergast, M. L., Podus, D., Chang, E., & Urada, D. (2002). The effectiveness of drug abuse treatment: A meta-analysis of comparison group studies. *Drug and Alcohol Dependence, 67,* 53-72.

Project MATCH Research Group. (1997). Matching alcoholism treatment to client heterogeneity: Project MATCH posttreatment drinking outcomes. *Journal of Studies on Alcohol, 58,* 7-29.

Rawson, R. A., Huber, A., McCann, M., Shoptaw, S., Farabee, D., Reiber, C., et al. (2002). A comparison of contingency management and cognitive-behavioral approaches during methadone maintenance treatment for cocaine dependence. *Archives of General Psychiatry, 59,* 817-824.

Regier, D. A., Farmer, M. E., Rae, D. S., Locke, B. Z., Keith, S. J., Judd, L. L., et al. (1990). Comorbidity of mental disorders with alcohol and other drug abuse: Results from the Epidemiologic Catchment Area (ECA) study. *Journal of the American Medical Association, 264,* 2511-2518.

Reich, R. R., & Goldman, M. S. (2005). Exploring the alcohol expectancy memory network: The utility of free associates. *Psychology of Addictive Behaviors, 19,* 317-325.

Ridenour, T. A., Maldonado-Molina, M., Compton, W. M., Spitznagel, E. L., & Cottler, L. B. (2005). Factors associated with the transition from abuse to dependence among substance abusers: Implications for a measure of addictive liability. *Drug and Alcohol Dependence, 80,* 1-14.

Robinson, T. E., & Berridge, K. C. (2001). Incentive-sensitization and addiction. *Addiction, 96,* 103-114.

Roll, J. M., & McSweeney, F. K. (1999). Within-session changes in response rate: Implications for behavioral pharmacology. *Psychological Record, 49,* 15-32.

Roll, J. M., McSweeney, F. K., Johnson, K. S., & Weatherly, J. N. (1995). Satiety contributes little to within-session decreases in responding. *Learning & Motivation, 26,* 232-341.

Salzinger, K. (2003). On the verbal behavior of relational frame theory: A post-Skinnerian account of human language and cognition. *The Analysis of Verbal Behavior, 19,* 7-9.

Sanchez-Craig, M. (1986). Is it useful to think of alcohol dependence as a continuum? *British Journal of Addiction, 81,* 187-190.

Schuckit, M. A. (1994). A clinical model of genetic influences in alcohol dependence. *Journal of Studies on Alcohol, 55,* 5-17.

Schuckit, M. A. (1999). New findings in the genetics of alcoholism. *Journal of the American Medical Association, 281,* 1875-1876.

Schuster, C. R., & Thompson, T. (1969). Self administration of and behavioral dependence on drugs. *Annual Review of Pharmacology, 9,* 483-502.

Seeman, M., & Seeman, A. Z. (1992). Life strains, alienation, and drinking behavior. *Alcohol: Clinical and Experimental Research, 16,* 199-205.

Sher, K. J., & Trull, T. J. (1994). Personality and disinhibitory psychopathology: Alcoholism and antisocial personality disorder. *Journal of Abnormal Psychology, 103,* 92-102.

Shiffman, S., Ferguson, S. G., & Gwaltney, C. J. (2006). Immediate hedonic response to smoking lapses: Relationship to smoking relapse, and effects of nicotine replacement therapy. *Psychopharmacology, 184,* 608-618.

Shiffman, S., Waters, A., & Hickcox, M. (2004). The nicotine dependence syndrome scale: A multidimensional measure of nicotine dependence. *Nicotine and Tobacco Research, 6,* 327-348.

Shiffman, S., & Waters, A. J. (2004). Negative affect and smoking lapses: A prospective analysis. *Journal of Consulting and Clinical Psychology, 72,* 192-201.

Siegel, S. (1999). Drug anticipation and drug addiction: The 1998 H. David Archibald lecture. *Addiction, 94,* 1113-1124.

Siegel, S. (2001). Pavlovian conditioning and drug overdose: When tolerance fails. *Addiction Research and Theory, 9,* 503-513.

Siegel, S. (2005). Drug tolerance, drug addiction, and drug anticipation. *Current Directions in Psychological Science, 14,* 296-300.

Siegel, S., & Ramos, B. M. (2002). Applying laboratory research: Drug anticipation and the treatment of drug addiction. *Experimental and Clinical Psychopharmacology, 10,* 162-183.

Slutske, W. S., Heath, A. C., Madden, P. A., Bucholz, K. K., Statham, D. J., & Martin, N. G. (2002). Personality and the genetic risk for alcohol dependence. *Journal of Abnormal Psychology, 111,* 124-133.

Smith, J. E., Meyers, R. J., & Delaney, H. D. (1998). The community reinforcement approach to homeless alcohol-dependent individuals. *Journal of Consulting and Clinical Psychology, 66,* 541-548.

Sobell, L. C., Ellingstad, T. P., & Sobell, M. B. (2000). Natural recovery from alcohol and drug problems: Methodological review of the research with suggestions for future directions. *Addiction, 95,* 749-764.

Sobell, M. B., Wagner, E. F., & Sobell, L. C. (2003). Substance-related use disorders: Alcohol. In M. H. Hersen & S. M. Turner (Eds.), *Adult psychopathology and diagnosis (4ᵗʰ ed.)* (pp. 192-225). New York: John Wiley & Sons, Inc.

Solomon, R. L., & Corbit, J. D. (1974). An opponent-process theory of motivation. I. Temporal dynamics of affect. *Psychological Review, 81,* 119-145.

Stewart, J., & Vezina, P. (1991). Extinction procedures abolish conditioned stimulus control but spare sensitized responding to amphetamine. *Behavioral Pharmacology, 2,* 65-71.

Stice, E., Barrera, M., Jr., & Chassin, L. (1993). Relation of parental support and control to adolescents' externalizing symptomatology and substance use: a longitudinal examination of curvilinear effects. *Journal of Abnormal Child Psychology, 21,* 609-629.

Stokes, T. F., & Baer, D. M. (1977). An implicit technology of generalization. *Journal of Applied Behavior Analysis, 10,* 349-367.

Stretch, R., Gerber, G. J., & Wood, S. M. (1971). Factors affecting behavior maintained by response-contingent intravenous infusions of amphetamine in squirrel monkeys. *Canadian Journal of Physiological Pharmacology, 49,* 581-589.

Substance Abuse and Mental Health Services Administration (SAMHSA), Office of Applied Studies (1998). *Preliminary results from the 1997 National Household Survey on Drug Abuse.* Rockville, MD: US Department of Health and Human Services.

Substance Abuse and Mental Health Services Administration (SAMHSA), Office of Applied Studies (2006). *Preliminary results from the 2004 National Household Survey on Drug Abuse.* Rockville, MD: US Department of Health and Human Services.

Tarter, R. E., Kirisci, L., Mezzich, A., Cornelius, J. R., Pajer, K., Vanyukov, M., et al. (2003). Neurobehavioral disinhibition in childhood predicts early age at onset of substance use disorder. *American Journal of Psychiatry, 160,* 1078-1085.

Tate, J. C., Stanton, A. L., Green, S. B., Schmitz, J. M., Le, T., & Marshall, B. (1994). Experimental analysis of the role of expectancy in nicotine withdrawal. *Psychology of Addictive Behaviors, 8,* 169-178.

Teasdale, J. D., Scott, J., Moore, R. G., Hayhurst, H., Pope, M., & Paykel, E. S. (2001). How does cognitive therapy prevent relapse in residual depression? Evidence from a controlled trial. *Journal of Consulting and Clinical Psychology, 69,* 347-357.

Tiffany, S. T. (1990). A cognitive model of drug urges and drug-use behavior: Role of automatic and nonautomatic processes. *Psychological Review, 97,* 147-168.

Tiffany, S. T., & Conklin, C. A. (2000). A cognitive processing model of alcohol craving and compulsive alcohol use. *Addiction, 95,* S145-153.

Titchener, E. B. (1916). *A text-book of psychology.* New York: MacMillan.

Tsuang, M. T., Bar, J. L., Harley, R. M., & Lyons, M. J. (2001). The Harvard Twin Study of Substance Abuse: What we have learned. *Harvard Review of Psychiatry, 9,* 267-279.

Vakalahi, H. F. (2001). Adolescent substance use and family-based risk and protective factors: A literature review. *Journal of Drug Education, 31,* 29-46.

Vega, W. A., Aguilar-Gaxiola, S., Andrade, L., Bijl, R., Borges, G., Caraveo-Anduaga, J. J., et al. (2002). Prevalence and age of onset for drug use in seven international sites: Results from the international consortium of psychiatric epidemiology. *Drug and Alcohol Dependence, 68,* 285-297.

Vuchinich, R. E., & Heather, N. (2003). *Choice, behavioural economics, and addiction.* Oxford, UK: Elsevier Ltd.

Vuchinich, R. E., & Tucker, J. A. (1988). Contributions from behavioral theories of choice to an analysis of alcohol abuse. *Journal of Abnormal Psychology, 97,* 181-195.

Wall, T. L., Shea, S. H., Chan, K. K., & Carr, L. G. (2001). A genetic association with the development of alcohol and other substance use behavior in Asian Americans. *Journal of Abnormal Psychology, 110,* 173-178.

Wang, Y. C., & Hsiao, S. (2003). Amphetamine sensitization: Nonassociative and associative components. *Behavioral Neuroscience, 117,* 961-969.

Waters, A. J., Shiffman, S., Bradley, B. P., & Mogg, K. (2003). Attentional shifts to smoking cues in smokers. *Addiction, 98,* 1409-1417.

Weintraub, E., Dixon, L., Delahanty, J., Schwartz, R., Johnson, J., Cohen, A., et al. (2001). Reason for medical hospitalization among adult alcohol and drug abusers. *American Journal on Addictions, 10,* 167-177.

Wenzlaff, R. M., Wegner, D. M., & Klein, S. B. (1991). The role of thought suppression in the bonding of thought and mood. *Journal of Personality and Social Psychology, 60,* 500-508.

West, R. (2006). *Theory of addiction.* Oxford, UK: Blackwell Publishing.

Wiers, R. W., Sergeant, J. A., & Gunning, W. B. (2000). The assessment of alcohol expectancies in school children: Measurement or modification? *Addiction, 95,* 737-746.

Wikler, A. (1977). The search for the psyche in drug dependence: A 35-year retrospective survey. *Journal of Nervous and Mental Disease, 165,* 29-40.

Wikler, A. (1984). Conditioning factors in opiate addiction and relapse. *Journal of Substance Abuse Treatment, 1,* 279-285.

Wills, T. A., & Cleary, S. D. (1996). How are social support effects mediated? A test with parental support and adolescent substance use. *Journal of Personality and Social Psychology, 71*, 937-952.

Wilsnack, R. W., Vogeltanz, N. D., Wilsnack, S. C., Harris, T. R., Ahlstrom, S., Bondy, S., et al. (2000). Gender differences in alcohol consumption and adverse drinking consequences: cross-cultural patterns. *Addiction, 95*, 251-265.

Wilson, K. G., & Hayes, S. C. (2000). Why it is crucial to understand thinking and feeling: An analysis and application to drug abuse. *The Behavior Analyst, 23*, 25-43.

Wilson, K. G., Hayes, S. C., Gregg, J., & Zettle, R. D. (2001). Psychopathology and psychotherapy. In D. Barnes-Holmes, S. C. Hayes, & B. Roche (Eds.), *Relational frame theory: A post-Skinnerian account of human language and cognition* (pp. 211-238). New York: Kluwer Academic/Plenum Publishers.

Witkiewitz, K., & Marlatt, G. A. (2004). Relapse prevention for alcohol and drug problems: That was Zen, this is Tao. *American Psychologist, 59*, 224-235.

Woolverton, W. L. (1996). Intravenous self-administration of cocaine under concurrent VI schedules of reinforcement. *Psychopharmacology, 127*, 195-203.

Yetnikoff, L., & Arvanitogiannis, A. (2005). A role for affect in context-dependent sensitization to amphetamine. *Behavioral Neuroscience, 119*, 1678-1681.

Young, R. M., Lawford, B. R., Nutting, A., & Noble, E. P. (2004). Advances in molecular genetics and the prevention and treatment of substance misuse: Implications of association studies of the A1 allele of the D2 dopamine receptor gene. *Addictive Behaviors, 29*, 1275-1294.

Zettle, R. D., & Hayes, S. C. (1986). Dysfunctional control by client verbal behavior: The context of reason-giving. *The Analysis of Verbal Behavior, 4*, 30-38.

Zettle, R. D., & Hayes, S. C. (1987). Component and process analysis of cognitive therapy. *Psychological Reports, 61*, 939-953.

Chapter 10

Eating Disorders:
A New Behavioral Perspective and
Acceptance-Based Treatment Approach

Georg H. Eifert
Chapman University
Laurie A. Greco
University of Missouri-St. Louis
Michelle Heffner
West Virginia University
Ashleigh Louis
Chapman University

We begin this chapter by briefly discussing diagnostic criteria for anorexia, bulimia, and binge eating and describing correlates and risk factors that have been linked to the development and maintenance of this class of disorders. Next, we describe existing cognitive-behavioral theoretical models and then outline a functional behavioral approach that posits experiential avoidance and control efforts as the basis for eating disorders. Based on this functional formulation, we outline the core components of an Acceptance and Commitment Therapy approach to the treatment of eating disorders.

Diagnostic Definitions

Anorexia and bulimia are the two most widely studied eating disorders. According to the Diagnostic and Statistical Manual for Mental Disorders (DSM-IV-TR; American Psychiatric Association, 2000), a person diagnosed with anorexia demonstrates extremely low body weight, self-starvation, fear of weight gain, body image disturbance, and amenorrhea for at least 3 consecutive menstrual cycles. The amenorrhea criterion is not applicable for women using a hormonal birth control method regulating the menstrual cycle (Walsh & Garner, 1997). DSM-IV-TR specifies two types of anorexia. Restricting type is characterized by caloric restriction alone, whereas binge-purge type is characterized by caloric restriction plus binge eating and engagement in compensatory behaviors such as self-induced vomiting, laxatives abuse, diet pills use, and/or diuretics.

Bulimia is characterized by heightened body image concerns, binge eating, and compensatory behavior. Based on the type of compensatory behavior, DSM-IV-TR (APA, 2000) specifies purging and non-purging types. Purging type bulimia involves compensatory behavior in which caloric intake is purged through vomiting, laxatives, enema use, and diuretics whereas non-purging type involves compensatory behavior such as fasting or excessive exercise. Purging type is more common and is associated with an earlier age of onset as well as more severe patterns of depression, anxiety, substance use, and sexual abuse histories compared to non-purging type (Garfinkel, Lin, Goering, & Spegg, 1996).

DSM-IV-TR (APA, 2000) describes binge eating disorder (BED) as recurrent binge eating without engagement in compensatory behavior. Individuals diagnosed with BED often eat rapidly even when satiated, binge in private to avoid embarrassment, and feel guilt or shame after binging. BED is often associated with obesity, although not all binge eaters are obese, and not all obese people are binge eaters (Bulik, Sullivan, & Kendler, 2003). Finally, eating disorder NOS refers to individuals who demonstrate "sub-clinical" levels of anorexia or bulimia or who exhibit binge eating behavior (Mizes & Sloan, 1998).

Eating disorders are associated with high mortality rates. Anorexia has been described as the most lethal of all psychological disorders, with a death rate five times greater than that of same-age and same-gender peers in the general population (Harris & Barraclough, 1998). Many anorexia-related fatalities are attributed to physical complications secondary to malnutrition (e.g., multiple organ failure). Suicide is another major cause of death associated with anorexia: Individuals diagnosed with anorexia are 33 times more likely to commit suicide than their same-age and same-gender peers in the general population. Although bulimia is less fatal than anorexia, the death rate for individuals diagnosed with bulimia is higher than the death rate for same-age and same-gender peers in the general population (Harris & Barraclough, 1998). Death can also result from the adverse side effects of excessive vomiting, such as electrolyte imbalance or heart conditions. Binge eating is associated with medical morbidity, especially Type II diabetes, and binge eating can jeopardize health even if the binge eater is not obese (Bulik & Reichborn-Kjennerud, 2003).

Etiological and Maintaining Factors

Eating disorders are likely caused by multiple factors stemming from individual, familial, and cultural influences (e.g., Garfinkel & Garner, 1982). Although the exact causes are unknown, researchers have identified possible etiological factors contributing to the development and maintenance of disturbed body image and unhealthy eating behavior. For example, a prospective study of 803 women found that low self esteem, low perceived social support from the family, high levels of body concern, and high use of escape and avoidance coping strategies increased risk for eating disorders (Ghaderi, 2003). The following section is a brief overview of available data to suggest possible individual, familial, and cultural factors that may be related to the development of eating disorders.

Individual Characteristics: Genetics, Temperament, and Neurological Findings

Genetics. Although there is some support for a genetic basis of eating disorders, the extent to which genetic influences contribute to the development of eating disorders remains unclear. Reviews examining research on the heritability of eating disorders (Bulik, 2003; Fairburn & Harrison, 2003) discuss the considerable variation in the numbers reported across studies. Fairburn and Harrison advise caution in interpreting these findings because of methodological and statistical limitations, which may hinder the detection of shared environmental effects.

It is apparent and much less controversial that genetics play a substantial role in determining body shape and size (Bulik, 2003). The interaction between an individual's inherited body type and perceived body image might play a role in the development of eating disorders. When examining a sample of middle and high school students, researchers found that adolescents with a compact or robust, muscular body type desired a lower body weight than individuals with a tall, thin body type (Neumärker, Bettle, Bettle, Dudeck, & Neumärker, 1998). Men and women may be striving for an ideal physique that is not physically possible given their inherited bone structure and body type. As noted by Brownell (1991), it is important for people with body size and weight concerns to take note of basic genetic facts rather than fight their biological make-up to the point of starvation.

The fight against biology is also common when weight gain and psychosexual changes occur during puberty. Risk factors for bulimia include early menarche for females, either early or late onset of ejaculation for males, and early age of sexual activity for both genders (Kaltiala-Heino, Rimpel, Rissanen, & Rantanen, 2001). However, Fornari and Dancyger (2003) caution there are no consistent findings regarding the role of puberty and psychosexual changes as risk factors for eating disorders. As with any other individual characteristic, puberty interacts with other risk factors and is neither a necessary nor a sufficient condition for the development of eating disorders.

Temperament. Individuals with eating disorders tend to have specific patterns of temperamental characteristics that differentiate them from healthy controls. Studies investigating various temperament variables have shown that individuals with eating disorders score higher on measures of harm avoidance and neuroticism and lower on measures of self-directedness compared to healthy controls (Diaz Marsa, Carrasco, & Saiz, 2000; Fassino, Amianto, Gramaglia, Facchini, & Abbate Daga, 2004). These studies found that individuals with anorexia scored high on measures of persistence and self-directedness compared to individuals with bulimia, who in turn scored relatively higher on harm avoidance, impulsivity, and novelty seeking than those with anorexia. A recent study that compared patients with acute eating disorders with recovered patients and found that individuals in both groups scored similarly on measures of temperament and personality. These findings suggest that temperamental characteristics precede and therefore likely contribute to the genesis of these disorders (Klump et al., 2004). In a longitudinal study that examined the relationship between childhood temperament and later development of eating and body concerns in adolescence, Martin et al. (2000) found that high negative emotionality and low persistence were associated with increased risk for disordered eating. This finding suggests that temperamental characteristics in early childhood play a significant role in predicting later body image and eating behaviors and further supports the theory that temperamental qualities contribute to the development of eating disorders.

Converging evidence also points to the overlap between eating disorders and anxiety disorders such as obsessive-compulsive disorder, social phobia, and generalized anxiety disorder (see Bulik, 1995). Overlapping clinical features include obsessive thinking, compulsive behavior, fear of negative evaluation, and excessive worry across multiple domains. High co-morbidity rates between the anxiety and eating disorders have been documented in clinical and epidemiological studies, co-occurring in approximately 50-75% of cases (e.g., Braun, Sunday, & Halmi, 1994; Kendler et al., 1995; Kessler, McGonagle, Zhao, Nelson, Hughes, Eshleman et al., 1994). Among individuals with co-morbid anxiety and eating disorders, clinically significant anxiety almost always *precedes* the onset of body image and eating concerns, thereby implicating anxiety as a possible risk factor for eating disorders (e.g., Deep, Nagy, Weltzin, Rao, & Kaye, 1995). Most studies focus on adult populations and are retrospective in nature. However, recent longitudinal data in a school-aged community sample suggests that anxiety in the Fall semester predicts body image concerns and problematic eating in the Spring (Greco & Blomquist, 2006). Of particular relevance to this chapter, acceptance-related processes were found to mediate the link between early anxiety and later eating problems. Future prospective research is needed to identify the role of anxiety, acceptance, and other psychological processes in the development of eating disorders.

Neurological findings. Although hypothalamic and brain stem lesions were previously believed to be at the core of the neurobiological etiology of eating disorders, Uher and Treasure (2005) found that damage to the right frontal and temporal lobe may also be associated with eating disorders. Brain imaging techniques have been used to determine any damage to the brain as the result of a pattern of starvation and extreme nutritional deficiency characteristic of anorexia (Kingston, Szmukler, Andrews, Tress, & Desmond, 1996). The documented problems anorexic people experience with attention, concentration, memory, and visual-spatial ability could be related to structural neural changes caused by severe starvation. Specifically, among women with anorexia, studies have found enlarge-ments of the lateral ventricles as well as reductions in gray and white matter volume in the brain (Dolan, Mitchell, & Wakeling, 1988).

Brain-derived neurotrophic factor (BDNF) has not only been linked to brain development, function, neural plasticity and survival, but also appears to play a role in regulating eating behavior. For example, BDNF was found to be significantly lower in patients with anorexia and bulimia compared to diagnosis-free adults (Hashimoto, Koizumi, Nakazato, Shimizu, & Iyo, 2005; Nakazato et al., 2003).

Monteleone and associates (2004) suggest that alterations in BDNF may be a secondary mechanism that compensates for the energy balance alterations associated with eating disorders. This conclusion is supported by a positive correlation between body weight and BDNF levels. For instance, individuals with anorexia have significantly lower BDNF levels compared to people with bulimia, who in turn have significantly increased BDNF compared to healthy controls (Monteleone, Brambilla, Bortolotti, & Maj, 2000).

A growing body of scientific research points to alterations in neuronal pathways as playing a role in anorexia. For instance, several studies have shown that some individuals with anorexia have serotonin deficits (Wolfe, Metzger, & Jimerson, 1997). This neurotransmitter helps regulate mood and behavior and has been shown to play a role in chronic anxiety, obsessions, and perfectionism, which also characterize anorexia. Some neuropathological changes (e.g., white matter volume deficits) return to normal after weight gain. There is evidence, however, that other types of damage, such as gray matter volume deficits, may be more long-lasting (Katzman, Zipursky, Lambe, & Mikulis, 1997). Serotonin abnormalities also appear to persist after recovery and weight has returned to normal levels. Such continuing serotonin abnormalities could contribute to the long-term anxiety, obsessionality, and perfectionism that characterize individuals with anorexia. Likewise, some cognitive impairments (e.g., concentration, attention, and memory deficits) resolve with weight gain, whereas others do not. The results of most of these studies, however, are not conclusive because it has usually not been possible to study the brain *before* the onset of the eating disorder. Moreover, it is difficult to separate neuroendocrine abnormalities induced by weight loss and malnutrition from those related primarily to the disorder itself (O'Dwyer, Lucey, & Russell, 1996).

Traumatic Events

Environmental events such as exposure to trauma may increase risk for abnormal eating behavior (Connors & Morse, 1993). Sexual abuse, for example, is more common among women with anorexia (23%) than among women without an eating disorder (7%; Deep, Lilenfeld, Plotnicov, Pollice, & Kays, 1999). Research suggests that up to 50% of anorexia inpatients report a history of sexual abuse (Hall, Tice, Beresford, Wooley, & Hall, 1989). McFarlane, McFarlane, and Gilchrist (1988) noted that excessive dieting may develop in reaction to trauma because weight control functions to increase the client's perception of control and reduces feelings of helplessness and victimization. Fairburn, Shafran, and Cooper (1999) espoused a similar view in their cognitive-behavioral theory of eating disorders, arguing that individuals restrict eating to compensate for the traumatic loss of control in other areas of their life and to regain a sense of control. These notions support the more general theory that dieting may function as an avoidance strategy to cope with aversive unwanted thoughts and feelings that result from trauma exposure.

Familial Influences

Other research has focused on the association between eating disorders and family dynamics. Some of the earliest eating disorder theorists cast blame on parents, especially mothers. Stitzel (1948), for example, proposed that bottle-fed infants could not form an intimate bond with their mother, and such improper feeding caused a child to refuse food later in life. More contemporary theorists and researchers have found that families of eating disorder clients tend to be unsupportive, over-involved, have difficulty resolving conflict, and are eager to maintain harmony by denying or ignoring problems. Studies have also shown the families of women with anorexia to be hard driven and very concerned about success and appearances (Mizes, 1995; Vandereycken, Kog, & Vanderlinden, 1989).

Parental behavior may also contribute to body image concerns, unhealthy eating patterns, and excessive dieting among young people. For example, mothers who express dissatisfaction with their own weight, use extreme weight loss techniques, and comment on their child's weight are likely to have a daughter who diets (Benedikt, Wertheim, & Love, 1998; Keel, Heatherton, Harnden, & Hornig, 1997). Pike and Rodin (1991) found that mothers of girls with eating disorders want their daughters to lose weight whereas mothers of girls without eating disorders want their daughters to gain weight. Additionally, mothers of daughters with eating disorders were more likely to rate their daughter as less attractive than the daughter rated herself. A related study found mothers of students with bulimia were more likely than mothers of non-bulimic students to encourage weight loss, dieting, and exercise (Moreno & Thelen, 1993). These findings suggest eating disorders may develop as a way of coping with familial pressure to be "good enough."

Cultural Influences

Socio-cultural factors such as media glamorization of thinness have been linked to the development of eating disorders. One study found that exposure to 15 issues of a fashion magazine led teen-age girls with social support deficits to experience increased body dissatisfaction, dieting, and bulimic symptoms (Stice, Spangler, & Agras, 2001). Similarly, college women who viewed slides of fashion models reported more anger and depression relative to women who viewed slides without human figures (Pinhas, Toner, Ali, Garfinkel, & Stuckless, 1999).

Eating disorders are most prevalent in affluent Western culture, which increasingly equates being thin with being successful. Eating disorders are less prevalent in non-Western societies and may become more common with increasing exposure to Western media and values. For instance, Pakistani researchers found exposure to Western culture positively correlated with the occurrence of eating disorders in Pakistani women (Suhail & Nisa, 2002). Within Western culture, women living in a warm climate, compared to those in cooler climates, have lower body weight, report more binging/compensatory behavior, and report more body image concerns (Sloan, 2002). This finding may be due to heightened body image awareness based on the norm to wear more revealing clothing in warmer weather.

In general, the literature on cultural influences suggests dieting can function as means to gain social acceptance and/or avoid social judgments and public embarrassment.

Barlow and Durand (2004) describe eating disorders as the most culturally specific psychological disorders. Although the impact of the social context on any disorder is difficult to quantify, this impact seems particularly powerful and destructive in the case of eating disorders. What is considered the ideal body image as portrayed by major media outlets has changed dramatically in less than 40 years. For instance, data collected from *Playboy* magazine centerfolds and from *Miss America* contestants from 1959 to 1988 show substantial decreases in weight and size measures (Wiseman, Gray, Mosimann, & Ahrens, 1992). This change was accompanied by a striking increase of articles in major women's magazines on exercise and diet in the same time period. One of the most disturbing findings of the study was that 69% of the *Playboy* centerfolds and 60% of *Miss America* contestants weighed 15% or less than normal for their age and height and thereby met one of the current DSM criteria for anorexia. By associating slenderness with success and high approval, the media teaches women through vicarious learning that losing weight is likely to lead to positively valued outcomes. As demonstrated by the chronic and often debilitating nature of eating disorders, our culture's "glorification of slenderness" (Levine & Smolak, 1996) is pervasive and difficult to break free from.

Existing Theoretical Models

Cognitive Models

Cognitive models view cognitive distortions, negative core beliefs, and appraisal deficits as causal variables, which may lead to the development and maintenance of eating disorders. According to Vartanian, Polivy, and Herman (2004), these cognitions include irrational thoughts related to eating and body weight and shape, as well as the meaning associated with being thin (e.g., self-control, beauty) and with being fat (e.g., being flawed, being a failure, being alone). These cognitions are believed to be "implicit," which means, they occur automatically and are not under conscious control. Such automatic thoughts and cognitive activities are performed smoothly and efficiently, and they are resistant to change. Women with eating disorders also show selective (biased) attention to food and body-shape-related information (Stewart, 2004). It is important to note, however, that this attentional bias pertains to a wider range of stimuli for individuals with bulimia, but is limited to only body weight stimuli for individuals with anorexia (Dobson & Dozois, 2004). Clients with eating disorders also demonstrate different categorization processes than normal subjects. Individuals with eating disorders tend to categorize food-related material by functional properties such as nutritional content and digestibility, whereas healthy individuals base their food categorizations on structural properties such as what foods are made of or what they are used for (Urdapilleta, Mirabel-Sarron, Meunier, & Richard, 2005).

Research has shown that women with anorexia report more negative beliefs about themselves and hold more distorted assumptions about weight and body shape when compared to other dieters and a control group, (Cooper & Turner, 2002). Christiano and Mizes (1997) describe a model of stress, appraisal, and coping related to eating disorders based on the stress and coping model developed by Lazarus and Folkman (1984). This theory emphasizes the negative consequences of engaging in avoidance-related coping to deal with stress. For example, compared to non-bingers, binge eaters tend to perceive inter-personal and academic situations as stressful (Hansel & Wittrock, 1997). Among the possible stress coping strategies, binge eaters appear to prefer avoidance-based strategies despite the fact that this type of coping is typically ineffective (Christiano & Mizes, 1997).

Body dissatisfaction (or negative body image) is a key variable in causal models of eating disorders (Vartanian et al., 2004). Stewart (2004) provides an interesting cognitive account of the role of body image distortion in understanding eating disorders, which has implications for an acceptance-based approach to treatment (see also Williamson, White, York-Crowe, & Stewart, 2004). Stewart proposes that the information gathering of people with a negative body image is biased by automatic thoughts and rigidly held beliefs. From a perceptual perspective, the experience of body image disturbance involves a habitual selective interpretation bias to overestimate one's body size ("I am obese"). As a consequence, when persons with body image disturbances are presented with different information about their body (e.g., a friend commenting, "you're looking good"), they are not open to such an alternative perspective and continue to focus on their negative body experience.

Stewart (2004) suggests a mindfulness-based behavioral treatment to help clients develop a different way of relating to their body image without making any attempts to change or challenge the core beliefs directly. Instead, the goal of mindfulness-based body image therapy is for clients to develop an "observer perspective" in order to be aware of and accept alternative perspectives of themselves both in terms of body shape and self worth.

From a practical clinical perspective, Stewart's (2004) approach is intriguing and points to the importance of helping clients with eating disorders develop a different relation to their thoughts and feelings. At a conceptual level, however, the dilemma remains that we cannot fully explain one type of behavior (e.g., excessive dieting) with another type of behavior (e.g., particular thoughts or beliefs). The critical issue is that behavior is a dependent variable that is itself in need of explanation. Thus, if we were to accept core beliefs and faulty schema as explanations, we still need to answer the crucial question of how one dependent variable causes another (Forsyth, Lejuez, Hawkins, & Eifert, 1996). In contrast to what many cognitive critics suggest, as behavior analysts we are interested in events people experience within the skin such as thinking and feeling. Yet we need to understand how these behaviors come about as a function of the circumstances that give rise to them and what functions they serve. Such analyses will give us important insights as to how we can best treat problems associated with them.

Cognitive-Behavioral Models

Despite significant personal and family distress and potentially fatal conse-quences, eating disorders are persistent and often resistant to change. Cognitive-behavioral models of eating disorders posit that cognitive disturbances character-istic of individuals with eating disorders (including cognitive distortions, negative body image, and poor coping strategies) combined with powerful social and self-reinforcement contingencies contribute to the development and maintenance of eating disorders (Fairburn, 2002). In addition to these cognitive disturbances, eating disorders are maintained because the reinforcing consequences of dieting, purging, and binging outweigh the punishing effects associated with such behavior (Farmer, Nash, & Field, 2001). Both positive and negative reinforcement have been implicated in the development and maintenance of eating disordered behavior (Garner, Vitousek, & Pike, 1997).

Cognitive-behavioral theory suggests that the tendency of people with anorexia and bulimia to define themselves and evaluate their self-worth based on their body size and eating behaviors is the fundamental cognitive disturbance and core process variable in the development and maintenance of eating disorders (Fairburn, 2002; Vitousek, 2002). Specifically, Fairburn (1997) proposes a vicious cycle model of bulimia where perfectionistic tendencies and dichotomous thinking interact with low self-esteem and overvalued concerns about food and body shape. This vicious cycle consists of extreme dietary restrictions that give way to minor slips that threaten the individual's sense of self-control, which, along with negative affect, set the stage for a binge episode. Binging reinforces the individuals' obsession with issues of self-control, food, and body image, thereby encouraging adherence to strict dietary rules and increasing the risk of future binge episodes.

Cognitive-behavioral models of anorexia, like those for bulimia, revolve around the dominant notion that self-worth is determined by body weight and shape. Models of anorexia, however, stress the reinforcement value of control, feeling special, being competitive, and having strong moral conviction as contributing factors in the maintenance of the disorder (Vitousek, 2002). Vitousek (2002) reports that individuals with eating disorders can be distinguished from other individuals by the content and intensity of their core beliefs about food and body-related material as well as their tendency to think in black-and-white terms. Yet she also points out that there is no convincing research that bulimia and anorexia can be differentiated from each other in terms of these cognitive factors.

Social reinforcement often plays a role in the development and maintenance of anorexia. Although social praise may positively reinforce healthy weight loss in normal individuals, increased attention to and compliments about physical appearance may lead to extreme weight loss for people with predisposing factors for anorexia. Praise alone, however, does not explain why unhealthy eating behavior is maintained, especially when clients with anorexia reach a weight that is lower than is socially acceptable and face criticism for being "too thin" (Garner et al., 1997). A more crucial reinforcer appears to be a sense of control or success resulting from strict adherence to calorie limits or achievement of weight goals. Fairburn et al. (1999) suggest that clients with anorexia may perceive themselves as having little or no control across important areas of life (e.g., work, school, etc.). As a result, these patients may resort to restrictive eating in order to control dietary intake.

Excessive dieting, binging, weight loss, or purging can also be maintained via negative reinforcement when these behaviors result in the avoidance of an aversive stimulus or event, such as weight gain and negatively evaluated thoughts or feelings. Escape-avoidance coping has been identified as a prospective risk factor for developing eating disorders (Ghaderi, 2003). Compared to a control group without eating disorders, clients with anorexia, bulimia, or BED experience more negatively evaluated emotional states and more frequently engage in avoidance-based coping (Christiano & Mizes, 1997; Henderson & Huon, 2002; Isnard et al., 2003; Soukup, Beiler, & Terrell, 1990; Webber, 1994). For binge eating, negatively evaluated affective states often precipitate a binge episode (Arnow, Kenardy, & Agras, 1992), and binging could be viewed as an attempt to change such affective states and to suppress painful emotions (Webber, 1994). Some researchers found purging to be a more salient negative reinforcer than binging and suggest that during the course of bulimia, purging eventually replaces binging as a means of reducing negatively evaluated affective states (Mizes & Arbitell, 1991). Further, Farmer and colleagues (2001) found the frequency of purging, but not binging, was positively correlated with sensitivity to operant reinforcement contingencies in participants with eating disorders.

A Functional Behavioral Approach to Eating Disorders

The Nature of Emotion Regulation

Emotion regulation simply refers to a heterogeneous set of actions that are designed to influence which emotions we have, when we have them, and how we experience and express them (Gross, 2002). Such actions include, but are not limited to, phenomena captured by terms such as reappraisal, distraction, avoidance, escape, suppression, emotion and problem-focused coping, and use of substances to enhance or blunt emotional experience. Each of these domains subsumes numerous actions that can be applied to both positive and negative emotional states.

In the context of aversive emotional states, emotion regulatory processes share a common functional goal, namely to avoid or minimize the frequency, intensity, duration, or situational occurrence of internal feeling states, associated thoughts, and physiological processes such as tension, heightened arousal, and abdominal discomfort. Some regulatory processes may be relatively autonomic or habitual, occurring inside or outside of awareness, whereas others may be more purposeful or deliberate (e.g., blame, rumination, suppression, avoidance). Most processes, however, can be characterized by actions (automatic or controlled) that aim to alter the form or frequency of emotional responding or the events that precede or follow an emotional response. The former has been described as response-focused emotion regulation, whereas the latter refers to antecedent-focused emotion regulation.

Implications of Experiential Avoidance and Control for Eating Disorders

Experiential avoidance (EA) is a form of emotion regulation where an individual attempts to avoid, suppress, or otherwise control the form and/or frequency of painful private events such as bodily sensations, emotions, thoughts, worries, and memories (Hayes, Wilson, Gifford, Follette, & Strosahl, 1996). The function of experiential avoidance is to control or minimize the impact of aversive internal experiences. Experiential avoidance can produce immediate, short-term relief from negatively evaluated thoughts and emotions, which negatively reinforces such behavior. Behaviors such as dieting, binging, and vomiting may reduce the immediate experience of weight- and food-related discomfort. In the long term, however, such experiential avoidance strategies may lead to serious psychosocial and health consequences and become sources of suffering themselves. Hayes, Luoma, Bond, Masuda, and Lillis (2006) conducted a meta-analysis investigating the relation between experiential avoidance (as measured by the Acceptance and Action Questionnaire, AAQ; Hayes, Masuda, Bissett, Luoma, & Guerrero, 2004) and various aspects of psychopathology and quality of life. The results from 32 studies and 6,600 participants show that higher levels of experiential avoidance and lower levels of psychological flexibility are consistently associated with poorer quality of life and outcomes.

According to relational frame theory (Hayes, Barnes-Holmes, & Roche, 2001), the ability of humans to engage in experiential avoidance is greatly facilitated by language. Despite ample evidence (e.g., Suomi, 1999) that primates experience and express pain and chronic states of arousal, there is no indication that they suffer about the experience of having pain and arousal. Rhesus monkeys exposed to uncontrollable and unpredictable aversive stimulation experience alarm responses followed by long-term anxious arousal. They will learn to avoid the source and context of aversive stimulation, but as best we can tell, they do not act deliberately to regulate their emotional experience. Humans, by contrast, can and do suffer about their own emotional pain. Humans respond to this pain with evaluative verbal behavior and thinking (e.g., "God, this is awful," "I look terrible") and by engaging in efforts to suppress, avoid, or escape emotional pain and related thoughts. Thus, humans can become depressed about their looks or worried about the future, agonize about the past, and struggle to avoid or escape from unpleasant thoughts, feelings, behavioral tendencies, and the circumstances that have evoked them or *may* evoke them in the future. According to RFT, language and social contingencies regarding the experience and expression of emotion make this possible (Forsyth, Eifert, & Barrios, 2006; Staats & Eifert, 1990).

For individuals with eating disorders, behaviors such as dieting, vomiting, and binging function to avoid, escape from and reduce the impact of negatively evaluated thoughts and emotions, which may be triggered by reflecting on past situations (e.g., "I am worthless because I failed my exam") and worrying about future events (e.g., "I will never be accepted if I stay so fat."). The concept of fusion may help to explain why thoughts become so threatening to people that they are prepared to engage in behavior that is clearly detrimental to their health and general well-being.

Cognitive fusion is a process that involves fusing with or attaching to the literal content of our private experiences. The event or stimulus (e.g., "I") and one's thinking about it ("am fat") become one and the same--they are so fused as to be inseparable, which creates the impression that verbal construal is not present at all (Hayes et al., 2004). When fusion occurs, a thought is no longer just a thought, and a word is no longer just a sound; rather, we respond to words about some event as if we were responding to the actual event the words describe. Individuals with eating problems appear to fuse with their perceptions and evaluations of their weight, appearance, and body shape.

For example, when taken literally, the thought "*I am fat and worthless*" would be threatening for anyone. When a client thinks or says, "*I am* fat and worthless" rather than "*I am having the thought that* I am fat and worthless" she connects worthlessness both with fatness and her as a person. Fatness, worthlessness, and she fuse together--they become one and the same. At that point, fat and worthless are no longer just two words. The person reacts to the words or the thought as if she is the embodiment of fatness and worthlessness--she is it. Wilson and Roberts (2002) provided a similar example: If an individual had the thought, "I can't stand being fat," and responds only to the literal content of that thought, she *must* do something to alter that state of affairs (e.g., starving herself to alleviate the insufferable state). Also, as a result of relational learning, the word or physical act of "eating" and the mere sight of food can themselves become bidirectionally connected with gaining weight, fatness, worthlessness, disgust and so on.

Although anorexia, bulimia, and BED refer to different patterns of behavior, rigid and inflexible patterns of emotional and experiential avoidance (including behavioral and covert forms of avoidance) appear to be the common functional link connecting these eating-related problems. For example, when a woman with anorexia starves herself, she is engaging in a form of experiential avoidance because starving is designed to reduce the intensity of painful emotions. Purging is another example of experiential avoidance because it serves to reduce feelings of anxiety and guilt after eating. Distraction from and suppression of distressing thoughts that may follow binging also are types of experiential avoidance. All these strategies may produce short-term relief by reducing unwanted thoughts and feelings. Yet, in the long term, thoughts like "I am a failure" or "I am ugly and fat" eventually resurface and prompt further types of experiential avoidance. This can become a vicious cycle in which problematic behaviors such as restricting and purging are used to get rid of weight-related thoughts and painful feelings.

Empirical Findings

Effects of thought suppression. Research has shown that thought suppression, a form of experiential avoidance, produces a "rebound effect" marked by an increase in the intensity and frequency of the avoided thought or emotion. For instance, Davies and

Clark (1998) asked study participants to stop thinking about negatively evaluated thoughts. Although the upsetting thoughts did in fact decrease, the decrease was short-lived. The authors noted a rebound in the number of upsetting thoughts such that participants were experiencing more upsetting thoughts at the end than at the beginning of the experiment. In a similar study, Harvey and Bryant (1998) tested people who had been in a car accident. Half of the accident victims were told to stop thinking about the accident, and the other half was not given this instruction. Before the different instructions were given, both groups reported the same amount of accident-related thoughts. After the instructions, the group who had been asked to suppress their thoughts actually experienced more thoughts about the accident than the uninstructed group.

Rebound effects have also been observed with negatively evaluated emotions. Mizes and Arbitell (1991) asked women with bulimia to monitor their mood before, during, and after each binge and purge episode. Although an immediate reduction in negatively evaluated mood states occurred during a purge, the negative emotions rebounded to higher levels after purging than were reported before binging. A common finding in the thought suppression literature is that the nature of the target thought affects the magnitude of the rebound effect as well as the subjective experience associated with it (Abramowitz, Tolin, & Street, 2001; Purdon & Clark, 2001). Purdon and Clark found that participants instructed to suppress obsessional thoughts reported more discomfort and negative mood than those instructed to suppress more positive or neutral thoughts. Suppression of neutral thoughts has also been demonstrated to produce negative affect, including feelings of failure and irritability (Belloch, Morillo, & Gimenez, 2004). Moreover, Brewin and Smart (2005) found that performance on working memory tasks is negatively correlated with thought suppression, suggesting that attempts to inhibit unwanted thoughts negatively affects working memory.

One study using a Stroop task with college women who scored high on an eating disorder inventory showed that such women avoided eating disorder-related words more compared to women who scored lower on this measure (Meyer, Waller, & Watson, 2000). Other laboratory results demonstrate the ineffectiveness of experiential avoidance strategies in relation to eating behavior. Johnston, Bulik, and Anstiss (1999) examined how asking people to stop thinking about food affects eating behavior by instructing half of their participants not to think about chocolate while participating in a computer task to earn chocolate candies. Results indicated that those instructed to suppress thoughts of chocolate earned more candy than participants who were not instructed to suppress. These findings suggest instructions to suppress food-related thoughts may have paradoxical effects on eating behavior and that mental control, therefore, is not likely to be an effective behavioral control strategy.

Dieting. Much like with thought suppression, restricting caloric intake often leads to increased preoccupation with food. In fact, most individuals with anorexia do not lose their appetite as the term anorexia (literally "without appetite") incorrectly implies. They often experience intense cravings and food-related obsessions and rituals. A classic finding was reported by University of Minnesota researchers who examined the effects of semi-starvation (Franklin, Schiele, Brozek, & Keys, 1948). Healthy volunteers who were maintained on 3500 calories per day were limited to 1500 calories for 6 months. While in a state of semi-starvation, participants experienced physical symptoms that resemble those found in persons with anorexia, such as intolerance to cold temperatures, dreams about food, conversations about food, and chewing gum as a food substitute. Some of the participants never lost their obsession with food even after unlimited access to food was restored.

Restricting caloric intake may not only lead to increased preoccupation with food, it may also lead to binging behavior. In a study with 200 obese women, Telch and Agras (1993) found that these women demonstrated marked increases in bingeing during and after rigorous dieting. Binge episodes following periods of intense dieting may explain the fact that dieting often does not result in weight loss and that weight loss attributed to dieting is rarely maintained over time (O'Connell, Larkin, Mizes, & Fremouw, 2005). Likewise, Herman and Mack (1975) found that restrained eaters engaged in "counterregulatory eating" such that following a high-calorie milkshake they consumed increased amounts of ice cream compared to unrestrained eaters who decreased their ice cream consumption. Herman and Mack explain this finding in terms of the disinhibitory effect that the milkshake had on restrained eaters since they already "broke" the rules of their diet. This counterregulatory eating pattern is highly associated with binge eating and obesity. Moreover, unrestrained eaters tend to be better at suppressing food-related thoughts and exhibit less of a rebound effect following suppression that restrained eaters (Oliver & Huon, 2001). Collectively, these studies show that the more people restrict how much they eat, the harder it is for them to stop thinking about food, eating, and body image, and the more likely binge behaviors will occur.

Dieting is also associated with labile affect, difficulties concentrating, heightened irritability, negative mood states, fatigue, and unrealistic weight goals (Anderson, Lundgren, Shapiro, & Paulosky, 2003; Polivy & Herman, 2002). Anderson and colleagues suggest that unrealistic weight loss goals often lead to rigid dietary restrictions because each successive level of dietary restraint fails to result in achieving the target weight. In addition, Polivy and Herman found that, compared to non-dieters, people who diet reported higher levels of insecurity and scored higher on cognitive measures of irrational beliefs. Dieters were also more reliant on external cues regarding hunger and satiety and endorsed beliefs that food can counteract negative affect and that losing weight will lead to self-improvement. In the presence of other risk factors, dieting may also make individuals more vulnerable to developing eating disorders and obesity (Lowe, 2002). In light of these findings, dieting may not only lead to negative side-effects such as negative mood, heightened fatigue, and concentration difficulties, but may also serve as the first step in the development of an eating disorder for individuals with other predisposing factors.

Effects of control efforts. There is growing evidence pointing to the issue of control as a central problem among people with eating disorders. For instance, Cockell, Geller, and Linden (2002) conducted extensive interviews with hundreds of women with anorexia. The authors noticed two recurring themes in the statements they collected. The first theme was that many women diet to cope with stressful situations and bad feelings about themselves. The function of dieting was to gain a sense of empowerment and achievement and as a way to cope with difficult life events, such as a divorce. Thus, women appeared to use dieting and weight control to gain or regain control over their lives. The second theme in those statements was an assessment of the long-term failure of this coping strategy. Many women noted that dieting did not lead to lasting control over painful thoughts. As time went on, these women became caught in a vicious cycle of continuously managing their weight as a way of regaining transient control over their feelings. Also, dieting was causing them to suffer physically because they felt weak and unable to do things they wanted to do. In effect, the women's attempts to change how they feel by changing how they look were not only unsuccessful in producing the desired outcomes; these attempts also led to further problems and life restrictions.

Consistent with findings of earlier studies showing that attempts to avoid aversive private events are largely ineffective and may be counterproductive (Hayes et al., 1996), there is increasing evidence that encouraging acceptance rater than suppression or control of private events leads to more positive outcomes and at times paradoxical side effects. For instance, several experimental studies have shown that acceptance-based coping methods enhanced willingness to experience negatively evaluated experiences relative to control-oriented methods (Eifert & Heffner, 2003; Hayes, Strosahl, & Wilson, 1999; Levitt, Brown, Orsillo, & Barlow, 2004). A study by Spira, Zvolensky, Eifert, and Feldner (2004) found acceptance-based coping strategies were associated with less emotional distress than avoidant coping strategies (e.g., denial, mental disengagement, substance abuse). A related study showed that greater predispositions toward emotional avoidance (as assessed by the AAQ), including the deliberate application of instructed emotion regulation strategies (i.e., emotion suppression), results in more acute emotional distress (Feldner, Zvolensky, Eifert, & Spira, 2003). This study was the first to show that emotional avoidance and emotion regulation strategies may potentiate acute episodes of emotional distress.

Greco and Blomquist (2006) conducted a school-based study to identify possible risk factors of body image and eating concerns in a sample of 255 girls (M = 13.1 years). Experiential avoidance and cognitive fusion were assessed with the Avoidance and Fusion Questionnaire for Youth (AFQ-Y; Greco, Murrell, & Coyne, 2005), a psychometrically sound measure developed specifically for children and adolescents. Results showed that peer relationship variables such as high dating likelihood and conflict within best friendships predicted body image disturbance and unhealthy eating patterns, as did high levels of anxiety and somatic complaints. Notably, scores on the AFQ-Y made incremental and unique contributions to body image and eating concerns after controlling for the effects of these predictor variables. Furthermore, experiential avoidance and cognitive fusion as measured by the AFQ-Y mediated the link between the aforementioned predictor variables (e.g., dating likelihood, anxiety) and body image concerns and eating behavior assessed five months later. These findings provide some evidence for the role of experiential avoidance and cognitive fusion in the development of eating disorder problems.

Treatment of Eating Disorders

Conventional Treatments for Eating Disorders

Cognitive Behavior Therapy (CBT) and Interpersonal Psychotherapy (IPT) remain the most established approaches for the treatment of eating disorders. CBT utilizes techniques such as self-monitoring, exposure, and cognitive restructuring. IPT does not address eating disordered behavior directly, but instead focuses on the identification and improvement of interpersonal problems. Garner and Needleman (1997) found that clients with bulimia respond more quickly to CBT than IPT, although both treatments were equally effective at follow-up. Garner and Needleman recommend CBT as a standard initial treatment over IPT because CBT works significantly faster. This finding was replicated in a multi-site study by Agras, Walsh, Fairburn, Wilson, and Kraemer (2000) involving 220 clients with bulimia. After 19 sessions of treatment with either CBT or IPT, 45% of clients in the CBT group were completely recovered, and a total of 67% were improved but still had some problems, whereas only 8% of IPT clients were recovered and a total of 40% were improved. Interestingly, these differences were no longer apparent at a one-year follow-up because some patients in the IPT group continued to improve and some patients in the CBT group had relapsed. The bottom line is that both CBT and IPT interventions eliminate binging and purging in only approximately 25–30% of treated cases, achieve improvements without full recovery in about 45% of cases, and at least one out of every four clients will drop out of treatment (Mizes, 1995; Wilson, Fairburn, & Agras, 1997).

Although there is a manualized treatment for bulimia (Agras & Apple, 1997), there is no manualized treatment for clients with anorexia. Treatment for anorexia is focused mainly on achieving weight gain goals, with some research demonstrating up to 50 % relapse rates following weight-restoration interventions (Mizes, 1995). With much lower long-term recovery rates, results for CBT treatments of anorexia are poorer than for bulimia. (Herzog, Dorer, Keel, Selwyn, Ekebad, Flores et al., 1999). In summary, the "best interventions" currently available often fall short, demonstrate high attrition and relapse rates, and often fail to produce clinically meaningful change.

We suspect one of the main problems with traditional interventions has been their over-reliance on reestablishing normal eating as the primary treatment goal while at the same time not sufficiently addressing the functions of restrictive and other types of abnormal eating. We will now describe a treatment approach to eating disorders that focuses on the functions of abnormal eating behavior.

Acceptance and Commitment Therapy (ACT)

Acceptance and Commitment Therapy (ACT) is a contemporary behavior therapy, which targets more directly the function of restrictive eating and the experiential avoidance and control efforts of individuals with eating disorders. The ACT approach suggests the development and maintenance of abnormal eating behavior stems from paradoxical control and avoidance-based coping strategies. ACT seeks to undermine unproductive and often detrimental levels of experiential avoidance that exacerbate human suffering. Primary goals in ACT are to promote client willingness to experience naturally occurring private events and to reduce unnecessary suffering caused by experiential avoidance strategies.

Acceptance involves a counterintuitive approach toward constructive living in which clients are encouraged to give up their struggle of changing what cannot be changed for the sake of promoting change in valued domains of their life where change is possible. The basic idea is to let go of ineffective and unworkable change agendas to open the door for genuine, fundamental change to occur (Greco & Eifert, 2004; Hayes, 2002). ACT utilizes cognitive defusion techniques (e.g., metaphors, mindfulness exercises) to teach clients to respond less literally to eating-related thoughts and emotions, and separate themselves from their thoughts and feelings (Hayes et al., 1999).

In the next five sections, we briefly discuss how the core components of ACT can be adapted to treat clients with eating disorders. More details and specific suggestions on how to use ACT for clients with eating disorders can be found in a workbook by Heffner and Eifert (2004).

Creative hopelessness. Binge eaters may enter psychotherapy with a history of failures, which may include hypnosis, attending Overeaters Anonymous, fad diets, and medication. Clients with anorexia are likely to have tried excessive dieting and exercise in the pursuit of thinness. The purpose of creative hopelessness exercises is to let clients experience that despite putting forth tremendous effort, they are still not satisfied with their body weight, appearance, and life in general. By letting people experience the futility of such control efforts, the therapist instills a sense of hopelessness, which is creative and motivational because the situation is only hopeless if nothing changes. The key is to let go of ineffective efforts to control private events and to take responsibility in areas of life that can be controlled.

Control is the problem. This component builds upon creative hopelessness by bringing clients into experiential contact with the futility of their current control agenda. It is vital for clients to experience that dieting, vomiting, and binging are not solutions and that these behaviors are problems themselves. Past attempts to control unwanted private events have not worked and have been costly in terms of poor health and personal well-being.

Acceptance. ACT introduces mindful acceptance as a skillful way of approaching life experiences. Specifically, ACT encourages active acceptance of private events such as thoughts and feelings. This is an important aspect of treatment because thoughts and perceptions about body size experienced by individuals with an eating disorder are known to be especially resistant to change. Clients who evaluate their body and appearance as disgusting often do not change their views and evaluate their bodies more positively even after their actual eating behavior has been changed successfully (Wilson, 1996).

Specific applications of mindfulness for eating disorders include observing thoughts and feelings during eating and body-related exposure exercises (Heffner & Eifert, 2004). For example, clients are asked to notice what thoughts and feelings arise while viewing their body in a full-length mirror or to engage in mindful eating as an alternative to binge or mindless eating, in which a client eats so rapidly that she fails to notice the quality or quantity of food consumed. Through such exercises clients learn to assume an observer perspective in relation to their body-related and other unwanted feelings and thoughts. The larger goal is to undermine the tendency to react to anxious thoughts and sensations, including avoiding situations where concerns about weight and their looks may show up.

Defusion. The ultimate purpose of acceptance and mindfulness exercises is to foster cognitive defusion, a process that involves undermining the fused or attached link between private events and our evaluations of such events. Defusion methods are used to create a healthy distance between clients and the content of their private experience. Instead of responding to the literal content of a thought, clients learn to respond to thoughts as just a thought that can simply be observed. ACT uses a variety of defusion techniques to uncouple or disentangle words and thoughts from the actual events or experiences that such words and thoughts refer to. For instance, rather than saying or thinking "I am fat and worthless" clients can learn to say *"I am having the thought that* I am fat and worthless."

Cognitive-behavioral therapists may mistake defusion as a form of cognitive restructuring. Yet defusion is not aimed at changing the content or accuracy of a client's thoughts and feelings—the goal of cognitive defusion is to help the client forge a new relationship with their private experience (Orsillo & Batten, 2002). For instance, defusion is not aimed at correcting the cognitive distortion or erroneous perception that an 18-year-old adolescent weighing 100 pounds is fat and ugly, but rather at helping the client recognize and experience the evaluative thought or image for what it is: a thought that can simply be observed and need not be corrected or struggled with.

Focus on values rather than eating. ACT is a constructive approach to behavior change with a focus on enhancing quality of life. Clients are encouraged to think about what they *want to do,* not what they *don't want to do, have, or feel.* This re-orientation is achieved by helping clients define what they want their lives to be about in key life domains such as family, friends, romantic relationships, leisure, spirituality, health, career, education, and community (Dahl & Lundgren, 2006; Hayes et al., 1999; Heffner, Eifert, Parker, Hernandez, & Sperry, 2003). For example, in the case of an anorexic client who values friendship, treatment is aimed not at reducing body dissatisfaction, but at increasing the client's vitality such that she can learn to socialize with friends, even when feeling too ugly or embarrassed to be seen in public.

As clients identify values, they often recognize that eating disorder behaviors are in stark contrast to chosen life values. For example, dieting, binging, and purging may lead to energy depletion and serious health conditions, which hinder participation in numerous valued domains such as sports, relationships, academics, and community activities. Rather than continue to devote more time and energy to dieting, binging, and purging in a life consumed by food, eating, and weight management, clients are encouraged to choose to approach previously avoided stimuli and engage in previously avoided activities to reach a personal goal. For instance, when an anorexic adolescent girl decides she wants to excel on her school's swimming team, she needs to eat enough to have the physical strength to keep up with the physical demands of her training schedule.

Taking valued action and overcoming barriers. After identifying valued directions, the most important next steps involve taking action. Almost invariably, barriers arise as clients pursue valued directions. The final phase of ACT aims to help clients be with and move with barriers while remaining committed to their values. The case example of a 15-year old girl (Heffner, Sperry, Eifert, & Detweiler, 2002) shows how, in this context, excessive dieting itself can come up as a barrier to valued living.

Before embarking on an ACT treatment program, Mary thought there were no greater values than being attractive, slim, and feeling good about herself. After completing some of the values exercises, she started to wonder if she would ever become the person she wanted to be if she continued to diet and lose more weight. After completing a list outlining the ways dieting interferes with her pursuit of valued directions, Mary experienced much anxiety over the thought of actually having to eat more in order to be able to do what she wanted to do. With the use of mindfulness and exposure exercises, Mary learned to move in her valued directions *and* eat *and* have the fear about the effects of eating—all at the same time. Again, unlike conventional treatments, the goal is not to reduce the fear directly, but to live a life filled with valued rewards (Heffner & Eifert, 2004).

Outcome data and future directions. Although there are quite a number of clinical studies examining the efficacy and effectiveness of ACT (Hayes, Masuda, Bissett, Luoma, & Guerrero, 2004), research examining the efficacy of ACT with eating disorders is limited. We conducted a single-case study that documents the effectiveness of using ACT to treat an adolescent client for anorexia (Heffner et al., 2002). Another case study (Baer, Fischer, & Huss, 2005) successfully applied mindfulness-based cognitive-behavioral therapy to binge eating disorder. Both of these studies illustrate interesting points about the relationship between acceptance and change in ACT compared to CBT. Unlike traditional CBT approaches to eating disorders, acceptance-based treatments involve careful observation of thoughts, emotions, perceptions, and the relationships among them, and allowing these to be as they are, without trying to change or eliminate them. These treatments did not emphasize eating or exercise behavior (e.g., what or how much to eat, how or when to exercise) and made no attempts to teach clients to identify, dispute and replace cognitive distortions.

Due to the limited clinical outcome data to support the use of ACT with eating disorder populations, further research is necessary. Specifically, we need to investigate the efficacy of ACT compared to the current standards of care. Randomized-controlled clinical trials are imperative to demonstrating the short- and long-term effects of ACT relative to wait list and other treatment conditions such as pharmacotherapy and traditional CBT. Furthermore, component analyses will be important in determining the necessary and sufficient ingredients of ACT.

There is also a need for research focusing on the use of ACT with child and teen populations. To date, conceptual and empirical attention has focused primarily on the application and effectiveness of ACT with various adult populations. Conversely, little is known about the effective application of acceptance-based strategies with children, teens, and families (e.g., Greco, Blackledge, Coyne, & Enreheich, 2006; Greco & Eifert, 2004). This is particularly pertinent for teenagers with eating disorders where such problems almost invariably involve the family and affect its functioning. Parents often attempt to change the teenager's eating behavior and end up in a futile power struggle with their child that eventually leads to an impasse where both sides are stuck in their unsuccessful struggle to control each others' behavior. Future research and practice might, for example, focus on age-appropriate adaptations and the integration of family members and other systems-level influences into ACT protocols. Research with adolescent populations is particularly relevant to eating disorders in view of the relatively high prevalence rates among teenage girls.

References

Abramowitz, J. S., Tolin, D. F., & Street, G. P. (2001). Paradoxical effects of thought suppression: A meta-analysis of controlled studies. *Clinical Psychological Review, 21*, 683-703.

Agras, W. S., & Apple, R. F. (1997). *Overcoming eating disorders: A cognitive-behavioral treatment for bulimia nervosa and binge-eating disorder.* San Antonio, TX: Graywind Publications.

Agras, W. S., Walsh, B. T., Fairburn, C. G., Wilson, G. T., & Kraemer, H. C. (2000). A multicenter comparison of cognitive behavioral therapy and interpersonal psychotherapy for bulimia nervosa. *Archives of General Psychiatry, 57*, 459-466.

American Psychiatric Association. (2000). *Diagnostic and statistical manual of mental disorders* (4th ed., text revision). Washington, DC: Author.

Anderson, D. A., Lundgren, J. D., Shapiro, J. R., & Paulosky, C. (2003). Weight goals in a college population. *Obesity Research, 11*, 274-278.

Arnow, B., Kenardy, J., & Agras, W. S. (1992). Binge eating among the obese: A descriptive study. *Journal of Behavioral Medicine, 15*, 155-170.

Baer, R. A., Fischer, S., & Huss, D. B. (2005). Mindfulness-based cognitive therapy applied to binge eating disorder: A case study. *Cognitive and Behavioral Practice, 12*, 351-358.

Barlow, D. H., & Durand, V. M. (2004). *Essentials of abnormal psychology* (4th ed.). New York: Wadsworth.

Belloch, A., Morillo, C., & Gimenez, A. (2004). Effects of suppressing neutral and obsession-like thoughts in normal subjects: Beyond frequency. *Behavior Research and Therapy, 42*, 841-857.

Benedikt, R., Wertheim, E. H., & Love, A. (1998). Eating attitudes and weight-loss attempts in female adolescents and their mothers. *Journal of Youth and Adolescence, 27*, 43-57.

Braun, D., Sunday, S., & Halmi, K. (1994). Psychiatric comorbidity in patients with eating disorders. *Psychological Medicine, 24*, 859-867.

Brewin, C. R., & Smart, L. (2005). Working memory capacity and suppression of intrusive thoughts. *Behavior Therapy and Experimental Psychiatry, 36*, 61-68.

Brownell, K. D. (1991). Dieting and the search for the perfect body: Where physiology and culture collide. *Behavior Therapy, 22,* 1-12.

Bulik, C. M. (1995). Anxiety disorders and eating disorders: A review of their relationship. *New Zealand Journal of Psychology, 24,* 51-62.

Bulik, C. M. (2003). Genetic and biological risk factors. In J. Kevin-Thompson (Ed.), *Handbook of eating disorders and obesity* (pp. 1-20). New York: Wiley.

Bulik, C. M., & Reichborn-Kjennerud, T. (2003). Medical morbidity in binge eating disorder. *International Journal of Eating Disorders, 34,* S39-S246.

Bulik, C. M., Sullivan, P. F., & Kendler, K. S. (2003). Genetic and environmental contributions to obesity and binge-eating. *International Journal of Eating Disorders, 33,* 293-298.

Christiano, B., & Mizes, J. S. (1997). Appraisal and coping deficits associated with eating disorders: Implications for treatment. *Cognitive and Behavioral Practice, 4,* 263-290.

Cockell, S. J., Geller, J., & Linden, W. (2002). The development of a decisional balance scale for anorexia nervosa. *European Eating Disorders Review, 10,* 359-375.

Connors, M. E., & Morse, W. (1993). Sexual abuse and eating disorders: A review. *International Journal of Eating Disorders, 13,* 1-11.

Cooper, M., & Turner, H. (2000). Underlying assumptions and core beliefs in anorexia nervosa and dieting. *British Journal of Clinical Psychology, 39,* 215-218.

Dahl, J., & Lundgren, T. (2006). *Living beyond your pain.* Oakland, CA: New Harbinger Publications.

Davies, M. I., & Clark, D. M. (1998). Thought suppression produces a rebound effect with analogue post-traumatic intrusions. *Behaviour Research and Therapy, 36,* 571-582.

Deep, A., Lilenfeld, L. R., Plotnicov, K. H., Pollice, C., & Kays, W. H. (1999). Sexual abuse in eating disorder subtypes and control: The role of co-morbid substance dependence in bulimia nervosa. *International Journal of Eating Disorders, 25,* 1-10.

Deep, A. L., Nagy, L. M., Weltzin, T. E., Rao, & Kaye, W. H. (1995). Premorbid onset of psychopathology in long-term recovered anorexia nervosa. *International Journal of Eating Disorders, 17,* 291-297.

Diaz Marsa, M., Carrasco, J. L., & Saiz, J. (2000). A study of temperament and personality in anorexia and bulimia nervosa. *Journal of Personality Disorders, 14,* 352-359.

Dobson, K. S., & Dozois, D. J. (2004). Attentional biases in eating disorders: A meta-analytic review of Stroop performance. *Clinical Psychological Review, 23,* 1001-1022.

Dolan, R. J., Mitchell, J., & Wakeling, A. (1988). Structural brain changes in patients with anorexia nervosa. *Psychological Medicine, 18,* 349-353.

Eifert, G. H., & Heffner, M. (2003). The effects of acceptance versus control contexts on avoidance of panic-related symptoms. *Journal of Behavior Therapy and Experimental Psychiatry, 34,* 293-312.

Fairburn, C. G. (1997). Eating disorders. In D. M. Clark & C. G. Fairburn (Eds.), *Science and practice of cognitive behaviour therapy* (pp. 209-243). Oxford, England: Oxford University Press.

Fairburn, C. G. (2002). Cognitive-behavioral therapy for bulimia nervosa. In C. G. Fairburn & K. D. Brownell (Eds.), *Eating disorders and obesity* (pp. 302-307). New York: Guilford.

Fairburn, C. G., & Harrison, P. J. (2003). Eating disorders. *The Lancet, 361,* 407-416.

Fairburn, C. G., Shafran, R., & Cooper, Z. (1999). A cognitive-behavioural theory of anorexia nervosa. *Behaviour Research and Therapy, 37,* 1-13.

Farmer, R. F., Nash, H. M., & Field, C. E. (2001). Disordered eating behaviors and reward sensitivity. *Journal of Behavior Therapy and Experimental Psychiatry, 32,* 211-219.

Fassino, S., Amianto, F., Gramaglia, C., Facchini, F., & Abbate Daga, G. (2004). Temperament and character in eating disorders: Ten years of studies. *Journal of Eating and Weight Disorders, 9,* 81-90.

Feldner, M. T., Zvolensky, M. J., Eifert, G. H., & Spira, A. P. (2003). Emotional avoidance: An experimental test of individual differences and response suppression during biological challenge. *Behaviour Research and Therapy, 41,* 403-411.

Fornari, V., & Dancyger, I. F. (2003). Psychosexual development and eating disorders. *Adolescent Medicine, 14,* 61-75.

Forsyth, J. P., Eifert, G. H., & Barrios, V. (2006). Fear conditioning in an emotion regulation context: A fresh perspective on the origins of anxiety disorders. In M. G. Craske, D. Hermans, & D.

Vansteenwegen (Eds.), *Fear and learning: Basic science to clinical application*. Washington, DC: American Psychological Association.

Forsyth, J. P., Lejuez, C., Hawkins, R. P., & Eifert, G. H. (1996). A critical evaluation of cognitions as causes of behavior. *Journal of Behavior Therapy and Experimental Psychiatry, 27*, 369-376.

Franklin, J. C., Schiele, B. C., Brozek, J., & Keys, A. (1948). Observations on human behavior in experimental semi-starvation and rehabilitation. *Journal of Clinical Psychology, 4*, 28-45.

Garfinkel, P. E., & Garner, D. M. (1982). *Anorexia nervosa: A multidimensional perspective*. New York: Brunner/Mazel.

Garfinkel, P. E., Lin, E., Goering, P., & Spegg, C. (1996). Purging and nonpurging forms of bulimia nervosa in a community sample. *International Journal of Eating Disorders, 20*, 231-238.

Garner, D. M., & Needleman, L. D. (1997). Sequencing and integration of treatments. In D. M. Garner & P. E. Garfinkel (Eds.), *Handbook for treatment for eating disorders* (pp. 50-66). New York: Guilford.

Garner, D. M., Vitousek, K. M., & Pike, K. M. (1997). Cognitive-behavioral therapy for anorexia nervosa. In D. M. Garner & P. E. Garfinkel (Eds.), *Handbook for treatment for eating disorders* (pp. 94-144). New York: Guilford.

Ghaderi, A. (2003). Structural modeling analysis of prospective risk factors for eating disorder. *Eating Behaviors, 3*, 387-396.

Greco, L. A., Blackledge, J. T., Coyne, L. W., & Enreheich, J. (2005). Acceptance and mindfulness-based approaches in childhood anxiety disorders: Acceptance and commitment therapy as an example. In S. M. Orsillo & L. Roemer (Eds.), *Acceptance and mindfulness-based approaches to anxiety: Conceptualization and treatment* (pp. 301-321). New York: Springer.

Greco, L. A., & Blomquist, K. K. (2006). *Body image and eating behavior among school-aged girls: Role of experiential avoidance and cognitive fusion*. Paper presented at the 40th Annual Convention of the Association of Behavioral and Cognitive Therapies, Chicago, IL.

Greco, L. A., & Eifert, G. H. (2004). Treating parent-adolescent conflict: Is acceptance the missing link for an integrative family therapy? *Cognitive and Behavioral Practice, 11*, 305-314.

Greco, L. A., Murrell, A. R., & Coyne, L. W. (2005). *Avoidance and Fusion Questionnaire for Youth (AFQ-Y)*. Unpublished measure, University of Missouri, St. Louis. (Available from Laurie A. Greco, Ph.D. and www.contextualpsychology.org)

Gross, J. J. (2002). Emotion regulation: Affective, cognitive, and social consequences. *Psychophysiology, 39*, 281-291.

Hall, R. C., Tice, L., Beresford, T. P., Wooley, B., & Hall, A. K. (1989). Sexual abuse in patients with anorexia nervosa and bulimia. *Psychosomatics: Journal of Consultation Liaison Psychiatry, 30*, 73-79.

Hansel, S. L., & Wittrock, D. A. (1997). Appraisal and coping strategies in stressful situations: A comparison of individuals who binge. *International Journal of Eating Disorders, 21*, 89-93.

Harris, E. C., & Barraclough, B. (1998). Excess mortality of mental disorder. *The British Journal of Psychiatry, 173*, 11-53.

Harvey, A. G., & Bryant, R. A. (1998). The effect of attempted thought suppression in acute stress disorder. *Behaviour Research and Therapy, 36*, 583-590.

Hashimoto, K., Koizumi, H., Nakazato, M., Shimizu, E., & Iyo, M. (2005). Role of brain-derived neurotrophic factor in eating disorders: Recent findings and its pathophysiological implications. *Progress in Neuropharmacology and Biological Psychiatry, 29*, 499-504.

Hayes, S. C. (2002). Acceptance, mindfulness, and science. *Clinical Psychology: Science and Practice, 9*, 101-106.

Hayes, S. C., Barnes-Holmes, D., & Roche, B. (2001). *Relational frame theory: A post-Skinnerian account of human language and cognition*. New York: Kluwer.

Hayes, S. C., Luoma, J. B., Bond, F. W., Masuda, A., & Lillis, J. (2006). Acceptance and commitment therapy: Model, processes, and outcomes. *Behaviour Research and Therapy, 44*, 1-25.

Hayes, S. C., Masuda, A., Bissett, R., Luoma, J., & Guerrero, L. F. (2004). DBT, FAP, and ACT: How empirically oriented are the new behavior therapy technologies? *Behavior Therapy, 35*, 35-54.

Hayes, S. C., Strosahl, K. D., & Wilson, K. G. (1999). *Acceptance and commitment therapy: An experiential approach to behavior change*. New York: Guilford.

Hayes, S. C., Wilson, K. G., Gifford, E. V., Follette, V. M., & Strosahl, K. (1996). Experiential avoidance and behavioral disorders: A functional dimensional approach to diagnosis and treatment. *Journal of Consulting and Clinical Psychology, 64,* 1152-1168.

Heffner, M., & Eifert, G. H. (2004). *The anorexia workbook: How to accept yourself, heal suffering, and reclaim your life.* Oakland, CA: New Harbinger Publications.

Heffner, M., Eifert, G. H., Parker, B. T., Hernandez, D. H., & Sperry, J. A. (2003). Valued directions: Acceptance and commitment therapy in the treatment of alcohol dependence. *Cognitive and Behavioral Practice, 10,* 379-384.

Heffner, M., Sperry, J., Eifert, G. H., & Detweiler, M. (2002). Acceptance and commitment therapy in the treatment of an adolescent female with anorexia nervosa: A case study. *Cognitive and Behavioral Practice, 9,* 232-236.

Henderson, N. J., & Huon, G. F. (2002). Negative affect and binge eating in overweight women. *British Journal of Health Psychology, 7,* 77-87.

Herman, C. P., & Mack, D. (1975). Restrained and unrestrained eating. *Journal of Personality, 43,* 647-660.

Herzog, D. B., Dorer, D. J., Keel, P. K., Selwyn, S. E., Ekebad, E. R., Flores, A. T., et al. (1999). Recovery and relapse in anorexia and bulimia nervosa: A 7.5-year follow-up study. *Journal of the American Academy of Child and Adolescent Psychiatry, 38,* 829-837.

Isnard, P., Michel, G., Frelut, M. L., Vila, G., Falissard, B., Naja, W., et al. (2003). Binge eating and psychopathology in severely obese adolescents. *International Journal of Eating Disorders, 34,* 235-243.

Johnston, L., Bulik, C. M., & Anstiss, V. (1999). Suppressing thoughts about chocolate. *International Journal of Eating Disorders, 26,* 21-27.

Katzman, D. K., Zipursky, R. B., Lambe, E. K., & Mikulis, D. J. (1997). A longitudinal magnetic resonance imaging study of brain changes in adolescents with anorexia nervosa. *Archives of Pediatric Adolescent Medicine, 151,* 793-797.

Kaltiala-Heino, R., Rimpel, M., Rissanen, A., & Rantanen, P. (2001). Early puberty and early sexual activity are associated with bulimic-type eating pathology in middle adolescence. *Journal of Adolescent Health, 28,* 346-352.

Keel, P. K., Heatherton, T. F., Harnden, J. L., & Hornig, C. D. (1997). Mothers, fathers and daughters: Dieting and disordered eating. *Eating Disorders, 5,* 216-228.

Kendler, K., Walters, E., Neale, M., Kessler, R., Heath, A., & Eaves, L. (1995). The structure of the genetic and environmental risk factors for six major psychiatric disorders in women: Phobia, generalized anxiety disorder, panic disorder, bulimia, major depression, and alcoholism. *Archives of General Psychiatry, 52,* 374-383.

Kessler, R. C., McGonagle, K. A., Zhao, S., Nelson, C. B., Hughes, M., Eshleman, S., et al. (1994). Lifetime and 12-month prevalence of DSM-III-R psychiatric disorders in the United States. *Archives of General Psychiatry, 51,* 8-19.

Kingston, K., Szmukler, G., Andrews, D., Tress, B., & Desmond, P. (1996). Neuropsychological and structural brain changes in anorexia nervosa before and after refeeding. *Psychological Medicine, 26,* 15-28.

Klump, K. L., Strober, M., Bulik, C. M., Thornton, L., Johnson, C., Devlin, B., et al. (2004). Personality characteristics of women before and after recovery from an eating disorder. *Psychological Medicine, 34,* 1407-1418.

Lazarus, R. S., & Folkman, S. (1984). *Stress, appraisal, and coping.* New York: Springer.

Levine, M. P., & Smolak, L. (1996). Media as a context for the development of disordered eating. In L. Smolak, M. P. Levine, & R. Striegel-Moore (Eds.), *The developmental psychopathology of eating disorders* (pp. 235-257). Mahwah, NJ: Erlbaum.

Levitt, J. T., Brown, T. A., Orsillo, S. M., & Barlow, D. H. (2004). The effects of acceptance versus suppression of emotion on subjective and psychophysiological response to carbon dioxide challenge in patients with panic disorder. *Behavior Therapy, 35,* 747-766.

Lowe, M. R. (2002). Dietary restraint and overeating. In C. G. Fairburn & K. D. Brownell (Eds.), *Eating disorders and obesity* (pp. 88-92). New York: Guilford.

Martin, G. C., Wertheim, E. H., Prior, M., Smart, D., Sanson, A., & Oberklaid, F. (2000). A longitudinal study of the role of childhood temperament in the later development of eating concerns. *International Journal of Eating Disorders, 27,* 150-162.

McFarlane, A. C., McFarlane, C. M., & Gilchrist, P. N. (1988). Post-traumatic bulimia and anorexia nervosa. *International Journal of Eating Disorders, 7,* 705-708.

Meyer, C., Waller, G., & Watson, D. (2000). Cognitive avoidance and bulimic psychopathology: The relevance of temporal factors in a nonclinical population. *International Journal of Eating Disorders, 27,* 405-410.

Mizes, J. S. (1995). Eating disorders. In M. Hersen (Ed.), *Advanced abnormal child psychology* (pp. 375-391). Mahwah, NJ: Erlbaum.

Mizes, J. S., & Arbitell, M. R. (1991). Bulimics' perceptions of emotional responding during binge-purge episodes. *Psychological Reports, 69,* 527-532.

Mizes, J. S., & Sloan, D. M. (1998). An empirical analysis of eating disorder, not otherwise specified: Preliminary support for a distinct sub-group. *International Journal of Eating Disorders, 23,* 233-242.

Monteleone, P., Brambilla, F., Bortolotti, F., & Maj, M. (2000). Serotonergic dysfunction across the eating disorders: Relationship to eating behaviour, purging behavior, nutritional status, and general psychopathology. *Psychological Medicine, 30,* 261-272.

Monteleone, P., Tortorella, A., Martiadis, V., Serritella, C., Fuschino, A., & Maj. M. (2004). Opposite changes in the serum brain-derived neurotrophic factor in anorexia nervosa and obesity. *Psychosomatic medicine, 66,* 744-748.

Moreno, A., & Thelen, M. H. (1993). Parental factors related to bulimia nervosa. *Addictive Behaviors, 18,* 681-689.

Nakazato, M., Hashimoto, K., Shimizu, E., Kumakiri, C., Koizumi, H., Okamura, N., et al. (2003). Decreased levels of brain-derived neurotrophic factor in female patients with eating disorders. *Biological Psychiatry, 54,* 485-490.

Neumärker, K. J., Bettle, N., Bettle, O., Dudeck, U., & Neumärker, U. (1998). The eating attitudes test: Comparative analysis of female and male students at the Public Ballet School of Berlin. *European Child & Adolescent Psychiatry, 7,* 19-23.

O'Connell, M. A., Larkin, K., Mizes, J. S., & Fremouw, W. (2005). The impact of caloric preloading on attempts at food and eating-related thought suppression in restrained and unrestrained eaters. *International Journal of Eating Disorders, 38,* 42-48.

O'Dwyer, A. M., Lucey, J. V., & Russell, G. F. (1996). Serotonin activity in anorexia nervosa after long-term weight restoration: response to D-fenfluramine challenge. Structural brain changes in patients with anorexia nervosa. *Psychological Medicine, 26,* 353-359.

Oliver, K. G., & Huon, G. F. (2001). Eating-related thought suppression in high and low disinhibitors. *International Journal of Eating Disorders, 30,* 329-337.

Orsillo, S. M., & Batten, S. V. (2002). ACT as treatment of a disorder of excessive control: Anorexia. *Cognitive and Behavioral Practice, 9,* 253-259.

Pike, K. M., & Rodin, J. (1991). Mothers, daughters, and disordered eating. *Journal of Abnormal Psychology, 100,* 198-204.

Pinhas, L., Toner, B., Ali, A., Garfinkel, P., & Stuckless, N. (1999). The effects of the ideal of female beauty on mood and body satisfaction. *International Journal of Eating Disorders, 25,* 223-226.

Polivy, J., & Herman, C. P. (2002). Experimental studies of dieting. In C. G. Fairburn & K. D. Brownell (Eds.), *Eating disorders and obesity* (pp. 84-87). New York: Guilford.

Purdon, C., & Clark, D. A. (2001). Suppression of obsession-like thoughts in nonclinical individuals: Impact on thought frequency, appraisal and mood state. *Behavior Research and Therapy, 39,* 1163-1181.

Sloan, D. M. (2002). Does warm weather climate affect eating disorder pathology? *International Journal of Eating Disorders, 32,* 240-244.

Soukup, V. M., Beiler, M. E., & Terrell, F. (1990). Stress, coping style, and problem solving ability among eating-disordered inpatients. *Journal of Clinical Psychology, 46,* 592-599.

Spira, A. P., Zvolensky, M. J., Eifert, G. H., & Feldner, M. T. (2004). Avoidance-oriented coping as a predictor of anxiety-based physical stress: A test using biological challenge. *Journal of Anxiety Disorders, 18,* 309-323.

Staats, A. W., & Eifert, G. H. (1990). The paradigmatic behaviorism theory of emotions: Basis for unification. *Clinical Psychology Review, 10,* 539-566.

Stewart, T. M. (2004). Light on body image treatment: acceptance through mindfulness. *Behavior Modification, 28,* 783-811.

Stice, E., Spangler, D. S., & Agras, W. S. (2001). Exposure to media-portrayed thin-ideal images adversely affects vulnerable girls: A longitudinal experiment. *Journal of Social and Clinical Psychology, 20,* 270-288.

Stitzel, E. W. (1948). Avoiding behavior problems: Anorexia. *Hahnemannian Monthly, 83,* 159-164.

Suhail, K., & Nisa, Z. U. (2002). Prevalence of eating disorders in Pakistan: Relationship with depression and body shape. *Eating and Weight Disorders, 7,* 131-138.

Suomi, S. (1999). *Serotonin and aggression in primates.* Paper presented at the annual meeting of the American Psychological Association, Boston, MA.

Telch, C. F., & Agras, W. S. (1993). The effects of a very low calorie diet on binge eating. *Behavior Therapy, 24,* 177-193.

Uher, R., & Treasure, J. (2005). Brain lesions and eating disorders. *Neurology, Neurosurgery and Psychiatry, 76,* 852-857.

Urdapilleta, I., Mirabel-Sarron, C., Meunier, J. M., & Richard, J. F. (2005). Étude du processus de catégorisation chez des patientes aux troubles des conduites alimentaires : une nouvelle approche cognitive de la psychopathologie [Study of the categorization process among patients with eating disorders: A new cognitive approach to psychopathology]. *Encephale, 31,* 82-91.

Vandereycken, W., Kog, E., & Vanderlinden, J. (1989). *The family approach to eating disorders: Assessment and treatment of anorexia nervosa and bulimia.* New York: PMA.

Vartanian, L. R., Polivy, J., & Herman, C. P. (2004). Implicit cognitions and eating disorders: Their application in research and treatment. *Cognitive and Behavioral Practice, 11.* 160-167.

Vitousek, K. B. (2002). Cognitive-behavioral therapy for anorexia nervosa. In C. G. Fairburn & K. D. Brownell (Eds.), *Eating disorders and obesity* (pp. 308-313). New York: Guilford.

Walsh, B. T., & Garner, D. M. (1997). Diagnostic issues. In D. M. Garner & P. E. Garfinkel (Eds.), *Handbook for treatment for eating disorders* (pp. 25-33). New York: Guilford.

Webber, E. M. (1994). Psychological characteristics of binging and nonbinging obese women. *The Journal of Psychology, 128,* 339-351.

Williamson, D. A., White, M. A., York-Crowe, E., & Stewart, T. M. (2004). Cognitive-behavioral theories of eating disorders. *Behavior Modification, 28,* 711-738.

Wilson, G. T. (1996). Acceptance and change in the treatment of eating disorders and obesity. *Behavior Therapy, 27,* 417-439.

Wilson, G. T., Fairburn, C. G., & Agras, W. S. (1997). Cognitive-behavioral therapy for bulimia nervosa. In D. M. Garner & P. E. Garfinkel (Eds.), *Handbook for treatment for eating disorders* (pp. 67-93). New York: Guilford.

Wilson, K. G., & Roberts, M. (2002). Core principles in acceptance and commitment therapy: An application to anorexia. *Cognitive and Behavioral Practice, 9,* 237-243.

Wiseman, C. V., Gray, J. J., Mosimann, J. E., & Ahrens, A. H. (1992). Cultural expectations of thinness in women: An update. *International Journal of Eating Disorders, 11,* 85-89.

Wolfe, B. E., Metzger, E. D., & Jimerson, D. C. (1997). Research update on serotonin function in bulimia nervosa and anorexia nervosa. *Psychopharmacological Bulletin, 33,* 345-354.

Chapter 11

Personality Disorders

Scott T. Gaynor & Susan C. Baird
Western Michigan University

Description of Problem

The term personality is generally used descriptively; that is, as a summary label for how someone has behaved and is likely to behave. For example, when it is said that someone has an extroverted personality what is meant is that in the past this person has been very outgoing and talkative and is likely to be so again. Thus, when psychologists and laypersons alike refer to personality what is often being communicated is the presence of a somewhat predictable pattern of behavior that is consistent across time and situations. This is apparent in the Diagnostic and Statistical Manual of Mental Disorders (DSM-IV-TR; American Psychiatric Association, 2000) which describes personality traits as "enduring patterns of perceiving, relating to, and thinking about the environment and oneself that are exhibited in a wide range of social and personal contexts" (p. 686).

According to the DSM (APA, 2000), personality traits become personality disorders (PDs) when the patterns of behavior deviate markedly from cultural norms and are so rigid and stable over time and across situations that they cause significant subjective distress or impairment in an important area of functioning. The DSM further clarifies that these patterns must be manifested in two (or more) of the following areas: cognition, affectivity, interpersonal functioning, and impulse control. Cognition is specified to mean perceiving and interpreting self, others, and events. Affect includes the range, intensity, and appropriateness of the emotional response. The DSM further specifies that a PD diagnosis requires report of a long-term pattern of similar functioning to ensure that the particular personality feature has been evident since adolescence or early adulthood. In addition, the personality features must not simply be a response to a particular stressor, a reflection of a theoretically more transient Axis I disorder, or the result of use of a substance or general medical condition (APA, 2000). As an illustration, consider an individual diagnosed with paranoid PD who is identified by a pattern of behavior indicative of disproportionate distrust and suspiciousness of others that is longstanding and occurs across a range of personal and interpersonal settings. The individual has few friends because of perceived mistreatment at their hands, which produces an immediate angry retort from him and the bearing of an ongoing grudge. At work the person assumes a financial bonus is a coercive attempt to enhance his performance;

a bank teller's error is a deliberate attempt to swindle money; and his spouse's failure to answer the telephone a sign that she is being unfaithful.

PDs are coded in the DSM on Axis II and are further grouped into three clusters. The two leftmost columns of Table 11.1, taken from the DSM-IV-TR (APA, 2000, p. 685), provide a brief description of each of the currently recognized personality disorders. As is apparent in the table, the clustering is based on proposed similarities. That is, Cluster A is characterized by odd and eccentric behavior and includes Paranoid, Schizoid, and Schizotypal Personality Disorders; Cluster B includes Antisocial, Borderline, Histrionic, and Narcissistic Personality Disorders and is typified by dramatic, emotional, or erratic behavior; Cluster C is characterized by anxious or fearful behavior and includes Avoidant, Dependent, and Obsessive-Compulsive Personality Disorder.

PDs warrant the attention of clinical behavior analysts for a number of reasons. PDs, as currently identified, are prevalent in clinical and non-clinical settings. A recent review of prevalence rates for PDs in non-clinical populations reported a median point prevalence of 11%, with estimates ranging from 7-18% across studies (Trull & Widiger, 2003; see also Lenzenweger, Loranger, Korfine, & Neff, 1997; Pilkonis, Neighbors, & Corbitt, 1999; Samuels, Bienvenu, Joseph, Brown, Costa, & Nestadt 2002). Thus, roughly 1 out of every 10 persons in the community meets criteria for at least one PD, rates that are commensurate with or exceed those of more recognizable Axis I disorders, such as major depression, the so-called common cold of mental illness. Among the PDs, Cluster B diagnoses appear modestly more common than the others (APA, 2000; Trull & Widiger, 2003).

While PDs are relatively prevalent in the community, they are highly prevalent in the clinic. Several sources indicated that the rate of PDs in outpatient samples is about 50% (Cloninger, 2000; Trull & Widiger, 2003). Thus, on average 1 out of every 2 of our clients may be so diagnosed. PDs are also highly comorbid with Axis I diagnoses and other PDs. Across studies, anywhere from 31-81% of depressed outpatients meet criteria for a PD diagnosis and rates of PDs among those diagnosed with anxiety and substance abuse disorders appear similarly high (Pilkonis et al., 1999). Moreover, recent estimates suggest about 50% of those diagnosed with one PD will likely also meet criteria for a second PD (Pfohl, 1999).

These prevalence statistics are especially striking when it is recognized that they are based on categorical diagnoses which require crossing a numerical threshold in terms of the number of symptoms present (3-5 across the various PDs) for the diagnostic label to be applied. These thresholds are surely arbitrary and many current researchers suggest that PDs are best conceptualized on a continuum with "normal" personality functioning (see Strack & Lorr, 1997). From this dimensional perspective, while PDs may represent an extreme variant, they are not qualitatively unique (Widiger, 2002; Costa & Widiger, 2002). Thus, there are surely large numbers of people in the community and clinic who would be considered to show significant PDs features despite being "subthreshold" for the diagnosis.

Personality Disorder	Core Feature(s)	Biological Etiology	Psychological Etiology
Cluster A (odd/eccentric)			
Paranoid	Distrust and suspiciousness such that others' motives are interpreted as malevolent.	Little research to indicate direct inheritance.	Parents were excessively critical, rejecting, withholding, and possibly abusive. Leads to paranoid beliefs that become self-perpetuating due to focus on signs of and evidence for malicious intentions.
Schizoid	Detachment from social relationships and a restricted range of emotional expression.	Little research to indicate direct inheritance.	Possibly sustained history of isolation during childhood with parental encouragement and modeling of interpersonal withdrawal, social indifference, and emotional detachment.
Schizotypal	Acute discomfort in close relationships, cognitive or perceptual distortions, and eccentricities of behavior.	Evidence for genetic correlation with schizophrenia. Poor performance on laboratory tasks of visual and auditory attention that correlate with CNS dysfunction possibly in the dopaminergic pathways.	Deficits in attention/perception disrupts evaluation of and relatedness to environment, which may lead to discomfort with social situations, misperceptions, suspicions, and social isolation.
Cluster B (erratic/dramatic)			
Antisocial	Disregard for, and violation of, the rights of others.	Support for genetic contribution to etiology. Deficits in behavioral inhibition system (hyporeactive electrodermal response to stress) associated with low arousal, anxiousness, and inhibition, which may contribute to risk-taking (stimulation seeking), impulsivity, and the lack of guilt and remorse.	Substantial data support contribution of family, peers, and other environmental factors. Parents model aggressive, exploitative behavior, use erratic discipline (overly lenient then excessively harsh), punish warmth/empathy and reward aggressiveness and exploitation, which leads to view of the environment as hostile.

Table 11.1. List and brief description of the currently recognized personality disorders (taken from the DSM-IV-TR, APA, 2000) and a summary of current research on the etiology of personality disorders (taken from Trull & Widiger, 2003; see also McGuffin & Thapar, 1992; Nigg & Goldsmith, 1994 cf. Trull & Widiger, 2003).

Personality Disorder	Core Feature(s)	Biological Etiology	Psychological Etiology
Borderline	Instability in interpersonal relationships, self-image, and affects, and marked impulsivity.	Possible genetic predisposition for affect-control and impulse-control problems (emotional instability).	Empirical support for history of abuse (physical or sexual) and maltreatment in relationships with significant others (e.g., parents). Such an invalidating environment may lead to malevolent view of others and failure to learn to regulate emotions and tolerate distress.
Histrionic	Excessive emotionality and attention seeking.	Some limited support for heritability (to the extent that there is overlap with extroversion).	Parents provision of love and attention was largely contingent on attractiveness and provocativeness, such that self-worth becomes centered around receipt of attention for these behaviors from others.
Narcissistic	Grandiosity, need for admiration, and lack of empathy.	Little research to indicate direct inheritance.	Child may find that attention, interest, and love from parents is contingent on achievements or successes. Fail to perceive parents valuing/loving him/her for his/her own sake and instead sees love and attention as conditional on successful accomplishments. Self-worth becomes dependent on recognition of achievements and successes.
Cluster C (anxious/fearful)			
Avoidant	Social inhibition, feelings of inadequacy, and hypersensitivity to negative evaluation.	Some support for heritability (to the extent that there is overlap with introversion and neuroticism). Excessive functioning of behavior inhibition system (anxious temperament).	Timidity and insecurity may be result of cumulative history of interpersonal embarrassment, rejection, and humiliation, which leads to beliefs of inadequacy/inferiority that then perpetuates inhibited behavior.
Dependent	Submissive and clinging behavior related to an excessive need to be taken care of.	Evidence for modest heritable influence, may involve anxious/fearful temperament.	Fearful temperament in interaction with insecure attachment to inconsistent, unreliable primary caretaker results in lack of sense of security, which is sought from others through excessive reassurance seeking, clinginess, and submissiveness.
Obsessive-compulsive	Preoccupation with orderliness, perfectionism, and	Some evidence of heritability of trait of obsessiveness.	Parents emphasize excessive, rigid control of feelings and impulses, which leads to rigidity

Table 11.1. Continued.

Interrater reliability for PD diagnoses is generally acceptable when structured instruments are used, but does appear to improve when dimensional judgments are employed (Maffei, Fossati, Agostoni, Barraco, Bagnato, Deboah et al., 1997). Recent reviews of the convergent validity of various PD assessment approaches more clearly points to the importance of a dimensional perspective. Widiger (2002) reports that across studies the median convergent validity for categorical measures is .25, while dimensional assessments (using symptom counts from semistructured interviews and scores on self-report measures) is .42, with self-report measures demonstrating the highest convergent validity. The low-to-modest estimates are seen not only across two measures administered to the same individual, but also when the identified client and an informant that knows the client are both interviewed (about the client) using the same measure (Klonsky, Oltmanns, & Turkheimer, 2002; Widiger, 2002). Furthermore, even if convergent validity could be achieved during an assessment at time A, the test-retest reliability of categorical PD diagnoses suggest that things may change by assessment point B. For instance, Zimmerman (1994) reviewed long-term (typically over 12-month) test-retest reliabilities and found a range from very low (.11) to quite high (.86), with STPD (.11) and DPD (.15) having the lowest and ATPD (.86), PPD (.57), and BPD (.56) having the highest. Recently, Shea, Stout, Gunderson, Morey, Grilo, McGlashan et al. (2002) reported that diagnoses were maintained across a 12-month period for 56% diagnosed with AVPD, 34% diagnosed with STPD, 41% diagnosed with BPD, and 42% diagnosed with OCPD. If the categorical thresholds are critical and PDs are rigid and stable over time, then such data are problematic. However, correlations between number of specific PD symptoms at baseline and 12-months were higher than .84 for all four PDs assessed, suggesting dimensional stability. Nonetheless, temporal stability and persistence of functional impairment do not appear to readily differentiate PDs from conceptually more transient Axis I disorders (Shea & Yen, 2003).

Thus, while PD features appear prevalent, how they should be categorized and assessed remains controversial. The growing recognition that PDs be viewed from a dimensional perspective appears a clear advance over a categorical approach (and the implicit medical model accompanying such an approach, see Follette & Houts, 1996). Indeed, a number of researchers have responded by attempting to correlate dimensional measures of PDs with dimensional measures of other personality traits. For instance, in a number of studies the correlations between PD measures and the "Big 5" personality traits (Extroversion, Conscientiousness, Agreeableness, Neuroticism, and Openness to Experience; Costa & Widiger, 2002) or the traits of sociotropy and autonomy (Morse, Robins, & Gittes-Fox, 2002) have been explored. These studies do an important service in uniting PD symptoms with constructs that are considered to be basic aspects of personality. Tying PDs to basic/normal aspects of personality implies that normal biological and psychological processes are relevant to understanding both. However, static correlations between PD symptoms and dimensional personality traits do not speak to the processes that might lead to or maintain the functioning described by the constructs.

Current Perspectives on Etiology

Determining the factors contributing to the etiology and maintenance of PDs is an area in which much work remains to be done. The most cohesive and empirically-based etiological accounts are for ATPD. A diagnosis of ATPD requires meeting criteria for a childhood diagnosis of Conduct Disorder (CD). CD involves engaging in a pervasive pattern of behavior that shows clear disregard for the property (e.g., fire-setting), physical well-being (e.g., abuse of animals or humans), or rules of others or society (e.g., truancy, armed theft, running away). Those most likely to progress to an ATPD diagnosis evince CD from an early age (prior to adolescence). This "early starter" pathway is considered to involve the interaction of a genetic diathesis, and possibly subtle neurological deficits, with exposure to an early environment marked by hostile, coercive interactions with caretakers (Moffitt, 1993; Patterson, DeBaryshe, & Ramsey, 1989; Snyder, 2002; Snyder & Stoolmiller, 2002). For instance, imagine parents routinely snap at their child to complete his homework, but when the child responds caustically they typically withdraw the demand, negatively reinforcing the child's oppositional responding. Over time, as the parents increase the intensity of their demands, the child increases the level of his oppositional behavior, which consistently removes the demands. These mutually coercive interactions with parents (and siblings) train the child to behave in increasingly noxious ways interpersonally in order to reduce demands and get his way. Inconsistently (e.g., after an embarrassing parent-teacher conference) the parents may employ harsh punishments. However, the inconsistency fails to alter the established pattern and the violent behavior serves to further model the value of hostile, aggressive, coercive behavior. This noxious interpersonal behavior learned in interaction with parents negatively influences early peer relationships. As poor school performance and aggressive/coercive interpersonal behavior reduces the range of potential friendships available to the child, he increasingly associates with other deviant peers who further reinforce delinquent behavior. This peer deviancy training leads to an escalation in delinquent behavior (substance abuse, skipping school, etc.) and further decreases contact with pro-social contexts (e.g., school) narrowing the teen's options and skills, and increasing the likelihood of contact with the criminal justice system and setting the stage for persistent offending (Patterson et al., 1989; Snyder, 2002; Snyder & Stoolmiller, 2002). Thus, for many the disregard for others and unlawful behavior characterizing adult ATPD is the endpoint in a developmental trajectory where such a repertoire was progressively, if unwittingly, molded. (Of note, alternative etiological accounts are offered for those with adolescent-onset CD [see Moffitt, 1993] or for a subset of those with child-onset CD, who may comprise a callous, unemotional subtype [see Frick & Ellis, 1999]).

The available etiological models for the remaining PDs are not nearly as well developed or consistently empirically supported. Indeed, as Trull and Widiger note, "one of the more remarkable gaps in knowledge is the childhood antecedents for PDs" (Trull & Widiger, 2003, p. 164). Thus, we will offer only a succinct summary of proposed etiological factors for the remaining disorders, which is provided in Table 11.1, and is based on a review of PDs by Trull and Widiger (2003).

The growing recognition in the field of PDs on the potential importance of a dimensional approach has implications for how one seeks to determine the etiological factors involved. First, if PDs are not categorically distinct and are highly comorbid with one another and other disorders, it is reasonable to ask if one should use the current PDs as a starting point for exploring etiology? When one accepts the PDs as currently defined then the outcome is determined and one is searching for the variables that lead to that outcome. But as a recent review suggests, the DSM provides only "a best approximation to date of a scientifically based nomenclature, but even its authors have acknowledged that its diagnoses and criterion sets are highly debatable. Well-meaning clinicians, theorists, and researchers could find some basis for fault in virtually every sentence, due in part to the absence of adequate research to guide its construction" (Widiger & Clark, 2000, p. 946). Given that the outcomes called PDs are currently poorly characterized, searching for the variables that lead to these distinct outcomes is less likely to be productive in the long run. That is, using the DSM as a starting point to guide research leads to a search for something that only appears (in "pure form") in the categorization system. Some have proposed focusing on the clusters rather than the specific disorders, but the data supporting the utility of the cluster arrangements is also equivocal at best. As stated in the DSM-IV-TR, the cluster approach "has serious limitations and has not been consistently validated" (APA, 2000, p. 686; see also Yang, Bagby, Costa, Ryder, & Herbst, 2002).

Second, if PDs are best understood as an extreme variant of normal personality functioning, then attempts to understand PDs as the result of unique, yet to be determined, abnormal/disordered processes also appears unlikely to be successful. Some have characterized how PDs fall according to normal personality dimensions (Costa & Widiger, 2002). While an advance in emphasizing the dimensional understanding of PDs, such an approach is open to criticisms for accepting the DSM as a starting point and not addressing the variables that lead to or maintain functioning at the extreme end of the normal continuum.[1] That is, we may simply end up exchanging one descriptive scheme (e.g., Avoidant PD) for another descriptive scheme (e.g., high introversion and high neuroticism). Thus, accepting that PDs lie on a continuum with normal personality traits is probably not enough. Instead, it may be more informative to examine how behaviors associated with PDs might be developed and maintained by empirically established psychological processes. The example of CD/ATPD is relevant. The proposed psychosocial sequence described above is based on decades of sophisticated research (summa-

---

[1]This approach is also open to criticism from within the DSM perspective in that it could be argued that while PDs have some dimensional features, this may not be the best strategy to understand truly clinical PDs because at the extreme end of the continuum there may be qualitative discontinuity.

rized in Reid, Patterson, & Snyder, 2002) outlining how basic principles of behavior (negative reinforcement characterizing coercive behavior in the home, positive reinforcement for antisocial behavior by deviant peers) are involved in the development and maintenance of unlawful behavior. Such an approach illustrates how an ultimately dysfunctional repertoire may be acquired and solidified and can be understood as simultaneously maladaptive yet entirely functional.

Based on the above considerations, we will not in this chapter attempt to develop a model of each of the currently described PDs, nor will we simply redescribe them in behavioral terms. Instead we will apply a contemporary behavioral approach to interpret core features that seem characteristic of PDs generally and several patterns of responding that are considered central features of particular PDs to illustrate how such responding may be developed and/or maintained. The classes of behavior selected for analysis are those that have received some consistent empirical support. The accounts offered will be necessarily speculative; however, our interpretation will begin with empirically established behavioral processes. The interpretations offered will go beyond the current empirical data, but the logic of the analyses will be tied to these processes. Before beginning this task it is necessary to describe existing behavioral and cognitive-behavioral approaches to personality and personality disorders and to then outline some critical features of Relational Frame Theory, the latter providing the perspective that will inform much of our analysis of the PD-relevant response patterns.

Existing Behavior Therapy Approaches

Cognitive Behavioral Theory and Personality Disorders

There are a variety of approaches that fall under the general heading of cognitive-behavioral. According to Dobson and Block (1988, p. 4), cognitive-behavioral approaches can be characterized by their common endorsement of three propositions: 1) cognitive activity affects behavior, 2) cognitive activity may be monitored and altered, and 3) desired behavior change may be affected through cognitive change. Thus, while not dismissing the role of environmental antecedents and consequences of behavior, the "fundamental propositions" of the cognitive-behavioral approach emphasize cognition, which is what is considered to differentiate the cognitive-behavioral position from the behavioral position (Dobson & Block, 1988).

Cognitive-behavioral approaches to PD employ a diathesis-stress model, suggesting that the behavior characteristic of individuals diagnosed with PDs is the result of a relatively stable cognitive diathesis that systematically biases how environmental events are processed (Beck, Freeman, & Associates, 1990). Specifically postulated is the presence of cognitive structures called schemas which determine how information will be processed and lead to a unique pattern of cognition, affect, and behavior. Beck et al. (1990) illustrate the pattern in the following example of how an individual might respond to a potentially threatening stimulus: "The person interprets the situation as dangerous (cognitive schema), feels anxiety (affective schema), wants to get away (motivational schema), and becomes mobilized to run away (action or instrumental schema)" (p. 34). This example illustrates the broad use of the concept of schemas and the specific importance of cognitive schemas in initiating the sequence.

Cognitive schemas consist of the individual's underlying beliefs, the specific rules that govern his/her information processing. Schemas are inferred from behavior or information gathered in clinical assessments and are considered the fundamental units of personality (Beck et al., 1990). Schemas are believed to be acquired over the course of development as innate characteristics (e.g., temperamental inhibition) interact with relevant experiences (e.g., overly critical familial environment). Thus, schemas are acquired because they are functional in the context in which they are formed but are expected to change with development. However, "some of the schema do not mature and are maintained at an earlier level of development. This is the beginning of an Axis II problem" (Freeman & Leaf, 1989, p. 408).

Thus, from a CBT perspective, PDs are characterized by the presence of pronounced maladaptive cognitive schemas that are activated across situations, bias information processing, and are difficult to control or change. Therefore, an individual with a PD may interpret even the most benign event in a dysfunctional way. For example, consider a situation where one's boss walks hurriedly past without a look or greeting. In most cases, one might come to a rather innocuous conclusion, such as the boss is late for an important meeting. In contrast, the sensitive, rejection-prone individual interprets this to mean, "My boss rushed past me because she is dissatisfied with my work." This is an example of a conditional schema (i.e., if my boss does not greet me, then she is unhappy with me). This type of belief then activates a progression of broader and more dysfunctional beliefs, such as "If my boss is displeased with me, she will fire me." "If she fires me, I will be unemployed forever." This example illustrates how the belief system not only characterizes the disorder, but also perpetuates it (Beck et al., 1990; Beck, Butler, Brown, Dahlsgaard, Newman, & Beck, 2001).

Beck and colleagues (1990) describe, based on their clinical observations and some initial empirical work (see Beck et al., 2001), specific cognitive profiles they believe are prototypical of most of the PDs. These are summarized in Table 11.2 which includes the core beliefs, associated overt behaviors, and the typical views of self and others associated with the PDs (Beck et al., 1990).

Clinical Behavior Analysis and Personality Disorders

Behavior analytic approaches involve interpreting the characteristic symptoms of PDs in terms of basic, well-established, behavioral principles. The behavior called personality disordered, like any behavior, is assumed to be a function of the individual's genetic endowment and past history of reinforcement in interaction with the current environmental context (Skinner, 1974). As such, a behavioral

Personality Disorder	Core belief	View of Self	View of Others	Core overt behavior
Paranoid	People are adversaries	Righteous, Innocent	Interfering, Malicious	Wariness
Schizoid	I need space	Self-sufficient, loner	Intrusive	Isolation
Schizotypal		No specific content proposed		
Antisocial	Others are there to be taken	Loner, autonomous, strong	Vulnerable, exploitable	Attack
Borderline		No specific content proposed		
Histrionic	I need to impress	Glamorous, impressive	Seducible, admirers	Dramatics
Narcissistic	I am special	Special, superior	Inferior, admirers	Self-aggrandizement
Avoidant	I may get hurt	Socially vulnerable and inept	Critical, superior	Avoidance
Dependent	I am helpless	Needy, incompetent	Nurturers, competent	Attachment
Obsessive-compulsive	I must not err	Responsible, competent	Irresponsible, incompetent	Perfectionism

Table 11.2. Characteristic profiles of individuals with specific personality disorders (adapted from Tables 2.1 and 3.2 in Beck et al., 1990).

framework leads one to look for environment-behavior relationships that lead to the patterns of behavior that occasion the use of the PD labels.

Behavioral approaches to personality and personality disorders. Much of the current behavioral writing as it relates to personality and personality disorders addresses how a behavior analytic approach could inform and be conceptually applied to the general domain of personality (Parker, Bolling, & Kohlenberg, 1998) and personality disorders (Follette, 1997; Koerner, Kohlenberg, & Parker, 1996). Such writing is important because behavioral approaches to personality and personality disorder in particular may initially appear oxymoronic or self-contradictory (Koerner et al., 1996; Nelson-Gray & Farmer, 1999) because of the trait and mental illness connotations associated with these terms. Clinical behavior analysts are indeed leery of using the DSM as the basis for understanding problem behavior and are especially careful when confronted with descriptive terms such as a personality disorder label or personality trait label to avoid reifying the label into a "thing" and using it as an explanation for the behavior it describes (Follette & Houts, 1996; Parker et al., 1998). However, clinical behavior analysts are interested in the patterns of behavior that lead to use of the labels and how best to understand and characterize these behavioral patterns. As described in the DSM, the patterns of behavior that occasion the use of "personality disorder" are ones that are enduring (i.e., longitudinally consistent), rigid (i.e., cross-situationally consistent), fall outside societal norms (i.e., reveal individual differences in responding that do not appear attributable to the situation itself), and are associated with distress (i.e., making them worthy of diagnosis).

From a behavior analytic perspective, current behavior is understood as the joint product of the current environment and the contingencies of reinforcement to which the person has been exposed in the past (i.e., his/her learning history). In other words, the current context has its effects (e.g., certain features functioning as discriminative stimuli) as a result of past experiences. Thus, if the current environment is functionally similar to that experienced in the past it would be expected that responding would be similar. Longitudinal consistency then can be understood, at least in part, as the result of a relatively consistent environment providing consistent contingencies over time (Parker et al., 1998). In addition to consistency over time, cross-situational consistency is another feature of PDs. From a behavioral perspective, behavior may be similar across situations if the situations are functionally similar. That is, the same behavior may be seen across a seemingly wide range of situations, if these situations share stimulus properties that in the past have led to reinforcement of a particular class of behavior (Nelson-Gray & Farmer, 1999; Parker et al., 1998). Thus, a behavioral approach is conceptually neutral as to whether behavior should or should not be consistent. Behavior is longitudinally or cross-situationally consistent or inconsistent depending upon the current and historical environment-behavior relations supporting such responding.

Behavior is often attributed to one's personality when two (or more) people are apparently exposed to the same stimulus (e.g., a holiday work party) but respond differently (e.g., looking forward to the party and interacting with others vs. dreading the party and withdrawing from contact with others). When the situation appears common to all respondents, it is logical to conclude that any differences observed are attributable to the person. Moreover, when the response of one of the individuals is seen as outside the cultural norm (e.g., in terms of social avoidance) it may be considered evidence of a PD (e.g., AVPD). As noted above, particular features of the current context have psychological functions as the result of past experiences. As Skinner (1953, p. 260) said "discriminative behavior waits upon the contingencies which force discriminations." Thus, to the extent that the individuals exposed to a similar situation have divergent reinforcement histories, the current situation, while apparently similar, will be experienced very differently (Parker et al., 1998). In response to a gregarious salesperson, one individual may be overly trusting because he/she has never been "taken advantage of" and thus does not discriminate interpersonal cues associated with illicit sales techniques. A second person, on the other hand, having been taken advantage of in the past, may be overly distrusting, to the point of discriminating generally innocuous cues as indicative of high risk.

One of the differences between cognitive-behavioral and clinical behavior analytic approaches is the willingness to use the DSM as the foundation for understanding problems in living, including those called PDs. Beck and colleagues (1990), for example, provide a comprehensive CBT account of the existing PDs. The DSM is put forth as an etiological descriptive classification scheme. That is, it is intended to describe what symptoms look like and what symptoms are likely to covary, but not why they occur. The goals of such an approach are to avoid alienating potential users by emphasizing a particular approach to etiology and to facilitate communication among professionals. Based on its widespread use, the DSM has doubtless been successful in this regard. Indeed, not alienating users and increasing communication are worthwhile, pragmatic goals. However, some problems with such an approach are also recognized (see Follette & Houts, 1996). One particular concern relates to the DSM's classification of behavior and patterns of behavior according to what it looks like (i.e., its form/appearance/topography) rather than its purpose (i.e., its function). Many behaviors may look alike (e.g., aggression) yet have different functions (e.g., attack versus self-defense) and, conversely, many behaviors may look different (e.g., self-mutilation, binge drinking, binge eating, casual sexual liaisons, derogation of others, etc.) yet serve the same function (e.g., to reduce contact with painful internal states). Behavior analysts have long suggested that behavior cannot be most meaningfully understood taken out of context and based solely on its appearance. Behavior qua behavior is not of interest (Keller & Schoenfeld, 1950; Skinner, 1938). What is of interest is determining the purpose (i.e., function) of the behavior, which requires analysis of environmental antecedents and consequences. All behaviors which serve the same function, regardless of what they look like, are considered to be members of the same response class (Follette, 1997). Focusing on the function of behavior provides an alternative to the structural approach taken by the DSM and the hypothetical cognitive structures proposed by Beck and colleagues (1990).

Attempt to understand the function of behavior. A fully developed functional classification system does not presently exist, but it seems that such a system would likely look very different from the current DSM (Bissett & Hayes, 1999; Follette & Houts, 1996; Hayes, Wilson, Gifford, Follette, & Strosahl, 1996). At present, practicing behavior therapists can simply add functional analysis to a DSM assessment, an approach which appears useful for pragmatic clinical purposes given the current marketplace (Farmer & Nelson-Gray, 1999; Nelson-Gray & Farmer, 1999; Scotti, Morris, McNeil, & Hawkins, 1996). However, such an approach may not be the best way to proceed in advancing clinical science. For example, it is hard to envision how such an approach would feed back to the DSM allowing the criteria to be revised (Bissett & Hayes, 1999).

This leaves a bit of a dilemma. How to write a chapter on PDs without assuming them a priori? Hayes et al. (1996) and Hayes, Strosahl, and Wilson (1999) have suggested that much psychopathology can be understood as indicative of restricted, narrow, rigid behavioral repertoires organized around experiential avoidance (i.e., removing or reducing contact with painful thoughts, images, or internal states). Thus, while many of these restricted repertoires will differ in appearance, they have a similar function, which is problematic to the extent that it prohibits/interferes with pursuit of important life goals. Experiential avoidance has been proposed as a functional diagnostic dimension; that is, a process common in the initiation and/ or maintenance of a range of topographically different problem behaviors (Hayes & Follette, 1992; Hayes et al., 1996). The approach outlined above provides a starting point for entering the PD literature – identify some patterns of responding that are generally agreed upon to be indicative of PD and try to determine the possible functions of these behaviors.

The approach taken here was two-fold. First, when possible, we relied on findings for which there appear to be some agreement and/or which come from research designs that are "behaviorally referenced" (see Bornstein, 2003). The latter refers to research where subjects were exposed to manipulated environments and their responses to these manipulated environments served as the dependent variable. Thus, while the subjects in these experiments were grouped according the elevations or lack there of on measures associated with PD diagnoses, we can focus on the differences or lack there of that were found in the study and how these might be explained from a behavioral perspective and what functional process(es) might account for the differences obtained. In other words, existing empirical findings will be treated as observations of clinically relevant behavior which will be interpreted from a behavioral perspective. This approach seemed the most likely to be fruitful in a field where the modal study involves correlating questionnaires with diagnostic interviews. Second, when data from self-report correlational studies were used we focused on identifying general factors or core characteristics that across studies seem to be predictive of PD functioning; thus, allowing us to remain consistent with the topic area of this chapter while not needlessly accepting the current diagnostic criteria.

Importance of language and cognition. Behavior analytic approaches reject explanations of behavior that require reference to hypothetical structures (e.g., schemas) that must be inferred based on behavior and, hence, are in principle unobservable. However, behavior analysis does not reject a role for private events (e.g., cognition) in the causal sequence. Behavior lies on a continuum: some is only privately observed (e.g., thinking, imagining), while some is publicly observed (e.g., movements), but all of it is in principle observable and hence amenable to analysis. Private responses are not dismissed but are also accorded no special status. Private responses are behavior. Thus, while the initiating causes of behavior are considered to be in the external environment, just as multiple public responses may participate in a chain leading to a terminal response, it is clear that multiple combinations of public and private responses (i.e., behavior-behavior relationships) can be part of a causal sequence (see Hayes & Brownstein, 1986; Malott & Malott, 1991; Skinner, 1945; 1974). Indeed, in understanding complex human behavior, much important responding appears to involve private verbal behavior.

Human beings attend to or disregard the world in which they live. They search for things in that world. They generalize from one thing to another.

They discriminate. They respond to single features or special sets of features as "abstractions" or "concepts." They solve problems by assembling, classifying, arranging, and rearranging things. They describe things and respond to their descriptions, as well as to descriptions made by others. They analyze the contingencies of reinforcement in their world and extract plans and rules which enable them to respond appropriately without direct exposure to the contingencies. They discover and use rules for deriving new rules from old. In all this, and much more, they are simply behaving, and that is true even when they are behaving covertly (Skinner, 1974, p. 245-246).

Relational Frame Theory (Hayes, Barnes-Holmes, & Roche, 2001) is a comprehensive attempt at extending behavior analysis further into the domains captured by the terms language and cognition and, thus, seeks to further our understanding of the complex discriminations, generalizations, verbal descriptions, and derived responding to which Skinner refers in the above quotation. Furthermore, because of RFT's connection to cognition and language, it is not surprising that application of RFT to some relevant PD dimensions will reveal some content overlap with existing cognitive-behavioral theorizing (i.e., Beck et al., 1990). However, to fully appreciate the approach, and because RFT is complex and technical, before applying it directly to relevant findings in the PD literature, a brief overview of some of the critical features is required.

Contemporary Behavioral Approach to PDs

Relational Frame Theory (Hayes et al., 2001)

A relation between stimuli is said to exist if the stimulus functions of one depends upon the stimulus functions of the other (Hayes & Wilson, 1993). Imagine a pigeon is confronted with two lighted response keys. Projected onto each response key is a square. However, one of the squares is larger than the other. Across numerous trials, the pigeon is shown many different sizes of squares, but in all cases one is larger than the other and selecting the larger is reinforced with access to grain. Over time this training will result in the pigeon reliably selecting the larger of the two squares. Such selections will be maintained during unreinforced probe trials using two novel squares and even when the particular large square in a trial is novel and the smaller square is one that has previously served as a larger square. These results suggest that responding is under the control of the relationships between the stimuli and not prior reinforcement for selecting any particular square.

Both nonhuman and human organisms can learn to respond to formal physical relationships between stimuli (e.g., larger, smaller, brighter, duller, same, different; see, Cook, 2002; Reese, 1968, cf. Hayes et al., 2001; Zentall, Galizio, & Critchfield, 2002). In these situations, where the discriminative stimulus involves a formal physical relation between stimuli, such control is considered *nonarbitrary* relational stimulus control (Hayes et al., 2001).

Given that organisms can come to respond to relations between stimuli, is it possible that some organisms (namely humans) learn to respond not only to nonarbitrary relations, but also to arbitrary relations (i.e., those that do not share formal similarities but are based on social convention)? Laboratory studies conducted over the past 30 years using an arbitrary/symbolic match to sample procedure suggest an answer in the affirmative.

Consider the following basic experiment (adapted from Devany, Hayes, & Nelson, 1986; Sidman, 1994). Imagine a child unfamiliar with basic numerals and number names is seated at a small table in front of an experimenter. The experimenter presents the child with various symbols (i.e., stimuli) printed on standard 3.5 by 5 inch index cards. For each trial 4 stimuli are presented on the wooden tabletop - a sample stimulus in the center and three comparison stimuli surrounding the sample. Across trials the children are reinforced for selecting the comparison symbol *one* (designated stimulus B1) rather than *two* or *three,* when in the presence of the sample symbol *1* (designated stimulus A1), the symbol *two* (designated stimulus B2) rather than *one* or *three* in the presence of the sample symbol *2* (designated stimulus A2), and the symbol *three* (designated stimulus B3) rather than *one* or *two* in the presence of the sample symbol *3* (designated stimulus A3). Similarly, selections of *uno* (designated stimulus C1) in the presence of the symbol *one* (B1), *dos* (designated stimulus C2) in the presence of the symbol *two* (B2), and *tres* (designated stimulus C3) in the presence of the symbol *three* (B3) are also reinforced. This match-to-sample (MTS) training continues until the child selects the correct English word conditional on the specific sample numeral and the correct Spanish word conditional on the specific sample English word. The alphanumeric designations representing these trained conditional relations are: A→B, B→C.

Here is where things get interesting. Children with basic language skills reverse the trained relations without any explicit reinforcement for so doing. That is, in the presence of the English names the subject selects the appropriate numeral, and in the presence of the Spanish names the subject selects the corresponding English name. The trained conditional relations are reversed (i.e., derived) without any explicit training, revealing a bi-directionality (i.e., A↔B, B↔C). Similarly, derived relations are also witnessed between the numerals and Spanish names. When Spanish names are used as samples, participants select corresponding numerals, and when numerals are used as samples, participants select the corresponding Spanish names. This occurs with no further training and no explicit reinforcement for so doing. Thus, the trained conditional relations are not only reversed but also become equivalence relations (A ↔ B, B ↔ C, A ↔ C, or A = B = C).

The result of training six conditional relations was that twelve additional relations were derived without explicit training and reinforcement. Such derived relations have been widely demonstrated following arbitrary/symbolic MTS training (Hayes et al., 2001; Horne & Lowe, 1996; Saunders & Green, 1999; Sidman, 1994; Tierney & Bracken, 1998) and suggest that humans can learn to respond not only to nonarbitrary stimulus relations, but also to *arbitrary* stimulus relations – those involving no formal physical similarity.

The suggestion is that this ability to respond to arbitrary stimulus relations is learned as a natural part of the conditioning histories typical of verbal human beings. For instance, a child may often hear things like *x* goes with, is similar to, or is equal to *y* and when as a listener he/she has responded to *x* in all (or many of) the ways he/she has responded to *y*, similar consequences have followed. Thus, across many particular *x*s and *y*s the common property (abstraction) is the way in which the stimuli are related (Hayes et al., 2001). What is learned is more than particular relations, but how to relate stimuli in particular ways. With respect to equivalence relations, the abstracted property can be represented by the following *frame:* _____ = _____. Once abstracted, such a frame can house any stimuli (it is arbitrarily applicable or generalizable) and given appropriate contextual cues ("Uno is equal to ____ ?") comes to control responding ("one"). Thus, verbally competent participants enter symbolic MTS training with the necessary history to readily derive equivalence relations.

The equivalence frame (or frame of coordination) captures one particular abstracted, arbitrarily applicable, way of relating stimuli, but there are numerous others. Through a similar process of multiple exemplar training, as described above, additional ways of relating stimuli may be developed (Dymond & Barnes, 1995; 1996; Hayes & Barnes, 1997; Steele & Hayes, 1991). These different ways of relating stimuli are captured via opposition, comparison, hierarchical, temporal, causal/conditional, and perspective-taking frames.

Once stimuli are framed relationally, conditioning relevant to one stimulus is made relevant to the other stimuli to which it is related. This is most easily recognized, and most well researched, with equivalence frames. Once equivalence frames have been established, any variable that has an effect on one member can have an effect on other related stimuli. For instance, building on the experiment previously described, if clapping is reinforced in the presence of '1' and waving in the presence of '2', presenting 'uno' will produce clapping and 'dos' will produce waving - a transformation of discriminative stimulus functions (Barnes et al., 1995). Similarly, if '1' is paired with negative feedback on a task, and '2' is paired with positive feedback, presenting 'uno' could now serve as a conditioned punisher and 'dos' as a conditioned reinforcer - a transformation of consequential functions (Hayes, Kohlenberg, & Hayes, 1991). Moreover, pairing '1' with electric shock produces a transformation of respondent functions such that 'uno' now elicits a galvanic skin response (Dougher, Augustson, Markham, Greenway, & Wulfert, 1994). These outcomes are described as indicative of transformation of function through relational frames.

Hayes et al. (2001) summarize RFT as follows: "RFT is a behavior analytic approach to human language and cognition. RFT treats relational responding as a generalized operant, and thus appeals to a history of multiple-exemplar training. Specific types of relational responding, [are] termed relational frames..."(p. 141).

Verbally competent humans learn not only specific relations between stimuli, but also, with experience, to relate stimuli generally in particular ways (e.g., an equivalence frame). These generalized relational frames can "house" any stimuli, allow untrained relations to be derived (e.g., if A=B and B=C then C=A), and reveal transformation of stimulus functions in accord with the frame (e.g., if B is paired with shock, presentation of A and C elicit a galvanic skin response). How stimuli are related, the relations that are derived, and the functions that are transformed, depend on the individual's history and the current environmental context. This basic conceptualization is the foundation upon which complex human behavior such as language and cognition is understood from an RFT perspective (Hayes et al., 2001). Indeed, what defines a stimulus as verbal from an RFT perspective is participation in derived stimulus relations, such as equivalence relations (Barnes-Holmes, Stewart, Dymond, & Roche, 2000; Hayes et al., 2001; Hayes & Wilson, 1993).

The MTS procedure and the resulting derived stimulus relations and transformation of stimulus functions are interesting in that they provide an experimental parallel to many aspects of natural language and cognition (Hayes et al., 2001; Sidman, 1994). Semantics is the study of words and their meanings. From an RFT perspective, words enter into equivalence frames with objects and events in the environment, such that words are now said to have meaning or to stand for the objects or events (e.g., "dog" means furry, four-legged, thing that pants and barks) and can occasion many of the responses generally evoked by the actual environmental events (e.g., hearing "bumble bee" can produce anxiety and hypervigilance similar to that produced by seeing a bumble bee).

As our experimental example illustrated, training six conditional relations yielded twelve derived relations, demonstrating the emergence of novel, productive performances, which are considered a hallmark of human language and cognition. A person familiar with the distinction between "good" and "bad" can be told that "benevolent" is similar to "good" (i.e., benevolent is put in an equivalence frame with good) and now use the word effectively and respond to it appropriately. Likewise, when told "malevolent is the opposite of benevolent" (a frame of opposition) the person would be able to derive, and respond effectively to, malevolent as "bad" (this process may be analogous to what linguistic researchers refer to as fast mapping). Also, to the extent that "good" has conditioned reinforcing properties and "bad" has conditioned aversive properties, these might be transferred to benevolent and malevolent, such that hearing "that was quite benevolent" following some response might serve a reinforcing function, while hearing "that was quite malevolent" following some response might serve a punishing function.

Combining equivalence frames (classes of nouns, verbs, and objects) with temporal frames (e.g., noun then verb then object) leads to entirely novel, grammatically correct utterances, "Dawson bombarded Timbuktu." Other combinations of frames may play a role in verbal self-regulation and self-denigration. For instance, if "studying" is in a causal frame with "getting good grades" and combined with a temporal frame of "study first then relax" playing video games before studying becomes less reinforcing. If one gets an *F* on an exam, he/she could conclude "I am a failure." This perspective-taking frame (I am a _____), places "I" and the evaluative term "failure" in a relation just as easily as it relates "I" and a purely descriptive term such as "female." In terms of the frame, these become equally "true." Thus, the arbitrary applicable nature of relational frames allows for much novelty, productivity, and indirect learning, but also has a potential downside in failing to promote certain discriminations (such as between evaluations and descriptions). Moreover, even factual descriptions can become reactive. "I am bald" is not just a description of my appearance, but because "bald" is related to other stimuli (e.g., unattractive, old) that have aversive functions, such self-knowledge, can be both descriptively accurate and psychologically painful.

RFT and Core Characteristics of PDs

RFT provides an empirical basis for understanding how verbal stimuli can come to share psychological characteristics with events and, thus, how thoughts/images/emotional states can become events to be avoided or from which to escape. RFT suggests that dominance by indirect (verbal) functions of stimuli is a fundamental quality of human language and not in-and-of-itself pathological. Indeed, in many domains the fact that symbols can substitute for actual events is adaptive. This is especially the case as it relates to the external environment. For example, verbal descriptions can be passed on from parent to child, mentor to student, writer to reader (e.g., don't touch the stove top when the burner is on), such that the latter can behave more effectively. That is, they can learn from the experiences of the former (who may have learned themselves from the experiences of someone else) without having to have the direct experiences themselves (e.g., touching a hot stove and getting burned). However, verbal descriptions can also be wrong and as such when followed inhibit contact with corrective direct experiences. This appears to be especially the case as it relates to the internal environment, such as when one attempts to escape/avoid thoughts and feelings, particularly because such thoughts or feelings are evaluated verbally as "bad" and are viewed as impediments that need to be removed or reduced in order to pursue ones goals in life (e.g., only after I feel motivated can I get and keep a job). The risk is that such an approach can lead to disproportionately internally-focused change efforts at the expense of attempts to change overt behavior or problematic circumstances directly. Indeed, Hayes and colleagues (Hayes et al., 2001; Hayes et al., 1996; Wilson & Blackledge, 2000) have suggested that much of psychopathology can be understood in the context of constricted, inflexible behavioral repertoires, which often appear centered around escaping/avoiding contact with negative thoughts, emotions, cravings, urges, images, etc. (i.e., experiential avoidance). Is there any evidence that such an analysis applies to PDs?

The available data, while limited and coming largely from cross-sectional, correlational studies, is not unsupportive and allows for identification of some general factors that across a range of studies seem to be predictive of PD functioning.

Neuroticism, as defined in the five-factor model, is a construct representing the tendency to experience a range of negative thoughts and feelings; that is, to experience anxiety, anger, depression, shame/embarrassment, and uncontrollable urges/cravings (Costa & Widiger, 2002). A number of studies have found that neuroticism is a general characteristic reported by individuals across PD categories (Schroeder, Wormworth, & Livesley, 2002; Trull, 1992). These data suggest pervasive aversive internal stimulation (chronic negative affect) is a prominent feature in a range of PDs. Moreover, studies relating coping styles to personality pathology indicate the prominence of dysfunctional, emotion-focused, rather than problem-focused, coping (Endler, Parker, & Butcher, 1993; Vollrath, Alnaes, & Torgersen, 1996). Across the PD categories escape/avoidance coping appears disproportionately prevalent (Watson, 2001; Watson & Sinha, 1999-2000). Examination of the items comprising escape and avoidance coping (on the Ways of Coping Questionnaire, see Folkman & Lazarus, 1985) suggest the use of strategies that function to reduce contact with both external (e.g., avoiding being with people) and internal (e.g., trying to make myself feel better by eating, drinking, smoking, using drugs or medication) events. Additionally, the remaining escape/avoidance strategies involve passive verbal strategies that are unlikely to be effective (e.g., hoping a miracle will happen, wishing the problem will go away, or refusing to believe the problem is occurring). Consistent with the neuroticism and escape/avoidance coping findings, Cloninger and colleagues (Cloninger, 2000; Svrakic, Draganic, Hill, Bayon, Przybeck, & Cloninger, 2002; Svrakic, Whitehead, Przybeck, & Cloninger, 1993), using outpatient and inpatient populations, have identified low self-directedness as a feature associated with all of the PDs (with the possible exception of schizoid). Low self-directedness is characterized by reports of purposeless, helplessness, poor self-acceptance, irresponsibility, and poor impulse control (Cloninger, 2000). Combining the neuroticism, escape-avoidance, and low self-directedness findings, a general picture of PD functioning emerges that is consistent with the trap set by pursuit of experiential avoidance. By the time the individual is identified as high on a dimension of PD, he/she is having chronic experiences of negative internal states, which are coped with ineffectively through the use of experiential avoidance or passive coping responses that fail to solve the problem that generated the negative arousal and further contributes to poor self-acceptance, purposelessness, and helplessness, and so on.

RFT and The Self

The preceding references to self-regulation, self-evaluations, self-knowledge, and self-directness set the stage for describing an RFT analysis of what is meant by the term "self" and why this may have some relevance to PDs.

In this chapter we are dealing with a behavioral perspective on disorders attributed to the person (i.e., *personality* disorders) or the self. From a behavioral perspective we do not approach the self as a thing/entity to be understood, but instead explore the variables that lead one to attribute something to the self (Parker et al. 1998; Skinner, 1974). We speak, for example, of self-awareness/self-knowledge when one can discriminate his/her own behavior and the variables that control it. Such a person "who has been 'made aware of himself'... is in a better position to predict and control his own behavior" (Skinner, 1974, p.35). For instance, Skinner distinguishes creative thinking from self-control based, in part, on awareness. That is, "in self-control the individual can identify the behavior to be controlled while in creative thinking he cannot" (Skinner, 1953, p. 229). Once the behavior to be controlled is identified (e.g., getting out of bed on time), the individual is then in a position to manipulate his/her environment (e.g., putting the alarm clock several feet away from the bed) to preempt control by the usual controlling variables (e.g., reaching out and hitting the snooze button). Likewise, a person who "knows" that he/she makes impulsive purchases may choose to leave credit cards or cash in the car while window shopping. In these circumstances, "the self which is concerned with self-knowing functions concurrently with the behavioral system which it describes" (Skinner, 1953, p. 287-288).

Self-as-context/perspective

RFT builds on this idea suggesting that a human sense of self occurs when an individual as a locus of action and his/her actions enter into relational frames (Barnes-Holmes, Hayes, & Dymond, 2001; Barnes-Holmes et al., 2000). To illustrate how this might develop, consider a game the authors' often play with their young son Malcolm. Malcolm is asked to identify his ongoing behavior and discriminate it from that of others. We ask things like "Who's standing up? Is Malcolm standing up? Is Mommy standing up? Who's wearing diapers? Is Malcolm wearing diapers? Is daddy wearing diapers? Who's playing with the cars? Is Malcolm playing with cars? Is Lenny (the cat) playing with the cars?" In all of these cases he must differentiate his own behavior (for whom the answers are affirmative) from that of others (for whom the answers are negative). He is learning self-awareness, to discriminate his own behavior, but he is also learning that his answers come from a specific locus. This specific locus is "Malcolm, I, me" and is in contrast to "Mommy, Daddy, Lenny, and you." Across many exemplars a generalized personal perspective taking frame can emerge. For instance, through Malcolm is standing, Malcolm is wearing diapers, Malcolm is playing cars, etc., etc., he learns not only to discriminate his own behavior (what is being spoken about) but also that it is Malcolm doing the discriminating.

Self-as-content/The conceptualized self

Once such perspective taking frames are abstracted the self as perspective can be related to a host of other stimuli or events. For instance, the descriptors, "I am bald, I am a male, I am 6 feet tall, I am wearing khaki pants and a white dress shirt" would be useful for someone meeting the first author at the airport. These are essentially factual descriptors of the self much like saying "the stop sign is red" is a factual description of that object. Consider the following set of descriptors, however: "I am a loser, I am a failure, I am worthless and good for nothing." These seem different from the preceding list and they are in the sense that they are evaluations (they would not help someone to pick one out at the airport) but notice that the nature of the frame is identical across instances – _____ (personal perspective) am _____ (descriptor or evaluation). The generic perspective taking frame does not distinguish factual descriptions from evaluations and because the frame is just as able to "hold" evaluations as it is factual descriptions we can easily fail to discriminate between the two. The result is that *I am a loser* can appear to be as much a real, inherent aspect of the individual as is *I am 6 feet tall*.

This distinction is important because evaluations often have psychological functions because of established relations with other stimuli. For instance, the term "loser" might have initially been learned as a derogatory term in peer interactions or in the context of failing to win at sports or in other competitive environments, which endowed the term "loser" with an aversive function. Such an aversive function would be expected, based on empirical demonstrations of transformation of function, to be present when the self is identified as a loser. Thus, we might expect one to want to escape from such an evaluation. Moreover, even "pure" descriptions (e.g., I am bald) can be altered when combined with evaluations (e.g., Bald men are unattractive) that lead to new derived relations (e.g., I am unattractive) and the accompanying aversive functions that may now be present (i.e., those associated with unattractiveness).

The sum of such evaluations and descriptions framed from the perspective of I/me/myself is referred to as the "conceptualized self" or "self-as-content." The conceptualized self is not a thing but a descriptive label. Much like the term *behavioral repertoire* is a summary label for all the behavior an organism is capable of emitting, even if it is not presently so doing (Catania, 1991), conceptualized self is the summary label for evaluations and descriptions framed from the perspective of I/me/myself. As described by Barnes-Holmes et al. (2001, p. 126-127):

> The conceptualized self is the most readily accessible verbal sense of self, virtually by definition. This sense of self is what we tell others or ourselves about ourselves. It tends to be well elaborated, multi-layered, and rigid. It is well elaborated because the conceptualized self touches on virtually every aspect of life as verbally known (e.g., history, situation, preferences, abilities, private events). It is multi-layered because there are strong social contingencies attached to self in this sense. If people are asked to speak about themselves, they will usually present a sanitized version of the story. It will typically be socially desirable (indeed it is a sign of psychopathology if it is not, Edwards, 1970), and relatively well worn. If pressed more negative or difficult material will be presented, but more material will exist that is only told to close friends, or to no one but onself. The conceptualized self is rigid because it is historical... History cannnot change in a literal sense, and a great deal of the conceptualized self purports merely to report what happened... This process of reporting is not seen... Further, the conceptualized self is used as a touchstone in verbal explanations and reasons given to others. The social/verbal community tends to punish the

speaker for changing these stories.... If the conceptualized self and its response implications change, the person is "wrong" – a fate that verbal humans avoid at all costs... Rigidity of the conceptualized self, and of behavior as it bears on the conceptualized self, is the result.

Defending the conceptualized self: Application to grandiose self-esteem, a central aspect of NPD. According to the DSM-IV-TR (2000), the core of NPD is a grandiose self-concept, accompanying need for admiration, and a lack of empathy. As the DSM arranges the items in the criteria sets for the PDs according to diagnostic importance, the first and, thus, most important feature for diagnosing NPD is this grandiose sense of self-importance.

A series of studies over the last decade has explored the differential responses of college students with elevated or low scores on the Narcissistic Personality Inventory (NPI) to various manipulations related to self-concept. Rhodewalt and Morf (1998) found that following positive feedback about performance on an intelligence test, high NPI subjects attributed their success to their ability more so than did control subjects. The high NPI subjects also reported greater increases in self-esteem following such success and, in a separate study, reported greater enjoyment and engaged in the intelligence test for a longer duration under "free choice" conditions (Morf, Weir, & Davidov, 2000). Moreover, when they subsequently received negative performance feedback, those with elevated NPI scores reported greater anger (Rhodewalt & Morf, 1998), were more likely to aggress against the peer who gave the negative evaluation (Bushman & Baumeister, 1998), and when told that a peer outperformed them, rated the peer more negatively (Morf & Rhodewalt, 1993). Interestingly, subsequent positive feedback resulted in greater increases in self-esteem compared to controls (Rhodewalt & Morf, 1998).

These results are illustrative for a number of reasons. First, they demonstrate the importance of understanding behavior in context: responding changed in accord with the environmental manipulations. For instance, those with elevated NPI scores rated peers more negatively only when outperformed by that peer (Morf & Rhodewalt, 1993) and showed heightened aggressive tendencies only in response to an insult and only toward the source of the negative evaluation (Bushman & Baumeister, 1998). In addition, while the authors focused on group differences, the data also often revealed general patterns of context sensitive responding. For instance, even low NPI participants tended to rate a better performing peer more negatively, attribute success to their ability, and show an increase in anger when a failure followed a success and a boost in self-esteem when a success followed a failure (Morf & Rhodewalt, 1993; Rhodewalt & Morf, 1998). Thus, the general pattern was not different for those with elevated NPI scores, just more extreme.

How might we account for the pattern observed? At a general level the role of reinforcing and aversive stimuli is apparent. Success is a potent conditioned reinforcer which might lead to increases in approach behavior and heightened esteem ratings. Failure is a strong aversive which might increase the reinforcing value of behavior that removes it, such as a subsequent success or degrading the better performing peer. To extend this line of reasoning, the group differences might be interpreted as indicative of differential reinforcer effectiveness. That is, while participants in general appeared sensitive to achievement-based feedback, those with elevated NPI scores were more sensitive. Just as food is more reinforcing to a food deprived organism, by analogy, success or failure relative to a peer might be especially reinforcing or punishing for high NPI participants.

The participants in the experiments received partial course credit for participation; thus, we can understand why showing up and completing the experiment would be important, but how is it that the feedback given during the experiment, that has no tangible consequences for the individual, becomes important? That it did suggests that the experimental events provoked verbal constructions that made particular consequences relevant. In other words, the experimental events provided a context for relating stimuli in a particular way (relational framing), which resulted in certain stimulus functions being transformed and, thus, made psychologically present during the experiment. Specifically, the experimental instructions established an evaluative context promoting perspective taking frames involving self-discriminations, i.e., identifying how one did on the task – "I performed well," "I performed poorly," "I succeeded," "I failed," etc. Doing well or poorly can be seen purely as a description, simply a self-discrimination, which should be non-reactive (e.g., in the same way accurately saying "I put on my shoes" would be non-reactive for most people reading this chapter). However, in an evaluative context the stimuli "succeeded" or "failed" for verbal humans have conditioned reinforcing and punishing functions and are likely in equivalence relations with many other stimuli, such that doing well or doing poorly allows for additional positive or aversive stimulus functions to be made relevant in the moment. In the context of an intelligence test, doing well would clearly evoke relations with intelligent, smart, etc., while doing poorly would evoke relations with unintelligent, dumb, etc., which likely have powerful psychological consequences associated with them. Thus, the initial straightforward descriptive discrimination "I did well" becomes the derived evaluative "I am smart." Furthermore, frames of comparison allow "I am smart" to blossom into "I am smarter than others." Substitute "poorly" for well and "dumb" for smart to understand how the same process occurs in the opposite direction.

Why would the evaluative context be more reactive for some (i.e., those called narcissists)? The answer from a behavioral perspective would, of course, have to lie in their reinforcement history and how that history impacted the derived relations and transformed stimulus functions made present in an achievement-oriented, evaluative context. Unfortunately, reinforcement history is a relatively neglected area in behavior analysis (Salzinger, 1996), but drawing from current psychological theories of NPD (see Table 11.1 above), a potentially relevant aspect might be a history involving a disproportionately high amount of reinforcement (praise, affection, etc.) for competence/achievement with less or little reinforcement that was not contingent on success in some comparative/competence-based context. This discrimination training could result in greater control by stimulus features involving interpersonal comparisons and transformation of consequential functions for coming out on top. In other words, interpersonal situations come to evoke stimulus relations characterized by frames of comparison (better than, smarter than, more competent than, etc), such that others come to be seen not as potential friends, sources of interpersonal connection and mutual affection, but rather as a sources of self-confirmation (someone to be better than, smarter than, more competent than, or admired by). Reinforcement then becomes akin to a zero-sum game – there is little to no transformation of positive consequential functions for doing one's best, reinforcement is contingent on besting the other. Indeed, Wallace and Baumeister (2002) recently found that those scoring high on the NPI underachieved under experimental conditions that did not allow them to readily distinguish their level of performance compared to others, but performed significantly better when task demands were changed such that good performances would readily distinguish the subject compared to others. These data further point to the importance of regular positive comparisons for these individuals. In addition, in the absence of such comparisons, there may become an incompleteness in the frame, and, hence, the conceptualized self. Remember, the conceptualized self is what one tells oneself about oneself. As such, when an important part of this involves telling oneself that one is better than others, lack of regular contact with objects/events/individuals that provide positive comparisons leaves little to be said. In this sense, the conceptualized self may become unstable. Consistent with this interpretation, Morf and Rhodewalt (2001) describe several daily dairy studies showing high NPI participants' self-esteem was more variable than controls and more highly correlated with social interactions that supported their sense of self than controls.

This need for social sources of evaluation does not come without risk, as there is no guarantee of success, and failure at some point seems almost guaranteed. When such a failure happens, and events are constructed in terms of frames of comparison such that the other person's gain is the NPI individual's loss, the self is now not simply incomplete, but is under attack. Here is where anger, aggression, and derogation of others are employed (Bushman & Baumeister, 1998). Just as admiration from others is especially reinforcing (see Wallace & Baumeister, 2002) because it is consistent with the verbally constructed self, criticisms or insults are highly aversive (see Bushman & Baumeister, 1998) and establish retaliatory aggression as highly reinforcing. Thus, a paradox of narcissism, how one can have an apparent grandiose self-concept and yet be very vulnerable to seemingly innocuous threats can be understood quite readily in RFT terms. It is interesting to note that while implicating different processes, this RFT interpretation shares much with Morf and Rhodewalt's (2001) self-regulatory processing model.

Self-as-process

If self-as-content is analogous to how one responds to the question "Tell me about yourself?" self-as-verbal process is how one responds to the question "What are you feeling, right now?" Self-as-verbal process involves frames of coordination between various internal and bodily states (perspiration, increased heart rate, feeling a hot flush, butterflies in the stomach) and conventional verbal labels for these states (e.g., "anxious") that then enter into frames of personal perspective (e.g., I am anxious; Barnes-Holmes et al., 2001).

The ability to identify and label internal states must be taught by the social/ verbal community. Such training is usually accomplished by those in the social/ verbal community through the use of public accompaniments to internal states (Skinner, 1953). For instance, during a long car trip a parent notices her child in the back seat of the car holding her stomach, grimacing, and moaning and asks, "Are you feeling sick to your stomach?" To the extent that the public accompaniments are correlated with internal stimulation the parent can reliably teach the child to tact the internal state. It is in this way that children are taught to label physical states with words such as "car sick," "nauseated," "hot," "cold," "tired," "hungry," etc. Such a repertoire is extremely beneficial both for the child and the parent. The child can now more effectively communicate with the parent and the parent is better able to respond and help the child manage or terminate such states. The child learns the importance the social/verbal community places on internal states and by using the label the child allows the parent to be a more effective problem solver on his/her behalf, helping not only to solve the immediate problem but also modeling effective problem-solving and prevention strategies.

The process is not a simple one; however, and there is little way to know how truly accurate one has been in teaching such verbal labels. This is because the parent only has access to the public accompaniments and these may be imperfectly correlated with the internal states (Skinner, 1953). When the public accompaniments are imperfectly correlated or when parents are inattentive or inconsistent, the training in identifying internal states is likewise inconsistent leading to the child speaking inconsistently about the presence of such internal stimulation.

Escaping self-as-process: Application to self-injury, a central aspect of BPD. Deliberate, intentional self-injury (or parasuicide) is not exclusive to borderline personality disorder, but represents the behavior pattern most commonly associated with a BPD diagnosis (Linehan, 1993). There is a growing literature suggesting that childhood sexual abuse, emotional neglect, and, possibly, physical abuse, are risk factors for adult self-harm (Gratz, 2003). Furthermore, it appears that those who engage in self-harm as adults do so because it functions to reduce negative emotions (Gratz, 2003). How might it be that childhood maltreatment contributes to the use of self-injury as a coping strategy in adulthood?

A repertoire for recognizing and labeling emotions must be taught in the same fashion as other internal state labels reviewed above. In typical development, emotional labeling begins early in life (2-3 yrs of age) as caretakers identify and model emotions and are responsive to children's affective displays (Bretherton, Fritz, Zahn-Waxler, & Ridgeway, 1986; Cicchetti & Beegly, 1987; Denham, Zoller, & Couchoud, 1994; Dunn, Bretherton, & Munn, 1987). However, in maltreating environments where caretakers are neglectful or abusive, the use of verbal labels may not be consistently reinforced in the presence of the relevant internal state. The result is incomplete or biased recognition of emotions (Pollak, Cicchetti, Hornung, & Reed, 2000) and difficulty speaking consistently about a range of emotional states – an outcome called alexithymia or "lacking words for emotions" (Sifneos, 1996; Taylor & Bagby, 2000). Zanarini, Frankenburg, Reich, Marino, Lewis, Williams et al. (2000) found that 84% of 358 BPD inpatients reported experiencing biparental child abuse or neglect, including both parents denying the validity of their thoughts and feelings. Linehan (1993) describes rearing conditions such as these, in which mention of negative emotions is met by erratic, inappropriate, and extreme responses, as an "invalidating environment." In an invalidating environment, it appears quite likely that the child will fail to acquire consistent emotional labels, which has the added consequence of the child failing to learn the social importance of such communications (in validating environments) or how to solve the problem that elicited the negative internal state.

Moreover, displays of negative affect, such as crying or signs of distress, may produce disapproval, avoidance, or further punishment, so that maltreated children increasingly attempt to inhibit emotional displays (Mash & Wolfe, 2002). When the parents are the cause of painful states, as often happens in cases of emotional, physical, or sexual abuse, another layer is added. By sexually, physically, and/or verbally assaulting the child, the parents produce negative emotions; however, these are often met with further invalidation. In the case of sexual abuse, the child's emotional reaction is secondary to keeping the secret, which may have to be done under threat. In the context of abusive discipline, the invalidation may be justified because the child "got what she had coming" for misbehaving (e.g., "Quit crying or I'll give you something to really cry about!" "You should feel lucky all you got was slapped, my father would have killed me."). The punishment of affective displays (and the co-occurring internal state) promotes suppression of affect and paradoxically contributes to internal states (even though not effectively labeled, but because of being correlated with punishment) becoming increasingly aversive and something to be avoided. The diffuse internal state becomes analogous to a warning stimulus in signaled shock avoidance paradigms. Thus, negative emotions do not come to occasion problem solving regarding the events that triggered the emotions, but rather the negative emotions become the problem to be solved.

While sometimes the child may experience physical punishment (e.g., being given something to cry about), often the punishment is verbal disapproval or derogation ("get control of yourself, calm down, quit being such a baby."). Among other effects, this verbal disapproval contributes to the internal state becoming verbally "wrong" or "bad." That is, a frame of coordination develops between affective displays and internal states and "wrong/bad," words that quickly in life (usually because they are used in discipline) have become conditioned punishers. Thus, the aversive functions of "bad, wrong" etc. can be made present when internal states occur. A physiological state of the body has now been rendered "bad." Moreover, as the internal states occur within the skin (it is the person who is having the "bad" emotions), "bad" can be readily extended through a personal perspective frame, such as *I am bad*, transferring its related verbal baggage to the self. That is, not only is the internal state "bad," but so too is the being, or locus referred to as I/me/myself, that is having the emotion. This process further supports the verbal castigation received from maltreating caretakers, and over time could become especially problematic because the being/locus can be "bad" even in the absence of the "bad" internal state. (The latter point may be related to an outcome seen clinically in which clients are described as having core low self-esteem, chronic negative self-attributions, or dysfunctional core beliefs, e.g., I am worthless, useless, unlovable, stupid, good for nothing, etc.).

The individual who has difficulty identifying emotions using conventional labels, such that social support and assistance regarding the events that produced the internal state cannot be effectively sought, and who has been shaped to suppress and avoid affect displays and labels internal states as "bad" is in a poor position to succeed in the larger social/verbal community. In fact, the learning history of such individuals is often such a poor fit with the norms of the larger social/verbal community that the problems are amplified rather than corrected. For instance, the social/verbal community supports the notion that lack of understanding and control over emotions is "bad" and negative emotions are something to be gotten rid of (e.g., they are a sign of pathology). Thus, the tendency toward emotional inhibition and escape from and avoidance of emotion persists (see Krause, Mendelson, & Lynch, 2003).

An individual with the above conditioning history is highly likely to lack the ability to recognize emotions, attempt to suppress or block contact with internal states, and, when contacted, identify such states as "bad," amplifying their aversive properties and extending them to the locus labeled self. Indeed, a comparison of BPD and non-BPD clients found those diagnosed with BPD were less able to differentiate feelings, less able to accurately identify emotions from facial expressions, and more intense in their reactions to negative emotions (Levine, Marziali, & Hood, 1997). Such a person may proceed through parts of life rather emotionally unaware and not in acute distress. However, when bad things happen, and they inevitably will, the individual is now placed in contact with the negative state and recognizes that such a state is "bad." Additionally, the individual has trouble clearly communicating about this state to others, and, furthermore, knows that such confusion and lack of control is itself "bad" as is the self that has such experiences. This is a powerfully aversive experience from which one would be expected to be eager to escape. Indeed, a recent case study found that bouts of self-injury were preceded by progressive increases in self-reported emotional arousal and corresponding increases in cortisol excretion (a biological marker of stress/arousal), which were temporarily decreased following bouts of self-injury (Sachsse, von der Heyde, & Huether, 2002). That understood, it is important to acknowledge the myriad layers involved. The individual may seek escape from confusion, escape from contact with the internal state, and/or escape from contact with her "bad, out of control, confused" self. Thus, any potent escape response would have to impact these overlapping, interwoven sources of aversive stimulation. Unfortunately, self-injury seems to contact these sources too, at least according to those who engage in such behavior. Studies asking individuals who self-injure to describe their reasons for the behavior reveal that an overwhelming majority indicate that self-injury provides a clear expression of anger/pain, a distraction from negative thoughts, an escape from bad feelings, a way of punishing oneself, and a way of establishing a sense of control (Brown, Comtois, & Linehan, 2002; Warm, Murray, & Fox, 2003). While data derived from self-reports of persons who engage in self-injury is not equivalent to a functional analysis, it certainly points to relevant purposes such behavior may be serving (Brown et al., 2002).

These data accord nicely with what might be expected given the current analysis which speculates on the history and potential mechanisms by which childhood maltreatment might be turned inward (Guralnik & Simeon, 2001; cf. Brown et al., 2002) or by which invalidation could lead to self-invalidation and emotional avoidance (Krause et al., 2003; Linehan, 1993). Specifically, the described functions of self-injury are consistent with the suggestion that negative emotions do not come to occasion problem solving regarding the events that produced the emotions, but rather the negative emotions become the problem to be solved. Thus, self-injury is one member of a class of behaviors (substance abuse, binge eating, sexual liaisons) that in the short-run may address negative affect, but leave the origin of the negative affect, and thus, the likelihood of future problems unchanged. Furthermore, these behaviors are frowned on socially and often produce later shame and guilt and have other negative long-term consequences (e.g., disfigurement).

Verbal constructions of others

Earlier it was suggested that arbitrarily applicable personal perspective taking frames occur as the result of a conditioning history with a verbal/social community that has consistently reinforced, across innumerable individual instances, speaking about experience and behavior from a consistent locus described as I/me/myself (Barnes-Holmes et al., 2001). The arbitrarily applicable nature of the personal perspective taking frame allows not only for events and behavior to be framed as something you did, are doing, or will do, but also allows attributions and evaluations to be framed as something you are (e.g., I am a good person). The sum total of the latter comprises the conceptualized self. In addition, the perspective taking frame contributes to one connecting I/me/myself as a locus with events occurring under the skin (e.g., I am anxious), resulting in what is described as self-as-process.

In our description of the proposed multiple exemplar training establishing I/me/myself as a locus of self, we have alluded to, but not specifically mentioned, the simultaneous training of you/other/yourself to refer to the locus of others. Across multiple instances, when referring to one's own behavior or experiences personal references are reinforced (and references to others are punished/corrected), while when referring to someone else's behavior or experiences references to the appropriate other are reinforced (and references to oneself are punished/corrected). The result is a generalized other perspective-taking frame (Barnes-Holmes et al.,

2001). The arbitrarily applicable nature of the other perspective-taking frame allows not only for events and behavior to be framed as something someone else did, is doing, or will do, but also allows attributions and evaluations to be framed as something they are (i.e., _____ is a good person). The sum total of the latter, with respect to a particular other or class of others (e.g., psychologists), comprises the conceptualized other.[2]

How another is conceptualized can alter how one behaves towards that person. Imagine a friend is going to introduce you to a new person ("Chad") who is described as being "a loose cannon." When meeting the physically large and vocally loud Chad you might find yourself "walking on egg shells," watching him very closely for signs of annoyance, and exiting the conversation as rapidly as possible after the introduction. The constructed nature of Chad is evident in that you are not simply responding to the stimulus properties of Chad (e.g., his size and vocal quality) but also to "loose cannon" and the stimuli that are in derived relations with "loose cannon" (which may or may not be based on a past history with actual "loose cannons"). That such responding is based, at least in part, on a verbal construction is also evident if we imagine that your friend now takes you aside and indicates he was "pulling your leg" and actually Chad is a "big teddy bear," which now results in greater interpersonal approach behavior from you.

The verbal stimuli (i.e., information) provided about Chad (that he is a "loose cannon" or "big teddy bear") impacts the relations that are derived with respect to him and alters Chad's stimulus properties. To further illustrate, imagine now that two people are introduced to Chad without hearing any prior characterizations of him. Person A responds privately to the physically large and vocally loud stimulus properties of Chad with "loose cannon," while Person B responds privately with "big teddy bear." When Person A responds to Chad as a "loose cannon" other stimuli in equivalence relations with "loose cannon" emerge (e.g., aggressive, unpredictable, dangerous, obnoxious) and the functions of these stimuli become present in the current environment (consistent with transformation of function), such that Person

---

[2]Interestingly, from this perspective PDs as currently defined can be viewed as representing generic constructed others of PD researchers and theoreticians (especially those associated with the DSM Task Force and Personality Disorders Work Group). To the extent that these constructed others are internally consistent (represent clusters of behaviors that tend to covary) recognizing one symptom as a member of a particular diagnosis may usefully lead to asking about other symptoms that may be present at higher than base rates (Farmer & Nelson-Gray, 1999). However, there may also be untoward effects. That is, seeing one behavior in terms of other behaviors within a particular diagnosis may also suggest the presence of features that are not present; thus, leading the clinician away from other important features that are present (Clarkin & Sanderson, 2000).

A feels unsettled, on-edge, and on-guard around Chad. On the other hand, when Person B responds to Chad as a "big teddy bear" stimuli in equivalence relations with "big teddy bear" emerge (e.g., harmless, friendly, good-natured) and the functions of these stimuli become present in the current environment (consistent with transformation of function), such that Person B feels comfortable and relaxed around Chad. The preceding example illustrates how two people apparently exposed to identical stimuli can react quite differently. In reality, the stimuli are only superficially identical. Given the conditioning histories of the individuals involved, the stimuli were experienced functionally quite differently leading to different initial verbal constructions which made unique stimulus functions present for each person.

Attracting verbally constructed others: Submissiveness, assertiveness, and interpersonal dependency. The DSM-IV-TR indicates the "essential feature of DPD is a pervasive and excessive need to be taken care of that leads to submissive and clinging behavior and fears of separation" (APA, 2000, p. 721). Such a conceptualization is consistent with the long history of emphasizing passivity in diagnosing DPD, which dates back to the DSM-I's "passive-dependent personality disorder" (APA, 1952). Despite the historical connection between passivity and interpersonal dependency, recent investigations emphasize the importance of contextual features in predicting whether those described as dependent or non-dependent will behave passively or actively.

In several studies (Baird, 2000; Bornstein, Riggs, Hill, & Calabrese, 1996) undergraduate females who scored high or low on the Interpersonal Dependency Inventory were asked to complete a "creativity test" being developed by two psychology professors. The participants were randomly assigned to either a condition where they were told their results would be reviewed in-person with a peer who was simultaneously taking the test or, a second condition, where their results would be both reviewed with the peer and evaluated by the two professors. Prior to beginning the creativity test, participants were given the opportunity to practice in order to enhance their performance. The number of practice items completed and the amount of time spent practicing were the primary dependent measures. If, as suggested in the DSM-IV-TR (APA, 2000, p. 666), dependent individuals are more likely to "present themselves as inept" and fear "appearing to be more competent" then it would be expected that they would engage in less practice across both conditions.

In the condition where their creativity test results were to be reviewed only with a peer, females scoring high in interpersonal dependency did indeed complete significantly fewer practice items and spent less time practicing than did controls. This finding is consistent with the description of dependency in the DSM emphasizing submissiveness, ineptness, and incompetence. However, when anticipating having their results not only compared face-to-face with a peer but also reviewed by the two professors, the females scoring high in interpersonal dependency now completed more practice items and practiced longer than controls. This reversal is inconsistent with dependency as described in the DSM and instead reveals an active attempt by those high in dependency to perform skillfully and competently (Baird, 2000; Bornstein et al. 1996).

These findings have led some to suggest that the primary feature of dependency is a motivation to maintain nurturing, protective relationships, a goal which will be pursued through a variety of active or passive behaviors depending on the situation (Bornstein, 1997). In certain situations it would facilitate a relationship to be passive, submissive, and modest, while in other situations active, assertive, self-promoting behaviors would facilitate the relationship. In other words, the behavioral variability in dependency might be organized according to its relationship-enhancing function (Baird, 2000), allowing the topographically different behaviors, because they serve the same function, to be understood as one response class.

These data are interesting in apparently demonstrating a situation where those high on a PD dimension apparently showed more behavioral variability compared to those who are low on the PD dimension. In other words, the behavior of those high in interpersonal dependency showed sensitivity to the experimental conditions, while the behavior of the controls did not. What might account for the apparent sensitivity of those reporting high levels of interpersonal dependency but not controls? As discussed in the Chad example, situations where the stimulus properties of a situation appear identical, yet participants respond differently, reveal that functionally the stimuli are not identical. The ultimate explanation for the different responding lies in the conditioning histories of the participants, which may lead them to verbally construct the apparently identical stimuli quite differently, providing a proximal explanation for the differences.

In interpreting the experiments of Bornstein and colleagues (1996) and Baird (2000), we might speculate that the relevant history involves differential reinforcement for construction of others as sources of support. That is, based on their reinforcement history, those who are high in interpersonal dependency may be more likely to construct others in terms of their ability to provide nurturance or support, while those lower in interpersonal dependency construct others more broadly. The experiments of Bornstein and colleagues and Baird involved taking a creativity test in the context of being told that the results will be reviewed with a peer or a peer and two professors that the participants had never met. There are many stimulus features that could impact responding; for instance, the situation could be framed as one involving competition (Am I better than my peer?), self-understanding (How creative am I?), interpersonal relations (What will impress the other?), artificiality (This is stupid and won't tell me anything!), etc. Our speculation is that individuals scoring high in interpersonal dependency were more likely to come under control of stimulus features involving interpersonal relating and, thus, to construct the others with whom they expected to interact in such terms. Indeed, when responding to a post-experiment questionnaire, high dependent subjects, across conditions, despite differing in their practice behavior, accorded greater importance to the reactions of the peers and professors than did controls (Baird, 2000). The verbally constructed nature of the others is apparent in that the participants in the study never met the hypothetical professors involved. Just as when giving a speech one anticipates the audience and tries to adjust his/her presentation accordingly, those high in dependency appeared to anticipate (verbally construct) their audience and adjust their behavior to that which appeared most likely to facilitate a relationship. With peers a balance is called for, performing too well or too poorly may isolate one from the peer; however, with the professors performing as competently as possible is the most relationship-enhancing approach.

Treatment of PDs

In practice, combined pharmacotherapy and psychotherapy is the standard approach in treating PDs (Gabbard, 2000). While the prevailing view is that psychotherapy is critical in the treatment of PDs, there is a lack of clinical outcome data, making it difficult to offer specific recommendations and rendering most conclusions tentative at best.

Empirical Status of Treatments for PDs

Several recent reviews, including studies using both controlled and naturalistic designs, suggest that cognitive-behavioral and psychodynamic psychotherapies appear superior to no treatment or standard care in the treatment of PDs (Crits-Christoph & Barber, 2002; Leichsenring & Leibing, 2003; Perry, Banon, & Ianni, 1999; Perry & Bond, 2000;). These data are important in challenging historical notions about the intractability of PDs. Moreover, the available data suggest that overall attrition rates, which averaged about 20%, appear commensurate with those found more generally in clinical trials, such that individuals with PDs are not necessarily more apt to discontinue treatment (although variables such as the therapeutic alliance and diagnosis may moderate this effect). It does appear that treatments for PDs will generally be lengthier (usually requiring a year or more) than is often the case in treatment outcome research; however, it is possible that some PDs (e.g., Cluster C) may show a more rapid response to treatment than others (e.g., Crits-Christoph & Barber, 2002; Leichsenring & Leibing, 2003; Perry et al., 1999; Perry & Bond, 2000).

BPD has received the most attention in studies of psychotherapy for PDs. Current randomized clinical trials support the efficacy of 6-12 months of Dialectical Behavior Therapy (DBT; Koons, Robins, Tweed, Lynch, Gonzalez, Morse et al., 2001; Linehan, Armstrong, Suarez, Allmon, & Heard, 1991; Linehan, Dimeff, Reynolds, Comtois, Welch, Heagerty et al., 2002; Linehan, Schmidt, Dimeff, Craft, Kanter, & Comtois, 1999) and 18 months of psychoanalytically-oriented partial hospitalization (Bateman & Fonagy, 1999; 2001) over standard care. While data from naturalistic studies support the above findings, only DBT has been tested in more than one randomized trial and by more than one research group. One randomized clinical trial found the effects of 10-weeks of behavior therapy (involving at a minimum graduated exposure, but for some participants social skills and intimacy training) superior to no treatment for AVPD (Alden, 1989). In addition, several studies using largely Cluster C samples have been supportive of relatively brief dynamic interventions (Crits-Christoph & Barber, 2002; Leichsenring & Leibing, 2003; Perry et al., 1999; Perry & Bond, 2000).

Clinical trial data are very limited with respect to other PDs. Indeed, as Crits-Christoph and Barber (2002) note: "No controlled treatment outcome studies have yet been performed for histrionic, dependent, schizotypal, schizoid, narcissistic, passive aggressive, antisocial, or paranoid personality disorder" (p. 617). There is speculation that the worst outcomes appear associated with Cluster A and ATPD diagnoses, which it is suggested may be due to both failure to seek treatment and lack of responsiveness to treatment. For example, some recent data suggest those with SPD and PPD are more likely to reject treatment than those with Cluster C diagnoses (Tyrer, Mitchard, Methuen, & Ranger, 2004). Additionally, a naturalistic study of day hospital treatment found those diagnosed with STPD failed to show improvement, unlike those with BPD or Cluster C diagnoses (Karterud, Vaglum, Friis, Irion, Johns, & Vaglum, 1992). However, a differential lack of responsiveness was not noted for those with Cluster A diagnoses in further naturalistic assessments of this day treatment program (Wilberg, Karterud, Urnes, Pedersen, & Friis, 1998). With respect to ATPD, lack of subjective distress, presence of psychopathy, and the fact that many are compelled into therapy complicate treatment provision and limit optimism about intervention effectiveness (Stone, 2000).

RFT Treatment Implications

Individuals identified as high on a dimension of PD experience chronic negative internal states, disproportionately employ escape/avoidance coping responses, and report low self-directedness; that is, poor self-acceptance, irresponsibility, purposelessness, and helplessness (Cloninger, 2000; Schroeder et al., 2002; Svrakic et al., 2002; Svrakic, et al., 1993; Trull, 1992; Watson, 2001; Watson & Sinha, 1999-2000).

While RFT provides an empirical model for the pervasiveness of aversive internal stimulation and why escape from these private experiences may be sought, RFT also makes clear that the private experiences are not the events for which they stand nor do they necessarily mean what one says they mean. As such, they need not dominate over direct experience nor compel escape and avoidance. Thus, RFT points to an alternative to emotion-focused, escape/avoidance-based coping strategies directed at modification of the content or frequency of negative thoughts/emotions. Instead of attempting to change negative private events, one can learn to identify them for what they are (e.g., thoughts, emotions, images, urges, etc.) and not what they say they are (e.g., statements of fact, evidence of weakness, strength, etc.). In other words, without changing the content of the private experiences, it may be possible to alter their function such that the reinforcing value of escape/avoidance is reduced. This suggestion from RFT converges with the common practices of several contemporary cognitive-behavioral approaches to treatment that share an acceptance/mindfulness component. For instance, proponents of Mindfulness-Based CT suggest that effective cognitive therapy for depression may help, in part, by allowing clients to experience negative thoughts/feelings as simply mental events, rather than as the self; thus, changing their relationship to the negative thoughts rather than changing their thought content (Teasdale, Moore, Hayhurst, Pope, Williams, & Segal, 2002).

The goal of acceptance/mindfulness is to decrease the need to engage in emotion-focused change efforts that while often successful in the short term are ineffective, dangerous, or life constricting in the long run. Acceptance/mindfulness is usually used in conjunction with strategies promoting active, goal-directed or problem-focused responses that often involve some distress in the short term but are more effective, adaptive, and life enhancing in the long run. DBT for BPD is the most well-articulated and empirically supported intervention in the PD literature and is exemplary of this approach. One of the core dialectics in DBT is between acceptance and change, and the treatment emphasizes both equally. The therapy is simultaneously supportive (clients are doing the best they can) and directive (clients must do more), validating (clients did not cause all of their problems) and problem-focused (clients have to solve their problems). This blend of acceptance and change is in the service of decreasing dysfunctional emotion regulation strategies (e.g., parasuicidal behaviors, substance use) and building a life worth living. One particularly relevant aspect for the present discussion is the teaching of mindfulness skills. As described by Linehan (1993, p. 63) the goal is to develop "a lifestyle of participating with awareness" an ability to contact "events, emotions, and other behavioral responses, without necessarily trying to terminate them when painful or prolong them when pleasant." The first step in this process is to learn that observations of an event and one's emotional reactions to an event are separate or different from the event itself. When observations are seen as such, when reactions are seen as such, they are less likely to evoke behavior designed to eliminate or reduce them. In this way, participation with awareness can help decrease emotion-focused (mood dependent) responding and create a greater opening for responding focused in the direction of goals or active problem solving (Linehan, 1993).

Acceptance and Commitment Therapy (ACT): An explicitly RFT-based approach to treatment

As described above, an RFT analysis provides one tool for understanding the potential utility of mindfulness/acceptance practice and how it may be used in conjunction with other strategies to decrease passive, ultimately ineffective, emotion-focused change efforts and support active, problem-focused, goal-directed behavior. ACT is one of several contemporary approaches that include an acceptance/mindfulness component. Thus, the relevance of ACT for some characteristics of PD functioning has already been articulated in the above section. What is unique about ACT is that it was developed in concert with RFT and, thus, follows directly from an understanding of RFT.

A full presentation of ACT is beyond the scope of this paper (see Hayes et al., 1999); however, a summary of the general approach followed by how it might be broadly relevant to the treatment of PDs is offered. In a sentence, ACT is designed to increase behavioral flexibility by helping clients contact internal experiences without engaging in unnecessary and ultimately ineffective escape/avoidance responses, and behave toward concrete goals based on their own personal values (Hayes et al., 1999). ACT seeks to weaken the link between private events and other responses that often seems to lead to rigid, narrow repertoires. For example, other things being equal, one who can feel a lack of self-confidence (which would usually lead to escape/avoidance) but still take on and pursue an important task evinces more flexibility than one who must feel confident before taking on an important task. Toward this end verbal formulations of events/situations are distinguished from the events themselves and descriptions are distinguished from evaluations. Verbal behavior is just behavior: words do not mean or are not the things to which they refer. Saying "This stress is intolerable!" (which, consistent with what is known about transformation of function, would likely increase felt stress and thereby encourage action directed at reducing the internal state) can be identified as a thought and not a literal factual description. Identified as a thought (specifically an evaluation) the stimulus functions of "This stress is intolerable!" may be altered such that the reinforcing value of escape is reduced and the emission of escape behavior less probable. Relatedly, ACT helps clients distinguish between self-rules (verbal descriptions of contingencies) that can and cannot be followed successfully. For example, in most areas of life the rule: "If I don't like it find out how to get rid of it, and get rid of it" can work, so the client has a great deal of experiences in which control works. However, when this approach is applied to private events, the results are often not as good. Direct attempts at control are not as effective or healthy (especially in the long run) in this domain. Here the rule of thumb is more "If you aren't willing to have it, you've got it" (Hayes et al., 1999). For example, consider an individual who is dissatisfied with being socially isolated, but is waiting to pursue interpersonal contacts until he/she feels socially adequate and no longer fears rejection, criticism, embarrassment. Such an approach is unlikely to work. In fact, the longer one waits for fears of rejection, criticism, and embarrassment to go away the worse they often seem to get, and more of his/her activities become directed at avoiding possible rejection, criticism, and embarrassment (an outcome that might be called AVPD). Thus, within a therapeutic relationship characterized by collaboration, validation, and support, ACT therapists attempt to create a therapy context that challenges the necessity of changing the content or form of private events in order to behave effectively.

When attempts to control private events are lessened, control efforts can then be directed at areas where control is generally most effective: the external world. At this point clients are helped to elucidate important personal values and to make a commitment to acting towards goals that are driven by these personal values (Hayes et al., 1999). For example, if leisure activities, family, and friendships are highly valued but currently are pursued only minimally, a client might make a commitment to increase time spent doing family outings or recreational activities with friends.

The goals are pursued even though thoughts and anxieties about wasting time, chores going undone, and work projects remaining imperfectly completed will likely arise during such activities.

In the space below we will describe how ACT may help address the low self-directedness reported among those meeting criteria for PD. Remember, self-directedness according to Cloninger and colleagues involves reports of lack of self-acceptance, helplessness, irresponsibility, and purposelessness. As Svrakic et al. (1993, p. 997) summarize their data, "patients are most often diagnosed as personality disordered if they are low in self-directedness: that is, most individuals with personality disorder have difficulty accepting responsibility, setting meaningful goals, resourcefully meeting challenges, accepting limitations, and disciplining their habits to be congruent with their goals and values."

Self-acceptance. Earlier we described how RFT distinguishes between self-as-content, self-as-process, and self-as-context or perspective. Evaluations and descriptions framed from the perspective of I/me/myself constitute the conceptualized self or self-as-content. That is, self-as-content is how one views him or herself. It is what clinicians collect on self-report measures and in clinical interviews. Moreover, because the conceptualized self appears generally stable, relatively rigid, internally consistent, and pervasive across life domains it captures a number of aspects generally associated with personality traits and disorders. As Trull and Widiger (2003) note: "people may consider many of their personality traits to be integral to their sense of self, and they may even value particular aspects of their personality that a clinician considers to be important targets of treatment." From an RFT perspective, if particular content is in a frame of coordination with I/me/myself then psychologically "I" and the content are at the same level (I = content). Thus, if the content is changed or lost, "I" might be lost as well. For instance, if "I" is in an equivalence frame with "very special person who is superior to others" and then I perform poorly on a task, not only is my evaluation of myself called into question but my very self is at risk to some degree. Similarly, if "I" is in an equivalence frame with "interesting and exciting person who needs others to pay attention to me and who cannot tolerate boredom" finding oneself alone and bored places the self in danger.

Helping the client to experience thoughts, emotions, images, urges, cravings, etc. for what they are – private events – can be useful in weakening the link between these responses and subsequent responses designed to alter or eliminate them. However, it can also be useful to weaken the relation between "I" and verbal content. That is, while learning to experience thoughts, emotions, images, urges, cravings, etc. for what they are – private events – a client can be helped to discriminate that it is him/her that is identifying, discriminating, and observing that the private event is occurring. Through experiential exercises the client is helped to contact this part of the self doing the identifying, discriminating, and observing that is separate from reactions and evaluations about the self. The client experiences that the person doing the thinking/feeling (I as context or perspective) can be distinguished from the thoughts and feelings. This is useful because once identified, "I" is now greater than content or process. Furthermore, "I" as a perspective or locus is always and has always been present (through success or failure, loneliness and connectedness, pain and joy, acceptance and rejection) even though it may have rarely been contacted. Once contacted, a sense of self is now available that is not at risk if content changes and, thus, need not be defended as such. As Hayes et al. (1999, p. 186) describe:

> This sense of observing self is critical to acceptance work because it means that there is at least one stable, unchangeable, immutable fact about oneself that has been experienced directly. That kind of stability and consistency makes it less threatening for a client to enter into the pain and travails of life, knowing that in some deep way that no matter what comes up, the "I" as the observing self will not be at risk.

Helplessness. As outlined earlier, a general feature of PDs is chronic negative affect. Its chronicity, by definition, indicates that attempts to eliminate negative internal experiences have been ineffective. As such, feelings of ineptness and helplessness are understandable and provide a point of entry in therapy because it suggests that at some level the client is in contact with the fact that their efforts at eliminating aversive internal states have not been working. What the client usually has not identified is that maybe these attempts cannot succeed (Hayes et al., 1999). Through a variety of metaphors and exercises the ACT client is helped to see that direct attempts to control private events does not work and may in fact be a significant part of the problem. When direct attempts to control private events have been identified as ineffective and problematic, control efforts can then be directed to where they are most effective. At this point taking responsibility might be discussed. The therapist might point out that "responsible" used to be written as "response able," referring to one's ability to respond. The client has the ability to respond (i.e., he/she is physically capable) and will be asked to commit to responding in domains where control can work. Because the client is able to respond change is possible. This is an opposite message to one of ineptness and helplessness. Thus, while being asked to take responsibility for one's behavior is often cast as a pejorative, here there is an attempt to alter the typical stimulus functions of "responsibility" by pointing out and having the client experience the necessity of being able to respond for things to be different.

Purposelessness. Purposelessness captures a quality of lacking direction in life and reporting a loss of meaning in life (Svrakic et al., 1993). Recent research on the relationship between values and behavior suggests that when values are cognitively activated and central to one's self-concept they help give meaning to events and situations and contribute significantly to value-congruent behavior (Verplanken & Holland, 2002). In other words, discriminating one's values can alter the evocative effects of stimuli and the reinforcing value of behavior that is congruent or incongruent with the identified values. One component of ACT that is directly relevant here is the values assessment and clarification. During this portion of the treatment, the client's values in the domains of family, intimate relations, parenting, social life, work, education, recreation, spirituality, citizenship, and physical health are assessed and the discrepancy between the importance placed on each value and the client's current action toward that value determined. This assessment serves as the basis for deriving goals toward which the client verbally commits to behave. So while much of the treatment focuses on weakening verbal control that promotes experiential avoidance, verbal control is now promoted in an attempt to strengthen values-based behavior change. Articulation of personal values, verbally committing to take action in pursuit of these values, and then taking said action appears directly relevant to the problem of purposeless in PD clients as articulated by Svrakic and colleagues (1993).

In sum, ACT seeks to remove barriers to pursuing values by weakening unhealthy relations between private events and escape/avoidance behavior and by strengthening relations between stated values and approach behavior. As such, ACT can be viewed as a therapy that promotes self-directedness. Clients are helped to contact a sense of self that is stable and not at risk, to set goals that are based on personal values, and then to commit to their pursuit.

The preceding analysis shows how ACT may be relevant to some of the core characteristics identified among samples with PD. However, ACT has not been employed in clinical outcome studies designed to directly test its efficacy with any particular PD nor has PD functioning been a major focus of measurement in ACT studies. ACT has been used in a number of controlled clinical outcome studies showing positive effects across areas as seemingly diverse as depression, anxiety, polysubstance abuse, smoking cessation, psychosis, chronic pain, and work-site stress (see Hayes, Masuda, Bissett, Luoma, & Guerrero, 2004 for a review). Many of these are problems that are highly comorbid with PDs. In addition, ACT has been used in a clinical field trial demonstrating that HMO therapists, with relatively brief training, could incorporate ACT strategies effectively and with good outcome across a diverse client population (Strosahl, Hayes, Bergan, & Romano, 1998). Furthermore, ACT has some significant conceptual and technical overlap with DBT, the treatment with the most empirical support in the PD literature.

Conclusion

In this chapter we tried to outline what a contemporary behavioral approach might offer to our understanding of PDs. This has not been a major area of focus within clinical behavior analysis and, as such, much of the material in the chapter was drawn from other sources. We interpreted this material through the lens of behavioral psychology, and RFT in particular, in an attempt to articulate how such an approach might accommodate these data. In so doing we speculated about the function and controlling variables of some PD relevant behavior and how this might relate to the treatment of PDs. These post-hoc interpretations benefited from knowing the results of the studies cited in advance and need to be viewed with this major limitation in mind. They are not akin to an experimental analysis and are no substitute for more rigorous empirical tests. In addition, much research remains to be done both on the PDs and on RFT. While RFT emerges from the behavioral tradition and is linked to empirical data, it is complicated and broad in scope. As such, there is some risk for misapplication and overreaching extensions. Therefore, this chapter should be seen as the beginning of an attempt to apply RFT to some relevant features of PDs. There may be other RFT consistent approaches that could be taken, new data may point in different directions, and certainly many relevant areas were missed. That said, at the level of behavioral process, no boundary is assumed between normal and abnormal behavior. As such, behavioral psychology should have something to say about the problematic intrapersonal and interpersonal behavior associated with PD diagnoses. Toward this end, the application of RFT seems to expand the breadth of the conversation and to provide some promise of potentially moving it forward.

Author Note

We thank Jimmy Anderson, Rebecca Arvans, Jay Clore, Dawn Dore, and Amanda Harris for helpful comments and feedback on earlier versions of this manuscript.

References

Alden, L. (1989). Short-term structured treatment for avoidant personality disorder. *Journal of Consulting & Clinical Psychology, 57,* 756-764.

American Psychiatric Association. (1952). *Diagnostic and statistical manual of mental disorders (1ˢᵗ ed.).* Washington, DC: Author.

American Psychiatric Association. (2000). *Diagnostic and statistical manual of mental disorders (4ᵗʰed., text revision).* Washington, DC: Author.

Baird, S. C. (2000). Interpersonal dependency and self-presentation strategies. *Dissertation Abstracts International, 60*(8-B), 4200.

Barnes-Holmes, D., Hayes, S. C., & Dymond, S. (2001). Self and self-directed rules. In S. C. Hayes, D. Barnes-Holmes, & B. Roche (Eds.), *Relational frame theory: A post-Skinnerian account of human language and cognition* (pp. 119-139). New York: Kluwer Academic/Plenum Publishers.

Barnes-Holmes, D., Stewart, I., Dymond, S., & Roche, B. (2000). A behavior-analytic approach to some of the problems of the self: A relational frame analysis. In M. J. Dougher (Ed.), *Clinical behavior analysis* (pp. 47-74). Reno, NV: Context Press.

Bateman, A., & Fonagy, P. (1999). Effectiveness of partial hospitalization in the treatment of borderline personality disorder: A randomized controlled trial. *American Journal of Psychiatry, 156,* 1563-1569.

Batemen, A., & Fonagy, P. (2000). Effectiveness of psychotherapeutic treatment of personality disorder. *British Journal of Psychiatry, 177,* 138-143.

Beck, A. T., Freeman, A. M., & Associates. (1990). *Cognitive therapy of personality disorders.* New York: Guilford.

Beck, A. T., Butler, A. C., Brown, G. K., Dahlsgaard, K. K., Newman, C. F., & Beck, J. S. (2001). Dysfunctional beliefs discriminate personality disorders. *Behaviour Research & Therapy, 39,* 1213-1225.

Bissett, R. T., & Hayes, S. C. (1999). The likely success of functional analysis tied to the DSM. *Behaviour Research & Therapy, 37,* 379-383.

Bornstein, R. F. (1997). Dependent personality disorder in the DSM-IV and beyond. *Clinical Psychology: Science & Practice, 4,* 175-187.

Bornstein, R. F. (2003). Behaviorally referenced experimentation and symptom validation: A paradigm for 21st-century personality disorder research. *Journal of Personality Disorders, 17,* 1-18.

Bornstein, R. F., Riggs, J. M., Hill, E. L., & Calabrese, C. (1996). Activity, passivity, self-denigration, and self-promotion: Toward an interactionist model of interpersonal dependency. *Journal of Personality, 64,* 637-673.

Bretherton, I., Fritz, J., Zahn-Waxler, C., & Ridgeway, D. (1986). Learning to talk about emotions: A functionalist perspective. *Child Development, 57,* 529-548.

Brown, M. Z., Comtois, K. A., & Linehan, M. M. (2002). Reasons for suicide attempts and nonsuicidal self-injury in women with borderline personality disorder. *Journal of Abnormal Psychology, 111,* 198-202.

Bushman, B. J., & Baumeister, R. F. (1998). Threatened egotism, narcissism, self-esteem, and direct and displaced aggression: Does self-love or self-hate lead to violence? *Journal of Personality & Social Psychology, 75,* 219-229.

Catania, A. C. (1991). Glossary. In I. H. Iversen & K. A. Lattal (Eds.), *Experimental analysis of behavior (Part 2)* (pp. G1–G44). Amsterdam: Elsevier.

Cicchetti, D., & Beeghly, M. (1987). Symbolic development in maltreated youngsters: An organizational perspective. *New Directions for Child Development, 36,* 47-68.

Clarkin, J. F., & Sanderson, C. (2000). Personality disorders. In M. Hersen & A. S. Bellak (Eds.), *Psychopathology in adulthood (2nd ed.)* (pp. 348-365). Needham Heights, MA: Allyn & Bacon.

Cloninger, C. R. (2000). A practical way to diagnosis personality disorder: A proposal. *Journal of Personality Disorders, 14,* 99-108.

Cook, R. G. (2002). The structure of pigeon multiple-class same-different learning. *Journal of the Experimental Analysis of Behavior, 78,* 345-364.

Costa, P. T. Jr., & Widiger, T. A. (2002). *Personality disorders and the five-factor model of personality (2nd ed.).* Washington, DC: American Psychological Association.

Crits-Christoph, P., & Barber, J. P. (2002). Psychological treatments for personality disorders. In P. E. Nathan & J. M. Gorman (Eds.), *A guide to treatments that work (2nd ed.)* (pp. 611-623). London: Oxford University Press.

Denham, S. A., Zoller, D., & Couchoud, E. A. (1994). Socialization of preschoolers' emotion understanding. *Developmental Psychology, 30,* 928-936.

Devany, J. M., Hayes, S. C., & Nelson, R. O. (1986). Equivalence class formation in language-able and language-disabled children. *Journal of the Experimental Analysis of Behavior, 46,* 243-257.

Dobson, K. S., & Block, L. (1988). Historical and philosophical bases of the cognitive-behavioral therapies. In K. S. Dobson (Ed.), *Handbook of cognitive-behavioral therapies* (pp. 3-38). New York: Guilford.

Dougher, M. J., Augustson, E., Markham, M. R., Greenway, D. E., & Wulfert, E. (1994). The transfer of respondent eliciting and extinction functions through stimulus equivalence classes. *Journal of the Experimental Analysis of Behavior, 62,* 331-351.

Dunn, J., Bretherton, I., & Munn, P. (1987). Conversations about feeling states between mothers and their young children. *Developmental Psychology, 23,* 132-139.

Dymond, S., & Barnes, D. (1995). A transformation of self-discrimination response functions in accordance with the arbitrarily applicable relations of sameness, more-than, and less-than. *Journal of the Experimental Analysis of Behavior, 64,* 163-184.

Dymond, S., & Barnes, D. (1996). A transformation of self-discrimination response functions in accordance with the arbitrarily applicable relations of sameness and opposition. *The Psychological Record, 46,* 271-300.

Endler, N. S., Parker, J. D. A., & Butcher, J. N. (1993). A factor analytic study of coping styles and the MMPI-2 content scales. *Journal of Clinical Psychology, 49,* 523-527.

Farmer, R. F., & Nelson-Gray, R. O. (1999). Functional analysis and response covariation in the assessment of personality disorders: A reply to Staats and to Bissett and Hayes. *Behaviour Research & Therapy, 37,* 385-394.

Folkman, S., & Lazarus, R. S. (1985). If it changes it must be a process: Study of emotion and coping during three stages of a college examination. *Journal of Personality & Social Psychology, 48,* 150-170.

Follette, W. C. (1997). A behavior analytic conceptualization of personality disorders: A response to Clark, Livesley, and Morey. *Journal of Personality Disorders, 11,* 232-241.

Follette, W. C., & Houts, A. C. (1996). Models of scientific progress and the role of theory in taxonomy development: A case study of the DSM. *Journal of Consulting and Clinical Psychology, 64,* 1120-1132.

Freeman, A. M., & Leaf, R. (1989). Cognitive therapy applied to personality disorders. In A. Freeman, K. M. Simon, L. E. Beutler, & H. Arkowitz (Eds.), *Comprehensive handbook of cognitive therapy* (pp. 403-433). New York: Plenum Press.

Frick, P. J., & Ellis, M. (1999). Callous-unemotional traits and subtypes of conduct disorder. *Clinical Child and Family Psychology Review, 2,* 149-168.

Gabbard, G. O. (2000). Combining medication with psychotherapy in the treatment of personality disorders. In J. G. Gunderson & G. O. Gabbard (Eds.), *Psychotherapy for personality disorders* (pp. 65-94). Washington, DC: American Psychiatric Publishing.

Gratz, K. L. (2003). Risk factors for and functions of deliberate self-harm: An empirical and conceptual review. *Clinical Psychology: Science & Practice, 10,* 192-205.

Guralnik, O., & Simeon, D. (2001). Psychodynamic theory and treatment of impulsive self-injurious behaviors. In D. Simeon & E. Hollander (Eds.), *Self-injurious behaviors: Assessment and treatment* (pp. 175-197). Washington, DC: American Psychiatric Publishing.

Hayes, S. C., & Barnes, D. (1997). Analyzing derived stimulus relations requires more than the concept of stimulus class. *Journal of the Experimental Analysis of Behavior, 68,* 225-233.

Hayes, S. C., Barnes-Holmes, D., & Roche, B. (2001). *Relational frame theory: A post-Skinnerian account of human language and cognition.* New York: Plenum Press.

Hayes, S. C., & Brownstein, A. J. (1986). Mentalism, behavior-behavior relations, and a behavior-analytic view of the purposes of science. *The Behavior Analyst, 9,* 175-190.

Hayes, S. C., & Follette, W. C. (1992). Can functional analysis provide a substitute for syndromal classification? *Behavioral Assessment, 14,* 345-365.

Hayes, S. C., Kohlenberg, B. K., & Hayes, L. J. (1991). The transfer of specific and general consequential functions through simple and conditional equivalence classes. *Journal of the Experimental Analysis of Behavior, 56,* 119-137.

Hayes, S. C., Masuda, A., Bissett, R., Luoma, J., & Guerrero, L. F. (2004). DBT, FAP, and ACT: How empirically oriented are the new behavior therapy technologies. *Behavior Therapy, 35,* 35-54.

Hayes, S. C., Strosahl, K. & Wilson, K. G. (1999). *Acceptance and commitment therapy: An experiential approach to behavior change.* New York: Guilford.

Hayes, S. C., & Wilson, K. G. (1993). Some applied implications of a contemporary behavior-analytic account of verbal events. *Behavior Analyst, 16,* 283-301.

Hayes, S. C., Wilson, K. G., Gifford, E. V., Follette, V. M., & Strosahl, K. (1996). Emotional avoidance and behavioral disorders: A functional dimensional approach to diagnosis and treatment. *Journal of Consulting and Clinical Psychology, 64,* 1152-1168.

Horne, P. J., & Lowe, C. F. (1996). On the origins of naming and other symbolic behavior. *Journal of the Experimental Analysis of Behavior, 65,* 185-241.

Karterud, S., Vaglum, S. Friis, S., Irion, T., Johns, S., & Vaglum, F. (1992). Day hospital therapeutic community treatment for patients with personality disorders: An empirical evaluation of the containment function. *Journal of Nervous & Mental Disease, 180,* 238-243.

Keller, F. S., & Schoenfeld, W. N. (1950). *Principles of psychology.* New York: Appleton-Century-Crofts.

Klonsky, E., Oltmanns, D., & Turkheimer, T. F. (2002). Informant-reports of personality disorder: Relation to self-reports and future research directions. *Clinical Psychology: Science & Practice, 9,* 300-311.

Koerner, K., Kohlenberg, R. J., & Parker, C. R. (1996). Diagnosis of personality disorder: A radical behavioral alternative. *Journal of Consulting & Clinical Psychology, 64,* 1169-1176.

Koons, C. R., Robins, C. J., Tweed, J. L., Lynch, T. R., Gonzalez, A. M., Morse, J. Q., et al. (2001). Efficacy of dialectical behavior therapy in women veterans with borderline personality disorder. *Behavior Therapy, 32,* 371-390.

Krause, E. D., Mendelson, T., & Lynch, T. R. (2003). Childhood emotional invalidation and adult psychological distress: The mediating role of emotional inhibition. *Child Abuse & Neglect, 27,* 199-213.

Leichsenring, F., & Leibing, E. (2003). The effectiveness of psychodynamic therapy and cognitive behavior therapy in the treatment of personality disorders: A meta-analysis. *American Journal of Psychiatry, 160,* 1223-1232.

Lenzenweger, M. F., Loranger, A. W., Korfine, L., & Neff, C. (1997). Detecting personality disorders in a nonclinical population: Application of a 2-stage procedure for case identification. *Archives of General Psychiatry, 54,* 345-351.

Levine, D., Marziali, E., & Hood, J. (1997). Emotion processing in borderline personality disorders. *Journal of Nervous & Mental Disease, 185,* 240-246.

Linehan, M. M. (1993). *Cognitive-behavioral treatment of borderline personality disorder.* New York: Guilford.

Linehan, M. M., Armstrong, H. E., Suarez, A., Allmon, D., & Heard, H. L. (1991). Cognitive-behavioral treatment of chronically parasuicidal borderline patients. *Archives of General Psychiatry, 48,* 1060-1064.

Linehan, M. M., Dimeff, L. A., Reynolds, S. K., Comtois, K. A., Welch, S. S., Heagerty, P., et al. (2002). Dialectical behavior therapy versus comprehensive validation therapy plus 12-step for the treatment of opioid dependent women meeting criteria for borderline personality disorder. *Drug & Alcohol Dependence, 67,* 13-26.

Linehan, M. M., Schmidt, H., Dimeff, L. A., Craft, J. C., Kanter, J., & Comtois, K. A. (1999). Dialectical behavior therapy for patients with borderline personality disorder and drug-dependence. *American Journal on Addictions, 8,* 279-292.

Maffei, C., Fossati, A., Agostoni, I., Barraco, A., Bagnato, M., Deboah, D., et al. (1997). Interrater reliability and internal consistency of the Structured Clinical Interview for DSM-IV Axis II Personality Disorders (SCID-II), version 2.0. *Journal of Personality Disorders, 11,* 279-284.

Malott, R. W., & Malott, M. E. (1991). Private events and rule-governed behavior. In L. J. Hayes & P. N. Chase (Eds.), *Dialogues on verbal behavior* (pp. 237-254). Reno, NV: Context Press.

Mash, E. J., & Wolfe, D. A. (2002). *Abnormal child psychology (2nd ed.).* Belmont, CA: Brooks/Cole-Wadsworth.

McGuffin, P., & Thapar, A. (1992). The genetics of personality disorder. *British Journal of Psychiatry, 160,* 12-23.

Moffitt, T. E. (1993). Adolescence-limited and life course persistent antisocial behavior: Developmental taxonomy. *Psychological Review, 100,* 674-701.

Morf, C. C., & Rhodewalt, F. (1993). Narcissism and self-evaluation maintenance: Explorations in object relations. *Personality & Social Psychology Bulletin, 19,* 668-676.

Morf, C. C., & Rhodewalt, F. (2001). Unraveling the paradoxes of narcissism: A dynamic self-regulatory processing model. *Psychological Inquiry, 12,* 177-196.

Morf, C. C., Weir, C., & Davidov, M. (2000). Narcissism and intrinsic motivation: The role of goal congruence. *Journal of Experimental Social Psychology, 36,* 424-438.

Morse, J. Q., Robins, C. J., & Gittes-Fox, M. (2002). Sociotropy, autonomy, and personality disorder criteria in psychiatric patients. *Journal of Personality Disorders, 16,* 549-560.

Nelson-Gray, R. O., & Farmer, R. F. (1999). Behavioral assessment of personality disorders. *Behaviour Research & Therapy, 37,* 347-368.

Nigg, J. T., & Goldsmith, H. H. (1994). Genetics of personality disorders: Perspectives from personality and psychopathology research. *Psychological Bulletin, 115,* 346-380.

Parker, C. R., Bolling, M. Y., & Kohlenberg, R. J. (1998). Operant theory of personality. In D. F. Barone, M. Hersen, & V. B. Van Hesselt (Eds.), *Advanced personality* (pp. 155-171). New York: Plenum Press.

Patterson, G. R., DeBaryshe, B. D., & Ramsey, E. (1989). A developmental perspective on antisocial behavior. *American Psychologist, 44,* 329-335.

Perry, C. J., Banon, E., & Ianni, F. (1999). Effectiveness of psychotherapy for personality disorders. *American Journal of Psychiatry, 156,* 1312-1321.

Perry, C. J., & Bond, M. (2000) Empirical studies of psychotherapy for personality disorders. In J. G. Gunderson & G. O. Gabbard (Eds.), *Psychotherapy for personality disorders* (pp. 1-31). Washington, DC: American Psychiatric Publishing.

Pfohl, B. (1999). Axis I and Axis II: Comorbidity or confusion? In C. R. Cloninger (Ed.), *Personality and psychopathology* (pp. 83-98). Washington, DC: American Psychiatric Association.

Pilkonis, P. A., Neighbors, B. D., & Corbitt, E. M. (1999). Personality disorders: Treatments and costs. In N. E. Miller & K. M. Magruder (Eds.), *Cost-effectiveness of psychotherapy: A guide for practitioners, researchers, and policymakers* (pp. 279-290). London: Oxford University Press.

Pollak, S. D., Cicchetti, D., Hornung, K., & Reed, A. (2000). Recognizing emotion in faces: Developmental effects of child abuse and neglect. *Developmental Psychology, 36,* 679-688.

Reese, H. W. (1968). *The perception of stimulus relations: Discrimination learning and transposition.* New York: Academic Press.

Reid, J. B., Patterson, G. R., & Snyder, J. (2002). *Antisocial behavior in children and adolescents: A developmental analysis and model for intervention.* Washington, DC: American Psychological Association.

Rhodewalt, F., & Morf, C. C. (1998). On self-aggrandizement and anger: A temporal analysis of narcissism and affective reactions to success and failure. *Journal of Personality & Social Psychology, 74,* 672-685.

Sachsse, U., von der Heyde, S., & Huether, G. (2002). Stress regulation and self-mutilation. *American Journal of Psychiatry, 159,* 672.

Salzinger, K. (1996). Reinforcement history: A concept underutilized in behavior analysts. *Journal of Behavior Therapy & Experimental Psychiatry, 27,* 199-207.

Samuels, J. E., Bienvenu, W.W., Joseph III, O., Brown, C., Costa, P. T., & Nestadt, G. (2002). Prevalence and correlates of personality disorders in a community sample. *British Journal of Psychiatry, 180,* 536-542.

Saunders, R. R., & Green, G. (1999). A discrimination analysis of training-structure effects on stimulus equivalence outcomes. *Journal of the Experimental Analysis of Behavior, 72,* 117-137.

Schroeder, M. L., Wormworth, J. A., & Livesley, W. J. (2002). Dimensions of personality disorder and the five-factor model of personality. In P. T. Costa Jr. & T. A. Widiger (Eds.), *Personality disorders and the five-factor model of personality (2nd ed.)* (pp. 149-160). Washington, DC: American Psychological Association.

Scotti, J. R., Morris, T. L., McNeil, C. B., & Hawkins, R. B. (1996). DSM-IV and disorders of childhood and adolescence: Can structural criteria be functional? *Journal of Consulting and Clinical Psychology, 64,* 1177-1191.

Shea, T. M., Stout, R., Gunderson, J., Morey, L. C., Grilo, C. M., McGlashan, T., et al. (2002). Short-term diagnostic stability of schizotypal, borderline, avoidant, and obsessive-compulsive personality disorders. *American Journal of Psychiatry, 159,* 2036-2041.

Shea, T. M., & Yen, S. (2003) Stability as a distinction between Axis I and Axis II disorders. *Journal of Personality Disorders, 17,* 373-386.

Sidman, M. (1994). *Equivalence relations and behavior: A research story.* Boston: Authors Cooperative, Inc.

Sifneos, P. E. (1996). Alexithymia: Past and present. *American Journal of Psychiatry, 153,* 137-142.

Skinner, B. F. (1938). *The behavior of organisms.* Englewood Cliffs, NJ: Prentice-Hall.

Skinner, B. F. (1945). The operational analysis of psychological terms. *Psychological Review, 52,* 270-277.

Skinner, B. F. (1953). *Science and human behavior.* New York: Free Press.

Skinner, B. F. (1974). *About behaviorism.* New York: Knopf.

Snyder, J. (2002). Reinforcement and coercion mechanisms in the development of antisocial behavior: Peer relationships. In J. B. Reid, G. R. Patterson, & J. Snyder (Eds.), *Antisocial behavior in children and adolescents: A developmental analysis and model for intervention* (pp. 101-122). Washington, DC: American Psychological Association.

Snyder, J., & Stoolmiller, M. (2002). Reinforcement and coercion mechanisms in the development of antisocial behavior: The family. In J. B. Reid, G. R. Patterson, & J. Snyder (Eds.), *Antisocial behavior in children and adolescents: A developmental analysis and model for intervention* (pp. 65-100). Washington, DC: American Psychological Association.

Steele, D., & Hayes, S. C. (1991). Stimulus equivalence and arbitrarily applicable relational responding. *Journal of the Experimental Analysis of Behavior, 56,* 519-555.

Stone, M. H. (2000). Gradations of antisociality and responsivity to psychosocial therapies. In J. G. Gunderson & G. O. Gabbard (Eds.), *Psychotherapy for personality disorders* (pp. 95-130). Washington, DC: American Psychiatric Publishing.

Strack, S., & Lorr, M. (1997). The challenge of differentiating normal and disordered personality. *Journal of Personality Disorders, 11,* 105-122.

Strosahl, K. D., Hayes, S. C., Bergan, J., & Romano, P. (1998). Assessing the field effectiveness of acceptance and commitment therapy: An example of the manipulated training research method. *Behavior Therapy, 29,* 35-64.

Svrakic, D. M., Draganic, S., Hill, K., Bayon, C., Przybeck, T. R., & Cloninger, C. R. (2002). Temperament, character, and personality disorders: Etiologic, diagnostic, treatment issues. *Acta Psychiatrica Scandinavica, 106,* 189-195.

Svrakic, D. M., Whitehead, C., Przybeck, T. R., & Cloninger, C. R. (1993). Differential diagnosis of personality disorders by the seven-factor model of temperament and character. *Archives of General Psychiatry, 50,* 991-999.

Taylor, G. J., & Bagby, R. M. (2000). An overview of the alexithymia construct. In R. Bar-On & J. D. A. Parker (Eds.), *The handbook of emotional intelligence: Theory, development, assessment, and application at home, school, and in the workplace* (pp. 40-67). San Francisco: Jossey-Bass.

Teasdale, J. D., Moore, R. G., Hayhurst, H., Pope, M., Williams, S., & Segal, Z. V. (2002). Metacognitive awareness and prevention of relapse in depression: Empirical evidence. *Journal of Consulting & Clinical Psychology, 70,* 275-287.

Tierney, K. J., & Bracken, M. (1998). Stimulus equivalence and behavior therapy. In W. T. O'Donohue (Ed.), *Learning and behavior therapy* (pp. 392-402). Needham Heights, MA: Allyn & Bacon.

Trull, T. J. (1992). DSM-III-R personality disorders and the five-factor model of personality: An empirical comparison. *Journal of Abnormal Psychology, 101,* 553-560.

Trull, T. J., & Widiger, T. A. (2003). Personality disorders. In G. Stricker & T.A. Widiger (Eds.), *Handbook of psychology (Vol. 8): Clinical psychology* (pp. 149-172). New York: John Wiley & Sons, Inc.

Tyrer, P., Mitchard, S., Methuen, C., & Ranger, M. (2004). Treatment rejecting and treatment seeking personality disorders. *Journal of Personality Disorders, 17,* 263-267.

Verplanken, B., & Holland, R. W. (2002). Motivated decision making: Effects of activation and self-centrality of values on choices and behavior. *Journal of Personality & Social Psychology, 82,* 434-447.

Vollrath, M., Alnaes, R., & Torgersen, S. (1996). Coping in DSM-IV personality disorders. *Journal of Personality Disorders, 10,* 335-344.

Wallace, H. M., & Baumeister, R. F. (2002). The performance of narcissists rises and falls with perceived opportunity for glory. *Journal of Personality & Social Psychology, 82,* 819-834.

Warm, A., Murray, C., & Fox, J. (2003). Why do people self-harm? *Psychology, Health & Medicine, 8,* 71-79.

Watson, D. C., & Sinha, B. K. (1999-2000). Stress, emotion, and coping strategies as predictors of personality disorder pathology. *Imagination, Cognition & Personality, 19,* 279-294.

Watson, D. C. (2001). Stress and personality disorder. In F. Columbus (Ed.), *Advances in psychology research, Vol. III* (pp. 127-149). Hauppauge, NY: Nova Science Publishers, Inc.

Widiger, T. A. (2002). Personality disorders. In M. M. Antony & D. H. Barlow (Eds.), *Handbook of assessment and treatment planning for psychological disorders* (pp. 453-480). New York: Guilford.

Widiger, T. A., & Clark, L. A. (2000). Toward DSM-V and the classification of psychopathology. *Psychological Bulletin, 126,* 946-963.

Wilberg, T., Karterud, S., Urnes, Ø., Pedersen, G., & Friis, S. (1998). Outcomes of poorly functioning patients with personality disorders in a day treatment program. *Psychiatric Services, 49,* 1462-1467.

Wilson, K.G., & Blackledge, J. T. (2000). Recent developments in the behavior analysis of language: Making sense of clinical phenonmena. In M. J. Dougher (Ed.), *Clinical behavior analysis* (pp 27-46). Reno, NV: Context Press.

Yang, J., Bagby, M., Costa, P. T., Jr., Ryder, A. G., & Herbst, J. H. (2002). Assessing the DSM-IV structure of personality disorder with a sample of Chinese psychiatric patients. *Journal of Personality Disorders, 16,* 317-331.

Zanarini, M. C., Frankenburg, F. R., Reich, D. B., Marino, M. F., Lewis, R. E., Williams, A. A., et al. (2000). Biparental failure in the childhood experiences of borderline patients. *Journal of Personality Disorders, 14,* 264-273.

Zentall, T. R. Galizio, M., & Critchfield, T. S. (2002). Categorization, concept learning, and behavior analysis: An introduction. *Journal of the Experimental Analysis of Behavior, 78,* 237-248.

Zimmerman, M. (1994). Diagnosing personality disorders: A review of issues and research methods. *Archives of General Psychiatry, 51,* 225-245.

Chapter 12

Sexual Disorders

Bryan Roche
National University of Ireland, Maynooth
Ethel Quayle
University College Cork, Ireland

Over the past half-century behavior analysts and behavior therapists have shown both industry and creativity in applying the principles of learning to the analysis and treatment of a variety of sexual disorders. In so doing, a small but respectable body of literature on the behavioral treatment of sexual disorders has emerged. Nevertheless, given the enormous prevalence of sexual problems in the general population as suggested by the prevalence of child pornography on the internet (e.g., Quayle & Taylor, 2002a), the frequency of child molestation (Johnson, 2004), and rape against adults (Ullman, 2004), there is a relative paucity of research into specifically behavioral treatments of human sexual disorders.

Perhaps the dearth of sex research within behavior analysis can be partly explained by the assumption that sexual behavior will submit to the same principles of learning already established with other forms of behavior, and with non-human animals (e.g., Alford, Plaud, & McNair, 1995; Laws & Marshall, 1990). Indeed, the basic principles of behavior have been applied very widely in the treatment of sexual disorders, often with considerable effect. Nevertheless, researchers appear to have abandoned the attempt to deal with complex sexual problems from a behavioral perspective, with the result that cognitive-behavioral approaches have become the standard against which newly emerging sex-therapies are judged (Maletzky, 2002).

The modern behavioral approach to human sexuality and sexual disorders that will be outlined here represents an extension of the traditional behavioral perspective insofar as it introduces the concepts of derived relational responding and transformation of function. This new approach is supported by a small but growing body of empirical research into the emergence of novel and highly complex patterns of sexual arousal. Before we consider this new approach, however, we need to consider the typology of sexual disorders and its most popular treatment paradigms.

Sexual Disorders

The term 'sexual disorder' represents a very broad concept and is a blanket term used for at least three types of sexual problems. The first of these is the sexual dysfunctions, which include such problems as erectile failure, premature ejaculation, lack of sexual desire, and vaginisimus. The second is the sexual identity disorders, including transexualism and transvestism. It is interesting to note that homosexuality also appears in the Diagnostic and Statistical Manual (DSM-IV; American Psychiatric Association, 1994) as a sexual disorder, but only for cases in which it is ego-dystonic, or in which it causes significant distress to the individual. The third category of sexual disorder is the paraphilias. While much of what is discussed in this chapter relates directly to the paraphilias, the same conceptual framework can be used in the treatment of other sexual disorders. Nevertheless, the lion's share of the behavioral contribution to the treatment of sexual disorders has been made in the treatment of paraphilias. For this reason we will outline the nature of paraphilic sexual disorders, as defined by DSM-IV, before considering a new and modern behavioral approach to their understanding and treatment.

People find many ways of expressing and fulfilling sexual needs and desires without infringing the limits set by their society, and vary greatly in what they find arousing. Behaviors that infringe societal mores are often categorized as paraphilias, perversions, or deviations, and result in a diagnostic label. DSM-IV is used to generate a diagnosis of such behavior and to suggest a relevant etiology. As ever, the diagnostic criteria employed by DSM-IV do not lend themselves to exact definitions but rather serve as guidelines to be informed by clinical judgment. These concerns notwithstanding, paraphilias can be described as sexual activities that involve nonhuman objects, non-consenting adults, suffering or humiliation by one's partner, or children. The major paraphilias include:

- Fetishism (using inanimate objects as the preferred or exclusive source of sexual arousal)
- Transvestitism (dressing in the clothes of the opposite sex as a primary means of becoming sexually aroused)
- Sexual sadism (sexual gratification through inflicting pain and humiliation)
- Sexual masochism (sexual gratification through experiencing pain and humiliation)
- Voyeurism (compulsively and secretly watching another person undressing, bathing, engaging in sex or being naked)
- Exhibitionism (sexual gratification by exposing one's genitals to involuntary observers)
- Frotteurism (sexual gratification through rubbing one's genitals against or fondling the body parts of a non-consenting person)
- Pedophilia (gratification by engaging in sexual activities with children)

In DSM-IV a set of definitional characteristics have to be met for a person to be diagnosed as having a paraphilia. According to DSM-IV, to meet the definition, a person must show "recurrent, intense sexually arousing fantasies, sexual urges, or behaviors" (APA, 1994, p. 522). As Doren (2002) has indicated, such a definition is confusing as it is unclear as to whether the phrase "sexually arousing" applies only to fantasies or to sexual urges and behaviors. With regard to pedophilia in particular, confusion is caused by the fact that it is unclear what constitutes a child. A child may be defined by chronological age, level of sexual development, emotional maturity, or whether the person is still under the care of an adult. In addition, this definition will vary across cases and jurisdictions.

For an individual to receive a paraphilia diagnosis, the duration of fantasies, urges and behaviors has to occur over a period of at least six months, and be the cause of clinically significant distress or impairment in social, occupational, or other important areas of functioning. However, it is unclear as to how the six months are counted or as to how the clinician might assess the occurrence of fantasies and urges if not disclosed by the individual or evidenced by other behaviors (such as stories, images, or a collection of memorabilia). Self-reports of such activities are at best unreliable and as with other socially unacceptable behaviors may be only partially disclosed (Hammond, 2004).

Interestingly, there is no separate diagnostic grouping for rape, which appears to be subsumed under the most controversial of the DSM-IV categories of 'Paraphilia, Not Otherwise Specified, Nonconsent'. Objective data about rape are conflicting (see Groth, Hobson, & Gary, 1982; Knight & Prentky, 1990). Physiological measures of arousal, such as penile plethysmographs, yield inconsistent data, suggesting that not all men who have engaged in nonconsensual sexual activity are aroused by physical violence against women. These findings may be due to methodological difficulties in selecting stimuli that fit with the sexual script of the individual, or ensuring that the intensity or duration of the stimuli is sufficient to produce arousal. Of course, this also raises questions about whether or not rape is in fact a sexual behavior at all, or can be conceived of more readily as an act of dominance and violence that falls along a continuum of normal male heterosexual behavior (e.g., Brownmiller, 1975; Sculy & Marolla, 1985). While some researchers have attempted to generate reliable and valid adult and child rapist typologies the broader impact of their efforts is limited (Knight & Prentky, 1990).

Access to reliable information regarding the etiology and development of sexual disorders is a pressing problem for those interested in the typology of paraphilia. The differentiation of pedophiles and child molesters serves as a case in point. Specifically, both DSM typology and popular treatments of pedophiles are based on the assumption that all pedophiles desire to make a contact offense against a child. However, newly emerging qualitative data suggest that some users of Internet child pornography may not be specifically sexually interested in children *per se*. When the image collections of convicted child pornography users are analyzed it is often found that either a very small number of child-related images are possessed or that such images comprise only a small part of a larger collection of other 'pornographies' that do not involve children (Quayle, Holland, Linehan, & Taylor, 2000; Sullivan & Beech, 2004). Even when the specific focus of sexual interest is children, it is not yet clear whether or not the use of Internet child pornography might function as blueprint for the commission of a contact offense, or even in some cases as a substitute for the molestation of children (Quayle & Taylor, 2002b).

Another prominent issue relevant to the psychological analysis of sexual behavior is the need to clarify the biological processes that underlie both acceptable and deviant sexual activities. The idea that deviant sexual preferences reflect an underlying biological abnormality is attractive insofar as it holds out the possibility that unacceptable sexual behavior is 'sick' rather than 'bad', but also that the sexual deviance may be 'cured', or at least managed. This belief has led to the prescribing of many drugs, such as Depo-provera, centrally active hormonal agents, and serotonin-active antidepressants to control deviant sexual arousal and behavior (Maletzky & Field, 2003), and the search for a congruent theoretical model to explain how these drugs might work.

Authors such as Flor-Henry (1987) have argued that "sexual deviations are, overwhelmingly, a consequence of the male pattern of cerebral organization" (p. 79). In effect, sexual deviation is sometimes seen as the natural outcome of an over-active sexual response system. Indeed, sex researchers have argued for some time that while some people commit sex offences in response to intense, unconventional sexual urges, biological factors such as hormone levels or chromosomal makeup sometimes play a major role (Berlin, 1983). Thus, the assumption underlying much of the antiandrogen treatments for deviant sexual behavior is that the offender's sex drive is out of control because his level of sex hormones (plasma testosterone) is too high. Despite the popularity of these biologically based treatments, however, the results of systematic research into the relationship between hormone levels and sexual activity remain sparse and equivocal (Lanyon, 1991; Maletzky & Field, 2003). It is only for the most aggressive or dangerous of sex offenders that significantly elevated levels of plasma testosterone have been reliably found (Rada, Laws, Kellner, Stivastava, & Peake, 1983).

Marshall and Barbaree (1990) generated a global theory of deviant sexual behavior, which suggested that for males, biological factors cause a ready and unlearned propensity for sexual aggression. This propensity has to be overcome by a process of socialization, which inhibits the expression of such behavior. The presence of factors such as poor parenting places the male at risk. Secondary risk factors include negative socio-cultural attitudes, an example of which would be exposure to or the use of pornography. Thus, the model attempted to integrate the factors that were thought to be central in causing sex offending.

More recent research has examined the evidence for elevated non-right-handedness in sex offenders as a measure of underlying developmental or central nervous system abnormalities (Bogaert, 2001). Taylor and Quayle (2003) have argued that while such correlations are interesting, they do little to move us away from models emphasizing associations between a variety of biological factors and the emergence of behavior that is socially labeled as deviant.

Cognitive and Behavioral Approaches

In an important and influential paper Marshall (1996) described the historical development of psychological approaches to the treatment of sex offenders, from a Freudian conceptualization, which equated problematic sexual behavior with a form of deviant personality, to accounts that were more behavioral or 'motivational'. More specifically, it emerged from Marshall's analysis that respondent conditioning processes, as variously conceived and ill-conceived by researchers over the past century, found their way into mainstream treatments of sexual disorder. According to Marshall, behavioral treatment approaches emphasize that when sexual arousal and masturbation are paired with a 'deviant' stimulus (such as a child or a non-sexual object), the deviant stimulus can itself become the primary context for sexual arousal. The opportunity for such conditioning can be fortuitous or may be provided on a regular basis through the use of pornography (see Seto, Maric, & Barbaree, 2001). While early behavioral treatments made some considerable advances in the elimination of sexual deviance (e.g., Bancroft, 1969; Colson, 1972; Feldman & MacCulloch, 1971; Mandell, 1970; McConaghy, 1970; Rachman, 1961) they were dogged by controversy over the ethical nature of aversion treatments and were criticized for merely eliminating deviant arousal, rather than eliminating any assumed underlying cause or managing the overall problem behavior.

More recently there has been a growth in the interest in cognitions as important influences on sexual behavior. This has led to considerable growth in therapies whose focus is challenging or changing dysfunctional cognitive processing. While the initial focus of cognitive therapies was the treatment of emotional distress, such techniques were later adapted to moderate sexually aggressive behavior. What has emerged is a generic cognitive behavioral model for the treatment of sexual disorder, which moves the focus from some inherent psychopathology to examining the offense-specific cognitions, emotions, and behaviors that are deemed both to be part of the etiology of the offense (underlying schemata) and to maintain the offending process. One influential cognitive-behavioral treatment model has been adapted from the work of Fisher and Beech (1999). The model addresses four components: denial, offense-specific behaviors, social inadequacy, and relapse prevention skills.

Cognitive accounts of paraphilia focus on factors such as empathy, social skills, and cognitive processes as a way of understanding, and hopefully changing, sex offender behavior. These models imply that there is something problematic in the way in which sex offenders view or interpret their social world. Such 'cognitive distortions' are most often defined as attitudes and beliefs that offenders use to deny, minimize, and rationalize their behavior (Geer, Estupinan, & Manguno-Mire, 2000). In the context of offenses against children, cognitive distortions include beliefs such as: if children fail to resist advances, they must want sex; sexual activity with children is an appropriate means to increase the sexual knowledge of children; if children fail to report sexual activity, they must condone it; in the future, sexual activity between adults and children will be acceptable, if not encouraged; if one fondles, rather than penetrates, sex with children is acceptable; any children who ask questions about sex really desire it; and one can develop a close relationship with a child through sexual contact (see Horley, 2000). A fundamental assumption of the cognitive approach is that these inaccurate beliefs play a major role in both precipitating and maintaining offending behavior (Abel, Lawry, Karlstrom, & Osborn, 1994).

Risk management is also a universal part of both assessment and intervention with sex offenders within the dominant cognitive-behavioral treatment paradigms. While risk management efforts may make intuitive sense in the case of potentially dangerous sex offenders, the appropriateness of such strategies for some offenders is in fact not yet clear. More specifically, it may be argued that much sex offending is in fact ego-syntonic insofar as it is usually pleasurable for the offender. Risk management requires the offender to curtail activities that are highly reinforcing and accept in their place a way of living that is less so. According to LoPiccolo (1994):

> The emotional valence of the emotions and behaviors involved in a paraphilia is quite the opposite of what the patient experiences in an anxiety or depressive disorder. Sexual desire is a pleasurable emotion, and the approach behaviors motivated by it result in sexual arousal and orgasm, which are intrinsically rewarding... For many paraphilic patients, their deviation is ego syntonic, and it is only the societal consequences of their behavior which causes them distress. (p. 150)

Traditional Behavioral Models of Paraphilia

The traditional behavioral approach to understanding patterns of sexual responding rests largely on the well-worn principles of respondent and operant conditioning (Barnes & Roche, 1997; Roche & Barnes, 1998; see also Alford et al., 1995; Laws & Marshall, 1990). In one of the earliest investigations of learning principles in human sexual arousal, Lovibond (1963) demonstrated that electrodermal responses of homosexual males could be conditioned, using film clips of nude males as unconditioned stimuli (USs) and abstract symbols as conditioned stimuli (CSs). Later, using male volunteers, Rachman (1966) established a conditioned sexual response (this time measured by penile plethysmography) to a pair of female boots by repeatedly projecting slides of the boots on a screen immediately prior to the presentation of slides of attractive nude females. What Rachman called his "laboratory induced fetish" generalized to physically similar stimuli and extinguished with repeated presentations in the absence of the US (i.e., the nude females). In another early study, McConaghy (1970) demonstrated conditioned penile volume increases in two groups of heterosexual and homosexual males using film clips of nude females and males, respectively, as USs (the CS was a red circle in both cases). Other demonstrations of the classical conditioning of human sexual arousal in male subjects were reported by Langevin and Martin (1975), McConaghy (1969), and Rachman and Hodgson (1968).

While some respondent conditioning research has continued to be conducted with non-human animals (e.g., Kippin, Talianakis, & Pfaus, 1997; Pfaus, Kippin, & Centeno, 2001; see also Domjan & Holloway, 1998), only a handful of studies have been conducted on the role of respondent processes in human sexual arousal in recent decades. In one study, Lalumière and Quinsey (1998) paired slides of partially nude females with video clips of heterosexual interactions. The researchers reported an increase in penile tumescence in response to the slides following the pairing procedure. In another study, Plaud and Martini (1999) employed 9 subjects in a well-controlled study which examined three different conditioning paradigms (i.e., short delay, backward conditioning, and random CS-US presentation). Sexually explicit images were employed as the unconditioned stimuli (US), and a neutral slide of a penny jar was employed as the conditioned stimulus (CS). Results indicated that participants showed systematic maximum increases in penile tumescence (measured using a penile plethysmograph) from baseline using the short delay conditioning procedure, but not using the other two control procedures.

Only two published studies have attempted to demonstrate the conditioning of a sexual arousal response in human female subjects. The first study was reported by Letourneau and O'Donohue (1997). These researchers used the illumination of a light bulb as a conditioned stimulus that was paired contingently with the presentation of erotic film clips. The conditioning paradigm failed to show conditioned genital or subjective responses to the conditioned stimulus. In the second of these studies, Hoffmann, Janssen, and Turner (2004) reported the conditioning of sexual arousal in both male and female subject groups using both biologically relevant and irrelevant conditioned stimuli.

The respondent conditioning paradigm for the understanding of human sexual response patterns has been explicitly harnessed in several successful behavioral treatments for paraphilia (e.g., LoPicollo & Stock, 1986). One of the more popular behavioral methods for the alteration of unwanted sexual responses is covert sensitization. This procedure typically involves instructing clients to imagine aversive stimuli (e.g., vomiting) at the onset of a sexual response to "inappropriate" experimental stimuli. In one early, albeit politically sensitive demonstration of the technique, Barlow, Agras, Leitenberg, and Callahan (1972) successfully used the technique to reduce sexual responsivity to same-sex models in a group of homosexual males. In another study, Maletzky (1980) combined covert sensitization with olfactory aversion in the treatment of 38 homosexual pedophiles and 62 exhibitionists. The treatment consisted of having each client relax and imagine one in a series of sexual scenes arranged in increasing order of sexual potency. When sexual arousal to the scene occurred the client was instructed to imagine a specific aversive event and was simultaneously presented with the odor of rotting tissue. The sexual scenes were presented in each session and tape recordings were made for home practice across a 24-week period. Follow-up outcome assessments (at 6, 13, 18, 24, and 36 months) included measures of the frequency of inappropriate sexual fantasies or acts, penile circumference changes to paraphilic stimuli, reports of progress by significant others, and legal records of charges or convictions. Improvements were recorded in all cases, with only 8 clients re-offending during the follow-up period.

Despite the existence of promising data to support a respondent conditioning approach to human sexual arousal, there is a dearth of new data on the role of respondent processes in the development of sexual response patterns. Nevertheless, the respondent conditioning paradigm has continued to be offered as a conceptual framework for the behavioral analysis of human sexual activity (see Alford, et al., 1995; O'Donohue & Plaud, 1994).

While analyses of human sexual responding within a respondent conditioning paradigm have been sparse, operant analyses have been almost non-existent. In one study, Quinn, Harbison, and McAllister (1970) used a pleasant drink to reinforce minimal erectile responses to slides of nude females in a group of liquid-deprived homosexual males (dehydration was achieved through an 18 hour abstinence period and the administration of a powerful diuretic). By gradually increasing the minimum erectile response required for reinforcement, the researchers were able to enhance heterosexual responsivity for their subjects. These authors suggested that erectile responses are susceptible to reinforcement, although no follow-up studies were ever conducted.

In another study, Rosen, Shapiro, & Schwartz (1975) reported that 12 subjects had demonstrated increased penile tumescence to a discriminative stimulus when monetary reinforcement was available for such responding. These responses were in contrast to those of a control group that received noncontingent reinforcement in the presence of the same discriminative stimulus.

Schaefer and Colgan (1977) tested the idea that ejaculation could be used as a reinforcer for erectile responses elicited by reading sexually explicit material. In that study two groups of subjects were required to read long passages of sexually explicit literature in each of six sessions held over a two-week period. At the end of each session the experimental subjects were allowed to ejaculate while subjects in the control group were required to read nonsexual material until penile detumesence was observed on a penile plethysmograph. The researchers reported that penile tumescence increased over trials when reading of the sexually explicit material was followed by ejaculation.

Finally, in a study by Cliffe and Parry (1980), sexual stimuli were used to test the matching law (Herrnstein, 1970). In that study a male pedophile was exposed to three concurrent variable-interval schedules of reinforcement. The first involved choosing to view either slides of women or men, the second, between slides of men or children, and the third between women and children. The matching law was found to accurately describe the subjects' behavior in the first two conditions. That is, a matching relation was found between the overall number of responses and the overall relative number of reinforcement presentations.

The role of operant processes in human sexual behavior has been more widely studied in the context of treatments for paraphilia. In a rare laboratory-standard aversive conditioning procedure, Rosen and Kopel (1977) used the sound of an alarm buzzer as an aversive stimulus presented when subjects demonstrated an erectile response to an inappropriate stimulus. Specifically, as penile tumescence increased to a sexually arousing stimulus, the aversive alarm sound also increased. This procedure produced a reduction in penile tumescence responses to the sexual stimulus. In one well-cited demonstration of aversive conditioning, Feldman and MacCulloch (1971) administered electric shocks to a group of male homosexuals during the final 0.5 seconds of exposure to visual "homosexual" stimuli that were 2 seconds in duration. A subsequent decline in responsivity to nude males was recorded. In a more recent study, the administration of a noxious olfactory stimulus (ammonia) was successfully used to punish sexual responses towards children in a male pedophile (Earls & Castonguay, 1989). The reduction in responsivity was still significant one year after therapy had ceased. A combination of electric shocks and noxious olfactory stimuli was used by another group of researchers to eliminate "deviant" sexual thoughts in a group of pedophile outpatients (Marshall & Barbaree, 1988).

While traditional behavioral treatments have generally supported a behavioral approach to the paraphilias, the jury is still out on the overall efficaciousness of a behavioral treatment paradigm. The primary reasons for this are twofold. Firstly, much of what we know about the role of respondent and operant processes in human sexual arousal has been obtained from early applied research into the alteration of homosexual patterns of sexual responsivity. Not only does this raise ethical concerns for our field, but it also poses conceptual problems for the theoretical integrity of our accounts. More specifically, a behavioral approach must be built from the ground up within the context of a healthy synergy between applied and basic research efforts. In the case of human sexuality, our knowledge base is overwhelmingly influenced by findings from the applied setting.

Perhaps of greater concern is the fact that some researchers, including pioneers of the behavioral approach to human sexuality, have long questioned the explanatory scope of respondent and operant processes. Indeed, as much as 35 years ago, researchers who were experienced in the behavioral analysis and treatment of sexual dysfunction were beginning to suspect that respondent and operant processes were insufficient in explaining sexual behavior in the world outside the laboratory (see Bancroft, 1969; McConaghy, 1969). Since that time it has become apparent that convincing analogs of deviant arousal cannot be easily created through traditional laboratory conditioning procedures (Laws & Marshall, 1990; LoPiccolo, 1994). Moreover, new data are beginning to suggest that widely used aversive conditioning procedures are less than satisfactory in producing long-term changes in sexual behavior. For instance, in one recent study, Maletzky and Steinhauser (2002) reviewed the treatment of 7,275 sex offenders over a 25-year period. These researchers found that failure rates from sex therapy as a whole, including failure to complete therapy, are sufficiently high to warrant serious concern to clinical practitioners. In addition, as traditional behavioral techniques, such as aversion therapy, fall into decline, sex therapists are increasingly turning to cognitive methods in the treatment of sexual dysfunction (Maletzky & Steinhauser, 2003). Indeed, cognitive-behavioral treatments for sexual disorders continue to be developed and applied with relative success while behavioral researchers increasingly watch from the sidelines.

A Derived Relations Approach to Paraphilia

One obvious response to the lack of confidence in behavioral treatments of sexual disorders might be to more thoroughly investigate the relevance of traditional behavioral processes to the understanding and treatment of the paraphilias. This has been the response of some researchers, who continue with the effort to carefully identify the optimal parameters of sexual conditioning (e.g., Plaud & Martini, 1999) and the trajectory of habituation to sexual stimulation (Plaud & Gaither, 1997). While such a response is indeed merited, another more progressive response may be to consider additional learning processes that may extend our traditional behavioral understanding of human sexual activity. Relational Frame Theory (RFT; Hayes, Barnes-Holmes, & Roche, 2001) provides such an opportunity in suggesting a framework for the analysis of derived stimulus control, the derivation of reinforcing functions, and the emergence of subtle contextual control over both.

As with other aspects of psychological functioning, analyses in terms of derived stimulus relations allow us to account for what might otherwise appear as generative or novel behavior. The literature on paraphilia is filled with examples of what appears to be highly novel behavior. For instance, Bourget and Bradford (1987) outlined two case-studies of fire fetishism (also known as pyrolangia or sexual arson; see Cox, 1979). The individuals in question were brought to the attention of authorities because of the sexual pleasure they derived from lighting fires. While such topographically unique behavior may appear difficult to account for in terms of a history of direct stimulus association or the fortuitous reinforcement of sexual arson, Roche and Barnes (1998) outlined one possible relational account of the emergence of fire fetishism. Those authors suggested that the emergence of a fire fetish might be understood in terms of the overlap between sexual terms and fire terms used in daily discourse. For instance, both sexual arousal and fire are spoken of as "explosive" and "hot". In romantic fiction lust is sometimes referred to as "burning desire" and love as a "flame." In effect, sexual and fire terms often participate in frames of coordination with each other, and we might therefore expect to observe, at least occasionally, a derived transformation of fire terms and fire events in terms of the relation these events and terms bear to other sexual terms and events.

Interestingly, psychoanalysts have also noted the overlap between terms pertaining to fire and sex. Cox (1979) identified the semantic overlap between sex and fire in such phrases as "my best flame" and "you set me on fire" as possible sources of fire fetishism. What is particularly exciting about the RFT approach, however, is that it provides a technical and functional-analytic nomenclature with which to conduct such interpretive analyses.

The idea that established sexual arousal stimulus functions can transform the functions of novel and arbitrary stimuli in accordance with derived relations was first tested by Roche and Barnes (1997; Experiment 1). In that study, seven subjects were trained on a series of conditional discrimination tasks (i.e., see A1 pick B1, see B1 pick C1, see A2 pick B2, see B2 pick C2, see A3 pick B3, see B3 pick C3, where all stimuli were nonsense syllables). Training on these tasks led to the emergence of the following equivalence relations during testing; A1-B1-C1, A2-B2-C2, and A3-B3-C3. Sexual and nonsexual functions were then established for the C1 and C3 stimuli, respectively, using a respondent conditioning procedure. The acquisition of sexual/emotional functions by the conditioned stimuli was monitored and assessed in terms of phasic skin resistance responses (SRRs). Following 12-18 conditioning trials, subjects showed differential conditioning (i.e., C1 produced significantly greater SRRs than C3). Moreover, these respondent functions spontaneously transformed the functions of the A1 and A3 stimuli, in the absence of any further respondent conditioning or reinforcement. Specifically, five of seven subjects showing significantly greater SRRs to C1 over C3 also showed a significant arousal response differential to A1 over A3. This effect was also demonstrated for subjects who had not received the equivalence test until after the probes for the derived transformation of functions. In a further experiment (Experiment 3), Roche and Barnes (1997) examined the robustness of the derived sexual responses phenomenon by demonstrating a derived transformation of sexual arousal in accordance with a five-member, four-node, equivalence relation.

The foregoing findings support a relational control approach to understanding paraphilia. Specifically, the findings of Roche and Barnes (1997) demonstrated that, at least under laboratory conditions, human subjects are capable of responding sexually to any given stimulus in terms of a sexual one to which it is arbitrarily related. The explanatory power of such findings is immediately apparent. For instance, Roche and Barnes (1998) used the foregoing findings to construct a possible relational account of the emergence of cross-dressing in a young boy. In their words:

> Consider a boy who learns verbally (e.g., is told by his classmates) that "bizarre" behaviors are often considered sexually arousing... If this boy is then told at another time (e.g., a week or a month later) that it is "weird" or "bizarre" to dress in the clothes of the opposite sex (it is fair to argue that many children learn this), the words "sexual arousal" may be related to the words "cross-dressing," in a suitable context, by virtue of a derived frame of coordination. More importantly, though, the words 'sexual arousal' and the words "cross-dressing" also participate in socially established frames of coordination with actual sexual arousal and actual cross-dressing, respectively. The operation of these relations makes it likely that, in some contexts, the functions of actual sexual arousal will transfer to actual cross-dressing... (p. 42)

The foregoing analysis illustrates that a behavioral account of the emergence of sexual stimulus functions for arbitrary stimuli may indeed be supplemented by an analysis of the derived transformation of functions in accordance with equivalence relations or frames of coordination. It is important to appreciate, however, that the greatest contribution of RFT to this arena of research is its ability to disentangle complex histories of learning involving relations other than equivalence. More specifically, while an individual may indeed respond to two equivalent stimuli in terms of each other, they may also respond to one stimulus in terms of its relation of opposition, difference, or comparison to another. For instance, if a boy learns that men and women are opposites, and that men are sexually aggressive, the child may spontaneously respond to women as sexually submissive (see also Roche & Barnes, 1996, 1998). In practice, when this boy develops heterosexual response patterns he may find himself sexually attracted to submissive women, and less so, or not at all, to sexually aggressive or domineering women. Thus, RFT may help us to specify the psychological process according to which social narratives may transform the sexual behavior of individuals.

Roche and Barnes (1997; Experiment 4) tested the idea that complex relational networks involving relations other than coordination could control sexual responses to arbitrary stimuli. In that study, subjects were first exposed to a relational pretraining preparation. Specifically, subjects were trained to relate same stimuli (e.g., a large line with a large line) in the presence of one contextual cue, opposite stimuli (e.g., a large line with a small line) in the presence of a second contextual cue, and different stimuli (e.g., a small line with an oval) in the presence of a third contextual cue. Training across a range of such tasks led to the establishment of contextual control functions of Same, Opposite, and Different for each of three abstract stimuli.

Subjects were then trained on the following contextually controlled conditional discriminations; Same/A1-[B1-B2-N1], Same/A1-[C1-C2-N2], Opposite/A1-[B1-B2-N1], Opposite/A1-[C1-C2-N2], where all stimuli were nonsense syllables and underlined comparisons indicate reinforced choices. The N1 and N2 stimuli were included as comparisons but were not employed during any further training or testing phase. The test probes were as follows; Same/B1-[C1-C2-N2]; Same/B2-[C1-C2-N2]; Opposite/B1-[C1-C2-N2]; Opposite/B2-[C1-C2-N2]. During this phase, subjects related B1 with C1 in the presence of Same (i.e., B1 and C1 are both the same as A1 and therefore the same as each other); B2 with C2 in the presence of Same (i.e., B2 and C2 are both opposite to A1 and therefore the same as each other); B1 with C2 in the presence of Opposite (i.e., B1 is the same as A1, and C2 is opposite to A1, and therefore B1 is opposite to C2); and B2 with C1 in the presence of Opposite (i.e., B2 is opposite to A1, and C1 is the same as A1, and therefore B2 is opposite to C1). Thus, the relations; [Same] B1-C1 and [Same] B2-C2 were derived during testing.

The experimenters then exposed subjects to a respondent conditioning procedure in which the two nonsense syllables, B1 and B2, were paired with sexual and nonsexual film clips, respectively (for some subjects the functions of these stimuli were reversed). Conditioned sexual responses were assessed in terms of skin resistance responses during the nonsense syllable-film clip interval. Within approximately 18 conditioning trials, subjects generally showed differential conditioning, insofar as B1 produced significantly greater SRRs than B2. When the C1 and C2 stimuli were subsequently presented alone, four of the five subjects who showed a response differential to B1 and B2, also showed a transformation of sexual arousal functions. That is, subjects who showed greater arousal to B1 over B2 also showed significantly greater autonomic arousal to C1 over C2 in the absence of any direct association between C1 and a sexual stimulus. In addition, those subjects who showed greater autonomic arousal to B2 over B1 also showed significantly greater autonomic arousal to C2 over C1.

These findings extend the explanatory power of a relational control analysis of sexual arousal by bringing even more complex forms of derived sexual arousal (i.e., under Same and Opposite contextual control) within the remit of the experimental analysis of behavior. Specifically, these data provide the empirical evidence that it is possible for an individual to become sexually aroused when presented with a stimulus that is the "opposite of the opposite of" a sexual stimulus. It is reasonable to assume, therefore, that sexual arousal in the world outside the laboratory may on occasion be moderated and controlled by relational contextual cues. Such findings go some way towards justifying the introduction of the RFT framework to the behavioral sex research agenda.

While the Roche and Barnes (1997) studies clearly demonstrate the role that language processes (i.e., derived relational responding) may play in the etiology of sexual arousal patterns in the world outside the laboratory, one further dimension of derived sexual arousal needs to be considered. Specifically, according to RFT, all derived relational responding is controlled in any given instance by a contextual cue. The contextual cue may be explicit, as it normally is in experimental contexts, or it may be extremely subtle (e.g., smells, settings, tones of voice, etc.). This cue sets the occasion for specific types of relational activity (i.e., C_{rel}) and selects the specific functions that are transformed (i.e., C_{func}). For instance, while reading an explicit description of a sexual scenario, an individual may produce an erectile response. Nevertheless, the context of reading operates as a contextual cue that controls the transformation of some of the functions of sexual arousal, but not all. Thus, according to RFT, the individual will not produce all of the operant responses involved in the complex chain of activities required in order to actually copulate. If we are to fully understand the transformation of sexual stimulus functions in the real world, therefore, we must first establish that the derived functions of arbitrary stimuli are indeed subject to modulation by higher-order levels of contextual control. This idea was first investigated by Roche, Barnes-Holmes, Smeets, Barnes-Holmes, and McGeady (2000).

In the Roche et al. (2000) study, nine male subjects were first exposed to a relational pretraining procedure in order to establish contextual functions of Same and Opposite for two arbitrary stimuli. These stimuli were then employed in the subsequent arbitrary relational training phase. More specifically, subjects were exposed to the following relational training tasks; Same/A1-[B1-B2-N1], Same/A1-[C1-C2-N2], Opposite/A1-[B1-B2-N1], Opposite/A1-[C1-C2-N2], Same/X1-[Y1-B1-N3], Same/X1-[Y2-C1-N4], Opposite/X1-[Y3-B2-N3], Opposite/X1-[Y4-C2-N4], where underlined comparison stimuli indicate reinforced choices.

The relational test probed for the spontaneous emergence of the following relations: Same/B1-[C1-C2-N2]; Same/B2-[C1-C2-N2]; Opposite/B1-[C1-C2-N2]; Opposite/B2-[C1-C2-N2]. During testing, subjects chose B1 given C1 in the presence of Same (i.e., B1 and C1 are both the same as A1 and therefore the same as each other), chose B2 given C2 in the presence of Same (i.e., B2 and C2 are both opposite to A1 and therefore the same as each other), chose B1 given C2 in the presence of Opposite (i.e., B1 is the same as A1, and C2 is opposite to A1, and therefore B1 is opposite to C2), and chose B2 given C1 in the presence of Opposite (i.e., B2 is opposite to A1, and C1 is the same as A1, and therefore B2 is opposite to C1). Subjects were also exposed to a respondent conditioning procedure in order to establish B1 and B2 as sexual and nonsexual stimuli, respectively (although this was reversed for some subjects). The critical test for a contextually controlled derived sexual arousal response involved repeatedly presenting the C1 and C2 stimuli for 3 seconds each in the presence of either the Same or Opposite contextual cue and recording subjects' arousal responses in terms skin resistance levels.

The results showed that C1 produced greater arousal than C2 when both were presented in the presence of the Same contextual cue. However, in the presence of the Opposite contextual cue, C1 produced *less* arousal than C2. In other words, the derived sexual arousal functions of C1 were subject to modulation by the contextual cues. These results suggest, therefore, that derived sexual responses are determined by the participation of the relevant stimuli in derived relations, the nature of those relations and contextual control over the transformation of functions.

The Roche et al. (2000) data demonstrate the remarkable flexibility of human sexual responses and their susceptibility to highly complex forms of stimulus control. Such findings support the interpretation of paraphilic activity in relational terms. As an example of how such functional-analytic interpretive exercises might proceed, let us consider the example of pedophilia. From a traditional stimulus control perspective, we might expect to observe sexual arousal responses to children in some individuals within a sufficiently large population. More specifically, both adult women and young girls share several anatomical features (i.e., primary sexual characteristics) and several social characteristics (e.g., names, clothes) that may allow for an account of pedophilic arousal in terms of stimulus generalization from adults to children. While a traditional stimulus control account must figure in any behavioral approach to pedophilia, RFT takes the analysis of stimulus generalization one step further by considering the arbitrary continua along which stimuli may acquire sexual stimulus control functions. More specifically, while female children do indeed share several anatomical features with adult females, arbitrary relations that are established by the wider culture also obtain between adults and children. For instance, if social stereotypes portray adult women as dependent and in need of men's care, then children are *more* feminine than adult females in this regard (i.e., they are *more* dependent). Furthermore, if social stereotypes suggest that feminine adult women should be submissive to their partners, then children are also more feminine than adult women in this regard. In effect, relations of comparison may obtain between adult women and (female) children such that a small number of the stimulus functions of femininity will be amplified for children in the context of certain social stereotypes (i.e., they are even more submissive, innocent, docile, and dependent). The relevant stereotypes are those that place women and men in frames of opposition with each other, and women and children in frames of comparison, such that children possess in abundance some of the socially desirable character-istics of an adult female. Indeed, a concern over the cultural infantalization of women has formed a major theme in the feminist literature over the past thirty years (e.g., see Kilbourne & Pipher, 2000). Thus, RFT can provide a technical account of how pedophilic interest in children can emerge, at least in part, from the normal verbal contingencies operating in Western communities.

Several empirical and conceptual questions remain regarding the optimal conditions for the derived transformation of sexual arousal functions and the robustness of the effect across time in the world outside the laboratory. For instance, no published study to date has examined the transformation of sexual reinforcing functions. In other words, we do not yet know if arbitrary stimuli can be used reliably as sexual reinforcers. Answering this question would help us to move some way towards a more complete account of novel sexual behaviors (e.g., fire fetishism) where access to the fetish object appears as an end in itself and where conventional sexual gratification (e.g., orgasm) is entirely absent in its presence (e.g., as in many cases of transvestism). In one study, however, Hayes, Kohlenberg, and Hayes (1991) showed that when a consequential function was established for one stimulus in a derived relation, it transformed other members of the relation such that they too functioned as punishers or reinforcers. If this same effect can be established for sexual reinforcers it will further emphasize the relational flexibility of human sexual arousal patterns. More specifically, if sexual reinforcers can be arbitrarily determined and derived the number of processes according to which unusual topographies for sexual behavior emerge (e.g., fire fetishism) will be enormously expanded.

A recent study reported by Dymond and Roche (in press) attempted to demonstrate that the nonarbitrary properties of primary sexual reinforcers might transform the arbitrary functions of the discriminative stimuli that signal their availability. In that study, subjects were exposed to a simple discrimination procedure in which red, green, and blue circles presented on a computer screen were established as discriminative stimuli for a mouse-click, which was in turn consequated with the presentation of a sexually explicit image for 5 seconds. One of three sizes of image was presented on the computer screen following each operant response; large, small, or medium. We will refer to these sexual images as A1, A2, and A3, respectively. Moreover, the size of the image presented was always correlated with the particular discriminative stimulus presented on that trial (i.e., green circle – mouse click – A1, red circle – mouse click – A2, blue circle – mouse click – A3). However, the content of sexual images was randomized from trial to trial.

Subjects were then exposed to a free-operant testing phase in which they were presented with all three discriminative stimuli on every trial. Subjects could use the computer mouse to click on any discriminative stimulus to receive the associated reinforcer. By allowing the experimenters to track the frequency of responses to each of the three discriminative stimuli, this phase established that the A3 stimuli were the most reinforcing for the subjects. Following this, subjects were exposed to Bigger than/Smaller than relational pretraining in order to establish the contextual functions of Bigger than and Smaller than for two arbitrary cues, respectively. During relational pretraining the correct comparison on each trial was always physically bigger or smaller than the sample, depending on the contextual cue present (e.g., in the presence of the Bigger than arbitrary contextual cue, and given the image of a medium-sized chair as a sample, subjects should pick the bigger-sized chair from a comparison array containing a small chair, a medium-sized chair, and a large chair).

In the next phase, subjects were exposed to a linear equivalence training procedure in which the following three relations were established among the sexual reinforcers (A stimuli) and a series of nonsense syllables (B and C stimuli): A1-B1-C1, A2-B2-C2, and A3-B3-C3. Some subjects were then tested for equivalence relations between the A and C stimuli, whereas others were not. Finally, subjects were exposed to a relational testing phase which tested for derived relations of Bigger than and Smaller than among the discriminative stimuli and nonsense syllables. Results showed that subsequent to the equivalence training, subjects responded to the discriminative stimuli in arbitrary relational terms. That is, they responded to the green circle as Bigger than both the red and blue circles, the red circle as Smaller than the green and blue circles, and the blue circle as Bigger than the red circle but Smaller than the green circle. This pattern was consistent across five out of seven subjects, despite the fact that the colored circles were identical in physical size. The same pattern of responding was observed to all of the B and C stimuli (i.e., nonsense syllables). In effect, the nonarbitrary functions of the primary sexual reinforcers had transformed the entire relational network such that all of the participating stimuli and the discriminative stimuli associated with them were responded to in terms of the arbitrary comparative relations among those reinforcers. Even more surprising, was the fact that during a subsequent free operant phase in which the C1, C2, and C3 stimuli were presented simultaneously, subjects consistently clicked on the C1 stimulus (because it was equivalent to A1, which was a large sexual reinforcer).

The observed pattern of simple discrimination emerged spontaneously and was not consequated by any reinforcers at any stage. In effect, the sexual discriminative functions of the A stimuli transformed the functions of the C stimuli such that they too began to function as discriminative stimuli for sexual reinforcement. Such findings strongly suggest that operant responses or response chains leading to sexual reinforcement are subject to transformation because of the participation of the relevant discriminative stimuli in relational networks. This, once again, points to the impressive flexibility and arbitrariness of human sexual behavior. More importantly, however, it points to the fruitfulness of the RFT account from which such research questions emerged and the explanatory scope of its theoretical framework.

A Relational Approach to Sexual Behavior Change

One of the biggest challenges to sex therapists over the past several decades has been the development of interventions that can produce lasting behavior change (Maletzky, 1991). Traditional interventions based on counter-conditioning may not be successful in the long-term elimination of complex and derived sexual arousal responses because such strategies leave the verbal relations and the attendant derived transformation of function intact (Roche & Barnes, 1998). Research into derived relational responses, however, may help us to understand why derived and conditioned sexual responses are so resistant to permanent change. In one study,

Roche, Barnes, & Smeets (1997) trained subjects on a matching-to-sample procedure that led to the formation of the equivalence relations A1-B1-C1 and A2-B2-C2 during testing. Sexually arousing film clips were then paired with two nonsense syllables, A1 and C2, in a respondent conditioning paradigm. Similarly, nonsexual film clips were paired with A2 and C1. In other words, the experimenters established incongruous sexual functions for stimuli that participated in common derived equivalence relations. The researchers found that when subjects were re-exposed to the equivalence test they re-produced the original equivalence relations. In effect, the stimulus pairing procedure failed to disrupt the laboratory created equivalence relations. The relations even failed to shift following several exposures to the incongruous stimulus pairing procedure.

Roche et al. (1997) also wondered what would happen if subjects were first exposed to the stimulus pairing procedure followed by the incongruous equivalence training. They found that the subsequent incongruous stimulus equivalence training failed to produce equivalence relations. Instead, subjects matched stimuli during the equivalence test on the basis of their sexual or nonsexual functions (i.e., match A1 with C2 and A2 with C1) that were established during the stimulus pairing procedure. In effect, once a stimulus relation has been established between two sexual stimuli using a respondent conditioning procedure, it is difficult to disrupt that relation by attempting to reorganize the relevant stimuli into distinct equivalence relations. Conversely, when a derived relation is established it dominates over subsequent stimulus relations established using stimulus pairing procedures.

The foregoing findings sit well with more recent data showing that functional stimulus classes are not easily reorganized using stimulus equivalence training and testing procedures. Specifically, Tyndall, Roche, and James (2004) exposed fifty subjects to a simple discrimination-training procedure during which identical discriminative stimulus (S+) functions were established for each of six arbitrary stimuli, and identical extinction stimulus (S-) functions were established for six additional stimuli. Following this training, each participant was exposed to equivalence training and testing under one of five conditions (i.e., using only the six S+ stimuli; using three S+ and three S- stimuli, with each set of three corresponding to the trained equivalence relations; using three S+ and three S- stimuli, each assigned to their roles as samples and comparisons in a quasi-random order; using all six S- stimuli; using a set of six novel stimuli for which no functions had been established). The researchers reported that participants required significantly more testing trials to form equivalence relations when the stimuli involved were functionally similar rather than functionally different. Put simply, the researchers found that is difficult to create two equivalence relations from an array of stimuli that already form a single functional class.

The foregoing findings are consistent with a small body of research from outside the sex research field illustrating that derived relations may be resistant to reorganization in several experimental situations. In one early study, Pilgrim and Galizio (1990) trained adult subjects on a series of conditional discriminations (i.e.,

A1-B1, A2-B2, A1-C1, A2-C2) that led to the emergence of two three-member equivalence relations during testing (i.e., A1-B1-C1, A2-B2-C2). Following equivalence testing, subjects received further training in which the original A-C relations were reversed (i.e., A1-B1, A2-B2, A1-C2, A2-C1). This led to alterations in the symmetry responding of three of four subjects, but none of them responded in accordance with the predicted transitive relations (see also Pilgrim, Chambers, & Galizio, 1995; Saunders, Saunders, Kirby, & Spradlin, 1988; Spradlin, Saunders, & Saunders, 1992). Wirth and Chase (2002) also reported a series of experiments that illustrated that both functional classes of stimuli and equivalence relations are resistant to reorganization and that both are highly persistent across time. However, research by Smeets, Barnes-Holmes, Akpinar, and Barnes-Holmes (2003) found that derived relational responding is sensitive to novel reinforcement contingencies under specific conditions. Those authors point out that full equivalence reversal has been reported in studies involving class-specific reinforcers (e.g., Dube, McIlvane, Mackay, & Stoddard, 1987) but not in others (Pilgrim, Chambers, & Galizio, 1995; Pilgrim & Galizio, 1990; Roche et al., 1997; Saunders, et al., 1988). These latter studies showed that the reversal of baseline conditional discriminations relations often leads to a reversal of symmetry relations but not symmetric transitivity performances.

Experiment 4 of the Roche et al. (1997) study also suggested one specific way in which resistant derived relations or functional classes of stimuli might be disrupted. Specifically, the authors found that subjects' test performances could be altered by a prior history of exposure to the types of contingencies that would later serve as incongruous contingencies in the experiment. For instance, consider a subject who was exposed to a stimulus pairing procedure and matching-to-sample test followed by an incongruous stimulus equivalence training and testing phase. Roche et al. found that the final test performance of such a subject could be controlled by the immediately preceding equivalence training contingencies (i.e., thereby over-riding the initial stimulus pairing) if the subject had previously been exposed to an irrelevant stimulus equivalence training and testing phase. Thus, given a prior history of equivalence training using novel stimuli, subjects were more likely to alter stimulus function-based matching patterns when incongruous equivalence training was introduced. Similarly, subjects provided with a prior history of stimulus pairing and testing with novel stimuli were more likely to alter equivalence-based test performances when a subsequent incongruous stimulus pairing procedure was introduced. In effect, the researchers decreased the resistance to change of stimulus classes by first increasing the flexibility of the test performances using novel stimuli in a pre-experimental phase.

The authors suggested that this finding might help us build a behavioral technology for sexual attitude change. More specifically, they suggested that sexual attitudes would not be easily changed by repeated contradiction or logical argument (i.e., attempts to reorganize verbal relations). What is needed instead is a history of reinforcement for behavior change in the intervention context. Thus, we might expose an individual to a form of 'pretraining' in which the formation of verbal relations, unrelated to sexuality is reinforced. If the individual is a non-smoker, for example, the therapist might discuss the many disadvantages of smoking and reinforce consensus on the topic. By reinforcing already-established verbal relations, the therapist may establish her verbal behavior as an effective contingency of behavior change. Given this 'pretraining' further behavior change efforts may be more effective. Alternatively, we may employ as a behavior-change agent an individual who has already acquired some form of behavioral control over the individual (e.g., a community leader or family member). While these strategies have already been supported in the applied literature (Kelly, St. Lawrence, Diaz, Stevenson, Hauth, Brasfield et al., 1991; Kelly, St. Lawrence, Stevenson, Hauth, Kalichman, Diaz et al., 1992; Wulfert & Biglan, 1994), RFT helps us to provide a functional-analytic, experimentally supported rationale with which to investigate and build upon these applied practices.

While the foregoing provides a functional-analytic interpretation of one sexual behavior change process, what is urgently needed is a systematic program of behavioral sex research that will fully explicate the role of verbal and derived relational processes in human sexual functioning. Only such a program of research will inform us fully as to how to proceed in changing the persistent dangerous sexual behaviors presented in the clinical context. The truth is that the behavioral approach, and its aversive methods in particular, is considered to have had only limited success in the treatment of sexual dysfunction (e.g., rape; see Maletzky, 1991). Consequently, an increasing number of sex therapists are employing impulse control interventions and risk management techniques (see Bancroft, 2000). In the following section we will briefly consider these methods and consider their relevance to the RFT research agenda.

Relational Frame Theory in Mainstream Sex Therapy

Acceptance and Commitment Therapy (ACT; Hayes, Strosahl, & Wilson, 1999) is a functional-analytic psychotherapy that has emerged in tandem with the theoretical framework of RFT. One important concern of ACT is the suggestion that derived relations, once established, are resistant to reorganization. Thus, in ACT, the therapist makes no attempt to reorganize verbal relations, but rather teaches the client to respond differently to both overt and covert discriminative stimuli. In technical terms, we might describe this as altering the context for the transformation of functions. That is, while the relevant verbal relations stay intact and the context for relational responding (i.e., C_{rel}) is unaltered, the specific functions that transform in accordance with those relations is changed in an increasing variety of settings (i.e., C_{func}). This process is what ACT therapists refer to as *acceptance*.

The relevance of acceptance strategies to treating problematic sexual behaviors becomes apparent when one considers the ever-widening effects of the transformation of stimulus and response functions. Specifically, over time well-established verbal relations may emerge between a range of stimuli, such as thoughts, feelings and overt responses. For instance, a compulsive child pornography user may respond verbally to the natural and repeated sequence of physical sexual urges, followed or accompanied by specific thoughts (e.g., "I want to download"), followed by specific responses (e.g., viewing child pornography), followed by further specific feelings (e.g., sexual relief) and thoughts ("I am ashamed"). When this verbal relation is well rehearsed by virtue of the repeated tacting of the foregoing sequence (e.g., "here I go again, there's that feeling and I'm going to download to feel better and end up feeling worse") we should expect to observe a considerable transformation of functions across the relevant stimuli such that they become functionally substitutable for each other. Thus, whatever the original discriminative stimulus for offending, the deviant response may now occur in the presence of any of the other events in the relation (e.g., the urge). Of course, the idea that covert events may function as discriminative stimuli is nothing new to radical behaviorists (see Tourinho, 2006). What is new is the idea that verbal relations may be derived between a range of covert stimuli such that each can produce the deviant response and the psychological functions of each other (see Roche & Barnes, 1998). When this occurs, the thought "I want to download" is psychologically (verbally) fused with other thoughts and feelings and the ultimate problem behavior (e.g., "I feel like downloading so I will").

Acceptance strategies, as conceptualized in ACT, aim to alter the fusion of verbal relations by increasing contextual control over them. For instance, the therapist may ask the compulsive child pornography user to imagine alternative responses to sexual urges. The client may also be encouraged to stay in the presence of thoughts such as "I want to download" while remaining relaxed and responding to that thought as "just another thought". This experience is thought to widen the contextual control over problematic verbal relations such that a wider range of response options presents itself in an ever-widening variety of contexts. The offender gets to keep their urges to offend but "rides them out" until the response functions for actual offending are extinguished in the presence of overt (e.g., a computer terminal) and covert discriminative stimuli (e.g., specific thoughts and urges). In essence, when private behaviors need not be changed, their controlling effects over overt behavior are reduced considerably (Kohlenberg, Tsai, & Dougher, 1993). This method is also typical of those used in a wide range of other mindfulness and acceptance-based therapies (Segal, Williams, & Teasdale, 2002).

Deliteralization is one specific technique used to extinguish several of the derived emotional responses to stimuli while leaving the relevant network of related stimuli intact (e.g., Masuda, Hayes, Sackett, & Twohig, 2004). This is a technique designed to reduce the needless domination of language. Deliteralization exercises often proceed by asking a client to repeat aloud a word or phrase that is discriminative for problematic behavior and which is often avoided by the client. For instance, an ego-dystonic pedophile who is struggling with urges to offend may avoid sexual thoughts involving minors for fear of becoming aroused. To achieve deliteralization the therapist may ask the client to repeat a sexually arousing phrase that is frightening or which usually serves as a discriminative stimulus for offending behavior. The client is simultaneously taught to remain in the presence of that thought and to experience it without avoiding or acting upon it. In this way the functions of overt offending behavior can extinguish and cease to be produced by the relevant verbal discriminative stimuli. In simpler terms, deliteralization changes the context in which the individual experiences sexually deviant thoughts, which in turn alters the relation between deviant stimuli and sexual gratification (LoPiccolo, 1994). Consequently, deviant thoughts or overt stimuli need no longer be avoided because a repertoire of acceptable behavior has been established in their presence.

Very little research exists to support the idea that acceptance-based approaches may be suitable for the treatment of paraphilias. Nevertheless, anecdotal evidence has been provided by LoPiccolo (1994) that acceptance of paraphilic urges can help to dissipate the danger of actual offending in incarcerated sex offenders. Other researchers (Paul, Marx, & Orsillo, 1999) have reported success in the use of ACT in the treatment of exhibitionism in a single-case design. (See also Quayle, Vaughan, & Taylor, 2006).

In addition, several existing behavioral sex therapy techniques appear to adopt similar strategies to ACT. Impulse control and risk management training, for instance, often form part of relapse prevention programs for sex offenders. The aim of these techniques is to teach clients to respond to sexual impulses in a more productive way and to recognize the onset of dangerous covert and overt situations that may lead to problem sexual behavior. Furthermore, clients are taught that the consequences of offending may cause great distress to themselves in the long term.

Interestingly, sex therapists have had some success in the application of a technique known as verbal satiation (DiCaprio, 1970; Gray, 1995; Kaplan, Morales, & Becker, 1993; Laws, 1995) that is surprisingly similar to deliteralization. The technique is not unlike a form of covert desensitization in which the therapist attempts to extinguish the functions of sexual stimuli in their absence. This is achieved by requiring the client to repeat words or phrases referring to sexually arousing paraphilic stimuli until the sexual arousal response has been extinguished. It is important to appreciate, however, that while verbal satiation may prove useful in the sex therapy context, a functional process-based account of this techniques is still required. RFT provides just such an account in terms of derived relations and changes in the context for the transformation of function.

Challenges for a Relational Control Account

Given the dearth of behavioral laboratory research into human sexual behavior and dysfunction, much of the descriptive analysis provided in the current chapter is necessarily speculative. Our reliance on speculation at this point, however, is not in itself a shortcoming. If research findings such as those presented here are to have real-world application, it behooves us to build conceptual bridges from our own domain to that of the applied scientist and to that of researchers in other fields. An important part of this endeavor will always be the construction of extrapolations. Of course, testing these extrapolations may stretch the limits of our account, but if this is the challenge that presents itself, we must rise to it.

One of the first challenges for the current research agenda will be to establish whether or not humans do in fact produce derived sexual responses under normal social conditions. In other words, in order to support a relational control account of human sexual behavior we need to show that derived relational responding is a necessary (if not sufficient) condition for the development of complex patterns of sexual responding. This will be no easy task and will have to begin with a concerted effort by basic laboratory researchers to work with and speak to the concerns of the sex therapist and to conduct their research using real sex offender populations. This work has only just begun (see Roche, O'Riordan, Ruiz, & Hand, 2005).

Even if it can be shown that derived relational responding is an important process in the acquisition of complex sexual response repertoires in the real world, it still remains to be established whether or not verbal contingencies can sometimes dominate over direct contingencies in the production of sexual behavior. This will have important implications for sex therapy. More specifically, if it emerges that derived relational process can establish novel sexual responses repertoires but not over-ride old ones, we will likely be at loss in any attempt to eliminate direct contingency-shaped sexual behavior patterns using verbal contingencies (e.g., talk therapies). Alternatively, if verbal contingencies can dominate over direct contingencies of reinforcement, it may be possible to eliminate directly established response repertoires using entirely verbal contingencies and with little or no need for aversion or traditional extinction and exposure techniques. Of course, direct and derived contingencies are not orthogonal to each other and the distinction we draw here is somewhat false. Derived responses can quickly come under the control of direct reinforcement contingencies and directly established response patterns may participate in verbal relations once an individual learns to verbally discriminate their own behavior. Nevertheless, it is important to ask the question as to whether or not an effective behavior therapy for paraphilia might proceed without recourse to the concepts of derived relational responding and the transformation of function. Furthermore it is important to investigate the relative roles of direct and verbal contingency control in various instances of paraphilic behavior in an attempt to establish the likelihood of derived sexual behavior occurring in a given instance and the stability that behavior is likely to display over time. This should cast light on why it is that many individuals can participate in a verbal community whose practices support the emergence of a specific paraphilia (e.g., fire fetishism), while only a small number develop that paraphilic behavior pattern.

A related area of uncertainty in the current analysis is the degree to which verbal relations can control sexual response patterns across time in the absence of direct reinforcement. For instance, can derived sexual arousal responses be maintained across time in the absence of sexual reinforcement or will unreinforced derived sexual responses decrease in the sexual response repertoire? It may emerge that verbal contingencies (e.g., stories, stereotypes) may lead to the emergence of derived sexual response patterns in the real world. However, it may also be the case that the role of verbal contingencies is simply to bring novel sexual responses under the control of primary reinforcers (e.g., orgasm) rather to maintain them in the long term.

The foregoing considerations notwithstanding, RFT has provided behavior analysts with an immense opportunity to conduct experimental and conceptual analyses of even the most complex forms of human sexual activity. While much work is required to assess the full utility of the approach, the limited data available to date suggest that a relational approach may be our most promising avenue for the analysis and treatment of human sexual disorders.

References

Abel, G. G., Lawry, S. S., Karlstrom, E., & Osborn, C. A. (1994). Screening tests for pedophilia. *Criminal Justice and Behavior Special Issue: The assessment and treatment of sex offenders, 21*, 115-131.

Alford, G. S., Plaud, J. J., & McNair, T. V. (1995). Sexual behavior and orientation: Learning and conditioning principles. In L. Diamant & R. D. McAnulty (Eds.), *The psychology of sexual orientation, behavior, and identity: A handbook* (pp. 121-135). Westport, CT: Greenwood Press.

American Psychiatric Association. (1994). *Diagnostic and statistical manual of mental disorders* (4th ed.). Washington, DC: Author.

Bancroft, J. (1969). Aversion therapy of homosexuality. *British Journal of Psychiatry, 115*, 1417-1432.

Bancroft, J. (2000). *The role of theory in sex research*. Bloomington, IN: Indiana University Press.

Barnes, D., & Roche, B. (1997). Relational frame theory and the experimental analysis of human sexuality. *Journal of Applied and Preventive Psychology: Current Perspectives, 6*, 117-135.

Barlow, D. H., Agras, W. S., Leitenberg, H., & Callahan, E. F. (1972). The contribution of therapeutic instructions to covert sensitization. *Behavior Research and Therapy, 10*, 411-415.

Berlin, F. S. (1983). Sex offenders: A biomedical perspective and a status report on biomedical treatment. In J. G. Greer (Ed.), *The sexual aggressor: Current perspectives on treatment* (pp. 83-123). New York: Van Nostrand Reinhold.

Bogaert, A. F. (2001). Handedness, criminality, and sexual offending. *Neuropsychologia, 39*, 465-469.

Bourget, D., & Bradford, J. M. (1987). Fire fetishism, diagnostic and clinical implications: A review of two cases. *Canadian Journal of Psychiatry, 36*, 459-462.

Brownmiller, S. (1975). *Against our will: Men, women, and rape*. New York: Simon & Schuster.

Cliffe, M. J., & Parry, S. J. (1980). Matching to reinforcer value: Human concurrent variable-interval performance. *Quarterly Journal of Experimental Psychology, 32*, 557-570.

Colson, C. E. (1972). Olfactory aversion therapy for homosexual behavior. *Journal of Behavior Therapy and Experimental Psychiatry, 3*, 1-3.

Cox, M. (1979). Dynamic psychotherapy with sex-offenders. In I. Rosen (Ed.), *Sexual deviation* (pp. 306-350). Oxford, England: Oxford University Press.

DiCaprio, N. S. (1970). Essentials of verbal satiation therapy: A learning-theory-based behavior therapy. *Journal of Counseling Psychology, 17*, 419-424.

Domjan, M., & Holloway, K. S. (1998). Sexual learning. In G. Greenberg & M. M. Harraway (Eds.), *Comparative psychology: A handbook* (pp. 602-613). New York: Garland.

Doren, D. M. (2002). *Evaluating sex offenders*. Thousand Oaks, CA: Sage.

Dube, W. V., McIlvane, W. J., Mackay, H. A., & Stoddard, L. T. (1987). Stimulus class membership established via stimulus-reinforcer relations. *Journal of the Experimental Analysis of Behavior, 47*, 159-175.

Earls, C. M., & Castonguay, L. G. (1989). The evaluation of olfactory aversion for a bisexual pedophile with a single-case multiple baseline design. *Behavior Therapy, 20*, 137-146.

Feldman, M. P., & MacCulloch, M. J. (1971). *Homosexual behaviour: Therapy and assessment*. Oxford, England: Pergamon Press.

Fisher, D., & Beech, A. R. (1999). Current practice in Britain with sexual offenders. *Journal of Interpersonal Violence, 14*, 240-256.

Flor-Henry, P. (1987). Cerebral aspects of sexual deviation. In G. D. Wilson (Ed.), *Variant sexuality: Research and theory* (pp. 49-83). Baltimore, MD: The Johns Hopkins University Press.

Geer, J., Estupinan, L., & Manguno-Mire, J. (2000). Empathy, social skills and other relevant cognitive processes in rapists and child molesters. *Aggression and Violent Behavior, 5*, 99-126.

Gray, S. R. (1995). A comparison of verbal satiation and minimal arousal conditioning to reduce deviant arousal in the laboratory. *Sexual Abuse: Journal of Research & Treatment, 7*, 143-153.

Groth, A. N., Hobson, W. F., & Gary, T. S. (1982). The child molester: Clinical observations. In J. Conte & D. A. Shore (Eds.), *Social work and child sexual abuse*. New York: Haworth.

Hammond, S. (2004). The challenge of sex offender assessment: The case of internet offenders. In M. C. Calder (Ed.), *Child sexual abuse and the Internet: Tackling the new frontier*. Dorset, England: Russell House Publishing.

Hayes, S. C., Barnes-Holmes, D., & Roche, B. (2001). *Relational frame theory: A post-Skinnerian account of human language and cognition*. New York: Kluwer Academic/Plenum.

Hayes, S. C., Kohlenberg, B. S., & Hayes, L. J. (1991). The transfer of specific and general consequential functions through simple and conditional equivalence relations. *Journal of the Experimental Analysis of Behavior, 56,* 505-518.

Hayes, S. C., Strosahl, K., & Wilson, K. G. (1999). *Acceptance and commitment therapy: An experiential approach to behavior change*. New York: Guilford.

Herrnstein, R. J. (1970). On the law of effect. *Journal of the Experimental Analysis of Behavior, 13,* 243-266.

Hoffmann, H., Janssen, E., & Turner, S. L. (2004). Classical conditioning of sexual arousal in women and men: Effects of varying awareness and biological relevance of the conditioned stimulus. *Archives of Sexual Behavior, 33,* 43-53.

Horley, J. (2000). Cognitions supportive of child molestation. *Aggression and Violent Behavior, 5,* 551-564.

Johnson, C. F. (2004). Child sexual abuse. *The Lancet, 364,* 462-470.

Kaplan, M. S., Morales, M., & Becker, J. V. (1993). The impact of verbal satiation of adolescent sex offenders: A preliminary report. *Journal of Child Sexual Abuse, 2,* 81-88.

Kelly, J. A., St. Lawrence, J. S., Diaz, Y. E., Stevenson, L. Y., Hauth, A. C., Brasfield, T. L., et al. (1991). HIV risk behavior reduction following intervention with key opinion leaders of a population: An experimental community-level analysis. *American Journal of Public Health, 81,* 168-171.

Kelly, J. A., St. Lawrence, J. S., Stevenson, L. Y., Hauth, A. C., Kalichman, S. C., Diaz, Y. E., et al. (1992). Community AIDS/HIV risk reduction: The effects of endorsements by popular people in three cities. *American Journal of Public Health, 82,* 1483-1489.

Kilbourne, J., & Pipher, M. (2000). *Can't buy my love: How advertising changes the way we think and feel*. Columbus, OH: Free Press.

Kippin, T. T., Talikanakis, S., & Pfaus, J. G. (1997). The role of ejaculation in the development of conditioned sexual behaviors in the male rat. *Social Behavioral Neuroendocrinology Abstracts, 1,* 38.

Knight, R. A., & Prentky, R. A. (1990). Classifying sexual offenders: The development and corroboration of taxonomic models. In W. L. Marshall, D. R. Laws, & H. E. Barbaree (Eds.), *Handbook of sexual assault: Issues, theories, and treatment of the offender* (pp. 23-52). New York: Plenum Press.

Kohlenberg, R. J., Tsai, M., & Dougher, M. J. (1993). The dimensions of clinical behavior analysis. *Behavior Analyst, 16,* 271-282.

Lalumière, M. L., & Quinsey, V. L. (1998). Pavlovian conditioning of sexual interests in human males. *Archives of Sexual Behavior, 27,* 241-252.

Langevin, R., & Martin, M. (1975). Can erotic responses be classically conditioned? *Behavior Therapy, 6,* 350-355.

Lanyon, R. I. (1991). Theories of sex offending. In C. R. Hollin & K. Howells (Eds.), *Clinical approaches to sex offenders and their victims* (pp. 35-54). Chichester, England: Wiley.

Laws, D. R. (1995). Verbal satiation: Notes on procedure, with speculations on its mechanism of effect. *Journal of Research & Treatment, 7,* 155-166.

Laws, D. R., & Marshall, W. L. (1990). A conditioning theory of the etiology and maintenance of deviant sexual preference and behavior. In W. L. Marshall, D. R. Laws, & H. E. Barbaree (Eds.), *Handbook of sexual assault: Issues, theories, and treatment of the offender* (pp. 209-229). New York: Plenum Press.

Letourneau, E. J., & O'Donohue, W. (1997). Classical conditioning of female sexual arousal. *Archives of Sexual Behavior, 26,* 63-78.

LoPiccolo, J. (1994). Acceptance and broad spectrum treatment of paraphilias. In S. C. Hayes, N. S. Jacobson, V. M. Follette, & M. J. Dougher (Eds.), *Acceptance and change: Content and context in psychotherapy* (pp. 149-170). Reno, NV: Context Press.

LoPiccolo, J., & Stock, W. (1986). Treatment of sexual dysfunction. *Journal of Consulting and Clinical Psychology, 54*, 158-167.

Lovibond, S. H. (1963). Conceptual thinking, personality and conditioning. *British Journal of Social and Clinical Psychology, 2*, 100-111.

Maletzky, B. (1980). Self-referred versus court-referred sexually deviant patients: Success with assisted covert sensitization. *Behavior Therapy, 11*, 306-314.

Maletzky, B. M. (1991). *Treating the sexual offender*. Newbury Park, CA: Sage.

Maletzky, B. M. (2002). The paraphilias: Research and treatment. In P. E. Nathan & J. M. Gorman (Eds.), *A guide to treatments that work* (2nd ed.) (pp. 525-557). London: London University Press.

Maletzky, B. M., & Field, G. (2003). The biological treatment of dangerous sexual offenders: A review and preliminary report of the Oregon pilot depo-Provera program. *Aggression & Violent Behavior, 8*, 391-412.

Maletzky, B. M., & Steinhauser, C. (2002). A 25-year follow-up of cognitive/behavioral therapy with 7,275 sexual offenders. *Behavior Modification, 26*, 123-147.

Maletzky, B. M., & Steinhauser, C. (2003). Olfactory aversion: Notes on procedure, with speculations on its mechanism of effect: Comment. *Sexual Abuse: Journal of Research & Treatment, 15*, 215-217.

Mandell, K. H. (1970). Preliminary report on a new aversion therapy for male homosexuals. *Behavior Research and Therapy, 8*, 93-95.

Marshall, W. L., & Barbaree, H. E. (1988). An outpatient treatment programme for child molesters. *Annals of the New York Academy of Sciences, 528*, 205-214.

Marshall, W. L., & Barbaree, H. E. (1990). An integrated theory of sexual offending. In W. L. Marshall, D. R. Laws, & H. E. Barbaree (Eds.), *Handbook of sexual assault: Issues, theories and treatment of the offender*. New York: Plenum.

Marshall, W. L. (1996). Assessment, treatment and theorizing about sex offenders: Developments during the past twenty years and future directions. *Criminal Justice and Behavior, 23*, 162-199.

Masuda, A., Hayes, S. C., Sackett, C. F., & Twohig, M. P. (2004). Cognitive defusion and self-relevant negative thoughts: Examining the impact of a ninety year old technique. *Behaviour Research and Therapy, 42*, 477-485.

McConaghy, N. (1969). Subjective and penile plethysmograph responses following aversion-relief and apomorphine aversion therapy for homosexual impulses. *British Journal of Psychiatry, 115*, 723-730.

McConaghy, N. (1970). Penile response conditioning and its relationship to aversion therapy in homosexuals. *Behavior Therapy, 1*, 213- 221.

O'Donohue, W., & Plaud, J. J. (1994). The conditioning of human sexual arousal. *Archives of Sexual Behavior, 23*, 321-344.

Paul, R. H., Marx, B. P., & Orsillo, S. M. (1999). Acceptance based psychotherapy in the treatment of an adjudicated exhibitionist: A case example. *Behavior Therapy, 30*, 149-162.

Pilgrim, C., Chambers, L., & Galizio, M. (1995). Reversal of baseline relations and stimulus equivalence: II. Children. *Journal of the Experimental Analysis of Behavior, 63*, 239-254.

Pilgrim, C., & Galizio, M. (1990). Relations between baseline contingencies and equivalence probe performances. *Journal of the Experimental Analysis of Behavior, 54*, 213-224.

Pfaus, J. G., Kippin, T. T., & Centeno, S. (2001). Conditioning and sexual behavior: A review. *Hormones and Behavior, 40*, 291-321.

Plaud, J. J., & Gaither, G. A. (1997). The long-term habituation of sexual arousal in human males: A crossover design. *Psychological Record, 47*, 385-398.

Plaud, J. J., & Martini, J. R. (1999). The respondent conditioning of male sexual arousal. *Behavior Modification, 23*, 254-268.

Quayle, E., Holland, G., Linehan, C., & Taylor, M. (2000). The internet and offending behavior: A case study. *Journal of Sexual Aggression, 6*, 78-96.

Quayle, E., & Taylor, M. (2002a). Child pornography and the internet: Perpetuating a cycle of abuse. *Deviant Behavior, 23*, 331-362.

Quayle, E., & Taylor, M. (2002b). Pedophiles, pornography and the internet: Assessment issues. *British Journal of Social Work, 32*, 863-875.

Quayle, E., Vaughan, M., & Taylor, M. (2006). Sex offenders, internet abuse images and emotional avoidance: The importance of values. *Aggression & Violent Behavior, 11*, 1-11.

Quinn, J. T., Harbison, J., & McAllister, H. (1970). An attempt to shape penile responses. *Behavior Research and Therapy, 8*, 27-28.

Rachman, S. (1961). Aversion therapy: Chemical or electrical? *Behavior Research and Therapy, 2*, 289-299.

Rachman, S. (1966). Sexual fetishism: An experimental analogue. *The Psychological Record, 16*, 293-296.

Rachman, S., & Hodgson, R. J. (1968). Experimentally-induced "sexual fetishism": Replication and development. *The Psychological Record, 18*, 25-27.

Rada R. T., Laws D. R., Kellner, R., Stivastava L., & Peake G. (1983). Plasma androgens in violent and nonviolent sex offenders. *Bulletin of the American Academy of Psychiatry and the Law, 11*, 149-158.

Roche, B., & Barnes, D. (1996). Arbitrarily applicable relational responding and sexual categorization: A critical test of the derived difference relation. *The Psychological Record, 46*, 451-475.

Roche, B., & Barnes, D. (1997). A transformation of respondently conditioned stimulus function in accordance with arbitrarily applicable relations. *Journal of the Experimental Analysis of Behavior, 67*, 275-301.

Roche, B., & Barnes, D. (1998). The experimental analysis of human sexual arousal: Some recent developments. *The Behavior Analyst, 21*, 37-52.

Roche, B., Barnes, D., & Smeets, P. (1997). Incongruous stimulus pairing and conditional discrimination training: Effects on relational responding. *Journal of the Experimental Analysis of Behavior, 68*, 143-160.

Roche, B., Barnes-Holmes, D., Smeets, P. M., Barnes-Holmes, Y., & McGeady, S. (2000). Contextual control over the derived transformation of discriminative and sexual arousal functions. *The Psychological Record, 50*, 267-291.

Roche, B., & Dymond, S. (in press). A transformation of functions in accordance with the non-arbitrary relational properties of sexual stimuli. *The Psychological Record*.

Roche, B., O'Riordan, M., Ruiz, M., & Hand, K. (2005). A relational frame approach to the psychological assessment of sex offenders. In M. Taylor & E. Quayle (Eds.), *Viewing child pornography on the internet: Understanding the offense, managing the offender, and helping the victims* (pp. 109-125). Dorset, England: Russell House Publishing.

Rosen, R. C., & Kopel, S. A. (1977). Penile pletysmography and bio-feedback in the treatment of a transvestite-exhibitionist. *Journal of Consulting and Clinical Psychology, 45*, 908-916.

Rosen, R. C., Shapiro, D., & Schwartz, G. (1975). Voluntary control of penile tumescence. *Psychosomatic Medicine, 37*, 479-483.

Saunders, R. R., Saunders, K. J., Kirby, K. C., & Spradlin, J. E. (1988). The merger and development of equivalence classes by unreinforced conditional selection of comparison stimuli. *Journal of the Experimental Analysis of Behavior, 50*, 145-162.

Schaefer, H. H., & Colgan, A. H. (1977). The effect of pornography on penile tumescence as a function of reinforcement and novelty. *Behavior Therapy, 8*, 938-946.

Scully, D., & Marolla, J. (1985). Riding the bull at Gilley's: Convicted rapists describe the rewards of rape. *Social Problems, 32*, 251-263.

Segal, Z.V., Williams, J. M. G., & Teasdale, J. D. (2002). *Mindfulness-based cognitive therapy for depression*. New York: Guilford.

Seto, M. C., Maric, A., & Barbaree, H. E. (2001). The role of pornography in the etiology of sexual aggression. *Aggression and Violent Behavior, 6*, 35-53.

Smeets, P. M., Barnes-Holmes, Y., Akpinar, D., & Barnes-Holmes, D. (2003). Reversal of equivalence relations. *The Psychological Record, 53*, 91-119.

Spradlin, J. E., Saunders, K. J., & Saunders, R. R. (1992). The stability of equivalence classes. In S. C. Hayes & L. J. Hayes (Eds.), *Understanding verbal relations* (pp. 29-42). Reno, NV: Context Press.

Sullivan, J., & Beech, A. J. (2004). Assessing internet offenders. In M. C. Calder (Ed.), *Child sexual abuse and the internet: Tackling the new frontier* (pp. 69-83). Dorset, England: Russell House Publishing.

Taylor, M., & Quayle, E. (2003). *Child pornography: An internet crime.* London: Brunner-Routledge.

Tourinho, E. Z. (2006). Private stimuli, covert responses, and private events: Conceptual remarks. *The Behavior Analyst, 29,* 13-31.

Tyndall, I., Roche, B., & James, J. E. (2004). The relationship between stimulus function and stimulus equivalence: A systematic investigation. *Journal of the Experimental Analysis of Behavior, 81,* 257-266.

Ullman, S. E. (2004). Sexual assault victimization and suicidal behavior in women: A review of the literature. *Aggression and Violent Behavior, 9,* 331-351.

Wirth, O., & Chase, P. (2002). Stability of functional equivalence and stimulus equivalence: Effects of baseline reversals. *Journal of the Experimental Analysis of Behavior, 77,* 29-47.

Wulfert, E., & Biglan, A. (1994). A contextual approach to research on AIDS prevention. *The Behavior Analyst, 17,* 353-363.

Chapter 13

Clinical Behavior Analysis and Health Psychology Applications

Ann D. Branstetter & Christopher C. Cushing
Missouri State University

Health psychology involves the application of psychological principles and research findings to the treatment of psychosocial needs of individuals with illness, to the prevention of future illness, and to the enhancement of overall quality of life (Straub, 2002). Within the field, many subspecialities exist. Some are focused on promoting, understanding barriers to, and improving compliance with recommended health screening behaviors, such as mammography, colorectal cancer screening, or HIV testing. Others are dedicated to reducing high-risk health behaviors (e.g., smoking or unsafe sexual practices) or developing interventions to promote positive health behaviors such as exercise, good diet, and oral hygiene.

Many of these health-focused interventions and programs are effective. However, in the field of coping with chronic disease, pain, and terminal health status, empirical support remains weak. There is a strong need for the development of theoretical and data-based approaches for psychosocial interventions with these populations. Although the various chronic diseases and causes of chronic pain and disease vary, individuals suffering from these conditions tend to share similar experiences and respond with similar ways of coping, which can result in poor behavioral and emotional outcomes.

Contemporary behavior analysis is in the position to understand the coping behaviors of persons with chronic terminal health conditions and to derive effective treatment strategies aimed at aiding in the care of those with such conditions. In addition, contemporary behavior analysis may also improve current methods of addressing health behavior and treatment adherence. To illustrate this point, we have chosen three common targets of health psychology (i.e., chronic pain, treatment adherence, and chronic/life-threatening disease) and summarized the presenting problems and commonalities, while emphasizing the role of contemporary behavior analysis. Behavioral and cognitive-behavioral treatment strategies are briefly reviewed for each of these areas, and an overview of the available research is presented. In addition, we will discuss the potential role of contemporary behavior analysis as applied to these areas of health psychology, along with current supportive research.

Chronic Pain

Chronic pain is defined as pain lasting for 6 months or longer which is relatively unresponsive to treatment and may progress in severity over time (Taylor, 2003). At any given time, it is estimated that at least 50 million people in the United States are suffering from chronic pain (American Chronic Pain Association, 2006). The pain itself may be related to a disease, such as cancer, or may be of an unknown or undetectable etiology, such as is often the case with lower back pain. Chronic pain results in a variety of negative psychological events, including low self-esteem, insomnia, hopelessness, anger, and depression (Straub, 2002). These negative outcomes are particularly likely to occur among individuals who tend to catastrophize their situations, who withdraw socially, and who receive external rewards for their pain related behavior (Hassinger, Semenchuk, & O'Brien, 1999; Osterhaus, Lange, Linssen, & Passchier, 1997).

Not only does pain result in devastating psychological costs, it also produces a high cost to society through missed work days, disability pay, medication costs, hospitalization, and other treatment costs. It is estimated that the yearly costs of chronic pain in the United States may be as much as $100 billion dollars (Straub, 2002). For treatment providers, chronic pain is often frustrating to diagnose due to an inability to physically detect and measure nociceptive (pain) sensation and its subjective nature. For example, two individuals who have similar injuries or diagnoses may report vastly different levels of associated pain. Such clinical examples contribute to the growing belief that pain is not only an individual experience but also a contextually-based psychological phenomenon.

Despite the phenomenological and contextual nature of pain, research consistently indicates that greater levels of physical disability due to a chronic pain condition are reported among individuals who cope through avoidance of feared pain stimuli and pain related events (Asmundson, Norton, & Allerdings, 1997; Verbunt, Seelen, Vlaeyen, van de Heijde, Heuts, Pons et al., 2003; Vlaeyen, Kole-Snijders, Boeren, & van Eek, 1995). Such avoidance also predicts greater interference with life activities and psychological distress (Geisser, Robinson, & Henson, 1994). Furthermore, the use of avoidance and passive coping strategies, such as "wishing it would go away," is correlated with depression among pain patients (Weickgenant, Slater, Patterson, Atkinson, Grant, & Garfin, 1993).

Treatment Adherence

Adherence to treatment regimens is less than ideal across almost all medical disorders, but is especially problematic among diseases which require adherence currently, in order to potentially prevent further disease or exacerbation in the future. This pattern is clearly evident in the recommendations for individuals with diabetes.

Diabetes

Diabetes, a disease which involves the body's inability to produce or properly use insulin, is the third most common chronic disease in the United States, affecting almost 6% of the population (Taylor, 2003). This disease is of interest to health psychologists due to the behavioral risk factors which contribute to the onset of Type II (adult-onset) diabetes, the relationship between stress and diabetes, the psychological consequences of living with a chronic disease, and adherence to treatment programs.

For those who receive a diagnosis of diabetes, it is common to first experience a variety of emotional responses, including shock, anger, depression, and denial (Jacobson, 1996). This response may continue for some time, given that research indicates that depression and anxiety are more common among individuals with diabetes as compared to the general population (Katon & Sullivan, 1990). This impacts not only psychological functioning, but also physiological functioning, as distress has been shown to lead to increasing difficulty in the regulation of blood-sugar levels (Brand, Johnson, & Johnson, 1986).

Similar to findings within the cancer literature, research indicates that diabetes sufferers who engage in avoidant coping behaviors tend to also report poorer quality of life and greater levels of depression (Boey, 1999; Coelho, Amorim, & Prata, 2003; Grey, Cameron, & Thurber, 1991). In response to this, treatment providers are advised to encourage patients to acknowledge and accept their disease and new lifestyle, rather than avoiding and potentially creating additional stress as it relates to their health status.

Like many chronic diseases, diabetes care is dependent on adherence to treatment recommendations. When adherence occurs, the disease can often be well controlled. However, adherence to self-management programs is very low. Across numerous studies, it appears that only about 15% of patients with diabetes follow their full prescribed treatment regimen (Taylor, 2003). Such nonadherence has serious health consequences, including potential blindness, numbness, neuropathy, and limb loss. Despite these very real threats, individuals continue to struggle to follow their recommended guidelines. Nonadherence is especially common among those who cope through more avoidant mechanisms (Hanson, Cigrang, Harris, Carle, Relyea, & Burghen, 1989; Hunt, Pugh, & Valenzuela, 1998). Avoidance is most likely used to create a false sense of comfort and distance from the disease, but in so doing, the person is less attentive to their physical needs, and less likely to engage in disease management behavior.

Chronic/Terminal Illness

A diagnosis of a serious and potentially fatal illness is a universal stressor. It creates unique psychological and emotional experiences for each individual. In the United States, one of the most common terminal diagnoses is cancer.

Cancer

Each year, over 1,000,000 individuals are diagnosed with, and nearly 600,000 die from cancer in the United States (American Cancer Society, 2005). Progression through the cancer experience, from time of diagnosis, through treatment, to survivorship or death is emotionally difficult. Although the exact numbers of patients who experience a clinically significant level of depression, anxiety, or general psychological distress differs based upon the site and type of cancer (Zabora, Brintzenhofeszoc, Curbow, Hooker, & Piantadosi, 2001), approximately 50% will experience psychiatric disorders at some point during the course of illness (Derogatis, Morrow, & Fetting, 1983). The most common diagnoses include adjustment disorders, depressive disorders, and less frequently, anxiety disorders. In addition, an unknown number will experience psychological distress, yet not report it to treatment providers.

Providing appropriate treatment for the psychological concerns of cancer patients is important for at least two reasons. First, to maximize quality of life, it is important to ensure that patients cope effectively with their disease with respect to the related emotional sequelae, their ability to make decisions, speak freely and deliberately with loved ones, and engage in any necessary planning activities. Second, because of the increasing amount of data linking both depression (Irwin, 1999) and chronic anxiety (Herbert & Cohen, 1993) to impaired immune functioning, it is in the best interest of their physiological health and response to treatment that they enter their regimen free of stress-related psychopathology.

The cancer experience is often one of uncertainty. Individuals live day to day, treatment to treatment, not knowing if the cancer is progressing or shrinking. The cancer journey is also unpredictable. At first diagnosis the tumor may appear small enough to remove surgically, yet the patient may awaken from surgery to be told that the cancer was far more progressed than first assumed, and that a complex and experimental approach may be the best treatment option. As a result of this varied and unpredictable course, the disease places an extreme psychological burden on the patient and family. Patients react to this stress in a variety of ways. One finding, however, is increasingly clear. Individuals who cope with the cancer experience through avoidance of emotional content and external stimuli are more likely to experience psychological distress as compared to individuals who cope through the use of emotional social support and emotional expression (Stanton, Danoff-Burg, Cameron, Bishop, Collins, Kirk et al., 2000).

Summary

Across the three clinical health psychology patient populations discussed, one consistent theme is that avoidance based coping tends to be associated with negative outcomes, including poor adherence, poor quality of life, and increased incidence of psychological distress, depression, and anxiety. However, avoidance has not always been a focus of treatment. As illustrated in the following models, only recently have researchers identified the contribution of avoidance to poor outcomes. As such, empirically based methods of intervention, relevant to avoidance, have been lacking.

Traditional Behavioral Models

Chronic Pain

Traditional behavioral models have been effectively utilized in understanding and treating individuals with chronic pain. This model focuses on observable pain behaviors in both assessment and targeted interventions, and there is no attempt to identify or alter the emotional experiences related to chronic pain conditions (Fordyce, Roberts, & Sternbach, 1985). Assessment, for example, focuses on observations and ratings of objective pain behaviors, such as slow response time, limping, position shifts, grimacing, sounds, and pain statements (Follick, Ahern, & Aberger, 1985). The interventions are designed to produce changes in these outward indicators of pain, as well as to increase the individual's participation in life activities. This is illustrated by Fordyce and colleagues (1985), who stated, "Behavioral pain methods do not have as their principal objective the modification of nociception, nor the direct modification of the experience of pain...Rather, behavioral methods in pain-treatment programs are intended to treat excess disability and expressions of suffering" (p.115). The logic is that chronic pain sufferers do not necessarily need to be free from pain to enjoy life.

Operant treatment programs which targeted objective pain behaviors were developed largely based upon the model program at the University of Washington (Fordyce, Fowler, Lehman, & DeLateur, 1968). The Washington program consisted of a one-to-two month inpatient stay, during which pain behavior was systematically extinguished (such as no attention or empathic responses from staff in response to complaining). Simultaneously, the staff was also trained to reinforce adaptive behaviors, such as socialization, by providing various reinforcing stimuli, including verbal attention and medication, contingent upon the performance of the targeted adaptive behavior. Such operant pain treatment programs were found to result in significantly fewer pain reports by patients, and significant decreases in use of pain medications (Fordyce & Steger, 1979). The success of these interventions, led to them being considered empirically supported treatments for chronic back pain and headache (Compas, Haaga, Keefe, Leitenberg, & Williams, 1998).

Treatment Adherence

Traditional behavioral models have also led to effective treatments for modifying adherence behaviors. According to this model, nonadherence is a product of inadequate immediate reinforcement of adherence behaviors (Rapoff, 1999). Patients often have difficulty perceiving the relation between adherence (e.g. taking one's medication everyday) and the ultimate health outcome (e.g., limited disease progression), as adherence typically produces a very distal reinforcer. Because of the weak link between behavior and consequence, interventions may be more effective when a more immediate reinforcer for adherence behavior is presented. Many self-management programs attempt to build on this, by encouraging individuals to administer their own reinforcement based upon behavioral performance, rather than outcome (e.g., Bellack, 1976; Murray & Hobbs, 1981).

Based on this model, operant interventions, particularly token economies, have been proposed to increase adherence (Rapoff, 1999). These interventions have been shown to be effective, especially among children. For example, using a point economy system along with verbal praise contingent on the occurrence of targeted behavior, researchers were successful in modifying diet and exercise behavior, and increasing monitoring behavior among children with insulin-dependent diabetes (Epstein, 1981). When applied to adults, the bulk of the research concerning token economies has been conducted with individuals who are confined to an inpatient setting and/or who are of limited intellectual functioning. Although these protocols appear to be effective, it is likely, that such interventions are arduous and limited in success for normal functioning adults in less well-controlled environments (Winkler, 1985).

Chronic/Life-Threatening Illness

Despite these advances in some areas of health psychology, traditional behavioral models of treatment have offered little to address the emotional pain and suffering associated with the experience of cancer and other life-threatening diseases. The behavioral model for depression suggests that depression is the result of decreased access to reinforcers, and/or the presence of uncontrollable aversive stimuli (Ferster, 1973; Lewinsohn, 1974; see Chapter 6 of this volume by Kanter and colleagues). This model may be useful in helping to conceptualize depression among individuals who, due to their medical status, have become unable or unwilling to engage in previously enjoyable activities, such as work, or daily life activities, and who may now be limited in ability to participate in social interactions. For example, many cancer patients with progressive disease become increasingly homebound, with decreased mobility and independence. This would result in fewer opportunities to engage in positive social interactions and desired physical activities, and limited exposure to natural reinforcers.

Treatment based upon the traditional behavioral model includes behavioral activation, a process of scheduling enjoyable and masterful activities into each day to increase the individual's exposure to natural reinforcers, and thereby, gradually decrease depression. This approach has been shown to be effective in treating depression among psychiatric samples (Dimidjian, Hollon, Dobson, Schmaling, Kohlenberg, Addis et al., 2006). A variant of behavioral activation, Behavioral Activation Treatment for Depression (BATD; Lejeuz, Hopko, & Hopko, 2001) has been developed for depressed individuals previously diagnosed with cancer. BATD is distinct in that it requires only 10-12 sessions, focuses exclusively on activation-based interventions, and includes a comprehensive assessment of values, goals and objectives borrowed from Acceptance and Commitment Therapy (ACT; Hayes, Strosahl, & Wilson, 1999). In an open trial of 6 depressed individuals previously diagnosed with cancer who were receiving treatment in a primary care setting, patients demonstrated significant pre–post improvement across a variety of outcome measures with strong effect sizes, and patient and clinician satisfaction with the treatment was strong (Hopko, Bell, Armento, Hunt, & Lejuez, 2005). Currently, a randomized trial comparing BATD to another active treatment and treatment-as-usual in primary care is occurring.

Although traditional behavioral activation is highly effective in general populations, and current data indicates that BATD may also be highly effective, both are limited in applicability to chronically ill populations, and may be less appropriate when disease progression is so severe that mobility and activity is prohibited.

Cognitive Behavioral Models

The Cognitive-Behavioral (CB) model of treatment is based on the cognitive model which suggests that an event or situation does not determine how a person reacts, but that the actual determining factor is how a person perceives the event or situation (Beck, 1964). From this perspective, the situation does not create an emotional response, but rather the perception or cognitive construction of the situation leads to the emotional response. The CB model suggests that behaviors, thoughts, and emotions are related to each other through a positive feedback loop, and that by creating change in behavior or in thought, the entire cycle may be modified.

Applications of this treatment for medical populations have been instrumental in reducing patient distress, improving psychological adjustment of those with problem health conditions, and increasing the quality of life among patients with chronic and life-threatening disease (Gatchel, 1999). Here we briefly review the content and efficacy of CB treatment packages for chronic pain, treatment adherence, and chronic/life threatening illnesses.

Chronic Pain

Similar to the traditional behavioral model of chronic pain, the CB model suggests that the behavioral disability experienced by pain sufferers is of primary clinical concern (Lethem, Slade, Troup, & Bentley, 1983). However, the focus is on the cognitive and emotional components of fear (Vlaeyen et al., 1995). It has been suggested that even acute pain conditions, such as musculoskeletal injuries, can lead to long-term pain disability if the individual begins to fear and avoid the painful stimuli (Lethem et al., 1983). Likewise the CB model suggests that the pain and disability cycle is further mediated by the individual's cognitive catastrophization of the pain experience (Vlayen et al., 1995). For example, individuals with pain who ruminate about how awful the situation is, how it will never improve, and how the pain has interfered with everything, are more likely to fear and avoid the pain, leading to increasingly higher levels of disability (Hill, Niveen, & Knussen, 1995; Robinson, Riley, Myers, Sadler, Kvaal, Geisser et al., 1997). Treatment packages focus on helping patients to change their beliefs about the pain, solve problems related to the pain condition, monitor and identify the relationships between thoughts, emotions, and behaviors, and develop adaptive ways of thinking about and responding to pain

(Bradley, 1996). Others have suggested that modifying cognition, in the form of distraction from the pain, is useful (Schmitz, Saile, & Nilges, 1996).

Treatment Adherence

Given the significant problem of nonadherence among individuals whose health conditions require self-monitoring, taking medication as directed, or other lifestyle modifications, researchers and clinicians have attempted to apply the CB model to develop successful adherence interventions. These interventions often involve assessing thoughts about the treatment regimen that may interfere with adherence. Typical cognitive barriers emerging from such an assessment include believing that one could not be successful in completing the target behavior, believing that the behavior is unnecessary or insignificant, or a failure to understand what is expected. Based upon this information, the clinician and patient work to modify those thoughts. Such interventions have been utilized to improve several adherence behaviors, such as flossing (McCaul, O'Neil, & Glasgow, 1988), diabetes monitoring (see Lemanek, Kamps, & Chung, 2001 for review of empirically supported literature), and diet and exercise programs within the context of treatments for obesity (Cooper, Fairburn, & Hawker, 2003).

Chronic/Life-Threatening Illness

Several cognitive-behavioral interventions have been proposed to facilitate effective coping with cancer (Jacobsen & Hann, 1998). Among these packaged programs, the cognitive-behavioral techniques most frequently included are cognitive restructuring, coping self-statements, distraction, relaxation, and activity planning. The general conclusion based upon review of numerous studies indicates that compared to receiving no intervention, cognitive-behavioral interventions result in improved psychological functioning (see Jacobsen & Hann, 1998 for a full review).

Although efficacy data are generally supportive, reliance on restructuring of cognitions may be a problem for some patients in this population. The issue is that, when performed poorly, restructuring interventions may be seen as invalidating or counter-productive. Take for example an emotionally distressed patient in palliative care with thoughts of "I'm going to die" or "I don't want to die." Under the circumstances, there is limited ability to modify these thoughts, for although catastrophic, they indeed represent an accurate perception of their current situation. Such thoughts are not inaccurate or illogical, therefore not readily addressed by traditional identification of dysfunctional thoughts and cognitive restructuring.

Under these circumstances, many CB treatment providers encourage patients to actively work to not think about (distract from) their pain or health situation as a way of coping if the patient reports feeling better when they do so. However, recent research suggests that this distraction may be counterproductive. For example, use of distraction has been shown to be predictive of higher levels of reported pain severity (Hill, 1993; Hill et al., 1995) and disability (Robinson et al., 1997) among chronic pain patients.

As we discuss below, the contemporary behavioral model suggests that such forms of distraction may function as experiential avoidance, which occurs when an individual desires to avoid a thought or sensation and takes steps to behaviorally or cognitively limit their interaction with the event (Hayes, Strosahl, & Wilson, 1999). In fact, research on experiential avoidance indicates that within a short period of time, this avoidance often results in increasing levels of painful stimuli as evidenced by lower pain endurance and tolerance (Feldner, Hekmat, Zvolensky, Vowles, Secrist, & Leen-Feldner, 2006). Despite these findings highlighting the key role of avoidance, most treatments do not attempt to directly address or modify avoidance. The contemporary model, however, emphasizes the role of experiential avoidance in psychological distress and offers a conceptualization of how this may be applied within health populations.

Contemporary Behavioral Model

Contemporary behavior analysis has great potential within the field of health psychology. Relational Frame Theory (RFT; Hayes, Barnes-Holmes, & Roche, 2001), provides a contemporary behavioral theory of language and cognition and may provide a useful platform for understanding avoidance behavior as well as the pervasive nature of pain behavior. In addition, ACT (Hayes et al., 2001) provides a promising clinical intervention to address and modify avoidance behavior, reduce distress, and assist individuals in living valuable and productive lives in the context of illness.

Chronic Pain

Although the Fordyce model of pain (1985) and associated interventions are clearly effective in modifying overt behavior, they focus on a limited set of behaviors. In addition, the model fails to recognize that pain behavior is subject to language and cognitive abilities. Alternatively, the contemporary model is built upon the concept that due to the pervasive and chronic nature of pain conditions, virtually every aspect of an individual's life can become linked with pain through arbitrary learning processes. Instinctually, humans avoid stimuli and activities which produce pain. If touching a flame produces pain, then one is less likely to place one's hand in the fire and experience tissue damage and possible infection and/or demise. Likewise, if one's ankle hurts when one runs, then one is likely to stop running. In such acute pain situations, avoidance is functional and serves to protect one's physical well-being. However for the individual with a chronic and pervasive pain condition, such avoidance may be less functional and, to the extent it is rule-based, may prevail over other direct contingencies. For such an individual, pain may be experienced in virtually every activity. A rule to avoid pain quickly narrows the field of potential behavioral choices and activities. As a result, it is common to encounter patients who are virtually bed-ridden, devoid of meaningful life events and relationships, all in the service of avoiding pain. This is illustrated by the consistent findings that individuals with chronic pain report lower quality of life (e.g. Laursen, Bajaj, Olesen, & Delmar, 2005) and are more likely to attempt and commit suicide compared to those without chronic pain (Fishbain, 1999).

Treatment Adherence

RFT may also add to our understanding of nonadherence. Suppose that "diabetes" has been related through verbal contextual historical experiences to "sickness," or "disability," or "physical inadequacy." It is unlikely that one would be excited to use this stimulus class as a personal descriptor. As such, a rule may be generated to avoid "diabetes." What other stimuli are likely to be mutually entailed within this class through a history of arbitrarily derived relations? No doubt the class contains stimuli such as medication, insulin injections, blood glucose monitoring tools and rules for disease management. If the unstated rule is to avoid feeling inadequate, and to therefore avoid thoughts related to having diabetes, the individual is likely also to not engage in prescribed health behaviors which logically may serve to actually maintain health and wellness. In such a case, operant conditioning programs, such as token economies, do not address or attempt to break-up the relations among the members of the stimulus class, therefore should not generalize to other adherence related behaviors in the class that are not directly targeted.

Chronic/Life-Threatening Illness

RFT similarly adds to our understanding of phenomena related to chronic illness. For example, why is it that talking about one's cancer diagnosis is emotionally painful? Based upon an operant model, talking to a friend about one's health status and treatment should take on the reinforcing functions of the friend offering reassurance and comfort (Wilson & Blackledge, 2000). In fact, despite the emotional difficulty associated with talking about aversive events, including health concerns and fears, current evidence has amassed that that the simple activity of "languaging" about the topic produces positive outcomes. However, individuals frequently find such discussions emotionally painful and full of stimulus cues for avoidance. A treatment based on RFT designed to treat distress among individuals with chronic or terminal disease would target experiential avoidance through attempts to break up these relational networks. Clinicians might encourage the patient to engage in behavioral experiments to test "rules" and allow opportunities to contact natural contingencies. In so doing, experience rather than rules may inform behavioral choices.

RFT may serve to provide health psychologists with a new and fresh conceptualization of health-related behaviors and the psychological experience of the medical patient. For example, it is culturally and contextually reinforcing for human beings to be perceived as physically and psychologically healthy. Imagine a task in which participants are asked to quickly write all the words that come to mind when visually presented the word "cancer." It is likely that many of the responses would be rather negative in nature. Words such as "disabled," "contagious," "disease," "pity," "death," and "ill" may come quickly to mind. Behaviorally, we suggest that these words may represent a stimulus equivalence class and the aversive or avoidance functions of any member of the class may transfer to any other member. Given the statement, "you have cancer," many people will actively work to avoid contact with the stimulus "cancer" based upon its equivalence with the numerous "bad" private events previously noted. Unfortunately, just as the individual works to avoid any experience with stimuli in this class, the class may be expanding with each person who asks about the cancer, with each visit to the physician, with each medication, and with each new person the individual encounters in the process of treating this avoided stimulus. It is not that these events are formally related in any way, but the verbal/cognitive activity of "avoiding cancer" brings them together. Thus, to the extent that the RFT analysis is correct, previously innocuous or even pleasurable events (such as speaking with a friend) may gain new stimulus control functions. Similarly, providing a verbal report of one's health state can result in the emotional experience of pain as great as when one first received the statement, "you have cancer."

A further consideration is rule-governed behavior, specifically rules related to experiential avoidance that may be culturally reinforced and quite prevalent in our culture (Hayes et al., 1999). Such rules, combined with the logic of expanding equivalence classes, may be quite detrimental. For example, rules that one must avoid feeling bad may result in further rules that one must avoid thinking about cancer. In order to do that, one can no longer talk with friends, as friends will inquire about the cancer. The unfortunate effect is that the individual never comes directly into contact with what really would happen if he/she did in fact socialize with friends. The rule simply serves to create further problems and constriction in life quality. Even though the rule may be not be accurate, in the pragmatic sense the individual who engages in experiential avoidance will not actually experience naturally occurring consequences so the inaccuracy of the rule will never become salient.

Existing Empirical Support for the Contemporary Model

Though not originally designed to support or test the contemporary model of behavior analysis, a growing body of literature supports a relationship between verbal expression of one's emotions, particularly emotions and concerns which are unpleasant, and one's overall psychological and physical well being.

Emotional Expression Literature

Although a few empirical studies indicate that emotion-focused coping is psychologically maladaptive to the process of dealing with stressful situations, the majority of findings indicate that when confronted with health and medical concerns, individuals fare better overall when they cope through actively processing and expressing their emotional responses and experiences (e.g., Classen, Koopman, Angell, & Spiegel, 1996; Stanton et al., 2000). Several randomized controlled trials have been conducted to examine the effect of "forced" emotional expression on physical health and psychological well-being.

For example, an influential study by Spiegel, Bloom, and Yalom (1981) examined the psychological effects of participation in support groups among women with Stage IV breast cancer. Fifty women were randomly assigned to a treatment condition which included attending a 90-minute support group each week. Thirty-six women were assigned to a standard treatment condition, which did not include any psychological intervention. Participants in the experimental condition met in groups of 7-10 and were encouraged by the group facilitator to verbally and openly express painful emotions related to the disease experience, impending death, the effect of their illness and death on their family, and what it was like to live under these unique and stressful circumstances. The women in the intervention group reported significantly higher quality of life, less psychological distress, and actually survived longer than women in the control condition. A replication attempt found that intervention women were significantly improved in quality of life, psychological distress and mood but did not demonstrate lengthened survival (Goodwin, Leszca, Ennis, Koopmans, Vincent, Guther et al., 2001). These findings provide further support for the notion that emotional expression of difficult subject matter has a positive impact on life quality and psychological adjustment.

In an alternative experimental paradigm of emotional expression, Pennebaker (2003) has employed a writing task, in which participants are instructed to write about their deepest thoughts and feelings related to a traumatic or emotionally painful event. These studies consistently produce significant differences in health and psychological outcomes as compared to control groups, such that individuals who are asked to express painful emotions experience greater health, and less psychological distress. For example, Pennebaker, Colder, and Sharp (1990) investigated the potential health benefits of written emotional expression for students beginning their college experience. Students who wrote for 20 minutes over the course of 3 sessions had significantly fewer health center visits and reported fewer physical and psychological complaints as compared to the control group, which was instructed to write about neutral topics. Similar findings have resulted in positive health outcomes among asthma and rheumatoid arthritis patients (Smyth, Stone, Hurewitz, & Kaell, 1999), cancer patients (Stanton, 2002), and general healthy samples (Austenfeld, Paolo, & Stanton, 2006).

The question remains as to why a simple intervention such as writing for 20 minutes about an emotionally painful topic would yield such dramatic and reliable findings. It may be that through the continual cognitive contact with stressors or difficult emotions, the participant habituates to the stimuli. The individual may be repeatedly engaging in exposure to the content, experiencing the emotions as they would normally occur, but instead of immediately engaging in avoidance strategies (e.g., distraction, thought suppression, etc.) the participant maintains intimate contact with these emotions for at least 20 minutes. Based on learning principles, this exposure technique, paired with the experience of a non-threatening reality should, over time, result in a decrease in the amount of physical arousal and/or psychological distress experienced in response to the instructional content (Foa & Kozak, 1986).

A recent study attempted to determine the specific nature of exposure to account for the above findings (Stanton, Danoff-Burg, Sworowski, Collins, Branstetter, Rodriguez-Hanley et al., 2002). This study involved women newly diagnosed with early stage breast cancer. The participants were randomly assigned to one of three writing conditions. The first condition was based on the traditional Pennebaker instruction to write about thoughts and feelings related to the experience of breast cancer, with an emphasis on "things you may have tried to not think about or haven't shared with others." In the second condition, the women were instructed to write about and describe the facts and events related to their disease, such as date of diagnosis, types of treatment, and physician appointments. The instruction was specific to not include your thoughts and feelings, but to specifically focus on the facts related to the breast cancer diagnosis and treatment. Finally, the third condition instructed women to write about all the positive thoughts and feelings regarding the breast cancer experience. This may include things they believe they have gained as a result of the experience, such as new knowledge or friendships built as a result of the experience. Of the three experimental conditions, women who engaged in written emotional expression of thoughts and feelings related to the cancer experience demonstrated greater physical outcomes and significantly decreased psychological distress as compared to the remaining two conditions. Thus, this study demonstrates the importance specifically of expression of and exposure to the potentially avoided emotional content. This is consistent with the ACT perspective, in that decreased avoidance eventually leads to less psychological distress and greater levels of adjustment.

Emotional Avoidance Literature

Other researchers have concentrated more on the effects of emotional avoidance and avoidant coping in medical populations. The construct of avoidance is not consistently defined in the literature. While some use the term synonymously with denial, others distinguish between types of avoidance, such as behavioral avoidance and cognitive avoidance (Carver, Scheier, & Weintraub, 1989). For the purposes of this discussion, it is most fitting to employ a broad functional definition, such that avoidance refers to both behavioral and cognitive efforts which serve to prevent aversive thoughts and memories from entering one's conscious awareness (Primo, Compas, Oppedisano, Howell, Epping-Jordan, & Krag, 2000).

A link between avoidant coping style and distress has been clearly identified in samples of cancer patients. For example, in a prospective study of breast cancer patients, researchers examined coping and distress from diagnosis to six months post-diagnosis. Cognitive avoidance consistently predicted distress, both concurrently and prospectively (Stanton & Snider, 1993). In a later study, Stanton and colleagues (2000) again reported that breast cancer sufferers who engaged in avoidant coping techniques became more distressed across the three months following initial diagnosis, as compared to those who engaged in less avoidance.

In addition to being linked with psychological distress, avoidance as a method of coping with other chronic diseases consistently is associated with negative outcomes. For example individuals with chronic pain conditions who are highly avoidant of engaging in any behavior which they perceive as being related to increasing pain intensity have significantly higher rates of pain disability, and report greater distress (Sorbi, Peters, Kruise, Maas, Kerssens, Verhaak et al., 2006). Avoidance is also, as noted previously, correlated with nonadherence to medical regimens (Hanson et al., 1989).

Alternatively, previous research indicates that acceptance of pain is statistically associated with lower anxiety, depression, physical and psychosocial disability and reported pain intensity (McCracken, 1998). Acceptance of pain has also shown to be a positive and significant predictor of whether or not an individual will return to work following disability. This remains a predictor even when controlling for pain intensity ratings (McCracken & Eccleston, 2003). Furthermore, acceptance of pain also predicts mental health and psychological well-being despite level of pain severity (Viane, Crombez, Eccleston, Poppe, Devulder, Van Houdenhove et al., 2003).

Problems with Contemporary Model and Verifiable Hypotheses

Currently, the most glaring problem for the contemporary model within health psychology is the lack of basic empirical support for the role of relational framing and derived relations. For example, do disease-related words share class membership with negatively valanced words? Does this occur more frequently among those individuals who engage in avoidant forms of coping? Can this relationship be experimentally demonstrated?

One hypothesis that may be derived from the RFT literature is that as a stimulus equivalence class of "avoid pain" expands, antecedent cues for avoidance behavior should increase and behavioral repertoires should narrow. Likewise, longer durations of pain should result in larger equivalence classes, more avoidance behavior and narrower repertoires.

According to RFT, pain behavior in adults is partially a product of strict rule following (i.e., "avoid pain"). Therefore, very young children with limited verbal ability should be more likely to persist in laboratory pain tasks. It may be assumed that before the development of firm rules dictating the avoidance of pain, child would not have the "avoid pain" rule producing behavioral avoidance. Furthermore, pain behavior is thought to be in equivalence relations with "suffering" descriptors and innocuous pain descriptors. If this learning has not taken place the individual should show fewer pain avoidance behaviors. While children are at a stage with limited stimulus equivalence classes, it should be possible to more effectively train abstaining from making value judgments about thoughts and feelings not yet part of an avoidant equivalence class.

We would also expect that successful cognitive defusion of equivalence classes would reduce behavioral avoidance. For example, a cancer patient who avoids conversing with friends because such conversations, through equivalence relations, evoke suffering might be taught to defuse these two stimulus events. Upon successful defusion, the sufferer would not only be expected to demonstrate reduced behavioral avoidance of conversing with a friend, but also exhibit less behavioral avoidance related to all other bidirectionally related stimuli.

This suggests the importance of developing treatment interventions that address the specific needs of health populations. Only a limited number of treatment protocols have been proposed (e.g., Gregg, Callaghan, Hayes, & Glenn-Lawson, in press; Wicksell, Dahl, Magnusson, & Olsson, 2005), and evaluations of those protocols are lacking. Ideally, model-based protocols should be compared to the existing treatment modalities through randomized controlled trials.

Treatment Implications

The contemporary model of behavior analysis provides a link between theory, basic science, and the development of clinical psychosocial interventions. RFT explains expansive avoidance behaviors that are so prevalent and detrimental to health populations. It also provides a direction for treatment development. Given the research reviewed earlier concerning emotional avoidance and emotional exposure, a treatment that focuses on decreasing avoidance may be a viable option for treating the psychological distress and behavioral concerns of health populations. Acceptance and Commitment Therapy (ACT; Hayes, Strosahl, & Wilson, 1999) may be such an option. ACT is a behavior analytic treatment, developed in conjunction with emerging empirical support for RFT, which facilitates acceptance of one's thoughts, emotions, personal history, and other uncontrollable events. ACT proposes that as acceptance occurs, behavioral options expand and avoidance of aversive stimuli becomes less frequent. Patients should decrease their reliance on avoidant coping strategies, producing a decrease in the incidence of negative outcomes associated with such strategies.

To date, one randomized trial has compared ACT to traditional CBT with patients who were undergoing treatment for late stage ovarian cancer (Branstetter, Wilson, Hildebrandt, & Mutch, 2004). In this trial, 60 women, many of whom were also clinically depressed and/or anxious, were randomly assigned to one of the two therapy conditions and participated in 12 sessions of individual therapy. Measures of psychological distress, depression, anxiety, coping style, thought suppression, and emotional control were completed at baseline, after four sessions, eight sessions, and at the completion of the intervention. Results indicated that women in the ACT condition demonstrated significantly greater decreases in depression, anxiety, and distress compared to women in the CBT condition. Furthermore, avoidant coping styles mediated the effects of therapy, with ACT participants demonstrating a decrease in avoidant coping while CBT participants demonstrated an increase in cognitive and behavioral avoidance throughout therapy.

An ACT approach to chronic pain in individuals in a rehabilitation setting recently has been developed (Dahl, Wilson, Luciano, & Hayes, 2005). This approach begins with an assessment of patient's values. Behavioral goals are developed based on these stated values and both the goals and values are discussed frequently throughout the brief intervention. The values become a context and motivating force for the next steps of the protocol, and serve to facilitate a shift in perspective away from symptom alleviation and onto living one's life as fully as possible.

The second focus of the intervention is based on exposure principles. Behaviors which were previously avoided for fear of inducing or exacerbating pain are identified and targeted in a process of gradual exposure, completed in a manner reflective of the patient's values. For example, if family outings are a valued experience, and the patient has avoided such outings for fear of increased pain, the exposure exercise is chosen and facilitated as a means of refocusing the patient's life on his/her own values. As part of the exposure exercise, the patient is encouraged to acknowledge and accept, as opposed to attempting to control or suppress various bodily signals such as pain. It is suggested that such signals may be present and negative thought content may occur ("I can't do it"), but that obeying this content is not necessary.

Although these protocols appear promising, much more research is needed. Current literature clearly indicates that that avoidance plays a role in health behaviors and psychological distress. In addition, it appears that function-based interventions, which include acceptance as a contextual tool and which seek to undermine literal language, rules, and potentially expanding stimulus classes, may prove useful for decreasing avoidant health behaviors. By doing so, the overall physical health and psychological well-being of the individual coping with difficult health concerns may be improved. It is our hope that contemporary behavior analysis offers these advantages and that as researchers and clinicians we may use these tools to ameliorate the current standard treatment and associated desired outcomes.

References

American Cancer Society. (2005). *Cancer facts and figures 2005.* Atlanta, GA: Author.

American Chronic Pain Association. (2005, May 5). *Current News.* Retrieved April 14, 2006, from http://www.theacpa.org/md_01.asp.

Asmundson, G. J. G., Norton, G. R., & Allerdings, M. D. (1997). Fear and avoidance in dysfunctional chronic back patients. *Pain, 69,* 231-236.

Austenfeld, J. L., Paolo, A. M., & Stanton, A. L. (2006). Effects of writing about emotions versus goals on psychological and physical health among third-year medical students. *Journal of Personality, 74,* 267-286.

Beck, A. T. (1964). Thinking and depression: Theory and therapy. *Archives of General Psychiatry, 10,* 561-571.

Bellack, A. S. (1976). A comparison of self-reinforcement and self-monitoring in a weight reduction program. *Behavior Therapy, 7,* 68-75.

Boey, K. W. (1999). Adaptation to type II diabetes mellitus: Depression and related factors. *International Medical Journal, 6,* 125-132.

Bradley, L. A. (1996). Cognitive-behavioral therapy for chronic pain. In R. J. Gatchel & D. C. Turk (Eds.), *Psychological approaches to pain management: A practitioner's handbook* (pp. 131-147). New York: Guilford.

Brand, A. H., Johnson, J. H., & Johnson, S. B. (1986). Life stress and diabetic control in children and adolescents with insulin-dependent diabetes. *Journal of Pediatric Psychology, 11,* 481-495.

Branstetter, A. D., Wilson, K. G., Hildebrandt, M., & Mutch, D. (2004). *Improving psychological adjustment among cancer patients: ACT and CBT.* Paper presented at the annual conference of the Association for the Advancement of Behavior Therapy, New Orleans, LA.

Carver, C. S., Scheier, M. F., & Weintraub, J. K. (1989). Assessing coping strategies: A theoretically based approach. *Journal of Personality and Social Psychology, 56,* 267-283.

Classen, C., Koopman, C., Angell, K., & Spiegel, D. (1996). Coping styles associated with psychological adjustment to advanced breast cancer. *Health Psychology, 15,* 434-437.

Coelho, R., Amorim, I., & Prata, J. (2003) Coping styles and quality of life in patients with non-insulin-dependent diabetes mellitus. *Psychosomatics: Journal of Consultation Liaison Psychiatry, 44,* 312-318.

Compas, B. E., Hagga, D. A., Keefe, F. J., Litenberg, H., & Williams, D. A. (1998). Sampling of empirically supported psychological treatments from health psychology: Smoking, chronic pain, cancer, and bulimia nervosa. *Journal of Consulting and Clinical Psychology, 66,* 89-112.

Cooper, Z., Fairburn, C. G., & Hawker, D. M. (2003). *Cognitive-behavioral treatment of obesity: A clinician's guide.* New York: Guilford.

Dahl, J., Wilson, K. G., Luciano, C., & Hayes, S. C. (2005). *Acceptance and commitment therapy for chronic pain.* Reno, NV: Context Press.

Derogatis, L. R., Morrow, G. R., & Fetting, J.R. (1983). The prevalence of psychiatric disorders among cancer patients. *Journal of the American Medical Association, 249,* 751-757.

Dimidjian, S., Hollon, S. D., Dobson, K. S., Schmaling, K. B., Kohlenberg, R. J., Addis, M. E., et al. (2006). Randomized trial of behavioral activation, cognitive therapy, and antidepressant medication in the acute treatment of adults with major depression. *Journal of Consulting and Clinical Psychology, 74,* 658-670.

Epstein, L. H. (1981). The effects of targeting improvements in urine glucose on metabolic control in children with insulin dependent diabetes. *Journal of Applied Behavior Analysis, 14,* 365-375.

Feldner, M. T., Hekmat, H., Zvolensky, M. J., Vowles, K. E., Secrist, Z., & Leen-Feldner, E. W. (2006). The role of experiential avoidance in acute pain tolerance: A laboratory test. *Journal of Behavior Therapy and Experimental Psychiatry, 26,* 146-158.

Ferster, C. B. (1973). A functional analysis of depression. *American Psychologist, 28,* 857-870.

Fishbain, D. A. (1999). The association of chronic pain and suicide. *Seminars in clinical neuropsychiatry, 4,* 221-227.

Foa, E. B., & Kozak, M. J. (1986). Emotional processing of fear: Exposure to corrective information. *Psychological Bulletin, 99,* 20-35.

Follick, M. J., Ahern, D. K., & Aberger, E. W. (1985). Development of an audiovisual taxonomy of pain behavior: Reliability and discriminant validity. *Health Psychology, 4,* 555-568.

Fordyce, W. E., Fowler, R., Lehmann, J., & DeLateur, B. (1968). Some implications of learning in problems of chronic pain. *Journal of Chronic Disabilities, 21,* 179-190.

Fordyce, W. E., Roberts, A. H., & Sternbach, R. A. (1985). The behavioral management of chronic pain: A response to critics. *Pain, 22,* 112-125.

Fordyce, W. E., & Steger, J. C. (1979). Chronic pain. In O. F. Pomerleau & J. P. Brady (Eds.), *Behavioral medicine: Theory and practice* (pp. 125-153). Baltimore, MD: Williams & Wilkins.

Gatchel, R. J. (1999). Perspectives on pain: A historical overview. In R. J. Gatchel & D. C. Turk (Eds.), *Psychosocial factors in pain: Critical perspectives* (pp. 3-17). New York: Guilford.

Geisser, M. E., Robinson, M. E., & Henson C. D. (1994). The coping strategies questionnaire and chronic pain adjustment: A conceptual and empirical reanalysis. *The Clinical Journal of Pain, 10,* 98-106.

Goodwin, P. J., Leszca, M., Ennis, M., Koopmans, J., Vincent, L., Guther, H., et al. (2001). The effect of group psychosocial support on survival in metastatic breast cancer. *The New England Journal of Medicine, 345,* 1719-1726.

Gregg, J. A., Callaghan, G. M., Hayes, S. C., & Glenn-Lawson, J. L. (in press). Improving diabetes self-management through acceptance, mindfulness, and values: A randomized controlled trial. *Journal of Consulting and Clinical Psychology.*

Grey, M., Cameron, M. E., & Thurber, F. W. (1991). Coping and adaptation in children with diabetes. *Nursing Research, 40,* 144-149.

Hanson, C. L., Cigrang, J. A., Harris, M. A., Carle, D. L., Relyea, G., & Burghen, G. A. (1989). Coping styles in youths with insulin-dependent diabetes mellitus. *Journal of Consulting and Clinical Psychology, 57,* 644-651.

Hassinger, H., Semenchuk, E., & O'Brien W. (1999). Appraisal and coping responses to pain and stress in migraine headache suffers. *Journal of Behavioral Medicine, 22,* 327-340.

Hayes, S. C., Barnes-Holmes, D., & Roche, B. (Eds.). (2001). *Relational frame theory: A post-Skinnerian account of human language and cognition.* New York: Plenum Press.

Hayes, S. C., Strosahl, K. D., & Wilson, K. G. (1999). *Acceptance and commitment therapy: An experiential guide to behavior change.* New York: Guilford.

Herbert, T. B., & Cohen, S. (1993). Stress and immunity in humans: A meta-analytic review. *Psychosomatic Medicine, 5,* 364-379.

Hill, A. (1993). The use of pain coping strategies by patients with phantom limb pain. *Pain, 55,* 347-353.

Hill, A., Niven, C. A., & Knussen, C. (1995). The role of coping in adjustment to phantom limb pain. *Pain, 62,* 79-86.

Hopko, D. R., Bell, J. L., Armento, M. E. A., Hunt, M. K., & Lejuez, C. W. (2005). Behavior therapy for depressed cancer patients in primary care. *Psychotherapy: Theory, Research, Practice, and Training, 42,* 236-243.

Hunt, L. M., Pugh, J., & Valenzuela, M. (1998). How patients adapt diabetes self-care recommendations in everyday life. *Journal of Family Practice, 46,* 207-215.

Irwin, M. (1999). Immune correlates of depression. *Advances in Experimental Medicine and Biology, 461,* 1-24.

Jacobson, A. M. (1996). The psychological care of patients with insulin-dependent diabetes mellitus. *New England Journal of Medicine, 334,* 1249-1253.

Jacobsen, P. B., & Hann, D. M. (1998). Cognitive-behavioral interventions. In J. C. Holland (Ed.), *Psycho-oncology* (pp. 717-729). New York: Oxford Press.

Katon, W., & Sullivan, M. D. (1990). Depression and chronic medical illness. *Journal of Clinical Psychiatry, 51,* 12-14.

Laursen, B. S., Bajaj, P., Olesen, A. S., & Delmar, C. (2005). Health related quality of life and quantitative pain measurement in females with chronic non-malignant pain. *European Journal of Pain, 9,* 267-275.

Lejuez, C. W., Hopko, D. R., & Hopko, S. D. (2001). A brief behavioral activation treatment for depression: Treatment manual. *Behavior Modification, 25,* 255-286.

Lemanek, K. L., Kamps, J., & Chung, N. B. (2001). Empirically supported treatments in pediatric psychology: Regimen adherence. *Journal of Pediatric Psychology, 26,* 253-275.

Lethem, J., Slade, P. D., Troup, J. D., & Bentley, G. (1983). Outline of a fear-avoidance model of exaggerated pain perception: I. *Behavior Research and Therapy, 21,* 401-408.

Lewinson, P. M. (1974). A behavioral approach to depression. In R. J. Friedman & M. M. Katz (Eds.), *The psychology of depression: Contemporary theory and research* (pp.157-178). Oxford, England: Wiley.

McCaul, K. D., O'Neil, H. K., & Glasgow, R. E. (1988). Predicting the performance of dental hygiene behaviors: An examination of the Fishbein and Ajen model and self-efficacy expectations. *Journal of Applied Social Psychology, 18,* 114-128.

McCracken, L. M. (1998). Learning to live with pain: Acceptance of pain predicts adjustment in persons with chronic pain. *Pain, 74,* 21-27.

McCracken, L. M., & Eccleston, C. (2003). Coping or acceptance: What to do about chronic pain? *Pain, 105,* 197-204.

Murray, R., & Hobbs, S. A. (1981). Effects of self-reinforcement and self-punishment in smoking reduction: Implications for broad-spectrum behavioral approaches. *Addictive Behaviors, 6,* 63-67.

Osterhaus, S., Lange, A., Linssen, W., & Passchier, J. (1997). A behavioral treatment of young migrainous and nonmigrainous headache patients: Prediction of treatment success. *International Journal of Behavioral Medicine, 4,* 378-396.

Pennebaker, J. W., Colder, M., & Sharp, L. K. (1990). Accelerating the coping process. *Journal of Personality and Social Psychology, 58,* 528-537.

Primo, K., Compas, B. E., Oppedisano, G., Howell, D. C., Epping-Jordan, J. E., & Krag, D. N. (2000). Intrusive thoughts and avoidance in breast cancer: Individual differences and associations with psychological distress. *Psychology and Health, 14,* 1141-1153.

Rapoff, M. A. (1999). *Adherence to pediatric medical regimens.* New York: Plenum.

Robinson, M. E., Riley, J. L., Myers, C. D., Sadler, I. J., Kvaal, S. A., Geisser, M. E., et al. (1997). The coping strategies questionnaire: A large sample, item level factor analysis. *Clinical Journal of Pain, 13,* 43-49.

Schmitz, U., Saile, H., & Nilges, P. (1996). Coping with chronic pain: Flexible goal adjustment as an interactive buffer against pain-related distress. *Pain, 67,* 41-51.

Smyth, J. M., Stone, A. A., Hurewitz, A., & Kaell, A. (1999). Effects of writing about stressful experiences on symptom reduction in patients with asthma or rheumatoid arthritis: A randomized trial. *Journal of the American Medical Association, 28,* 1304-1309.

Sorbi, M. J., Peters, M. L., Kruise, D. A., Maas, C. J. M., Kerssens, J. J., Verhaak, P. F. M., et al. (2006). Electronic momentary assessment in chronic pain II: Pain and psychological pain responses and predictors of pain disability. *Clinical Journal of Pain, 22,* 67-81.

Spiegel, D., Bloom, J. R., & Yalom, I. (1981). Group support for patients with metastatic cancer: A randomized prospective outcome study. *Archives of General Psychiatry, 38,* 527-533.

Stanton, A. L., Danoff-Burg, S., Cameron, C. L., Bishop, M., Collins, C. A., Kirk, S. A., et al. (2000). Emotionally expressive coping predicts psychological and physical adjustment to breast cancer. *Journal of Consulting and Clinical Psychology, 68,* 875-882.

Stanton, A. L., Danoff-Burg, S., Sworowski, L. A., Collins, C. A., Branstetter, A. D., Rodriguez-Hanley, A., et al. (2002). Randomized, controlled study of written emotional expression and benefit finding in breast cancer patients. *Journal of Clinical Oncology, 20,* 4159-4168.

Stanton, A. L., & Snider, P. R. (1993) Coping with a breast cancer diagnosis: A prospective study. *Health Psychology, 12,* 16-23.

Straub, R. O. (2002). *Health psychology.* New York: Worth Publishers Inc.

Taylor, S. E. (2003). *Health psychology.* New York: McGraw Hill.

Verbunt, J. A., Seelen, H. A., Vlaeyen, J. W., van de Heijde, G. J., Heuts, P. H., Pons, K., Knottnerus, J. A. (2003). Disuse and deconditioning in chronic low back pain: Concepts and hypotheses on contributing mechanisms. *European Journal of Pain, 7,* 9-21.

Viane, I., Crombez, G., Eccleston, C., Poppe, C., Devulder, J., Van Houdenhove, B., et al. (2003). Acceptance of pain is an independent predictor of mental well-being in patients with chronic pain: Empirical evidence and reappraisal. *Pain, 106,* 65-72.

Vlaeyen, J. W. S., Kole-Snijders, A. M. J., Boeren, R. G. B., & van Eek, H. (1995). Fear of movement (re)injury in chronic low back pain and its relation to behavioral performance. *Pain, 62,* 363-372.

Weickgenant, A. L., Slater, M. A., Patterson, T. L., Atkinson, J. H., Grant, I., & Garfin, S. R. (1993). Coping activities in chronic low back pain: Relationship with depression. *Pain, 53,* 95-103.

Wicksell, R. K., Dahl, J., Magnusson, B., & Olsson, G. L. (2005). Using acceptance and commitment therapy in the rehabilitation of an adolescent female with chronic pain: A case example. *Cognitive and Behavioral Practice, 12,* 415-423.

Wilson, K. G., & Blackledge, J. T. (2000). Recent developments in the behavioral analysis of language: Making sense of clinical phenomena. In M. J. Dougher (Ed.), *Clinical behavior analysis* (pp. 27-46). Reno, NV: Context Press.

Winkler, R. (1985). Twenty years of token economies in psychiatric institutions: Some basic issues. *Behaviour Change, 2,* 111-118.

Zabora, J., Brintzenhofeszoc, K., Curbow, B., Hooker, C., & Piantadosi, S. (2001). The prevalence of psychological distress by cancer site. *Psycho-Oncology, 10,* 19-28.

Chapter 14

A Behavioral Perspective on Adult Attachment Style, Intimacy, and Relationship Health

Abigail K. Mansfield & James V. Cordova
Clark University

Couples come to therapy in distress and seeking help for a variety of problems in their relationships. Most of the problems couples encounter cannot be classified in terms of DSM IV disorders. Instead, the symptoms of marital ill-health include chronic relationship distress, thoughts of divorce, frequent bitter arguing or withdrawal, and a sense of being either chronically at war with each other or completely emotionally numb. From the perspective of adult attachment theory, these problems can result from the complex interplay between individual partners' attachment histories and bids for nurturance and closeness within the current relationship that have gone awry.

Given that the purpose of the current volume is to explore contemporary behavioral perspectives on behavior disorders, this chapter will focus on disorders of attachment and intimacy in couple relationships. The goal of this chapter is to explore the potential contributions to attachment theory that might be derived from application of contemporary behavioral theory and research. Although early attachment researchers clearly understood and identified the key role played by a mother's responsiveness to a child's signals in the development of different attachment styles, we argue that these researchers did not take full advantage of behavioral theory and research to aid their understanding of attachment as a developmental phenomenon. Drawing principally on evolutionary-ethological and psychodynamic theories, and more recently on cognitive and cognitive-behavioral theories, attachment researchers have missed a potentially rich source of information about the shaping of behavior provided by decades of basic operant research.

A behavior analytic (BA) perspective on attachment focuses on the development of the person in the context of her learning history and the lawful development of attachment repertoires shaped by that learning history. In contrast, traditional attachment theory, while acknowledging individual history, focuses on internal mechanisms as causal agents (i.e., cognitive maps and working models). We will not wage the standard partisan battle here between contextualists and mechanists, because in the case of the attachment literature, that debate is unlikely to be fruitful.

Rather than oppose traditional theory, we would like to suggest that because of BA's solid foundation in empirically observed behavioral phenomena, it can function to provide a much more active dialogue with the data provided by Harlow, Bowlby, Ainsworth, Main, and other attachment scientists. The potential outcome of such a dialogue is a fresh perspective on attachment and new testable hypotheses.

In this chapter, we will explore how a behavioral perspective can foster a rich understanding of adult attachment styles and how such styles can contribute to distress between partners. We review the literature on attachment relationships and then spell out how a behavioral perspective can provide a compelling framework for understanding how attachment styles develop as well as how they influence adult relationships. We then apply a behavioral perspective to understand how patterns of vulnerability and intimacy in couples emerge and how some such patterns become problematic for couples. Finally, we will offer an account of how Integrative Behavioral Couples Therapy (IBCT) can be used to help couples move beyond the difficulties they experience.

Origins and Background of Attachment Theory

John Bowlby laid the foundation of attachment theory with his three volume tome, *Attachment and Loss* (1969, 1973, 1980). Influenced by the evolutionary biologist Konrad Lorenz and by Harlow's work with rhesus macaque monkeys (e.g., Harlow, 1958), Bowlby rejected the idea that attachment was a product of drive reduction. More specifically, he rejected the idea that attachment between mother and child developed because mothers meet their infants' need (drive) for food. Harlow (1958) was instrumental in refuting the drive-reduction theory of attachment. In experiments with macaque monkeys, he found that monkeys spent more time with a warm, soft dummy-mother that did not provide food than with a wire cage dummy-mother that provided food. This finding validated Bowlby's sense that attachment relationships were more complex than drive-reduction theory allowed. With this information in tow, Bowlby proceeded to develop the argument that attachment relationships have survival value because they keep infants close to caregivers who can provide protection in the face of danger (Bowlby, 1969, 1973, 1980, 1988). Thus, he came close to offering a functional analytic explanation of attachment in which the function of attachment eliciting behavior (e.g., crying, bids for physical closeness) is ultimately the protection of infants. Had he embraced this position more fully, the field might not have taken the psychoanalytic turn that now characterizes it. However, Bowlby had strong philosophical commitments to the psychoanalytic paradigm and eschewed the idea that attachment theory was a version of behaviorism (Bowlby, 1988). As a result, the operant underpinnings of attachment theory were minimized and attachment became a subfield within psychodynamic theory. Within this subfield, many researchers have made valuable contributions.

Mary Ainsworth and her colleagues (Ainsworth, Blehar, Waters, & Wall, 1978) expanded on Bowlby's work through intensive observational studies of mothers and infants in Uganda and the United States. Through these observations, particularly those conducted in the United States, Ainsworth developed the laboratory based "strange situation" procedure, which she used to characterize styles of attachment relationships. In the "strange situation," researchers observe the caregiver and child in several different scenarios: with the caregiver and the child alone in an observation room together, next with a stranger in the room with them, then with the baby alone with the stranger and then briefly reunited with the caregiver, and finally, with the child alone in the room. After each shift, researchers noted how the infant responded and whether he or she was distressed or apathetic. They also noted how easily the infant was soothed by his or her caregiver.

Ainsworth and colleagues (1978) used their extensive observations of infant-mother interactions, both in naturalistic settings and in the "strange situation," to develop a three-tiered classification system of attachment styles. They termed the three types of attachment relationship A, B, and C styles, each of which will be described in turn.

Style A, sometimes referred to as an avoidant attachment style, is characterized by infants who show practically no response to being alone in the "strange situation" (Ainsworth et al., 1978). When the caregiver leaves the room, the infant does not appear distressed, and when the caregiver returns, the infant does not greet or approach him or her. Similarly, when the stranger enters, infants with avoidant attachment styles either ignore him or her or are *more* friendly toward the stranger than toward the caregiver. Furthermore, Ainsworth et al. noted that infant avoidance is linked to caregiver behavior: Infants who display avoidant behavior tend to have caregivers who either directly reject attachment behavior (i.e., ignore bids for physical closeness, ignore infants' greetings, etc.) or report resentment at having to care for the infant.

Attachment style B, often termed the "secure" attachment style, is characterized by infants who show distress at being separated from their caregivers, who greet or approach caretakers after their return from separation, and who are easily comforted by caregivers when distressed by the separation (Ainsworth et al., 1978). As with the avoidant attachment style, Ainsworth et al. noted that caregiver behavior is linked to the secure attachment style. Indeed, caregivers of securely attached infants are likely to respond quickly and appropriately to their infant's needs and to be comforting to the infant when the infant is in distress.

Finally, attachment style C, also known as the resistant/ambivalent attachment style, is characterized by infants who appear to *both* seek *and* resist contact with the caregiver after reunions in the "strange situation." In addition, style C infants are often uncomfortable and distressed in the "strange situation" from the beginning, even before any separation from the caretaker has occurred (Ainsworth et al., 1978). When the caregiver leaves the room, the "resistant/ambivalent" infant tends to become very distressed, and when the caregiver attempts to soothe the infant, the infant usually continues to cry or fuss. Interestingly, Ainsworth et al. noted that this style of attachment is *not* related to maternal rejection, but rather to inconsistency and insensitivity in the caregiver's ability to meet and respond to his or her infant's bids for closeness and comfort.

Mary Main and her colleagues (1985) posited that the attachment behaviors exhibited in the "strange situation" procedure become internalized as "working models of attachment." According to Main's theory, these representations of what a person expects from relationships are unconscious but modulate a person's expectations about the feelings, thoughts, and experiences that surround interpersonal relationships (Main, Kaplan, & Cassidy, 1985). While Main and other attachment theorists (e.g., Ainsworth et al., 1978) concede that attachment styles can change when, for example, severe economic strain or emotional difficulty drastically limit the time and quality of attention a caregiver can provide, they contend that attachment styles tend to be stable over time.

To examine the stability of attachment styles, Main et al. (1985) examined children at ages one and six and administered the Adult Attachment Interview (AAI; George, Kaplan, & Main, 1985) to their caregivers. The AAI was designed to measure adults' internal working models of attachment and classifies adults into three attachment categories: secure-autonomous, dismissing, and preoccupied (George et al., 1985). Secure-autonomous adults tend to have securely attached children. They are able to speak articulately and objectively about their attachment figures. Equally important, whether their own caregivers were consistent or appropriate is irrelevant to whether an adult is classified as secure-autonomous; it is the ability to speak clearly and objectively, and in a way that values the importance of attachment figures, that matters. According to George and colleagues, adults classified as "dismissing" tend to have children classified as avoidant. Their narratives concerning their own attachment experiences tend to minimize the importance of attachment figures and to ignore negative events. Such narratives often have a very positive tone, but when probed, interviewees cannot explain what exactly was positive about their upbringing or attachment relationships. Over the course of their work, Main and colleagues (1985) argued that the attachment behavior of 12-month-old infants becomes codified into an "internal working model" of relationships, accounting for the large association between the attachment styles of children at 12 months and 6 years. They also found that adult working models of attachment are closely related to their children's working models of attachment.

In addition to her work on "internal working models" of relationships, Main made another major contribution to attachment theory: She explicated a fourth distinct style of attachment. First recognized by Ainsworth and Eichberg in 1991, the fourth style of attachment was known as style D, which Main referred to as "disorganized." According to Main (2000), disorganized infants tend to respond to reunions during the "strange situation" with contradictory and sometimes difficult to understand behaviors, such as staring blankly, closing the eyes, engaging in undirected or misdirected movements, freezing, or appearing apprehensive at the sight of the parent. Main found that disorganized infants are most at risk for developing lapses in the ability to reason, becoming aggressive or disruptive, and for developing dissociative disorders (Main, 2000). In addition, she found that infants exhibiting a disorganized attachment style tended to have either witnessed an event in which the caregiver was frightened due to a traumatic event or to have been traumatized directly by the caregiver. Main used this information to expound on Bowlby's theory that attachment has survival value. She posed the question: What happens when the person an infant comes to in distress becomes "a source of alarm?" (Hesse & Main, 2000). As with Bowlby's evolutionary theory of attachment, there are hints of an operant understanding of attachment relationships in Main's work, a point to which we shall return later in this chapter.

Bartholomew and Horowitz (1991) contested the idea that attachment styles are categorical. They suggested that attachment is the product of an individual's positioning on two continua: the degree to which a person feels positively about oneself and the degree to which a person feels positively about other people. Feeling positive about oneself is much the same as the construct of self-esteem. Feeling positive about others refers to the degree to which an individual trusts or feels confident in the ability of others to support, nurture, care for, or otherwise be present in relationships. Bartholomew and Horowitz proposed four distinct styles of attachment corresponding to the four quadrants formed by their two orthogonal continua. The first, referred to as secure attachment, results from a positive sense of self and a positive sense of others in a relationship. The second style, called preoccupied, results from a negative sense of self and a positive sense of others and is similar to the AAI's preoccupied style. People with this style tend to devote a great deal of energy to thinking about their relationships. They tend to seek affirmation and acceptance from others and to vest their hopes for security and safety in attaining these things. The dismissing attachment style, which results from a positive view of oneself and a negative view of others in relationship, is similar to Main's dismissing style. People who exemplify this style of attachment tend to avoid closeness and intimacy. In addition, they tend not to value close relationships with others. Finally, Bartholomew and Horowitz suggested a fourth style, much like Main's (2000) disorganized style. They termed this fourth attachment style "fearful," and theorized that it results from a negative model of both self and others in relationships. They asserted that people with fearful attachment styles are highly dependent on affirmation and acceptance from others but that they avoid intimacy in order to avoid pain. Thus, they are in the difficult position of valuing and wanting closeness as well as avoiding it so as to protect themselves from rejection and pain.

Hazan and Shaver (1987) linked adult romantic relationships with attachment processes. Following Bowlby, they described romantic love as a biological process which functions to keep prospective and actual parents connected so that they will provide reliable nurturance and protection for their children. Hazan and Shaver found that insecurely attached adults reported more negative thoughts and experiences of love than their securely attached counterparts.

A Behavioral Conceptualization of Adult Attachment Relationships

Like Hazan and Shaver (1987), we contend that couple relationships are contexts for attachment processes and take this as a foundation for developing our own behavioral conceptualization of attachment and its function in couple relationships. We believe that a behavioral perspective offers a compelling theoretical base from which to conceptualize the existing empirical evidence and generate new, unique, and testable hypotheses. We have great respect for the scientists who have done, and continue to do, pioneering work in attachment, and we do not wish to challenge the quality of their work. Instead, it is our position that a behavioral perspective on attachment contributes to the field by highlighting the basic behavioral processes through which attachment processes develop and proceed through time. In addition, we believe that a behavioral perspective on attachment connects seemingly incompatible claims about attachment and allows for an enriched understanding of how attachment styles play out in romantic relationships. Finally, a behavioral perspective posits the potential existence of additional, and as yet unidentified, attachment styles.

As we discussed earlier, we believe that Bowlby's work on attachment contained underpinnings of an operant understanding of attachment. Bowlby described attachment behavior as an operant that functions to bring caregivers to the infant and thus protect the infant from danger. This view is compatible with a behavioral perspective, and we will develop it further by exploring how attachment behavior can be differentially reinforced to yield distinct attachment styles. We contend that each episode of attachment behavior begins with the same operant class: a bid for nurturance, closeness, or protection. In order to explore this idea, we will investigate how different consequences and various reinforcement schedules allow for the development of different attachment styles. It is important to note that although attachment patterns vary in a more continuous rather than categorical way, we are most interested in clearly identifiable patterns of behavior. We therefore acknowledge but do not get sidetracked by the fact that attachment behavior varies continuously and contextually.

Extending Basic Principles of Behavior to Attachment Theory

The first step in extending basic principles of behavior to attachment theory is to identify the operant in question. In other words, what is the specific class of behavior involved in attachment events? Attachment often refers to "internal working models," presumably derived from histories of interactions with primary caretakers. Bowlby (1969, 1973, 1980) referred to those behaviors that functioned to provide proximity between the infant and the caregiver, thus providing protection and, presumably, nurturance such that the infant was more likely to survive to pass on his or her own genes. Although originally discussed as a "behavioral system" (consisting of the innate attachment-relevant behaviors of both infant and mother) based on Bowlby's ethological perspective, we will frame attachment behavior specifically as a behavioral class shaped by its operant function of obtaining nurturance (broadly defined). From our perspective, Bowlby correctly asserted that the history of the species has shaped an inclination for infants (and adults) to seek attachment and for caregivers (including other adults) to respond by providing protection and nurturance. In addition, a BA perspective recognizes that the exact topography of the attachment repertoire is shaped by each individual's unique reinforcement history. It is this individual-level reinforcement history that we are most interested in for the current analysis.

Attachment Transactions

When we observe attachment transactions as they unfold in the natural environment or in the strange situation, what do attachment-seeking behaviors look like? Principally, they involve approaching or calling to the caretaker or partner for nurturance. We will equate attachment behavior with nurturance-seeking and define the class of behavior as comprised of a range of behaviors including bids for closeness, companionship, comfort, protection, caretaking, reassurance, and sustenance. Each of these emerges from a particular state of deprivation or threat but generally represents the inclination to seek protection and resource-sharing from others assumed to have evolved over the history of the species. In short, we are born inclined to seek out and attach ourselves to those who protect and nurture us. Bowlby, from his ethological perspective, focused more narrowly on the protection-seeking function of the attachment-seeking repertoire, because evolutionary theory stresses the survival of the individual in the service of reproductive success. We have broadened the emphasis somewhat to take into account the range of reinforcers that are most likely associated with the overarching protection goal. Just as feelings of hunger and the experience of flavor are associated with the overarching goal of eating to survive, feelings of closeness, comfort, reassurance, and desire for caretaking are associated with the overarching goal of acquiring protection.

Given nurturance-seeking, the key to exploring attachment transactions and the resulting attachment repertoires from a behavior analytic perspective lies in examining the variety of ways in which those bids for nurturance can be consequated or completed between partners. To put it simply, bids for nurturance can be (a) reinforced, (b) punished, or (c) ignored, and the different ratios of those three types of consequences, including variability in schedules of reinforcement, should determine the attachment repertoire that the person develops in relation to actual and potential attachment figures. Put another way, the manner in which an attachment figure tends to respond to bids for nurturance can be represented as a three-part ratio consisting of the probability that nurturance-seeking will be reinforced, punished, or ignored. Each bid for nurturance is a reach into a probability bag containing those three possible responses, with the expected odds of pulling any particular response depending entirely on that dyad's previous history of attachment transactions. The behavior that is shaped by that history constitutes the person's attachment repertoire. Depending on the historical mix of these three types of responses, the person will develop a repertoire in relation to others (potential attachment figures) that should resemble previously described attachment categories, while at the same time highlighting the "spaces between" those categories. In the following sections, we will describe the various probability ratios formed by the three possible consequences of nurturance bids and the repertoires most likely to result from those ratios.

Ratios highest in reinforcement. Initially, it should be noted that nurturance-seeking as a category of behavior will vary in strength depending on conditions of deprivation and threat. In other words, people are not always strongly seeking nurturance from others. A person's need for nurturance will vary with the circumstances. A person is more likely to seek nurturance after a period of deprivation, separation, or threat than during times when that "need" has been satiated.

Histories in which bids for nurturance are reinforced more frequently than they are punished or ignored should result in a stable, well-defined, and secure attachment repertoire characterized by a tight association between deprivation, an available attachment figure, and confident nurturance-seeking. Evidence from the extensive attachment literature demonstrates that such secure attachment styles are the most commonly occurring. Ainsworth et al. (1978) noted that the mothers of more securely attached infants "tend to be substantially more sensitive, accepting, cooperative, and psychologically accessible to the babies" (p. 146). In addition, Ainsworth's studies found that the mothers of more securely attached children responded more promptly to their babies' cries, handled their babies more affectionately and tenderly, and responded to their babies' cues more contingently. In those circumstances in which reinforcement of nurturance-seeking is substantially more probable than either punishment or ignoring, nurturance-seeking under the appropriate conditions of deprivation or threat, and in the presence of an appropriate discriminative stimulus (i.e., attachment figure), should occur consistently and lawfully. In other words, a person will develop a strong repertoire of nurturance-seeking from identifiable attachment figures, and the person will reliably seek nurturance when he or she needs it. Histories rich in reinforcement for nurturance-seeking teach a person that attachment figures are responsive and can be counted on and that the world of close others is stable and reliable. From a behavior analytic perspective, a secure attachment style is a repertoire for nurturance-seeking that results from a reliable reinforcement history. More technically, such highly contingent responding by the mothers to their infants' bids for nurturance should result in strong stimulus control by the mother over the infant's nurturance-seeking behavior under conditions of deprivation. This relationally situated stimulus control constitutes the infant's attachment to her "attachment figure."

Although stimulus control under such circumstances is extremely strong, a related characteristic of rich reinforcement contingencies is that the resulting behavior tends to generalize rather well to similar circumstances. Accordingly, one would expect people raised with high degrees of responsiveness to nurturance bids to form positive attachment relationships with sufficiently similar others fairly easily. In fact, results from some of Main's early work (as cited in Ainsworth et al., 1978) suggest that more secure babies are more positively sociable with relatively unfamiliar adults than babies categorized as more insecure. Additionally, the literature on adult attachment has consistently reported a robust association between secure attachment style and capacity to form close intimate relationships.

Although it is unlikely that any person has ever been raised in circumstances that provided reinforcement for nurturance-seeking on a strictly continuous reinforcement schedule, schedules rich in reinforcement are apparently the most probable. It is likely that all schedules of reinforcement for nurturance-seeking are essentially intermittent and vary in terms of the probability of reinforcement over punishment or ignoring. Some circumstances may nearly approximate a continuous reinforcement schedule, while others may be increasingly intermittent. Ainsworth et al. (1978) noted that among mothers of securely attached infants, there are mothers who respond very sensitively and consistently as well as mothers whom they describe as inconsistently sensitive, mixing in both periods of ignoring and interfering.

Like Bartholomew and Horowitz (1991), the BA perspective proposes that one result of variance in the probability of reinforcement is that attachment repertoires are continuous or dimensional rather than strictly categorical. For example, within the broad category of "securely attached," there should exist a continuum spanning the range from ratios that approximate continuous reinforcement schedules to those that mix in substantially higher probabilities of ignoring (but little or no punishment).

Theoretically, therefore, within the broad category of securely attached individuals, there should be some variability with regard to how well individuals tolerate periods in the relationship in which the partner is less responsive to attachment bids. The closer a reinforcement schedule is to continuous (the larger the ratio of reinforcement to ignoring), the more vulnerable is the resulting repertoire to extinction. The smaller the variable ratio is the more extinction-resistant it becomes. Thus, within the range of securely attached individuals, some will be more resistant to the extinction of their nurturance-seeking repertoires than others. For example, if a person has been raised by parents that respond very consistently every time she approaches them seeking nurturance and then as an adult she becomes involved with a partner that tends to ignore her bids for nurturance, she is likely to stop seeking nurturance from that partner fairly quickly (following perhaps a brief extinction burst). In other words, she will be unlikely to stay with someone that tends to ignore her attachment needs. On the other hand, if a person has been raised by parents who often provided nurturance on demand but also ignored those bids from time to time, that person would learn to tolerate some lack of responsiveness from an attachment partner. Thus, as an adult, that person would be more likely to tolerate the occasional lack of responsiveness from a partner without ceasing bids for attachment altogether.

BA theory predicts that some otherwise securely attached individuals should be fairly extinction-vulnerable and relatively more likely to leave a partner that does not consistently respond to bids for nurturance, whereas other securely attached individuals should be much more tolerant of occasional or intermittent nonresponsiveness. Speculatively, the more extinction-resistant secure individuals may be those that are more capable of forming stable relationships with avoidantly attached partners, whereas the more extinction-vulnerable secure individuals may be much more selective of consistently bid-sensitive partners. Regardless, neither "type" of secure individual should be particularly prone to developing disordered relationships. In fact, in adult couples, the most frequent pairing is of two securely attached partners, and the next most common pairings are between one securely attached and one insecurely attached individual (Brennan & Shaver, 1995). This simple frequency, along with other evidence from the literature, suggests that not only are more securely attached individuals less susceptible to relationship dysfunction, but they may actually function as a stabilizing force in pairings with more insecurely attached individuals.

Ratios highest in reinforcement, but also high in ignoring. As implied by the continuum discussed above, ratios involving mostly reinforcement can theoretically include large amounts of ignoring, up to and beyond the point where the result is greater extinction-resistance within a primarily secure attachment style. At the point where ignoring begins to be almost as probable as reinforcement, the resulting repertoire should begin to look more and more relentless and clingy, with bids for nurturance becoming fairly constant and invariable. Such large variable ratio schedules tend to produce behavior that occurs at a very high rate with virtually no post-reinforcement pause. Thus, a person whose bids for nurturance resulted about equally in ignoring as reinforcement would be expected to develop a repertoire in which he would tend to make bids for nurturance at a fairly high rate and would be undeterred from making those bids, regardless of a partner's nonresponsiveness. In addition, even given a reinforcing response, the person would be likely to continue making bids for nurturance with little sign of a post-reinforcement pause. It is also likely that it would be difficult for that person to feel satiated for long by nurturing responses, given a history of reinforcement that taught him that nurturing is fairly unreliable. This style of persistent nurturance and reassurance seeking has been described in the attachment literature as a "preoccupied" attachment style characterized by preoccupation with the attachment partner, clinginess, and a pervasive sense of anxiety about the availability of continued nurturance (Main, 2000).

One expectable characteristic of a large variable ratio schedule, as noted above, is that it produces a very high rate of behavior with little post-reinforcement pause, thus leaving little time and energy for other behaviors. One of the central facets of Bowlby's (1969, 1973, 1980) attachment theory is that an infant must feel relatively assured of the responsiveness of an attachment figure before he or she will feel comfortable exploring and learning from the rest of the environment. Among infants and adults classified as securely attached, exploration of the environment occurs regularly and consistently. Such individuals have learned that their attachment partners will respond with contingent nurturing if and when needed, and therefore they can turn their behavior to other priorities. However, for individuals such as those described here, for whom the history of reinforcement for nurturance-seeking has been very inconsistent, so much time and energy becomes devoted to seeking reassurance and nurturance (with little post-reinforcement pause), that little time and energy remains for engaging effectively with the rest of the environment. As a result, the focus of attachment behavior narrows to only one time-consuming relationship. In addition to being potentially relationally dysfunctional, this type of repertoire is also likely to be depressogenic (Scott & Cordova, 2002). Narrow and rigid repertoires have been argued to create a particular vulnerability to developing depression specifically because they provide few, and easily disrupted, opportunities for engaging in effective behavior (Cordova & Gee, 2001). In terms of relationship dysfunction, the preoccupation and clinginess that characterize a preoccupied style can generate a great deal of stress within a relationship because it feeds demand-withdrawal patterns between partners, emphasizes differences in needs for closeness versus distance, and generally contributes to an underlying chronic sense of dissatisfaction with the amount of nurturing provided by the partner. Preliminary evidence does suggest, however, that these repertoires can be modified so that more preoccupied adults can form more securely attached relationships with adult partners (Scott, 2002). At the same time, repertoires are built, not replaced, and so it is likely that in the absence of opportunities to build new repertoires, such individuals will maintain an enduring vulnerability predisposing them to preoccupied behavior.

The general principle at work in building such "preoccupied" repertoires is that the higher the proportion of nonresponsive to reinforcing responses, the greater the tolerance or extinction resistance the person develops to being ignored by an attachment figure. On the secure end of the spectrum, this presents few problems and may actually confer some strength to the secure attachment style by making it more resilient to periods of neglect that may characterize difficult periods in an adult long-term relationship. The transition to parenthood, with its associated decrease in time available for nurturing the parents' relationship, is one such example. On the preoccupied end of the spectrum, increased extinction-resistance also comes with an anxiety-driven persistence or clinginess that is chronically uncomfortable for the person experiencing it and difficult to tolerate for the partner.

Ratios highest in reinforcement, but also high in punishment. Following from the same general principle discussed above, if a person's bids for nurturance are sometimes reinforced and sometimes punished, that person will learn to tolerate punishment to get his nurturance needs met. The punitiveness involved need not necessarily be abusive, but can, and most likely often does, include noxious interactions with a caregiver around occasions of nurturance. For example, Ainsworth and colleagues (1978) describe mothers of ambivalent infants as sometimes engaging in inappropriately controlling behavior and, for example, "resist[ing] any effort the baby made to feed himself. The babies who were treated thus tended to rebel, so that feedings were unhappy and occasions for struggle" (p. 146). In this example, nurturance and punitiveness are occurring simultaneously in response to the child's bid to be shown care. The affective side effect should be anxiety about punishment or reciprocated anger. Thus, if a person cannot predict whether a bid for nurturance will result in being nurtured or punished, then simply needing nurturance should elicit anxiety and fear, and approaching the attachment figure should intensify that feeling. In addition, the three standard responses to applied punishers are (a) aggression, (b) escape, and (c) avoidance. So, theoretically, given a need to be nurtured and the presence of an attachment figure, the person should feel (a) fear, (b) anger, (c) a desire to approach, and (d) a desire to run away. That exact mix of motivations has been observed by Ainsworth and others in children they have classified as "anxious-ambivalent." From the BA perspective, anxious-ambivalent attachment styles should result directly from histories in which bids for nurturance are almost equally likely to be met with punishment as reinforcement. As we will discuss later, as more and more punishers are added, the repertoire should move from looking like anxious-avoidance to looking like what has been described as a "disorganized" attachment style.

The BA perspective suggests that current attachment theory may merge two potentially quite different attachment styles, preoccupied and ambivalent, into the one category of "anxious-ambivalent." At the same time, it should also be noted that early attachment researchers, including Ainsworth, made distinctions between several subgroups within each of the original three attachment styles and recognized that there was lawful variability that remained to be discerned and studied. A BA analysis suggests that if reinforcement is most probable, even if only slightly more probable than other responses, the individual will learn to tolerate whatever else is in the mix, regardless of whether the rest of that mix consists mostly of being ignored or of being punished. If having nurturance bids ignored is a significant probability and punishment is not, then the person should develop an attachment style that looks preoccupied and anxiously persistent. If punishment is a significant probability (again with reinforcement being most probable), then the person should develop an attachment style that looks anxious and genuinely ambivalent. Thus, a genuine distinction should exist between a "preoccupied" attachment style and an "anxious-ambivalent" attachment style, two styles that are potentially confounded in current attachment theory. The difference should be the source of the experienced anxiety. One might expect anxiously-ambivalent individuals to report an approach-avoidance conflict about attachment figures and preoccupied individuals to report a more simple sense of yearning for attachment figures. In other words, the anxiously-ambivalent should genuinely experience and be able to report the ambivalence about attachment figures that the category term has always implied, whereas preoccupied individuals should experience a much less ambivalent craving for nurturance from others. In addition, because of that strong sense of ambivalence about others, anxiously-ambivalent individuals may report that they only genuinely feel at ease when alone, whereas preoccupied individuals may report that they easily "lose themselves" in relationships. A sense of only being genuinely comfortable when alone may also characterize fearfully-avoidant individuals due to the punitive nature of their history with attachment figures, as we will discuss later.

Another important characteristic of punishment, repeatedly demonstrated in the basic BA literature, is that punishment suppresses behavior without extinguishing it. Put another way, the individual remains just as motivated to seek nurturance but suppresses the behavior associated with that need in order to avoid punishment. The implication is that the experienced desire for nurturance remains strong in anxious-ambivalent individuals and the behavior, bids for nurturance, is likely to rebound strongly at any signal that reinforcement (nurturance) might be available. This would account for the high degree of vigilance in anxious-ambivalent individuals, as well as for their potentially high tolerance for the punishment of nurturance bids.

An additional principle that has been derived from the work of behavior analysts regarding punishment is that punishment does not generalize well. Indeed, punishment tends to be rather tightly associated with the specific source of punishment and the punished behavior quickly reemerges when the source of the punishment changes or is removed. Extending that principle to attachment theory suggests that individuals whose bids for nurturance are frequently punished are likely to associate punishment with the specific person who has applied punishment and with the specific circumstances under which punishment occurred. If a new person enters the scene, then nurturance-seeking behavior should quickly reemerge to the extent that the new person is perceptibly different from the punishing person. Ainsworth et al. (1978) noted that the avoidant infants in their sample were quite willing to respond positively to the close bodily contact of the visitor-observer in the strange situation, despite the fact that those same infants generally avoided contact with their own mothers. One may also see this phenomenon in the particularly passionate relationships formed by individuals with abusive histories. In addition, even given the same punishing partner, if the circumstances surrounding punishment for nurturance-seeking change, then nurturance-seeking should again quickly reemerge, depending on how different the circumstances are and whether or not those specific circumstances have been previously associated with punishment.

Ratios highest in punishment. In those circumstances where a child's caretakers are frequently punitive or abusive, bids for nurturance are more likely to result in punishment than either nurturance or neglect. Ainsworth et al. (1978) noted that, "a highly rejecting mother frequently feels angry and resentful toward her baby. She may grumble that he interferes unduly with her life, or she may show her rejection by constantly opposing his wishes or by a generally pervasive mood of scolding or irritation" (p. 142). Ainsworth's studies also showed that these mothers demonstrated a strong aversion to physical contact with their babies, despite the fact that they tended to hold their babies as much as other mothers (usually toward instrumental ends determined by the mother). Ainsworth et al. (1978) noted that such mothers "provide their babies with unpleasant, even painful experiences associated with close bodily contact" (p. 151). Under such circumstances, according to basic behavioral principles, the individual will learn to avoid, escape from, and/ or aggress against those punishers, resulting in either fearful or aggressive attachment styles.

On the one hand, an individual may develop a "fearful-avoidant" attachment repertoire, such as that described by Bartholomew and Horowitz (1991), characterized by fearful avoidance of others, along with a chronic desire for nurturance. On the other hand, an individual may develop what might be called an "aggressive" attachment repertoire, characterized by defensively aggressive nurturance-seeking. Such a person might act out their nurturance needs by being domineering, possessive, threatening, and generally abusive in response to the assumed aversiveness of attachment transactions. In other words, because someone who has developed an aggressive attachment repertoire has learned that attachment figures are usually punitive, and because punishment does not extinguish nurturance-seeking, he or she may react to needing nurturance by lashing out in response to expected or perceived threat from available attachment figures.

If punishment is the most probable contingency, but the probability of reinforcement is also relatively high, then the resulting repertoire may be akin to that described by Hesse and Main (2000) as "disorganized," or one in which the individual, in response to the need for nurturance, becomes stuck in an approach-avoidance response. Ainsworth et al. (1978) noted that even the most rejecting mothers in their studies at least occasionally interacted with their babies in tender and affectionate ways, providing their babies with a history of nurturance mixed with both punishers and reinforcers. Under circumstances in which an individual does not know whether a bid for nurturance is going to be punished or reinforced, the resulting behavior is likely to be a confusing mix of approach, avoidance, and aggression. The availability of periodic nurturance should maintain nurturance-seeking by the individual, but since punishment is more likely than reinforcement, that nurturance-seeking should come with a great deal of fear and anger. In addition, the individual would learn that punishment has to be tolerated in order to receive any nurturance at all. The person genuinely becomes attached to her punitive caretaker, and expectations for what nurturing relationships should look like may generalize into adult relationships, setting the stage for the person to tolerate abusive relationships. Ainsworth et al. noted that "most family-reared infants do become attached, even to unresponsive or punitive mother figures" (p.18).

Punishers can vary in intensity and severity. When we refer to punishers as contingent responses to bids for nurturance, we do not usually make reference to the severity of those punishers. The technical definition of punisher is that it is a contingent response that decreases the probability of subsequent occurrences of the target behavior. More informally, we generally think of punishers as noxious events contingent upon a particular behavior. For the most part, in the context of naturally occurring responses to bids for nurturance, the punishers that most people encounter are likely to be mild, including signs of irritation, frustration, anger, and rejection.

In other words, punitive responses do not have to be abusive in order for them to serve their function as punishers in shaping an individual's attachment repertoire. At the same time, punishers do vary in intensity from mild to severely abusive. Currently, the effects of that variability in severity on the formation of attachment repertoires are unclear. However, it is assumed that more noxious punishers result in greater aversion.

Ratios highest in ignoring or noncontingent responding. Ignoring leads to extinction of attachment seeking. Thus, high probabilities of ignoring place nurturance-seeking on an extinction schedule, theoretically resulting in the actual removal of nurturance-seeking from the repertoire. Perhaps the most dramatic circumstances in which ignoring is the most likely response to bids for nurturance is in orphanage institutions. As noted by Ainsworth et al. (1978):

> ...an infant reared for a long period..., in an institutional environment in which he has so little consistent interaction with any one potential attachment figure that he fails to form an attachment may, when subsequently fostered and thus given an opportunity to attach himself, be unable to attach himself to anyone (p. 9).

However, given that the inclination to seek nurturance is fundamental to the species, extinction or near-extinction schedules are unlikely to remove nurturance-seeking from the repertoire altogether. Rather, they are likely to drastically weaken nurturance-seeking. More commonly, ignoring occurs within normal family settings characterized by unresponsiveness. Ainsworth et al. (1978) noted that "the inaccessible or ignoring mother is often so preoccupied with her own thoughts and activities that she does not even notice her baby, let alone acknowledge his signals" (p. 143). The resulting attachment repertoire should be akin to the "dismissive avoidant" style described by Bartholomew and Horowitz (1991), characterized by a virtual absence of nurturance-seeking, but by little, if any, anxiety about others. The person learns that other people do not provide nurturance and therefore does not seek it from them. This likely creates a self-fulfilling prophecy that follows individuals into adult life, providing them with little opportunity to receive nurturance from their social network. Again, this style should exist on a continuum, with higher levels of ignoring resulting in greater dismissiveness.

Even though a rigid extinction schedule should remove nurturance-seeking from an individual's repertoire, it will not destroy nurturance as a powerful reinforcer. In fact, one would expect such individuals to exist in a constant state of nurturance deprivation that may not only be palpable but chronically aversive and distracting. In the same way that certain circumstances extinguish an individual's efforts to find food without extinguishing the basic survival value of food or "hunger," other circumstances can extinguish an individual's efforts to find nurturance without changing the survival value of nurturance-seeking.

Ainsworth et al. (1978) described some ignoring mothers as not ignoring bids for nurturance, but instead as providing nurturance according to the mother's schedule and terms, rather than in response to the baby's signals (noncontingent nurturing). Under such circumstances, one would expect the child's nurturance bids to extinguish (since they are not contingently responded to) and for the child to either develop a passive nurturance-seeking repertoire, or a superstitious nurturance-seeking repertoire, given that noncontingent reinforcement has been shown to shape superstitious behavior. Ainsworth et al. noted that "because the C2 infant [a subcategory of ambivalently attached] could rarely experience a consequence contingent on his own behavior, it is not surprising that he behaved very passively both in the strange situation and at home" (p. 237).

Although the effects of noncontingent responding should be similar to simple nonresponding, there are relatively few naturally occurring cases in which attachment figures are genuinely nonresponding in a neglectful and abusive sense. Instead, the type of attachment relationships observed to give rise to ambivalent attachment styles were not necessarily neglectful (the mothers did provide adequate care for their children) but provided care only on the caretaker's terms and schedule and not in response to bids from the child. Under such circumstances, a person learns that how and when they are provided nurturance is out of their control, resulting in the extinction of a great deal of the nurturance-seeking repertoire and a generally passive relationship to attachment figures. One might imagine such individuals passively falling into adult attachment relationships (because they have been sources of noncontingent nurturance in the past), but subsequently providing attachment partners with few, if any, cues about their own attachment needs, passively expecting to be nurtured without knowing how to ask for it. This repertoire would likely manifest itself not as active avoidance of close adult relationships, but as a passive nonpursuit of intimacy accompanied by a normal desire to be nurtured.

An analysis from a BA perspective comes to the same general conclusion as that argued by Bartholomew and Horowitz (1991) regarding avoidant attachment styles: that the original category of avoidant attachment (or style A children) described by Ainsworth and colleagues likely includes children shaped by two distinguishable histories, one in which frequent punishment suppresses approach behavior (fearful avoidance in Bartholomew and Horowitz's terms) and one in which frequent ignoring essentially extinguishes approach behavior (dismissive avoidance). In addition, an adult style that may look insecure, much like an avoidant attachment style, may actually be characterized by a learned, passive nonpursuit of attachment relationships that are actively desired, rather than by either fear of potential attachment figures or a conviction that others are not nurturing (quite the opposite, in fact).

Summary of Attachment Repertoires

In sum, an examination of attachment phenomenon from a contemporary behavioral perspective suggests a variety of possible attachment repertoires developing out of histories in which bids for nurturance are responded to with combinations of contingent reinforcement, punishment, ignoring, and noncontingent responding. See Table 14.1 for a summary of ratios of reinforcement and the resultant attachment styles.

Ratio of Reinforcement to Ignoring to Punishment	Resulting attachment repertoire/style	Description	Likely behavior in couple relationship
High reinforcement Low ignoring Low punishment	Secure, extinction vulnerable	Individuals with this attachment repertoire tend to have secure relationships with close others. They tend to trust attachment figures and to have faith in them. They also tend to have children who are more likely to be secure in their attachment relationships.	Generally form positive attachment relationships, and have healthy relationships. The closer the reinforcement schedule with the primary caregiver was to continuous, the less tolerant of ignoring responses these individuals will be in couple relationships. Thus, individuals with this style tend to have little tolerance for partners who are inattentive, and are likely to stop seeking nurturance/closeness or even to end relationships that are not adequately responsive.
High reinforcement Moderate ignoring Low punishment	Secure, extinction resistant	Same as above.	Generally form healthy relationships as adults. These individuals tend to be more tolerant of periods of inattention from their partners and thus tend to cope well with relationships in which their bids for closeness/nurturance are usually met but sometimes ignored.
High reinforcement High ignoring Low punishment	Preoccupied	Preoccupied style characterized by a high rate of bids for nurturance with little post-reinforcement pause between bids. Tend to yearn for attention from caregivers.	Potentially dysfunctional and depresogenic because almost all of a person's energy is focused on maintaining a secure connection, at the expense of devoting energy to other relationships or activities. Individuals tend to be jealous, fearful, and clingy. Demand-withdraw patterns may be common.
High reinforcement Low ignoring High punishment	Anxious-Ambivalent	Anxious-ambivalent style in which person may feel fear, anger, and a desire to run away from potential providers of nurturance due to a history of receiving both punishment and reinforcement for nurturance-seeking. Because of the mixed reinforcement and punishment history, people may report feeling at ease only when alone.	Approach-avoidance patterns are common. Nurturance-seeking behavior has been partially suppressed but is likely to re-emerge strongly given reinforcement. Vigilant monitoring of partner's behavior is common. Short-term passionate relationships occur frequently, but tend to end early due to fearful or angry responses to interpersonal hurt.
Low reinforcement High ignoring Low punishment	Avoidant-Dismissive	This style is characterized by a virtual absence of nurturance seeking. The individual has learned that bids for nurturance are almost never met, and therefore nurturance-seeking behavior is practically extinct.	Individuals have learned that other people do not provide nurturance and therefore they do not seek it out. This can lead to a self-fulfilling prophecy in which individuals do not expect nurturing and therefore do not try to attain it. As a result, such individuals are often not in couple relationships as adults, and may be lonely.

Table 14.1. Description of Attachment Styles.

Ratio of Reinforcement to Ignoring to Punishment	Resulting attachment repertoire/style	Description	Likely behavior in couple relationship
Low to moderate reinforcement (non-contingent nurturance) High ignoring Low punishment	Avoidant-Passive	Individuals with this reinforcement history may be interested in intimacy but often have no practical repertoire for pursuing it. Their attachment figures tended to respond non-contingently to their bids for nurturance, so they have little experience seeking out nurturance but do expect others to provide it.	As adults, these individuals may be lonely because they yearn for closeness, but do not know how to pursue it. These individuals may also be in relationships where they passively expect nurturance but in which they are relatively poor nurturers.
Low reinforcement Moderate ignoring High punishment	Fearful-Avoidant	This style appears generally avoidant of attachment relationships. Bids for nurturance were most often either ignored or punished, and as a result, individuals learn to avoid close others in order to minimize the threat they pose.	Tend to have great difficulty forming and maintaining close couple relationships. They sometimes move quickly from relationship to relationship in pursuit of nurturing but leave quickly in order to avoid pain. Nurturance-seeking has been suppressed and is likely to rebound strongly when reinforced. However, as the relationship becomes more emotionally threatening, the person is likely to re-suppress nurturance-seeking, creating a situation in which the person may withdraw from the relationship suddenly.
Moderate reinforcement Low ignoring High punishment	Fearful-Disorganized	Bids for nurturance are occasionally reinforced, but often punished. The availability of periodic reinforcement maintains nurturance seeking but involves fear. The resulting behavioral repertoire includes approach, avoidance, and aggression.	Individuals with this history tend to experience the prospect of nurturance as both noxious and appealing. Nurturance-seeking behavior comes with a great deal of fear and anger, which often results in a powerful approach-avoidance pattern. Individuals may tolerate abusive treatment in adult couple relationships and may also be abusive in relationships.
Low reinforcement Low ignoring High punishment	Fearful-Aggressive	People with this history of reinforcement have learned to associate seeking nurturance with punishment. They therefore often relate to close others in an aggressive fashion.	Tend to form abusive relationships in which they behave aggressively and are treated aggressively. Since these individuals have not learned to associate nurturance-seeking with reinforcement, they tend to lack a repertoire of nurturing behavior.

Table 14.1. cont'd Description of Attachment Styles.

Mostly secure attachment repertoires should theoretically vary in terms of their extinction resistances. Such variance should depend on the ratio of reinforcement versus ignoring responses to bids for nurturance, with greater probabilities of ignoring building greater extinction resistance. As noted earlier, mostly secure attachment repertoires have been shown to be associated with greater relationship health, and the distinction we draw here should theoretically have its impact on stability of adult relationships during times of decreased responsiveness. For example, one might predict that more extinction-resistant secure repertoires would be more resilient during periods in which partners are forced to be apart (e.g., during military deployment). One might also expect people with more extinction-vulnerable repertoires to be more selective of mates, and therefore, to move quickly out of relationships that are not adequately responsive. In general, however, one would expect secure attachment repertoires to confer greater relationship health and stability.

What have traditionally been categorized as ambivalent attachment styles should, according to the current analysis, consist of two distinguishable repertoires. The first should be characterized primarily by a preoccupation with attachment-seeking and anxiety about abandonment, and the second should be characterized by fearful approach-avoidance. The first type of repertoire is theoretically shaped by histories consisting mostly of ignoring with some low-to-moderate probability of contingent reinforcement for nurturance-seeking. As adults, individuals with this type of repertoire should be clingy, fearful of abandonment, jealous, and in great need of reassurance. However, there is some preliminary evidence that these individuals can form more secure styles as adults if they find contingently nurturing partners (Scott, 2002).

The second, more genuinely ambivalent, type of repertoire is theoretically shaped by histories consisting of a somewhat equal mix of punishment and reinforcement for nurturance-seeking. As adults, individuals with this type of repertoire are constantly faced with an approach-avoidance dilemma in attachment relationships. On the one hand they want and seek nurturance and on the other hand, they are afraid of and therefore avoid closeness. Ultimately, fearfulness should limit intimacy within adult relationships, creating a chronic, if mild-to-moderate, sense of dissatisfaction and disconnection for both partners. Again, the repertoire will continue to be shaped by transactions with current attachment partners, either toward more secure or more insecure styles. Even among those shaped toward more attachment security, those with a history of ambivalent attachment should continue to have a unique vulnerability to developing approach-avoidance relationships.

From the current perspective, attachment styles traditionally categorized as avoidant may contain two distinguishable dismissive attachment repertoires and three distinguishable fearful attachment styles. Dismissive attachment styles may include both genuinely dismissive repertoires resulting from the near-extinction of nurturance-seeking and passive attachment repertoires resulting from noncontingent nurturing. Within adults, the dismissive attachment repertoire should be characterized by a genuine disinterest in intimate relationships with little anxiety about other people. The passive attachment repertoire should be characterized by a genuine interest in and longing for intimacy but no effective repertoire for actively pursuing it. Both repertoires are likely to result in loneliness and difficulty finding and maintaining intimate relationships.

Fearful attachment styles may include three distinguishable repertoires. First, a genuinely fearful repertoire should result from histories consisting primarily of punitive consequences for nurturance-seeking and should be characterized in adults as consistent fearful avoidance of intimate relationships accompanied by genuine longing for closeness. This type of fearful repertoire is the most likely to be sustained by negative reinforcement, since avoidance of feared others functions to eliminate a threat. Consequently, one might expect individuals with fearful-avoidant repertoires to have great difficulty forming and maintaining intimate relationships. One might also predict that individuals with fearful-avoidant repertoires might move quickly in and out of emotionally intense relationships, because suppressed nurturance-seeking is likely to rebound strongly when the person is made to feel safe. Similarly, nurturance-seeking is likely to resuppress as the relationship becomes more emotionally threatening, akin to the behavior of those with borderline personality disorder.

The next type of fearful repertoire is shaped by a history consisting of a mix of punishing and of reinforcing consequences, with punishing consequences being more probable than reinforcing ones. The resulting repertoire should be like an ambivalent attachment style in that it is characterized by an approach-avoidance conflict. In some cases, when the history consists primarily of punishment, the resulting behavior may look much more disorganized. In this case, the level of deprivation required to elicit an approach would have to be quite powerful to overcome a strong inclination to avoid a feared attachment figure. As adults, individuals with this type of history likely experience the desire for nurturance as both attractive and noxious, creating an approach-avoidance paradox much more powerful than that experienced by the ambivalently attached, resulting in emotional chaos. These individuals may be particularly susceptible to finding themselves in abusive relationships because they have learned to associate nurturance with punitiveness.

Finally, an aggressive attachment repertoire is also a likely outcome of histories consisting of large probabilities of punishment for nurturance-seeking. This may constitute a unique repertoire or it may be a facet of all attachment repertoires shaped by some mix of punitive consequences. Regardless, some individuals with histories of being punished regularly for seeking nurturance may develop repertoires in which they relate to potential intimates in a uniquely aggressive fashion. Having learned to associate nurturance with punitiveness, they may be particularly susceptible to forming abusive relationships. Whether an individual develops a disorganized style or an aggressive style may be culturally mediated.

Addressing Adult Attachment Insecurities in Couple Therapy

Although attachment histories cannot be erased, they can be shaped by the addition of new learning opportunities; for many people, stable responsive adult intimate relationships provide just the type of new learning experiences that can shape more secure attachment styles. At the same time, the enduring vulnerabilities created by insecure attachment repertoires are likely to manifest themselves in adult intimate relationships in fairly predictable forms.

Attachment Difficulties in Relationships

Insecure attachment interferes with the intimacy process through several routes. Histories of punishment for nurturance-seeking (fearful, disorganized, aggressive, and ambivalent attachment repertoires) make nurturance-seeking dramatically more interpersonally vulnerable than is the case for more securely attached individuals. As a result, fearfully and ambivalently attached individuals have more difficulty initiating intimate events because interpersonal vulnerability is substantially more threatening for them. In addition, the deepening of intimacy necessarily results in more frequent intimate hurts because intimate partners are more vulnerable to each other and more capable of being both intentionally and unintentionally hurtful (Cordova & Scott, 2001). As a result, maintaining close intimate connections requires an ability to tolerate occasional emotional hurt in non-relationship-destructive ways. However, these individuals are much more likely to respond to the inherent slings and arrows of intimacy with powerful urges to withdraw or counterattack. Thus, individuals with punitive attachment histories are not only less likely to initiate intimate events, they are also more likely to terminate the intimacy process.

Individuals with histories of having nurturance-seeking ignored or noncontingently responded to are substantially less likely to initiate intimate events because active nurturance-seeking has nearly been extinguished from their overall repertoire. The genuinely dismissive are not only less likely to initiate intimate events, but are also unlikely to reinforce the interpersonally vulnerable behavior of others and therefore are unlikely to culminate intimate events. Depending on how thoroughly nurturance and nurturance-seeking have been removed from the repertoire, the dismissively attached may either fail to form intimate relationships entirely or may form relationships that consist of very little intimacy. In contrast, the passively attached may be unlikely to initiate intimate events but may be more capable of culminating them simply by virtue of the fact that they are much more comfortable and desirous of intimacy in general. Although they may be prone to depriving their partners of sufficient nurturing, they themselves may be perfectly content as long as they have partners who are willing to actively pursue closeness with them.

Finally, the preoccupied and ambivalently attached, due to the clingy and hyper-vigilant nature of their attachment bids, are likely to overwhelm even the most securely attached partners at times with their need for reassurance. The preoccupied may be so focused on getting their own intimacy needs met that they themselves make poor intimate partners and their relatively extreme vulnerability to feeling abandoned may contribute to something of a self-fulfilling prophecy. Ambivalent partners, by contrast, may withdraw at the first sign of rejection or hurt, leaving their partners with the task to figuring out what went wrong and how to repair the relationship.

Dysfunctional Relationship Themes

Three common "themes" (Jacobson & Christensen, 1996) in distressed couples can be accounted for by attachment styles that interfere with the intimacy process.

For the purpose of this paper, intimacy refers to a process in couples' interactions in which behavior made interpersonally vulnerable by a history of punishment by others is elicited and reinforced by another person (technically, an intimate event; Cordova, 2002; Cordova & Scott, 2001). The classic example of interpersonally vulnerable behavior is the sharing of past hurts, humiliations, failures, and other painful emotional experiences. Additional examples include most of those behaviors that we refer to as "just being ourselves" which generally include behavior that we do not usually share with others because they are interpersonally risky (e.g., caressing, kissing, and holding, as well as burping, cussing, and acting cranky). Being reinforced for interpersonally vulnerable behavior increases the probability of whole classes of interpersonally vulnerable behavior in relation to that reinforcing person. The reinforcing person gains stimulus control over our interpersonally vulnerable behavior, thereby beginning to establish him or herself as an intimate partner. Most fundamentally, the process results in the development of a relationship in which we are, more often than not, safe "just being ourselves." Thus, intimate events are the building blocks of intimate partnerships that become characterized by open interpersonal vulnerability and feelings of safety, acceptance, and comfort. This occurs if the intimacy process unfolds well and is not derailed by other factors. Below, we describe three common relationship themes resulting from insecure attachment styles' effects on the intimacy process.

The closeness/distance theme. In the closeness/distance theme, one member of a couple typically wants more contact and closeness than the other member. This theme often arises out of differences between partners in their desires for closeness, with one partner wanting more closeness and the other wanting more distance. The closeness-seeking member of the couple often complains that the other partner does not spend enough time with him or does not want to spend time together in the same way. For example, a closeness-seeking partner might not consider watching television together to be "together time." She might long instead for more frequent conversation and physical touch. Closeness-seeking partners often complain that they do not feel fully appreciated or validated by their partners and that they typically have to be the one to initiate contact. Distance-seeking partners, by contrast, tend to feel overwhelmed by their closeness-seeking partners. They often report feeling as though no matter how much time they spend with their partners, it is never enough. Sadly, the closeness-seeking behavior of one partner often becomes the discriminative stimulus for the other partner's distancing, which in turn serves as the discriminative stimulus for the first partner's increased demand for closeness, creating a self-perpetuating dysfunctional pattern.

What might be going on here, and how might an understanding of attachment theory be helpful? One way closeness/distance patterns can originate is through the mismatch of attachment styles. An adult with a preoccupied attachment style has a learning history which has taught him or her that others' nurturance is unpredictable and that closeness needs will not always be met. Such individuals engage in high frequency bids for closeness with little post-reinforcement pause. Adults with ambivalent attachment styles are also likely to engage in a great deal of reassurance-seeking driven by a chronic fear that their partner is angry. This pattern emerges from an attachment history in which punitiveness was common. For both of these types of styles, nurturance is not perfectly satiating because attachment figures signal both sources of nurturance and abandonment or rejection. The resulting clinginess and reassurance-seeking can overwhelm even securely attached partners, increasing the probability of falling into a closeness-distance pattern.

Chronically distancing partners, for their part, are likely to have avoidant attachment repertoires, characterized by dismissiveness or fear of closeness. Because their attachment histories have taught them that attachment figures are either generally nonresponsive or mostly punitive, maintaining closeness is either outside their repertoire or just plain scary. Individuals with avoidant repertoires often deprive even securely attached partners of optimal levels of closeness, thus these styles also increase the odds of setting in motion a closeness-distance pattern.

It should be noted that fearfully avoidant adults have had their nurturance-seeking behavior suppressed, not extinguished, and thus although closeness-seeking may be particularly scary for them, that repertoire may still be made available for shaping by a more reinforcing partnership. The genuinely dismissive, however, having had their nurturance-seeking repertoire extinguished (to varying degrees), may have the most difficulty forming intimate adult relationships without specific training in how to effectively seek and provide nurturance. The passively avoidant should fare relatively well with partners that actively pursue closeness with them because the passively attached genuinely want closeness and do not actively avoid it. They may, however, benefit from specific training in how to elicit and provide nurturance to their partners.

The parallel but separate lives pattern. Another common pattern evident in distressed couples is that of two people living separate lives in the same living quarters. Although the couple lives together, their lives do not appear otherwise intertwined; they may spend their leisure time separately, do household chores separately, and when home at the same time, are rarely to be found together. Such couples often state that they feel distant from each other or that they feel more like housemates than intimate partners. Working collaboratively as a couple is often a challenge for these couples, as their inclination is to divide up tasks and perform them individually, not as a couple.

From an attachment perspective, couples who find themselves in this pattern are likely to have learning histories that involve having had bids for closeness ignored or punished. As a result, when they perceive trouble in the relationship, they tend to withdraw and turn inward. Not surprisingly, people who have avoidant attachment styles are particularly susceptible to this relationship pattern. Once the pattern has been established, it often seems to gather momentum, and breaking out of it to seek contact or approach the other partner becomes less and less likely. When one or both partners have a history of having been punished for seeking closeness, the pattern is even more unlikely to be broken without professional help. Treatment for avoidance will be discussed at greater length later in this chapter, but the general approach to helping couples who experience the "parallel lives" pattern is to decrease avoidance by increasing comfort with intimate interactions. This is usually accomplished through acceptance, which will be discussed later. It is also important to note that this pattern may emerge for nonattachment-related reasons. One common trigger for this theme is the transition to parenthood, when partners have less time and energy to devote to their relationship. It seems likely that securely attached couples are most likely to recover easily from such a situationally induced pattern, while more insecurely attached couples are likely to struggle with the pattern for longer periods of time.

The blaming or mutually aggressive pattern. Couples who are caught in a blaming pattern tend to have frequent arguments which quickly devolve into mutual blame, retribution seeking, grudge holding, and avoidance. Over time, even attempts at reconciliation or closeness may be met with a punitive response. Couples in which one or both members have learning histories that involve a history of receiving punishment when making bids for closeness may be especially prone to this pattern; this applies especially to those who rarely experienced reinforcing responses to their requests for closeness or comfort. As noted earlier, besides avoidance and escape, aggression is the most predictable response to contact with aversive stimuli. For fearfully and ambivalently attached individuals, attachment and closeness have acquired aversive qualities from histories of punitive responses to attachment bids. In addition, nurturance-seeking is particularly interpersonally vulnerable for such individuals, and any hint of rejection or punitiveness by an intimate partner is likely to be especially painful, again eliciting either aggression or withdrawal. In short, individuals with punitive attachment histories are particularly vulnerable to reactive aggressiveness and blaming in their adult intimate relationships and are particularly likely to fall into mutual blame and mutual aggressiveness with even securely attached partners. Unfortunately, anger and aggression can escalate when a person feels blamed, so this pattern has the potential to become dangerous. The pattern of trading punishment (blaming responses) either in response to aversive stimuli or in self-defense creates a cycle in which punishment becomes the most probable outcome of interaction. Since neither member of the couple is reinforced in most interactions, it is difficult for either member to provide reinforcing responses to the other.

An Approach to Couples Therapy

We believe that Integrative Behavioral Couples Therapy (IBCT) is uniquely suited for working with couples struggling with relationship dysfunction caused by insecure attachment styles. Developed by Jacobson and Christensen (1996), IBCT was designed for use with couples who had special difficulty in working collaboratively. Christensen and Jacobson (1991) found that traditional behavior therapy for couples did not work well for couples who were very polarized because, although they sometimes could follow the rules prescribed by the therapist for problem solving and communication, they stopped following the rules almost as soon as they left therapy. In some cases, couples were so polarized that even with the help of a therapist, they could not collaborate well enough to attempt new techniques of communicating or solving problems together. For these particularly difficult couples, Christensen and Jacobson (1991) developed a new approach to therapy, designed especially for couples who have difficulty collaborating or moving beyond damaging patterns. The primary mechanism of change is, paradoxically, learning greater acceptance and developing deeper understanding of those aspects of the partnership that are unlikely to change. Although IBCT is a relatively new treatment, initial data suggest that it is more effective than traditional behavioral couples therapy in improving relationship satisfaction (Cordova, Jacobson, & Christensen, 1998; Jacobson, Christensen, Prince, Cordova, & Eldridge, 2000).

Using Acceptance Work in Therapy

Acceptance has been described with terms ranging from complete rejection of an event, through tolerance, to enthusiastic embracing (Cordova, 2001). Implicit in all definitions of acceptance, however, is the idea of giving up the struggle to change that which cannot be changed. Much like the oft repeated "serenity prayer" of Alcoholics Anonymous, the goal of acceptance work is to "accept the things (one) cannot change." As Christensen and Jacobson (2000) note, however, acceptance can be much more radical than simply tolerating that which one does not have the power to change. The ultimate form of interpersonal acceptance is empathy and compassion, the ability to notice one's partner's aversive behavior and to understand the lovable and sometimes even well-intentioned reasons behind it. As Christensen and Jacobson (2000) explain, "acceptance ... is tolerating aversive behavior because you see that behavior as part of a larger context of who your partner is and who you are" (p. 124).

The goals of IBCT in relation to insecure attachment issues are compassionate acceptance and active coping. Given the assumption that insecure attachment styles remain enduring vulnerabilities within intimate relationships (Karney & Bradbury, 1995), even when secure attachment between partners is achieved, we believe that it is necessary for both partners to thoroughly understand the roots of insecure attachment styles and the understandable ways in which those styles are likely to manifest themselves in intimate relationships. The theory is that compassion for both the self and the partner, as well as a willingness to collaborate on coping with enduring vulnerabilities, emerges out of genuine understanding by and for each member of a partnership. Attachment insecurities are treated as faultless, naturally occurring "flaws in the fabric" of a couple's relationship from which both partners suffer and toward which both partners can orient as a team with mutual compassion and active coping. How does a therapist help a couple achieve acceptance? Cordova (2001) suggests three strategies for fostering acceptance: targeting the discriminative stimulus, targeting the aversion behavior, and targeting the consequences of aversion.

Targeting the discriminative stimulus. Targeting the discriminative stimulus involves shifting the stimulus value of an initially aversive stimulus from aversive to more appetitive. For example, the avoidantly attached individual's inclination to avoid intimacy is often quite aversive and blameworthy to his partner when the couple first enters therapy. One approach to facilitating greater acceptance of that inclination is to help both partners more thoroughly understand the attachment history that shaped avoidance and the underlying fearful vulnerability that characterizes it. The goal, following from relational frame theory (e.g., Hayes, Barnes-Holmes, & Roche, 2001), is to shift the stimulus value of withdrawal from the aversiveness associated with descriptors like "cold" and "distancing" to the more compassion eliciting stimulus value of "scared" and "vulnerable." A successful shift in the stimulus value along this gradient should result in both partners actually experiencing the first partner's struggle with avoidance as more tolerable, understandable, and approachable, thus facilitating the intimacy process for both of them. The therapeutic process involves the repeated sharing of these more compassion eliciting reasons, which allows for the gradual shifting of stimulus value.

Targeting the aversion behavior. Targeting the aversion behavior means directly addressing how a partner responds to an aversive stimulus, most often his or her partner's behavior. Aversion usually takes the form of avoidance (e.g., withdrawing from an argument), so the therapeutic goal is most often to promote exposure and response prevention. The goal in targeting aversion behaviors is to change the stimulus value of the discriminative stimulus from aversive to more tolerable by facilitating experiences that undermine negatively reinforced avoidance and reinforce actively making contact. As with exposure and response prevention in the treatment of germ phobia, exposure to the aversive stimulus (e.g., dirt) in the absence of any harm should ultimately extinguish the avoidance response. In addition, if making contact with naturally occurring consequences is actually reinforcing (e.g., experiencing greater intimate safety), then not only is avoidance extinguished but an approach repertoire is established. As Cordova (2001) noted, the topography of the stimulus does not change, but its stimulus value does. Put another way, the aversive event that triggers avoidance does not change. Instead, the avoidant behavior is made to change, and through the resulting exposure, the stimulus value shifts from aversive to appetitive.

For example, for fearfully attached individuals, making bids for nurturance is scary and is therefore avoided. Greater acceptance can be facilitated by (a) facilitating a climate of compassionate understanding in therapy, and (b) encouraging the making of bids for nurturance and facilitating the partner's reinforcing response to those bids both in therapy and at home. The ultimate goal is for the naturally occurring contingencies to take hold and begin the process of shaping a more effective attachment repertoire. As Cordova (2001) noted, such exposure and response strategies rely on the fact that no harm comes from engaging in them. In a situation in which abuse or harm is possible, such techniques should not be used.

Targeting the consequences of aversion. The third way to promote acceptance in couples is through targeting the consequences of aversion. This means drawing attention to the negative consequences of aversion behavior while reinforcing efforts to approach and maintain contact. Borrowed from Functional Analytic Psychotherapy (FAP; Kohlenberg & Tsai, 1991), the goal of this strategy is to help shift the contingencies of reinforcement away from an automatic avoidance response and toward a more intimacy-producing response. Whereas targeting aversion behavior relies on exposure, targeting the consequences relies on reinforcing a new, more intimacy facilitative repertoire. For example, in the above scenario with the fearfully avoidant partner, new, naturally occurring approaches for nurturance are likely to be weak and difficult to discern, but the therapist and both partners can be taught to be vigilant for any behavior approximating interpersonal vulnerability and to increase the amplitude of naturally occurring reinforcing responses (e.g., "when you told me how you felt about that, it made me feel closer to you."). As those initially tentative attempts at intimate approach are naturally reinforced, the stimulus value of bids for closeness should shift from mostly fearful toward greater intimate safety.

Conclusion

In this chapter, we have reviewed the literature on attachment theory and have suggested that a behavioral analytic perspective provides a generative theoretical framework from which to understand and approach this body of research. We have used BA to explain the function of attachment behavior and to account for the variability in attachment "styles." Our account reframes attachment styles as repertoires that have been shaped by individual histories composed of different ratios of reinforcement, ignoring, and punishment in response to bids for nurturance. By extension, attachment repertoires are evoked in the context of adult intimate relating. Many common relationship distress patterns can be understood as originating from attachment repertoires that are not conducive to intimacy. Indeed, insecure adult attachment styles can contribute to common painful relationship patterns, and IBCT can be useful in helping such couples to create new, more rewarding patterns with each other. By helping couples to gain a deeper understanding about what has shaped their behavior in close relationships (histories of punishment, being ignored, etc.), couples therapists can help partners come to a deeper understanding of themselves and their partners. Such an understanding, called "acceptance," leads to intimacy-conducive behaviors and can both reduce relationship distress and improve relationship satisfaction. We hope that our interpretation of attachment repertoires will lead the field to reconsider how attachment styles have traditionally been understood and to undertake new research based on these new interpretations. In addition, we hope that our re-conceptualization of attachment will help guide clinical formulations and interventions, both in research and in practice.

References

Ainsworth, M. D., Blehar, M. C., Waters, E., & Wall, S. (1978). *Patterns of attachment: A psychological study of the strange situation.* Hillsdale, NJ: Erlbaum.

Ainsworth, M. D., & Eichberg, C. G. (1991). Effects on infant-mother attachment of mother's unresolved loss of an attachment figure on other traumatic life experience. In P. Marris, J. Stevenson-Hinde, & C. Parks (Eds.), *Attachment across the life cycle* (pp.160-183). New York: Routledge.

Bartholomew, K., & Horowitz, L. M. (1991). Attachment styles among young adults: A test of a four-category model. *Journal of Personality and Social Psychology, 61,* 226-244.

Bowlby, J. (1969). *Attachment and loss, Vol. I: Attachment.* London: Hogarth Press.

Bowlby, J. (1973). *Attachment and loss, Vol. II: Separation.* New York: Basic Books.

Bowlby, J. (1980). *Attachment and loss, Vol. III: Loss.* New York: Basic Books.

Bowlby, J. (1988). *A secure base: Parent-child attachment and healthy human development.* New York: Basic Books.

Brennan, K. A., & Shaver, P. R. (1995). Dimensions of attachment, affect regulation, and romantic relationship functioning. *Personality & Social Psychology Bulletin, 21,* 267-283.

Christensen, A., & Jacobson, N. S. (1991). *Integrative behavioral couple therapy.* Unpublished treatment manual, University of Washington.

Christensen, A., & Jacobson, N. S. (2000). *Reconcilable differences.* New York: Guilford.

Cordova, J. V. (2001). Acceptance in behavior therapy: Understanding the process of change. *The Behavior Analyst, 24,* 213-226.

Cordova, J. V. (2002). Behavior analysis and the scientific study of couples. *The Behavior Analyst Today, 3,* 412-420.

Cordova, J. V., & Gee, C. B. (2001). Couple therapy for depression: Using healthy relationships to treat depression. In S. R. H. Beach (Ed.), *Marital and family processes in depression* (pp. 185-204). Washington, DC: American Psychological Association.

Cordova, J. V., Jacobson, N. S., & Christensen, A. (1998). Acceptance vs. change in behavioral couples therapy: Impact on client communication processes in the therapy session. *Journal of Marital and Family Therapy, 24,* 437-455.

Cordova, J. V., & Scott, R. L. (2001). Intimacy: A behavioral interpretation. *The Behavior Analyst, 24,* 74-86.

George, C., Kaplan, N., & Main, M. (1985). *The adult attachment interview.* Unpublished manuscript, University of California at Berkeley.

Harlow, H. F. (1958). The nature of love. *American Psychologist, 13,* 673-685.

Hayes, S. C., Barnes-Holmes, D., & Roche, B. (2001). Relational frame theory: A précis. In S. C. Hayes, D. Barnes-Holmes, & B. Roche (Eds.), *Relational frame theory: A post-Skinnerian account of human language and cognition* (pp. 141-156). New York: Kluwer Academic/Plenum Publishers.

Hazan, C., & Shaver, P. (1987). Romantic love conceptualized as an attachment process. *Journal of Personality and Social Psychology, 53,* 511-524.

Hesse, E., & Main, M. (2000). Disorganized infant, child, and adult attachment: Collapse in behavioral and attentional strategies. *Journal of the American Psychoanalytic Association, 48,* 1097-1127.

Jacobson, N. S., & Christensen, A. (1996). *Acceptance and change in couple therapy.* New York: W. W. Norton & Company.

Jacobson, N. S., Christensen, A., Prince, S. E., Cordova, J. V., & Eldridge, K. (2000). Integrative behavioral couple therapy: An acceptance-based, promising new treatment for couple discord. *Journal of Consulting and Clinical Psychology, 28,* 351-355.

Karney, B. R., & Bradbury, T. N. (1995). The longitudinal course of marital quality and stability: A review of theory, methods, and research. *Psychological Bulletin, 118,* 3-34.

Kohlenberg, R. J., & Tsai, M. (1991). *Functional analytic psychotherapy: Creating intense and curative therapeutic relationships.* New York: Plenum.

Main, M. (2000). The organized categories of infant, child, and adult attachment: Flexible vs. inflexible attention under attachment-related stress. *Journal of the American Psychoanalytic Association, 48,* 1055-1096.

Main, M., Kaplan, N., & Cassidy, J. (1985). Security in infancy, childhood and adulthood: A move to the level of representation. *Monographs of the Society for Research in Child Development, 50,* 66-104.

Scott, R. L. (2002). *The association between adult attachment and attributions for romantic partners' negative behavior.* Unpublished doctoral dissertation, University of Illinois at Urbana-Champaign.

Scott, R., & Cordova, J. V. (2002). The influence of adult attachment styles on the association between marital adjustment and depressive symptoms. *Journal of Family Psychology, 16,* 199-208.

Chapter 15

Implications of Verbal Processes for Childhood Disorders: Tourette's Disorder, Attention Deficit Hyperactivity Disorder, and Autism

Michael P. Twohig, Steven C. Hayes, & Nicholas M. Berens
University of Nevada, Reno

Direct contingency principles have, for understandable historical and pragmatic reasons, dominated in the analysis of childhood problems from a behavioral perspective, and cognitive or verbal processes have often been ignored. New generations of behavioral concepts that are linked to verbal processes are receiving more attention in the field, particularly Relational Frame Theory (RFT; Hayes, Barnes-Holmes, & Roche, 2001). This chapter examines some of the implications of verbal processes for contemporary behavioral models of childhood behavior problems, specifically Tourette's Disorder (TD), Attention Deficit Hyperactivity Disorder (ADHD), and Autism. This chapter will consider the possible benefits of incorporating these data and the principles they imply into our existing behavioral conceptualizations of a set of childhood behavior problems. This chapter will not stand alone, and assumes some degree of familiarity with this set of concepts, which are covered in the initial chapters of the book and elsewhere (e.g., Hayes et al., 2001).

Tourette's Disorder

Tics are defined as sudden, repetitive, stereotyped movements and vocalizations (American Psychiatric Association, 2000). Children with tic disorders may present with simple or complex tics. Simple tics are relatively short and discrete in duration such as a cough or a hard eye blink, whereas complex tics are much more prolonged and may include tics such as twirling or singing. Tic disorders are categorized by tic type (motor or vocal), and the length of time the tics are present. The tic disorder is considered to be transient if the tics have been present for less than one year, and chronic if the tics are present for over a year. If both motor and vocal tics are present, a diagnosis of TD is warranted. Motor tics are those that involve contractions of muscle groups and vocal tics are those that involve repetitive sounds or vocalizations, although the distinction is imprecise because vocal tics certainly involve contractions of muscles necessary for vocalizations.

The prevalence of TD in the general population is approximately 1%, it is more common in males, the average age of tic development is around the ages of 6 or 7, and motor tics usually develop before vocal and simple tics develop before complex (Findley, 2001). Motor tics also generally develop in a top down fashion with the first tics usually being in the face and developing down the body (Leckman, King, & Cohen, 1999). TD is usually strongest in middle adolescence and then the tics usually decrease in frequency, where approximately 65% of children with TD no longer exhibit tics as adults (Leckman, Zhang, Vitale, Lahnin, Lynch, Bondi et al., 1998).

The distinctions between motor and vocal, and simple and complex tics used in the diagnostic literature are topographical, not functional. The function of tics is not entirely known, but as will be discussed below, the most likely behavioral function that develops is some type of environmental control of the premonitory urge, which occurs prior to tics and is relieved through the expression of tics. Almost all adults with tics can sense such an urge before the tic, and report their tics to be partially or wholly voluntary (Leckman, Walker, & Cohen, 1993).

Etiology of Tourette's Disorder

Research has implicated biological/neurological factors in the development of TD. Biological relatives of those with TD have increased rates of both tic disorders and OCD. First-degree family members of those with TD generally have high rates of TD (10-11%), chronic tic disorder (15%), and OCD (11-12%; Pauls, Alsobrook, Gelernter, & Leckman, 1999). It seems likely that several genes are associated with the development of this disorder (Findley, 2001). Neurological research has generally implicated the secondary motor cortex (SMC) and dopaminergic systems in the basal ganglia as central to tic disorders. Basal ganglia volumes are smaller in TD patients and excitement of the SMC produces premonitory urges (Peterson, Leckman, Arnsten, Anderson, Lawrence, Gore et al., 1999). It is also important to note that biology does not affect behavior outside of environmental influence and that it is more likely that these biological features might contribute or set the stage for the creation of the disorder, but not directly establish those functions. Furthermore, although they are not commonly given causal credit in the development in TD, environmental variables can strongly affect tic frequency and are involved in many of the most successful interventions for these problems.

Antecedent variable manipulations have shown that certain bodily states may cause an exacerbation in tics, including being upset, anxious, or fatigued (Bornstein, Stefl, & Hammond, 1990; Silva, Munoz, Barickman, & Freidhoff, 1995). Individuals who have TD may have a greater rate of vocal tics when engaged in a tic-related conversation (Woods, Watson, Wolfe, Twohig, & Friman, 2001), suggesting that the verbal/psychological context plays a role. There is also evidence indicating that socially mediated consequences may maintain tic frequency for some (Carr, Taylor, Wallander, & Reiss, 1996; Malatesta, 1990). It seems fair to conclude that both biological and psychological factors work together in the development of TD.

Traditional Behavioral Model of Tourette's Disorder

Azrin and Nunn (1973) presented the first behavior analytic account of tic disorders. They hypothesized that tics began as a normal reaction to an extreme event such as physical trauma or injury. For example, if one suffered damage to ones arm, shaking of the arm may reduce the pain from the damage. The shaking of ones arm is negatively reinforced through the removal of the pain and begins to occur more intensely and at higher rates, thus, becoming more tic-like. Normally, the tic would decrease as the individual matures because of the aversive social reaction that one receives, but for some, the behavior begins to occur out of awareness. If no social repercussions are present, the behavior blends into a response chain that seems automatic in nature. Because tics occur with such high frequency, they can begin to strengthen the muscles that are involved in the tic and make it more difficult to stop. This model of TD was very useful in developing a successful treatment for tics that involved awareness training, competing response practice, habit control motivation, and generalization training (Azrin & Nunn, 1973; Azrin, Nunn, & Frantz, 1980; Azrin & Peterson, 1990).

More recent behavioral theories of TD conceptualize tic disorders in bio-psychological terms. Biological predispositions, particularly in the development of the SMC and dopaminergic systems in the basal ganglia, create a context where the individual experiences particular stimuli (both public and private) that increases the likelihood of tics occurring. Tics are then maintained through a negative reinforcement paradigm: a particular negatively evaluated private event such as muscle tension or a feeling of "not being right" is decreased by engaging in the tic (Miltenberger & Woods, 2000). If so, the behavioral process in the development of tics may be psychological (negative reinforcement) while the specific establishing operations and reinforcers would be primarily biological (e.g., whatever biological processes establish urges and movements reduce those urges).

Implications of Verbal Processes for a Behavioral Model of Tourette's Disorder

Although Azrin and Nunn's original model of the development and maintenance of tic disorders was useful in developing a successful intervention, subsequent research has shown that it is not an adequate account of TD. First, research has not uncovered a common type of extreme environmental event that is associated with the onset of TD (e.g., physical injury). Second, survey research has indicated that although some tics occur out of awareness, a large percent of individuals indicate that they are aware of their tics and can predict and control when they are going to occur (Findley, 2001). This does not fit with Azrin and Nunn's model of TS which contains the idea that the tics occur out of awareness and therefore increase in strength because the individual is not controlling them. Azrin and Nunn also assumed that because the tics are out of awareness they are less susceptible to social punishers. Research has shown that individuals with tics can have social difficulties as a result of their tics (Woods, 2002; Woods, Koch, & Miltenberger, 2003), which may modify when and how the tics occur.

Third, research has demonstrated that maintenance of tics is not the result of the strengthening of muscles involved in the tics (Miltenberger & Fuqua, 1985; Sharenow, Fuqua, & Miltenberger, 1989; Woods, Murray, Fuqua, Seif, Boyer, & Siah, 1999). The HR procedure was originally assumed to decrease tics because it strengthened the muscles opposite those used in the tic, thereby increasing the strength to suppress the tic. However, competing responses that do not involve tic muscles (such as using legs muscles for an arm tic) are as successful as those that do involve them (Sharenow et al., 1989; Woods et al., 1999). For all of these reasons, the Azrin and Nunn model does not seem to adequately explain TD.

Including verbal processes in TD may help our theoretical understanding of the disorder, and expectantly inform our treatment practices. Of particular importance are the variables involved in the maintenance and exacerbation of tics, including conditions that occasion and maintain tics after tics are present.

Verbal Processes and the Regulation and Maintenance of Tic Occurrence

On the surface, tics seem involuntary because of the rate, speed, and manner in which they occur. These formal properties seem to explain the common sense view that tics occur outside of one's awareness or consciousness. Individuals with TD, however, indicate that they are usually aware of an urge to tic that occurs shortly before the tic and that engaging in the tic relieves that urge (Leckman et al., 1993). Researchers generally believe that this urge is present early on for children, but that their awareness or ability to discuss it seems to occur about three years after emergence of the tics (Leckman et al., 1993). The following section focuses on why, for some, it takes a period of time for children to develop an awareness of this feeling and why it is evaluated negatively.

How verbal processes help create psychological functions for the premonitory urge. Most children are taught to avoid feeling bad or uncomfortable and furthermore that when something feels physically wrong steps should be taken to change it. Considerable attention is paid by the social/verbal community to training children to detect, label, evaluate, and respond to physical sensations. Through multiple exemplars, children are often taught that abnormal feelings in the body are "bad," such as when the child has a sore throat, headache, fever, or scraped knee. In most such situations if a child has an uncomfortable feeling or even simply an unusual one, it might be necessary to address it. For example, a child coming to caregivers with a headache will typically be examined, and steps will be taken focused on the sensation (reassurance, aspirin administration, rubbing, cool cloths, rest, etc.). Even if the sensation is not obviously "bad," the same response may occur ("Mommy, I feel funny" may occasion similar responses to "Mommy, I hurt"). Given an extensive history of this sort, a child may build a repertoire of overt action focused on the removal of "unusual" and actually or presumptively "negative" sensations. In essence, each example is also an example of a verbal rule: when something odd or bad is felt, take steps to change it and you will feel more normal. In most cases taking steps to change negative or unusual bodily sensations will in fact work. This repertoire then can be applied to one's urges to tic.

When the premonitory urge first starts to come into the child's awareness it is likely felt as another bodily sensation, without evaluation tied to it. Though the sensation may not have been directly aversive (e.g., it may have felt more "tingly" than "painful"), prior history may be enough to place this unusual bodily sensation in a frame of coordination with "feeling bad" or at least "having a feeling that shouldn't be there." Engaging in the tic will remove the sensation for a short time, confirming its relation to the earlier rule promoted explicitly or implicitly by the social/verbal community ("when something odd or bad is felt, take steps to change it and you will feel more normal") and reinforcing the actions that removed the sensation. It is worth noting that this analysis would suggest that the negative reinforcement contingency itself may be in part verbal. The change in sensation may be reinforcing because it removes an "odd" sensation or because one now feels "more normal." Unfortunately, this reinforcement contingency also increases the stimulus control properties of the original sensations, the ease with which they are evaluated as odd or negative, and the relationship between the sensations and overarching rules about what to do with regard to unusual or negative sensations. This will make the original sensations more readily detected and more powerful in the establishment of the tic.

The elaboration of relational networks relevant to an initial sensation can lead the urge to become increasingly complex and verbal. The following are descriptions of premonitory urges provided by Leckman et al. (1993):

"I feel that I have too much energy and have to get some of it out so I do that." 12-year-old boy

"A need to tic is an intense feeling that unless I tic or twitch I feel as if I am going to burst. Unless I can physically tic, all of my mental thoughts center on ticking until I am able to let it out. It is a terrible urge that needs to be satisfied." 21-year-old woman

"I guess it's sort of an aching feeling, in a limb or a body area, or else in my throat if it precedes a vocalization. If I don't relieve it, it either drives me crazy or begins to hurt (or both)-in that way it is both physical and mental." 27-year-old woman

"I have to 'do it one more time' or 'complete something' or make something symmetrical." 71-year-old man (p. 102)

These descriptions of the premonitory urge show how complex, metaphorical, and evaluative urges can become. What may originally have been a slight sensation now part of a well-developed verbal network. As such, urges become more susceptible to other verbal events.

Premonitory urges occasioned through verbal behavior. Verbal relations can become involved in the expansion of this evaluative process. Verbal relations are bidirectional and combinatorial, and thus any event verbally related to the sensation or tic may occasion the urge. This helps explain why focusing one's own attention to the area of the body where the tic occurs, discussion of tics, or bringing public attention to one's tics will often increase their frequency (Findley, 2001; Woods et al., 2001). This process is sometimes a problem in school settings when other students learn the specific cues that occasion a classmate to tic. For example, if a child has a laughing tic, a short laugh or words like "funny," "isn't that funny," or "don't laugh" can cause the child with TD to tic.

RFT suggests that relational networks function in ways that are not always expected—verbal relations need not be similar to occasion specific responses. For example, the word "hot" will frequently occasion the word "cold." The two are tightly related, despite the fact that the relation is literally one of opposition. In a similar way, "quiet" may occasion "noisy" or "giggly." The relational frames of this kind may help explain why signs or suggestions to "please be quiet" or "don't make a sound," such as one would see or hear in a library, can cause an increase in verbal tics (Leckman, King, Scahill, Findley, Ort, & Cohen, 1999). Relations of mutual entailment of this kind can also participate in combinatorially entailed relations. Combinatorial entailment refers to a derived stimulus relation where two or more stimulus relations mutually combine. For instance, if A is related to B, and A is related to C, then C and B will be related based on the combination of the two mutually entailed relations. In this way, any of a number of other events related to silence (church, a funeral) might occasion the premonitory urge. As these processes of verbally established stimulus control occur, the rates of tics may increase in part because the tic relevant stimuli in the environment are increasing through processes of derived stimulus relations. Consider the child who has a verbal history where trying not to laugh is related to a laughing sound, the word "laugh," churches, funerals, and so on, may come to occasion tics. The function of trying not to laugh may transfer to other members of a larger network of stimulus relations, causing events that are more and more indirect to occasion the urge and the laughing tic. Merely talking about church or hearses may be enough to occasion the urge to laugh, for example. This may be the exact verbal process that was seen in the Woods et al. (2001) study where tic-related conversation increased tic occurrence over conversation about non-tic-related areas.

Experiential Avoidance and Tics

The previous section presents the hypothesis that tics are done in part in order to escape the premonitory urge, which has such functions in part because of its verbal qualities. It is also hypothesized that engaging in tics to decrease the urge has increased the functional importance of this urge. This could be an example of a larger class of functional relations knows as experiential avoidance (Hayes, Wilson, Gifford, Follette, & Strosahl, 1996). Experiential avoidance is defined as "the phenomenon that occurs when a person is unwilling to remain in contact with particular private experiences and takes steps to alter the form or frequency of these events and the contexts that occasion them" (Hayes et al., 1996, p. 1154), even when such avoidance causes harm to the individual. Many forms of psychopathology may be forms of experiential avoidance (see Hayes et al., 1996, for a review). It could be that experiential avoidance is involved in the maintenance and perhaps even the etiology of TD. Evidence from the treatment literature generally supports this hypothesis. The most effective nonpharmacological treatment for TD is HR (Chambless, Baker, Baucom, Beutler, Calhoun, Crits-Christoph et al., 1998) and the central component of which is the competing response (Miltenberger, Fuqua, & Woods, 1998; Peterson & Azrin, 1992; Twohig & Woods, 2001). HR structures a time when the child has to sit with the urge to engage in the tic until the urge subsides. In essence, the child is being told to not do the tic, instead do something else until the urge to do the tic is gone. Seen in this way, HR may be effective because it does not support experiential avoidance. From an experiential avoidance standpoint, if a child did not attempt to decrease or alleviate the urge to do the tic, the stimulus control exerted by the premonitory urge should gradually diminish. Over time, the child's tics and premonitory urge would extinguish.

If the competing response is a form of experiential exposure and an extinction procedure, it might be necessary to maintain exposure to the urge beyond a brief period. In an experimental evaluation of the most successful duration of the competing response, with adults who nail bite, this has been confirmed. When five-second, one-minute, and three-minute versions of the competing response have been compared, only the one- and three-minute competing response periods were effective in the long-term (Twohig & Woods, 2001). This general finding is consistent with findings in other interoceptive exposure-based interventions that a greater length of exposure is generally more effective (Chaplin & Levine, 1981). Similarly, it has been shown that Exposure with Response Prevention, which involves exposing the individual to the urge to tic while preventing the occurrence of the tic, is as effective as HR in decreasing tics (Verdellen, Keijsers, Cath, & Hoogduin, 2004). While this hypothesis has not been tested directly, it is plausible and leads to useful treatment approaches.

Problems with the Present Model

This model, while plausible, is based on an extension of RFT thinking into a disorder domain. There are many empirical holes that must be filled before the model can be widely adopted or used. For example, more research will be needed to see if the premonitory urge functions as an aversive event that is relieved through engaging in the tic. This might be done by deliberately occasioning the urge (e.g., through discussion of its features; through the presentation of stimuli deliberately associated with it previously, and so on) and assessing the rate of tics and effects of the tic on the urge. If these procedures work, the RFT analysis could be strengthened by deliberately constructing arbitrary relational networks that include events that occasion the urge, to see if derived stimulus relations provide a model for the cognitive/verbal relations that are thought to underly the process.

The impact of general emotional avoidance rules on tics might be examined by studying the relationship between emotional avoidance measures and tics. There is growing evidence that suggests a link between experiential avoidance and habit disorders. A survey of nonreferred hair pullers found that greater experiential avoidance was significantly related to more severe Trichotillomania; high avoiders had more frequent and more intense urges to pull over low avoiders; and high avoiders has less control over their urges and more distress than low avoiders (Begotka, Woods, & Wetterneck, 2004). Perhaps the highest test of the current model, however, is through its treatment implications. As a pragmatic/contextual theory, if these hypothesized processes do not lead to better treatment outcomes, the underlying model is not supported.

Treatment Implications from this Model

This model proposes that TD at least partially functions through experiential avoidance of private events, where the private events have acquired some of their aversive functions through verbal processes, and that the process of avoiding these private events is also verbally maintained as a result of strong rule following. From this model, cognitive-based intervention for TD should involve strategies aimed at decreasing the strength of control of verbal processes over the urge to tic, including rule following, and increase psychological acceptance of these types of feelings. Thus, if a person is willing to experience their urges to tic, and not tic to reduce that feeling, they are in a much better position to use behavioral management procedures to control their ticking. There is growing evidence that acceptance and mindfulness procedures can alter these verbal processes (Hayes, 2004), and that these types of procedures can be integrated with HR if needed (e.g., Twohig & Woods, 2004; Woods, Wetterneck, & Flessner, 2006). This analysis will focus on decreasing the role of verbal behavior in TD.

Procedures already exist to assist a person control his or her habit behaviors including TD (e.g., HR). For many, they possess the behavioral repertoire to engage, or not engage in a particular behavior, but certain private events make it very difficult to do so. For TD, this private event is usually the premonitory urge. According to the RFT account of TD, it is unlikely that one would be able to talk oneself out of the urge to do the tic. Because language is bi-directional, trying to not think about how strong the urge is to do the tic may be functionally equivalent to thinking about doing the tic. In the treatment of TD defusion and acceptance procedures taken from Acceptance and Commitment Therapy (ACT) (Hayes, Strosahl, & Wilson, 1999) may be useful in decreasing the strength of control that the premonitory urge has over one's ticking. Defusion, briefly, involves seeing one's thoughts, feelings, or bodily sensations as nothing more than thoughts, feelings, and bodily sensations. They are experienced as they are, without verbal evaluation. If one were to experience the premonitory urge from a defused stance, it would presumably exert less control over behavior. Once a person is somewhat defused from the verbal part of an experience, it is easier for that person to take an accepting stance toward that experience. Acceptance involves fostering a willingness to experience unpleasant private events as events actively and deliberately rather than taking steps to change them in any way. Both of these procedures directly contradict experiential avoidance and rules that one must not experience the premonitory urge. If a person approached the premonitory urge from a defused and accepting stance, he or she should be in a much more likely position to not tic when the urge to do so is there.

Acceptance of the urge could change its function from something to be avoided to something to be experienced. Through coming in greater contact with the urges to do the tic, but without resorting to them, the participant may a) experience that nothing bad actually happens, b) undermine overarching experiential avoidance rules, c) come into contact with the natural contingencies associated with not ticking such as improved social acceptance, d) extinguish the evocative effect of the urge, and reinforce the use of acceptance and defusion procedures through a decrease in tics.

In addition to its direct targets, ACT and other new behavior therapies may also be useful for some of the comorbid issues that are associated with TD or as an intervention for those who work with the child and may have stigmatizing attitudes towards him or her. First, children with TD often suffer from comorbid ADHD, OCD, and learning disorders, for which acceptance-based treatment may be useful. Second, children with TD generally fare better academically and socially when parents, schoolteachers, and other school personnel accept the child's disorder and do not blame or punish him or her for his or her tic symptomatology (Dykens, Sparrow, Cohen, Scahill, & Leckman, 1999). For that reason, work with both parents and teachers and other school staff to foster a more accepting approach towards their reactions to children with these disorders would likely foster a more healthy development for the child. ACT may be useful in this area.

To date, two studies have examined the impact of ACT on parents of disabled children (Biglan, 1989; Blackledge & Hayes, 2006). Both found positive results, but both are within subject studies.

Attention Deficit Hyperactivity Disorder

Attention Deficit Hyperactivity Disorder (ADHD) is defined by problems in "inattention" or "hyperactivity-impulsivity." To be diagnosed with ADHD according to the *Diagnostic and Statistical Manual of Mental Disorders* (DSM-IV-TR; APA, 2000) the child must show behavior problems of this kind for at least six months, the behaviors must be maladaptive or inconsistent with his or her developmental level, and the symptoms must have developed by the age of seven. The child can either meet the criteria under the "inattention" category, "hyperactivity" category, or both.

To meet the criteria under the inattention category, six of the nine following items must be endorsed. The child must (1) fail to give close attention or make careless mistakes on his or her schoolwork, work, or other activities, (2) exhibit difficulty sustaining attention in tasks or play activities, (3) not listen when spoken to directly, (4) not follow through on instructions and fail to finish schoolwork, chores, or duties in the workplace, (5) show difficulty organizing tasks and activities, (6) avoid, dislike, or be reluctant to engage in tasks that require sustained mental effort, (7) lose things necessary for activities, (8) be easily distracted by extraneous stimuli, and (9) be forgetful in daily activities. To meet the criteria under the hyperactive-impulsive category, six of the nine following items must be endorsed. The child must (1) fidget with his or her hands or feet or squirms in his or her seat, (2) leave the seat in classroom or in other situations in which remaining in the seat is expected, (3) often run about or climb excessively in situations in which it is inappropriate, (4) show difficulty playing or engaging in leisure activities quietly, (5) seem as if he or she is "on the go" or "driven by a motor," (6) talk excessively; or impulsivly (7) blurt out answers before questions have been completed, (8) exhibit difficulty waiting his or her turn, and (9) interrupt or intrude on others. The prevalence of ADHD is between 3-5% and is more common in males than females (APA, 2000).

Biological Etiology

Like TD, there is substantial research on neurological and genetic factors associated with ADHD. Brain damage was originally proposed as a cause of ADHD because of the similar behavioral characteristics between the two groups, but subsequent research showed that fewer than 5% of those with ADHD have neurology consistent with brain damage (Rutter, 1977). Research on neurological factors has shown differences between individuals with ADHD and controls in frontal lobe functioning including brain wave activity, cerebral blood flow, and size of the region (Barkley, 1997, 1998). Proponents of neurological theories of ADHD often provide support for their theory based on improvements seen as a result of pharmacotherapy (Barkley, 1998). Environmental factors that affect brain development including, abnormally low birth weight, complications during pregnancy or child birth, acquired brain damage, or the entrance of toxins during the brain's development are also associated with high rates of ADHD (Barkley, 1998). Individuals with ADHD share high rates of the disorder with their parents and siblings; adopted children with ADHD share higher rates of the disorder with biological relatives than adopted relatives; and greater rates are found between monozygotic twins than zygotic twins (Barkley, 1998). The relation between genetics, neurology and ADHD as provided by Barkley (1998) is one where the individual is genetically programmed to have a less developed prefrontal-striatal network, which is consistent with the general etiological theory of ADHD.

Existing Models of ADHD

Few behavioral theories of ADHD have been proposed (Block, 1977; Willis & Lovaas, 1977). Willis and Lovaas (1977) took a very traditional behavioral approach to ADHD by proposing that it is the result of poor stimulus control. Others have implicated parental management techniques as a causal factor in the production of ADHD (Carlson, Jacobvitz, & Sroufe, 1995; Jacobvitz & Sroufe, 1987). Even without a firm theory, however, behavior analysts have been able to demonstrate positive effects with contingency management procedures including: function guided interventions (Ervin, DuPaul, Kern, & Friman, 1998), peer tutoring (DuPaul, Ervin, Hook, & McGoey, 1998), peer mediated reinforcement and self prompts (Flood, Wilder, Flood, & Masuda, 2002), and fading procedures (Binder, Dixon, & Ghezzi, 2000; Neef, Bicard, & Endo, 2001).

The behavioral inhibition model. Likely, the most popular model of ADHD is the behavioral inhibition model proposed by Barkley (1997, 1998). This model proposes that behavioral inhibition is the central behavioral deficit that negatively influences other executive functions including: prolongation or working memory, self-regulation of affect, internalization of speech, and reconstruction. Behavioral inhibition involves the capacity to inhibit prepotent responses (selecting the immediate reinforcer), thus, creating a delay in the response to an event, the capacity to interrupt ongoing responses, and the protection of this delay in responding. In Barkley's approach, inhibition is dominantly biological, and leads to the major behavioral deficit of ADHD: lack of self-control.

Implications of Verbal Processes for a Behavioral Model of ADHD

Although there is no one current behavioral theory of ADHD, it appears that most applied behavior analysts also depict it as a problem self-control or impulsivity. Self-control is defined as behavior that results in access to a larger reinforcer after a longer delay, rather than impulsive behavior that results in a small reinforcer after a shorter or no delay (Schweitzer & Sulzer-Azaroff, 1988). Nonverbal animals have notable difficulties with self-control (Mazur & Logue, 1978), but increases in self-control are generally seen as individuals acquire language and mature (Schweitzer & Sulzer-Azaroff, 1988). The verbal process that seems most involved in self-control is the ability to follow rules.

The role of rule governance in ADHD. There seems to be broad agreement that ADHD is in part a rule-following disorder. Barkley (1998) pointed to five features of children diagnosed with ADHD that are indicative of a delayed rule following repertoire: 1) greater variability in response patterns in experimental preparations, 2) they do better under conditions where the reinforcers are immediate rather than delayed, 3) they have more difficulty on tasks when there are delays within the task, 4) the children show more difficulties in tasks when reinforcement schedules are thinned or changed from continuous to intermittent, and 5) they show greater difficulties in tasks when noncontingent reinforcers are added to the experiment. The specific deficit seems to be more one of rule-following than rule-generation. In Ryle's (1949) terms, the problem is one of "knowing how" not "knowing that." Children with ADHD may be able to state what they should do in a certain situation (knowing that), but lack the repertoire to engage in those described behaviors (knowing how). Barkley (1998) says that children diagnosed with ADHD have trouble "doing what they know rather than knowing what to do" (p. 106).

Given the broad agreement that ADHD involves a disorder in rule-following, what might a more modern behavioral approach to human language contribute to its understanding and treatment? The main contribution is that there are a range of steps that might be researched in programs designed to establish better rule-following. For example, unlike Barkley's analysis, in which poor rule-following is due to an irreparable biological deficit, RFT suggests that even if there is such a deficit, extraordinary environments may be arranged to establish behaviors that the natural environment, or treatments unguided by a basic understanding, may fail to establish. As a result, it is quite possible that extraordinary methods focused on the key verbal issues involved could help regulate ADHD. Behavioral interventions have targeted verbal processes, showing that distracting oneself by performing activities such as singing or talking to oneself helps prevent impulsive responding (Binder et al., 2000); or that the manner in which the contingency is specified to the child affects the child's ability to follow rules (Bicard & Neef, 2002). But these interventions have not been guided by a comprehensive behavioral theory of language and cognition and tell us little about how to increase rule following in a meaningful way.

An RFT model of self-control. Consider the following situation: a small reinforcer is immediately available, while an alternative response sequence would lead to a larger delayed reinforcer. This classic behavior model of self-control (Rachlin & Green, 1972) has been used in a wide variety of studies. In the absence of language, increased self-control (preference for the delayed larger consequence) is possible, but the effects are not large and the methods are difficult. They include hundreds of trials in which the larger reinforcer is very gradually delayed (Mazur & Logue, 1978); this results in the development of longer chains of responding linked to the delayed reinforcer.

Humans have a more complex self-control situation. Typically, a small reinforcer is immediately available through known behaviors, while a described alternative response sequence would lead to a described larger reinforcer after a described delay. Sometimes the "impulsive" behavior is itself first available in rule form, but for the purposes of this chapter we can model the key issues by assuming that the impulsive behavior is shaped and directly available, while the self-controlled response is available in the form of a rule of this kind or its variants: if (behavior) then (better consequence) after (delay). Sometimes this rule is given by others; other times it is self-generated.

We will assume in this analysis that the child is able to describe, understand, and generate the rule. In part this seems to comport with the data. If they are not present in a given case, the steps needed to establish the relational frames needed for rule-generation and understanding seem relatively clear from an RFT point of view.

What we are describing here as "the self-control rule" requires at least three relational frames: coordination, temporal (time or contingency), and comparison. For example, these relational frames will result in the statement "If you wait three minutes you can have the larger candy bar, or you can select the small one right now," having behavioral functions. Specifically, frames of coordination are primarily involved in the description of the behavior and consequence; frames of time and contingency in the if ... then and delay elements; and comparative frames is the evaluation of a consequence relative to another (e.g., the immediate consequence available by impulsive behavior).

For a self-control rule to work initially, the relative value of the consequences and behavioral costs relative to the self-controlled response *in the present* must be greater and equally or more likely than the consequences and behavioral costs for the impulsive behavior. Over time, however, self-control rules may come to control behavior in a more automatic fashion as larger and larger patterns of effective action are constructed, allowing relative response probability and more molar contingencies to take hold (Rachlin, 1995).

There are a variety of variables that can influence a self-control rule when it is conceptualized this way. Temporal relational frames must be well established so that the contingency descriptions and delayed consequences are tightly related to the present moment. According to RFT, frames of this kind require a relatively predictable environment; with a high rate of exposure to future oriented talk linked to desirable outcomes; beginning with short time frames and extending gradually to longer ones. If future events are relatively unpredictable (e.g., due to relatively chaotic social environments), acquisition of temporal frames will be weakened, and indeed self-control behaviors are notoriously weak in such environments (Mauro & Harris, 2000).

For the verbally contacted consequence to make a behavioral impact, there must also be a transformation of stimulus functions. A verbal rule can be understood and not followed, but the opposite is not true; a rule cannot be followed when it is not understood. The stimulus functions of the verbal rule must transform accordingly to give the rule meaning and emotional functions. Behaviorally, evidence that a rule is understood occurs when the individual responds appropriately to one. Verbal reports of understanding can be inaccurate. There is some evidence that transformation of stimulus functions is key to verbal motivation (Ju, 2001). Little is yet known about how to increase the transformation of stimulus functions beyond providing clear contextual cues. It makes sense that relatively basic perceptual functions would precede more abstract or arbitrary functions, and that abstract functions would depend on larger more elaborated relational networks. Thus, children for who rules do not have a behavior regulatory function will likely need additional training on particular relational networks.

Comparative relational frames must be well-established and must be able to bring a directly experienced immediate consequence into a comparative relation. When an individual verbally contacts the larger-later reinforcer the relative difference between it and smaller-immediate consequences must be evident. It is this comparative relation that helps "spoil the fun" of an immediate smaller reinforcer. In essence, this analysis suggests that part of the process of developing self-control is to bring unhelpful contingency-shaped events into relational frames.

These features set the stage for a kind of effective verbal understanding that can lead to successful patterns of rule-following. It is never enough to understand a rule: rule-following itself must be developed.

If this analysis is correct, then increased attention should be placed on the manner in which rule following is trained. Currently, children with ADHD are largely trained in pliance. That kind of training can only go so far because the environment that initially maintains pliance is confined to the situation where the training occurs. This is evidenced by the findings from the behavioral treatment of ADHD (large scale contingency management procedures): the treatment is moderately effective when the contingency is in place, but dramatic decreases in effectiveness are seen when the contingency is removed (Hinshaw, Klein, & Abikoff, 2002). A broader and more generalized rule following repertoire might be seen if the child is trained in the more advanced types of rule following. Possible methods for training rule following will be described in the treatment implication section.

In using self-control rules, it may also be helpful to learn how to diminish the immediate properties of short term reinforcers. Research has shown that children are able to wait longer if they engaged in other behaviors during the delay for the larger reinforcer (Dixon, Hayes, Binder, Manthey, Sigman, & Zdanowski, 1998; Mischel, Ebbesen, & Zeiss, 1972). One explanation of why engaging in other behaviors during the delay increases the time that the child waits, is that it decreases contact with the immediate reinforcer and thus reduces behavior evoked or elicited by that contact. This, in turn, may reduce the aversive private events that the child experiences due to self-control.

Engaging in self-control is not immediately reinforcing: it is immediately aversive, and thus patterns of experiential avoidance will undermine self-control in multiple ways. It has been shown that engaging in avoidance behaviors can strengthen the aversive private event by conditioning the avoidance behaviors to the avoided event, thus, at a later time, the avoidance behaviors will elicit the aversive private events (Bouton, Mineka, & Barlow, 2001). The research on thought suppression and avoidance strategies focused on emotion illustrate the paradox of direct attempts to control one's private events (Abramowitz, Tolin, & Street, 2001), although this has not been as thoroughly tested with clinical samples (Abramowitz et al., 2001; Purdon, 1999). This indicates that attempts at controlling the aversive private events through avoidance might be unsuccessful or punitive in the long-term (Hayes et al., 1996; Hayes et al., 1999). Teaching children how to sit with difficult emotions without avoidance could be helpful in promoting self-control immediately and in the long run.

Treatment implications from an RFT model. Relatively little is known about how to establish effective rule-following repertoires, and thus it is not so much that a focus on rule-following will impact ADHD as it is that a focus on ADHD might impact on our analysis of a specific type of rule-following. That, however, is part of the point of a speculative exercise: to see gaps in knowledge and possible ways that these might be filled.

This present analysis looks at ADHD as a problem of self-control or impulsivity that is linked to behavioral deficits in relational framing repertoires and rule following, and possibly exacerbated by an inability to experience certain private events. Increasing the strength and effective contextual control of underlying relational frames should help increase the generalized operants of this type of rule following. Multiple exemplar training involves multiple training trials where irrelevant stimuli are varied and key features correlate consistently with the contingencies. In the case of relational frames, the key is to increase the fluidity and contextual control of relational operants. These operants need to be controlled by abstracted features of the environment as well as by arbitrary social cues; they need to occur at high rates of speed and with high accuracy; they need to support transformations of stimulus functions; and to combine with other relational frames. For example, if one wanted to train a frame of comparison, one would use varying stimuli such as half a candy bar and a whole candy bar, or glasses filled to varying degrees. So that nonarbitrary features do not dominate, purely arbitrary examples (e.g., a nickel is "bigger" than a dime) would be trained to fluency. Arbitrary cues would be allowed to alter nonarbitrary ones: (e.g., "if whole were half and half were whole which candy bar would you want: this whole one or this half one?"). Acquisitions of given frames and their combination would be assessed through application to novel stimulus sets and situations. Training of this kind is important because it ensures that the listener has a history of deriving stimulus relations. This is the repertoire that allows the rule to be "understood" in a way that their functions are transformed and affect overt behavior.

Rule understanding is not enough. Rule following requires direct experience in the effects of guidance by verbal formulae. Because pliance is likely the easiest form to train, most training in rule following starts there. The tight behavioral programs commonly used with ADHD are good examples, but often not enough attention is given to rule-following per se. Transitioning pliance to tracking involves using rules that correspond to the natural environment, powerful natural reinforcers, and gradual removal of arbitrary social contingencies. Fading procedures, such as those used by Dixon et al. (1998), seem well suited to such a task. The child would be presented with a very simple rule, with very low response effort, that would allow the child to access reinforcement for following the rule. The complexity and response effort involved in the rule would gradually be increased until the child can follow more complex rules. Social consequences for rule-following per se would gradually be shifted to the nonarbitrary consequences accessed more efficiently by rules.

There are a number of lines of research that suggest how rule following repertoires should be focused in order to achieve higher levels of self-control. These include training in such areas as emotional acceptance (e.g., Gutiérrez, Luciano, Rodríguez, & Fink, 2004; Hayes et al., 1996), distress tolerance (e.g., Brown, Lejuez,

Kahler, & Strong, 2002), performance of longer and more difficult response chains (what has been termed "learned industriousness," e.g., Quinn, Brandon, & Copeland, 1996), and delay of gratification or delay discounting (Bickel & Johnson, 2003). The goal is to undermine rules that lead to impulsivity because they are focused on ineffective targets (e.g., emotional control rules), to build rule control in situations that demand high persistence, and to be mindful of the importance of basic elements of rule generation, understanding, and following.

Problems with existing model. The main assumption in this section is that children with ADHD have deficits in rule following or its contextual control and that these deficits can be alleviated with the proper training. While it may be the case that rule following is the core deficit in ADHD, other behavioral deficits may contribute to its proliferation. For example, a student who fidgets during classroom instruction may have academic skill deficits that make class participation difficult and possibly aversive. Thus, academic skill remediation may be beneficial for that individual. However, it is still probably beneficial to build rule control with this individual. Bicard and Neef (2002) found that the manner in which rules are presented affects how well rules are followed which suggests that contextual issues are of some importance. It may seem obvious that children diagnosed with ADHD have deficits in rule following because delays in following instructions are included in the diagnostic criteria, but a behavioral analysis adds possible components that might explain this deficit. A more functional and molecular research program might determine whether rule following deficits are related to delays in relational responding, poor contextual control over these relational operants, weak transformation of stimulus functions, poor temporal frames, failure to train distress tolerance, differences in what occurs privately while the child is waiting for a larger later reinforcer, or any of a dozen or more similar processes. The best manner in which to train rule following to children needs to be worked out, not just for ADHD children but for other children as well. It is not clear how children normally acquire rule following as a generalized operant. In that sense, the problems of ADHD point to a gap in our knowledge of normal language processes.

Autism

Another disorder which points to the same gap is autism, which is one of several pervasive developmental disorders. The prevalence of autism is 2-20 cases per 10,000 individuals and is four to five times more likely in males than females (APA, 2000). According to the diagnostic criteria, the onset of autism must be before the age of three, and deficits must be seen across social, communicative, and repetitive behavior/spontaneous play. Specific impairments in social interaction include: (1) impairment in nonverbal behaviors, (2) failure to develop peer relationships, (3) lack of spontaneous seeking to share enjoyment with others, and (4) lack of social or emotional reciprocity; impairments in communication include: (1) spoken language delays, (2) in those with adequate speech, delayed ability to initiate or maintain conversations, (3) repetitive use of language, and (4) lack of spontaneous make-believe play and restricted repetitive and stereotyped behaviors, interests, and activities include: (1) an intense interest or preoccupation that is abnormal or intense in focus, (2) inflexible adherence to specific nonfunctional routine or ritual, (3) repetitive overt behaviors, and (4) preoccupation with parts of objects.

To meet diagnostic criteria for autism, a child must exhibit a total of six or more behavior patterns, with at least two of them being from impairments in social interaction, one from impairments in communication, and one from the repetitive behavior category.

Current Research on Etiology

Evidenced by the diagnostic criteria, autism appears in the second or third year of life, and rarely after age three, although diagnoses are often made years after symptom onset. As the child matures, so do the behavior patterns, thus, autistic children have difficulties forming friendships and responding empathetically to others (Kanner, Rodriquez, & Ashden, 1972). When autistic children develop language abilities, their language is commonly thought of as deviant. For example, children with autism may exhibit monotonic speech delivery, often fail to give background to stories, and will often repeat words or sentences (Baron-Cohen, Tager-Flusberg, & Cohen, 2000). Most children with autism score in the mentally retarded range on intelligence tests (Smalley, Asarnow, & Spence, 1998) although they may have heightened skills in certain areas (APA, 2000).

Neurobiologically, autistic children are more likely to exhibit abnormalities on computerized assessments of brain activity, and an increased rate of seizures (Klin & Volkmar, 1999). Biological evidence of autism is supported because siblings of those diagnosed with autism have higher rates of the disorder than the general population, and monozygotic twins are more likely to than dizygotic twins to have the disorder (Klin, & Volkmar, 1999). Despite current evidence favoring a neurobiological mechanism of autism, a precise and identifiable mechanism has yet to be found (Klin & Volkmar, 1999).

Traditional Behavioral Model

There are at least four general behavioral theories of autism: Ferster's (1961) behavioral hypothesis theory, Lovaas and Smith's (1989) behavioral theory, Koegel, Valdez-Menchaca, and Koegel's (1994) social communication theory, and Bijou and Ghezzi's (1999) behavior influence theory. All four of these theories provide a comprehensive analysis of autism using behavior analytic principles. The main difference between these theories is in the origination of the disorder. Ferster (1961) attributes the cause of autism to faulty parenting. Lovaas and Smith (1989) attribute it to a mismatch between the child's nervous system and the child's environment. Koegle et al. (1994) attribute it to neurological delays that result in poor development of social skills. Bijou and Ghezzi (1999) point to delays in the children's sensory development causing the children to avoid or escape tactile stimulation which in turn does not allow the child to develop conditional positive social stimuli.

Applied behavior analytic interventions based on these theories have been particularly successful at training basic skills with the autistic population (Birnbrauer, & Leach 1993; Lovaas, 1987; McEachin, Smith, & Lovaas, 1993). Still, it has proven difficult to train generalized behavioral repertoires (Williams & Reinbold, 1999) or more complex behaviors that would be seen in the general population (McEachin et al., 1993). For example, McEachin et al. (1993) found, at follow-up, the group who received intensive behavioral training were functioning significantly better than the control group in school placement, intellectual functioning, adaptive and maladaptive scores, but not on scores representing personality functioning. Although these findings are very important, the experimental group scored at least one standard deviation below the standardized mean on all tests. Thus, significant improvements were seen in the intensive BA program over the control condition, but on average, the children were still clinically delayed.

Cognitive Model

Cognitive models have arisen in part to fill the perceived deficits in traditional behavioral models. One of the more popular cognitive theories of autism is the Theory of Mind (Baron-Cohen et al., 2000). Theory of Mind asserts that children acquire a mental interpretation of the world that is similar to the mental representations of others. They further learn that people's minds lead them to behave, and that understanding how other's minds function allows them to interact better socially. According to the Theory of Mind, these core understandings of other's minds enable individuals to engage in complex behaviors such as developing conceptions about people, relationships, groups, social institutions, conventions, manners, and morals. The theory also assumes that our everyday understanding of persons is fundamentally mentalistic: that we think of people in terms of their mental states such as beliefs, desires, or intentions. According to the Theory of Mind, children with autism lack this ability. This deficit is the root of their behavior problems.

It is difficult for Theory of Mind to account for the behavioral deficits that are seen low functioning autistic children who have not developed language (Klin & Volkmar, 1999). The theory does have broad appeal however particularly as applied to higher functioning children. The problem is that Theory of Mind is presented as a hypothetical construct, not a manipulable variable, and thus it is difficult to turn into an intervention program. Nevertheless, the idea of focusing on possible core cognitive deficits in these children might be useful if linked to a more useful theory that explains these deficits.

Autism and a Contemporary Behavioral Approach to Language

The behavioral analysis of the etiology of autism focuses on autism as a problem of skill deficits. At the severe pre-verbal level, deficits are in the areas of language and motivation for social contact. At the higher functioning end, are deficits in verbal behavior and more complex generalized social behavior. We will review some established behavioral theories on severe autism before conducting an analysis of the deficits seen in higher functioning autistic children.

Most behavioral theories of autism assume that the child's lack of interest in social interaction carries a large amount of the variance of the disorder (Bijou & Ghezzi, 1999; Koegel et al., 1994; Lovaas & Smith, 1989). This appears to be what it happening during the initial phases of autism where the child avoids certain types of stimulation, physical and social stimulation being the most common. Recent research suggests that this may be due to different habituation rates in autistic children when compared to their typically developing peers (Doney & Ghezzi, 2003). As a result, the child does not develop social stimuli as reinforcers, punishers, and discriminative stimuli. The developments of these social functions are necessary precursors for the verbal community to shape verbal skills, intellectual skills, or social interaction skills (Bijou & Ghezzi, 1999). Accordingly, children fail to develop basic skills that are necessary to function in a social community.

These delays in verbal skills will concurrently have a strong impact on the development of the child's relational responding repertoire. All well-developed behavioral intervention programs for autistic children include training in verbal behavior, but existing behavioral units (e.g., tacts and mands) only go so far in reducing verbal deficits. Typical behavioral models of intervention train language in a piecemeal fashion. Items to be taught are selected based upon a particular need in the individual's repertoire. While this approach has been more successful than any other, it often fails establish vocal repertoires that are contextually sensitive, display normal flexibility, and show the breadth of behavioral variability witnessed with typically developing peers. The primary impact of contemporary behavior analytic work on derived stimulus relations and relational frames is that it recasts the task of verbal training programs.

Research has indicated that language and a relational responding repertoire tend to covary (Barnes, McCullagh, & Keenan, 1990; Devany, Hayes, & Nelson, 1986; Lipkins, Hayes, & Hayes, 1993). Because the training usually does not focus on building a relational repertoire but does so coincidentally (Spradlin & Bradley, 1999), the relational responding repertoire is not very broad or advanced. Given this, autistic children who have not developed language will likely be delayed in relational responding. However, there is accumulating evidence that derived relational responding is indeed another form of operant behavior in that reinforcement contingencies will establish it when it is deficient. This has been established with frames of coordination (Barnes-Holmes, Barnes-Holmes, Roche, & Smeets, 2001a & b), exclusion relations (Carr, 2003), comparative frames (Barnes-Holmes, Barnes-Holmes, Smeets, Strand, & Friman, 2004; Berens & Hayes, in press), frames of opposition (Barnes-Holmes, Barnes-Holmes, & Smeets, 2004), deictic frames (Barnes-Holmes, et al., 2001; McHugh, Barnes-Holmes, & Barnes-Holmes, 2004; Rehfeldt, Dillen, Ziomek, & Kowalchuk, under review), and with derived manding skills (Rehfeldt & Root, 2005).

The apparent connection between derived relational responding and language, and the previously mentioned support for viewing such responding as operant behavior (see Chapter 3 in this text), is of major concern for clinicians doing language training with autistic individuals. These facts alone suggest means of providing language training that hits at the core of language. As was mentioned above, typical ABA programs often produce individuals whose vocal responding is rote. After years of intensive training, many autistic children have developed a large repertoire of simple discriminated operants that are readily emitted. Yet, their emission tends to be in rote form. Given the autistic child's initial prognosis, this is a major accomplishment. However, more sophisticated forms of verbal behavior such as understanding and creating metaphors, story telling, and problem solving are often noticeably deficient.

What has been missing from the behavioral language training with autistic children is a comprehensive functional approach to the specific units that need to be trained. Relational Frame Theory specifies over 40 levels of complexity in the relational repertoire of normal adults (Hayes et al., 2001). The earliest steps are readily linked to existing discrete trials verbal training, such as the training of contextually controlled mutual entailment in equivalence, or the training of comparative relational frames (e.g., Barnes-Holmes, Barnes-Holmes, Roche, & Smeets, 2001a; 2001b; Barnes-Holmes et al., 2004; Berens & Hayes, in press; Rehfeldt & Root, 2005). RFT language training programs of this kind are beginning to appear (e.g., Barnes-Holmes et al., 2001).

Recent work on the development of derived relational responding provides examples of programming that may be readily adapted with current training materials for use with autistic children (Barnes-Holmes, Barnes-Holmes, Roche, & Smeets, 2001a; 2001b; Barnes-Holmes et al., 2004; Berens & Hayes, in press; Rehfeldt & Root, 2005). One study enhanced the effects of an exclusion procedure with multiple exemplar training, using autistic children (Carr, 2003). In all of these studies, participants were exposed to multiple exemplar procedures whereby relational responding was directly trained. After a sufficient number of trials had been trained, individuals were able to emit a derived relational response in variety of untrained contexts.

A more advanced example of the possible benefits of uniting the advances made in behavioral language training with RFT is the recent work on perspective taking. This example is particularly apt in the present context, because perspective taking is one of the central issues of concern to Theory of Mind. Autistic children have notable deficits in perspective taking, which involves the ability to see that one sees the world from a perspective, to see that it differs from the perspective of others, and to have a sense of how the world would look from the perspective of another. For example, suppose a very young child is seated across the table from an adult. In front of the adult is a red spot; in front of the child is a green spot. If the child has acquired perspective taking, she would know that while she sees green then red, the adult sees red then green. Perspective taking of that kind is not only cognitively important, it is thought to be emotionally important. For example, empathy might involve being able to "see the world through another person's eyes." Thus, the deficits autistic children have in empathy might be related to their perspective taking deficits.

According to RFT, perspective taking is a result of deictic relational frames. Deictic frames are those such as I-YOU, HERE-THERE, and NOW-THEN. They can be trained only by demonstration relative to a speaker ("here" is not a specific place but a place in relation to the speaker). Deictic frames are acquired through multiple exemplar training that occurs in the normal social verbal community (McHugh et al., 2004). Children learn these frames through a history of responding to questions such as "what am I doing here?" or "what are you doing there?"

Recently, RFT researchers have begun to experimentally assess if these cognitive deficits could be treated as deficits in particular relational framing abilities (e.g., Barnes-Holmes et al., 2001; McHugh et al., 2004; Rehfeldt et al., under review). Barnes-Holmes et al. (2001) reported preliminary success training perspective taking in young children who lack the repertoire by training the underlying frames that are thought to be necessary to engage in these types of behaviors. This raises the possibility that a modern behavioral approach to language can not only address the content of cognitive theories such as Theory of Mind, but can do so in a way that links the analysis to intervention.

The clear relation between language and relational responding is beginning to be worked out (O'Hora, Paelez, & Barnes-Holmes, 2005). This research demonstrated the correlation between performance on the verbal sub-test of the WAIS-III and relational ability. However, more research needs to be conducted to show the effects of training on relational framing, language development, and the development of complex behaviors such as empathy and perspective taking.

The specific frames that the children need to be trained on depend upon the particular skills that they lack. Thus, specific deficits in relational responding must first be identified through a functional analysis. For example, if the child is delayed in social skills then training in deictic frames of I-YOU, HERE-THERE, NOW-THEN are likely necessary. However, for overall development, RFT suggests that all frames be trained. Hayes et al. (2001) provide a general outline of the fashion in which relational framing should develop. Accordingly, development of language begins with the simple components of relational framing, such as mutual entailment and combinatorial entailment, continues with the development of families of relational frames, the emergence of rules, and ends with the dominance of verbal functions.

Barnes-Holmes, Barnes-Holmes, and Cullinan (2001) indicate that RFT ads process to the analysis or teaching new skills. They go on to suggest that the combination of the behavioral focus on fluency training and the RFT focus are necessary to master specific relational repertoires. Specifically, to successfully train particular relational frames it is necessary to consider "(a) the arrangement of tasks that can only be mastered by specific relational responses, (b) variation of irrelevant dimensions of task performance, (c) expansion of the range and subtlety of contextual control over relational responding and the transformation of stimulus functions via relational responding, and (d) contact with the limitations of the relational task" (p. 163). Training in this fashion is consistent with an emphasis on training of the process of language rather than the specific content. An RFT analysis does not suggest that particular behaviors that are taught idiosyncratically are not important. Rather, the RFT analysis simply adds two components that may be missing from the current way that we conceptualize and work with autistic children.

First, it treats derived relational responding as operant behavior established by a history of reinforcement across multiple examples (see Chapter 3 in this text). Second, RFT orients clinicians to the arbitrary nature of language, such that programming of language instruction should be geared towards the development and measurement arbitrary applicability of relational responding (see Chapter 3 in this text). If the goal of language training with autistic children is to teach language and not just discriminated vocal operants then according to RFT, relational training that focuses on the flexible and fluent application of mutual and combinatorial entailment is necessary.

Conclusion

This chapter illustrates the possible role of verbal processes in childhood behavior problems. Although done on categorically distinct disorders, this analysis is functionally based therefore there is overlap between the analyses. The same verbal processes can have a functional impact on many categorically distinct disorders. Based on these functional analyses, treatment suggestions are provided. Some of the treatment suggestions are aimed at the verbal processes themselves, such as reducing cognitive fusion in children with tics, whereas others focus on behavioral deficits such as relational responding deficits seen in children with ADHD or autism. In addition to intervening at the individual level, treatment suggestions for the verbal community were provided because they have the ability to maintain or punish the behaviors being trained. This analysis is highly speculative in nature, but research on relational frames and derived stimulus relations is growing rapidly. As it does, it is worthwhile to attempt to apply these findings to clinical areas. Childhood behavior problems are a prime example. The value of this analysis will be determined by its usefulness in theory development and treatment, but much more awaits to be done before that determination can be made.

References

Abramowitz, J. S., Tolin, D. F., & Street, G. P. (2001). Paradoxical effects of thought suppression: A meta-analysis of controlled studies. *Clinical Psychology Review, 21,* 683-703.

American Psychiatric Association. (2000). *Diagnostic and statistical manual of mental disorders (4th ed., text revision).* Washington, DC: Author.

Azrin, N. H., & Nunn, R. G. (1973). Habit-reversal: A method of eliminating nervous habits and tics. *Behavior Research and Therapy, 11,* 619-628.

Azrin, N. H., Nunn, R. G., & Frantz, S. E. (1980). Habit reversal vs. negative practice treatment of nervous tics. *Behavior Therapy, 11,* 169-178.

Azrin, N. H., & Peterson, A. L. (1990). Treatment of Tourette syndrome by habit reversal: A waiting-list control comparison. *Behavior Therapy, 21,* 305-318.

Barkley, R. A. (1997). *ADHD and the nature of self-control.* New York: Guilford.

Barkley, R. A. (1998). *Attention deficit hyperactivity disorder: A handbook for diagnosis and treatment* (2nd ed.). New York: Guilford.

Barnes, D., McCullagh, P. D., & Keenan, M. (1990). Equivalence class formation in non-hearing impaired children and hearing impaired children. *The Analysis of Verbal Behavior, 8,* 19-30.

Barnes-Holmes, Y., Barnes-Holmes, D., & Cullinan, V. (2001). Education. In S. C. Hayes, D. Barnes-Holmes, & D. Roche (Eds.), *Relational frame theory: A post-Skinnerian account of human language and cognition* (pp. 181-196). New York: Kluwer Academic.

Barnes-Holmes, Y., Barnes-Holmes, D., Roche, B., Healey, O., Lyddy, F., Cullinan, V., et al. (2001). Psychological development. In S. C. Hayes, D. Barnes-Holmes, & B. Roche (Eds.), *Relational frame theory: A post-Skinnerian account of human language and cognition* (pp. 157-180). New York: Kluwer Academic.

Barnes-Holmes, Y., Barnes-Holmes, D., Roche, B., & Smeets, P. (2001a). Exemplar training and a derived transformation of function in accordance with symmetry. *The Psychological Record, 51,* 287-308.

Barnes-Holmes, Y., Barnes-Holmes, D., Roche, B., & Smeets, P. (2001b). Exemplar training and a derived transformation of function in accordance with symmetry: II. *The Psychological Record, 51,* 589-604.

Barnes-Holmes, Y., Barnes-Holmes, D., & Smeets, P. M. (2004). Establishing relational responding in accordance with opposite as generalized operant behavior in young children. *International Journal of Psychology and Psychological Therapy, 4,* 559-586.

Barnes-Holmes, Y., Barnes-Holmes, D., Smeets, P. M., Strand, P., & Friman, P. (2004). Establishing relational responding in accordance with more-than and less-than as generalized operant behavior in young children. *International Journal of Psychology and Psychological Therapy, 4,* 531-558.

Baron-Cohen, S., Tager-Flusberg, H., & Cohen, D. J. (2000). *Understanding other minds: Perspectives from developmental cognitive neuroscience* (2nd ed.). New York: Oxford University Press.

Begotka, A. M., Woods, D. W., & Wetterneck, C. T. (2004). The relationship between experiential avoidance and the severity of trichotillomania in a nonreferred sample. *Journal of Behavior Therapy and Experimental Psychiatry, 35,* 17-24.

Berens, N. M., & Hayes, S. C. (in press). Arbitrarily applicable comparatives: Experimental evidence for relational operants. *Journal of Applied Behavior Analysis.*

Bicard, D. F., & Neef, N. A. (2002). Effects of strategic versus tactical verbal instructions on adaption to changing contingencies in children with ADHD. *Journal of Applied Behavior Analysis, 35,* 375-389.

Bickel, W. K., & Johnson, M. W. (2003). Delay discounting: A fundamental behavioral process of drug dependence. In G. Loewenstein & D. Read (Eds.), *Time and decision: Economic and psychological perspectives on intertemporal choice* (pp. 419-440). New York: Russell Sage Foundation.

Biglan, A. (1989). A contextual approach to the clinical treatment of parental distress. In G. H. S. Singer & L. K. Irvin (Eds.), *Support for caregiving families: Enabling positive adaptation to disability* (pp. 299-311). Baltimore, MD: Brookes.

Bijou, S. W., & Ghezzi, P. M. (1999). The behavior interference theory of autistic behavior in young children. In P. M. Ghezzi, W. L. Williams, & J. E. Carr (Eds.), *Autism: Behavior analytic perspectives* (pp. 33-34). Reno, NV: Context Press.

Binder, L. M., Dixon, M. R., & Ghezzi, P. M. (2000). A procedure to teach self-control to children with attention deficit hyperactivity disorder. *Journal of Applied Behavior Analysis, 33,* 233-237.

Birnbrauer, J. S., & Leach, D. J. (1993). The Murdoch early intervention program after 2 years. *Behavior Change, 10,* 63-74.

Blackledge, J. T., & Hayes, S. C. (2006). Using acceptance and commitment training in the support of parents of children diagnosed with autism. *Child and Family Behavior Therapy, 28,* 1-18.

Block, G. H. (1977). Hyperactivity: A cultural perspective. *Journal of Learning Disabilities, 110,* 236-240.

Bornstein, R. A., Stefl, M. E., & Hammond, L. (1990). A survey of Tourette syndrome patients and their families: The 1987 Ohio survey. *The Journal of Neuropsychiatry and Clinical Neurosciences, 2,* 375-281.

Bouton, M. E., Mineka, S., & Barlow, D. H. (2001). A modern learning theory perspective on the etiology of panic disorder. *Psychological Review, 108,* 4-32.

Brown, R. A., Lejuez, C. W., Kahler, C. W., & Strong, D. R. (2002). Distress tolerance and duration of past smoking cessation attempts. *Journal of Abnormal Psychology, 111,* 180-185.

Carlson, E. A., Jacobvitz, D., & Sroufe, L. A. (1995). A developmental investigation of inattentiveness and hyperactivity. *Child Development, 66,* 37-54.

Carr, J. E., Taylor, C. C., Wallander, R. J., & Reiss, M. L. (1996). A functional-analytic approach to the diagnosis of a transient tic disorder. *Journal of Behavior Therapy and Experimental Psychiatry, 14,* 197-201.

Carr, D. E. (2003). Effects of exemplar training in exclusion responding on auditory-visual discrimination tasks with children with autism. *Journal of Applied Behavior Analysis, 36,* 507-524.

Chambless, D. L., Baker, M. J., Baucom, D. H., Beutler, L. E., Calhoun, K. S., Crits-Christoph, P., et al. (1998). An update on empirically validated therapists II. *The Clinical Psychologist, 51,* 3-21.

Chaplin, E. W., & Levine, B. A. (1981). The effects of total exposure duration and interrupted versus continuous exposure in flooding therapy. *Behavior Therapy, 12,* 360-368.

Devany, J. M., Hayes, S. C., & Nelson, R .O. (1986). Equivalence class formation in language-able and language-disabled children. *Journal of the Experimental Analysis of Behavior, 46,* 243-257.

Dixon, M. R., Hayes, L. J., Binder, L. M., Manthey, S., Sigman, C., & Zdanowski, D. M. (1998). Using a self-control procedure to increase appropriate behavior. *Journal of Applied Behavior Analysis, 31,* 203-210.

Doney, J. K., & Ghezzi, P. M. (2003, May). *Differential rates and patterns of habituation to auditory stimuli in children diagnosed with autism and their typically developing siblings.* Presented at the annual meeting of the Association for Behavior Analysis in San Francisco, CA.

DuPaul, G. J., Ervin, R. A., Hook, C. L., & McGoey, K. E. (1998). Peer tutoring with attention deficit hyperactivity disorder: Effects on classroom behavior and academic performance. *Journal of Applied Behavior Analysis, 31,* 579-592.

Dykens, E. M., Sparrow, S. S., Cohen, D. J., Scahill, L., & Lackman, J. F. (1999). Peer acceptance and adaptive functioning. In J. F. Leckman & D. J. Cohen (Eds.), *Tourette's syndrome: Tics, obsessions, compulsions: Developmental psychopathology and clinical care* (pp. 103-117). New York: John Wiley.

Ervin, R. A., DuPaul, G. J., Kern, L., & Friman, P. C. (1998). Classroom-based functional and adjunctive assessments: Proactive approaches to intervention selection for adolescents with attention deficit hyperactivity disorder. *Journal of Applied Behavior Analysis, 31,* 65-78.

Ferster, C. B. (1961). Positive reinforcement and the behavior deficits of autistic children. *Child Development, 32,* 437-456.

Findley, D. B. (2001). Characteristics of tic disorders. In D. W. Woods & R. G. Miltenberger (Eds.), *Tic disorders, trichotillomania, and other repetitive behavior disorders: Behavioral approaches to analysis and treatment* (pp. 53-72). Boston: Kluwer Academic Publishers.

Flood, W. A., Wilder, D. A., Flood, A. L., & Masuda, A. (2002). Peer-mediated reinforcement plus prompting as treatment for off-task behavior in children with attention deficit hyperactivity disorder. *Journal of Applied Behavior Analysis, 35,* 279-286.

Gutiérrez, O., Luciano, C., Rodríguez, M., & Fink, B. C. (2004). Comparison between an acceptance-based and a cognitive-control-based protocol for coping with pain. *Behavior Therapy, 35,* 767-783.

Hayes, S. C. (2004). Acceptance and commitment therapy, relational frame theory, and the third wave of behavioral and cognitive therapies. *Behavior Therapy, 35,* 639-665.

Hayes, S. C., Barnes-Holmes, D., & Roche, B. (2001). *Relational frame theory: A post-Skinnerian account of human language and cognition.* New York: Kluwer Academic/ Plenum Publishers.

Hayes, S. C., Gifford, E. V., Townsend, R. C., & Barnes-Holmes, D. (2001). Thinking, problem solving, and pragmatic verbal analysis. In S. C. Hayes, D. Barnes-Holmes, & B. Roche *Relational frame theory: A post-Skinnerian account of human language and cognition* (pp. 87-102). New York: Kluwer Academic.

Hayes, S. C., Strosahl, K. D., & Wilson, K. G. (1999). *Acceptance and commitment therapy: An experiential approach to behavior change.* New York: Guilford.

Hayes, S. C., Wilson, K. G., Gifford, E. V., Follette, V. M., & Strosahl, K. (1996). Emotional avoidance and behavior disorders: A functional dimensional approach to diagnosis and treatment. *Journal of Consulting and Clinical Psychology, 64,* 1152-1168.

Hinshaw, S. P., Klein, R. G., & Abikoff, H. B. (2002). Childhood attention-deficit hyperactivity disorder: Nonpharmacological treatments and their combination with medication. In P. E. Nathan & J. M. Gorman (Eds.), *A guide to treatments that work* (2nd ed.) (pp. 3-23). New York: Oxford University Press.

Jacobvitz, D., & Sroufe, L. A. (1987). The early caregiver-child relationship and attention-deficit disorder with hyperactivity in kindergarten: A prospective study. *Child Development, 58,* 1488-1495.

Ju, W. (2001). Toward an empirical analysis of verbal motivation: A possible preparation for distinguishing discriminative and motivational functions of verbal stimuli. *Dissertation Abstracts International: Section B: The Sciences and Engineering, 61,* 9-B, 4966.

Kanner, L., Rodriquez, A., & Ashden, B. (1972). How far can autistic children so in matters so social adaptation? *Journal of Autism and Developmental Disorders, 2,* 9-33.

Klin, A., & Volkmar, F. R. (1999). Autism and other pervasive developmental disorders. In S. Goldstein and C. R. Reynolds (Eds.), *Handbook of neurodevelopmental and genetic disorders in children* (pp. 247-276). New York: Guilford.

Koegel, L. K, Valdez-Menchaca, M. C., & Koegel, R. L. (1994). Autism: Social communication difficulties and related behaviors. In V. B. Hasselt & M. Hersen (Eds.), *Advanced abnormal psychology* (pp. 165-187). New York: Plenum Press.

Leckman, J. F., King, R. A., & Cohen, D. J. (1999). Tics and tic disorders. In J. F. Leckman & D. J. Cohen (Eds.), *Tourette's syndrome: Tics, obsessions, compulsions: Developmental psychopathology and clinical care* (pp. 23-41). New York: John Wiley.

Leckman, J. F., King, R. A., Scahill, L., Findley, D., Ort, S. I., & Cohen, D. J. (1999). Yale approach to assessment and treatment. In J. F. Leckman & D. J. Cohen (Eds.), *Tourette's syndrome: Tics, obsessions, compulsions: Developmental psychopathology and clinical care* (pp. 285-309). New York: John Wiley.

Leckman, J. F., Walker, D. E., & Cohen, D. J. (1993). Premonitory urges in Tourette's syndrome. *American Journal of Psychiatry, 150,* 98-102.

Leckman, J. F., Zhang, H., Vitale, A., Lahnin, F. Lynch, K., Bondi, C., et al. (1998). Course of tic severity in Tourette's syndrome: The first two decades. *Pediatrics, 102,* 14-19.

Lipkins, R., Hayes, S. C., & Hayes, L. J. (1993). Longitudinal study of derived stimulus relations in an infant. *Journal of Experimental Child Psychology, 56,* 201-239.

Lovaas, O. I. (1987). Behavioral treatment and normal educational and intellectual functioning in young autistic children. *Journal of Consulting and Clinical Psychology, 55,* 373-387.

Lovaas, O. I., & Smith, T. (1989). A comprehensive behavior therapy of autistic children: A paradigm for research and treatment. *Journal of Behavior Therapy and Experimental Psychiatry, 20,* 17-29.

Malatesta, V. J. (1990). Behavioral case formulation: An experimental assessment study of transient tic disorder. *Journal of Psychopathology and Behavioral Assessment, 12,* 219-232.

Mazur, J. E., & Logue, A. W. (1978). Choice in a "self-control" paradigm: Effects of a fading procedure. *Journal of the Experimental Analysis of Behavior, 30,* 11-17.

Mauro, C. F., & Harris, Y. R. (2000). Influence of child-rearing attitudes and teaching behaviors on preschoolers' delay of gratification. *Journal of Genetic Psychology, 161,* 292-306.

McEachin, J. J., Smith, T., & Lovaas, O. I. (1993). Long-term outcome for children with autism who received early intensive behavioral treatment. *American Journal on Mental Retardation, 4,* 359-372.

McHugh, L., Barnes-Holmes, Y., & Barnes-Holmes, D. (2004). Perspective-taking as relational responding: A developmental profile. *The Psychological Record, 54,* 115-144.

Miltenberger, R. G., & Fuqua, R. W. (1985). A comparison of contingent vs noncontingent competing response practice in the treatment of nervous habits. *Journal of Behavior Therapy and Experimental Psychiatry, 16,* 195-200.

Miltenberger, M. G., Fuqua, R. W., & Woods, D. W. (1998). Applying behavior analysis to clinical problems: Review and analysis of habit reversal. *Journal of Applied Behavior Analysis, 31,* 447-469.

Miltenberger, R. G., & Woods, D. W. (2000). Assessment and treatment of habit disorders. In J. Austin & J. E. Carr (Eds.), *Handbook of applied behavior analysis* (pp. 137-160). Reno, NV: Context Press.

Mischel, W., Ebbesen, E. B., & Zeiss, A. (1972). Cognitive and attentional mechanisms in delay of gratification. *Journal of Personality and Social Psychology, 21,* 204-218.

Neef, N. A., Bicard, D. F., & Endo, S. (2001). Assessment of impulsivity and the development of self-control in students with attention deficit hyperactivity disorder. *Journal of Applied Behavior Analysis, 34,* 397-408.

O'Hora, D., Palaez, M., & Barnes-Holmes, D. (2005). Derived relational responding and performance on verbal subtests of the WAIS-III. *Psychological Record, 55,* 155-175.

Pauls, D. L., Alsobrook, J. P., Gelernter, J., & Leckman, J. F. (1999). Genetic vulnerability. In J. F. Leckman & D. J. Cohen (Eds.), *Tourette's syndrome: Tics, obsessions, compulsions: Developmental psychopathology and clinical care* (pp. 194-212). New York: John Wiley.

Peterson, A. L., & Azrin, N. H. (1992). An evaluation of behavioral treatments for Tourette syndrome. *Behavior Research and Therapy, 30,* 167-174.

Peterson, B. S., Leckman, J. F., Arnsten, A., Anderson, G. M., Lawrence, S. T., Gore, J. C., et al. (1999). Neuroanatomical circuitry. In J. F. Leckman & D. J. Cohen (Eds.), *Tourette's syndrome: Tics, obsessions, compulsions: Developmental psychopathology and clinical care* (pp. 230-260). New York: John Wiley.

Purdon, C. (1999). Thought suppression and psychopathology. *Behaviour Research and Therapy, 37,* 1029-1054.

Quinn, E. P., Brandon, T. H., & Copeland, A. L. (1996). Is task persistence related to smoking and substance abuse? The application of learned industriousness theory to addictive behaviors. *Experimental and Clinical Psychopharmacology, 4,* 186-190.

Rachlin, H. (1995). Self-control: Beyond commitment. *Behavioral and Brain Sciences, 18,* 109-159.

Rachlin, H., & Green, L. (1972). Commitment, choice and self-control. *Journal of the Experimental Analysis of Behavior, 17,* 15-22.

Rehfeldt, R. A., Dillen, J. E., Ziomek, M. M., & Kowalchuk, R. K. (under review). *Assessing relational learning deficits in perspective-taking in children with high-functioning autism spectrum disorder.* Manuscript submitted for publication.

Rehfeldt, R. A., & Root, S. L. (2005). Establishing derived requesting skills in adults with severe developmental disabilities. *Journal of Applied Behavior Analysis, 38,* 101-105.

Rutter, M. (1977). Brain damage syndromes in childhood: Concepts and findings. *Journal of Child Psychology and Psychiatry, 18,* 1-21.

Ryle, G. (1949). *The concept of mind.* Chicago, IL: University of Chicago Press.

Schweitzer, J. B., & Sulzer-Azaroff, B. (1988). Self control: Teaching tolerance for delay in impulsive children. *Journal of the Experimental Analysis of Behavior, 50,* 173-186.

Sharenow, E. L., Fuqua, R. W., & Miltenberger, R. G. (1989). The treatment of muscle tics with dissimilar competing response practice. *Journal of Applied Behavior Analysis, 22,* 35-42.

Silva, R. R., Munoz, D. M., Barickman, J., & Freidhoff, A. J. (1995). Environmental factors and related fluctuation of symptoms in children and adolescents with Tourette's disorder. *Journal of Child Psychiatry, 36,* 30-312.

Smalley, S. L., Asarnow, R. F., & Spence, M. A. (1998). Autism and genetics: A decade of research. *Archives of General Psychiatry, 45,* 953-961.

Spradlin, J. E., & Bradley, N. C. (1999). Early childhood autism and stimulus control. In P. M. Ghezzi, W. L. Williams, & J. E. Carr (Eds.), *Autism: Behavior analytic perspectives* (pp. 49-65). Reno, NV: Context Press.

Twohig, M. P., & Woods D. W. (2001). Evaluating the necessary duration of the competing response in habit reversal: A parametric analysis. *Journal of Applied Behavior Analysis, 34,* 517-520.

Twohig, M. P., & Woods, D. W. (2004). A preliminary investigation of acceptance and commitment therapy and habit reversal as a treatment for trichotillomania. *Behavior Therapy, 35,* 803-820.

Verdellen, C. W. J., Keijsers, G. P. J., Cath, D. C., & Hoogduin, C. A. L. (2004). Exposure with response prevention versus habit reversal in Tourette's syndrome: A controlled study. *Behaviour Research and Therapy, 42,* 501-511.

Williams, W. L., & Reinbold, C. (1999). Conditional discrimination process, the assessment of basic learning abilities, and their relevance to language acquisition in children with autism. In P. M. Ghezzi, W. L. Williams, & J. E. Carr (Eds.), *Autism: Behavior analytic perspectives* (pp. 70-97). Reno, NV: Context Press.

Willis, T. J., & Lovaas, I. (1977). A behavioral approach to treating hyperactive children: The parent's role. In J. B. Millichap (Ed.), *Learning disabilities and related disorders* (pp. 119-140). Chicago, IL: Yearbook Medical Publishers.

Woods, D. W. (2002). The effect of video based peer education on the collateral acceptability of adults with Tourette's syndrome. *Journal of Developmental and Physical Disabilities, 14,* 51-62.

Woods, D. W., Koch, M., & Miltenberger, R. G. (2003). Impact of tic severity on the effects of peer education about Tourette's syndrome. *Journal of Developmental and Physical Disabilities, 15,* 67-78.

Woods, D. W., Murray, L. K., Fuqua, R. W., Seif, T. A., Boyer, L. J., & Siah, A. (1999). Comparing the effectiveness of similar and dissimilar competing responses in evaluating the habit reversal treatment for oral-digital habits in children. *Journal of Behavior Therapy and Experimental Psychiatry, 30,* 289-300.

Woods, D. W., Watson, T. S., Wolfe, E., Twohig, M. P., & Friman, P. C. (2001). An experimental analysis of the influence of tic-related conversation on vocal and motor tics in children with Tourette's syndrome. *Journal of Applied Behavior Analysis, 34,* 353-356.

Woods, D. W., Wetterneck, C. T., & Flessner, C. A. (2006). A controlled evaluation of acceptance and commitment therapy plus habit reversal as a treatment for trichotillomania. *Behaviour Research and Therapy, 44,* 639-656.

Index

acceptance, definition of, 59
Acceptance and Action Questionnaire (AAQ), 99, 135, 281
ACT (Acceptance and Commitment Therapy)
    for addictions, 259
    for anxiety disorders, 102, 106-108
    for chronic illness/pain, 374, 377, 381, 383
    for depression, 197-198, 203-205, 207
    for eating disorders, 287-290
    for OCD, 139, 141-146
    for personality disorders, 330-334
    for psychotic disorders, 228, 230-231
    for sexual disorders, 359-361
    for Tourette's Disorder, 424-425
    for trichotillomania, 176-177
agoraphobia, 83
anorexia, 271-280, 282-287, 289
    binge-purge type, 271
    restricting type, 271
antidepressant medication, 184
anxiety disorders
    see Agoraphobia, Generalized Anxiety Disorder, Obsessive Compulsive
    Disorder, Panic Disorder, Post Traumatic Stress Disorder, Specific
    Phobia, Social Phobia
anxiety sensitivity, 81, 99-100
Antisocial Personality Disorder, 298-299, 306, 329
arbitrarily applicable relational responding
    see relations, relational frame theory
assertiveness training, 42
attachment styles, 389-415
    aggressive, 402, 408
    anxious-ambivalent, 400-401, 405
    avoidant-dismissive, 391, 405
    fearful-avoidant, 402, 406, 408
    fearful-disorganized, 406
    fearful-aggressive, 406
    preoccupied, 392-393, 398-400, 405, 410
    secure, 391-393, 396-399, 405-408, 413
Attention Deficit Hyperactivity Disorder (ADHD), 417, 425-428, 430-432, 428
augmentals/augmenting

formative, 40, 68
motivative, 40, 68
Autism, 222, 224, 417, 432-435, 428
autonomic arousal/reactivity, 82-83, 166, 352
aversion therapy, 349
Avoidance and Fusion Questionnaire for Youth, 285
avoidant coping styles, 254, 383
Avoidant Personality Disorder, 298, 300, 303, 306
behavior therapy
    first wave, 11-13, 15
    second wave, 11, 12, 13
    third wave, 10, 15, 16, 49-50, 54, 106, 124, 125
behavioral activation system, 185, 214
Behavioral Activation, 16, 192, 196-198, 200, 203, 205, 374, 375
Behavioral Activation Treatment for Depression (BATD), 200, 203, 374
behavioral assessment, 202
behavioral economics, 243, 246
behavioral inhibition system, 98, 185, 299
behavioral marital therapy, 257
behavioral sex therapy, 361
behavioral theory, 48
binge eating disorder (BED), 272
biological factors
    in addictions, 238, 240, 242, 247
    in ADHD, 426-428
    in anxiety disorders, 86, 98-99
    in autism, 433
    in depression, 181, 183-184, 189
    in eating disorders, 273
    in OCD, 128, 130
    in personality disorders, 299-301, 323
    in psychotic disorders, 218-221
    in sexual disorders, 344
    in Tourette's Disorder, 418-419
    in trichotillomania, 159, 167, 169
Borderline Pesonality Disorder, 301, 321-323, 328-330
breathing retraining, 101, 105
bulimia, 271-277, 279-280, 282-283, 286
C func, 37-39, 353, 359
C rel, 37-39, 353, 359
cancer, 237, 369-372, 374, 376, 378-383
chronic pain, 145, 215, 334, 369-370, 373, 375-378, 382-383
chronic/life-threatening illness, 369, 374-376, 378

classical conditioning
 see respondent conditioning
cognitive fusion, 55, 57, 60, 132, 139, 142, 147, 229-230, 282, 285-286, 428
cognitive distortions/errors
 and drug taking, 251-253
 catastrophizing, 87, 100, 105, 132, 370, 375-376
 challenging/changing, 142, 229, 258, 287-288, 345
 restructuring, 105, 139-140, 176, 191-192, 286, 288, 376
 exaggerating, 43
cognitive behavioral theory
 of anxiety disorders, 105-108
 of chronic illness/pain, 383
 of depression, 383
 of eating disorders, 286, 289-290
 of OCD, 125, 138, 145, 146
 of personality disorders, 305, 308
 of psychotic disorders, 225
committed action, 55-57, 69-70, 72-73, 141,145
compulsions, 117-124, 127, 132, 134-135, 138, 145-146
Conduct Disorder, 240, 302, 303
contact with the present moment, 55-56, 63-65, 141, 144
context of literality, 60, 133
contextual cues, 33, 35-36, 194-195, 221, 224-225, 312, 353, 354, 429
contingencies
 direct and derived, 24, 40, 51, 53, 61, 64, 69, 90, 133, 168, 171-174, 362
 multiple, 86, 89
 natural, 41, 73, 92, 98, 135-137, 141, 143, 185, 255, 378, 414, 425
 related to verbal behavior, 23, 42, 51, 64, 90, 92, 103-104, 135-136, 224,
  254, 331, 355, 362, 377
contingency-shaped behavior, 39
counter-conditioning, 356
covert desensitization, 361
creative hopelessness, 204, 287
defusion, 50, 56, 60-62, 64, 68, 74, 141-143, 145, 204, 229-231, 258-259, 287-288,
 382-383, 424-425
delay discounting, 243-244, 432
delinquent behavior, 302
deliteralization, 230-231, 360-361
delusions, 217, 221-229, 231
Dependent Personality Disorder, 326, 335
depression
 see Major Depressive Disorder, Dysthymic Disorder
deviant sexual behavior, 344

Dialectical Behavior Therapy (DBT), 15, 16, 82, 102, 203, 328, 330, 334
dieting, 275-281, 283-285, 287, 289
dissociative disorders, 393
divorce, 186, 199, 285, 389
drive reduction, 390
Dysthymic Disorder (DD), 181-182
emotion regulation
    antecedent-focused, 94-95, 280
    consequence-focused, 95
    response-focused, 94, 96, 280
entailment
    combinatorial, 15, 35-39, 195, 422, 427-428
    mutual, 15, 35-36, 39, 195, 422, 426-428
establishing operations, 24, 29, 68, 163-164, 200, 247-248, 419
exhibitionism, 342, 361
experiential avoidance (EA), 17, 55, 57-59, 81, 82, 97-100, 102-105, 134, 135, 139,
    144, 146, 147, 166, 167, 171, 177, 181, 197, 198, 201, 204, 208, 251, 254,
    255, 271, 281, 283, 285-287, 308, 309, 314, 315, 334, 377-379, 422-425,
    430
exposure, 57, 59, 71, 75
    direct, 52
    imaginal, 105, 107, 262
    interoceptive, 59, 101, 104-105, 107, 139, 170, 174, 243, 247, 423
    in-vivo, 105, 107
    response prevention, 59, 105, 138, 142, 414, 423
extinction, 28-29, 87, 92, 104, 119, 133, 137, 139-141, 175-176, 201, 246, 252, 256,
    357, 362, 397-399, 403-407, 423
extinction burst, 29, 397
extraversion, 99, 239
fading procedures, 427, 431
fear
    acquisition, 89
    learning, 81-82, 87-90, 93-95, 97, 102-103, 109
fetishism, 342, 350, 355, 362-363, 366
flooding, 105
frames
    see relations
functional analysis, 48, 145, 193, 308, 324, 427
Functional Analytic Psychotherapy, 15, 49, 53, 73, 203, 206, 359, 414
functional assessment, 175, 192-194, 202-203, 207-208, 256
functional context (C func), 37-39, 132, 135, 353, 359
functional contextualism, 13-16

fusion, 55, 57, 60-62, 68, 92, 125-126, 132, 139, 142-143, 147, 204, 229-230, 281-282, 285-286, 360, 428
Generalized Anxiety Disorder (GAD), 84-85, 105, 144, 189, 274
guided imagery, 105
habit reversal (HR), 11, 146, 176-177, 420, 423-424
habituation, 176, 246-247, 350, 435
hair pulling
    automatic, 164, 166-168, 172-176
    childhood-onset, 159
    focused, 166-167, 172-175
hallucinations, 217, 221-230, 232, 238
health psychology, 369, 372, 374, 377, 382
Histrionic Personality Disorder, 298, 300, 306, 329
homosexuality, 342, 363
hyperactivity, 417, 425
imitation, 38, 40
impulse control, 297, 315, 359, 361
impulsivity, 55, 240-241, 244, 273, 299-300, 425, 427, 431-432
inattention, 405, 425
information processing, 87, 187, 221, 250, 305
Integrative Behavioral Couples Therapy, 102, 390, 412
Interpersonal Psychotherapy (IPT), 286, 290
intimacy, 206, 328, 389-390, 393, 404, 406-407, 409-410, 413-415
introversion, 300, 303
learned helplessness, 186, 191, 201
learning disorders, 425
Major Depressive Disorder (MDD), 181-183, 185, 240
mands/manding, 41-42, 435
masturbation, 345
matching law, 348
memory impairment, 127, 154
metaphor, 46, 104, 107, 143
middle level concepts, 47-48, 50, 54
mindfulness, 15, 49-50, 56, 60-61, 65-66, 72, 106, 143, 204-205, 278, 287-289, 329-330, 360, 424
motivation, 22, 29-30, 58, 144, 244, 327, 419, 429, 434
Narcissistic Personality Disorder, 318-319
negative reinforcement
    automatic, 164
neuroticism, 95, 98-99, 273, 300, 303, 315
obsessions, 117-123, 125-127, 132-135, 138-142, 144-147, 275, 284
Obsessive-Compulsive Disorder (OCD), 82, 101, 105, 117-147, 160-161, 163, 274, 418, 425

Obsessive-Compulsive Personality Disorder, 120, 298
opponent process theory, 244-245
pain treatment, 373, 375
panic attacks, 58, 64, 82-83, 85, 87, 100-101, 104-105
Panic Disorder, 64, 83, 100-101, 105, 107, 158
paranoia, 223
Paranoid Personality Disorder, 329
Paraphilias, 342, 349, 361
parasuicide, 321
pedophilia, 342-343, 354
personality disorders
    see specific disorders
perspective taking, 223-225, 227-228, 312, 314, 316-317, 319, 324-325, 426-427
Post Traumatic Stress Disorder, 31, 84
premature ejaculation, 341
premonitory urge, 418, 420-425
prevalence rates, 118, 157, 183, 290, 298
problem solving, 22, 38, 63, 66-67, 96, 130-131, 189, 192, 198-199, 205, 321-322,
    324, 330, 412, 426
psychodynamic, 191, 328, 389-390
psychological flexibility, 56-57, 75, 104, 107-108, 281
psychopathy
    see anti-social personality disorder
punishment
effectiveness of, 23, 25, 27-29, 32, 36, 41, 71, 122, 138, 163, 185-186, 191, 193,
    195-196, 198, 201, 322, 396-397, 399-402, 404-410, 412, 415
    negative, 25, 28
    positive, 25, 27-28
radical behaviorism, 13-14, 202
reinforcement
    negative, 25-27, 86, 109, 164, 174-175, 193, 198-199, 201, 242, 244-246,
        250, 256, 279-280, 304, 408, 419, 421
    intermittent, 29, 427
    deprivation model of depression, 189, 191
    schedules of, 29, 185, 244, 246, 257, 348, 394-395, 397-398, 403, 427
relapse prevention, 345, 361
relational context (C rel), 33, 36-39, 353, 359
Relational Frame Theory (RFT), 14-17, 35-39, 42, 50, 57-60, 62-63, 91, 131-133,
    135-137, 194-196, 198, 200, 202, 204, 223, 225, 251, 253, 255-257, 259-260,
    281, 304, 310, 312-316, 320, 329-330, 332, 334-335, 350-354, 356, 359,
    361-362, 377-379, 382-383, 414, 417, 422-424, 428-430, 426-428
relations/relational frames/frames
    coordination, 171, 312, 320, 322, 332, 350-352, 421, 428-429, 435

combinatorial entailment, 15, 35-39, 42, 422, 427-428
comparative, 38, 63, 131, 356, 429, 435-426
same and opposite, 36-37, 39, 92, 131, 166, 251
deictic, 62-63, 223, 435, 427
equivalence, 311-313, 319, 325-326, 332, 350-351, 356-358, 382
evaluative, 58, 60, 63-66, 91, 131, 133, 139
exclusion, 435
generalized, 35, 313, 316, 324, 431
temporal, 51, 63-65, 68, 71-72, 131, 133, 136, 139, 312-313, 428-429, 432
transformation of stimulus function, 37-39, 42, 131, 136, 251
mutual entailment, 15, 35-36, 39, 422, 426-427
probabilistic, 23, 69
relational stimulus control, 194
nonarbitrary, 310
relaxation, 94, 101, 144, 146, 191, 376
respondent conditioning, 31-32, 86, 345-348, 350-352, 354, 357
response generalization, 248
rule governed behavior
and experiential avoidance, 97-98, 177, 198, 201, 204, 251, 379
in ADHD, 426-428, 430-432
rule-behavior correspondence, 38, 40, 42-43, 131, 223
pliance, 40-42, 55, 69, 130-131, 430-431
tracking, 40-41, 55, 69, 74, 130-131, 168, 172, 431
rumination, 93, 189, 199, 205, 280
schemas, 188, 192, 196, 304-305, 309
Schizoid Personality Disorder, 298-299, 306, 315, 329
Schizotypal Personality Disorder, 219-220, 298-299, 306, 329, 339
Schizophrenia, 182, 217-225, 227-229, 299
selective serotonin reuptake inhibitors, 124, 161
self
as context, 33
conceptualized, 55, 62, 316-318, 320, 324, 332
self-awareness, 62, 316
self-control, 69-70, 279, 316, 427-431
self-discrimination, 319, 336
self-esteem, 158, 182, 187, 190, 197, 222, 231-232, 279, 318, 320, 323, 370, 393
self-harm, 321, 337, 340
self-monitoring, 72-73, 95, 286, 376
sexual abuse, 272, 275, 321-322
sexual conditioning, 350
Sexual Disorders
see Sexual Dysfunctions, Sexual Identity Disorders, Paraphilias
Sexual Dysfunctions, 341

Sexual Identity Disorders, 341
shaping, 32, 52-54, 73-74, 93, 136, 206, 389, 403, 411, 414
skills training, 52, 54
social cognition, 222
social desirability, 95, 135
social learning theory, 122, 248,-249
social phobia, 83, 274
social skills training, 31, 33, 191-192, 205
stereotypes, 354, 362
socialization, 344, 373
specific phobia, 83, 105
spirituality, 106, 288, 333
stimulus generalization, 247-248, 251, 256, 354
stimulus-behavior relations, 247, 257
substance abuse, 101, 217, 219, 237-238, 240-242, 245, 250, 254-255, 257, 259-
    260, 285, 298, 302, 324
substance dependence, 237-241, 244-245, 249
symptom substitution, 28
systematic desensitization, 11, 105, 145,
tact/tacting, 36, 43, 168-169, 200, 321
temperament, 98-99, 186, 241, 273-274, 300
Theory of Mind, 222-223, 225, 434, 426-427
therapeutic alliance/relationship, 15, 53, 73-75, 206, 208, 328, 331
thought action fusion, 125-126
thought suppression/stopping, 58-59, 125-126, 133, 135, 142, 199, 227-228, 282-
    283, 380, 383, 430
tics, 120, 160, 417-420, 422-425, 428
time-out, 28
token economies, 11, 374, 378
Tourette's Disorder, 119-120, 161, 417-420, 422-426
transvestitism, 342
trauma, 57, 84, 86, 275, 419
trichotillomania (TTM), 120, 123, 135, 138, 146, 157-177, 424
unconditional positive regard, 32
vaginisimus, 341
values, 50-51, 54-57, 67-74, 106-109, 122, 141, 144-145, 147, 204, 229, 231, 258-
    259, 276, 288-289, 331-334, 374, 383-384, 392
voyeurism, 342
willingness, 100, 108, 145-146, 166, 228, 230-231, 285, 287, 307, 413, 425
worry, 64, 82-85, 105, 126, 138, 228, 274